Statistical Reasoning in Law and Public Policy

Volume 2

Tort Law, Evidence, and Health

This is a volume in
STATISTICAL MODELING AND DECISION SCIENCE

Gerald L. Lieberman and Ingram Olkin, Editors
Stanford University, Stanford, California

Statistical Reasoning in Law and Public Policy

Volume 2

Tort Law, Evidence, and Health

Joseph L. Gastwirth
Department of Statistics
George Washington University
Washington, DC

ACADEMIC PRESS, INC.
Harcourt Brace Jovanovich, Publishers

Boston   San Diego   New York
Berkeley   London   Sydney
Tokyo   Toronto

ACADEMIC PRESS, INC.
1250 Sixth Avenue, San Diego, CA 92101

United Kingdom Edition published by
ACADEMIC PRESS INC. (LONDON) LTD.
24–28 Oval Road, London NW1 7DX

Library of Congress Cataloging-in-Publication Data

Gastwirth, Joseph L.
  Statistical reasoning in law and public policy.

  (Statistical modeling and decision science)
  Includes bibliographies and indexes.
  Contents: v. 1. Statistical concepts and issues of
fairness—v. 2. Tort law, evidence, and health.
  1. Forensic statistics—United States. 2. Statistics.
I. Title. II. Series.
KF8968.75.G37 1988   349.73'8021   87-33367
ISBN 0-12-277160-5 (v.1)
ISBN 0-12-277161-3 (v.2)

Printed in the United States of America
88 89 90 91   9 8 7 6 5 4 3 2 1

Contents

Chapter 9

Principles and Application of Scientific Sampling

1. Introduction

In previous chapters we have seen that accurate estimates of parameters of interest (e.g., the minority proportion of a work force, the average salary of employees of a firm, etc.) can be obtained from a random sample rather than a complete enumeration of the whole population. Indeed, the standard error of the estimate (Section 3.3) and the confidence interval (3.20) for the population mean μ provide us with a measure of the precision of our estimate of μ. In this chapter we describe some methods of properly selecting a sample in order that the results obtained are generalizable to the entire universe sampled and illustrate their use in several legal contexts, e.g., sampling to estimate economic loss due to overcharging or overpayment of taxes, determining market share in an antitrust action, food adulteration or mislabeling, trademark infringement and deceptive advertising. Although the population or universe sampled varies with the application—e.g., the bills or vouchers in question in a case involving improper overcharges, the shipment of food that has been adulterated or the potential buyers of the product in a trademark infringement case—the purpose of sampling is the same: to obtain an accurate picture of the whole population from a representative sample of it. The further one departs from analyzing records of economic transactions or items of food from a shipment in the direction of sampling the views or opinions of a human population, the more care one needs to take to assure then the sampling procedure and questions asked are proper and fair, because people in the desired sample may have moved and cannot be located or deliberately do not respond. Moreover, the questions asked the respondents may not be worded carefully, i.e., they may suggest a desired response or be misunderstood by a large portion of the respondents.

We begin the chapter by discussing some improper methods that have been used to select a sample and then project the results to the universe. A useful method for checking that a sample is (or is not) a representative one is described and illustrated. In Section 3, the major aspects of sample design are discussed, emphasizing the importance of carefully planning the survey measurements or questions and the selection of the sample by a probability mechanism (random sampling). The next two sections discuss the use of samples in Food and Drug Act cases and in cases involving economics (audits, market share). As almost all samples and censuses are incomplete in the sense that some of the data desired is missing, e.g., some persons are not counted in a census or do not answer the questionnaire completely, or administrative records that should exist somehow have been lost or destroyed;[1] we discuss the effect of nonresponse and missing data in Section 6. Some guidelines for assessing the seriousness of these problems are presented and applied to data from actual cases.

The next section is devoted to the use of samples of the public in trademark infringement and deceptive advertising cases. The necessity of following the principles of proper sample selection and questionnaire design is demonstrated by examining the judicial reception of survey evidence in these cases. The last section discusses other applications of sampling in the legal and policy areas focusing on the *Craig v. Boren*[2] case concerning the propriety of an Oklahoma statute mandating a different age for males to purchase 3.2% beer than females.

2. The Problems Inherent in Nonrepresentative and Nonrandom Samples and Checking a Sample for Representativeness

Since designing a proper random sample requires care, sometimes the media as well as researchers use a *convenience* sample. Examples of such samples are studies based on volunteers or voluntary responses or the reliance on the views of one city[3] or town as typical of the entire nation.

The persons who volunteer to participate in a study or respond to a mail survey may well be those who are most interested in the topic or who hold strong views on the subject. Thus, their responses may not be representative of the general population. Similarly, when a single place is used to represent the political views of a nation

(a) there is no way to judge the accuracy of the result, i.e., we cannot measure its reliability;

(b) even though the chosen place was typical in the past, there is no guarantee it will remain so.

Other examples of *convenience* samples are:

(1) Sampling a few items from the top of a train car of shipped goods, such as coal or food items, because they are easy to reach.

(2) Obtaining survey information on the characteristics of households in a city by visiting homes chosen by a proper random sample at convenient times for the interviewers, e.g., Monday–Friday, 10:00 a.m. to 4:00 p.m., and interviewing the first available adult.

The first method selects the items which are readily available for testing and may miss the harder to reach items. A shipper intent on cheating the purchaser could place the lower quality items at the bottom and the higher quality ones at the top. The convenience sample would yield an overestimate of the true quality of the shipped goods. By visiting homes at a convenient time and interviewing the first available adult, the sample obtained is likely to underrepresent working single people (living alone) and working couples. Moreover, most of the data for married couples with one working spouse will have been obtained from the spouse who is not working (in the market place). This example also illustrates how a properly designed sample survey may be severely compromised by the introduction of convenience elements which can cause the actual respondents to differ substantially from those the sample called for.

Another form of nonrandom sampling is a *judgment* sample based on asking several experts for their opinions. Unfortunately, it often happens that the experts disagree. For example, several experts were asked to estimate unemployment in the 1930s. The estimates for 1935 ranged from 6 to 14 million people, a far wider region than a 95% confidence interval derived from a proper sample survey. Indeed, the monthly estimate of the unemployment rate in the United States has a standard error[4] of about .12 of 1%, so that, when the government reports a monthly unemployment rate of 7.1%, the 95% confidence interval would be about 7.1 ± .24. The estimates produced by the experts were inaccurate because they were based on past economic relationships which were assumed to hold at the time (1935) of the depression, and the estimates of current values of the variables they were using to estimate the unemployment were themselves based on incomplete and inadequate data.

While both *judgment* and *convenience* samples are sensible ways to acquire some information about the population of interest, both methods have no built-in mechanism which generates a representative sample of the whole population. Thus, there is no way to measure the possible error inherent in the estimate derived from such samples. With random samples, however, we have seen that the probability that an estimate is within specified distance of the true parameter (e.g., mean) of the population can be calculated and, therefore, a sample of the size needed to yield an accurate estimate can be determined. The major characteristic of a random sample is that the probability (chance) that any member of the population will be in the sample is specified before the sample is selected. Quite often, samples are taken in a way guaranteeing that each member of the population has the same chance of being included in the sample. For some purposes, we can improve on a simple random sampling of the entire population by categorizing the population into important subgroups (strata) and taking a simple random sample from each strata. For example, in surveying the views of the nation about the Equal Rights Amendment, rather than taking a sample of 1000 adults, it may be preferable to sample 500 men and 500 women, as an individual's opinion concerning the desirability of such an amendment may depend on sex. Even when a stratified sample is taken, the fact that *before* the sample is chosen the probability of any member of the population being in it is known, enables us to derive confidence intervals and make tests of hypotheses.

The basic ideas in taking a random sample for a survey can be illustrated by considering a presidential poll. Suppose we had a list of all registered voters (say 100,000) in Washington, D.C. and desired to predict their preference in an upcoming election. To select a sample of 1000 people, theoretically, we could place all the names of registered voters in a huge box, mix them thoroughly and draw out our sample of people. Then we could ask the members of our sample to cooperate and answer our questionnaire. Notice that *every registered voter* has the same chance (1 in 100) of being in our sample. If all the people cooperate, statistical theory tells us that 95% of the time, the proportion of the sample favoring candidate A will be within 3% of the proportion of the entire population favoring candidate A.[5] In practice, one does not place the names of the registered voters in a big container and select them randomly from it. Rather each person is assigned a number, in our example 1, 2, ..., 100,000, and a sample is selected using a computerized random number generator which selects digits at random. The voters with these randomly chosen numbers form the sample.

In order to illustrate the difference between generalizations from a valid sample and those from an unrepresentative one, a brief summary of a famous unrepresentative sample is helpful. In 1936, the *Literary Digest* carried out a poll of voters and predicted that Landon would defeat President Roosevelt since he was favored by a majority of the respondents. This poor prediction resulted from two errors: first, the *Literary Digest* obtained the names of people to whom they mailed ballots from automobile lists, telephone directories, and other sources which were biased upwards in socioeconomic status (i.e., relatively well-to-do people were over-represented in their lists and the poor were severely under-represented, as over 25% of the households did not have a telephone). Thus, the people sampled were not a microcosm of the country's voters. Secondly, while 10 million ballots were mailed out, only about 20% were returned. This mail method was subject to distortion, because the better educated and more literate part of the population, as well as those who were higher on the economic scale, tended to return their ballots in greater proportion than those who had a lower educational level. Hence, the respondents weren't even representative of the population in the already biased list being sampled. Even though the *Literary Digest* based its forecast on a sample of about two million ballots it made a big error. This incident serves to remind us that in order to obtain reliable results *the size of the sample is not as important as its representativeness.*

In summary, probability-based samples are the only ones which are representative of the population and to which the mathematical laws of probability can be applied to determine the magnitude of sampling variability in the results derived from the sample.

a. Checking that a sample is really random

The feature of a random sample is that it is free of any *selection bias,* i.e., it should be representative of the entire population from which it is taken, and major subgroups of the population should be selected in proportion to their fraction of the population. Since there is a small chance that a truly random sample will have an odd character, statisticians often compare the sample with known characteristics of the population to check its representativeness. For example, the Institute of Mathematical Statistics polled its membership a few years ago to ascertain whether a new journal of Probability should be published separately from a journal of Statistics rather than as a combined journal. The questionnaire also asked respondents where they worked. The proportions of people answering who worked in university, government, and private industry settings, respectively, were compared with the data on place of employment submitted by all members at the time of joining the institute. In this way the committee made sure that all important segments of the membership were actually represented in the sample in their appropriate proportions.

In order for this procedure to be most useful as a check, one should know the *purpose* for which the results will be used and select the few characteristics of the population which could have an effect on the results for checking. We now turn to an analysis of the nonrepresentativeness of a sample offered to a court in an accounting case involving the claims of the Fort Belknap Indians.[6]

The major issue of the case concerned the dollar amount of damages possibly owed the Indian tribe because of improper expenditures of funds by U.S. agents over many years. A sample of the vouchers had to be examined to determine

(a) whether the expenditure was proper (i.e., in accord with the provisions of the treaty);

(b) the amount of money still owed the Indians from improper expenditures.

Because the detailed determination of whether an expenditure was in accordance with the treaty is a legal issue and may be costly to determine, one should first categorize the types of expenditures and take *random* samples of the major categories (strata) of expenditures. The simplest way of accomplishing this is to sample the vouchers in each category in a manner that the chance (probability) that any voucher is in the sample is proportional to its size in dollars. Thus, expenditures for $300 would be three times more likely to be sampled than those for $100. The fundamental question at the trial was whether the sample chosen by the plaintiffs (Fort Belknap Indians) was a proper statistical sample from which inferences about all expenditures can be made, or was it a nonrandom and, hence, unrepresentative sample?

In the report submitted by the plaintiffs' accountant, the vouchers sampled were selected as follows: "We then reviewed the fiscal years in which the largest expenditures were made. Where necessary and on the basis of information developed in the sample, we expanded our review to cover additional years and questionable items.'' From a statistical viewpoint, there are several problems with this approach.

(1) The proportion of vouchers to be studied in each fiscal year is not specified in advance. In some years all the vouchers were examined, while in others less than 20% were studied.

(2) The selection of only the years in which the largest expenditures were made may bias the results, as one big expenditure may dominate the sample. Moreover, other years had *no* chance of being examined. Most importantly, it is not clear that this rule was followed in each expenditure category.

(3) The expansion of the sample to cover additional years and "questionable" items was not accomplished by random selection but by judgment. Hence, the resulting sample is not a representative one but a judgmental one.

As the major expenditure category studied was provisions, let us examine the sample chosen by plaintiffs to see whether it was randomly selected from all the years of data. In order to check the representativeness of the sample for each year, we computed the proportion of all expenditures for provisions over the entire time period that were made during that year and the corresponding proportions in the sample. The results are reported in Table 9.1 and show that many years with substantial expenditures (e.g., 1889–90, 1892–96, 1898, and 1900) were completely excluded from the sample. As slightly more than half of the total expenditures for provisions occurred in the years noted, their omission from the sample could hardly be due to chance. On the other hand, some of the years studied (e.g., 1904 and 1906) are over-represented by a factor of four. Moreover, 1892, the year with the largest expenditures for provisions, was not in the sample studied, although the procedure described in the report stated that "we then reviewed those fiscal years in which the largest expenditures were made." This over-representation of a few years of data in the plaintiffs' sample occurred in almost all the categories of expenditures, e.g., clothing, education, pay of various workers, agricultural implements, etc.

Another way to check a sample for randomness is to see whether the proportion of expenditures in each category (or year) that were sampled are approximately equal as they would be if each dollar spent had the same chance of being sampled. In Table 9.2, we list the categories of expenditures, the total amount spent, the amount sampled, and the proportion of each category studied.

TABLE 9.1. Comparison of the Proportion of Expenditure for Provisions in Each Fiscal Year with the Proportion in Plaintiffs' Sample

Year	Percent of Total Population	Percent of the CPAs Study
1889	5.92	0.0
1890	7.08	0.0
1891	7.30	30.2
1892	8.85	0.0
1893	7.48	0.0
1894	6.91	0.0
1895	6.29	0.0
1896	5.40	0.0
1897	5.91	3.9
1898	6.06	0.0
1899	7.64	8.6
1900	6.57	0.0
1901	5.58	20.24
1902	6.27	16.76
1903	2.13	8.61
1904	1.66	6.75
1905	0.22	0.0
1906	1.15	4.78
1907	0.04	0.0
1908	0.04	0.0
1911	0.10	0.0
1912	0.03	0.0
1915	0.00	0.0
1917	0.02	0.0
1919	0.00	0.0
1920	0.18	0.0
1921	0.02	0.0
1922	0.03	0.0
1923	0.00	0.0
1924	0.01	0.0
1925	0.05	0.0
1926	0.14	0.0
1927	0.41	0.0
1928	0.18	0.0
1929	0.30	0.15
1930	0.007	0.0
1943	0.01	0.0

TABLE 9.2. Comparison of the Total Expenditure in Each Category with the Amount in Plaintiff's Sample

Category	Amount	Amount in Sample	Percent of Total in the Sample
Provisions	$662,794.60	$160,171.88	24.17
Education	210,243.60	68,528.21	32.60
Clothing	108,219.00	22,493.32	20.79
Indigent Indians	20,779.23	2,529.98	12.18
Agricultural aid	174,024.84	53,889.12	30.97
Agricultural implements	64,144.29	25,343.69	39.51
Agricultural aid:			
Clearing, breaking, fencing land	18,711.33	18,340.11	98.02
Seeds, fruit trees, fertilizers	31,633.72	27,788.17	88.16
Pay of farm laborers	10,282.62	1,272.15	12.37
Irrigation operations*	13,147.33	121.64	
Work and stock animals	89,035.00	88,065.00	98.91
Livestock, purchase of	18,806.78	15,427.60	82.03
Livestock, feed and care of	38,752.58	14,514.35	37.45
Tribal herd, erection and repair of fence	5,203.10	5,036.60	96.80
Pay of miscellaneous employees	72,276.30	15,674.52	21.69
Pay of harnessmakers	15,101.53	1,980.28	13.11
Pay of herders	12,334.70	1,735.67	14.07
Pay of mechanics	42,124.48	7,707.02	18.30
Pay of farmers	43,429.88	8,153.30	18.77
Household equipment and supplies	41,844.50	7,712.36	18.43
Hardware, glass, oils and paints	14,462.78	2,345.87	16.22
Fuel and lights	7,655.34	2,241.05	29.27
Roads and bridges	14,323.83	3,775.58	26.36
Medical attention	49,611.13	7,183.03	14.48
Industrial assistance reimbursable	53,870.03	37,679.24	69.94

* Because one major expense in 1918 dominated this category, we excluded it from our analysis.

While some variation in the proportions sampled is to be expected, as vouchers are for different amounts, the range from 12% to 93% is far too large to be due to chance alone. Furthermore, some of the categories which are over-represented in the study, such as clearing land, contained many small expenditures so that a proper random sample could have been taken.

The results of both comparisons of the sample of vouchers with known characteristics of the total population of vouchers indicates that the sample was *not* a representative one. Such unrepresentative samples which do not even approximate a random sample often have inherent biases so that one cannot safely generalize the results obtained from them to the entire population. In this example the method of "expanding" the sample to cover additional years and items was not carried out by random sampling but by the accountant's "judgment". This has the potential of allowing the individual taking the sample (perhaps subconsciously) to add vouchers with improper expenditures. Also one would expect that some Indian agents and administrators were more honest than others so that if many inappropriate expenditures were found in one year, the next year's expenditures might also have a higher than average rate of inappropriate ones (assuming the same agent was there). Thus, the accountant's procedure is likely to yield an overestimate of the true fraction of improper uses of funds.

3. An Introduction to the Design of Sample Surveys

When conducting a sample, either of persons or of records, one must define the *universe* (or population) for which the sample results will be valid. Then one needs to develop a list of all elements (people, workers, records, etc.) in the universe, called the *sampling frame*. The third stage is the design of a proper *sampling plan* which is based on *probability sampling,* i.e., the probability that any member of the universe will be in the sample is specified prior to conducting the sample. Indeed, the basis for establishing confidence intervals for a parameter, e.g., the mean of a population, discussed in Chapter 3, was the assumption that all members of the population had the same chance of being included in the sample. The survey form or *questionnaire* must be carefully worded in order to elicit answers relevant to the issue under study but not lead the respondent. The data must be collected properly, i.e., the interviewers should be properly trained so that they obtain reliable responses from as many of the designated (by the sampling plan) respondents as possible. Finally, the data needs to be properly coded and edited, and proper statistical methods used to summarize and analyze the results.

a. Defining the universe and sampling frame

Although the ideal *universe* for a study may be well defined, e.g., all persons who will vote at the next election, persons who have purchased a specific item in the last year or all persons who have applied for employment at a firm during the last five years, obtaining a precise list of the universe to use as the *frame* from which the sample is chosen in quite difficult. Indeed, even for the major government surveys of employment and unemployment, the frame, which is developed from lists of residential dwellings, is never quite complete. Since a frame rarely is perfect, one should be aware of the following possible problems:

(1) The frame may have substantial amount of *missing members* of the population, i.e., the frame does not cover the whole universe.

(2) The frame may be *incomplete* in that a well defined portion of the population that should be listed is not. For example, it may take a while before records of recently hired employees are put into the firm's computer data base or newly completed homes are listed on the real estate tax rolls.

(3) The frame may contain *non-universe* members, e.g., one may be able to obtain a list of all registered voters as of the previous election, but some of them may have moved away and are no longer eligible to vote.

If a substantial amount of the universe is missing from the frame, but the frame is reliable for a sizable portion of the universe, one may restrict the conclusions to that subpopulation and obtain useful information.[7] Otherwise one may use other frames to augment the original one. This approach, called multiple frame sampling,[8] has been studied[9] extensively and is quite useful, although the effect of possible duplicate listings of population members must be considered. The problem of an over-inclusive frame can often be handled by restricting the results to the relevant universe. This can be done if membership in the proper universe can be obtained from answers to a few questions.

b. Designing a random sample

For some purposes an approximately random sample of social security numbers can be made by selecting all numbers with a certain digit (selected at random) in the second or third place from the right.[10] Thus, a 10% sample of a large file could count all persons with a 6 in the second place from the right and a 1% sample could be selected by also requiring that the third digit from the right be a 2. When samples of a population are taken periodically at regular intervals, the integers used to decide the sample should be selected anew from a table of random numbers. This ensures that any lack of representativeness in one particular sample does not continue to bias the results.[11]

When sampling the nation's population, the Census Bureau uses lists of homes, apartment houses and other residences to create a frame and gives each residential unit approximately the same chance of being in the sample. Since units of the same size (whether measured in terms of square footage or by the number of rooms) have different numbers of persons living in them, the sample has to be adjusted (technically speaking, "weighted") to approximate random sampling.

At this time it is appropriate to mention some modifications of the formulas for confidence intervals and tests for the population mean, μ, when the sample of size n forms a sizable fraction of the entire population of N units. The standard error of the sample mean becomes

$$(9.1) \qquad \sigma(\bar{x}) = \frac{\sigma}{\sqrt{n}} \cdot \sqrt{\frac{N-n}{N-1}},$$

so a $100(1 - \alpha)\%$ confidence interval for the population mean μ is

$$(9.2) \qquad \bar{x} - z_{\alpha/2} \frac{s}{\sqrt{n}} \sqrt{\frac{N-n}{N-1}} < \mu < \bar{x} + z_{\alpha/2} \frac{s}{\sqrt{n}} \sqrt{\frac{N-n}{N-1}},$$

where s is the *sample standard deviation* (See Section 1.3) which estimates σ. Since one may be interested in the total $(N\mu)$ quantity in the population rather than its average, a confidence interval for $N\mu$ is obtained by multiplying both inequalities in (9.2) by N, as $N\mu$ is estimated by $N\bar{x}$. Specifically, a $100(1 - \alpha)\%$ confidence interval for the total is

$$(9.3) \quad N\bar{x} - Nz_{\alpha/2} \frac{s}{\sqrt{n}} \sqrt{\frac{N-n}{N-1}} < N\mu < N\bar{x} + Nz_{\alpha/2} \frac{s}{\sqrt{n}} \sqrt{\frac{N-n}{N-1}}.$$

The reason the standard error (9.1) of $\bar{x}$ is reduced by the factor $\sqrt{(N-n)/(N-1)}$ relative to formula (3.2) for independent samples is that the units sampled are no longer independent of one another. If a member with an especially large or small value is selected, the variability among the remaining units is smaller. Hence, there is a built in tendency for the sample to correct itself and have less variability than in the case of independent sampling. The reader will note a similar phenomenon occurred in our comparison of the variances of the binomial and hypergeometric models in Chapter 2. The factor $\sqrt{(N-n)/(N-1)}$ occurring in 9.3 is the square root of the extra term $(N-n)/(N-1)$ in the variance of the hypergeometric distribution (see formula 2.20) which models the number of objects of a particular type in a sample from a fixed (finite) total.

For determining the proportion p of the population of size N who possess characteristic A (e.g., the proportion of vouchers whose expenditure was proper), the fraction (a/n) of a sample of size n who belong to A (the number of A members among the N is denoted by A) is a natural estimate. Exact confidence intervals can be determined using the fact that a has a hypergeometric distribution. For our purposes we will estimate $p = A/N$ by $\bar{p} = a/n$, and estimate the

(9.4) $$\text{standard error of } \bar{p} = \sqrt{\frac{N-n}{N-1}} \sqrt{\frac{pq}{n}}$$

(by replacing p by $\bar{p}$, q by $1 - \bar{p}$ and use the normal approximation to the sampling distribution of $\bar{p}$) to obtain confidence intervals and tests.[12] Thus, an approximate $100(1-\alpha)\%$ confidence interval for the proportion $p = A/N$ of a finite population is

$$\frac{a}{n} \pm z_{\alpha/2} \sqrt{\frac{N-n}{n}} \cdot \frac{\sqrt{\left[\frac{a}{n}\left(\frac{n-a}{n}\right)\right]}}{n}$$

or

(9.5) $$\frac{a}{n} \pm z_{\alpha/2} \sqrt{1-f} \sqrt{\frac{\bar{p}(1-\bar{p})}{n}},$$

where $f = n/N$ is the fraction of the population sampled and $\bar{p} = a/n$. Notice that if f is $<.1$, the reduction in the *width* of the confidence interval (9.5) or equivalently the standard error of $\bar{p}$ compared to the binomial model is small, as $\sqrt{1-.1} = \sqrt{.9} = .95$. Thus, the formulas of Chapter 2 for tests and estimates based on sample means and proportions from observations which are independent of each other are often used for finite populations when the sample size is *less* than one tenth of the population.

In order to obtain more efficiency from sample data, one can often subdivide the population into groups, called *strata*, and take a simple random sample from each strata. The potential gain in precision of the sample mean can be seen by considering the following hypothetical situation. Suppose there are one million workers in an area, 40% of whom are female. Moreover, all women receive the same salary, say \$20,000, while male salaries are normally distributed with mean μ = $25,000 and standard deviation, σ = $5000. Now the overall mean

$$\mu^* = .4(20,000) + .6(25,000) = \$23,000,$$

and the standard deviation of the entire distribution of earnings is[13]

$$\sigma^* = \$4,582.58.$$

Suppose one can take a sample of 100 salary records, should one take a sample random sample of all one million salaries (or workers)? If one did this, the standard error of the sample mean would be

(9.6) $$\frac{\sigma^*}{\sqrt{n}} = \frac{4582.58}{\sqrt{100}} = 458.24.$$

However, one could be clever and use the information that all women have the same salary and select a sample of 1 female and 99 males. Then the sample estimate would be

(9.7) $$(.4)\bar{x}_f + (.6)\bar{x}_m,$$

where x_f and x_m denote the average of our sample means of the female and male strata. In this example

$$\bar{x}_f = 20,000$$

and has standard error 0, as σ_f = 0. The standard error of $\bar{x}_m$ is

$$\frac{\sigma_m}{\sqrt{99}} = \frac{5.000}{9.95} = 502.51,$$

and the *variance* of the estimator (9.7) of the overall mean μ^* is

$$(.4)^2 0 + (.6)^2 (502.51)^2 = 90905.87.$$

Hence, the estimator (9.7) which is a weighted average of $\bar{x}_f$ and $\bar{x}_m$ has standard error

(9.8) $$\sqrt{990905.87} = \$301.51,$$

which is two thirds the standard error ($458) of the unstratified sample.

   Using the knowledge that all women were paid the same leads to a more precise estimate of the overall population mean because we allocated more of the sample to the male subgroup whose salaries were more variable. This is the general idea underlying stratification. If we can split the whole universe into subgroups which are homogeneous (similar) with respect to the characteristic of interest, then a small sample is needed to obtain a precise estimate of the mean of each subgroup or strata. Since the standard deviation of the variable of interest *within* each strata is usually much smaller than its standard deviation in the entire population,[14] the total sample size needed to obtain an estimate of the population mean μ, based on a weighted average of the stratum estimates, is less than that needed to obtain an estimate of μ from a simple random sample. Indeed, in the present situation, a stratified sample of 50, one woman and 49 men, using (9.7) as the estimate would have a standard error of $428.57, which still is less than that of an unstratified sample using 100 observations.

A substantial literature exists on selecting optimal allocation of a total sample of size n among the strata, i.e., if there are k strata, n_i observations will be taken from the ith strata, $i = 1, ..., k$, and we need to decide the values of n, remembering that $\Sigma_{i=1}^{k} n = n$. For our purposes we mention that allocating the sample *in proportion* to the size of each strata will always yield an estimate of the population average which is at least as precise as the mean of a simple random sample. The general estimator of the form (9.7) for the population mean of a population divided into strata of size N_i, $i = 1, ..., n$ each of which a sample of n_i is chosen, is

$$(9.9) \qquad \sum_{i=1}^{k} w_i \bar{x}_i,$$

the weighted average of the stratum sample means, $\bar{x}_i$, where $w_i = N_i/N$ is the proportion of the whole population belonging to the ith stratum. When the sample fractions of each strata are small (i.e., $n_i/N_i < .05$), the standard error of the estimator (9.9) of the population mean is

$$(9.10) \qquad \sqrt{\sum w_i^2 \frac{s_i^2}{n_i}},$$

where s_i^2 is the sample variance of the sample taken from the ith stratum.

Another type of sampling strategy we need to mention is *cluster* sampling. In sampling accounts or expenditures, ideally we would like to consider each dollar as a member of the population and evaluate whether it was properly spent. However, the expenditures are naturally clustered, as one may be for $10 while another for $1000. A simple random sample of the *clusters,* e.g., the expenditure vouchers, is known to be rather imprecise unless the sample contains a substantial fraction of the population (which defeats the purpose of sampling). Thus, other procedures, such as sampling proportional to the size of the cluster rather than sampling each cluster with the same probability, yield more precise results, because larger expenditures should have a higher probability of being in an audit sample than smaller ones in order to obtain an accurate estimate of the total discrepancy.

Cluster sampling is often quite convenient, e.g., in sampling public opinion it is easier to select a sample of blocks in a city and interview several (often four to six) randomly preselected households (addresses). The disadvantage of this procedure is that the members of each cluster (dollars in an expenditure, residents of the same block) often may have the same or similar values of the variable of interest. Technically speaking, we say the values of the variable among members of the cluster are *correlated*.[15] Thus, the sample loses some of its representative quality, as the sample units are no longer independent of one another with regard to the variable of interest. For a cluster sample of any size, this implies that the standard error of the sample mean is *larger* than that of a simple random sample of the same size. This can be seen by considering the male and female salary example and imagining that males and females lived in two separate areas of the city, which we will call two clusters. Suppose we select one cluster with probability proportional to its share of the total population and then take a random sample of 100 persons. The sample average will be 20,000 with probability .4 (the chance the female cluster is selected), or will be normally distributed with mean $25,000 and standard deviation

$$\frac{5000}{\sqrt{100}} = \$500$$

if the male cluster is selected (which occurs with probability .6). Thus, the sample mean from this cluster sample has an expected value of

$$(.4)(20,000) + .6(21000) = 23,000.$$

It is an unbiased estimate of the population average but its standard error is[16]

$$\$1322.86,$$

which is much greater than that of the simple random sample of the whole population.

It is important to emphasize the distinction between stratified sampling, in which the population is divided into homogeneous subgroups and then a *random* sample is taken *within each* subgroup and the stratum means are weighted as in (9.7) to yield an estimate of the population mean (μ), and cluster sampling, where a *sample* of *clusters* is taken and then a random sample of units are taken from these clusters. Strata are usually selected using prior knowledge of the population, so each one contains a relatively homogeneous subpopulation. Thus, the stratum means can be accurately estimated from a sample of modest size. In contrast, clusters are typically taken because of cost considerations (it costs less to send an interviewer to one area of a city to obtain six interviews than six areas to obtain one interview in each). Hence, stratified samples can often be more efficient (yield the same precision with a smaller sample than a simple random sample), while cluster samples typically are less efficient than simple random samples would be (if it were possible to take a random sample). These conclusions ignore cost considerations which favor cluster samples, which is why they are often used.

c. Questionnaire design and data collection

The proper questioning of respondents is basic to the integrity of the results of the survey. Questions should be worded neutrally so as to elicit the respondents answer, *not* the answer that he or she thinks the interviewer desires. Often several questions can be used to probe for the answer, rather than just one question. An example of such a set of questions is the U.S. Government's labor force survey (reproduced in Exhibit 9.1) which establishes whether a person is employed, unemployed or out of the labor force. Notice that a person is not asked, "Did you look for work last month?", which is provocative, but rather, "What did you do?"

The interviewers should be trained to follow a set of clear and consistent instructions, and there should be a procedure for evaluating the quality of interviewing. We refer the interested reader to the statistics texts in the references for further discussion of the process of conducting surveys and now turn to the use of samples and surveys in a variety of legal applications.

4. The Use of Samples in Food and Drug Cases

The Pure Food, Drug and Cosmetic Act[17] prohibits the sale of adulterated, contaminated or misbranded products. According to the law, "A drug or device should be deemed to be adulterated ... (c) If ... its strength differs from or its purity or quality falls below, that which it purports or is represented to possess." Section 352 of the act provides that "A drug or

19. What was . . . doing most
of LAST WEEK—

{ Working
Keeping house
Going to school
or something else? ■

Working (Skip to 20A) . . WK ○
With a job but not at
work . . . . J ○
Looking for work . . . . . . LK ○
Keeping house . . . . H ○
Going to school . . . . S ○
Unable to work
(Skip to 24) . . . . U ○
Retired . . . . R ○
Other (Specify) . . . . OT ○

20C. Does . . . USUALLY work
35 hours or more a week
at this job?

Yes ○   What is the
reason . . . .
worked less
than 35 hours
LAST WEEK?

No ○   What is the
reason . . . .
USUALLY
works less than
35 hours a
week?

20. Did . . . do any work at all
LAST WEEK, not counting
work around the house?
(Note: If farm or business
operator in hh., ask about
unpaid work.)

Yes ○   No ○   (Go to   21)

20A. How many hours
did . . . work
LAST WEEK
at all jobs?

0 0
1 1
2 2
3 3
4 4
5 5
6 6
7 7
8 8
9 9

20B. INTERVIEWER
CHECK ITEM

49+ ○   (Skip to
item 23)

1–34 ○   (Go to
20C)

35–48 ○   (Go to
20D)

20D. Did . . . lose any time or
take any time off LAST
WEEK for any reason
such as illness, holiday
or slack work?

Yes ○   How many hours
did . . . take off?

On vacation . . . . . . ○
Bad weather . . . . . ○   ■
Labor dispute . . . ○

New job to begin
within 30 days ○   (Skip to
22B and
22C2)

Temporary layoff
(Under 30 days) ○

Indefinite layoff   (Skip
(30 days or more   to
or nor def. recall   }   22C3)
date) . . . . . . ○

Other (Specify) . . ○

21B. Is . . . receiving wages
or salary from his/her
employer for any of the
time off LAST WEEK?

Yes ○

No ○

21C. Does . . . usually work
35 hours or more a week
at this job?

Yes ○

No ○

because he/she lost or quit a
job or was there some other
reason?

● Lost job . . . . ○
● Quit job . . . . ○
● Left school . . . . . ○
● Wanted temporary
work . . . . ○
● Change in home
or family
responsibilities . . ○
● Left military service . ○
● Other (Specify in
notes) . . . . ○

22C. 1) How many
weeks has . . .
been looking for
work?   ■

0 0
1 1
2 2
3 3
4 4
5 5
6 6
7 7
8 8
9 9

2) How many
weeks ago did
. . start looking
for work?

3) How many
weeks ago was
. . . laid off?

22D. Has . . . been looking
for full-time or part-time
work?   ■

Full ○   Part ○

(Mark the appropriate reason)

Slack work ....○
Material shortage..............○
Plant or machine repair .....○
New job started during week...............○
Job terminated during week...............○
Could find only part-time work.............○
Holiday (Legal or religious)..○
Labor dispute.................○
Bad weather...................○
Own illness...................○
On vacation...................○
Too busy with housework, school, personal bus., etc..........................○
Did not want full-time work...○
Full-time work week under 35 hours............○
Other reason (Specify).......○

(Skip to 23 and enter job worked at last week)

(Correct 20A if lost time not already deducted; if 20A reduced below 35, correct 20B and fill 20C; otherwise, skip to 23.)

No ○

20E. Did ... work any overtime or at more than one job LAST WEEK?

Yes ○ How many extra hours did .... work?

(Correct 20A and 20B as necessary if extra hours not already included and skip to 23.)

No ■ (Skip to 23)

21. (If J in 19, skip to 21A.) Did ... have a job or business from which he/she was temporarily absent or on layoff LAST WEEK?

Yes ○ No ○ (Go to 22)

21A. Why was ... absent from work LAST WEEK?

Own illness ......

(Skip to 23 and enter job held last week)

22. (If LK in 19, Skip to 22A.) Has ... been looking for work during the past 4 weeks?

Yes ○ No ○ (Go to 24)

22A. What has ... been doing in the last 4 weeks to find work? (Mark all methods used; do not read list.)

Checked with—
pub. employ. agency ....○
pvt. employ. agency ....○
employer directly..........○
friends or relatives............○
Placed or answered ads ...○
Nothing (Skip to 24) ....○
Other (Specify in notes, e.g., JTPA, union or prof. register, etc.)...............○

22B. At the time ... started looking for work, was it

22E. Could .. have taken a job LAST WEEK if one had been offered?

Yes ○ No ○ Why not?
Already has a job .. ○
Temporary illness ... ○
Going to school ○
Other (Specify in notes) ○

22F. When did ... last work at a full-time job or business lasting 2 consecutive weeks or more?

Within last 12 months (Specify) .... ○

(Month)

One to five years ago ...... ○
More than 5 years ago ...... ○
Never worked full-time 2 wks. or more.. ○
Never worked at all.. ○
(SKIP to 23. If layoff entered in 21A, enter job, either full or part time, from which laid off. Else enter last full time job lasting 2 weeks or more, or "never worked.")

Source: Current Population Survey form for March 1986 obtained from the U.S. Bureau of the Census.

device is misbranded a) if its labeling is false or misleading in any particular.'' Similarly, the Federal Seed Act[18] requires that the seller inform the purchaser about the quality of the seed. One reason sampling is necessary in these situations is that the testing or checking process often renders the items unsalable. Who would buy a can of food that was already opened (even if the contents were found to be pure)? In this section we illustrate the use of samples mislabeling the quality of goods, adulterated goods and possible contaminated goods (excessive presence of mold indicating decomposition).

a.   E. K. Hardison Seed v. Jones:[19] *a case of mislabeling the quality of seed*

According to the Federal Seed Act, before agricultural seed can be shipped interstate each container must bear a label giving a) the percentage, by weight, of weed seeds, including noxious-weed seeds, b) the kinds of noxious-weed seeds and the rate of occurrence of each, which rate will not exceed the regulated amount determined by the state into which the seed is being transported, c) the weight of inert matter and d) the percentage of germination. On the basis of samples of six shipments of three different types of seeds, all of which indicated that the seeds Hardison Company shipped were of lower quality than labeled, the War Food Administrator found the firm in violation of the law. The petitioning company asserted that the lack of conformity in weed seed content (relative to the label) and the germination percentage in different samples taken from the same lot at different times were not sufficient evidence that the bags were falsely labeled.

Before describing two of the samples used by the government in the case, we note that the regulations required a representative sample to be selected by taking equal portions from evenly distributed parts of the total quantity of seed. Moreover, in lots containing five bags or less each bag was to be sampled, while in larger lots at least every fifth bag, but not less than five bags, should be sampled.

On October 22, 1942 the firm shipped eight bags of wheat seed to the Talladega County exchange in Alabama with labels representing that cheat seed was the only noxious-weed seed in the bag. An inspector from the Alabama State Department of Agriculture took samples from six of the bags and mailed the composite sample to the Seed Control Laboratory. The analysis showed that the bags contained an average of 41 corn cockles (a noxious weed) seed per pound. Although the opinion doesn't present the number of one pound samples analyzed, so we cannot obtain a confidence interval for the mean number (μ) of corn cockle seeds per pound, the fact that corn cockle seed was not even listed as one of the noxious-weed seeds clearly indicates mislabeling.

A second issue concerned the germination content of rye seeds. Samples from eight bags out of a shipment of 20 bags of rye seed labeled 90% germination showed a germination of 60%. An interesting aspect of the test for germination is that the regulations require that at least 400 seeds be tested by division into lots of less than 100. Moreover, if the subsample percentages differ by more than 10% or 15%,[20] then retests had to be made. This criterion is a check on the homogeneity or consistency of the sample estimates. Since the samples from the eight bags were aggregated into a composite sample before being mailed to the state, this check insures us that the eight bags of seed sampled were of similar quality so that the 400 seeds analyzed can be regarded as a sample from a common population. Although no data is presented in the case, we will assume that 240 of 400 seeds tested germinated. Using (4.8) we can make a test of the hypothesis that the probability, p, of any seed germinating is .9, against the alternative that $p < .9$, obtaining

$$(9.11) \qquad Z = \frac{240 - .9(400) + .5}{\sqrt{400(.9)(.1)}} = \frac{-119.5}{\sqrt{36}} = 19.9,$$

which is strong statistical evidence that the true fraction of germinating seeds is less than .9. While one might quibble with this analysis because seeds from the same bag *might* be more similar than seeds from different bags, i.e., each bag is like a cluster, the fact that the four subsamples of 100 seeds did not differ by more than 15% in germination quality indicates that there was little variation in seed quality among the bags. Moreover, even if the standard error of an estimate based on a cluster sample was three times that of a simple random sample, it would not change our inference, since the Z value would change from -19.9 to -6.63.

b.   U.S. v. 43 1/2 Gross of Rubber Prophylactics, etc.[21]

This case concerned the propriety of the government's condemning[22] an entire shipment of prophylactics a manufacturer in Akron sent to a concern in Minneapolis on or about June 19, 1945 because approximately 7.4% of the devices tested were defective. The opinion noted that "the articles consist of certain rubber devices sold ostensibly for the purpose of preventing venereal disease" and that the government's medical witnesses testified that the defective devices (which contained holes) would fail to prevent the transmission of the disease. Actually the shipment consisted of 43-1/2 gross[23] of Xcello brand prophylactics and 112-1/2 gross of the Silver-Tex brand, both made by the same manufacturer. Before the seizure of 108 Xcello brand devices were tested, 8 of which were defective, while 12 of 108 Silver-Tex brand were defective. The details of the pre-seizure sampling methods apparently were not presented to the court. After the seizure the FDA chose one dozen items from each of 36 gross cartons of Xcello items and then randomly selected 72 of them for testing and found 6 defectives. A similar sampling system was used for the Silver-Tex brand and 4 out of 120 of these devices were found to be defective. The court combined the samples, first noting that 14 of the 180 Xcello brand items were found defective and 16 of the 228 Silver-Tex brand were defective, and concluded that 30 of 408 or 7.35% of the sampled devices were defective. The manufacturer claimed that out of the entire shipment containing about $144 \times 126 = 22,464$ devices only 30, or *less* than 1%, were found defective, so the entire shipment should not be seized.

The court realized that failure to accept representative sampling would mean every item would have to be tested when it said, "It should be pointed out that apparently the only practical tests which the government representatives are able to make with the facilities available to them results in the articles being rendered useless after the test has been made." Thus, there were two questions it had to decide.

(a) Was the observed proportion of defective items sufficiently large to justify condemning the shipment?

(b) Was the sampling procedure carried out properly so that the sample was an accurate reflection of the entire shipment?

The court discussed the *meaningfulness* of 7.35% of prophylactics sold to the public being defective by stating that it was not permitted to establish a formula for an allowable tolerance of defects in every libel[24] proceeding before it conceded that the government met its burden of proof. It then observed that if the sample rate (7.35%) existed in the entire shipment, then over 1500 $(.0735 \times 22,464 = 1651)$ defective items would be sold to the public. Such a large number would constitute a potential threat to public health in light of the asserted purpose of the item. One may question the completeness of this analysis, as the potential health problem also depends on the fraction of persons who buy and use the items who have venereal disease. If even 5% of the purchasers had the disease, then the defective items would be expected to expose $.05 \times 1650 = 82.5$ people to the disease.[25] This calculation shows that when a large population is exposed to a risk of low probability, the expected number of cases may be substantial.

Although the sampling method used by the government was not questioned, and both brands had about the same proportion of defective items, examining the fractions of defectives in each of the four samples (Xcello: pre-seizure 8/108 = .074, post-seizure 6/72 = .083; Silver-Tex: pre-seizure 12/108 = .111, post-seizure 4/120 = .033) suggests[26] that the samples of Silver-Tex devices differ too widely to be considered as being from the same population, and a further sample should have been taken. Rather than test each pair of proportions separately[27] in the present application (to a shipment of items manufactured by the same firm at about the same time), it seems preferable to make *one* test to check that all four sample proportions can be considered as being from the same population. That procedure described in Appendix 9.A yielded a nonsignificant result (p value = .19).

In this case the court avoided making a public policy decision, which presumably the legislative and executive branches should have made, namely, what rate of defectives should be tolerated, since no manufacturer can realistically be required to produce perfect items 100% of the time. As we saw in Chapter 7, the tolerable rate will depend on several factors such as the seriousness of the disease and the number of persons exposed. Once these have been determined from reliable data, one has to translate the requirement into a workable framework to incorporate the uncertainty inherent in making decisions based on samples. For the present problem it is reasonable to require that the interval $(0, r)$, where r is the maximum tolerable rate of defectives has a 90% or 95% confidence of containing the true rate, i.e., the upper endpoint of a one-sided confidence interval (3.27) for the true rate should be *less* than r. The sample size could then be determined so that the estimated proportion of defective items would be sufficiently precise.

c. U.S. v. 499 Cases containing tomato paste[28]

The gravamen of this case was whether a shipment of tomato paste had such an amount of mold indicating decomposition that it should be deemed adulterated according to the Food, Drug and Cosmetic Act, which states that food shipped in interstate commerce is subject to condemnation "if it consists in whole or in part of any filthy, putrid or decomposed substance, or if it is otherwise unfit food." The shipment arrived on

April 9, 1951, and The Federal Security Agency took some samples for inspection and approved the food. The importer then paid for the goods, however, a government inspector, checking the warehouse in July noticed that several of the cases of tomato paste had been recoppered and some cans resoldered. Therefore, the government retested the contents of the shipment and found an excessive amount of mold in the tomato paste.

We now describe the method of measuring the prevalence of mold, called the Howard mold count from the contents of a sample of cans. A small amount of duly mixed tomato paste is put on a slide with 25 fields of view, i.e., the slide is divided into 25 equal area units (like graph paper) and the percentage of the fields which contain mold filaments are calculated. A total of four slides or 100 fields are used to analyze the sample from any one can. It should be emphasized that this procedure does not estimate the total amount of mold, as the number of mold filaments in each field is not counted. Rather, it estimates a variable (number of fields with mold) that is highly correlated with the amount of mold and is easy to measure.

The counts on the 30 cans sampled by the government and the importer are reported in Table 9.3. The court noted that there was decomposed matter in all the cans sampled and that the *average* count exceeded the government's allowance of 40%.[29] The count averaged the 40 counts on the 30 sampled cans, obtaining 43.6%. In doing this, the court missed the fact that the ten cans in the government's post-seizure sample had two counts apiece and are *overweighted* in the overall average. Had the court used the average count of the two analysts as the estimate of the mold count in each of these ten cans, the *overall* average count would have been 41.6%. This difference of two counts might have been meaningful in a closer situation in which the first average had slightly exceeded the 40% allowance.

Another aspect of the government's post-seizure data is that the second analyst's counts are higher than the first one's. We will discuss methods of analysis of such matched data (two measurements on the same or similar item in Chapter 11). For now we simply note the appearance of a systematic measurement differential, which may be due in part to inadequate mixing of the sampled cans as well as differences between the analysts. With such a large discrepancy it would have been useful to have all the analysts count several identical slides to ascertain the degree of measurement error. The sampling procedure was not described in the opinion. Indeed, the sampling was judged to be fair because in the post-seizure sample the claimant selected a sample of ten cans and the govern-

TABLE 9.3. Howard Mold Count Data of the 30 Cans of Tomato Paste Sampled in *U.S. v. 499 Cases* etc.

U.S. Government Counts			
Sample Taken at Import	Sample Taken at time of Seizure	Post-Seizure Sample (Analyst I)	Post-Seizure Sample (Analyst II)
8	42	42	60
38	33	46	60
38	61	57	56
30		46	54
34		38	58
		48	70
		55	54
		27	44
		61	60
		12	44
Avg. 29.6	45.3	43.2	56.0

Claimant's Counts		
Sample Taken at Import	Sample of 10 cans Taken at Seizure	
38	42	24
	42	46
33	50	37
	37	38
	49	32
Avg. 35.5	39.7	

Source: The data are taken from the opinion 212 F.2d 567 at 574. It should be noted that the 10 cans in the government's post-seizure sample were analyzed by two separate analysts.

ment selected a can next to it. This may not be a wise procedure if one expects substantial variation in the mold counts among the various cases, as well as among the cans, since the cases would then be a cluster for sampling purposes.

An interesting aspect of the opinion is the dissent of Judge Frank, who pointed out that the government's approving the shipment first and then rejecting it was unfair to the importer who paid for the shipment after the first approval. Had the standard deviation of the mold count in the five cans the government checked at the time of importation been calculated ($s = 12.52$) it might have been realized that the 95% of two-sided confidence interval[30] for the true mean μ is 29.6 ± 2.78(6.0)

$$\text{or } 95\% \text{ CONF}(\mu; 12.92, 46.28)$$

contains 40 and is quite long. Thus, a larger sample should have been taken. Moreover, there is substantial variation among the analysts performing the counts, which also indicates that a larger sample should be examined at import.

The three cases we discussed in this section were chosen because they demonstrate that sampling methods have been accepted by courts for many years. For more recent information about the government's inspection and regulatory programs, we refer the reader to recent articles from the *Food, Drug and Cosmetic Law Journal.*

Problems

1.*   How might the sampling methodology used in the rye seed study be improved so as to withstand an explanation that every once in a while, by accident, one bag containing inferior seeds passes through the firm's quality control system and, if it happens to be among the bags sampled, the entire shipment appears mislabeled?

2.   From the sample data in *43-1/2 Gross,* form an approximate 95% upper confidence interval (one-sided) for the proportion of defective items. Repeat the calculation for the post-seizure Silver-Tex sample. Why is a one-sided upper confidence interval appropriate for public policy?

Answers to Selected Problems

1.   Rather than forming a *composite* sample of the sample from the eight bags, perhaps the samples from each bag should be sent. Then between 50 and 100 seeds from each bag should be analyzed. If this approach of testing 50 seeds from each bag were taken, the homogeneity check might need to allow a difference of 15% to 25% in the proportions, because *more* units (bags) are being sampled individually and a greater fluctuation in the percentages occurs because the sample size per bag is less than before.

5. Using Sampling Techniques to Determine Damages and Market Share

A fairly straightforward use of sampling techniques occurs in auditing payment vouchers if the audit is done promptly and the entire universe is available. A random sample of the vouchers can be taken and the sample average overpayment (or underpayment) multiplied by the total number, N, of vouchers can be used to estimate the total discrepancy. We describe a few applications and use the confidence intervals given by (9.3 or 9.4) to account for the fact that a substantial fraction of the population of vouchers or records may be sampled.

a. Illinois Physicians Union v. Miller.:[31] *auditing medical bills*

In July 1975, the Illinois Department of Public Services conducted a routine audit of the records of one of its participating doctors. From a total of 1302 records, a random sample of 353 were examined for discrepancies such as the department being billed for a service which was not listed on the patient's medical chart. The audit process found that the doctor had received an overpayment of $5018 or an average of

$$\frac{5018}{353} = \$14.215,$$

per payment and estimated the total overpayment by multiplying this average by the number of payments (1302), obtaining $18,508.[32]

The individual doctor and the medical association asserted that a complete audit of all 1302 records should have been conducted. The Seventh Circuit's opinion rejected this assertion noting that it was impractical for the department to audit every payment claim presented to it and cited another case which accepted similar sampling methods.

There are two interesting statistical aspects of this decision. Since the determination of any over- or underpayment takes the time of a knowledgeable auditor, a careful analysis of a sample of records may yield a more accurate estimate of the total due than a full scale audit. Indeed, in a related case[33] the court noted that a qualified medicare clerk conducted the study.

There is one medical reimbursement case, *Daytona Beach General Hospital Inc. v. Weinberger*[34] which rejected the estimation procedure because the audit was based on a 10% sample. The basic statistical issue, however, is the *accuracy of the estimate,* which depends on the *standard deviation* of the characteristic being studied in the population as well as the sample size. Thus, the major question should be how large is the estimated standard error of the mean, which we recall from (9.1) equals

$$(9.12) \qquad \frac{s}{\sqrt{n}} \sqrt{\frac{N-n}{N-n}},$$

relative to the estimated mean ($\bar{x}$). The ratio

$$(9.13) \qquad \frac{\left[\dfrac{s}{\sqrt{n}} \sqrt{\dfrac{N-n}{N-n}}\right]}{\bar{x}}$$

estimates the *coefficient of variation* (CV), which reflects the *relative accuracy* of the sample mean. It measures the precision of the sample mean ($\bar{x}$) as an estimate of the population mean (μ) by an analog of percentage error, the ratio of the standard error to the estimate ($\bar{x}$). Of course, the precision required varies with the application. For example, a CV of .15 is typically sought by the U.S. Bureau of the Census, while the Consumer Product Safety Commission requires a CV of .33 or less for its estimates of the number of accidents. In the present application involving a payment of funds, a CV of .05 or .10 might be desirable. Some courts and agencies[35] use the *lower* endpoint of the 95% confidence interval for the total as an estimate of the disallowed expenses, rather than the point estimate $N\bar{x}$, as the dollar figure that providers of medical services should reimburse the government. The rational for this is that the point estimate has a 50% chance of being too high (or too low), and it is unfair for a single provider to bear such a large risk of overpayment. For the government, which audits many providers, $N\bar{x}$ would be more appropriate, as the sampling variability would average out over all providers in that over the long run half the reimbursements the government would receive would be too low and half too high. From a statistical viewpoint the use of a two-sided 95% confidence interval really means that a provider has only a $2\frac{1}{2}\%$ chance (or probability of .025) of being asked to pay more than they owe. Perhaps the one-sided 95% confidence interval,

$$(9.14) \qquad \mu \geq \bar{x} - (1.645)\frac{s}{\sqrt{n}} \sqrt{\frac{N-n}{N-n}}$$

would be a fairer allocation of the errors inherent in the sampling process. The use of a confidence interval puts the burden of conducting an accurate sample on the state governments and provides an incentive for them to improve their sampling procedures.

b. Sears, Roebuck & Co. v. City of Inglewood: determining the amount of a tax refund

We next review the *Sears, Roebuck and Co. v. City of Ingelwood* case described by Sprowls.[36] The case involved a claim by Sears for a sales tax refund from the city, which imposed a sales tax of 1/2 of 1% on all sales made by stores within the city limits. However, sales made to persons not living in the city limits were not subject to tax. During a routine audit Sears noticed that it overpaid its tax because of an erroneous definition of what constituted an out of city sale.

To support its claim of a refund of $27,000, Sears conducted a random sample of sales slips for 33 of the 826 working days of the 11 quarter period. The sampling was done by randomly choosing three days per quarter in order to assure that all quarters were represented. The sales slips of these 11 days were classified as being to an in or out of city addresses by locating the address of the purchaser on a map of the surrounding area. The estimated fraction, p, of out of city sales to all sales was .3669 (or 36.7%) and a 95% confidence interval for p was

(9.15)   .367 ± .03   or   95% CONF(p;.337,.397).

Since Sears had paid the city about $76,975, its estimated overpayment was

$$.367 \times \$76,975 = \$28,250,$$

and a 95% confidence interval for the overpayment is obtained multiplying the total tax paid, $76,975, by the limits of the confidence interval (9.15) yielding

(9.16)   ($25,940, $30,559).

It should be mentioned that the original claim for a refund of $27,000 was not based on the probability sample which was taken later to buttress the claim.

Although testimony of accounting experts was presented to justify the use and acceptability of sampling methods in auditing, the judge did not accept the sample results because the sales tax return called for a sale by sale computation. He did permit Sears to make a complete audit, which yielded an overpayment of $26,750.22. This overpayment is slightly low due to missing sales slips for about one month. Even with this bias,[37] the complete audit yielded a value inside the 95% confidence interval (9.16), and the overpayment based on the complete audit agrees well with the original claim.

The major advantage of the sampling procedure is saving time and money. The complete audit required 3384 person-hours, an expense of about $3500, in contrast with 300 hours and an approximate cost of $475 for the sample. An implicit advantage of sampling is that due to cost considerations more qualified personnel can be employed to check the records from a sample than can be used to perform a complete audit. In this and other situations, a well designed sampling audit may yield a more accurate estimate than a less carefully carried out complete audit or census.

c. U.S. v. United Shoe Machinery Corp.:[38] *determination of market dominance in an antitrust case*

In this case, the market share United Shoe Machinery Corporation (USMC) held for a wide variety of machines used in the shoe industry was an issue. Although the firm itself had reports from its own agents about its fraction of the market of the various machines, the judge suggested that the government obtain data on the make of the machines used by shoe manufacturers from a sample of the manufacturers.

The judge made up an approximate random sample by taking a directory of manufacturers and suggesting that the following firms compose the sample:

The first 15 whose names begin with A, the first letter of the alphabet.
The first 15 whose names begin with the 11th letter of the alphabet.
All 8 whose names begin with the 21st letter of the alphabet.
The first 7 whose names begin with the 22nd letter of the alphabet.

While the sample is not a true random sample in the sense that each manufacturer was not assigned a number, such as in its alphabetic order, and a random set of 41 numbers selected out of the total, in all likelihood it was approximately random, as the alphabetical list of manufacturers should not be related to the brand of machine they use. There is, however, a form of clustering inherent in this sampling procedure, namely data was collected on over 2000 machines used by 41 firms. Since a firm would often purchase several machines of the same type, presumably from the same manufacturer, one should not use the number of machines as the sample size n. We will be very cautious in our discussion and assume that each company buys all its machines of a specific type from the same manufacturer and use $n = 41$ in our calculations.

In Table 9.4 we reproduce the sample estimates of the market share (in fractions, rather than percentages) USMC held for ten of the categories of machinery as well as the data USMC had obtained from its representatives two years earlier. Notice that there is a general agreement. The only category in which the 95% two-sided confidence interval derived from the sample fails to contain USMC's count is for cement machines, where the confidence interval is

$$\bar{p} \pm (1.96) \frac{\sqrt{\bar{p}(1 - \bar{p})}}{\sqrt{n}} = .41 \pm (1.96) \frac{\sqrt{(.41)(.59)}}{\sqrt{41}}$$

(9.17)

$$= .41 \pm .151, \quad \text{or } 95\% \text{ CONF}(p; .26, .56),$$

which does not include .63. This is not surprising, as one should not expect all ten 95% confidence intervals to be perfect, especially as two

TABLE 9.4. Comparison of USMC's Data on its Market Share with Subsequent Sample for 10 Types of Machines

Machine Type	USMC data as of 5/1/47			Judges Sample, 1949		
	USMC	TOTAL	Fraction Made by USMC	USMC	TOTAL	Fraction Made by USMC
1. Clicking	16,346	16,885	.97	568	578	.98
5. Lasting	12,561	13,357	.94	403	420	.96
6. Welt	1,470	1,510	.97	36	36	1.00
10. Outsole stitching	3,537	3,846	.98	100	104	.96
17. Heel attaching	3,168	3,398	.93	110	116	.95
19. Cement	3,415	5,525	.63	95	234	.41
22. Fitting room	13,555	23,285	.58	587	1,313	.45
23. General	19,416	27,197	.71	993	1,305	.76
24. Goodyear	7,722	8,797	.88	191	229	.83
29. Pulling over	4,138	4,276	.97	160	167	.96

Source: 110 F.Supp. 295(1953) at 305-6.

years separated the data collections and recently purchased machines undoubtedly replaced some older ones counted in USMCs data. Moreover, the sample estimate differed from the firm's data by less than .03 in six types, exceeded .03 in one type and was below .03 in three types, which reflects a general consistency in both data sets. We used the margin of .03 to allow for the inherent discreteness of the sample fractions or percentages. Had we just counted whether the sample fraction was above or below USMCs fraction, we would find it exceeded USMCs for five of the ten types in Table 9.4. A similar analysis of the full set of 30 machine types used in the case also leads to the conclusion that the sample was proper.

The judge (at p. 307 of the opinion) summarized the data as follows: "In short it is not inaccurate in this market to say United has a 75–95% share, and it probably would be accurate to say an approximately 85% share". It is interesting to note that in this case Judge Wyzanski is allowing for sampling error in his conclusion and suggests that a proper confidence interval should be presented when possible. Only if several adjacent (alphabetically) manufacturers were related, e.g., subsidiaries of the same large firm, could the judge's sample be quite unrepresentative, as firms with the same parent firm may be more likely to purchase the same type of machine.

d.   *Hamilton v. United States:*[39] *estimation of the tax on wagering owed the IRS*

The U.S. Government levied a tax of $385,491.71 on Hamilton for failure to pay the 10% excise tax on wagers he allegedly handled during the period July 1, 1961 to May 21, 1965. The plaintiff filed suit to enjoin the government from collecting the tax assessment. The statistical aspects of the case concerned the determination of the assessment.

Although the law[40] provided that each person liable for the tax should keep a daily record of the gross amount of wages they handle, the plaintiff had not kept such a record. Thus, the only available data were for the three-day period May 19–21, 1965, which were seized subject to a search warrant. All the three days data for the "3 digit number" bets totaling $5715.99 and two days of complete data for "single action slips" totaling $1077.40 were seized. Thus, the daily averages of the two types of wagers were

$$\frac{5715.99}{3} = \$1905.33 \quad \text{and} \quad \frac{1077.40}{2} = \$538.70.$$

The government estimated the average daily wagering amount as their sum, $2443.03 and multiplied it by the number of days (six per week) for the time Hamilton admitted he accepted wagers, to project a total amount of wagering activity of $2,883,955, 10% of which, plus interest, etc., was owed the government.

Judge Mansfield noted that using the average revenues for a three-day period would not necessarily be representative of the plaintiff's business for the four-year period, however, such a projection was not arbitrary or irrational. Furthermore, he emphasized that the method had to be used because the plaintiff had failed to keep the required records and cited several cases where previous courts accepted similar calculations from incomplete records.

Had the plaintiff kept reasonable records, one probably would have simply added all the daily totals to determine the total daily wagers. If the daily receipts had not been totaled, i.e., all wagers were listed, then a sample of days could be taken. A proper approach would be similar to the one used in *Sears*, where a few days from each month would be selected. This has the advantage of accounting for seasonal fluctuations in receipts, which are very important in retail trade (Christmas) but might also occur in wagering activity. Indeed, a similar calculation of a wagering tax assessment was not accepted in *U.S. v. Washington*[41] because the seasonal pattern was not incorporated.

The decision in *Hamilton* and similar cases, e.g., *Pinder v. U.S.*,[42] to rely on an incomplete or small nonrandom sample when one party fails to preserve the basic data, is not unreasonable. Because gambling may be illegal, the destruction of records is inherent in the wagering operation, so a proper sample could never be obtained. This topic leads us to think about the effect missing data or incomplete data may have on statistical inferences derived from samples or surveys in other applications, which we discuss in the next section.

6. The Problems of Nonresponse and Missing Data

Suppose a sample is properly designed as a probability sample of the relevant population and letters or calls made to potential human respondents, or the randomly selected records requested from the holder of an administrative file. Can we simply accept the questionnaires or records returned and routinely apply statistical techniques and form conclusions from the data? The answer depends on how large a proportion of the *designated* sample responds (or desired records are available) and on the characteristics of the nonrespondents.

a. The potential effect of nonresponse on the accuracy of statistical estimates

Most of the discussion of the bias that nonresponse can introduce into generalizations derived from a sample will be in terms of the *difference* between the nonrespondents and respondents, and the nonrespondent *proportion* of the desired sample. The reason for this can be seen if we subdivide the population into potential respondents (containing $100p\%$ of the population) and nonrespondents (forming $100(1 - p)\%$). Assume that the *means* of the two groups in the population are μ_1 and μ_2, respectively. Thus, the overall mean of the population which we are trying to estimate is

$$(9.18) \qquad \mu = p\mu_1 + (1 - p)\mu_2.$$

Suppose our sample perfectly reflects this situation so that our sample mean, $\bar{x}_1$, actually equals μ_1 (the mean of the potential respondents). Then the difference between the sample mean ($\bar{x}_1$) and the true population mean μ is

$$(9.19) \qquad \bar{x}_1 - \mu_1 = \mu_1 - \mu = (1 - p)(\mu_1 - \mu_2).$$

The difference (9.19) is the *bias* or expected difference between the sample mean derived from the respondents and the overall population mean. Notice that it is the *product* of the *fraction* $(1 - p)$ of the population who are nonrespondents and the difference $\mu_1 - \mu_2$ between the means of the respondents and nonrespondents. Thus, there is a trade-off between the magnitude of the difference between the true means of the nonrespondents and respondents that is tolerable and the proportion of nonresponse. In particular, when the pattern of nonresponse and missing data (e.g., some questions are not answered) is completely random, implying that $\mu_2 = \mu_1$, one can consider the responses as a random sample of smaller size than originally desired. However, one must learn the reasons for or causes of the nonresponse to be sure that the proportion and characteristics of nonrespondents do not bias the ultimate statistical inference. In this section we discuss some of the reasons for nonresponse and present some general guidelines which should assist the readers in evaluating the reliability of inferences drawn from sample data. Then these guidelines are applied to data introduced in several cases.

Although samples of administrative records or of human populations are subject to the same statistical requirement of representativeness of the population studied, the reason for nonresponse or missing items often differ. When sampling people, some common reasons for nonresponse are

(1) A potential respondent simply forgets to answer a mail survey or loses the questionnaire.

(2) The person is unavailable, e.g., is in a hospital, on vacation, etc.

(3) The person is not at home when contacted, and the interviewer cannot obtain information from a family member or neighbor as to a more appropriate time to contact the desired respondent.

(4) A potential respondent refuses to answer a particular question.

Notice that while the first reason is likely to be randomly distributed over the population, the second and third reasons appear to be random but may affect the usefulness of the survey if they apply to a significant fraction of the original sample. For example, wealthier persons are more likely to be on extended vacations than the average person. The third reason is more likely to apply to single persons (living alone) than to persons residing in a family or group quarters. Indeed singles typically have three times the "not at home" rate in U.S. Bureau of the Census surveys as family members. Thus, one needs to assess the degree of nonresponse and the possible relationship of the characteristics of the nonrespondents to the purpose of the survey. The fourth category, refusals, often are not typical members of the universe, so when they form a moderate fraction of the desired sample a serious bias may result. For instance, in surveys of income, both the lower and upper income groups have higher refusal rates than the middle class. This is especially true for nonwage income, e.g., unemployment insurance and welfare payments in lower income households and interest and dividend income for upper income households. Failing to account for this could lead one to underestimate both the average income and the variation among incomes in an area.

When sampling administrative records, nonresponse and missing entries often arise from lost or damaged records and illegible entries. A related problem can stem from erroneous entries. These may be difficult to correct in administrative files if the original data was collected several years prior to the time the sample is taken. If possible and proper, one should take a small sample of records and check the information in them with another source, e.g., the individual who filled out the form.

Since a substantial degree of nonresponse and/or missing data introduces the possibility of significant biases in the data, with a consequent decrease in the reliability of any conclusions drawn, before making the assumption that an incomplete sample can be treated as a truly representative random sample one should check that the respondents' characteristics reflect those of the entire population, the proportion of refusals was small and that the overall proportion of nonresponse was not too large. While one cannot guarantee with certainty that data satisfying these requirements is truly a random sample, experience has shown that such samples are reliable.

In order to quantify the concept of a tolerable level of nonresponse, we shall rely, in part, on the guidelines for statistical surveys issued by the former Office of Statistical Standards of the U.S. Government. Before an agency could sponsor a survey it had to state that a response rate of 75% or more was expected. If a lower response rate was expected, a special justification of the usefulness of the survey results was required. Rarely, would surveys with an expected response rate of less than 50% be cleared (allowed to be carried out).

In general, samples with response rates of 90% or more are quite reliable, and one can treat them as random samples of the overall population. Response rates in the 75% to 90% range usually yield reliable results, but checks of the representativeness of the sample should be made. Estimates from samples with response rates in the 50% to 75% range have potentially far greater bias, and the representativeness of such sample data should be checked carefully. It is especially important that the sample be representative with respect to characteristics likely to affect the subject under study (e.g., race and sex and occupational mix in an employment discrimination case, the spectrum of property values in a jurisdiction in a tax-equity case). Estimates from samples with less than a 50% response rate should be regarded with *much caution*. Not only should representativeness be checked, but documentation that such low levels of response are usual in that type of survey and experience has shown that the pattern of nonresponse is likely to be random, should be provided.

One way to enhance the acceptability of samples with a high nonresponse rate is to conduct a further survey of the nonrespondents and show that

(a) the results of the old and new survey agree, so both samples can be combined, and

(b) the characteristics of the respondents are representative of the general population.

This is not always feasible because most surveys send a follow-up mailing (or interviewer) to nonrespondents so that obtaining a reasonable response rate from the nonrespondents may require an inordinate amount of effort, e.g., visits by interviewers rather than phone calls or mail.

Since the guidelines concerning nonresponse and missing data were developed primarily from experience with sample surveys conducted at a fixed time, one must be careful in using them when data for several years is being combined into one sample. Unless the random pattern of nonresponse or missing data is constant over all years of data, one may be misled when time plays a role in the analysis, even though a relatively small fraction (15%) of the total data is missing.

Let us consider the effect of two types of patterns of missing data on hypothetical data on new hires during a three-year period in an employment discrimination case where the data will be used to study equal pay and promotion issues. In Table 9.5 we present the data for three years. Pattern A of attrition corresponds to about a 20% attrition rate in each year (i.e., 40% of the hires in the first year have left by the end of the third year, 20% of the hires in the second year left, while none of the current year's hires have left). The attrition pattern B arises from females leaving at a high rate (80%) early in the period and leaving at a lower rate later, due to the fact that the firm opened up more opportunities to women in the middle of the second year. In pattern B, we assume that the same fraction (84.4%) of the males hired in each year still are employed so that the same fraction of new hires of each sex, during the entire period, are currently employed.

Notice that the pure random attrition pattern A led to a slightly higher proportion of females among currently employed persons because their share of new hires increased sharply during the period. On the other hand,

TABLE 9.5. Hypothetical Hiring and Remaining Data, by Sex, under Two Patterns of Attrition

	Hired			Remaining (A)			Remaining (B)		
	F|	M|	%F	F	M	%F	F	M	%F
Year 1	10	90	10.0	6	54	10.0	2	76	2.56
Year 2	30	70	30.0	24	56	30.0	24	59	28.92
Year 3	50	50	50.0	50	50	50.0	50	42	64.35
Total	90	210	30.0	80	160	33.3%	76	177	30.04

if employees were legitimately required to have two years of experience before being promoted, so that persons hired in the first year remaining in the work force is the appropriate group to use to study the promotion issue, as the attrition pattern A was the same for both sexes. In contrast, pattern B, although yielding about the same fraction of females in the remaining data (currently employed) as they were in the overall hiring data, contains a biased sample of employees hired two years earlier, as the female share of such employees (now eligible for promotion) has decreased from 10% to 2.6%. Similarly, a pay study using seniority as a factor could also be biased by the missing data in pattern B. When faced with a pattern of nonresponse or missing data which varies differently over time for relevant subgroups of the study population, one should assess its affect on a planned study and also attempt to understand why the patterns differ. In our hypothetical example, if a change in the firm's hiring and promotion practices could be substantiated (e.g., a charge was filed in the middle of the second year, and the female share of new hires and promotions increased sharply soon after) then one should not pool the pre- and post-charge data into one sample to study the firm's employment practices. If pattern B occurred for other reasons, e.g., by coincidence more of the women hires left the area for personal reasons, we could not infer that the firm's past practices caused the higher female attrition rate in the early period. The remaining sample, with only two females, would probably be too small for an analysis of the promotion issue.

To summarize, in order for a statistical study based on a portion of a desired random sample or population to be valid, the pattern of nonresponse and/or missing data should be the same for all subgroups in each relevant time period and be independent of the issue(s) under study. Since most real data sets are not perfect random samples in practice, one should not ignore imperfect data but should assess the seriousness of the problem and its potential effect on the ultimate statistical conclusion.

b. Examples of judicial treatment of nonresponse and missing data

A careful and thoughtful discussion of the issue of missing data appears in *Vuyanich v. R.N.B*,[43] a race and sex discrimination case in which both sides challenged the validity and reliability of the data used by the opposite side. Judge Higgenbotham noted that a heavy burden must be met before a statistical analysis should be totally rejected on the basis of errors or omissions in the data. Rather, the weight given the conclusions should be affected by any deficiencies in the data, and the party challenging the data should demonstrate that the errors and omissions are not distributed randomly and that they introduce a bias which has a meaningful impact on the statistical inferences drawn from the data.

In the opinion, the judge cited checks of representativeness. He noted that blacks formed 11.7% of all nonexempt employees and 10.24% of those employees whose records had some data missing. Using similar comparisons he concluded that the errors appeared to be randomly distributed among all races and sexes.

On the other hand, the educational data in the case had a greater percentage of errors (averaging 27%) and omissions (about 10%) so that more care had to be used in evaluating studies based on this characteristic. However, since 59% of all files were present and contained correct data, the deficiencies were not serious enough to warrant completely disregarding analyses using the educational data, especially as the proportions of employees of each race and sex category whose educational data was unavailable for use were similar.

Another example of the proper use of these statistical guidelines and checks occurred in *Rosado v. Wyman.*[44] The Supreme Court had remanded the case, which involved the level of welfare payments in New York State for a determination of the monetary value of about 20 special services which the state no longer provided welfare recipients so that their checks would be increased by the appropriate amount, and the Court had recommended that this amount be determined by statistical averaging. Since the total population contained 186,629 records it was decided to determine the average due from a random sample of 5344 records. Since there was an appreciable time lapse between the time of the original complaint and the taking of the sample, only 3343 (62.6%) records were found to be usable and complete. Judge Weinstein noted that the average payment and distribution of recipient family size in the sample approximated those known characteristics of the whole population and properly accepted the sample as valid.

It is important to emphasize that, in both of the above cases, the response rate was in the 50% to 75% region, requiring more care, and the judges checked the sample to assure its representativeness with respect to the factors at issue. Moreover, in the *Rosado,* case one began with a properly designed random sample, and the major reason for the unavailability of data was due to the passage of time, which should have an approximately random character and not introduce a serious bias.

In *EEOC v. Eagle Iron Works,*[45] Judge Stuart rejected statistical data which constituted 60% (1200 of 2000) of current and former employees, as *all* the missing racial data was for former employees (the race of only 55% of whom was known). A major issue in the case was whether blacks were assigned to foundry work (a less desirable job than work in the fab shop) due to their race, and the judge noted that the racially identified formed a much higher percentage of foundary workers than fab shop workers. Thus, the pattern of missing data was related to the issue under study and the judge was properly skeptical of an expert who gave the data more reliability than would most statisticians.

The possible impact of criticisms of data was shown to have a minor effect on the conclusions in *Douglas v. Hampton*.[46] The case concerned the racial impact of the federal employment exam, and the application forms did not ask for racial identification. Plaintiffs introduced a study which compared the pass-fail rates of applicants from predominantly black colleges to those from predominantly white colleges. The difference in pass rates was quite large, 11.5% for blacks versus 57.8% for whites, where a school was classified as black or white if 99% or more of its students were of one race. Although applicants from such schools formed only one third of all applicants, the large difference in pass rates clearly was relevant. Moreover, the opinion noted that even if 10% of the students from black colleges who took the exam were white and all failed, the pass rate for blacks would only be increased to 12.8%, so the difference in pass rates would still be substantial. This type of calculation is very useful in appraising whether an alleged defect in the data, in this instance, possible misidentification of an applicant's race due to the use of college attendance as proxy for it, could seriously affect the ultimate statistical inference.

The opinion in *McCarther v. Camelot Inn*,[47] emphasized the deficiencies in sampling procedures and noted that it is absolutely essential that the starting point for such a sampling technique be chosen on a random basis. Furthermore, the opinion noted that checking a sample already improperly drawn against certain known characteristics cannot have the effect of verifying that the sample is representative. This view is probably too strong, although any nonrandom sampling procedure must be examined carefully to make sure that it does not contain hidden biases, and the possible effects of missing data need to be assessed. The data rejected by Judge Eisele in *McCarther* suffered from ambiguous definitions and exclusion of a large number of unclassified persons, in addition to not having been selected according to a probability (random) mechanism. In such race discrimination cases, the existence of a large number of racially unidentified employees or applicants, combined with possible misclassification of an applicant's race, can affect the ultimate statistical conclusion, especially in statistically close situations.

In *Bristol Myers v. F.T.C*[48] the Federal Trade Commission ordered the company to cease advertising that "twice as many dentists use Ipana as another dentifrice" as well as that more dentists recommend Ipana than any other dentifrice because these claims were not supportable by the survey they were based on and would convey a misleading impression to the typical consumer about the dental profession's support of the brand. Bristol Meyers asked a random sample of 10,000 dentists from a population of 66,000 subscribers to two dental magazines which toothpaste they used and which one(s) they recommended to their patients. Of the 10,000 only 1983 answered the questionnaire. Of these, 621 said they used Ipana while 258 used the second most frequently mentioned brand. Similarly, 461 dentists recommended Ipana in contrast to the 195, 125, 106 and 94 recommendations of the next four brands. Although the advertising claims were derived from the survey results, the F.T.C action was upheld because the 20% response rate clearly indicated the survey's inadequacy. A question that was not raised was the adequacy of the *frame*, subscribers to two magazines. What fraction of all dentists subscribed to the magazines? If a substantial portion of dentists did not subscribe to either magazine, then their characteristics (income, geographic location) should be compared with those sampled to assess whether the frame could be regarded as a representative sample of all dentists. Finally, we note that a follow-up study of the nonrespondents does not appear to have been conducted.

c. The most conservative treatment of missing data

Sometimes one can still draw valid inferences by assuming that the missing data were distributed in the *least favorable* manner (for a proponents desired conclusion). We give an example of this technique as used in *Berger v. Ironworkers, Local 201*[49] The case involved alleged discrimination against blacks who desired to become union members.

One issue concerned the admission rate of persons with the requisite experience. Although two different experience criteria were used in the case, we report the admission rate of all persons with 2500 hours of experience at the times the union took in new members from June 1971 through October 1972 in Table 9.6. Using the test statistic (5.6) for a difference between proportions on the 139 persons whose race was known in Table 9.6, yields a Z of -3.87 or a p-value of .0001. To make

TABLE 9.6. Admission Rates of Persons with 2500
Hours of On-the-Job Experience, by
Race, from *Berger v. Ironworkers*

Race	Accepted	Not	Total	% Accepted
White	24	39	63	38.10
Black	7	69	76	9.21
Unknown	0	14	14	0.0

Source: The author's copy of one of the exhibits the plaintiffs placed into evidence at the trial.

sure that the missing data could not explain this difference or reduce it to
statistical insignificance, the plaintiffs assumed that all 14 persons whose
racial data missing were white, as none of them were admitted into the
union. By doing this the white admission rate was made as small as
possible. The resulting 2 × 2 table is given in Table 9.7. The same statistical test yielded Z of -3.18, which remained significant (p value $= .0015$)
at the usual .05 level (one or two-sided).

This method of allocating the missing data in the least favorable way is
ultraconservative or safe. Unless there is reason to assume that the missing data differs substantially from the available data, it is preferable to
analyze the available data. Another possibility is to make a probability
model for the missing data. In the present situation one might feel, if the
union staff (primarily white) was making the racial identifications, that a
higher proportion of the missing data were black than white because the
staff would have been less likely to meet and socialize with black workers. Of course, when the least favorable allocation yields a significant
result, a great deal of potential argument about the composition of the
missing data is avoided.

TABLE 9.7. Least Favorable Allocation for the Plaintiffs of the Persons for whom Race was
Unknown for the Data in Table 9.6

Race	Accepted	Not	Total	% Accepted
White	24	53	77	31.17
Black	7	69	76	9.21
Total	31	122	153	20.26

7. The Use of Survey Evidence in Lanham Act Cases

The use of a trademark can constitute a violation of the Lanham Trademark Act when it is so similar to a trademark already used by another
company that potential purchasers could believe that the goods or services come from the same source. According to McCarthy (1973 at p.
524), in order to prevail on a claim of unfair competition based on an
unregistered trademark the plaintiff (the firm claiming that its mark was
infringed upon) must prove:

> (1) that the public recognizes plaintiff's symbol as identifying his goods or
> services and distinguishes them from those of others, and (2) that defen-
> dant's actions cause a likelihood of confusion among the relevant buyer
> class. (a) that (1) [can] be shown in either of two ways: (a) that plaintiff's
> symbol was inherently distinctive or (b) that even if not inherently distinc-
> tive, the symbol achieved customer recognition and 'secondary meaning'.

A "secondary meaning" is acquired by a trademark when, because· of
extensive use and advertising, the public has come to identify a particular
product or service with a particular source.[50]
   Carefully designed sample surveys can provide evidence that potential
customers are likely to be confused by asking them to distinguish the
original product from the alleged infringer. Before we discuss three cases
illustrating the usefulness of surveys in establishing the likelihood of confusion as to source, that a name is understood as a brand name or that an
advertisement is misleading, it should be emphasized that the criteria
used in these cases differs slightly among the circuits. For example, the
Sixth Circuit uses the following eight factors

(1) strength of the trademark
(2) relatedness of the mark
(3) similarity of the goods
(4) evidence of actual confusion
(5) marketing channels used
(6) likely degree of purchaser use
(7) defendants intent in selecting the mark
(8) likelihood of plaintiff's expansion of the product lines.

While the first five criteria appear to be used in most circuits, the sixth
(purchaser care) was not among those used by the Fifth Circuit.[51] This
factor is important when designing a survey as the universe should repre-

sent the ''reasonably prudent buyer'' or ''ordinary purchasers buying with ordinary caution''.[52] Of course, the frequency with which a product is purchased, as well as its price, are factors which can be considered in deciding upon the level of care or thought a customer is likely to give to a purchase. The product itself may appeal to specialists (sophisticated home computers or tools) or to relatively inexperienced consumers (children's toys). When the potential purchasers are not clearly defined; e.g., the item is often bought as a gift,[53] it is helpful to survey a subpopulation of likely potential buyers in addition to the general public. This is accomplished by oversampling this subgroup. One method of showing customer confusion is to present survey evidence indicating that people associate the two trademarks with the same company or product, e.g., upon seeing the new trademark a significant portion of the survey believe the new product is the old one. Similarly, secondary meaning is indicated when the respondents believe that the product is made by or authorized by the producer of the original item. In assessing survey evidence the courts have focused on whether the sample is representative of the appropriate universe (potential consumers of the product) and whether the questions were properly designed and asked. Eight criteria typically used by courts and listed in the *Handbook of Recommended Procedures for the Trial of Protracted Cases* are:

> (1) that the proper universe was selected and examined; (2) a representative sample was drawn from that universe; (3) a fair and correct method of questioning the interviewees was used; (4) the persons conducting the survey were recognized experts; (5) the data gathered was accurately reported; (6) the sample, the questionnaire and the interviewing were in accordance with generally accepted standards of objective procedure and statistics in the field of such surveys; (7) the sample and the interviews were conducted independently of the attorneys in the case; (8) the interviewers were adequately trained in the field and had no knowledge of the litigation purposes for which the survey was to be used.

We now illustrate the use of survey evidence in establishing the likelihood of confusion in two cases from the Fifth Circuit which approved the use of the above eight criteria in *Amstar Corp. v. Domino's Pizza, Inc.* 615 F.2d 252 at 264 (5th Cir. 1980).

An example of a statistically valid survey is the one introduced by Exxon[54] when it sued a Texas auto repair company. The court noted that while the retail outlets differed there was a strong similarity in the customers of both concerns, the driving public. Since a technically proper frame (list of all drivers) was not available, Exxon interviewed 515 individuals between 10 a.m. and 6 p.m. at two high-traffic shopping centers on four days. All persons interviewed were licensed drivers, and all age groups and a wide variety of occupations were represented. Since 15% of the respondents associated the *Texon* sign with Exxon and another 23% associated it with gasoline, a gas station or an oil company, while only 7% mentioned the defendant's business the court concluded that the survey constituted strong evidence indicating a likelihood of confusion. In Exhibit 9.2 we reproduce the survey form. Notice that the form was designed not only to obtain the answer to the question at issue, whether there was a likelihood of confusing the two trademarks, but also to enable us to check its statistical validity. Moreover, the proportion of nonrespondents (refusals) could be obtained as well as the demographic characteristics of the respondents. This information enabled Exxon's expert witness to check that the sample was a representative one and that the missing data (nonrespondents) did not reach a level that could seriously affect the results.

In *Amstar Corp. v. Domino's Pizza Inc.,*[55] the Fifth Circuit overturned a finding of trademark infringement, in part, due to the inadequacy of plaintiff's survey. The plaintiff, producers of Domino sugar, attempted to show that the public might believe that Domino's Pizza was related to their line of products by conducting a survey of females who were responsible for making food purchases for their household. Each respondent was shown a Domino's Pizza box and was asked if she believed the company that made the pizza made any other product. If she answered yes, she was asked what other products were made by the company? Seventy-one percent of those answering the second question said sugar. However, there were three serious flaws with the survey. While housewives form the major portion of the purchasers of sugar in grocery stores, the primary customers of the pizza parlors are young, single, high school and college students. Thus, the sample introduced by the plaintiff excluded the persons most likely to purchase the defendant's product. Secondly, the survey was conducted in ten cities, eight of which had no Domino Pizza store so that most of the women sampled did not have an opportunity to see the defendant's mark, although they had been repeatedly exposed to plaintiff's mark. The third flaw was in the questionnaire design, as persons were asked whether the Domino Pizza mark brought anything else to mind, and thus it was more like a word association test. The questionnaire in the *Exxon* case did more than simply ask what the photograph of defendants sign brought to mind. A follow-up question attempted to find out what aspect of the sign caused the response. Thus, one could ascertain that a common property of both signs or marks caused the respondent's answer.

Many of the surveys introduced in trademark cases have been found inadequate by courts. Their major shortcoming has often been their fail-

---

EXHIBIT 9.2.   The Questionnaire Used by Exxon

COMPANY RECOGNITION STUDY

Hello, I'm _____ with Houston Interviewing a national marketing research and public opinion organization. We're conducting a research study of people's reactions to company logo's and signs. Are you a licensed driver and do you drive a car or truck? (IF NO, TERMINATE AND TALLY. IF YES, ASK . . . . .)

No _____
(Tally)

1a.   Are you . . .
         (READ)   Under 25   ( )
                  25–34   ( )
                  35–44   ( )
                  45–54   ( )
                  55 and over   ( )

1b.   (SIGHT CHECK)   Sex . . .
                  Male   ( )
                  Female   ( )

1c.   And, what is your occupation?
         Industry _____
         Job Title _____
         (ASK RESPONDENT TO PARTICIPATE IN THE STUDY AND TO COMPLETE THE INTERVIEW)

Refused _____
(Tally)

2a.   (SHOW RESPONDENT PHOTOGRAPH AND ASK . . . .)

First, would you please look at this photograph. Take as much time as you need and I'll ask you some questions.

What is the first thing that comes to mind when looking at this sign? (RECORD VERBATIM)

_____
_____
_____

EXHIBIT 9.2. (*Continued*)

2b. What was there about the sign that made you say that? (PROBE FULLY)

_____

_____

_____

3a. (IF A COMPANY NAME IS *NOT* MEN-TIONED IN QUESTION 2, ASK QUES-TION 3a. IF A COMPANY NAME *IS* MENTIONED, SKIP TO QUESTION 3b.)

What is the first *company* that comes to mind when you look at this sign? (RECORD NAME EXACTLY AS RESPONDENT STATES IT)

_____

3b. What was there about the sign that made you mention (COMPANY) ? (CLARIFY AND PROBE FULLY)

_____

_____

_____

Source: 628 F.2d (1980) 500 at 508.

ure to represent the *appropriate universe,* the potential or likely customers of the goods or services at issue. Poor questionnaire design that does not obtain the cause of the confusion or incorrect association (which should be the similarity in the trademarks if there is infringement) and does not ask for sufficient information to enable one to check that the sample is reasonably representative of the desired population are other common errors. On the other hand, some well designed surveys, using probability based sampling methods and questions focusing on the point at issue, have helped convince judges that trademark infringement has occurred.

We now discuss survey evidence from three cases. The first one discusses the use of survey evidence demonstrating that a name or trademark is associated with a particular product line and is not a common or generic[56] term as well as in assessing the likelihood of confusion. The serious flaws of a survey introduced to show secondary meaning leading to a likelihood of confusion are discussed in detail in the second case. Since the Lanham Act also prohibits misleading or deceptive advertising, the third case shows how a proper survey helped establish that an advertisement was misleading.

a. Dupont v. Yoshida:[57] The use of a survey to assess the likelihood of confusion and determine whether a name had become generic

In this case the plaintiff, Dupont, alleged that product named EFLON made by Yoshida's subsidiary, YKK Zipper, infringed on its trademark TEFLON for its nonstick products (cookware). Because the products were not similar and Dupont and YKK were not competitors in any product market related to the case, the scope of the protection of a trademark against an allegedly confusing similar mark was at issue. Therefore the gravamen of this action was whether YKK's mark, EFLON, was likely to cause confusion or mislead purchasers of the zippers as to the *source* or *origin* of the goods.

The criterion used in such cases in the Second Circuit originally were listed in Judge Friendly's opinion in *Polaroid v. Polarad Electronics*[58] and are listed below:

(1) strength of the mark
(2) degree of similarity of the marks
(3) proximity of the products
(4) the likelihood that the owner will bridge the gap (i.e., enter the alleged infringers market)
(5) actual confusion
(6) defendant's good faith in adopting the mark
(7) quality of defendant's product
(8) sophistication of the buyers of the product.

Notice that they are similar to the criteria used in the Sixth Circuit.

The opinion noted that to assess the fourth factor, the criteria is whether the ordinary purchaser could assume such a business expansion rather than the actual plans of the plaintiff. Since TEFLON was used in spacesuit zippers, it was reasonable to assume that it might be commercially usable to ease zipper sticking problems.

Dupont introduced the results of a random sample of 801 women, interviewed in their homes, all of whom had done some home sewing during the previous year, and 480 (59.9%) had purchased a zipper at retail in the past year. After answering basic demographic questions the women who had done some home sewing were shown a card which read

LAVORIS
EFLON
DRISTAN

and then asked:

(a) Describe the product.

(b) What does it remind you of (asked of those who did not respond to a)?

(c) Well, what do you think the product would be like? (asked only about EFLON).

Although only 6.6% of the respondents gave a TEFLON brand name or product-related identification in answering (a); when asked (b) an additional 26.5% of the respondents made such an identification indicating a possible confusion of product source in about 30% of the potential consumers. The defendant criticized the survey on the grounds that

(1) the responses were insufficient (numerically) and associational in nature and

(2) the interviews were not conducted in a purchasing environment.

The court concluded that the TEFLON mark or its nonstick features are fairly well known to a substantial minority of prospective zipper purchasers when confronted with the mark in a home environment.[59] Because the mark, TEFLON was a strong trademark deserving broad protection,[60] the high degree of similarity of the marks and the fact that zippers are bought infrequently by a homemaker, who would be expected to make such a purchase with relatively little scrutiny, the survey results were relevant as they indicated that a sizable fraction of purchasers might be confused as to the source of the item. Hence, the court found that the EFLON mark infringed on Dupont's.

Then the court turned to YKK's last defense, its assertion that TEFLON was generic. In order to document its claim YKK had to show that "*to the consuming public as a whole* the word has lost all to trademark significance." In its survey of adult women (90.6% of whom were aware of the existence of stick-free kitchen pots and pans), YKK asked the "aware" respondents:

(a) What is the name or names of these pots and pans?

(b) What name they would use to describe the pots and pans to a store clerk or friend.

Eighty-six percent of this group answered TEFLON or TEFLON II to question (a) and about 72% answered TEFLON or TEFLON II to (b). In contrast, only 7% of the "aware" respondents named Dupont as the manufacturer.

To counter the implication of YKK's survey, Dupont conducted two surveys. The first one described the fact that protective coatings were sometimes applied to household utensils to prevent food and grease from sticking to them and then asked, "Do you know a brand name or trademark for one of these coatings?" Those who said yes, were asked, "What is the brand name or trademark?" Of the 60% of all respondents who reached this last question, 80% answered TEFLON.

A second study first described the difference between a common (generic) name and a brand name using the example of automobile (car) as a common name in contrast with Chevrolet and then asked the respondent to classify eight product names as common or brand. The results given in Table 9.8 indicate that 68% of the respondents identified TEFLON as a brand name.

The court noted that the Dupont's second survey focused on the critical issue of the case, the way the general public understood the name TEFLON, and stated that "the public is quite good at sorting out brand names from common names." The survey introduced by YKK asked only for the name of the product and did not distinguish between a brand name and a common name. Thus, Dupont's survey evidence, in conjunction with evidence that it made an extensive effort to protect the distinctiveness of the TEFLON mark, helped persuade the judge that TEFLON had not become a generic term.

TABLE 9.8.   The Percent of Respondents Classifying Names of Eight Familiar Products as Brand Names

Name	Brand	Common	Don't Know
STP	90	5	5
Thermos	51	46	3
Margerine	9	91	1
Teflon	68	31	1
Jello	75	25	1
Refrigerator	6	94	—
Aspirin	13	86	—
Coke	76	24	—

Source: 393 F.Supp. at 526, taken from Plaintiffs Exh. 61.
Note: Some of the percentages do not add to 100 due to rounding.

b. Brooks Shoe Manuf. Co. v. Suave Shoe Corp.[61]

Plaintiff (Brooks) had sold running shoes with a "V" design for a number of years and sued Suave Shoe for infringement of its common law trademark.[62] The court adapted the standards we quoted from McCarthy's treatise. In particular, the opinion considered the distinctiveness or strength of the mark as well as its possible secondary meaning (similarity of product or mark might confuse prospective purchasers of the source of the item).

The court decided that "V" is not particularly fanciful or distinctive and then turned to the secondary meaning issue. It noted that Brooks shoes were high performance shoes designed to meet the needs of serious athletes, while Suave shoes were lower priced as selling for between $8 and $12, when Brooks sold for at least $25 so that the products were distinguishable, and then evaluated the plaintiffs survey according to the handbook criteria we reviewed previously.

The plaintiff's survey was based on a sample of 121 spectators and participants at three track meets in February–March, 1980. When shown a Brooks shoe with the name Brooks on the heel masked, 71% of them identified it as a Brooks shoe. Moreover, 33% of those recognizing the Brooks shoe attributed their recognition to the "V". The survey also showed the respondents a Suave shoe, and 39% of them identified it as a Brooks shoe (48% of them thought so because of the "V" sign).

There were a number of serious flaws in the plaintiff's survey noted by Suave's expert,[63] the major ones being that

(1) The universe selected for the survey consisted primarily of serious runners and their friends and family rather than the potential purchasers of the casual shoes sold by Suave.

(2) The respondents were not selected according to a random mechanism. These points were documented by comparing the percents of respondents who had some college education (78%), minority members ("very few blacks") with the corresponding percentages of the Baltimore-Washington area (Baltimore 18.4% some college, 21.9% black, Wash. D.C. 37.7% some college, 23.6% black). Thus, the results of the survey were of limited use in determining whether the "V" had secondary meaning to the public at large.

(3) The persons interviewed were chosen for convenient interviewing (a parent of a crying child would not be interviewed, persons who were curious would not be interviewed).

(4) There was no quality control mechanism, such as reinterviewing a

portion of the original respondents. Indeed, in the second part of the survey in which 39% of the respondents identified the Suave show as a Brooks one, one of the five shoes used was actually made by *Brooks*.

(5) Some of the questions (reproduced in Exhibit 9.3) were leading and suggestive. Question 5 suggests to the respondent that the above is a brand name one, which tends to bias the respondent towards answering a brand name. A better question would have read:

Q5a I am going to *hand* you a shoe. Do you know the source of the shoe, that is, who makes or sells it? (Take out shoe and hand to respondent, toe pointed toward respondent)

Yes _____   No _____ (go to question 8)

Q5b (If yes) Who makes or sells it?

_____

EXHIBIT 9.3.   Survey Questions Used by *Brooks Co.* in its Attempt to Demonstrate Likelihood of Confusion

(1) Are any members of your family in any of the following businesses?
   (a) Automobile Dealer
   (b) Shoe or Running Shoe Retailer—If yes terminate
   (c) Shoe or Running Shoe Manufacturer or Wholesaler—If yes terminate
   (d) Advertising Agency
   (e) Market Research Company
   (f) Department Store
(2) How old are you?
(3) Which of the following types of products did you buy or were bought for you in the past two years?
   (a) Warm up or sweat suits
   (b) Running shoes
   (c) Jeans
   (d) Sweaters
   (e) Athletic Shorts
(4) Sex of person being interviewed.
(5) I am going to hand you a shoe. Please tell me what brand you think it is? (Pull out shoe)
(6) If Brooks is mentioned, ask:
   What is it about this shoe that made you say it is Brooks?
(7) How long have you known about Brooks Running Shoes? (Put shoe away)

EXHIBIT 9.3. (*Continued*)

(8) Do you do any running?

(9) Do you own running shoes? (If yes ask question 10)

(10) (a) Which brand of running shoes do you own?

    (b) What are the chances you will purchase a pair of running shoes in 1980?

(11) Who selected the particular running shoe that you own?

(12) During the past 12 months, did you, yourself, shop at a K-Mart Store?

(13) How about during the past 2 years, did you, yourself shop at a K-Mart?

(14) During the past 12 months did you, yourself, shop at a Montgomery Wards or Wards Store?

(15) How about during the past 2 years, did you, yourself, shop at a Montgomery Ward or Wards Store?

(16) During the past 12 months, did any member of your family other than yourself, shop at a K-Mart Store?

(17) How about during the past 2 years, did any member if your family, other than yourself, shop at a K-Mart Store?

(18) During the past 2 months, did any member of your family other than yourself, shop at a Montgomery Wards Store?

(19) How about during the past 2 years, did any member of your family, other than yourself, shop at Wards or Montgomery Wards Store?

(20) Are you currently attending school?

(21) What year of school are you in?

(22) What was the last grade of school you completed?

(23) What is your occupation/job title?

(24) May I please have your:

Name: _____

Address: _____

City: _____ State: _____ Zip: _____

Phone Number: _____

Similarly, Question 7 mentions the name Brooks, which suggests to the respondents and interviewers that Brooks Company is taking the survey. This is especially important when the interviews are being taken at a few locations or events, as the first few respondents may discuss their answers with their friends at the same meet, some of whom undoubtedly were selected for a later interview. For these and other reasons,[64] the court did not give plaintiff's survey much weight. Even the fact that 71% of the respondents identified the Brooks shoe (with its name covered) only established that Brooks shoes with a "V" were known to serious runners, not the potential purchasers of Suave shoes.

The defendant also introduced a survey of 404 persons screened from a proper random sample of the general population using the criterion that they had purchased an athletic shoe, of any type, during the last year. Of these only 2.7% recognized a masked Brooks shoe (the shoe was covered except for the entire V-design pattern) as made by Brooks. This convinced the court that the public's association between the "V" and Brooks shoes was *de minimus.*[65]

c.   *Eastern Airlines v. New York Airlines:*[66] *using surveys to establish misleading or confusing advertisements*

This case concerned three claims Eastern Airlines (EAL) made for trademark infringement, misappropriation of commercial goodwill and false advertising. Since survey evidence was used to assess the nature of the advertisement campaign New York Air Lines (NYA) used we emphasize this issue.

As background we note that EAL owned two service marks for the name and design "Air-Shuttle" registered in the U.S. Patent Office in 1966 and had instituted a shuttle service between New York and Washington and New York and Boston in 1961. The main features of this service were

(a) Seats on air shuttle flights were guaranteed by EAL's providing a back-up aircraft.

(b) Passengers did not need to make reservations.

(c) Flights departed every hour on the hour from 7:00 a.m. to 9:00 p.m. on weekdays.

(d) Tickets could be purchased on board the plane. Moreover, EAL had aggressively promoted its Air-Shuttle, emphasizing the convenience and reliability of its service to residents of its market area.

In 1982 New York Airlines, which had commenced service between the same cities in 1980, initiated an advertising campaign which was designed in part to attract business from EAL. The opinion notes, "Particular advertisements, read ordinarily not analytically, readily implied that amenities associated with the Air-Shuttle were exceeded by the features to be found on NYA's planes." A specific ad listed, side by side, the features of the services of both airlines such as price, flight attendants who attend, an assigned seat and free drinks. EAL based its claim of misleading advertising on

(a) the fact that NYA's price comparisons did not indicate that NYA's lower fare did not apply at all times and

(b) NYA's service did not have the attributes that the public associates with the work "shuttle," as it does not have back-up aircraft.

In order to substantiate its claim, EAL commissioned a survey which sampled 500 persons who had flown between La Guardia airport in New York and either Boston or Washington and showed them the specific comparative advertisements mentioned. After the survey respondents had the opportunity to read the advertisement, they were asked, "What came closest to their understanding of which airline offers which special features?" Forty seven percent of the respondents answered that they were sure or thought that NYA provided a guaranteed seat with a back-up airplane in reserve to insure departure at or a short while after the scheduled time. In comparison, 53% of all respondents thought or were sure EAL provided such service. For the subgroup of frequent travelers, the corresponding percentages were 41% and 66%, respectively. A second example of the advertisement's misleading nature was revealed when the respondents were asked whether the statement "New York Air offers all that Eastern offers, plus more" was conveyed by the ad. Ninety-one percent of all respondents and 94% of the frequent fliers said that this was the impression conveyed by the ad.

Since a significant feature of EAL's shuttle service is its guarantee of a departure at or shortly after the scheduled time, the suggestion of NYA's advertisements that it provided equivalent or superior service were found to be misleading. The opinion noted[67] that Section 43 of the Lanham Act prohibits more than literal falsehoods and "covers the" sophisticated deception "that may be created by clever use of innuendo, indirect intimations and ambiguous suggestions *American Home Products Corp. v. Johnson and Johnson*, 577 F.2d 160, 165 (2d Cir. 1978)." The opinion also emphasizes that the tendency of an ad to confuse, mislead or deceive the public should be tested on the public, especially those persons who are likely to use or purchase the product or service.

From a statistical viewpoint we stress the care with which EAL's survey restricted itself to respondents who were potential users of the air service in question and asked questions directed at finding what the respondent's understood after reading NYA's comparative advertisement. Finally, it should be mentioned that the survey did not aid EAL in its attempt to prove secondary meaning, because only 10% of the individuals surveyed identified Air-Shuttle with Eastern, had the judge decided that "shuttle" was a descriptive rather than a generic word.[68]

Problems

1. *In American Basketball Assoc. v. AMF Voit*[69] the judge gave little weight to a survey which estimated that 42% of respondents associated the basketball at issue with the ABA because the universe sampled was limited to young men who had played basketball within a year of the survey rather than actual *purchasers* of basketballs.

(a) How could one try to demonstrate that the universe was adequate?

(b) If you had to develop a survey for a similar case, how would you do it?

2. Assume that you are working for the defendant, a manufacturer of running shoes, in a trademark infringement suit. What advice would you give your client if plaintiff introduced one of the following studies:

(a) The plaintiff's clerical staff of ten attended one running meet and each person interviewed 50 persons they met to see whether the two brands of shoes were similar enough to be confusing. Assume the questioning was fair.

(b) The plaintiff's clerical staff noticed that in the market area, say a state, there were five major jogging/running clubs and went to the annual meet of each club and then interviewed 50 persons they met.

(c) Same as (b) except that the staff was instructed *not* to select people haphazardly but to interview every tenth person walking through the gate and to keep a record of the persons who refused to be interviewed.

(d) Same as (c) but the proportion of refusals is known to be less than 10%.

(e) From a list of all stores selling running shoes of a quality comparable to those made by the plaintiff, a random sample of stores was selected and 50 randomly chosen purchasers of shoes in each of the stores were interviewed to assess whether they find the brands sufficiently similar to be confusing. The sample of size 50 was taken on several days of the week, and half the sample were interviewed on the weekend, as it is known that half of all sales of running shoes occur on the weekend.

In answering these questions, assume that in each example 25% to 30% of the respondents confused the defendant's brand with the plaintiff's.

3.* Suppose that a judge felt that a likelihood of confusion between two brands would be established if a proper survey showed that 10% or more of the potential customers might be confused by a similarity between the trademarks. Suppose a survey based on 600 answers for us showed that 20% (120) of the respondents were confused. How many additional persons could have refused to answer the question without affecting the usefulness of the survey in meeting the judge's criteria? Answer the same question if the data showed a 15% rate of confusion.

4.   Read the *Union Carbide v. Ever-Ready* 531 F.2d 366 (7th Cir. 1976) and *General Motors v. Cadillac Marine* and *Boat Co.* 226 F.Supp. 716 (W.D. Mich. 1964) cases. Discuss why the survey in the first case was accepted while that in the second was not. Emphasize the careful definition of the universe, sample size, proper questionnaire design and conduct of the survey.

5.   Examine a number of cases in which surveys were used and try to find the minimal level of confusion and/or secondary meaning courts require in order to find infringement. Some cases are:

Burrough v. Beefeater 540 F.2d 266 (7th Cir. 1976).

NFL v. Governor of the State of Delaware 435 F.Supp. (D. Del. 1977).

Boston Hockey v. Dallas Cap and Emblem Mfg. Inc. 510 F.2d 1004 (5th Cir. 1975).

World Carpets, Inc. v. Dick Littrell's New World Carpets. 438 F.2d 482, 489 (5th Cir. 1971).

Zippo Mfg. Co. v. Rogers Imports Inc. 216 F.Supp. 670 (S.D. N.Y. 1963)

Girl Scouts v. Personality Posters Mfg. Co. 304 F.Supp. 1228 (S.D. N.Y. 1969)

Holiday Inns, Inc. v. Holiday Out in America, 481 F.2d 445 (5th Cir. 1973)

Miles Laboratories, Inc. v. Frolich 195 F.Supp. 256 (S.D. Cal. 1961)

Roto Rooter Corp v. O'Neil 513 F.2d 44 (5th Cir. 1975)

Sears Roebuck and Co. v. Allstate Driving School Inc. 301 F.Supp. 4 (E.D. N.Y. 1969)

Volkswagenwerk Aktiengesellschaft v. Rickard, 492 F.2d 474, 478 (5th Cir. 1974)

National Football League Properties, Inc. v. Wichita Falls Sportswear, Inc. 532 F.Supp. 651 (W.D. Wash. 1982)

Henri's Food Products Co. v. Kraft Inc. 717 F.2d 352 (7th Cir. 1983)

Answers to Selected Problems

1.   (a) One might try to establish by testimony of owners of sporting good stores that most basketballs are bought for young men, even if their

parents pay for them. Also one would try to document that the brand liked by the young players was usually the one purchased, perhaps by surveying sellers of the basketballs.

(b) One would sample purchasers at retail outlets selling the product. One should sample a variety of different types of outlets, e.g., sporting goods stores, and department stores, and sample at various times of the day over a period of at least a week.

3.*   (a) If we assume the worst case allocation of the nonrespondents for the plaintiffs assertion, i.e., all refusals were not confused, the maximum *total* sample size would have to yield a 10% confusion rate. As there were 120 confused responses, the *total* sample could be 1200. Thus, there could have been up to 600 refusals without affecting the conclusion that at least 10% of the sample were confused.

8.   *Craig v. Boren:*[70] A Case Concerning the Constitutionality of a Gender-Based Classification

The constitutionality of an Oklahoma statute which prohibited the *sale* of "nonintoxicating"[71] 3.2% beer to males under the age of 21 and to females under the age of 18 was challenged by Craig, a male between 18 and 21 years of age, and Whitener, a licensed vendor of 3.2% beer, on the grounds that the law discriminated against males 18 to 21. A prior case *Reed v. Reed*[72] had established that statutory distinctions in the treatment of males and females were "subject to scrutiny under the Equal Protection Clause" and a series of related cases[73] established that gender based classifications

(a) must serve important governmental objectives and

(b) must be substantially related to the achievement of these objectives in order to be consistent with the Constitution.

A three judge panel upheld the law, finding that the state's objective of enhancing traffic safety was important and concluded that the statistics introduced by Oklahoma established that the gender-based distinction was substantially related to achieving the goal. The Supreme Court reversed this decision, and we now turn to the statistical evidence offered by the state.

First, Tables 9.9 and 9.10 together demonstrated that 18–20-year-old males were arrested more frequently for alcohol related offenses than females of the same age in Oklahoma. Similarly, youths aged 17–21 were

TABLE 9.9. Persons Arrested by Age and Sex From September 1, 1973 through December 31, 1973 for Alcohol-Related Offenses in Oklahoma

	Driving Under the Influence				All Persons Arrested	All 21 and Over
	18	19	20	18–21 Total		
Male	152	107	168	427	5,400	4,973
Female	14	2	8	24	499	475
	Drunkenness					
Male	340	321	305	966	14,713	13,747
Female	39	33	30	102	1,278	1,176

Source: Defendant's Exhibit 1 reproduced in 399 F.Supp. at 1314. The information came from the Sheriff's and Police Departments covering 84% of the population of Oklahoma.

found to be over-represented among those killed or injured in traffic accidents with males substantially exceeding females. The results of a random roadside survey of drivers of vehicles on the streets and highways of Oklahoma City during August 1972 and August 1973 were introduced. The total number of interviews taken was 1600 in 1971 and 1510 in 1973. A summary of the results is given in Table 9.11.

The Court noted[74] that the most focused statistical data showed that 2% of males and .18% of females were arrested for driving under the influence of alcohol. Apparently these rates were obtained by adding the number of males (females) in the 18–20 age group who were arrested for driving

TABLE 9.10. The Population of Oklahoma in 1970 by Sex and Age Groups

	18–20	21 and Over	All Ages
Male	69,688	749,051	1,246,355
Female	68,507	835,241	1,312,874
Total	138,195	1,584,292	2,559,229

Source: Table 20: Age by Race and Sex: 1970 on p. 49–50 in Part 38 (Oklahoma) of 1970 Census of Population (1973) *Characteristics of the Population*, Volume 1.

under the influence (424 males, 24 females) to the corresponding number arrested for drunkenness (966 and 102) in Table 9.9 and dividing the total by the corresponding population figures in Table 9.10. For example, the male rate is $1393/69688 = .01999 \simeq .02$. Technically, one could question whether the four monthly counts for the two separate offenses should be added together to form the numerator. Perhaps the data on arrests for driving under the influence should be multiplied by 3 to form an annual[75] estimate. If that had been done, the male rate would have been $1281/69688 = .0184$ or 1.84% and the female rate would have been $81/68507 = .0012 = .12\%$. With either set of rates, the probability of a male 18–20 being arrested for driving under the influence is about 10 times that of a female of the same age.

At first glance such a large relative risk would support the state's assertion concerning traffic safety. However, calculating the same rates used in the opinion (arrests for driving under the influence and drunkenness divided by population) for persons 21 years of age and older yields $18,720/749,051 = 2.5\%$ for males and $1651/835,241 = .2\%$ for females, indicating a relative risk of 12.5. Thus, it is difficult to discern a rationale for isolat-

TABLE 9.11. Number and Percent of Roadside Survey Respondents Who Consumed Alcohol at Various Amounts by Age and Sex

	Males Less than 20 years		All Male		Females Less than 20 years		All Females	
	1972	1973	1972	1973	1972	1973	1972	1973
Total numbers	243	238	1,246	1,161	70	68	354	349
Drink alcohol	171	180	941	873	48	48	354	349
% who drink	70.4%	75.6%	75.5%	75.2%	68.6%	70.6%	59.9%	60.2%
Consumed alcohol in last 2 hours	40	37	264	251	8	8	50	38
%	16.5%	15.5%	21.2%	21.6%	11.4%	11.8%	14.1%	10.9%
BAC > .01	35	20	218	194	8	5	38	27
%	14.4%	8.4%	17.5%	16.7%	11.4%	7.4%	10.7%	7.7%
BAC > .05	10	10	112	101	1	0	14	11
%	4.1%	4.2%	9.0%	8.7%	1.43%*	0.0%	4.0%	3.2%
Avg. miles in year driven	15,670	16,794	19,360	10,642	10,471	10,456	10,803	11,399
Avg. days a week driving	6.8	6.7	6.7	6.7	6.7	6.5	6.5	6.4

Source: Table 1 on p. 1316 of 399 F.Supp. (1975). Only percentages were given, and we tried to reconstruct the basic data. Thus, there may be slight discrepancies due to rounding. The only major change is that Table 1 reports the percentage of persons whose BAC exceeded .01 and whose BAC also exceeded .05, while we report the percentage of all respondents whose BAC exceeded .05.

ing the 18–20-year-old males. While the Court realized that the arrest data undoubtedly under-estimated the number of persons who actually drove under the influence, it also noted that the data included arrests for excessive drinking of *all* alcoholic beverages not just 3.2% beer, which was the subject of the law in question. Moreover, the opinion remarked that the arrest data may be misleading, as males are more likely to drive than females, especially when they are going out together and perhaps having a drink.[76]

The random roadside survey showed that about 80% of the drivers 20 or under of the sampled vehicles were male and a slightly higher percentage of males preferred beer than females. Examining the blood alcohol concentration (BAC) data in Table 9.11 the Court noted that in 1972 14.6% of young males sampled had a BAC of at least .01 compared with 11.5% of the females, an insignificant difference. Even the lower court's opinion[77] noted that the under-20 age group generally showed a lower involvement with alcohol in terms of having drunk within the past two hours or having a significant BAC but also said that a legislature could address a part of a problem while neglecting other aspects, citing *Jefferson v. Hackney,* 406 U.S. 535 at 546. The Supreme Court opinion, however, stated that the random roadside "survey provides little support for a gender line among teenagers and actually runs counter to the imposition of drinking restrictions based upon age". Our computations confirm this.[78] Finally the Supreme Court's opinion noted "that proving broad sociological propositions by statistics is dubious business and one that is inevitably in tension with the normative philosophy that underlies the Equal Protection Clause. Suffice to say that the showing offered by the appellees does not satisfy us that sex represents a legitimate, accurate proxy for the regulation of drinking and driving. In fact, when it is further recognized that Oklahoma statute prohibits only the selling of 3.2% beer to young males and not their drinking the beverage ..., the relationship between gender and traffic safety becomes far too tenuous to satisfy *Reed's* requirement that the gender-based difference be substantially related to achievement of the statutory objective."

It is interesting to ask how the random roadside survey could have been improved in order to provide more relevant data. First, all occupants of the cars could have been tested. Secondly, the type and amount of alcohol most recently consumed could have been requested in addition to each person's general preference. In this way one could check whether young males having drunk beer and driving alone had the highest BAC levels (which would have supported the state) or whether the females accompanying the young male drivers also had similar BAC levels (which would corroborate the Court's conjecture that the data were biased, as females who drink are chivalrously escorted home).

Even had a more careful survey been taken, it is doubtful that it could have persuaded the majority, because the gender-based distinction was so easily circumvented that it was virtually meaningless[79] and therefore did not bear a fair and substantial relation to the legitimate objective of the state. This case again illustrates the importance of ensuring that statistical data is focused on the major issue, whether restricting the sale of 3.2% beer to young males would reduce accidents and drunk driving arrests. If several states actually had such a statute, then the accident and alcohol related arrest data of those states could be compared with that of similar[80] states without such a law, or the accident rates in those states in years subsequent to the laws passage and enforcement could be compared with prior years. How much *lower* the accident rates in the states with the relative to the rates in states allowing the sale of 3.2% beer, or how large a decrease in post and pre-law accident rates would have to be in order for the Court to accept such a statute, is a legal rather than statistical question.

Comment. There is one statistically confusing statement in the opinion concerning the meaning of the fact that 2% of 18–20-year-old males were arrested for alcohol related offenses. The opinion, at p. 202, notes that a correlation of 2% must be considered a tenuous "fit" and proceeds to mention that differences in the rates of business experience of males and females which were greater than 2% were not substantial enough to justify a gender-based distinction in *Reed vs. Reed*. In Chapter 5, we discussed several measures of the difference in proportions and one of these, e.g., the difference $p_1 - p_2$, relative risk p_1/p_2 or odds ratio should usually be chosen. The term "correlation" relates to how much of the variation in one variable (e.g., college grade point average) can be explained or pre-dicted by another variable (e.g., college entrance exam scores). The Court in *Craig v. Boren* was dealing with a comparison of two rates rather than a correlation and determining whether a 2% difference between rates of alcohol related offenses was legally meaningful. Since the relative risk is used to assess the association between exposure to an agent (chemical, radiation) and the subsequent development of a disease, and correlation measures the degree to which the variations from their respective average values of two continuous characteristics such as height and weight are associated, it is easy to understand the Court's use of wrong terminology.

Problems

1. (a) Using the Mantel-Haenszel procedure of Chapter 5, test whether the proportion of males under 20 whose BAC exceeded .01 is significantly different from the corresponding proportion of females under 20.

(b) why is the Mantel-Haenszel statistic appropriate for this data set?

2. (a) Compare the proportion of males aged 20 and under, whose blood alcohol levels exceeded .05 with

(1) the proportion of males 21 and over whose BAC exceeded .05

(2) the proportion of females 21 and over whose BAC exceeded .05.

(b) Assuming that a BAC over .05 typically causes diminished alertness. What relevance might these comparisons have?

9. Further Uses of Statistical Surveys

In this chapter we illustrated the use of a statistical data in a variety of legal applications. We now briefly mention some other uses of surveys in the legal process, often citing articles for the reader wishing to pursue a particular application.

(a) In petitioning for a change of venue for a trial on grounds of prejudicial pretrial publicity, a survey of residents of the geographical area from which jurors will be selected can be used to estimate the fraction of persons who know about the crime or relevant events as well as their views concerning the innocence or guilt of the accused. This type of data was used to obtain a change of venue in the case of Joan Little (McConahay, Mullin and Frederick, 1977). A similar attempt to obtain a trial by a judge instead of a jury trial is described in the article by Dietz and Sussman (1984).

(b) Attitudinal surveys of the population of prospective jurors are being used to help lawyers decide how to allocate their peremptory challenges on *voir dire*. This application and references to the literature are given in the article by Frederick (1984).

(c) In certifying a class action case one needs to establish that the class of plaintiffs is sufficiently large so that separate trials would be impractical. A survey establishing that the number of women exposed to DES in utero met the numerosity requirement was submitted as evidence in *Payton v. Abbott Labs*. 83 F.R.D. 382 (D. Mass. 1979).

(d) When a contract is signed, both parties should understand its main provisions or that both "minds have met." In *Swards v. Lennox,* 314 F.Supp. 1091 (E.D. Pa. 1970) a survey showing that only 14% of Philadelphia debtors signing a contract knew that it contained a confession of judgment clause was helpful in obtaining a permanent injunction against its enforcement upon a class of low income renters.

(e) Survey evidence as to the degree of similarity of two works may be useful in copyright infringement cases, although they have not been introduced very often. Kegan (1985) describes how the type of surveys used in trademark litigation may be used in such cases. In order for infringement to be found, a substantial similarity of both the ideas and the expression of them in works, such as books, songs or computer programs must be demonstrated. As this is often best accomplished by comparing the two, original and alleged infringer, side-by-side, we will discuss two cases in Chapter 11, which deals with matched data sets. We should note that use of copyrighted material is allowed under the fair use provisions of the Copyright Law[81] provided the use does not affect the potential market and is for educational rather than commercial purposes. Survey evidence of the way owners of video tape recorders (VTRs) use them was introduced in *Sony Corp. v. Universal City Studios*[82] to demonstrate that the majority (75.4%) of owners use their machine at least half the time for time-shifting purposes. Moreover, over 80% of the respondents said that they watched at least as much regular television as they did before owning a Beta VTR. The percentage of respondents who indicated that their attendance at movies was unaffected by having a VTR was 83.2%. Thus, there was little evidence that the public was using their video recordings in a way that seriously impacted the regular TV and movie industries. Moreover, some programs are in the public domain, and some copyright holders stated that they had no objection to the public copying the program for later home viewing.

(f) Since the Supreme Court in *Miller v. California,* 413 U.S. 15 (1973) stated that the criteria for determining whether a book or movie is obscene is the reaction of "the average person, applying community standards," one would think that survey evidence might be helpful in determining the reaction of a community to a film. A potential problem in this area of application is that in order to decide that a work is obscene and has no redeeming social value, respondents need to sit through the entire movie or read the whole book (or at least a substantial portion) in order to validly reach such a conclusion concerning the production in question.

(g) In allocating royalty fees that are paid to copyright owners by cable TV systems, the *Copyright Royalty Tribunal* uses the Nielsen survey to measure the estimate the number of hours viewers see their programs. The notice allocating the 1983 distribution in the *Federal Register* (1986) 51, 12792 discusses various attitude surveys of each operator and subscribers as well as the Nielsen data. It emphasizes the fact that the Nielsen numbers are not as hard and fast as they appear, due to the effect of seasonal factors on sports programmers, possible viewing of Canadian stations, the lumping of specialty stations into one category and discrepancies between diary records and metered TV sets. In spite of these and other concerns, the *Tribunal* considered the Nielsen data more relevant than the attitude or preference surveys because the Nielsen data measures actual behavior (TV viewing) and the other surveys were conducted in 1984 and 1985 while the Nielsen data concerned the year, 1983, at issue.

Finally, we emphasize that the major use of statistical surveys in public policy is to obtain important economic, health and social data. The Labor Department's monthly data on Consumer Prices and Employment and Unemployment are an essential part of the data base relied on by economic policymakers. In addition, the Price Index is an often used inflation indicator in contracts with escalator clauses. The Census Bureau provides data on retail sales, industry structure, characteristics of owners and sole proprietors, as well as data on income and poverty. Other sources of data, often a sample of the relevant population or an administrative file, are the Department of Agriculture, the Internal Revenue Service, the National Center for Health Statistics, the National Center for Educational Statistics and the Statistical Reporting Service of the Department of Agriculture. As most of these agencies publish a short bulletin describing how their data is collected and analyzed, including an estimate of the standard errors of the published estimates, we will not describe the surveys here.

Problems

1. Using the article by Lamont and the following cases: *Commonwealth v. Robin,* 421 Pa. 70, 218 A. 2d. 546 (1966), *Commonwealth v. Trainor,* 374 Mass. 796, 74 N.E. 2d. 1216 (1978) and *People v. Thomas,* 37 Ill. App. 3d. 320, 46 N.E. 2d. 190 (1976), write a short report on the usefulness of survey evidence in obscenity cases. If you were defending a seller or producer of an allegedly obscene book or home video, how might you use a survey to assist your case? What precautions would you take to insure that the survey was relevant to the issue and your sample was sufficiently representative of the community?

2.   Read the article by Zeisel (1973) which demonstrated that the FBI's improper sampling method led to an overestimate of the proportion of released criminals who are caught again. How could the FBI have created a proper sampling strategy?

3.   Are there other areas of the law where sample data might be useful? If so, describe one example.

Answers to Selected Problems

3.   In tax assessment cases one could use a study of the assessment-sales (A-S) ratios of homes in an area to demonstrate that the complainant's house is assessed at a significantly higher than typical ratio and/or that the variation in the A-S ratios is so large that the assessment process is inherently unfair. Another example is in validating the propriety of signatures on a petition supporting the placement of a referendum on a ballot. For instance, a state law might require a certain fraction of the population or of registered voters to sign the petition. If 300,000 signatures of reported voters are required and a petition with 400,000 signatures is submitted, a sample of 5% to 10% of the names can be verified. If the percentage of verified signatures exceeds 75%, then the petition may be considered valid. This example illustrates the practical advantage of verifying a sample rather than the whole population.

APPENDIX

The Chi-Square Test of Homogeneity for Binomial Data

The data for defective contraceptive devices can be organized in the following format:

Sample	Defective	Good	Total	Fraction Defective
1	8	100	108	.0741
2	6	66	72	.0833
3	12	96	108	.1111
4	4	116	120	.0333
Total	30	278	408	.0735

In order to justify considering the four samples as a single sample from a large population of items, we need to check that the differences in the fractions of items found defective in each sample are consistent with the usual sampling variability found in four samples from the same binomial population.

If we just desired to check that the first sample was consistent with a prespecified p_0, say, we would use the binomial model of Chapter 3 or the normal approximation. Thus, we consider the statistic

(A.1) $$Z = \frac{\text{observed} - \text{expected}}{\text{standard deviation}},$$

and, as we are making a two-sided test, one can square Z and just examine whether it is too large. Since a two-sided test at the .05 level rejects if Z is less than -1.96 or greater than $+1.96$, the corresponding test with Z^2 rejects if Z^2 exceeds $(1.96)^2 = 3.84$. The distribution of Z^2 is called the chi-square distribution with one degree of freedom (because we are squaring just one standard normal variable). If one adds the squares of k independent standard normal variables, one obtains the chi-square variable with k degrees of freedom (df). We write this as

$$\text{chi-square } (k) = Z_1^2, + \dots + Z_k^2,$$

where the Z_i are independent standard normal variables of the form (A.1) for each of the k samples.

A natural extension of the test based on the square of (A.1) would be

(A.2) $$\sum_{i=1}^{k} \left(\frac{\text{observed minus expected number in } i^{\text{th}} \text{ sample}}{\text{standard deviation in the } i^{\text{th}} \text{ sample}} \right)^2,$$

which is just the *sum* of the squares of the k individual test statistics (A.1). Since (A.1) was calculated under the *assumption* that p was known, the test statistic (A.2) could be used to assess whether the minority composition of the juries of several judges was consistent with a *known* minority fraction, p, of persons eligible for jury service.

In our data, however, the fraction, p, of defectives is *unknown*. Under the null hypothesis that all four samples are from the same population is true, the natural estimate of p is $\bar{p} = 30/408 = .0735$, the fraction of all items examined that were defective. Thus, it is sensible to calculate the expected number of defectives in the ith group by the sample size (n_i) times $\bar{p}$ and its variance by $n_i \bar{p}(1 - \bar{p})$. When we do this the individual statistics Z_i are no longer statistically independent of one another, as $\bar{p}$ is estimated from all k ($k = 4$ in our example) samples.

To assess the effect of estimating the common value of p under the null hypothesis, recall that when we estimated a population mean from the mean, x, of a sample of n observations we realized that

$$\sum (x_i - \bar{x}) = 0.$$

This implied that $(n - 1)$ values $(x_i - \bar{x})$ determined the last one, so we only had the equivalent of $(n - 1)$ independent observations on the spread of the data about its mean. In the present situation the *sum* of the deviations

(observed count − estimated expected count)

over all groups will also be zero, i.e., using the data to estimate the common but unknown value of p means that we have the equivalent of $(k - 1)$ independent estimates of the spread or variability of the separate sample counts from their expected value. In more formal statistical terms, we say that the sampling distribution of the statistic (A.2) is the same as the sum of $(k - 1)$ independent squared standard normal variables. Therefore, we compare the result of our calculation to tables of this distribution called the chi-square with $(k - 1)$ degrees of freedom (df).

We now calculate the statistic (A.2) on the data set. Since $\bar{p}$ is .0735, the expected value of the number of defective items in the first sample is

$$n_1\bar{p} = (108)(.735) = 7.941.$$

Similarly, the expected values in the other three samples are 5.2941, 7.941 and 8.8235, respectively. Since the variance of a binomial variable is npq, the variance of each sample count is its expected value $(n_i\bar{p})$ times $\bar{q} = 1 - \bar{p} = 1 - .0735 = .9665$, where n_i is the number of observations in the ith sample. For our data the statistic becomes

$$\frac{(8 - 7.941)^2}{(7.941)(.9265)} + \frac{(6 - 5.2941)^2}{(5.2941)(.9265)} + \frac{(12 - 7.941)^2}{(7.941)(.9265)}$$

$$+ \frac{(4 - 8.8235)^2}{(8.8235)(.9265)} = 5.19.$$

From tables of the chi-square distribution with $3df$, we find that the upper 80% point is 4.64, i.e., there is probability .2 that an observation from this distribution would exceed 4.64. The upper 90% point is 6.25, and the value 5.19 of our data has a p-value of about .19, which is not close to significance at the usual .05 level.

We should note that when using statistical tests to check on basic assumptions, some statisticians use higher levels than .05. Thus, a test at the .10 level might be appropriate. The four rubber prophylactic samples would still be accepted as coming from a common population using this more stringent criteria. One reason for using the higher level, .10, instead of .05 is that the power of the test depends on the nature of the alternative. Unlike the binomial model used in discrimination cases where there is one natural alternative ($p_1 < p_0$), for homogeneity tests one might consider alternatives such as:

(1) All but one p_i are the same (one may or may not have a specific p_i in mind as the deviant one).

(2) The p_i's are spread evenly about a central value.

(3) Half the p_i's are equal to one value (p_1), while the other p_i's equal another value (p_2).

No single test can be very powerful against all of these possible alternatives. The test based on (A.2) is a general one, but other procedures have more power against some specific alternatives.

NOTES

1. One should ascertain whether the records were destroyed according to a regular routine, e.g., after a fixed number of years, or were destroyed because they contained information that might be detrimental to the holder. We will see how courts handle this issue in wagering cases.

2. 429 U.S. 190, 97 S.Ct. 451 (1975).

3. Readers may recall that the media often took Peoria, Ill. as a typical town and discussed proposed policies in terms like, "How will it play in Peoria?"

4. For a complete discussion of the sampling error and reliability of the monthly labor market data, see the explanatory notes in *Employment and Earnings,* issued monthly by the Bureau of Labor Statistics of the U.S. Department of Labor.

5. Recall that the standard error of a sample proportion is $\sqrt{(pq/n}$ and that a safe choice of p is 1/2. Hence, the standard error of the sample proportion is $\sqrt{(1/2 \cdot 1/2)/1000} = .0158$, and multiplying this by (1.96) to obtain a 95% confidence interval for p yields a margin of ±.031 or about 3%.

6. The case was ultimately settled, so we cannot discuss how the judge dealt with the issue.

7. In *Douglas v. Hampton,* 512 F.2d 976 (D.C. Cir. 1975), the court limited its discussion of the pass rates of whites and blacks to the subpopulation of racially identifiable applicants.

8. The need for multiple data sources or multiple frames to compile a representative list of prospective jurors is discussed in the paper by Kairys, Kadane and Lehoczky in the list of references in Chapter 4.

9. See the paper by Kairys, Kadane and Lehoczky listed at the end of Chapter 4 for references to these studies.

10. The reason we did not choose one of the first three digits from the left is that they indicate the place where one received the number.

11. Since it is impossible to guarantee that a particular sample is totally representative, it is safest to take new samples. Furthermore, the frequency interpretation of probability and the concept of a confidence interval are based on repeated samples from the population.

12. Here we make inferences on the proportion, p, of a finite population possessing a certain characteristic. Also, we note that in formula (9.4) we used $(N - n)/N$ in place of

$(N - n)/(N - 1)$, as N is usually large (otherwise, we would not need to use a sample). For further discussion of these results see Chapter 3 of the text by Cochran (1977).

13. This is obtained as follows: If X denotes a randomly selected person's earnings, then (in \$1000's)

$E(X - \mu^*)^2 = E(X^2) - (\mu^*)^2$

$= (.6) \, E(\text{square of a male salary}) + .4 \, E(\text{square of a female salary}) \text{ minus } (23)^2$

$= (.6) \, [(25)^2 + 25] + (.4) \, [(20)^2] \text{ minus } 529 = 21.$

The standard deviation is $\sqrt{21} = 4.5826$ and is multiplied by 1000, as we expressed everything in 1000 units. We also recall that since the variance of a random variable (X) is defined as

$\text{Var}(X) = E(\text{square of } X) \text{ minus the square of the mean of } X(\mu^2 \text{ or } [E(X)]^2),$

so that $E(\text{square of } X)$ or $E(X^2) = \text{Var}(X) + [E(X)]^2.$

14. In our example the standard deviation of male salaries did exceed (by about 10%) the standard deviation of salaries in the total population. This occurred because the standard deviation of female salaries was zero. Stratification allows us to allocate more of our sample to the strata where the characteristic has wide variability and less to the strata in which it has little variability.

15. Correlated is the technical term for two random variables which vary together. In Chapter 8, we formally defined it in terms of how much of the variation in one of the variates can be explained by the other. Thus, we can often improve our predictions of a variable (a student's grade point average) using knowledge of another variable (the student's IQ) which is correlated with it.

16. From a calculation similar to the one given in footnote 13. Recall that the expected value or mean of the sampling distribution of an unbiased estimate equals the parameter it is estimating.

17. The first act was Pub. L. No. 59-384, 34 Stat. 768 (1906) and the current one is in 21 U.S.C. enacted in 1976.

18. Federal Seed Act of Aug. 9, 1939, 7. U.S.C.A. at 1551 et seq.

19. 149 F.2d 252 (6th Cir. 1945).

20. The allowable range depended on the estimated germination percentage.

21. 65 F.Supp. 534 (D. Minn. 1946).

22. In the present context the condemnation of a shipment means that the government does not allow the items to be sold. The owner may obtain the items and screen out the defective ones and sell the remaining good ones.

23. A gross is 12 dozen or 144 items.

24. In admiralty law the term "libel" refers to the seizing of goods rather than slander.

25. This expectation is calculated assuming that the 5% of the purchasers have the disease, while their partners are disease-free. Hence, the expected number of disease transmissions is $np = 1650 \times .05 = 82.5$. If one modeled the mate selection process as two random selections from a population in which 5% were infected, then the chance that *at least one* member of a pair was infected would be

$1 - Pr(\text{neither is diseased}) = 1 - (.95)^2 = .0975.$

Since the probability that both members were diseased $= (.05)^2 = .0025$, the probability of transmission of the disease to a new person is $.0975 - .0025 = .095$. Under this assumption the expected number of newly infected individuals due to public use of the 1650 defective devices would be $np = 1650 \times .095 = 156.75$. Notice that the way one describes the process of partner selection has a big effect on the estimated number of disease transmissions.

26. This observation appears in the article by Kennedy (1951) in the references.

27. This is done in the article by Kennedy (1951). As we discussed earlier, when several tests are calculated (especially on independent data sets) the probability that *at least* one yields a significant result is *greater* than the level, α, used for the individual tests. Thus the chance that one of the two pre- and post-samples would yield a significant difference at the .05 level is .0975.

28. 212 F.2d 567 (2d Cir. 1954).

29. The opinion does not describe how the 40% allowance was established, however, it seems to have been accepted by all parties in the case.

30. Calculated assuming the mold count follows a normal curve.

31. 675 F.2d 151 (7th Cir. 1982).

32. Our calculations differ slightly from those reported in the opinion. These discrepancies are not worth worrying about for our purpose of illustrating the statistical ideas.

33. 446 F.Supp. 404 (N.D. Ga. 1977).

34. 435 F.Supp. 891 (M.D. Fla. 1977).

35. See the paper by Heiner, Wagner and Fried (1984) as well as the California Department of Health Services Administrative hearing in Greater El Monte Community Hospital, audit appeal – HA 2-1276-03.

36. See the references cited at the end of the chapter.

37. We are using the term "bias" in its statistical sense, i.e., an estimate is unbiased if its sampling distribution is centered on the true value of the parameter (more technically speaking, we say the expected value of the sample estimate is the parameter it is designed to estimate). An estimate is biased if its sampling distribution is centered on a point which is greater (or less) than the true parameter. In the present setting, omitting some receipts yields a downward bias, as Sears undoubtedly had some outside sales on these days and paid too much tax.

38. 110 F.Supp. 295 (D. Mass. 1953).

39. 309 F.Supp. 468 (S.D.N.Y. 1969).

40. 26 U.S.C. 440.

41. 251 F.Supp. 359 (E.D. Va. 1966) affirmed 402 F.2d 3 (4th Cir. 1968).

42. 330 F.2d 119 (5th Cir. 1964).

43. *Vuyanich v. Republic Nat'l Bank* 505 F.Supp. 224 (N.D. Tex. 1980).

44. 322 F.Supp. 1173 (E.D.N.Y. 1970).

45. 424 F.Supp. 240, 246–47 (S.D. Ia. 1976).

46. 512 F.2d 976 (D.C. Cir. 1975).

47. 513 F.Supp. 355 (E.D. Ark. 1981).

48. 185 F.2d 258 (4th Cir. 1950).

49. 42 FEP Cases 1161 (D.C. D.C. 1985), 843 F.2d 1395 (D.C. Cir. 1988).

50. *United Carbide v. Eveready Inc.* 531 F.2d 366 (7th Cir. 1976) *cert. denied* 429 U.S. 830, 97 S.Ct. 91 (1974).

51. *Continental Motors Corp. v. Continental Aviation Corp.* 375 F.2d. 857 (5th Cir. 1967), *Rotor-Rooter Corporation v. O'Neal*, 513 F.2d 44 (5th Cir. 1975).

52. See the treatise by McCarthy, v. 2 at 89.

53. While a product may be intended for a group, e.g., children or women, it may frequently be purchased by another segment of the population (parents, men).

54. 628 F.2d 500 (5th Cir. 1980).

55. 615 F.2d 252 (5th Cir. 1980).

56. A generic name is one that is used by the public in referring to a product rather than a particular brand. Examples of generic terms are "aspirin" and "cellophane."

57. 393 F.Supp. 502 (E.D.N.Y. 1975).

58. 287 F.2d 492 (2nd Cir. 1961).

59. A substantial amount of criticism of the surveys used in infringement and related cases has been directed at the issue of whether persons questioned at home are representa-

tive of people at the time they purchase an item. In the present case the survey was restricted to respondents who had purchased a zipper recently and did home sewing. In view of the price of the item, it does not seem plausible that a prospective purchaser would have conducted extensive research prior to purchasing another zipper. For expensive items, more detailed screening of respondents may be needed to insure that they represent serious prospective purchases.

60. The determination of the strength of the trademark relies on the judgment of the trier of fact. Original and fanciful words or designs are typically classified as strong marks.

61. 533 F.Supp. 75 (S.D. Fla. 1981).

62. Footnote 1 of the opinion, *supra* note 61, discusses the relevant patent. For our purposes it suffices to know that the mark was not registered so that Brooks did not formally possess the mark for exclusive commercial use. Unregistered trademarks, however, also receive protection when the public associates them with the product in question.

63. Professor Arthur Kirsch (who kindly provided the author with his detailed report).

64. The court also noted that the lawyer was overly involved in the design of the survey and the interviewers were inadequately trained, which violates the 7th and 8th criteria in the *Handbook*.

65. The term *de minimus* means that the effect is so small that it is legally unimportant.

66. 559 F.Supp. 1270 (S.D. N.Y. 1983).

67. The opinion, *supra* note 66, at p. 1278.

68. The opinion contains an interesting discussion of the history of the word "shuttle."

69. 385 F.Supp. 981 (1973).

70. 429 U.S. 190 (1976).

71. This is noted in the opinion, *supra* note 70 at p. 203, citing the relevant Oklahoma statute.

72. 404 U.S. 71 (1971).

73. At p. 198, the Supreme Court opinion, *supra* note 71, cites *Stanley v. Illinois* 405 U.S. 6454 (1972) and *Frontiero v. Richardson* 419 U.S. 498 (1973) among others.

74. *supra*, note 70 at 201.

75. While this is a reasonable approximation, one should obtain several years of data to see whether there are seasonal patterns in alcohol consumption and related arrests. In particular, the Christmas and New Year's Day season may be atypical but is included in the four months of arrest data in Table 9.9.

76. See footnote 14 of the opinion, *supra* note 70 at 202.

77. *Walker v. Hall* 399 F.Supp. 1304 (W.D. Okla. 1975).

78. See footnote 16 at p. 203 of the opinion, *supra* note 70.

79. See the concurring opinion of Justice Powell at p. 211, *supra* note 70.

80. In order for a proper estimate of the effect of the law to be made, other factors related to the frequency of accidents, such as traffic density, maximum speed limits, etc. should be similar in the states compared.

81. 17 U.S.C. 107.

82. 104 S.Ct. 774 (1984).

REFERENCES

Statistics Texts

COCHRAN, W. G. (1977). *Sampling Techniques,* 3rd ed., New York: Wiley. (This may well be *the* classic text for the basic sample survey course taught in most universities in the United States.)

KISH, L. (1965). *Survey Sampling*. New York: Wiley.

STUART, A. (1968). *Basic Ideas of Scientific Sampling*. New York: Hafner.

SUDMAN, S. AND BRADBURN, N. M. (1982). *Asking Questions*. San Francisco: Jossey-Bass. (A practical guide to questionnaire design with many examples illustrating the proper questionnaires for mail and telephone surveys and various approaches to measuring attitudes.)

WILLIAMS, W. (1978). *A Sampler on Sampling*. New York: Wiley.

Legal Treatises

Handbook of Recommended Procedures for the Trial of Protracted Cases (1960). 25 F.R.D. 351, 425–430.

Manual for Complex Litigation (1973). No. 4975, Chicago: Commerce Clearing House.

McCARTHY, J. T. (1984). *Trademarks and Unfair Competition* 2nd ed. Rochester: Lawyers Cooperative Publishing Company (The first (1973) edition of this comprehensive work is cited in numerous opinions).

General Articles on Sampling in Law and Public Policy

DEMING, W. E. (1954). On the Presentation of the Results of Sample Surveys as Legal Evidence. *Journal of the American Statistical Association* **49,** 814–825. (A valuable article based on the experiences of a leading statistician in court).

McCOID, A. H. (1956). The Admissibility of Sample Data Into a Court of Law: Some Further Thoughts. *UCLA Law Review* **4,** 233–250.

SPROWLS, R. C. (1956). The Admissibility of Sample Data Into a Court of Law: A Case History. *UCLA Law Review* **4,** 222–232. (This article and the previous one provide a comprehensive background to the use of sample data in legal cases.)

Office of Management and Budget (1988). Guidelines for Federal Statistical Activities; Notice, *Federal Register* **53** 1542–1552. (The most recent government guidelines for surveys and related statistical activities.)

Articles Relating to the Use of Samples in Food and Drug Cases and the Regulation of Food and Drugs

HUTT, P. B. AND HUTT, P. B. II (1984). A History of Government Regulations of Adulteration and Mislabeling of Food. *Food, Drug and Cosmetic Law Journal* **39,** 2–73. (An interesting history of the evolution of the law.)

KENNEDY, F. R. (1951). Sampling by the Food and Drug Administration 6. *Food, Drug and Cosmetic Law Journal* **6,** 759–774.

McNUTT, K. W., POWERS, M. E., AND SLOAN, A. E. (1984). Consumer Perceptions of Consumer Protection. *Food Drug and Cosmetic Law Journal* **39,** 86–98. (Reports the result of a survey of 200 women from a pool of readers of *Good*

Housekeeping magazine. The results indicate that these consumers desired protection from economic fraud as well as being assured of the safety and quality of the food supply.)

Articles Referring to the Use of Survey Evidence in Trademark Infringement and Related Cases

BOAL, R. B. (1983). Techniques for Ascertaining Likelihood of Confusion and the Meaning of Advertising Communications. *The Trademark Reporter* **73**, 405–435.

CAUGHEY, R. E. (1956). The Use of Public Polls; Surveys and Sampling as Evidence in Litigation, and Particularly Trademark and Unfair Competition Cases. *California Law Review* **44**, 539–546.

KEGAN, D. L. (1985). Survey Evidence in Copyright Litigation. *Journal of the Copyright Society of the U.S.A.* **32**, 283–314.

LAVIDGE, R. J. (1985). Survey Research in Trademark Cases. *Chicago Bar Record* **66**, 236–285.

LEISER, A. W. AND SCHWARTZ, C. R. (1983). Techniques for Ascertaining Whether a Term is Generic. *The Trademark Reporter* **73**, 376–390.

PALLADINO, V. N. (1983). Techniques for Ascertaining if there is Secondary Meaning. *The Trademark Reporter* **73**, 391–404.

REINER, J. P. (1983). The Universe and Sample: How Good is Good Enough? *The Trademark Reporter* **73**, 366–375.

ROBIN, A. AND BARNABY, H. B. (1983). Trademark Surveys—Heads You Lose, Tails They Win. *The Trademark Reporter* **73**, 436–445.

SHRYOCK, R. F. (1967). Survey Evidence in Contested Trademark Cases. *The Trademark Reporter* **57**, 377–384.

SORENSON, R. C. (1983). Survey Research Execution in Trademark Litigation: Does Practice Make Perfection? *The Trademark Reporter* **73**, 349–365.

Articles Relating to the Use of Sample Data in Audit and Antitrust Cases

HEINER, K. W., WAGNER, N. L. AND FRIED, A. C. (1984). Successfully Using Statistics to Determine Damages in Fiscal Audits. *Jurimetrics* **24**, 273–281.

KAYSEN, C. (1956). *United States v. United Shoe Machinery Corporation: An Economic Analysis of an Anti-Trust Case.* Cambridge, Harvard University Press. (This book describes the problems inherent in defining the appropriate market for the machines made by the company at 28–40. The author, an economist, served as a legal clerk to Judge Wyzanski.)

KECKER, R. E. (1955). Admissibility in Courts of Law of Economic Data Based on Samples. *Journal of Business* **28**, 114–127.

KING, B. F. (1977). Auditing Claims in a Large-Scale Class Action Refund—The Antibiotic Drug Case. *The Antitrust Bulletin* **22**, 67–93.

Articles Dealing with Other Applications

BARNES, D. W. (1983). The Significance of Quantitative Evidence in Federal Commission Deceptive Advertising Cases. *Law and Contemporary Problems* **46**, 25–47. (A general discussion of statistical evidence in a variety of cases. Guidelines for the presentation and interpretation of data analyses are presented.)

BAILAR, B. A. (1985). Some Uses of Probability Sampling for Public Policy. *1985 Proceedings of the Social Statistics Section, American Statistical Association,* 11–15. (A variety of important surveys, such as the Current Population Survey used to estimate unemployment and employment and the Survey of Asbestos in Buildings are described.)

DIETZ, S. R. AND SISSMAN, P. L. (1984). Investigating Jury Bias in a Child Molestation Case. *Behavioral Sciences and the Law* **2**, 423–434.

FREDERICK, J. T. (1984). Social Science Involvement in *Voir Dire:* Preliminary Data on the Effectiveness of "Scientific Jury Selection". *Behavioral Sciences and the Law* **2**, 375–394.

MCCONAHAY, J., MULLIN, C. AND FREDERICK, J. (1977). The Uses of Social Science in Trials with Political and Racial Overtones: The Trial of Joan Little. *Law and Contemporary Problems* **41**, 205–229.

ZEISEL, H. (1973). The FBI's Biased Sampling. *Bulletin of the Atomic Scientists* **29**, 38–42.

REFERENCES FOR THE APPENDIX

GUENTHER, W. C. (1977). Power and Sample Size for Approximate Chi-Square Tests. *American Statistician* **31**, 83–85. (This article illustrates how to make sample size and power calculations for the test based on (A.2) from existing statistical tables.)

MOSTELLER, F. M. AND ROURKE, R. E. K. (1973). *Sturdy Statistics*. Boston: Addison Wesley. (A readable intermediate text. The discussion of the chi-square test for homogeneity and its application to the jury composition in the trial of Dr. Spock is excellent.)

Chapter 10

Small Probabilities: Calculation and Interpretation of Accident and Disease Rates

Many public policy issues, such as transportation safety and health risks due to exposure to potentially toxic substances, require the consideration of small probabilities. For instance, the chance of an accident occurring during a single airline trip is so small as to be virtually negligible, however, the fact that approximately five million airline departures are made each year in the U.S. suggests that the total risk to the public may not be negligible. Thus, the FAA promulgates a variety of safety regulations and inspects planes for violations of them. In this chapter, we discuss several extensions of the concept of the probability of an event which are useful in considering accident and disease rates. After discussing some basic concepts, we illustrate their use in an epidemiologic study introduced in a hearing concerning the fitness of an individual with a heart problem to be certified as an airman. Then we present some formal statistical techniques for analyzing accident and disease rate data and use them to analyze data on airplane accidents and birth defects. Some issues involved with the design and interpretation of cancer mortality and health studies are discussed in the last two sections, and the importance of the concept of statistical power is illustrated on two planned studies.

1. Defining an Appropriate Rate

The concept of the probability of an event occurring at any one trial (repetition) is logically related to the *proportion* of times the event occurs in a long sequence of similar trials. To make this connection, we assumed that the probability, p, that the event occurs on any trial remains the same for all trials and that the outcome of one trial is independent of the other trials. When defining an accident or disease rate, care must be taken to assure that the underlying notion of independent, identical repetitions of the same experiment or trial is preserved in definition of a rate.

Three different rates for airline accidents are reported by the National Safety Board: accidents per million revenue passenger miles, accidents per million aircraft miles and accidents per departure. In calculating each of these rates, the same numerator, the number of accidents that occur in one year, is divided by a different denominator. The first rate considers the total miles passengers fly as the base and uses this total mileage (in millions) as the denominator in calculating the rate. Implicitly, this rate assumes that the chance of an accident is the same for each mile a passenger travels. Notice that if the number of passengers on each flight had been lower, the total passenger miles flown would have *decreased*, implying a higher accident rate, even though the number of accidents was unchanged. The second rate, accidents per 100,000 aircraft miles, assumes that the chance of an accident is the same during each mile of flight. We know, however, that most accidents occur on takeoff or landing, which is the basis of the third rate, the number of accidents per 100,000 departures. For airplane passengers wanting to know the risk they are taking, this rate is the most informative. The reason three rates are reported is that no single one is appropriate for all purposes. For example, a company insuring airplanes for physical damage might be concerned with the number of accidents per 100,000 aircraft miles, while a firm insuring passengers would be more interested in accidents per million passenger miles and accidents per 100,000 departures.

Similar considerations apply to the reporting and interpretation of statistics concerning the rate of disease in a population exposed to a toxic chemical or radiation and to general health statistics. The risk of contracting a disease is most easily understood in terms of the *number of new cases* that occur in a *fixed period of time* (e.g., a year). In order to properly interpret this number, we need to compare it to the size of the population studied. The incidence rate[1] is defined as $\hat{p} = d/n$, where a total of n persons are at risk and d new cases are observed during the time period in which the population (of size n) is studied.

When one observes a group of individuals over a reasonably lengthy time period (e.g., ten years) some persons leave the study (e.g., move to a new job) and those who get the disease do so at various times during the study period. Thus, the denominator n of the incidence rate is not constant throughout the study. If we assume that there is a constant (approximately) probability of contracting the disease per year (or other time unit), then the total amount of time (measured in years) the ith individual is observed and is disease-free is his person-time at risk and is denoted by t_i. The sum $t = \Sigma\ t_i$, of the person times for all individuals at risk is the total person-time at risk and the person-time incidence rate is given by

$$(10.1) \qquad\qquad \bar{p} = \frac{d}{T}.$$

The rate $\bar{p}$ can be considered as an estimate of the probability of contracting the disease per year, provided this probability does not change much with age. Because a specific disease occurs relatively rarely, person-time incidence rates are often reported in terms of the number of cases per 1000 persons per year.

Comment. The incidence rate $\hat{p}$ really estimates a risk or probability, as it is the proportion of persons who become ill during a fixed time frame and is not a true rate but a simple ratio. In science courses, rates usually are related to the time dimension, e.g., a car travels at 55 miles per hour. Notice that this rate will vary over the course of a trip, but at any point in time the speedometer indicates how fast one is driving by converting the current speed into miles per hour. Similarly, an incidence rate can be regarded as the instantaneous potential of a nondiseased person becoming ill. The person-time incidence rate $\bar{p}$ estimates the average of this instantaneous rate over the study period. We will not emphasize these distinctions, but the reader should be aware of their existence when reading the literature. In particular, the proportion $\hat{p}$ is often referred to as the *cumulative incidence rate,* as it is the proportion of the original group of n persons who contracted the disease during the total time of the study.

In health studies, characteristics such as the age distribution or smoking habits of the sample studied may affect the incidence of disease. Thus, a typical study would report the incidence rate $\hat{p}$ and/or the person-time

TABLE 10.1.   Incidence of Heart Disease in 12-Year Follow-Up Period

Age (at initial exam)	Number at Risk	Number of Heart Problems	Incidence Rate ($\hat{p}$)	Person-time Incidence Rate ($\bar{p}$) (per 1000 person-years)
30–39	789	40	.051	4.3
40–49	742	88	.119	10.5
50–62	656	130	.198	18.3
TOTAL	2187	258		

Source: J. Schlesselman (1982) p. 29, adapted from Truett, J., Cornfield, J. and Kannel, W. (1967). A Multivariate Analysis of the Risk of Coronary Heart Disease in Framingham, *Journal of Chronic Diseases* **20**, 511–524.

incidence rate $\bar{p}$ by age categories, as in Table 10.1, which reports the incidence of heart disease in a study of a sample of men in Framingham, Massachusetts.

The data in Table 10.1 reflect the fact that both measures of incidence increase with age. Had the study population not been classified by age group, the cumulative incidence rate would have been $\hat{p} = 258/2187 = .118$, which estimates the average (overall age groups) probability of contracting heart disease and is really a weighted average of the age-specific rates. Reporting the specific age-group incidence rates is very important for comparative purposes, since the age distributions in the populations (or samples) being compared may differ. For example, suppose that a similar 12-year follow-up study was made on males employed in an occupation exposing them to a potentially harmful substance in order to assess whether exposure was related to heart disease. Table 10.2 reports hypo-

TABLE 10.2.   Hypothetical Data on Exposed Workers

Age (at initial exam)	Number at Risk	Number of Heart Problems	Incidence Rate ($\hat{p}$)
30–39	1500	120	.080
40–49	450	63	.140
59–62	150	50	.333
TOTAL	2100	233	.111

thetical data obtained in a city in Massachusetts which is similar to Framingham.

If one simply compared the total incidence rates (.111 and .118) of the two groups, one would conclude that the rate of heart disease in the two groups was the same and would miss the fact that the exposed group (Table 10.2) had a higher incidence of new heart problems in all three age categories than the general population (Table 10.1) had. The reason for this anomaly is that the exposed population had a different (younger) age distribution. One way of accounting for this is to calculate an *age-adjusted* or *standardized rate*. Assuming that the age distribution in Table 10.1 was proportional to that for the state of Massachusetts, one calculates the age adjusted rate for the data in Table 10.6 by applying the fractions, f_i, of the population (from Table 10.1) in each age category to the rates in Table 10.2. The fractions, f_i, are 789/2187 = .361, 742/2187 = .339 and .300, so the age-adjusted (to the state male population 30–62) rate for the data in Table 10.2 is:

$$(10.2) \quad \sum f_i p_i = (.361 \times .080) + (.339 \times .140) + (.300 \times .333) = .176,$$

which is about one-and-a-half times the incidence rate (.118) of the general male population. The *standardized* rate estimates what the Massachusetts (or Framingham) overall incidence rate would be if the age-specific rates in Table 10.2 were valid for the corresponding age groups in Table 10.1. Equivalently, the standardized rate estimates the incidence rate for an exposed population with the age distribution of Framingham (or the state).

Usually rates are standardized using the age distribution of the nation (sometimes a state or county). The factors, f_i, used in our calculation (10.2) would then be determined from census data for the U.S., and the age-specific incidence rates in both tables would be weighted by these fractions to obtain nationally adjusted standardized rates. Standardized rates are especially useful for comparative purposes since they enable us to examine rates which have accounted for differences in the age distribution of the groups being compared. Nevertheless, one should also examine the age-specific rates to see whether they also follow the same pattern as the summary standardized rates.

The conclusion that the workers in Table 10.2 had a higher incidence of heart problems than the general population (Table 10.1) is on firmer grounds when the age-specific rates are all in the same direction (higher) as the standardized rates. Had one of the age-specific rates in Table 10.2 been much lower than the corresponding rate in Table 10.1, further study of the two groups would need to be carried out, as they may have had different distributions of smoking or other risk factors which also are related to heart problems.

Problems

The National Transportation Safety Board (NTSB) released the accident data given in Table 10.3 for the 10-year period 1973–1982.

1. In its press release, the NTSB noted that "despite the upturn in the fatality toll and fatal accident rate of the airlines, accident statistics in all

TABLE 10.3.   Airline Accidents, Fatal Accidents, Total Fatalities and Their Corresponding Rates

	Accidents				Accident Rates Per 100,000 Departures	
Year	Total	Fatal	Total Fatalities	Number of Departures	Total	Fatal
1973	36	8	221	5,133,816	.701	.158
1974	43	7	460	4,725,783	.889	.127
1975	31	2	122	4,704,052	.659	.043
1976	22	2	38	4,835,138	.455	.041
1977	21	3	78	4,934,094	.426	.061
1978	21	5	160	5,015,939	.419	.100
1979	24	4	351	5,379,852	.446	.074
1980	15	0	0	5,352,927	.280	.000
1981	25	4	4	5,197,971	.481	.077
1982	16	5	235	4,969,000	.302	.080

Source: NTSB 1982 Accident Rate Safety Information in a press release of January 7, 1983. The data for 1982 was preliminary. The data reported in Table 10.3 is for scheduled airlines (excluding commuter flights).

Note: the rates per 100,000 departures are obtained by dividing the number of accidents (total or fatal) by the number of departures in 100,000 units, which is just the number of departures divided by 100,000. To obtain the total accident rate per 100,000 departures for 1973, one divides 5,133,816 by 100,000 yielding 51.33816. The rate then becomes 36/51.338 = .701.

categories of civil aviation generally continued long-term downward trends. The accident rates of airlines in 1973 were more than twice their rates last year.''

(a) Was it statistically proper for the NTSB to buttress its claim that long-term accidents rates were declining (for all civil aviation) by comparing the 1982 data with the 1973 data? Explain.

(b) Calculate the *fatal accident* rate per 100,000 departures over the entire 10-year period. Do you think the 1982 rate (.080) differs meaningfully from it?

2. A critic[2] of the policy of airline deregulation which went into effect in 1978 asserted that the *number* of fatalities had nearly doubled since deregulation. His assertion was based on comparing the average number of fatalities (78) for the *three* year prior to deregulation (1975 through 1977) with that (150) for the *five*-year period 1978 to 1982.

(a) Would the results of the critic have changed had he used a five-year period for the pre- as well as post-deregulation period?

(b) Suppose the critic had used the average number of all accidents or fatal accidents as his criteria. Would these have substantiated his point as much? What if the five-year period had been used?

(c) From your answers so far, do you think that deregulation had a major impact on airline passenger safety?

(d) Since the number of fatalities in a year depends on the number of fatal accidents (or equivalently the fatal accident rate) and the number of passengers on a flight, which is also a *random* variable, would you expect that the number of fatalities in a year is *more* or *less* variable than the number of accidents (or the accident rate per 100,000 on departures)? Verify your belief by calculating the standard deviation of the yearly fatality counts given in Table 10.3.

Comment.   The previous two problems illustrated how data can be mishandled in order to prove or disprove an assertion. Readers should be wary of manipulations of data, such as shifting time periods or excluding several years of relevant data from an analysis, as well as conclusions which are reached by ignoring the *variability* (sampling or naturally occurring) inherent in the data.

3. Can you think of other public policy issues or legal cases in which accident rate data might play a role?

2. Using the Results of an Epidemiological Study in an Administrative Hearing

In 1980, the Federal Aviation Administration (FAA) denied Mr. H. A. Keinetz a third class airman medical certificate based upon his history of glaucoma and chronic atrial fibrillation (AF is an arrhythmic heartbeat), even though he was receiving medication for both conditions. He appealed the denial of his medical certificate and an evidentiary hearing was held in July 1981.[3]

The government's cardiologist relied on the Framingham epidemiological study to support his conclusion that the petitioner's cardiac condition was not only dangerously disqualifying, but also had increased his statistical probability of leading to a major acute incapacitating event, such as heart attack, stroke or partial paralysis. The Framingham study is an extensive, prospective (or cohort) study of the population of Framingham, Massachusetts aged 30 to 62, who had not had a stroke prior to the commencement of the study. The 5184 men and women were followed for 24 years and examined every two years.

A portion of the data from the study report which was used in the hearing is given in Table 10.4. The expected rate for each group (AF and non-AF) is a *standardized rate* where the *national rates of stroke incidence* for each age and blood pressure level category are applied to each such category in the two groups. Thus, the national rates are standardized to the age and blood pressure distributions of the study populations. This is necessary, as the likelihood of developing AF increases with age and blood pressure (hypertensive status). Since the chance of developing heart problems also increases with age and hypertension, the expected rate (7.43) for the AF group is larger than that (3.11) of the non-AF group. Only an observed rate exceeding 7.43 would indicate that AF (and not age or hypertension status) is associated with a higher incidence of stroke.

Comparing the observed rate of strokes for persons with AF, with its expected rate shows that persons with AF had a rate of strokes $41.48/7.43 = 5.6$ times that of men and women in the general population with the same age and blood pressure distribution as the AF group. Because of the standardization procedure, the increased risk of stroke in the AF group cannot be due to the age or hypertension characteristics possessed by the AF group. In light of these results, Judge Reilly concluded that the petitioner was at a much greater risk than the general population not having his condition of chronic AF and upheld the FAA's denial of medical certification.

TABLE 10.4. Comparing the Actual Rate of Strokes Per 1000 Person-Years with Expected in the Framingham Study

Group (1)	Person Years of Observation (2)	Number of Stroke Events (3)	Observed Rate (4)	Expected Rate (5)
no AF	109,051	311	2.87	3.11
AF	481	20	41.48	7.43

Source: Adapted from Table 2 of Wolf, P. A., Dawber, T. R., Thomas, H. E. Jr. and Kannel, W. B. (1978). Epidemiologic Assessment of Chronic Atrial Fibrillation and Risk of Stroke: The Framingham Study. *Neurology* **28,** 973–977.

It is important to note that it would have been misleading to compare the observed rate (41.48) of persons with AF to the observed rate (2.87) of the non-AF group. Such a comparison would have shown an exaggerated (14.4) risk of stroke for persons with AF relative to those without AF than the proper comparison, because the AF and non-AF populations had different distributions of age and hypertension characteristics.

Another significant aspect of the data is the fact that the observed rate (2.87) of the non-AF group agrees closely with its expected value (3.11) calculated by applying the national age and hypertension category rates to the age-hypertension status distribution of the Framingham study population. This reassures us that the control (non-AF) group is typical of the general population so that no special characteristics of the Framingham area appear to be influencing the data.

The ratio of the observed number of new cases (incidences) to its expected number determined by standardization using the national rates in each age-sex hypertensive status group is called the *standardized incidence rate* (SIR) and is an estimate of a relative risk, i.e., the *risk* of contracting the illness a member of the study population has *relative* to the general population accounting for the effect of the factors (e.g., age, hypertension status) used in the standardization procedure.

In some studies, deaths from a specific disease in a study population are compared to a standardized mortality rate (SMR), where the national age-specific mortality rates are used instead of the corresponding incidence rates. The methodology for calculating the estimated relative risk of death from the disease is the same as that used in comparing the incidence rates, and the method is called SMR comparison. The formal statistical test of significance in both types of studies is usually based on a model described in the next section.

Comment.   It should be noted that different procedures for standardizing rates were used in the two examples. Formula (10.2) applied the age-specific incidence rates observed in the study population to the age distribution of the national (or other standard) population. This procedure is called *direct* standardization. In order to use the direct method the age-specific rates in the study group need to be accurate. This implies that the population studied is reasonably large. When these age-specific rates are unavailable or unreliable, one can apply the age-specific rates of the (large) standard or reference population to the age distribution of the study group to obtain the number of cases one would expect to occur in the study group if the standard (e.g., national) age-specific rates were applicable to the study group. The ratio

$$\frac{\text{observed number of incidents in the study group}}{\text{expected number of incidents}}$$

is the Standardized Incidence Rate (SIR). It measures the risk of contracting the disease in the study group relative to that of the standard population. This procedure is called *indirect* standardization. The purpose of both methods is to eliminate the difference in the age distributions of the study group and the reference population from our comparison of the incidence rates. The methods assume that the distribution of other risk factors for the disease are similar in the study and standard populations. When this is not the case, these factors should also be incorporated in the standardization procedure. This is why the national rates by *age* and *hypertension* category were used in the AF study reported in Table 10.4. Had hypertensive status not been used in the standardization process one might not know whether the increased rate of heart problems in the AF group was due to the persons having AF or their having higher hypertension levels.

Finally, we mention that a third method is used in some studies of mortality rates when neither the direct nor the indirect standardization procedure can be used due to lack of appropriate data. In occupational health studies one may only know who worked in a particular job and presumably was exposed to the agent under study. From death certificates in years subsequent to employment, one can obtain the total number of deaths that occurred among the workers and the proportion due to a specific cause, e.g., heart failure or lung cancer, over a set time period.

The ratio

$$(10.3) \quad \frac{\text{observed deaths from the specific cause among the workers}}{\text{expected deaths from that cause among the workers}},$$

where the *expected number* of deaths is calculated by multiplying the *fraction* of all deaths in the age-adjusted standard population due to the cause by the *total* of all deaths occurring among the workers. The ratio (10.3) is then called the Proportional Mortality Rate (PMR). The PMR is similar in form to the Standardized Mortality Rate (SMR). The main difference is in the determination of the expected number of deaths due to the specific cause. Epidemiologists usually consider the PMR less reliable than the SMR, as the PMR for one cause of death is *not* independent of the PMR for other causes. Note that, if an unusually high proportion of workers die from one cause, the PMRs for other causes will be lowered. This occurs because the total number of deaths in the study (worker) group is increased. When this total is multiplied by the usual fraction of deaths to another cause, a larger number will be obtained than would be the case if the worker group had the normal overall death rate. When the distribution of *other* causes of death in the study group (workers) is similar to that of the standard population, the PMR is a reasonable proxy for the SMR.

Problems

1.   Although we did not discuss the statistical significance of the fivefold increase in risk of stroke for persons with AF, the data was significant. Regardless of the technical issue of statistical significance, does this degree of increased risk pose a *meaningful* excess risk to the petitioner and to the public?

2.   The use of the standardized (age and hypertension adjusted) rates indicated *less* of a risk than a simple comparison of the observed rates in the two groups.

     (a) If you represented a similar petitioner, how could you use the results of this study if the government presented a more recent epidemiological study which failed to use standardized rates and indicated that there was a fivefold increase in risk comparing the observed rates in the two groups?

     (b) To buttress your points, what characteristics of the study sample would you need to point out?

3.   In equal employment cases we were concerned with incorporating the major factors influencing a person's ability to do their job. The technique of standardization accomplishes this in epidemiologic studies. To what measure(s) discussed in Chapters 5 and 6 is the *standardized incidence rate* related? Explain.

Answers to Selected Problems

1.   A fivefold increase is quite a meaningful one, especially as stroke is not that rare. Moreover, should a solo pilot have a stroke, there is great risk to the public due to a crash.

2.   The *crude* or *unadjusted* comparison indicated an RR of 14 and standardization reduced it to 5. If the government presented an unadjusted study indicated RR of 5 you might argue that a proper standardization would reduce it to about 5/3, as standardization reduced the estimated RR in the AF study by a factor of 3. You would need to verify that the study group had a different (older) age distribution than the general population and therefore more cases would be expected to occur. Of course, other related factors besides age should also be considered.

3.   The standardized incidence rate is related to the selection ratio. Because we have essentially stratified the study group and general population to which the incidence in the study group will be compared into age (and other) subclasses, it is analogous to the summary odds ratio developed for binomial data in the appendix of Chapter 5. Remember that the odds and selection ratios are practically identical in the case of small probabilities.

3.   A Statistical Model for Accident and Rare Disease Data

Although the number of accidents in Table 10.3 varied from 15 to 43, the number of departures in each year varied by less than 10% from its average value (5.025×106). It seems reasonable, therefore, to consider a probability model which assumes that the same accident generating mechanism operates in each year. If there is a common, small probability, p, of an accident on any flight and accidents are independent of each other, then the number of accidents in each year can be regarded as a binomial distribution with parameters p and n (where n is the number of flights per year, approximately five million).

As calculating the exact distribution of the number of accidents would be quite tedious when the number of independent trials is in the millions, statisticians have developed an accurate approximate distribution, the Poisson. The idea underlying the derivation of the Poisson distribution is that its *mean,* λ, should equal the binomial mean np. Since the mean λ of a Poisson distribution is a finite number (representing the average number of accidents in a year), the probability p of an accident occurring on one of the n flights must be λ/n, i.e., p is very small. Notice that the variance of the binomial model we are approximating is $np(1 - p)$ and if p is very small, $1 - p$ is essentially *one* so that the mean and variance of the binomial variable indicating whether an accident occurs on a flight are virtually identical. This property will hold for the Poisson distribution which is an approximation to the binomial when p is small. The exact probability that k events from a Poisson distribution with mean λ occur is given by

$$(10.4) \qquad P(X = k) = \frac{e^{-\lambda}\lambda^k}{k!}, \qquad k = 0, 1, 2, \ldots$$

where e is a mathematical constant (2.71828) and λ is the mean or expected number of occurrences. It can be shown that the variance of the Poisson variable with mean λ also equals λ.

To illustrate the shape of a Poisson variable, we present the exact probabilities for $\lambda = .6$ and $\lambda = 1.0$ in Table 10.5, below. From the probabilities in Table 10.5, we see that the Poisson variable with mean 1 gives greater probability to the larger outcomes (1, 2, 3, etc.) than the Poisson variable with mean .6.

Before using the Poisson distribution on modern-day data, it is instructive to reproduce a famous set of data on the number of soldiers acciden-

TABLE 10.5. Poisson Probabilities for the Number of Events

k (number)	$\lambda = .6$	$\lambda = 1.0$
0	.54881	.36788
1	.32929	.36788
2	.098786	.18394
3	.019757	.061313
4	.002964	.015328
5	.0003556	.003066
6		.000511

TABLE 10.6. Record of Soldiers Dying From Kicks from a Horse

Number of deaths per year	Number of years in which deaths occurred (2)	Expected frequency (3)
0	109	109.76
1	65	65.86
2	22	19.76
3	3	3.95
4	1	.59
5	0	.07

Source: Derived from Table 5.5.1 of Fisz, M. (1963). *Probability Theory and Mathematical Statistics*. New York: John Wiley. The data originally appeared in a book by Bortkiewicz, cited by Fisz.

tally killed by the kick of horses in the Prussian cavalry per year for over a 200-year period. The *actual* observations are given in the second column of Table 10.6.

Since there were 122 deaths during the 200-year period, the rate per year = 122/200 = .61. For ease in calculation, we fit the data to a Poisson random variable with mean λ = .60 rather than λ = .61. Thus, we obtain the expected frequencies (column 3) in Table 10.6 by multiplying the probabilities in Table 10.5 by 200. Then, the expected number of years in which 0 deaths occur is 200 × .5488 = 109.76, the expected number of years in which one death occurs is 200 × .3292 = 65.86, etc. Comparing the actual frequency counts (number of years) with their expected frequencies calculated from the Poisson distribution in column 3 of Table 10.6 indicates that the Poisson model fits the data quite closely. This conclusion can be confirmed by calculating the variance of the observations and showing that it is near the average .61 (problem 1).

In the next section, we discuss statistical methods for estimating λ and for comparing two Poisson data sets, e.g., testing whether both means, λ_1 and λ_2, are equal. Whenever the Poisson distribution is used in the analysis of data, it is important to remember that, as in the binomial model, the occurrence of an event (e.g., accident or death) in one trial or time period (year) does not affect the probability of the occurrence of a similar event at another trial or time period.

Problems

1. Calculate the variance of the data on deaths resulting from kicks by a horse and show that it is close to the mean, λ = .61.

2.   Assume an accident (e.g., airline or cavalry death) occurs one day. How reasonable is the assumption that the occurrence will *not* affect the probability of a similar accident the next day?

Answers to Selected Problems

1. $s^2 = .521$.

2.   Undoubtedly people are more careful shortly after an accident. This increased caution often diminishes with time, so the degree of dependence (or lack of independence) between the outcomes of contiguous trials is relatively small. The fact that accident rate data is reported yearly also implicitly adjusts for seasonal variations, etc. Nevertheless, when examining accident rate data, it is useful to look for possible clusters of accidents which may be due to a common cause (such as bad weather).

4.   Statistical Methods for Analyzing Data from a Poisson Distribution

In this section, we describe statistical procedures for obtaining an estimate of the mean and its associated confidence interval and for testing the equality of two means (rates per year). The methods will be based on fact that the variance of a Poisson distribution equals its mean and will use the normal approximation (or central limit theorem). Therefore, the methods should be considered as yielding approximate results, especially in small samples.

Since the parameter λ is the *mean* or *expected* number of accidents per year (or other time unit), a natural estimate is the average overall years of relevant data. Indeed, this is how we found the Poisson distribution that fit the Polish cavalry data. For the airline accident data (Table 10.3), the average number of fatal *accidents per year* was

$$\bar{X} = \frac{40}{10} = 4.$$

From Chapter 3, recall that an approximate 95% confidence interval for a *population mean* is given by

(10.5) $\bar{X} + (1.96) \dfrac{s}{\sqrt{n}}$

where s is the sample estimate of the standard deviation of the population, and n is the sample size.

Since the mean and variance of a Poisson variable are equal (to λ), the standard deviation, the square root of the variance, equals $\sqrt{\lambda}$, so s may be replaced by $\sqrt{\overline{X}}$, in equation (10.5). For the fatal accident data in Table 10.3, $\sqrt{\overline{X}} = \sqrt{4} = 2$ so an approximate 95% CONF for λ is

$$4 + (1.96)\,\frac{\sqrt{5.77}}{\sqrt{10}} = 4 + 1.49; \qquad \text{i.e., 95\% CONF } (\lambda; 2.51, 5.49).$$

(10.6)

Because the sample size (number of years of data) is small (10), the length of the confidence interval is rather wide, and the normal approximation should be considered as a crude one.

For the data in Table 10.6, which spanned 200 years, we found $\overline{X} = .61$, so our estimate of the standard deviation is $\sqrt{.61} = .781$, and the confidence interval (10.5) becomes

$$.61 \pm (1.96) = \sqrt{.61} \pm .108 \qquad \text{or} \qquad \text{95\% CONF } (\lambda; .502, .718).$$

(10.7)

Notice that the confidence intervals (10.6) and (10.7) depend on the assumption that the data comes from a Poisson distribution. If one is unsure of that assumption, one can use the sample standard deviation $s = \sqrt{(1/n - 1)\,\Sigma_i(x_i - \bar{x})^2}$ instead of $\sqrt{\overline{X}}$. Indeed, statistical procedures that check whether the data comes from a Poisson distribution are based on the agreement (within sampling error) of $\overline{X}$ and s^2.

In order to test whether two sets of data come from the Poisson distributions with the same parameter λ against the alternative that their underlying rates (or mean numbers of yearly occurrences) differ, a useful procedure is based on the statistic

(10.8)
$$\frac{\overline{X}_2 - \overline{X}_1}{\sqrt{\dfrac{\overline{X}_1}{n_1} + \dfrac{\overline{X}_2}{n_2}}} \sim Z,$$

where $\overline{X}_1$ and $\overline{X}_2$ are the average number of accidents per year in the two data sets which refer to data for n_1 and n_2 years, respectively. The basis of the statistic (10.8) is that each sample mean is approximately normal, with mean λ_i and variance $\lambda_i (i = 1, 2)$. Under the null hypothesis (both means are equal to λ, say), the difference $\overline{X}_2 - \overline{X}_1$ has mean 0 and variance $\lambda/n_1 + \lambda/n_2$, as the variances of both Poisson distributions are the same, λ. Thus, we replace λ by $\overline{X}_1$ for the data from the first sample and by $\overline{X}_2$ for the data from the second sample in forming the normalized statistic (10.8).

Let us apply this method to see whether the data supports the claim that deregulation increased the rate of fatal accidents, by comparing the mean yearly rates of accidents reported in Table 10.3 for the five-year period 1973 through 1977, with that of the succeeding five-year period, 1978 through 1982. In the first period, the total number of fatal accidents was 22, so the average rate was 4.4. Similarly, there were 18 fatal accidents or an average rate of 3.6 in the second period. The statistic (10.8) equals

$$(10.9) \qquad Z = \frac{3.6 - 4.4}{\sqrt{\dfrac{3.6}{5} \quad \dfrac{4.4}{5}}} = \frac{-.8}{\sqrt{.72 + .88}} = \frac{-.8}{1.27} = -.63$$

Since a standard normal variable has probability .2643 of being less than $-.63$, the difference is not even close to statistical significance at the .05 level. Hence, the null hypothesis that the rate of fatal accidents for both time periods is the same is accepted, implying that the assertion of the critic that deregulation increased the rate of fatal accidents is not supported by the data.

Problems

The following table reporting the number of bank failures in the United States appeared in *The Economist*.

Time Period	Average Number of Bank Failures Per Year
1946–50	5.0
1951–55	4.6
1956–60	4.0
1961–65	6.6
1966–70	6.4
1971–75	6.8
1976–80	9.8
1981	10.0
1982	42.0
1983	48.0

Source: Taken from the issue of Sept. 22, 1984 (page 40) of The Economist which reported data from the F.D.I.C.

1. A number of bank regulations were removed during the 1980–1981 time period as part of a general trend to deregulate business. Assuming

that the number of bank failures follows a Poisson distribution, does the data for the years 1982 and 1983 have the *same* rate as that for 1976–80 (we delete 1981 as it was a transition year)?

2. The government might argue that the 1981 should have been included in the post-regulation period so that our conclusion in problem 1 was erroneous. Would recalculating the statistical test change the ultimate statistical inference that more banks failed after deregulation than did in the previous five-year period?

3. The 1981–82 time period is considered as a recessionary one. Could this fully explain the rise in bank failures in the data? What other data might you wish to analyze to study this issue?

4. Suppose the *number* of banks had risen *dramatically* during the time frame of the data. Would the Poisson model be appropriate?

Answers to Selected Problems

1. Comparing the 1976–80 data ($\overline{X}_1 = 9.8$) with that of 1982–83 ($\overline{X}_2 = 45$) using (10.8) yields a

$$Z = \frac{45 - 9.8}{\sqrt{\dfrac{9.8}{5} + \dfrac{45}{5}}} = \frac{35.2}{\sqrt{24.46}} = 7.117,$$

which is quite significant (the *p*-value is less than .0001).

2. If the 1981 data is included, X_2 becomes 33.3 and n increases to 3 so our test statistic is

$$Z = \frac{33.33 - 9.8}{\sqrt{\dfrac{9.8}{5} + \dfrac{33.3}{3}}} = \frac{35.2}{3.615} = 6.51,$$

which remains quite significant. Thus, the suggested explanation does not refute the conclusion.

3. We need to ascertain the effect of recessions on bank failures in earlier recessions. To do this one needs to obtain yearly data from the FDIC. Judging from the sharp jump in bank failures, the recession may only explain part of the increase, especially as recessions occurred in

some of the earlier time periods included in the data. The data for 1984 would also shed light on the issue, as it was a good year for the economy. An additional complication is the fact that weak banks are often allowed to be taken over by stronger ones to avoid failing. Data on such bank mergers might be obtained, and banks which were near failure might be included with the failures.

4.   The simple Poisson model counting bank failures would no longer be appropriate. Related methods using bank failure rates (per 1000 banks in operation) should be used.

5.   Further Use of the Poisson Model in Epidemiological and Environmental Studies

In Section 2, we assessed the effect of AF on the likelihood of a person having a stroke by comparing the rate of occurrence of strokes in persons with AF to the corresponding rate of a control group (a population of non-AF individuals with the same age-sex and hypertensive status characteristics). In such studies, the control group often is much more numerous than the study group so that we can ignore the fact the normal incidence rate λ_0 is subject to random error and simply test the hypothesis that the incidence rate λ of the experimental study group equals λ_0 against the alternative that it exceeds λ_0. In this section, we discuss this one sample test and its Mantel-Haenszel type extension to stratified samples.

   The basic test statistic again uses the normal approximation to the Poisson, i.e., if X has a Poisson distribution with mean λ_0, then X is approximately normally distributed with mean λ_0 and standard deviation $\sqrt{\lambda_0}$. To test whether $\lambda = \lambda_0$, we compute

$$Z = \frac{\text{actual count minus expected}}{\text{standard deviation}} = \frac{\text{actual minus expected}}{\sqrt{\text{expected}}} = \frac{X - \lambda_0}{\sqrt{\lambda_0}},$$

(10.10)

because the standard deviation of a Poisson variable is the square root of its mean and see if it is less than the approximate critical value, (e.g., 1.645 for a 5% level test against the alternative $\lambda > \lambda_0$). For the data in Table 10.3, the rate of 7.43 per 1000 person years means that of the 481 persons with AF, we expect

$$\frac{7.43}{1000} \times 491 = 3.57$$

to have a stroke, i.e., if the AF group has the same incidence of stroke as the general population of a comparable age and hypertensive status, the number of strokes would follow a Poisson distribution with mean $0 = 3.57$. However, we observed $X = 20$ strokes. The corresponding Z value (10.10) is

$$(10.11) \qquad Z = \frac{20 - 3.57}{\sqrt{3.57}} = \frac{16.53}{1.889} = 8.696,$$

which is far greater than the critical values 1.645 or 1.96, corresponding to one-sided and two-sided 5% significance levels. Indeed, the probability of observing such a large value from standard normal variable is less than one in a million. Thus, we conclude that the AF groups have a significantly greater incidence of strokes than the non-AF group. This formal statistical test reinforces the conclusion of the formal hearing that the fact that persons with AF had a relative risk of stroke 5.6 that of the comparable non-AF population constitutes an important difference between the two groups, as we know that such a large relative risk could not be due to chance.

Recall that the relative risk of exposure is the ratio of the probability, p, of getting the disease if exposed to the corresponding probability, p_0, of a nonexposed person (control group member) getting the disease. In the Poisson model, the mean λ represents np in the binomial model so that the relative risk is

$$\frac{p}{p_0} = \frac{np}{np_0} = \frac{\lambda}{\lambda_0}.$$

Usually the value λ for the study group is estimated by the observed number of cases, while λ_0 is the number of cases that are expected to occur in a nonexposed or control group of similar size (n). Again, the estimated relative risk is of the form

$$(10.12) \qquad \frac{\text{observed number of cases in the study group}}{\text{expected number}},$$

where the expected number is determined by one of the standardization procedures. For the data in Table 10.4, the relative risk of 5.6 is obtained by dividing the observed number of cases (20) in the study group by its expected number 3.57. Of course, this calculation agrees with the ratio of the rates per 1000 person years derived earlier. This alternative calculation of the relative risk is useful when verifying results from studies which just report the national rate from which λ_0 is derived.

The Framingham study is a cohort or follow-up study in which a large population was studied over a number of years. Such a process is time consuming, and the Poisson model is also used to analyze historical data where the observed count of cases or deaths over a previous time period are compared to their expected numbers calculated by applying the national age-sex rates to the age-sex distribution of the study population. If a large period of time is involved, the expected number of cases may be calculated for each of several subperiods and then summed. This ensures that changes in the age-sex composition of the study population during the time frame is accounted for.

An example of an historical mortality ratio analysis assessing the possible effect of exposure to electromagnetic fields on the job to mortality from leukemia will now be described. Death certificates of all males over 20 years of age residing in the state of Washington were coded by cause of death and occupation.

The actual number of deaths from leukemia that occurred during the years 1950–1979 in each of the relevant occupations were compared to their expected numbers. Due to the long time-period examined, the proportionate mortality standardization procedure was carried out for several subperiods in determining the expected numbers. The results of the study are reported in Table 10.7. Notice that the relative risk of 1.37 of *all* workers in the occupations indicates that workers exposed to electromagnetic fields have a somewhat increased risk of leukemia. To assess whether the observed relative risk could have occurred by chance we use the test statistic (10.10)

$$(10.13) \quad \frac{\text{observed deaths} - \text{expected}}{\sqrt{\text{expected}}} = \frac{136 - 99.2}{99.2} = \frac{36.8}{9.96} = 3.69,$$

which is clearly statistically significant (one-sided p value $< .001$).

Notice that the data is also reported for the individual job categories. In 10 of the 11 categories the PMR (estimated relative risk) exceeded one, although statistical significance at the .01 level was obtained in only three categories. This is probably due to the relatively small numbers of men employed in those jobs. Moreover, the PMR for the one group (welders) with a PMR less than 1.0 was *not* statistically significantly less than 1.0. Had it been, one might question whether all the occupations should be considered as exposed or exposed to the same degree and, consequently, whether it is statistically proper to pool all the data as we did in our test (10.13) of significance.

The basic idea underlying historical PMR analysis is similar to the

TABLE 10.7.   Leukemia Mortality in Men Occupationally Exposed to Electrical and Magnetic Fields. (Washington State White Males, 1950–1979)

Occupation	Mortality from All Leukemia		
	observed	expected	PMR
Electronic technicians	6	4.0	1.49
Radio and telegraph operators	5	4.5	1.11
Electricians	51	37.0	1.38*
Linemen (power and telephone)	15	9.4	1.59
Television and radio repairmen	5	3.2	1.57
Power-station operators	8	3.1	2.59*
Aluminum workers	20	10.6	1.89*
Welders and flame cutters	12	17.9	.67
Motion picture projectionists	4	1.7	2.34
Electrical engineers	7	6.1	1.14
Streetcar and subway motormen	3	1.7	1.75
ALL	136	99.2	137

Source: Extracted from Table 1 with the same title in Milham, S. Jr. (1982). Mortality from Leukemia in Workers Exposed to Electrical and Magnetic Fields. *New England Journal of Medicine* **307,** 249.

Note: Based on standardized mortality for Washington State white males. (PMR values are exact; expected values have been rounded off.) The PMR is the ratio of the observed to expected number of deaths, where the expected number is derived by assuming that the proportion of all deaths that are due to leukemia should be the same as that of all persons of the same age and sex of the workers. An * indicates that the *p*-value of a one-sided test is <.01.

binomial model in discrimination litigation. There is a small fraction, p, of the general population in each age-sex category that will naturally contract (or die from) a particular disease in a set time period. We compare the observed number of cases or deaths, in an exposed group with their expected number calculated by assuming they have the same chance of mortality as the general population. The test statistic (10.10) is the analog of standard deviation analysis. The difference between the observed and expected number is an absolute measure of the effect of the exposure studied, while the PMR (relative risk) is a relative measure. The standardization procedure used in determining the expected number (λ_0) of deaths adjusts for the effect of other known factors, just as we used factors such as geographic proximity, occupation and earnings to determine the appropriate minority share of the qualified work force available to an employer. The statistical tests assess whether the observed data (minority hires, deaths from a specific disease) can be considered as a representative random sample from the *relevant* population (qualified work force or general population with the same age-sex composition as the study group).

Combining the workers in all exposed occupations into one sample, as in our discussion of the data in Table 10.7, is an illustration of the fact that the *sum* of independent Poisson variables is also Poisson with mean $\sum_i \lambda_i$, the sum of the means (λ_i) of the component variables, i.e., the expected total count is the sum of the expected counts. Furthermore, the standard deviation of the total number is $\sqrt{\sum \lambda_i}$, since the *variance* of a Poisson variable equals its mean. We now turn to a slightly different application of these ideas.

A land management course at the George Washington University Law School was concerned with claims citizens opposing a proposed location of an airport might raise at a public hearing. Several epidemiological studies were reviewed concerning differential rates of mental illness and birth defects between areas near airports which were impacted by noise and comparable control areas which were not. The results of a study[4] on birth defects are summarized in Table 10.8. The noise area consisted of persons living in census tracts in the Los Angeles area which were exposed to noise levels of 90 decibels or more from the Los Angeles airport. The remainder of Los Angeles County was taken as the control group. The data in Table 10.8 is reported separately for each race because it is known that racial and ethnic groups have different rates of some types of birth defects. This also enables us to see whether the effect of noise is similar (i.e., increases or decreases or has no effect on the rate of birth defects) in the two races.

TABLE 10.8, Distribution of Births for the Years 1976, 1971 and
1972 in the Noise and Control Areas of Los Angeles
Metropolitan Area

	Total Births	Defects	Incidence Rate (Fraction)
White			
Noise	2,522	30	.0119
Control	172,690	1,493	.0086
Black			
Noise	2,545	36	.0141
Control	47,389	546	.0115

Source: Taken from Table 1 from Jones, F. N. and Tauscher, J. (1978).
Residence Under an Airport Landing Pattern as a Factor in Teratism.
Archives of Environmental Health **33,** 10–12.

Although the data is presented for both the study (noise area) and
control groups so that the Mantel-Haenzel (Section 5.6) statistic could be
calculated, it is easier to use the Poisson model. The reason for this is that
the sum of *independent* Poisson variables is also Poisson with mean the
sum of the means (λ_i) of the component variables. Thus, we can use the
test statistic (10.10) and the corresponding estimate of relative risk (observed divided by expected number of cases). Under the null hypothesis,
the expected number of cases of birth defects in the noise area is calculated by assuming that both races in the noise area have the same rate of
birth defects as in the control area. Thus, the expected number of cases
in the white population is (.0086) (2522) = 21.69, and the expected number in the black population is (.0115) (2545) = 29.27, so $\lambda_0 = 21.69 +
29.27 = 50.96$. As a total of 66 birth defects in the study (noise) area
occurred in the study period, the test statistic (10.11) is

$$(10.14) \qquad Z = \frac{\text{observed} - \text{expected}}{\sqrt{\text{expected}}} = \frac{66 - 50.96}{50.96} = 2.11,$$

implying that the excess number of birth defects occurring in the noise
area is statistically significant (at the two-sided .05 level). Again, the
overall measure of relative risk is obtained by calculating the ratio of
observed cases (66) in the noise area to its expected number (50.96),
yielding the value 1.295 or about 1.3. These results indicate that noise

does have an effect on the likelihood of a child having a birth defect, but the increased risk is not very great.

This data is also instructive from a statistical viewpoint, as we can study the effect of ignoring the sampling variability in a very large control group. Calculating the Mantel-Haenszel test for the data in Table 10.8 yields a Z of 2.05 instead of 2.11. The closeness of these results illustrates the accuracy of the Poisson approximation.[5]

So far we have focused on the statistical methods used in drawing inferences from data reporting accident and disease rates. In the context of litigation and public policy, the quality of the basic data and the choice of control or comparison group are especially important. In the teratism (birth defects) study, both the noise and control areas were shown to have comparable demographic profiles (i.e., similar age distribution and income levels of residents). This type of comparison is essential, as it reassures us that any observed difference is due to exposure to noise and not to another factor or characteristic in which the two areas differed. For example, suppose that the control area in the teratism study had both a higher level of income and a larger proportion of doctors in the population. Then the increase in teratism in the noise area might have reflected a difference in the quality of prenatal care rather than exposure to noise. Even when standardized rates which incorporate various factors such as sex and age differences between the study and control groups are used, the choice of the control group from which the expected number of cases in the study group is determined can create a serious problem. Usually *national* disease incidence or mortality rates for each age-sex category are used in developing the expected number or rate, however, these numbers may be too high (biased upwards) in occupational health studies, as the employed population is healthier than the general population. Without adjusting for this healthy worker effect, the risk of exposure in occupational studies is underestimated; therefore, OSHA in its regulatory deliberations has rejected[6] studies which do not account for this effect.

A difficulty in SMR and SIR analyses, such as the Washington State leukemia and teratism studies, is that complete comparability on all relevant confounding variables (covariates or influential factors) is virtually impossible to achieve. In an ideal research experiment, we would randomly assign people to the control and exposed groups to assure that the proportions of persons in the control and study groups with a particular factor, or set of factors, were approximately equal. In real life we cannot tell people where to live or work, rather we can only observe what happens. Thus, people living near an airport may differ from those living far away for a variety of reasons. Thus, even when a statistically significant, slightly increased relative risk in the range of 1.2 to 1.5 or so is observed after major confounders (age, race, sex) have been incorporated in the standardization process, it is still possible for one or more of the omitted factors or statistical errors in the data to explain the increased risk.

Comment.   Statisticians distinguish between *controlled experiments* and *observational studies* such as the teratism one. In a *controlled* investigation the researcher assigns persons to the treated (exposed) and the control groups in a way that assures that the groups are likely to be balanced with respect to other factors that may influence the response (i.e., whether one develops the disease under study). Typically, this is achieved by randomly assigning the subjects in the experiment or control group. Several controlled clinical trials will be discussed in Chapter 13. In observational studies, the effect of other factors related to the response being studied usually has to be accounted for in the analysis of the data. Indeed, stratification of the data into homogeneous subgroups and combining the results of the individual subgroups into a summary one such as the Mantel-Haenszel method and standardization methods are required for a careful analysis of observational data. Of course, these methods are used in the analysis of controlled experiments when stratification is appropriate.

Before concluding that a statistical association should be regarded as epidemiologic evidence of causalty or even a real relationship, several studies adjusting for the major covariates should be conducted in a variety of communities. If they show a consistent pattern of an increased relative risk of reasonable magnitude, then it is unlikely that a new factor could explain the association, since the proportion of people with this extra factor will probably vary widely among the study areas. Not only would the new factor need to possess a relative risk exceeding the observed one to satisfy Cornfield's first criterion, it would need to be sufficiently prevalent in each study group relative to its control group to satisfy the second criterion.

Another problem that arises in these studies concerning disease incidence or mortality is the ascertainment of all cases and their correct diagnosis. One may be fairly confident that almost all serious birth defects are correctly diagnosed and reported to the proper public health authorities for children born in hospitals; however, one is less certain about the reporting of teratism in children born outside hospitals. Indeed, the increased risk of teratism due to airport noise was not confirmed in a subsequent study[7] in Atlanta, perhaps due to differential reporting of various types of defects in one or both studies. These problems are even more serious in studies of the effect of occupational exposure to chemicals where diseases (e.g., cancer) take many years to develop. Over time, employees may not only leave the plant they worked in, they may move to another region of the country, making it quite difficult to determine their current health status. This problem of loss to follow-up occurs in a variety of medical studies, but careful studies often can minimize the problem.

We should note that prospective or follow-up studies, such as the Framingham one, or historical perspective studies where the subjects (and their parents) are alive and available to be interviewed about confounding factors, such as the Love Canal study, have a better opportunity to obtain needed information than SMR or PMR studies. In particular, information on smoking habits which enabled us to stratify the Love Canal data in Table 5.11 is usually not available in SMR studies relying on age-sex adjusted mortality rates. Since smoking is a major cause of cancer, heart and lung problems, and for a number of diseases has a relative risk of 5 or more, it is possible that differences in smoking patterns may explain an observed association or at least introduce a bias in the estimated SMR (or PMR).

Since questions can be raised about the quality of data in any large-scale study, it is important to report the p-value of the statistical tests carried out and an estimate of the relative risk or similar measure of the difference between the study and control groups. One can then assess whether a small amount of missing data or a few errors of misdiagnosis could alter the ultimate conclusion. While a moderate difference in access to medical care might explain the difference in rates of teratism between the noise impacted area and the rest of Los Angeles County to statistical insignificance (at the .05 level), since the value of the Z statistic was only 2.11, it is very unlikely that a modest difference in access to or quality of medical care between the AF and non-AF populations could reduce the Z value 8.9 of the test statistic to insignificance or reduce the estimated fivefold increase of stroke in AF patients to a minimal level.

Problems

1.   In our analysis of the totality of data in Table 10.8, we found that overall relative risk of having a baby born with a defect was about 1.3. From Table 10.8 calculate the relative risk for each racial group separately. Are they both reasonably close to the summary measure of 1.3?

2.   The data in Table 10.8 suggest that blacks in either area have a higher incidence of birth defects than whites. From this data can one conclude that the difference is genetic in origin?

3.   Another study[8] linked airport noise to higher mortality by comparing the death rate of persons in the noise-exposed area with that of a control area and found a relative risk of about 1.20. Although the authors attempted to choose a control region which was comparable to the exposed area, i.e., the race-sex composition and the economic status of the residents of both areas were similar, it is difficult to have all these factors balance out. A subsequent article[9] re-analyzed this data by comparing the observed deaths in each area to an *expected number* of deaths calculated by applying the Los Angeles County age, race and sex specific death rates to the corresponding population data. The new study found no evidence of increased mortality.

   (a) Read the two studies. Describe how the methods used for standardization differ.

   (b) The second study also questioned the validity of the conclusion of the teratism study. It apparently characterized the findings in Table 10.8 as not being statistically significant for either race separately and then criticized the first study for not accounting for other possible confounding variables such as mother's age or parity.

   (1) Was it correct for the authors of this second study to require a statistically significant increased risk of teratism for each race?

   (2) Is it plausible that mother's age or parity status could explain the finding of increased teratism?

   (3) Suppose the estimated relative risk of teratism for residents in the noise impacted area was 2.2 rather than 1.3. Do you think differences in maternal age and parity status could explain the results?

4.   (a) Compare the statistical characteristics of the Washington State occupational health study with the Los Angeles teratism study considering the following issues:

   (1) The number of covariates or confounding variables the methodology accounted for

   (2) The reliability of the case or death diagnosis.

   (3) The magnitude of the estimated relative risk.

   (4) The consistency of the results across relevant strata.

   (b) What other studies might you wish to see carried out before accepting the association between noise exposure and teratism as an estab-

TABLE 10.9.   Black Hires by Republic National Bank in Exempt Job Categories in 1970–1973

Job Groups	Total Hires	Black Availability	Black Hires	Expected Black Hires
A–H	31	.0141	0	.4371
I–K	85	.0318	1	2.7030
L–P	89	.0261	0	2.3229
Q–W	135	.0351	3	4.7385
X–Z	81	.0074	1	.5994
AA–CC	48	.0301	0	1.448
DD–II	18	.0206	0	.3708
JJ–MM	55	.0288	3	1.584
			8	14.2005

Source: 505 F.Supp. 224 (1980) at footnote 189.

lished risk to the public? What requirements would you introduce in the new studies?

5. Although we illustrated the combination of Poisson variables on epidemiologic data, it can also be used in EEO cases when the parameters p_i in each of the occupational categories are small so that the Poisson approximation is valid. Use the combination method of this section to analyze defendant's hires of blacks in exempt positions in *Vuyanich v. Republic National Bank*. Table 10.9 reports the data in this opinion, and an extra column, expected number of black hires, is included to assist your computation.

Since the availability figures were the bank's and tended to be low, use a one-sided test at the .05 level. Suppose the judge decided that the bank's availability fractions included some persons already employed in higher paying jobs in the same occupation and therefore underestimated black availability by about 20%. Multiply the availability figures in Table 10.9 by 1.25 and recalculate the test statistic. What happens to the *p*-value?
Hint: Since we are using the Poisson approximation in all job categories to obtain the new expected number (λ_0), just multiply the old one by 1.25.

Answers to Selected Problems

1. For whites, RR = .0119/.0086 = 1.384 and for blacks RR = .0141/.0015 = 1.226. They are reasonably close to the overall measure.

2.   No. There are other social and economic factors which may have caused the small difference.

3.   b. (1) No, a combined test is sufficient, especially when the expected number of cases is small and both sets of data show an effect in the same direction (increased risk)
3.   b. (2) By Cornfield's result, the fraction of persons in the higher age (risk) group in the airport would have to be at least 1.3 times the fraction of higher age persons in the control area. This is possible, however, the critics would be on sounder grounds had they offered data indicating that the age distributions of females of child-bearing ages in the two areas were different.
3.   b. (3) Probably not, especially as the age distributions of the two areas were not very different (see the original study).

4.   (a) The occupational health study was able to control for age, sex and occupation, while the teratism study only considered the race of the child. Of course, the teratism study did have a complete count of the actual number of births in the period from which those with defects came, while the census data on occupation is only based on a complete census every ten years, and the labor force questions are only given to a sample (15% or 20%) of respondents. The diagnosis of death due to cancer is probably more reliable than reported birth defects, and the magnitude of relative risk is higher in the leukemia study. On the other hand, the smoking pattern of the workers was unavailable and this can be a major confounder.

(b) A case-control study comparing the residence of a baby with a defect to several other children born in the same large metropolitan area the same day or week would be useful background data on the effect of age and parity of the mother. Family characteristics, such as income and whether or not the family members have a regular physician and the amount of prenatal care received by the mother, could also be obtained.

6.   Statistical Power and Related Considerations in Planning Epidemiologic Studies

In this section we discuss how the concept of power plays a basic role in designing an SIR or SMR study. First, the use of the statistical power in determining the sample size of a study concerning the incidence of a respiratory disease in coal miners is described. We then present a short table which demonstrates how the power of a study depends on the relative risk R deemed important to detect, i.e., the alternative value of $\lambda_1 = R\lambda_0$, where λ_0 is the number, E, of cases expected to occur when the null hypothesis is true. Once the values of λ_1, λ_0 are specified, then the only way to increase the power of a study of a .05 (or any predetermined desired type I error) level test is to increase E, the expected number of cases that should occur naturally. This may entail taking a larger sized sample from a big population or, if the exposed population is relatively small, increasing the time period of the study.

As part of its mandate under the Federal Mine Safety and Health Act,[10] the U.S. Department of Health and Human Services is required to schedule a process of "reducing the average concentration of respirable dust in the mine atmosphere ... to a level of personal exposure which will present no incidences of respiratory disease and the further development of disease in any person." An important disease of the lung which arises from exposure to coal mine dust is coalworker's pneumoconiosis (CWP), which occurs first in a benign state (named stage 1) and can progress to more serious stages 2 and 3, which may lead to progressive massive fibrosis that is often disabling and can cause premature death. Therefore, in 1972 the government set a standard of 2 mg/m3[11] for the maximum allowable concentration of dust in a mine.

The standard was established from a dose response curve derived from a study[12] which showed that there would be a very small probability of moving from the no disease category to a stage 2 or greater category in 35 years, assuming a person was exposed to an average concentration of 2 mg/m^3 of dust during those years. Thirty-five years was chosen, as it is typically the working period of an underground miner. The British data indicated that if the 2 mg/m^3 standard were enforced, only 2% of the miners would be expected to develop a stage 1 (benign) case of CWP, which was not likely to progress further. Hence, virtually *no* cases of the more serious stages would be expected to occur. To monitor the effectiveness of the standard, the government studies the health of underground coal miners.

In designing the monitoring study, it was decided that a 50% excess incidence of stage 1 or simple CWP among the miners would be important to detect, as this would indicate that there was non-negligible chance of miners contracting a more serious stage of the disease. In this situation the null hypothesis is that $p_0 = .02$ and *alternative* is that $p_1 = .03$, where p is the probability a miner contracts stage 1 CWP over a 35-year worklife.

An approximate formula for the *sample size* needed to keep both type I and type II error probabilities at the .05 level is given in the appendix to this chapter. In the mining context the required sample is about 2500. This sample size is necessary because under H_0 we expect only $.02 \times 2500 = 50$ cases, and the *critical point* (i.e., the number of cases that would need to be observed to reject the null hypothesis at the .05 level of significance) is about

$$(10.15) \qquad 50 \times (1.645)\sqrt{50} = 61.63 \qquad \text{or} \qquad 62.$$

Under the alternative hypothesis ($p = .03$), we expect $.03 \times 2500 = 75$ cases. From the normal approximation to the Poisson (8.10), there is only a 5% chance that we would observe *fewer* than

$$(10.16) \qquad 75 - (1.645)\sqrt{75} = 60.75 \qquad \text{or} \qquad 61$$

cases. Thus, using the rule, reject the null hypothesis if 62 or more cases are observed yields a one-sided .05 level test criteria having an approximate power of 95% of detecting the predetermined alternative, $p_1 = .03$.

Similar calculations showed that if the true incidence rate was double the rate expected under the federal guideline, i.e., $p_1 = .04$, then the study would have power exceeding .99%, i.e., the study would almost certainly detect it. On the other hand, if the true incidence rate was $p_1 = .0225$ (a 25% excess rate), then the power of the study would only be .44. Of course this alternative is quite close to the null hypothesis and an incidence rate of 2.25 stage 1 cases per 100 workers might not lead to a substantial increase in the expected number of serious cases.

In the coal miner study the Poisson model was used to analyze the data, as the probability, p, any single worker has of getting stage 1 CWP is quite small. Notice that the expected number (λ) of stage 1 cases was determined by translating the legal standard into an allowable incidence of benign cases based on prior scientific studies. In order to see the interplay between the relative risk (R) deemed important and the expected number (E) of cases under the null hypothesis ($R = 1.0$), in Table 10.10 we present the approximate power of a 5% one-sided test based on (10.10) to detect various alternative values of R as a function of E.

From Table 10.10 it is evident that for any fixed expected number of cases under the null hypothesis ($R = 1$), the power of the test increases rapidly as the alternative value of R gets further away from 1.0. Similarly, the power of a study to detect a specified alternative value of R increases with the expected number of cases when under the null hypothesis ($R = 1$). When planning a study the value of E will depend on the normal

TABLE 10.10.   Approximate Power of the One-Sided .05 Level Test used in SMR and Related Studies as a Function of the Expected Number of Deaths Under the Null Hypothesis and the Alternative Relative Risk (R)

Expected Number (E) of Cases Under the Null-Hypothesis $(R = 1)$	Power at Various Alternative Values Values of R				
	1.5	2.0	3	4	10
1	.13	.21	.43	.64	.99
2	.16	.32	.66	.87	.99+
4	.23	.50	.90	.99	.99+
6	.29	.65	.97	.99+	.99+
8	.35	.76	.99	.99+	.99+
10	.41	.84	.99+	.99+	.99+
20	.64	.98	.99+	.99+	.99+
50	.94	.99+	.99+	.99+	.99+

Source: The approximate powers were calculated using the formula in Beaumont and Breslow (1981) described in the appendix to this chapter.

incidence rate, the size of the population studied and the length of time the study population is observed.

An inherent difficulty in studies of relatively small groups (employees in a plant) is that even if there is a high relative risk of exposure, say $R = 4$, we may not expect to observe even one case in a reasonable time period if the normal incidence rate holds. On the other hand, even when a *single* study finds a significant increased risk due to the occurrence of a few cases, there is often some doubt as to whether all the excess cases can be attributed to the exposure under study. In the next section we describe an approach to assessing the results of several studies. We close this section by illustrating some statistical problems that arose in evaluating a planned small scale study.

In the 1970s a plant using a chemical now suspected as a possible cause of bladder and related cancers closed down after this fact became known. In response to community concern, a two-stage study was proposed. First, the number of cases of bladder cancer among the former workers would be observed for a period of 20 years and compared with the expected number of cases, assuming the normal incidence rate (standardized to the age-sex composition of the workers). If a significant excess risk was observed, then a case-control study would be conducted comparing the exposure level of cases to those of a control group of workers who did not get the disease. Such a control group may be quite different from the population-based control groups typically used in the case-control studies (see Chapter 6). Moreover, in order for such a case-control study to be informative, there would have to be a wide range of exposure levels amongst the workers. Otherwise, we could not observe a difference between the exposure levels of the cases and controls (workers of similar age as the cases but who worked in a different part of the plant). Thus, if it were reasonable to conduct the case-control study, a sizable fraction of the original workforce would have had to have little or no exposure. In the original plan of the basic cohort study, however, *all workers* were assumed to have been exposed. Intuitively, *including nonexposed workers* in such a study *as exposed* should dilute its power, thereby making it less likely to detect an increased risk of bladder cancer. We next indicate the magnitude of this loss in power.

Since only about 500 workers were employed by the firm at the time of major exposure, a 20-year follow-up of *all* workers was planned. Due to some loss due to death by accidents and unrelated illnesses, as well as difficulty in locating all the workers, it was assumed that after 20 years the total person years of exposure studied would be 9000, rather than the optimum $500 \times 20 = 10,000$. From the national incidence of bladder and related cancers, it was determined that the age-adjusted probability of contracting the cancer under study per person-year would be

$$p = .000167$$

for a cohort of unexposed persons with the same age distribution as the workers. Hence, if the chemical was unrelated to cancer, then we would expect to find

$$9000 \times .000167 = 1.5$$

cases among the workers during the 20-year follow-up period. On the other hand, similar chemicals had been shown to have relative risks of about 4.0, which means that if the chemical under study also has a relative risk of 4, then one would expect to observe 6 cases. Thus, the original study planned to use the critical region:

(10.17)   Reject if the observed number of cases is 5 or more.

This corresponds to a level, α, of about .02 for a one-sided test. The power of the test criteria (8.17) to detect a fourfold relative risk is the probability that a Poisson variable with mean, $\lambda = 6$, yields an observed value 5 or more which equals[13]

.715.

Now suppose that one third of the workers had little or no exposure to the chemical but those who were exposed had a fourfold increased risk of bladder and related cancer. What is the *true power* of the original study using the rejection region (10.17) of detecting a significant excess risk?

Now the expected number of cases is the sum of the expected number of cases occurring in the 6000 person-years of truly exposed workers, $6000 \times 4 \times .000167 = 4.00$, plus the expected number of cases from the 3000 person-years of unexposed workers, $3000 \times .000167 = .501$. Thus, under the alternative of a fourfold increase in risk due to exposure we expect 4.509 cases, which we will round to 4.5. The probability that a Poisson variable with mean 4.5 exceeds 5 is only .468 or .47. Thus, the inclusion of the nonexposed workers in the first standardized incidence comparison *decreases* the expected power to about two thirds of its original value.

Suppose that a *revised study plan* for the cohort study uses a questionnaire to classify all workers by their exposure level and only considers the two thirds of the work force with moderate to heavy exposure as the study group. We need to determine the critical region anew. Under the null hypothesis of *no* effect, we would expect to observe

$$6000 \times .000167 = 1.002 \text{ cases,}$$

or about one case. A one-sided critical region with probability .02 under the null hypothesis is

(10.18)   Reject if the observed number of cases is 4 or more,

as the probability a Poisson variable with mean 1 is 4 or more is .019.

The power of this statistical test to detect a *fourfold* excess risk is the probability that a Poisson variable with mean 4 assumes a value of at least 4. This probability is .567, which is a meaningful improvement over .47. Thus, by restricting the SIR study to a smaller group of definitely exposed workers, we increase the power relative to the original study plan that included persons who had little or no exposure to the chemical.

Comment.   An additional advantage of the revised study plan is that the case-control study can be carried out at the same time as the cohort study. Whenever a case occurs, its exposure level can be compared to that of several appropriate controls. The case and its controls can be interviewed while the case is still alive so that information on relevant covariates such as smoking and exposure to other carcinogens can be obtained. By waiting until the cohort study is completed to carry out the case-control study, the original study design risks losing this information, especially from the first cases that develop.

Problems

1. Suppose an increased risk is observed in the modified small sample study using the critical region given by (10.18) because six cases are observed at the end of the 20-year observation period. How much additional information will be gained from the proposed case-control study? Would your answer change if four cases had been observed?

2. (a) Suppose that in the mining study 800, or about one third, of the 2500 miners really had *no* exposure, what is the true power of the test using the original critical region (reject the null hypothesis of no effect if the number of cases is 62 or more) to detect a relative risk of 1.5 among the exposed workers?

   (b) How does the loss in power of this study compare with that of the smaller study? Explain.

7. Assessing the Results of Several Studies

Because of the lack of knowledge of exposure the study group had to possible confounding variables inherent in standardized mortality and incidence studies, it is advisable to rely on several studies before concluding that there is an association between exposure to a substance and a disease. A useful approach is to summarize the results of the various studies in a table which reports the size of the exposed cohort, observed and expected number cases (or deaths) under this hypothesis of no effect ($R = 1$), p-value and power.

   In Table 10.11 we enumerate the results of four independent SMR studies of the effect of exposure to vinyl chloride on a worker's risk of contracting liver cancer. The studies involved workers in different locations. The deaths occurring in each plant were compared to their expected number of deaths calculated by standardizing national rates by year and sex of the workers in the plant.

   The results in Table 10.11 show that three of the four studies yielded a significant excess of liver cancer deaths at the .05 level (one-sided). The one study which did not yield a statistically significant result had an SMR of 2.44, which is consistent with an increased risk due to exposure. Notice

TABLE 10.11. Results of Several SMR Studies of the Relationship of Exposure to Vinyl Chloride and Liver Cancer

Study authors	Cohort size	Expected deaths assuming $R = 1.0$	Observed deaths	SMR	Significant at .05 Level	p-values	Power when $R = 5.0$
Fox and Collier	7717	1.64	4	2.44	—	.0844	.93
Waxweiller	4806	2.34	10	4.27	+	.0002	.98
Byran et al.	750	.97	4	4.13	+	.0172	.80
Reinl et al.	7021	.79	12	15.23	+	.0000	.76

Source: Adapted from Tables 1 and 2 of Beaumont and Breslow (1981) Power Considerations in Epidemiologic Studies of Vinyl Chloride. *American Journal of Epidemiology* **114**, 725–734. The p-values were obtained from exact tables of the Poisson distribution. The expected deaths in Table 10.11 were carried to two decimal places and were obtained by dividing the observed deaths by the SMR reported in Beaumont and Breslow.

the power of each of the four studies to detect an RR of 5.0 were reasonably high (.76 to .98), but the power to detect an RR of 3.0 would be much less. In light of this data it is reasonable to conclude that exposure to vinyl chloride increases one's chance of contracting liver cancer. The estimated SMRs ranged from 2.4 to 15.23 with a median of 4.2. The estimated SMR of 15 in one study seems unusually large, so the median is preferable to the mean as an overall estimate.

The data in Table 10.11 were quite clear, as all studies indicated an increased risk due to exposure. In situations where there are several significant studies and several nonsignificant ones, the concept of power can assist our interpretation of the overall pattern. If the *negative*[14] findings were based on studies of low power, while the findings of an increased SMR were based on studies of relatively high power and if most of the studies had an SMR greater than 1, then one can feel safe in concluding that there is an increased risk due to exposure. On the other hand, if the studies with negative results had high power and most of the studies did not yield SMRs much greater than 1.0 and some were less than one, we should doubt the existence of a real association between the agent in question and the disease. We refer the reader to the paper by Beaumont and Breslow (1981) for details. Our major point is that the concept of power has an essential role in the interpretation of several studies, each of which is based on a small study population.

In our discussion of the relation between vinyl chloride exposure and liver cancer (Table 10.11), we suggested that the median SMR of 4.2 be used as a summary relative risk estimate. Another possible summary estimate of relative risk is

$$(10.19) \qquad \frac{\sum x_i}{\sum \lambda_i} = \frac{\text{total observed in all studies}}{\text{total expected in all studies}},$$

which is based on the fact the sum of independent Poisson variables is also a Poisson variable. For the studies summarized in Table 10.11 this estimate yields

$$\frac{30}{5.74} = 5.23.$$

It exceeds 4.2 because of the single study which yielded an estimated SMR of 15.23. When we combine relative risk estimates (SMRs) from several studies, we are assuming that they all are estimating the same relative risk of exposure after accounting for the same confounding variables. This is not always the case, as the studies may have been carried out in different geographical locations so that exposure to other chemicals or pollutants and dietary patterns may have varied between the studies. If the standardization procedure in each of the studies used city or state-wide, age-sex incidence rates rather than nationwide mortality or incidence rates, then the main effect of these geographically varying confounders would be accounted for. On the other hand, if national rates were used in the standardization process then the simple estimate (10.19) might not be statistically valid. Before using (10.19) one should check whether the SMRs are relatively homogeneous.[15] In the present situation one might prefer the median risk or perhaps one might simply conclude that the overall relative risk of liver cancer due to exposure to vinyl chloride is in the range of 4.2 to 5.2.

Another potential problem in obtaining a summary relative risk estimate from several studies is that the amount or duration of exposure to the chemical may vary among the studies. In this situation we look for a dose-response relationship, i.e., persons exposed to a high level of exposure should have a higher relative risk. An example of such a dose-response relationship is apparent from the data in Table 1.14 (volume 1) reporting the results of a study of the relationship between arsenic exposure and respiratory cancer deaths by exposure levels (low, high) and duration (in 10-year periods). Notice that for each duration period, the highly exposed workers had an increased SMR and that for workers exposed to either exposure level, the SMR usually increased with length of time exposed. One cannot expect to see a perfect dose response relationship in such studies because of the relatively small number of workers in each group and the fact that important confounders such as smoking are often not controlled for.

Problems

1. Suppose a policymaker reviewing the results of the vinyl chloride studies reported on Table 10.11 felt that *all* four studies should be significant at the .05 level. Assuming that the studies were completely independent of one another, what is the level of significance that the policymaker is actually requiring? What mistake is being made?

2. Another measure of risk to the public that policymakers consider is the expected number of cases or deaths attributed to the exposure, i.e., if an exposure has a relative risk $R > 1$ and the normal lifetime (or other

preset time period) probability of getting a disease is p, and n persons are exposed, then the excess number of expected cases due to exposure is

(10.20) $n(R - 1)p.$

Notice that (10.20) is an absolute measure rather than a relative measure.

(a) Suppose a population of 1000 persons is exposed to a substance with an $R = 9$ of causing bladder cancer. How many excess deaths do we expect to be due to exposure in a 20-year period?

(b) Suppose 100 million people are exposed to a substance with an $R = 1.5$ of causing bladder cancer. How many excess deaths do we expect in a 20-year period?

(c) Comment on the merits of the absolute effect measure (10.20) and the relative risk for public policy purposes.

Answers to Selected Problems

1.   The person is requiring significance at level $(.05)^4 = .00000625$. This mistake is analogous to the problem of fragmentation discussed earlier.

TECHNICAL APPENDIX

An Approximate Formula for the Power of the One-Sample Poisson Test to Detect an Increased Relative Risk and Its Use in Determining the Sample Size of a Study

When we test a null hypotheses, e.g., $\lambda = \lambda_0$ against an alternative $\lambda_1 = R\lambda_0$ with $R > 1$ our test statistic, the observed number (X) of cases of the disease, has a *different* distribution depending on which hypothesis is true. If the null hypothesis is true, then X is Poisson with mean λ_0, while if the alternative is true, X is Poisson with mean, $\lambda_1 = R\lambda_0$. In our presentation we often used a normal approximation to the Poisson distribution, however, there is a more accurate approximation using the fact that for a Poisson variable with mean λ, $\sqrt{x}$, the *square root* of the observed number of cases, is approximately normally distributed with mean $\sqrt{\lambda}$ and variance 1/4. Using this procedure a one-sided test of size α (type I error $= \alpha$) has this *critical region.*

(10A.1)   Reject if $\sqrt{X} > \sqrt{\lambda_0} + \dfrac{z_\alpha}{2},$

where z_α is the point on the normal curve satisfying $P[Z \geq z_\alpha] = \alpha$. Under the alternative hypothesis that the number of cases is Poisson with mean $\lambda_1 = R\lambda_0$, the *power* of the test is the probability that the square root of the Poisson variable with mean λ_1 exceeds

$$\sqrt{\lambda_0} + \left(\frac{1}{2}\right) z_\alpha.$$

This probability is calculated by the methods given in Chapter 3, i.e.,

$$P\left[\sqrt{\bar{X}} > \left(\lambda_0 + \frac{1}{2} z_\alpha\right)\right]$$

(10A.2)
$$= Pr\left[\sqrt{\bar{X}} - \sqrt{\lambda_1} > \sqrt{\lambda_0} - \sqrt{\lambda_1} + \frac{z_\alpha}{2}\right].$$

As $\sqrt{\bar{X}} - \sqrt{\lambda_1}$ has variance $1/4$, we multiply both sides by 2 to make the *variance* of this normal variable 1, so we obtain

(10A.3) $\quad P[\sqrt{2}(\sqrt{\bar{X}} - \sqrt{\lambda_1}) \geq z_\alpha + 2(\sqrt{\lambda_0} - \sqrt{\lambda_1})].$

Now the variable in the left of (10A.3) is a standard normal, and the probability it exceeds the transformed *critical value* $z_\alpha + 2(\sqrt{\lambda_0} - \sqrt{\lambda_1})$ is approximately equal to the probability that a standard normal variable exceeds

(10A.4) $\quad z_{1-\beta} = z_\alpha + 2(\sqrt{\lambda_0} - \sqrt{\lambda_1}) = z_\alpha - 2(\sqrt{RE} - \sqrt{E}),$

where $\lambda_0 =$ the expected number E, of cases under the null hypotheses and RE is the expected number of cases if the substance has relative risk R. The right side of (10A.4) can be simplified by factoring out $\sqrt{E}$ so we obtain

(10A.5) $\quad z_{1-\beta} = z_\alpha - 2(\sqrt{R} - 1)\sqrt{E}.$

Let us illustrate the use of formula (10A.5) by finding the power of a study that expects nine cases to occur to detect a relative risk of 2 using a one-sided .05 level test. Now $z_\alpha = 1.645$, $R = 2$ and $\sqrt{E} = \sqrt{9} = 3$. Substitution yields

$$z_{1-\beta} = 1.645 - 2(\sqrt{2} - 1)3 = -.84.$$

Thus, the power is the probability that a standard normal variable *exceeds* $-.84$ and is obtained from Table A as approximately .80.

The approximation shows that the essential parameters determining the power of a study are the *expected number* of cases under the null hypothesis (H_0) and the *relative risk, R* one desires to detect. The expected number of cases under H_0 depends on the normal incidence or mortality rate and the number of subjects studied, so the only way to increase the power is to increase the number of subjects studied or the length of time of the study.

We can use formula to (10A.5) to determine the sample size needed to have a study attain prespecified small type I and type II levels. We illustrate this in the coal miner study where the objective was to keep both possible errors, at the .05 level. Then $z_\alpha = 1.645$, so this test statistic has only a .05 probability of exceeding z_α if the null hypothesis is true and $z_{1-\beta} = -1.645$, which implies the test has a 95% probability of exceeding the critical value when the *alternative* hypothesis is true. Thus, (10A.5) implies that the expected number, E, of cases under the null hypothesis must satisfy

$$-1.645 = 1.645 - 2(\sqrt{1.5} - 1)\sqrt{E}$$

or

$$2\sqrt{1.5} - 1)\sqrt{E} = 3.29$$

or

$$\sqrt{E} = \frac{3.29}{2(.2247)} = 7.32.$$

Thus, E should be $(7.32)^2 = 53.58$. When the null hypothesis ($p_0 = .02$) is true, the expected number of cases among n miners is np_0. Hence, the number, n, of miners that should be studied is given by

$$np_0 = 53.58 \qquad \text{or} \qquad n = \frac{(53.58)}{.02} = 2679.$$

Thus, approximately 2700 miners should be surveyed for evidence of stage 1 (benign) CWP. We used 2500 for computational convenience in the text.

NOTES

1. In defining the incidence rate, the persons studied should not have the disease at the beginning of the study. Otherwise, they could not become new cases. Technically speaking, the incidence rate estimates the *conditional* probability of contracting the disease *given* an individual was free of the disease at the beginning of the study.

2. Kaus, R. M. (1983). Cheap Seats and White Knuckles. *Washington Monthly*, December, 45–48.

3. Petition of Keinetz for review of the denial by FAA of an Airman Medical Certificate, National Transportation Board Hearing, docket SM 2685, Manitowac, Wisconsin (IV Cir-

cuit), July 29, 1981. I am indebted to Dr. R. Abbott, the government's expert witness, for kindly informing me of this application of statistics and providing me with the underlying report.

4.   Jones, F. N. and Tauscher, J. (1978). Residence Under an Airport Landing Pattern as a Factor in Teratism. *Archives of Environmental Health* 33, 10–12.

5.   Recall that the Poisson distribution was introduced as an approximation to the binomial when p was small. When n is large, as in the control population, the variability of the estimated incidence rate (p) is very small and we can ignore it and consider it as a known constant leading to a known λ.

6.   *Federal Register,* Volume 48, No. 196, 45956 at 45962.

7.   Edmonds, L. D., Layde, P. M. and Erickson, J. D. (1979). Airport Noise and Teratogensis. *Archives of Environmental Health* 34, 243–247.

8.   Meecham, W. C. and Shaw, N. (1979). Effects of Jet Noise on Mortality Rates. *British Journal of Audiology* 13, 77–80.

9.   Frerichs, R. R., Beeman, B. C. and Coulson, A. H. (1980). Los Angeles Noise and Mortality—Faulty Analysis and Public Policy, *American Journal of Public Health* 70, 357–362 and the exchange of letters on pages 543–544 of the same volume.

10.   Public Law 91-173 as amended in PL95-164.

11.   Milligrams per cubic meter.

12.   Jacobsen, M., Rale, S., Walton, W. H. and Rogan, J. M. (1971). The Relation Between Pneumoconosis and Dust Exposure in British Coal Mines. In: Walton, W. H. (ed). *Inhaled Particles III.* Old Working, Surrey: Unwin Brothers, 903–919.

13.   Because of the small value of λ reflecting the small expected number of cases in this part of the text, the probability of rejection under the null hypothesis and the power of the test were obtained from tables of the Poisson distribution rather than from the normal approximation. Because counts can only be integers, the closest significance level to the usual .05 one was .02. Adding another integer to the critical region would make the level (α) of the test exceed .05.

14.   In medical studies a finding of no relationship or association is called a *negative result* in analogy to medical tests for agents in blood, etc.

15.   Remember that even if the true relative risk, R, is the same for all studies, we expect the individual estimates to vary around this true value due to sampling fluctuations. Statistical tests for homogeneity to see whether the variation among several estimates of R may be due to sampling error can be used to check this assumption before making a summary estimate such as (7.9). These tests are usually based on the squares of the differences between the observed data and what would be expected if the summary estimate R_s were true, i.e., now the expected number of cases in each study would be $R_s x E$. Specific formulas are given in the article by Beaumont and Breslow (1981). A useful test for whether several binomial samples can be regarded as having a common p is discussed in Mosteller and Rourke (1973) and is illustrated in the Appendix to Chapter 9.

REFERENCES

Attfield, M., Reger, R. and Glenn, R. (1984). The Incidence and Progression of Pneumoconiosis Over Nine Years in U.S. Coal Miners: I and II. *American Journal of Industrial Medicine* **6**, 407–415 and 417–425. (These papers provide further background on the pneumoconiosis study.)

Beaumont, J. J. and Breslow, N. E. (1981). Power Considerations in Epidemiologic Studies of Vinyl Chloride Workers. *American Journal of Epidemiology* **114**, 725–734.

BLOT, W. J., FRAUMENI, JR. J. F., MASON, T. J. AND HOOVER, R. N. (1979).
Developing Clues to Environmental Cancer: A Stepwise Approach With the
Use of Cancer Mortality Data. *Environmental Health Perspectives* **32,** 52–58.
(A useful guide to the ways in which cancer mortality data is used in developing
possible associations between exposure to agents and cancer, with references
to a variety of studies and sources of data.)

CORNFIELD, J., HAENSZEL, W., HAMMOND, E. C., LILLIENFELD, A. M.,
SHIMKIN, M. B. AND WYNDER, E. L. (1959). Smoking and Lung Cancer:
Recent Evidence and a Discussion of Some Issues. *Journal of the National
Cancer Institute* **22,** 173–203. (A classic paper on summarizing the results of
many studies and assessing the possible effect of omitted variables, measure-
ment error, etc.)

OLKIN, I., GLESER, J. J. AND DERMAN, C. (1980). *Probability Models Applications.* New York: MacMillan. (A probability text requiring a year of calculus,
emphasizing the wide variety of applications of probability. Its section on the
Poisson distribution presents data on wrong telephone connections and radioactive counts and mentions other applications to the number of misprints, vacan-
cies in the Supreme Court and biology.)

Chapter 11

Comparison of the Characteristics of Two Populations Using Matched or Paired Data

1. Introduction

Many of the methods described in the previous chapters were originally designed to compare the central values (averages) or success rates (proportions) of two distinct populations. They were designed for the analysis of independent random samples from each population or for studying the entire population using the concept of randomization. If other factors, e.g., age, education, in addition to group membership, may affect the characteristics studied, as in comparing wage data or health status, then one can stratify the data into comparable subgroups and use one of the combination methods discussed previously to obtain a summary statistic, or one can develop an appropriate regression model. This chapter discusses an approach based on matching each member of one group, usually the treatment or experimental one, with one (or more) members of the other group (often called the control group) possessing similar characteristics with respect to major relevant factors. For example, if one matched each newly hired female to a newly hired male, with similar prior experience and educational background, the difference between their salaries is an estimate of the effect of sex on initial salary, that controls for any difference with regard to the factors of experience and education which legitimately affect salary. The average of these differences in a sample of such matched pairs enables us to draw an inference about the employer's treatment of women relative to men. Similarly, in health research one should control for age, smoking habits and other factors which affect one's chances of contracting the disease being investigated.

Although finding a good match may be difficult, the technique is quite useful when one population is small relative to the other, so matches are usually available. Indeed, it is a basic method in the analysis of epidemiological data, where one compares the proportion of cases (ill) who were exposed to a chemical or substance being studied for a possible toxic effect to the corresponding proportion of controls (persons of similar prior health status who did not get the disease). By matching the case and its control on factors such as age and prior smoking history, these factors are automatically controlled for in our comparison of exposure rates. The purpose of matching is to make the groups being compared as similar as possible with respect to other factors which affect the variable or outcome of interest. Ideally we would like to have two clones differing only with respect to group status (e.g., ill or healthy in an epidemiologic study). Matching can be regarded as an approximation to this situation.

Before we discuss several statistical methods and their application to real data sets, it is useful to consider a model matched pair study, the comparison of the efficacy of a new skin ointment relative to a currently used one. Assume that a skin infection affects both hands of the patient, then we can use each patient as their own control or match by treating one hand (randomly selected) with the new treatment and the other hand with the old one. A hypothetical matched data set is presented in Table 11.1. The average of the differences in length of time to cure of all the pairs is an estimate of the average treatment effect in the population and forms the basis of the t-test described in Section 2. The median of all the pairwise differences is another estimate of the treatment effect and is the basis of the sign test described in Section 3. The analog of the Wilcoxon test is also presented in Section 3. When the pairwise differences have a normal distribution, the t-test is the most powerful procedure. However, in small samples it is difficult to validate the assumption that the differences have a normal distribution and, as the Wilcoxon procedure is nearly as powerful as the t-test on normal data, it is recommended for general use. The sign test which compares the number of positive and negative differences yields a quick indication of the direction or sign of the effect, Δ, but lacks power because it ignores the magnitudes of the differences.

Sections 4 and 5 are devoted to several important applications of the

TABLE 11.1. Matched Pair Data on Days to Cure

Pair	New Method (X)	Old Method (Y)	Difference ($Y - X$)
1	4.5	8.0	+3.5
2	3	6	+3.0
3	4	6.5	+2.5
4	7	9	+2.0
5	4	5.5	+1.5
6	2	3	+1.0
7	7.5	8	+0.5
8	3.5	3	−0.5

Note: For convenience, the data was ordered by the size of the difference.

methods of Sections 2 and 3. Special techniques for 0-1 responses (binary data) are discussed in Section 6 and illustrated on data arising in a survey used in a deceptive advertising case, discrimination cases and a case-control study. Section 7 is devoted to modifications of the methods to allow for matching one case (or minority person) with several controls. This procedure has greater power than matched pair tests, especially in small samples. Moreover, it enables one to use all the available information. The final section describes several special topics, including the use of regression analysis with matched pairs.

It should be emphasized that the purpose of matching is the same as that of stratifying a population or sample, namely, to eliminate the possible influence of other factors on our estimate of the difference between two groups with respect to the particular outcome or variable of interest. Although the statistical methods for analyzing matched studies and those for combining stratified samples are discussed in separate chapters, they are quite similar. Indeed, stratified samples can be considered as matched groups of individuals. When sampling from a large population, it may be easier to stratify the population into relevant subpopulations and take samples within each one rather than match individuals. On the other hand, in equal pay cases, it may be easier for a judge to compare the wage of the plaintiff with that of a few employees whose assignments and responsibilities are closest to those of the complainant[1] rather than all employees in the same occupation or department. Matching an individual in this manner may enable the judge to incorporate more factors than can be used to stratify a work force into groups which are comparable with

590   **Statistical Reasoning in Law and Public Policy**

respect to many factors, as the size of each strata would become quite small. If that happens, almost all of the observations in some strata may come from only one of the two populations being compared, thereby decreasing the precision of the estimated difference and the power of the test to determine its statistical significance.

2. Statistical Inference From Paired Data Using the Average Difference Between the Matched Pairs: The t-Test

The data available to us in a matched pair analysis consist of pairs (x_i, y_i) $i = 1, ..., n$ of measurements, where x_i is the value of the variable of interest (e.g., time to cure, salary) of the member of the ith pair from one group (called the control group) and y_i the corresponding value of the member of the pair from the second group (often called the *treatment* or study group). The difference $d_i = y_i - x_i$ can be regarded as one observation of the difference, Δ, between both populations which controls for all the factors used in the matching process. This parameter Δ is often referred to as the *treatment* effect, as in medical studies it represents the difference in time to cure, say between the treated and control group. When used in the equal pay context, it measures the gender effect (as the matching process presumably eliminates the effect of other job-related characteristics).

Given observations (x_i, y_i) from n matched pairs, the average difference $\overline{d} = (\Sigma_{i=1}^n d_i)/n$ is the natural estimate of Δ. As in Chapter 3, we make inferences about Δ from the sampling distribution of $\overline{d}$ which is centered around the true value of Δ. The statistical analysis is based on the assumption that each pairwise difference, d_i, can be considered as an independent observation from a population with mean Δ and variance σ^2. A typical frequency function for this population is drawn in Figure 11.1.

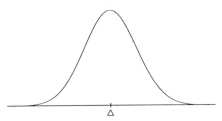

FIGURE 11.1.   A typical distribution of differences when they are normally distributed about the value Δ.

In many applications we desire to assess whether the treatment really has an effect and then estimate the magnitude of the effect. To determine that the treatment is effective, we test the null hypothesis that it has *no* effect of $\Delta = 0$ against the alternative $\Delta > 0$ (or $\Delta < 0$ or $\Delta \neq 0$, if they are appropriate). Only if the data shows that the observed $\bar{d}$ is sufficiently far from 0 that it was unlikely to have occurred if there was no effect ($\Delta = 0$), do we reject the null hypothesis and conclude that the treatment is effective.

In order to measure the variability of the differences, d_i, about their average $\bar{d}$, we use the sample standard deviation

$$(11.1) \qquad s_d = \sqrt{\frac{1}{n-1} \sum (d_i - \bar{d})^2}$$

to estimate the standard deviation, σ, of the distribution of differences, just as we did in developing confidence intervals for sample averages in Chapter 3. The average difference, $\bar{d}$, is a sample mean and has a probability distribution centered around Δ, but with standard deviation $\sigma/\sqrt{n}$. Using s_d (11.1) in place of σ suggests that a 95% confidence interval for the average treatment effect, Δ, is given by

$$(11.2) \qquad 95\% \ \text{CONF}\left(\Delta;\ \bar{d} - \frac{(1.96)\,s_d}{\sqrt{n}},\quad \bar{d} + \frac{1.96\,s_d}{\sqrt{n}}\right).$$

Formula (11.2) is valid in large samples by the Central Limit Theorem. In large samples ($n > 50$) we test the null hypothesis $\Delta = 0$ by using the standard normal variate:

$$(11.3) \qquad t = \frac{\text{observed } \bar{d} \text{ minus expected } \bar{d} \text{ under } H_0}{\text{standard error}} = \frac{\bar{d} - 0}{\dfrac{s_d}{\sqrt{n}}}$$

as in Chapter 3.

Example.   Suppose a manufacturer claimed that his product, A, enabled people to clean floors faster than the "leading Brand B". A sample of 100 households was taken, and the time it took the person who typically did the task to clean the floor was observed on two separate occasions (in half of the houses the new product was used first, and the other half used Brand B first). If the average difference, $\bar{d}$, in time to completion between the brands was two minutes and the standard deviation of these differences was nine minutes, then the test statistic using (11.3) is

$$(11.4) \qquad\qquad t = \frac{2 - 0}{\frac{9}{\sqrt{100}}} = 2.22 > 1.96,$$

implying that the average of two minutes saved is statistically significant at the .05 level and is unlikely to have occurred by chance. The 95% confidence interval (11.2) for the *difference* in the time taken to clean with the products is (.236, 3.764) minutes which adds a measure of uncertainty to the conclusion that two minutes are saved by using the new product. As in Chapter 3, the width of the confidence interval depends on the sample size, n. As n increases, the sample standard deviation, s_d, becomes a more accurate estimate of σ, which is why we can ignore the use of s_d in (11.2) and (11.3) when n is 100 or more. When a 95% confidence interval or 5% level significance test is desired, the z-value of 1.96 is replaced by t-values of 3.1825 if $n = 4$, 2.571 if $n = 6$, 2.086 if $n = 21$, 2.009 if $n = 51$ and 1.984 if $n = 101$. The fact that 2.01 is only slightly larger than 1.96 justifies the use of the standard normal, Z, value in samples of 50 or more. A short table of the critical t-values for commonly used significance levels is given in Appendix B. The statistic (11.4) is referred to as the *t-test for paired comparisons* in the statistical literature. Indeed, the large sample version (11.3) is also called the t-test, since the normal curve really approximates the distribution of the t-test statistic.

Problems

1.*   Rather than use a matched pair design, the manufacturer of the new floor cleaner in our example might have taken two samples of households and compared their average times to clean the floor. Why might the matched design be preferable?
Hint: Think of all the factors that might affect the time to complete the task. Is a random sample likely to be perfectly balanced (have identical proportions of people with all these characteristics)?

2.   Suppose you represented the manufacturer of Brand A and the FTC claimed your ad was deceptive because your study did not describe the size of the rooms used.
    (a) How could you check your data to show that the size of the room was not a factor?
    (b) How could you check your data to verify that the size of the living rooms sampled was typical of the area in which the ad ran?

3. Suppose that the manufacturer in our example had not ensured that the same person in the household cleaned the floor both times. Could that have affected the outcome? How might one assess the possible impact of such an error on the study?

Answers to Selected Problems

1. We can consider the time it takes for a randomly chosen person to accomplish a task as having two components, a) the natural variation among people and b) the fact that the time a particular person requires to finish a job also varies from week to week. When the variation (a) among people is *large* relative to the second source of variability (b), the average ($\bar{x}$) of a random sample of the population has substantial sampling variability (SE = $\sigma/\sqrt{n}$), so that the t-test of Chapter 7 may not be very powerful unless the sample sizes of the two groups are large. Matching eliminates most of the first source of variability, as the same person is measured twice so that a more precise estimate of the difference due to the factor under study can be obtained. In the present context, the time required to complete the task would depend on the size of the room as well as the age, physical condition and prior experience of the cleaner. These covariates presumably have wide variations among households which is why a matched design is useful.

3. Yes, it could have affected the outcome, especially if by chance in most of the pairs the more efficient household member was given one of the products. To assess the possible impact on the study, one could compare the estimated change, $\bar{d}_1$, from the matched pairs in which the same household member cleaned both floors with the $\bar{d}_2$ calculated for the households in which different members did the job. If these averages differed, then one should restrict the statistical analysis to those pairs in which the same person performed the task.

3. Two Distribution-Free Procedures for the Analysis of Matched Pair Data

Although the method in the previous section which is based on the average difference between the members of each pair is readily understood, we noted that in small samples, the validity of the confidence interval for the difference between the treatment and control groups and the associated statistical test required that the pairwise differences d_i have a normal

distribution about the true difference, Δ, between the two matched populations. In small samples the assumption of normality is difficult to check,
and we now present two methods which only require that each difference
d_i has a distribution which places the same probability of being a units
below Δ, as being a units above Δ, i.e., deviations from the mean of the
same magnitude in both directions have the same probability. Distributions obeying this assumption are called *symmetric,* and symmetry is a
natural assumption for most types of random measurement error. The two
methods, the sign and Wilcoxon tests, are distribution-free because they
are valid whenever the differences d_i have a symmetric[2] distribution. The
sign test is a useful indicator of the direction of an effect but is usually *not*
as powerful as the Wilcoxon procedure. We now describe the two tests of
the null hypothesis, $\Delta = 0$, i.e., there is no treatment effect first and then
present the estimate of the effect, Δ, associated with each test.

If there is *no treatment effect,* then each d_i has a symmetric distribution
of about 0. In particular, each d_i has probability 1/2 of being positive and
the same probability of being negative. Thus, we would expect about half
$(n/2)$ of the d_i to be positive. The *sign* test counts the number, S, of
positive differences and compares S to its expected value, $n/2$. Under the
null hypothesis, the number of positive differences has the same probability distribution as the number of heads obtained when a fair coin is tossed
n times, i.e., it has a binomial distribution with parameters n and 1/2.
Thus, (see Chapter 2) S has mean $n/2$ and variance $n/4$. When n is 25 or
more the normal approximation is adequate and we use the statistic

$$Z = \frac{\text{observed minus expected number of positive differences}}{\text{standard error}}$$

(11.5)

$$= \frac{S - \dfrac{n}{2}}{\sqrt{\dfrac{n}{4}}},$$

where S is the number of positive differences. The statistic S is called the
sign test because it only depends on the sign ($+$ or $-$) of each difference
and not on its magnitude. Sometimes a continuity correction of 1/2 is used
in formula (11.5), as in the normal approximation to the binomial model in
Chapter 2.

To illustrate the calculation, suppose that in the floor product example,
in 65 of the 100 pairs, the new product took *less* time to use than the old

product. There are 35 (100 − 65) positive differences, hence

(11.6)
$$Z = \frac{35 - 50}{\sqrt{25}} = \frac{-15}{5} = -3.0,$$

again a statistically significant result (two-sided p-value = .0026) implying that the observed difference is not likely to be due to chance.

The sign test can also be used to test a claim such as "the new product typically saves *two* minutes of work." Now we would count the number of differences (old-new) greater than 2, which should now have the same distribution as the sign test, i.e., one expects half of these differences to be greater than 2 if the assertion is true.

Just as the average difference is the estimate of Δ that corresponds to the t-test, the median, $\hat{m}$, of the n differences, d_i, is the estimate of Δ associated with the sign test. To see this, consider testing the hypothesis that $\Delta = \hat{m}$ using the sign test. By definition the number, S, of differences exceeding $\hat{m}$ is $n/2$ so the observed number equals its expected number. This indicates the best possible agreement between the data and the hypothesis.

Because the sign test *does not use* the *magnitude* of the differences, it is not as powerful as the t-test when the differences follow a normal distribution. Another distribution-free test, the Wilcoxon test, is more powerful than the sign test on normal data and is valid under the assumption that the differences have a symmetric distribution about their center will now be described.

Suppose that there is no treatment effect, so that each difference has a symmetric distribution about 0. Then the average of any two differences d_i and d_j, should also have a symmetric distribution about 0. Now consider all possible averages of two differences (including taking each difference with itself). Since each average is symmetric, when the null hypothesis is true we *expect* half of these averages of two differences to be positive and half to be negative since there are[3]

(11.7)
$$\binom{n}{2} + n = \frac{n(n - 1)}{2} + n = \frac{n(n + 1)}{2}$$

such pairwise averages, the number V, of them that are expected to be positive is $n(n + 1)/4$. Although V is defined analogously to the sign test, its sampling distribution is more complex because the averages $(d_i + d_j)/2$ are no longer independent of one another, as each difference d_i is averaged with all $(n - 1)$ other differences and itself. It can be shown that the variance of V is given by

$$n(n + 1) \frac{(2n + 1)}{24}.$$

The fraction, $\overline{P}$, of all the averages, $(d_i + d_j)/2$, which are positive is the Wilcoxon statistic for this problem, i.e., $\overline{P} = V/n(n + 1)/2$. It is analogous to the two-sample Wilcoxon test discussed in Chapter 7. Under the null hypothesis, its expected value is 1/2. In the present situation, its variance is $(2n + 1)/6n(n + 1)$ and the normal form of the Wilcoxon test for paired data is

$$Z = \frac{\text{observed } (\overline{P}) \text{ minus expected value } \left(\frac{1}{2}\right)}{\text{standard error}}$$

(11.8)

$$Z = \frac{\dfrac{V}{n(n + 1)} - 1/2}{\sqrt{\dfrac{(2n + 1)}{[6n(n + 1)]}}} = \frac{V - \dfrac{n(n + 1)}{4}}{\sqrt{\dfrac{n(n + 1)(2n + 1)}{24}}}.$$

By analogy with the sign test, the estimate of the treatment effect, Δ, associated with the Wilcoxon test is the median, $\hat{m}$, of all the averages $(d_i + d_j)/2$. Since the number of averages $(d_i + d_j)/2$ becomes quite large as the sample size n increases, the calculation of the Wilcoxon test and associated estimate are usually done with the aid of a computer. We illustrate the Wilcoxon test on the hypothetical data set on time days to cure for two skin ointments given in Table 11.1.

Let us carry out a two-sided test of the null hypothesis $\Delta = 0$ against the alternative $\Delta \neq 0$. There will be $n(n + 1)/2 = (8 \times 9)/2 = 36$ averages of pairs of differences. A convenient way to obtain them is to compute each average with itself and all *smaller* differences. For instance, the differences which include the observation 3.5 are calculated as $(3.5 + 3.5)/2 = 3.5$, $(3.5 + 3.0)/2 = 3.25$, $(3.5 + 2.5)/2 = 3.0$, etc. and then placed on the same line. The procedure is repeated until all 36 averages have been calculated. This process is carried out in Table 11.2, where we see that the number (V) of positive averages is 34.5.

Because the averages on the line next to each difference only relate to the averages of that difference with itself and smaller ones (its average with larger differences appears on one of the preceding lines), the number of averages on each line decreases by one as we go down the table. An

TABLE 11.2. Calculation of the Wilcoxon Test on the Data in Table 11.1

Differences	Averages	Number of Positive Averages
3.5	3.5, 3.25, 3.0, 2.75, 2.50, 2.25, 2.0, 1.5	8
3.0	3.0, 2.75, 2.50, 2.25, 2.0, 1.75, 1.25	7
2.5	2.5, 2.25, 2.0, 1.75, 1.50, 1.0	6
2.0	2.0, 1.75, 1.5, 1.25, .75	5
1.5	1.5, 1.25, 1.0, .5	4
1.0	1.0, .75, .25	3
.5	.5, 0	1-1/2
−.5	−.5	0
		TOTAL 34.5

average of 0 is counted as 1/2 since it can be regarded as half negative and half positive (like the ties in the two-sample Wilcoxon test). The normal form (11.8) of the test is calculated as follows:

$$(11.9) \qquad Z = \frac{\bar{P} - \frac{1}{2}}{\sqrt{\frac{(2n+1)}{[6n(n+1)]}}} = \frac{\frac{34.5}{36} - .5}{\sqrt{\frac{17}{[423]}}} = \frac{.4583}{.1984} = 2.31.$$

Thus, the data indicate a statistically significant (at the .05 level) result implying that the observed treatment effect cannot be attributed to chance (two-sided p-value = .022) and that the new treatment cures the disease faster.

To obtain an estimate of the effect, Δ, we need to find the median of the 36 averages in the table, i.e., the average of the eighteenth and nineteenth largest entries in the table. As these averages are roughly ordered along the diagonal, counting them in increasing order shows that both the eighteenth and nineteenth largest observations equal 1.75 so that $\hat{m} = 1.75$.

Although the sign test is also applicable to the data in Table 11.1, it is *not* a very powerful test in small samples. Indeed, the exact two-sided p-value (i.e., the probability of obtaining 7 or 8 positives or 0-1 positive signs, corresponding to 8 or 7 negative signs) is .07 and was obtained from tables of the binomial distribution. Although this result is not statistically significant at the .05 level it is close to significance, so the sign test really does not contradict our previous finding. The sign test, S, has low power because the range of possible values of the statistic is small in small samples. In our example S can take on only the values 0 thru 8. Since in a two-sided test possible values equally distant from the expected value are paired, i.e., 0 and 8, 1 and 7, etc. differ from the expected value (4) of S by the same amount, only if all the signs had been positive (or all negative) could the sign test have detected the treatment effect found by the Wilcoxon and t-test (see problem 2). Since, the probability of obtaining 0 or 8 positive signs is only .008, we only have two potential levels of .008 and .07 near .05, so a precise 5% level test on the data is not possible.

In contrast with the sign test, the Wilcoxon statistic, V, the number of positive averages, $(d_i + d_j)/2$ or $\overline{P}$ has 36 possible values. Hence, if the exact distribution of V (or $\overline{P}$) is used, there are more significance levels available so that the .01 and .05 levels can be approximated more accurately. For small samples, problem 2, shows that the normal approximation to the distribution of V or $\overline{P}$ is not that accurate and should only be relied on for definitive results when n is at least 20. One should use tables of the exact distribution of the Wilcoxon or signed rank statistic which appear in Lehmann (1975) when analyzing data from samples of size less than 20.

If a court were faced with two different analyses of the data in Table 11.1, one using the sign test and the other the Wilcoxon test, then the power of each method to detect one (or more) value(s) of Δ indicating a difference, e.g., $\Delta = 1$, should be considered and the most powerful test used. Unless one had evidence that the differences were very far from normally distributed or there were a number of unusual observations, the Wilcoxon test should be more powerful than the sign test. As we learned in our discussion of the *Capaci* case in Chapter 7, failure to consider the power of the statistical tests advocated by both sides has led courts to accept analyses which failed to find meaningful differences when they probably existed.

Comment. Recently courts have shown some awareness of this problem. In *Coates v. Johnson and Johnson,*[4] the opinion disallowed aggregating all years of data into a single sample but first noted that the sample size in each year of data was sufficient to detect a difference so that the circuit distinguished this case from the fragmentation that occurred in *Capaci* in the defendants' year-by-year analysis of the hiring data in Table 4.6.

In order to assess the difference in the power of the three tests considered so far, we present their power to detect a shift Δ when the differences follow a normal distribution. Since the power of a test depends on both the sample size n and the magnitude of Δ (it is easier to detect a large shift than a small one), the powers were computed for a variety of values of n and amounts Δ. The results are presented in Table 11.3 in which the size of Δ is expressed in terms of its fraction of the standard deviation, $\sigma(d)$, of the distribution of differences. The calculations are based on the large sample approximation in Lehmann's text, *Nonparametric Statistics,* and should be considered as a rough guide for small sample sizes. Clearly the sign test is less powerful than the Wilcoxon.

TABLE 11.3. Approximate Power of the One-tailed .05 Level t, Wilcoxon and Sign Tests for Normal Data as a Function of Sample Size and the Magnitude, Δ, of the Average Difference

$$\Delta = \frac{\sigma(d)}{4}$$

Sample Size	t	Wilcoxon	Sign
20	.2992	.2844	.2185
30	.3914	.3740	.2827
40	.4746	.4552	.3430
50	.5489	.5284	.3998
75	.6985	.6778	.5263
100	.8038	.7852	.6315

$$\Delta = \frac{\sigma(d)}{2}$$

10	.4746	.4413	.3193
20	.7228	.6932	.5292
30	.8630	.8419	.6870
40	.9354	.9222	.7998
50	.9707	.9631	.8750
75	.9964	.9949	.9648
100	.9996	.9994	.9910

Source: The large sample approximate power calculations were based on formulas (4.44), (4.33) and (4.14) on pages 172, 168, and 160 of Lehmann's *Nonparametrics.*

Problems

1. For the data in Table 11.1, verify that the average difference is 1.6875 and the median is 1.75. (The fact that the median difference coincided with $\hat{m}$, the median of the pairwise averages, is an artifact of the data).

2. (Optional) Using the exact distribution of the Wilcoxon statistic given in Lehmann's text and interpolating between the values for V of 34 and 35 shows that the two-sided p-value of our data (3.4) is about .008. Contrast this with the normal approximation used in the text.

3.* Suppose one desired to have at least 50% power to detect a Δ equal to $\sigma(d)/4$. How many matched pairs would be needed if the sign test is used? If the Wilcoxon test is used? Assume the differences are normally distributed.

Answers to Selected Problems

2. The two-sided p-value corresponding to $Z = 2.31$ is .0208, indicating that the normal approximation to the Wilcoxon statistic (11.8) should also be checked with the exact tables when small samples ($n < 20$) are used. Exact tables are available in the texts by Lehmann, Gibbons and Siegel mentioned in Chapter 7. The most detailed tables are given in Wilcoxon, Katti and Wilcox (1973).

3. From Table 11.3 we see that nearly 75 pairs are required for the sign test but only 50 pairs are needed for the Wilcoxon test.

4. Application of Paired Data in Actual Cases and Health Studies

In this section we shall discuss several actual uses of the analysis of paired data. Although the legal issues vary, from a statistical viewpoint they all concern the issue of establishing or rebutting a hypothesis that there is an effect or a difference between two groups.

a. The quality of shipped goods

A contract specified that coal of a certain quality, expressed in terms of its BTU content (approximately 10,000) was to be shipped from the U.S. to a foreign buyer. Before the coal was shipped, a sample was taken by an independent laboratory to assure its quality met the standards. Upon arrival of each shipment, the purchaser took a sample and compared the results with the independent laboratory and, after a number of shipments, terminated the contract and sued for compensation because its samples showed the coal to be of lower quality than specified.

In this application, each shipment was its own control or match, as there were two separate estimates of BTU content of each shipment, although both measurements were based on a sample of the coal. Indeed, part of the dispute concerned whether the sample taken by the independent laboratory was truly representative of the entire shipment. The differences between the two measurements (independent laboratory minus purchaser) are presented in Table 11.4.

The differences are all positive, and all three procedures yield a significant result. Applying the t-test to the data yields

$$t = \frac{1888.2}{\frac{850}{\sqrt{10}}} = \frac{1888.2}{268.8} = 7.02,$$

which is not only significant at the .05 level (two-sided test), but has a *p*-value less than one in a thousand. The Wilcoxon procedure takes on its

TABLE 11.4. Differences in the Estimate BTU Content of Shipped Coal

Shipment	Difference
1	+754
2	+511
3	+2219
4	+2156
5	+2987
6	+2880
7	+2651
8	+1775
9	+1567
10	+1382
Total	18882
Average	1888.2
Standard deviation	850

Note: The average value of the independent laboratory measurements of BTU content was about 10,200.

most extreme value, $\overline{P} = 1$, as all 55 pairwise averages are positive. The exact probability that this could occur, under the null hypothesis, is $1/2^{10} = .0098 \simeq .001$, so the two-sided p-value is .002. For this data set, the sign test also yields a significant result, as the chance that all ten differences would be positive is $(1/2)^{10} \simeq .001$ so that the two-sided p-value of the sign test is .002, agreeing with the Wilcoxon procedure. Because of the extreme character of the data, all three tests indicate that the difference is significant at the .01 level. Had there been *one* negative difference which was smaller in absolute value than the nine positive differences (e.g., had +511 been −11), the two-sided p-value of the sign test on the data would be .021, while the Wilcoxon test would have a p-value = .004, yielding a more significant result. Again, this illustrates the potential loss of power that occurs when the sign test is used in small samples.

In the hearing, the purchaser submitted another matched pair analysis to substantiate the accuracy of its equipment and its BTU measurements. They took over 50 coal samples, split each sample in half and had the subsamples assayed by a university laboratory as well as its own. The differences were analyzed by the t-test, which showed that the pairs of measurements did not differ (at the .05 level) which verified the accuracy of their laboratory's results.

The statistical analysis demonstrated that the coal which arrived was of lower quality than the contract called for and that the BTU measurements of the independent neutral laboratory taken before shipment were significantly larger than the BTU measurements taken on arrival. By itself, the conclusion that the measurements in Table 11.4 were statistically significantly different cannot definitely establish that the independent laboratory had systematically overstated the BTU content of the coal before it was shipped, since the measurements were made at different times. Nevertheless, the burden of proof logically shifts to the shipper who asserted that a loss in BTU content would occur in transit due to exposure of the coal to water en route. The shipper did not present statistical data on the amount of BTU typically lost in shipment, and the arbitration panel decided that the original coal did not meet the contract's specification and the measurements of the original independent laboratory were unreliable. The magnitude of the difference (1900 BTU) relative to the specified content (about 10,000 BTU) indicates that the seller of the coal needed to document a substantial loss of BTU in transit and failed to do so.

b. *A case-control study of a possible relationship between coffee consumption by pregnant women and birth defects*

In epidemiological studies which are used to support government regulation, e.g., the requirement that cigarettes have a label warning of the health hazard of smoking, a sample of cases (persons with the disease) are matched with appropriate controls and their levels of exposure to the potential hazard (substance being studied) are compared. If the substance is harmful, the cases should have a significantly higher average level of exposure than the control group.

After a number of studies reported an association between coffee consumption and defective pregnancy outcome, and high doses of caffeine produced congenital defects in animal studies, the FDA removed caffeine from the "generally regarded as safe list"[5] and warned the public about the ingestion of coffee during pregnancy.

Because Finland leads the world in per capita coffee consumption, the government sponsored a study[6] of the potential harmful effects of coffee drinking on the outcome of pregnancy. As the reporting of all congenital defects is mandatory in Finland, a register of (virtually) all such cases was available and a sample of 755 mothers of cases were selected for interview. Each mother selected for the study was matched with a control mother whose delivery immediately preceded that of the study mother in the same maternity welfare district. Thus, the pairs were matched on the basis of geographic residence and time period of pregnancy. Of the 755 matched pairs, 35 pairs of mothers consumed only tea drinks, while inadequate answers to the question in 14 of the matched pairs rendered them unusable. Thus, the analysis was based on 706 matched pairs. The data is summarized in Table 11.5.

Notice that the *marginal* distribution of the number of cups of coffee consumed daily of the control mothers (right-hand column) agrees fairly closely with that of the case mothers (bottom row). Because of the large sample size, the t-test is valid even though the data is not normally distributed, since the Central Limit Theorem applies to the *average, $\bar{d}$,* of the differences. The *t*-statistic based on the case minus control differences was calculated from formula (11.4) and yielded -1.1, indicating that the difference in coffee consumption was *not* statistically significant.

The researchers also studied several specific types of birth defects and found no significant difference between the cases and controls in all in-

TABLE 11.5.   Coffee Consumption During Pregnancy of the Pairs of Case and Control Mothers (all Malformation Groups)

Cups of coffee a day	Control Mothers						
	0	1–3	4–6	7–9	10–15	23–25	TOTAL
Case Mothers 0	58	78	48	10	6	—	200
1–3	93	135	64	14	12	1	319
4–6	40	59	26	4	9	—	138
7–9	10	11	3	4	—	—	28
10–15	6	12	2	—	—	—	20
23–25	1	—	—	—	—	—	1
TOTAL	208	295	143	32	27	1	706

Source: Table 1 from Kurppa, K., Holmberg, P. C., Kuosma, E. and Saxen, L. (1983). Coffee Consumption and Selected Congenital Malformations: A Nationwide Case Control Study. *American Journal of Public Health* **73**, 1397–1399.

stances. This is reassuring, as there often is a specific linkage between exposure to a substance and a particular illness or defect.

Comment.   In view of the sample size of the study the fact that 14 pairs had to be disregarded because of faulty data could not seriously affect the conclusions of the study.

c.   The use of matched studies to assess the reliability and consistency of measurements

In our discussion of the coal shipment data we noted that the plaintiff submitted samples of the coal to a university laboratory in order to verify the accuracy of the company's findings. This use is also important in verifying the grading or evaluation process used in employment decisions.

The validity of a written exam which had a disparate impact on blacks was a major issue in *Gillespie v. State of Wisconson*,[7] a case involving a relatively senior level position in personnel management. Before discussing the validity issue, we report the results of the test. Of 403 whites who took the exam, 173 passed, while only 11 minority applicants out of 48 passed. Thus the *selection ratio* of $(11/48)/(173/403) = .229/.429 = .534$ was below the EEOC's four-fifths rule. The written exam in question had been developed by the state in order to have less of a disparate impact than previous tests had. Therefore, the new test used an essay exam rather than multiple-choice questions, which had a substantial adverse impact in a previous exam. The personnel specialist also devised a grading system, established the criteria for grading and trained the actual graders. Moreover, the 451 exams were graded by eight teams of two graders and, to check for consistency, 10 or 12 papers were distributed to all eight grading teams. Somewhat more sophisticated methods than we have discussed, but essentially based on the correlation of the score each team gave these exams, showed that all grading teams were consistent, as their scores were highly correlated. Moreover, the consistency of grading within each team was checked, probably by a matched pair analysis of the differences each grader in the team gave to the same exam. This analysis showed no significant difference between the graders.

After learning that he failed the written exam, the plaintiff lodged a complaint with the department, and his exam was re-evaluated by a different team, *unaware* that they were grading an exam that had been graded previously. They gave the paper a score three points less than the first team. Subsequently, the formal suit was filed. Although the trial court considered the relationship of the written exam to the job in order to decide whether it was a valid predictor of success, in the plaintiff's original letter complaining about the exam he did not question its job relationship. He questioned scoring methods, qualification of the raters and the entire grading process. Therefore, the matched analysis showing that the grading process was uniform was relevant.

Comment. In order to assess the consistency of each pair of graders, two statistical tests should be performed. The matched pair study using the methods of Sections 2 and 3 can determine whether the graders score each paper consistently or whether one grader is typically higher or lower than the other. If one grader in a pair is far more variable than the other, e.g., half the papers differ by $+10$ and the other half by -10, this might raise doubts about the propriety of using the team average. Thus, one should also use the correlation coefficient and related procedures presented in Chapter 8 to assure the exams graded above average by one grader were also graded above average by the other. The reliability study carried out by the state of Wisconsin probably was based on this idea (although it is not described in the opinion).

In our discussion of the data in Table 9.3 concerning the mold count of the tomato paste seized in *U.S. v. 499 Cases,* we noted that the counts of the two government analysts appeared to disagree. Assuming that the data was matched, i.e., the counts on the same line in Table 9.3 were made on samples taken from the same can, we find the following ten differences (II minus I)

$$18, 14, -1, 8, 20, 22, -1, 17, -1, 32$$

and now determine whether there is consistent bias in either direction between the counts of the analysts.

Since the average difference is 128/10 = 12.8, while the median, the average of the fifth (14) and sixth (17) ordered difference, is 15.5, the differences seem to have a central value near 14. There is a slight skewedness in the sense that the three -1 observations are furthest to the left of either central value, while there is only one large positive observation (32). Of course, in a sample of size ten, we cannot expect a perfect balance. The fact that the differences seem to lie in a neighborhood about 14, say, 14 ± 6, or are much further from 14, suggests that the differences might not follow a normal distribution. Therefore, we use the paired Wilcoxon procedure (11.8) and find

$$Z = \frac{\frac{49}{55} - \frac{1}{2}}{\sqrt{\frac{21}{660}}} = 2.19,$$

which is statistically significant (two-sided p-value = .03). This result indicates that there is a significant variation between the analysts, in addition to the variation in mold count between the various cans.

This data again illustrates the importance of the concept of power and its essential role in selecting an appropriate statistical procedure. Had the sign test been used to test whether or not the average difference was equal to zero, we would have found seven positive differences out of the ten. As the exact probability of observing seven or more successes in ten independent trials with success probability, $p = 1/2$ on each one is .1719, the two-sided p-value is .342, which is not even close to statistical significance. The reason the sign test *fails to find the difference* which seems *apparent in the data* is a difference of -1, which is given the same weight as one of $+18$ because the sign test ignores the magnitudes of the differences.

Comment.   The mold count data also illustrates a problem which occurs when exact probabilities of statistical tests are calculated from imprecise data. Had some of the -1's been 0 or $+1$, the p-value of the sign test would change far more than that of the Wilcoxon. When the basic measurements are not very accurate, one can assess the impact of the inference drawn by changing some of the data by a *small* amount. One should have more confidence in an analysis which is not sensitive to these small changes.

d. The need for careful matching in class action equal pay cases: Penk v. Oregon State Board of Higher Education[8]

As part of a broad claim of discrimination in employment, the plaintiffs alleged that the institutions in the Oregon State system paid women less than *similarly situated* male faculty members. In addition to regression analyses, matched studies were introduced. The opinion noted that while a matched study was easier to understand than a regression analysis, its relevance might be questionable unless the matched females were representative of the entire class. We now describe some of the matched studies used in the case which focused on employment actions occurring after July 21, 1979.

Plaintiffs first salary study matched 169 females to males on the basis of institution (same college or university), department, highest degree and service year. A regression adjustment was made for years since highest degree (we will discuss methods of combining regression and matching in Section 8). A significant difference at the .05 level (t-statistic = 2.33) was found, indicating that females were paid $677 less per year than their male counterparts. The plaintiffs also showed that the 169 matched females were representative of the entire class.

The defendants raised a number of questions concerning the validity of the study. The most serious were:

(a) The plaintiffs included 6 pairs with data errors, 9 pairs where both individuals received their highest degree *after* the relevant year (1979) and 35 pairs were support faculty who were not members of the class. Thus, 50 of the 169 matched pairs or about 30% of plaintiff's data was inappropriate or erroneous.

(b) The rank held by members of the pair could differ, i.e., rank was not one of the variables used in the matching process.

In order to demonstrate the effect of ignoring rank in the matching, the defendants showed that plaintiff's data restricted to those pairs with the same rank showed a nonsignificant average difference of $73 per year, with a t-statistic of .27, which is not even close to statistical significance (one-sided p-value $\simeq$ .40). In addition, defendants introduced their own study matching female faculty members to a male in the same institution and department with the same rank and time in rank (within two years). In three institutions, the number of matched pairs was too small, in three others the average difference was statistically insignificant, while a statistically significant difference appeared in two institutions. Thus, a general pattern of salary discrimination was not shown to exist.

Comment.   (1) The opinion also discusses the propriety of aggregating the results over all eight institutions and decided that the data for each institution should be examined separately, partly because the board had little influence over the employment decisions made at the individual schools. This may have placed a severe limitation on the use of matching studies, because a suitable match for a female might be a male in the same department in another institution of the system, provided that the institutions were comparable. It is plausible that the three state colleges were sufficiently similar for this purpose, and the two major research universities might also be considered together. This would have enabled more females to be matched and perhaps finding more than one match for some of them, thereby increasing the power of the ultimate statistical test.

   (2) Had the court allowed aggregation of the results of the defendant's matched pair salary study across the eight institutions, it might have asked what the probability is that two or more significant differences at the .05 level would have occurred by chance. As we realized earlier, this is the probability that a binomial random variable with parameters, $n = 8$, $p = .05$ would have a value of at least 2 and equals .058. Thus, the defendant's study does not seem quite as convincing, statistically speaking, as the opinion appears to indicate, since there is only a 6% chance that two or more of the eight matched studies would be significant at the 0.5 level if the null hypothesis of equal pay were true. Moreover, each test really concerned the one-sided alternative (females earned less than males), so the actual level of each test was .025. The probability that two or more out of eight tests would be significant at this level (.025) under the null hypothesis is about .015. While our discussion is somewhat circumscribed by the fact that we do not have the data or results of all eight studies, we considered all eight schools, even though the sample in three of them was too small (presumably this means that the power of the test used was very low in these schools). This also illustrates the advantage of properly combining the statistical results for each school rather than requiring a significant finding (at the two-sided .05 level) in each institution, which implies a very small type I error probability without any consider-

ation of power. Of course, the counting method we used, like the sign test, is *not* as sensitive as combination procedures using the *p*-values of the eight separate tests or average salary differences.

Problems

1. Compute the histogram of the distribution of the number of cups of coffee drank per day of the case and control mothers from data in Table 11.5. Compare the histograms by eye and judge whether mothers of the cases appear to have been heavier coffee drinkers than the control mothers.

2.* Suppose a similar study on birth defects was conducted on the relationship of a mother's cumulative exposure to x-rays over her lifetime (prior to pregnancy).

   (a) Suppose that a researcher suggested that the case mothers should also be matched on age. What affect might matching on age have on our estimate of the difference in x-ray exposure between the cases and control?

   (b) How reliable would a person's estimate of their lifetime exposure to x-rays be? Compare the reliability of this exposure information to that of the coffee study. Why is this topic important in case-control studies?

3. In *Penk*, the plaintiffs introduced a study matching 43 females in the class with males who had similar publication records and experience. Find the relevant portion of the opinion and comment on its evaluation of the sample size, the use of males in other departments and the vitae (resumes) used to create the pairs. How might the plaintiffs have improved upon the quality of the study? In light of power considerations and the court's view of the appropriateness of aggregating results across the eight institutions, should the plaintiffs have based a large portion of their case on the matched vita study?

4. Suppose the judge in *Penk* had decided that plaintiffs would have established a prima facie case if their salary study had shown a significant difference at the .05 level (one-sided test) in at least six institutions. Consult a table of the binomial distribution and find the actual level of significance he would be requiring. Do the same calculation replacing six by five, i.e., if plaintiffs were to show a significant difference occurred in majority of the schools were required.

5. How convincing would our binomial analysis of the defendant's matching study in Penk be if the females had a higher average pay than their matched male counterparts in the three institutions in which the defendant found a nonsignificant difference?

6. (Optional) In order to assess the sensitivity of the sign and Wilcoxon tests to small changes in the data resulting from imprecise measurements, first add $+2$ to the ten differences in the mold count data and compute the p-values of both tests. Then subtract 2 from each difference and compute both p-values. Which test is more sensitive? Why does this occur?

Answers to Selected Problems

2. (a) Age itself would be related with lifetime exposure to x-rays from dental and physical examinations as well as background radiation so matching on age would make it difficult to observe differences in exposure. On the other hand, maternal age is also related to the chance of the child having a birth defect, so it should be controlled for, either in the matching process or in a regression analysis of the matched pairs. The possible collinearity of age and exposure implies that a larger sample size is needed to estimate the relative risk of having a child with a birth defect due to higher than normal exposure to x-rays.

   (b) Because one drinks (or does not drink) coffee, etc. on a regular basis, the consumption data should be quite reliable. Indeed, studies show that people remember and reliably report their brands of commonly used household items such as soap, toothpaste, etc. On the other hand, most of us do not know the dosage of x-rays we have been given by dentists and doctors, etc., nor do we know the amount of background radiation we have been exposed to. In order to obtain more accurate data one should ask questions about the frequency of x-rays and exposure to the sun so that one can assess the quality of the data or make an estimate for each person based on the average dose of x-rays typically given by dentists and doctors. Sometimes one can obtain permission from the study group members to contact their physicians to obtain better data.

4. The probability that a binomial variable with parameters $n = 8$ and $p = .05$ yields six or more successes is .0000004, while the probability of five or more successes is .000154. The point here is that type I error for these test criteria are extremely small so that the power of the test to reject the null hypothesis also is very small, making the plaintiffs' task nearly impossible.

5.   As these differences are in the opposite direction to the two which determined our result, they suggest that a more complete analysis using the differences and p-values in all eight institutions would not yield a significant difference in the pay of similarly qualified men and women.

6.   The Wilcoxon test is less sensitive. As the sign test only considers whether or not a difference (d_i) is greater or less than 0, a small measurement error on observations near 0 can have a major effect on it.

5.   *Motor Vehicle Manufacturers Association v. EPA:* Testing the Environmental Equivalence of Fuels[9]

The Clean Air Act requires that before new fuels or fuel additives are sold in the United States, the producer must demonstrate that the emission products generated by the fuel will not cause or contribute to a failure of any emission control system or device to achieve compliance with the emission standards a vehicle has been certified as meeting. For practical purposes we can think of a new fuel, typically a gasahol blend, as being equivalent to the standard one when the amounts of air pollution generated by vehicles using the two fuels are quite close. When a new fuel is shown to have a similar effect as the usual ones, EPA grants the producer a waiver to sell the product. Before issuing a waiver the EPA conducts several tests,[10] two of which we shall discuss in detail.

a.   *A matched pair test for an effect on the level of emissions*

There is scientific evidence that some fuels will have only an instantaneous emission effect, i.e., there will not be a further degradation of a vehicle's pollution control equipment over a long period of time using the new fuel relative to the standard fuel (typically unleaded gas). Thus, the new fuel is expected to produce a small increment, Δ, in the emission levels of vehicles using it and if Δ is sufficiently small (close to 0), there will not be any violation of the compliance standards. To estimate Δ, or test its closeness to zero, a paired comparison technique, called back-to-back testing, of a sample of n cars is used. The same cars are first driven with the standard fuel and then with the new fuel, and the emission levels of several noxious gases are compared. We discuss the procedure for one gas. The differences, d_i, in the emission levels of the new and used fuels on the cars in the sample are the data used to estimate Δ, and the EPA constructs two 90% two-sided confidence intervals for Δ, one from the t-test and the other from the sign test. If 0 is contained in both intervals, then Δ is judged sufficiently small, as the estimate of Δ does not differ significantly from 0 at the two-sided .10 level. Recall that the 90% two-sided confidence interval contains all values of the parameter, Δ, which would be accepted when testing the null hypothesis $\Delta = 0$ at the level .10.

Since we are only concerned when $\Delta > 0$, indeed $\Delta < 0$ implies the new fuel pollutes less than the standard one, the problem can be considered as testing the null hypothesis H_0: $\Delta = 0$ versus the alternative hypothesis H_A: $\Delta > 0$, and a one-sided test at the .05 level will correspond to the .10 level two-sided test criteria used by EPA. We now illustrate the procedure on the data on the emission levels of nitrogen oxide (NO_x) considered in the Petrocal hearing and in subsequent litigation. The data and the paired differences are presented in Table 11.6.

TABLE 11.6.   Emission Data for NO_x from *Motor Vehicle Manufacturer's Association vs. EPA*

Emission Level			
Base Fuel(B)	Petrocal(P)	Difference(P − B)	Sign
1.195	1.385	+.190	+
1.185	1.230	+.045	+
.755	.755	0.0	tie
.715	.775	+.060	+
1.805	2.024	+.219	+
1.807	1.792	−.015	−
2.207	2.387	+.180	+
.301	.532	+.231	+
.687	.875	+.188	+
.498	.541	+.043	+
1.843	2.186	+.343	+
.838	.809	−.029	−
.720	.900	+.180	+
.580	.60	+.02	+
.63	.72	+.090	+
1.44	1.04	−.400	−
		AVERAGE .0841	

Source: Table 1 from Analysis of Emissions Data from Vehicles Tested with Petrocal. Prepared by Energy and Environmental Analysis, September 8, 1981.

We first discuss the sign test which is the simpler method. The data in Table 11.6 has one 0, which we will say is negative to favor the new fuel (Petrocal). Therefore, we need to calculate the probability of observing 12 or more positive differences out of a set of 16, where the probability of each difference being positive is 1/2. From exact tables of the binomial distribution, one finds that this probability is .038, which is *less* than .05. Thus, we reject the null hypothesis that $\Delta = 0$ in favor of the alternative $\Delta > 0$, i.e., the new fuel increases the level of NO_x emission. For comparative purposes we note that the normal approximation to the sign test (11.5), incorporating the continuity correction because of the small sample size (18) yields

$$Z = \frac{12 - 8 - \frac{1}{2}}{\sqrt{16 \left(\frac{1}{2}\right)\left(\frac{1}{2}\right)}} = \frac{3.5}{2} = +1.75,$$

giving an approximate p-value of .040, which is quite close to the true p-value, .038.

The analysis of the data by the t-test (11.4) requires the calculation of

$$s_d^2 = \frac{\sum (d_i - \bar{d})^2}{n - 1} = \frac{.4192}{15} = .0279,$$

and $s_d = \sqrt{.0279} = .1672$. The upper tail critical value of the t-test based on 16 observations is obtained from the table in Appendix B on the line for $n - 1 = 15$ degrees of freedom and is 1.753 (slightly larger than the value 1.645 for the normal curve, as it should be). Calculating the statistic (11.3) yields

(11.10)
$$t = \frac{\bar{d} - 0}{\dfrac{s_d}{\sqrt{n}}} = \frac{.084}{\dfrac{(.1672)}{\sqrt{n}}} = 2.01,$$

which exceeds 1.753, again implying that the null hypothesis $\Delta = 0$ should be rejected. The one-sided p-value of this result is about .03, which is slightly less than that of the sign test.

Although both statistical tests resulted in rejecting the null hypothesis, $\Delta = 0$, and the new fuel failed another statistical standard stated by EPA by a small amount, the EPA allowed a waiver of Petrocal, partly justifying its action on the fact that the estimated environmental effect, $\bar{d} = .084$, on NO_x levels seemed small and that Petrocal "narrowly missed" passing the other standard described later in subsection c. The Motor Vehicle Manufacturer's Association sued to have the sale of the new fuel disallowed and the appellate court reversed EPA's determination partly on the grounds that the agency had deviated from its announced statistical criteria. The opinion also noted that the percentage of alcohol in the Petrocal used in some of the vehicles tested was less than the percentage (15) requested in the waiver application so that the estimated effect obtained from the data was likely to be an understatement.

Comment.   Suppose a statistician ignored the fact that the data in Table 11.6 had been collected in matched pairs and treated the base and Petrocal fuel data as two independent samples of size ten and used the two-sample t-test statistic (7.17) to analyze the difference. This procedure yields a *t*-value of .3984 which is not even close to significance (two-sided *p*-value = .693). Notice that the emission levels in Table 11.6 for either fuel show a fairly wide variation, which is due to the variety of car models tested. Since the standard deviation of the sampled population enters in the two-sample procedure (7.17), one needs a larger sample in order to detect a modest, but meaningful, difference between the energy emission levels of the two fuels. The advantage of the paired or matched study is that the variation between car models is eliminated because each model is driven twice and the difference in emission levels of the fuels constitutes the observation for that model. Ignoring the matched design of the data collection in the data analysis means that the variation among car models which was controlled for by matching is reintroduced in the analysis, increasing the estimated standard error of the difference between the two averages. Although, $\bar{d} = \bar{P} - \bar{B}$ is the numerator of both formulas (11.4) and (7.17), their denominators, which are the standard errors, differ. Thus, it is important to analyze the data with a procedure consistent with the way it was collected. Otherwise, one may draw an erroneous inference.

b.   (optional continuation) A statistical problem inherent in EPA's use of two test statistics

The reason the EPA required that the sign test be used in conjunction with the t-test was to make sure that the t-test was not unduly influenced by very high or very low emission differences from a few vehicles. As we saw in Chapter 1, the average of a set of numbers is more sensitive to one or two extreme values than the median, and the t-test being based on the sample mean is similarly affected, especially when the distribution of the differences does not follow a normal curve. Looking at the data in Table 11.6 we see that this concern is justified, as half of the differences are between $-.09$ and $+.09$, but the next difference (in absolute value) is .18, which is too large a gap for normal data. The sign test is unaffected by the magnitude of the difference and tests for a general pattern of an effect. We now show that the EPA's procedure, which apparently is based on a one-sided .05 level test (or a two-sided .10 level test), actually has a *higher level* or *probability of rejecting* the null hypothesis, $\Delta = 0$, when it is true than .05.

The reason that the level of the *joint test* is greater than .05 is that now one rejects $H_0 : \Delta = 0$ if either

a) the .05 level t-test is significant

or

b) the .05 level sign test is significant.

If we denote the event in the sample space corresponding to (a) by A and the event corresponding to (b) by B, then the probability that the *joint procedure* rejects H_0 $P(A \cup B)$, is

(11.11) $\qquad P(A \cup B) = P(A) + P(B) - P(A \cap B)$

as in (2.1). Since both tests use the .05 level, under the null hypothesis $P(A) = .05$ and $P(B) = .05$. If both tests were *independent,* then $P(A \cap B)$ would be $.05 + .05 - (.05)^2 = .0975$ or nearly .10 or double the .05 level. However, the two procedures are not independent but are correlated or dependent when the null hypothesis is true, because a sample in which over half of the individual observations is positive also has probability greater than one half of having a positive average and vice versa. An approximation,[11] based on large sample theory, shows that the probability of rejecting $H_0 : \Delta = 0$ in favor of $H_A : \Delta > 0$ when $\Delta = 0$ is .075. Thus, the EPA is using a level of significance about .075 in their requirement rather than an .05 level test criteria.

The p-value of EPA's method is also affected. When *both* tests yield significant results at the .05 level, the p-value is $P(A \cap B)$ not just $P(A)$ or $P(B)$, and so the p-value of the joint test on the data in Table 11.6 is *less* than the p-value of *either test alone.* Since the p-values of both procedures were about .04, the same large sample approximation mentioned previously indicates that the p-value of EPA's joint procedure is about .02. This is stronger evidence against the null hypothesis of emission equivalence than either test yielded individually. In situations where one test yields significance and the other does not, a more refined calculation is needed to obtain the p-value of the joint method. In particular, the true p-value of the joint test need not lie between the two p-values of the individual tests.

Since only 16 cars were tested, the power of EPA's procedure to detect increased emissions may still be relatively low so that the *probability of failing to detect a meaningful increase,* say, $\Delta = .12$, may exceed .10. Unfortunately, the concept of power did not play a role in the decision or in EPA's description of this aspect of emission testing, but it does play an important role in a different part of EPA's emission testing standards which we discuss later.

As an alternative to using two procedures for testing $H_0: \Delta = 0$ versus $H_A: \Delta > 0$, one sensitive to extreme values and one ignoring the magnitudes of the differences, one should consider methods such as the Wilcoxon test and other robust tests which limit the influence of the data points (differences here) furthest from the center of the data. The Wilcoxon test does this by using the relative ranks of the observations rather than their actual values. On the emissions data, the paired comparison Wilcoxon statistic (11.8) yields

$$(11.12) \qquad Z = \frac{112.5 - 68}{\sqrt{374}} = 2.30,$$

a result which has a one-sided p-value of .0107. The advantage of using *one* test is that the probability of a type I error remains at the originally desired .05 level. Of course, the EPA could set the type I error rate of the individual tests at an appropriate value, about .035 to .04, thereby ensuring that the joint procedure has level .05.

Comment. Another consequence of EPA's failure to seriously consider the power of its procedure is that manufacturers might be encouraged to use *small* sample sizes, which would give a wide confidence interval for the difference, Δ. Such intervals might well include 0 even if Δ exceeded 0. If one wishes to establish criteria in terms of a confidence interval, based on the t-test, say, then one should specify a maximum tolerable value for $s_d/\sqrt{n}$, the standard error of d.

c. *EPA's deteriorated emission test: a test criteria specified in terms of the type II error or power*

In addition to assessing the effect of Petrocal use on the emission level of each specific pollutant, another procedure, the deteriorated emissions test, is carried out to determine whether a car model certified as meeting the government's emission standard when gasoline is used will still meet it when a substitute fuel is used. The test is accomplished by adding the observed difference in the emission levels of the paired test vehicles to the certified level of the model and then comparing this value to the standard that should be met. The idea is to see whether the incremental emission due to a substitute fuel such as Petrocal would cause the vehicle to fail its compliance standard. For example, the first car in the NO_x data in Table 11.6 had to meet a standard of 2.0 gm/mile but was certified as emitting only 1.6 gm per mile. As adding the difference +.19 to 1.6 yields 1.79, which is less than 2.0, EPA concludes that the model would meet its compliance standard with Petrocal. The sign test is used to determine whether the number, S, of compliance standard failures is too large.

In the present application one needs to determine the threshold or critical value of S, as the usual sign test procedure checks the data for consistency with a probability, p, of failure (or success) of 1/2. Clearly, the EPA desires that only a small fraction of car models would fail to meet their standard when driven with a substitute fuel. Hence, the critical region of the test based on the number (S) of failures of the cars driven with Petrocal is expressed in terms of the power or type II error. In fact, the critical region (number of failures) is determined to insure that the probability of being denied a waiver is at least 90% if 25% or more of the sample fleet *fails* to meet emission standards. Thus, the EPA does not specify an allowable fraction, p, of the population of cars which could fail to meet the emission standard and then test whether the sample data is consistent with it. Instead, the EPA desires a high probability that no more than 25% of all cars violate the standard. Before examining the NO_x data for the deteriorated emissions test, we should calculate the critical value of this sign test. As there were 16 pairs of cars tested for NO_x we need to find the value, k, satisfying

$$(11.13) \qquad\qquad P[S \geq k] \simeq .90,$$

where S is the number of models failing the criteria and has a binomial distribution with parameters $n = 16$ and $p = .25$. The value k in (11.13) defines the *rejection* region of the statistical test, and we desire its probability to be high (.9) when $p = .25$. From exact tables of the binomial distribution we find that

$$(11.14) \qquad P[S \geq 2] = .9365 \qquad \text{and} \qquad P[S \geq 3] = .8029$$

so that a power of exactly 90% is not possible to attain. The EPA adopted the critical region $S \geq 2$, which has over 90% power, to detect a probabil-

TABLE 11.7.   Deteriorated Emission Test Data for NO_x from *Motor Vehicle Manufacturer's Association vs. EPA*

Car Model	Standard	Certified	Difference	Increment Meets (0) or Fails (1) the Standard
1	2.0	1.6	+.190	0
2	2.0	1.2	+.045	0
3	1.0	0.79	.0	0
4	2.0	1.0	+.06	0
5	2.0	1.4	+.219	0
6	2.0	1.5	−.015	0
7	2.0	1.6	+.180	0
8	0.70	0.59	+.231	1
9	0.70	0.47	+.188	0
10	0.70	0.52	+.043	0
11	2.0	1.1	+.343	0
12	1.0	0.82	−.029	0
13	1.0	0.89	+.180	1
14	1.0	0.62	+.020	0
15	1.0	0.52	+.090	0
16	2.0	1.6	−.400	0

Source: The same as Table 11.6. Note that the certified emission level is determined by the manufacturer and the EPA prior to the use of the vehicle in the deteriorated emission test.

ity (p) of failure of .25, while allowing one test vehicle to fail the test. In Table 11.7 we reproduce the data for NO_x and see that two models failed the test.

It is interesting to determine the fraction, p, of cars manufacturers are permitted to make that do not satisfy the standard, i.e., there will be a high probability (around 90%) that only 0 or 1 cars in a sample of 16 would fail the incremental emissions test, so the cars will satisfy the test criteria. The complement of the event $[S \geq 2]$ or $[S \leq 1]$ corresponds to the cars passing the test and its probability depends on p. When $p = .25$, $P[S \leq 1] = .0635$; when $p = .20$, $P[S \leq 1] = .1407$; when $p = .10$, $P[S \leq 1] = .5147$; when $p = .05$, $P[S \leq 1] = .8108$ and when $p = .03$, $P[S \leq 1] = .9182$. Thus, the EPA's criteria is equivalent to testing the null hypothesis .03 against the alternative $p = .25$ where both type I and type II errors are approximately equal to .10. Because of the small sample size (16), the power of EPA's test against alternatives such as $p = .10$, which might also be considered meaningful, is not high (about 50%). The only way to have higher power to detect a fraction of cars (violating EPA standards) less than .25 is to increase the sample size.

We should mention that the results of the tests on all evaporated emissions had bigger roles in the ultimate outcome of the case than the tests on NO_x emissions. Data on all evaporated emissions was collected on only *nine* pairs of vehicles, which makes the task of obtaining a critical region with about 90% power more difficult due to the inherent discreteness of the binomial counting variable. Indeed, when $n = 9$ and $p = .25$,

$$P[S \geq 1] = .9249 \quad \text{and} \quad P[S \geq 2] = .6997.$$

Thus, the EPA would have been justified in using even one failure as its critical value as the rejection region $[S \geq 2]$ leads to a type II error rate of 30%, which far exceeds the desired 10% rate. In the actual case, three car models failed the evaporated emissions test, so the issue of whether one or two failures should be allowed never arose. Apparently the EPA originally used 2 as the critical value and they allowed the waiver even though three of the nine cars failed the evaporated emissions test. In effect, they changed the critical region $[S \geq 2]$ into reject if $[S \geq 4]$, which has a probability of occurring of only .1657 when $p = .25$ and $n = 9$. Thus, by not sticking to the original statistical criteria EPA used a test with a power of 16.6%, which is very far from their 90% criteria. Our analysis of the difference between the actual and officially announced power specification supports the appellate court's finding of a meaningful deviation from EPA's statistical standard. Even *without these calculations* the fact that the proportion of car models failing the evaporated emissions test, $(3/9) = 33.3\%$, exceeds the 25% figure that EPA desired to guard against implies that EPA's granting the waiver was inconsistent with its stated objective.

Problems

1.   After examining the differences between the certified levels and the emission standards for the cars certified as meeting the 2.0, 1.0 and .7 standard for NO_x in Table 11.7, explain the effect of the variation in these tolerances on the deteriorated emissions test. If you were a manufacturer, which of the three standards (.7, 1.0, 2.0) would you wish to be able to comply with?

2.*   A key step in the deteriorated emissions test is adding the estimated difference between the emission levels of the same car when driven with Petrocal and the base fuel to the certified emission level of the car model. How reliable is the estimated effect (difference) in the data used in the Petrocal case? What might be done to improve the reliability of the deteriorated emissions test?

3.   Look at the differences in Table 11.7. Do the ones for cars at the 2.0 standard appear to have the same distribution as those for cars certified at lower standards? If one believed that cars at the 2.0 standard had more variation in the differences, how might one create an appropriate test statistic?

Answers to Selected Problems

1.   The difference between the standard that had to be met and the certified emission level of the car models was much smaller for the models certified at .7 gm/mile than for those at the higher levels. This makes it more difficult for cars certified at the .7 (or 1.0) level to pass the test using a new fuel than cars certified at the 2.0 gm/mile level. Indeed, the two cars that failed the deteriorated emissions test had levels of .7 and 1.0, respectively. Furthermore, the actual level of NO_x emissions on these two test cars when driven with Petrocal did not exceed the standards.

2.   Since only one difference is estimated for each model and then added to the certified value, the method is not very reliable. The only measure of the standard error of the difference we can calculate requires us to assume that all the differences have the same standard deviation. This assumption is also required for the validity of the t-test and the Wilcoxon procedures, however, they remain valid (approximately) if the standard deviations of the distribution of the pairwise differences vary somewhat over the variety of car models. In situations where small samples are used, it would be preferable to have several paired observations on each model to estimate the effect (difference), especially as it is not reasonable to assume that the differences for cars certified at the 2.0 gm/mile standard have the same distribution as those of cars certified at the lower standards. Looking at Table 11.7 shows that the largest differences (ignoring the sign) seem to occur for cars certified at the 2.0 standard.

3.   The differences for the cars meeting the 2.0 standard seem larger in absolute value (magnitude disregarding the sign) and therefore may be

more variable. While this does not affect the sign test, it does affect the assumption that all differences have the same symmetric (normal) distribution required for the validity of the Wilcoxon (*t*) tests. If the standard deviations of the differences for cars at the different standards are truly different (say by a factor exceeding 2) then one could use a combined Wilcoxon procedure analogous to the one described in Chapter 7. We should mention that in the actual data underlying Table 11.6 a few models were tested with two pairs and the average difference reported. These average differences have smaller standard errors than the single differences, as the standard deviation of $(d_1 + d_2)/2$ is $\sigma/\sqrt{2}$, where σ is the standard deviation of one difference.

6. Testing for the Equality of Proportions Using Matched Pairs

In Chapter 5 we discussed methods for comparing the proportions of successes in two groups when the data consisted either of the whole population or random samples of each group. We illustrated their usefulness in the analysis of promotion and layoff (termination) data occurring in equal employment cases and noted that the Mantel-Haenszel procedure enables one to subdivide the data into groups of similar qualification levels and combine the statistical calculations for each subgroup into one statistical test and a summary measure of the odds faced by minority members relative to those of majority members. An alternative to stratifying the data into groups of similar qualification levels would be to match each minority group member to one (or more) majority members possessing similar qualifications.

In this section we discuss the use of matched pairs to analyze binary data, i.e., observations which are described by a 1 or 0 (promoted or not, exposed to a chemical or not) to decide whether two groups received the same proportion of 1's (e.g., promotions). Before proceeding to the description of the statistical methodology, we remind the reader that the matching process must be carried out carefully so that we are studying pairs which are similar with respect to other influential factors.

For purposes of exposition we shall describe the statistical procedure in the context of a promotion case. Suppose we have N matched pairs (x_i, y_i) of minority and majority members, some of whom are promoted (1) and some are not (0). We have four possible types of pairs:

(1,1) both promoted
(1,0) minority promoted, majority not promoted

(0,1) minority not promoted, majority promoted

(0,0) neither promoted.

The results of a study of matched pairs are summarized by the number of pairs of each type which are denoted by A, B, C, and D, respectively, and are presented in the format of Table 11.8.

Intuitively, pairs of the type (1,1) and (0,0) do not tell us much about the difference between the promotion rates of the groups, since both members have the same status with respect to having received a promotion. Thus, for purposes of comparing the rates, information is only contained in the B pairs of type (1,0) and C pairs of type (0,1), and the formal statistical analysis is based on the $B + C$ pairs in which the outcomes of the pair differ. Given that there are $B + C$ pairs with only one member promoted, we can ask in how many of them should the minority be the one promoted. Under a fair system each member should have probability 1/2 of being the promotee, so with this assumption (the null hypothesis) the number B of (1,0) pairs is a binomial random variable with parameters $n = B + C$ (number of trials) and success probability, $p = 1/2$. Thus, B has the same probability distribution as the sign test discussed earlier. In particular, when $B + C$ is reasonably large, the standard normal approximation to the exact distribution of the binomial ($n = B + C, p = .5$) variable applies so we can use

$$(11.15) \qquad Z = \frac{B - \dfrac{(B + C)}{2}}{\sqrt{\dfrac{(B + C)}{4}}} = \frac{\dfrac{B}{2} - \dfrac{C}{2}}{\dfrac{\sqrt{B + C}}{2}} = \frac{B - C}{\sqrt{B + C}}$$

to carry out the test for equality of the proportions in each group.

TABLE 11.8. Format Summarizing the Results of a Matched Study of N Pairs

		Control Group		
		+	−	Total
Experimental	+	A	B	A + B
Group	−	C	D	C + D
	Total	A + C	B + D	N

Note: In a promotion case (+) means promoted (−) denotes not promoted. In a case-control study (+) means exposed while (−) signifies nonexposed.

To illustrate the procedure, suppose that in 1980, 200 new minority hires were matched to 200 majority hires, and a year later we observe who has been promoted. The data is summarized in Table 11.9 and shows that $B = 30$ and $C = 70$, i.e., in 30 pairs the minority member was the one promoted, while in 70 pairs the majority member was. Since $B + C = 100$, under the null hypothesis of equal promotion rates we expect that minorities would have received $(B + C)/2 = 100/2 = 50$ of the promotions. Calculating the normal approximation (11.15) to the sign test statistic, we obtain

$$(11.16) \qquad Z = \frac{30 - 50}{\sqrt{\dfrac{100}{4}}} = \frac{-20}{5} = -4,$$

clearly a statistically significant result (p-value less than .0001).

Additional insight into the procedure is obtained by noting that each pair can be considered as a separate 2×2 table and the results combined using the Mantel-Haenszel procedure. The four possible tables are as follows:

	(1)		(2)		(3)		(4)	
	Prom	Not	Prom	Not	Prom	Not	Prom	Not
Minority	1	0	1	0	0	1	0	1
Majority	1	0	0	1	1	0	0	1

From formulas (5.14) and (5.15) the means and variances of the number of minority promotions in each of the four types of tables are given by (1,0); (1/2, 1/4); (1/2, 1/4) and (0,0). To illustrate the derivation look at a table of the first type:

	Prom	Not	Total
Minority	1	0	1
Majority	1	0	1
Total	2	0	2

In terms of the usual format of 2×2 tables we have $a = 1$, $b = 0$, $c = 1$ and $d = 0$. Hence, the expected number of minority promotions is

$$\frac{(a + c)(a + b)}{N} = \frac{2 \cdot 1}{2} = 1$$

and its variance is

$$\frac{(a + c)(b + d)(c + d)(a + b)}{N^2(N - 1)} = \frac{[1 \cdot 1 \cdot 0 \cdot 2]}{4.1} = 0.$$

TABLE 11.9. Frequency of Promotion in a Sample of 200
Matched Pairs

| | | Majority |||
		1 (Promoted)	0 (Not)	Total
Minority	1 (Promoted)	40	30	70
	0 (Not)	70	60	130
	Total	110	90	200

This result means that when both members of a pair are promoted we
know that exactly one minority and one majority member were promoted,
i.e., there is no variability at all, which implies that the variance of the
number of minority promotions equals 0. The results for the other tables
are obtained similarly.

Notice that the totality (A) of tables of the first type and those (D) of
the last type do not contribute to the MH statistic. They do not affect the
numerator, as they always equal their expectation since both members of
the first type of tables are promoted while neither member of the fourth
type is promoted. Also, the variance of the number of minority promotions is 0 in these tables, so they do not affect the denominator of the MH
statistic. Thus, the MH statistic (5.35) combining the B tables of the
second type and the C tables of the third type reduces to

$$(11.17) \quad \frac{\sum (\text{observed} - \text{expected})}{\sqrt{\sum V(A_i)]}} = \frac{\frac{B}{2} - \frac{C}{2}}{\sqrt{\frac{(B + C)}{4}}} = \frac{B - C}{\sqrt{B + C}},$$

the same statistic as before.

Full advantage of considering each pair as a separate table is gained
when we calculate the MH estimate of the odds ratio; the ratio of the odds
a minority faces to those faced by a majority member. Recalling formula
(5.36), i.e.,

$$(11.18) \quad \frac{\dfrac{\sum (a_i d_i)}{N_i}}{\dfrac{\sum (b_i c_i)}{N_i}},$$

and noting that all $N_i = 2$ and that only the tables of the second type enter the calculation of the numerator as $a_i \cdot d_i = 0$ for the three other types. For tables of the second type $a_i d_i = 1 \cdot 1 = 1$ so the numerator of (11.18) is $B/2$. Similarly, only tables of the third type have non-zero contribution $(b_i \cdot c_i)$ to the denominator. Each of the C tables (pairs) contributes 1/2 to the denominator so the denominator of 11.18 is $C/2$ and the MH statistic (11.18) equals

$$(11.19) \qquad \frac{\dfrac{B}{2}}{\dfrac{C}{2}} = \frac{B}{C}.$$

For the data in Table 11.9, the estimated odds ratio is $30/70 = .4286$ and is consistent with the sign test indicating the minorities had significantly less chance of promotion than majority members.

The matched-pair analysis of proportions can be generalized to allow for more than one majority member to be matched with a minority one. In the promotion context, failure to use multiple matching would entail a potentially serious loss of information and we discuss these procedures in Section 7.

We now illustrate the use of matched pair studies in cases involving fair housing, equal employment opportunity and a claim of deceptive advertising based on the results of a matched study.

a. A fair housing case: U.S. v. Youritan Construction Company [12]

One approach to demonstrating discrimination in housing by a real estate agent or apartment house manager is through the use of testers, i.e., pairs of black and white applicants for housing with virtually identical housing needs and financial condition. If the black applicants are consistently told that an apartment is not available or a background (credit) check must be made prior to their application being accepted, while the white applicants are told otherwise, a pattern of discriminatory treatment may be established.

In the *Youritan* case 14 pairs of testers were sent, usually on the same day, to an apartment building run by the defendant company. When possible, data was obtained on whether an apartment was available and, if so, whether a credit check was required. The data from the opinion is reproduced in Table 11.10 below. Unfortunately, the data in Table 11.10 is not

TABLE 11.10. Appendix B. Raw Data on the Experience of Testers in the *Youritan* Case

Name of Witness	Name of Apartment Complex	Date of Inquiry	Experiences of White and Black Testers and Black Bona Fides at Tan Apartment Complexes					Source of Supporting Testimony
			Was Witness Told Credit Check or Other Delay for Processing Application?		Was Witness Told That Type of Unit Asked for Was Available?		Actual Existence of Vacancies Per Defendants' Records	
			YES	NO	YES	NO		
WHITE WITNESSES								
Gross	Tan House	1-24-71		X	X			RT-I 173–175 (A-5)
Bredt	Tan House	9-11-69				X[1]		D. Ex. BA pp. 14–15 RT-II 123–127
Gross	Tan Manor	1-24-71		X	X			RT-I 174–175, 181, 195
Murphy	Tan Manor	7-14-71		X	X			RT-II 242–245
Gross	Tan Village	1-24-71		X	X			RT-I 174–179
Gross	Americana	2-7-71		X	X			RT-I 175–176, 234
Brandt	Americana	1-6-71		X	X			P. Ex. 4-a, RT WB-12-17, 52–53, 71–73
Smith	Americana	1-6-71		X	X			P. Ex. No. 4 (b)
Gross	Sunshine Gardens	2-7-71		X	X			RT-I 177–178, 212–213
Gross	Tan Plaza International	2-7-71		X	X			RT-I 179–180, 228–229
Gross	Tan Plaza	2-7-71		X	X			RT-I 180–181, 230–233
Smith	Tan Plaza	1-6-71		X		X		P. Ex. No. 4 (b)
Gross	Tan Plaza	2-7-71		X		X		RT-I 178–179, 222–227, 233
Smith	Continental Tan Plaza	1-6-71		X	X			P. Ex. No. 4 (b)

WITNESSES

Witness	Complex	Date				References
Johnson	Tan House	1-24-71		X	1	RT-II 187–188, 202; P. Ex. 1 (A-5)
Fitch	Tan House	9-11-69		X[2]		RT-II 81–87
Evans	Tan House	9-12-69		X[3]		D. Ex. AK, BA, & U; RT-II 150–155
Davenport	Tan House	mid. Aug. -70		X	1	P. Ex. 1 (B-1)
Johnson	Tan Manor	1-24-71	X			RT-II 188–190, 202
Wimberly	Tan Manor	7-14-71		X	10[4]	RT-II 270–273, P. Ex. 2; D. Ex. AS, pp. 25–26, 42–43
Johnson	Tan Village	1-24-71	X	X		RT-II 190, 202, P. Ex. 1(A4)
Davenport	Tan Village	mid. Aug. -70		X[6]	9[5]	P. Ex. 1 (B-2), see week of Aug. 9 and 16, 1970
Johnson	Americana	2-7-71	X	X	1	RT-II 190–192, 202
McCullen	Americana	1-6-71	X[7]	X		RT-AM 8–10, 12, 15–16; P. Ex. 4-c
Johnson	Sunshine Gardens	2-7-71	X	X		RT-II 192–193, 202
Johnson	Tan Plaza International	2-7-71	X	X		RT-II 194, 202
Johnson	Tan Plaza	2-7-71	X	X		RT-II 193, 202
McCullen	Tan Plaza	1-6-71	X	X		P. Ex. 4(c), RT-AM, pp. 16–18
Johnson	Tan Plaza Continental	2-7-71	X	X		RT-II 193–194, 202
McCullen	Tan Plaza Continental	1-6-71	X	X		D. Ex. AR, p. 65; P. Ex. 4(c), RT-AM, pp. 18–26

[1] Bredt was told that a 1-bedroom apartment would be available in 3 days and was invited back to see similar apartment next day.

[2] Fitch was told that a 1-bedroom apartment would be available in 16 days and quoted a rental price $20 higher than white witness in footnote 1.

[3] Evans requested a 1-bedroom apartment and was told that only a studio apartment was available. He was also told that a 1-bedroom apartment would not be available for 8 days. He also inquired about the price of a 1-bedroom apartment and was quoted a rent of $185 per month, which was $20 in excess of rent quoted to white witness. (See footnote 1.)

[4] In addition, four studios were to become vacant by 8-14-71.

[5] In addition, three 2-bedroom apartments were to become vacant by 2-8-71.

[6] Mrs. Roberts did not, however, tell Mrs. Davenport about Apartment No. 90/104, an unfurnished 1-bedroom apartment which was vacant at the time. (See P. Ex. 1, Part B(2). Particular reference should be made to the weekly vacancy reports for August 9 and 16, 1970.)

[7] McCullen was quoted a security deposit which was $40 more than the two white testers (i.e., Brandt and Smith) who went to the Americana on the same day.

TABLE 11.11   Approximate Matched Pairs for the *Youritan* Data

No. Date	Place		Credit Check	Told Apt. Available	Name of Tester
1) 1/24/71	Tan House	W	No	Yes	Gross
		B	?		Johnson
2) 9/11/69	Tan House	W		No*	Bredt
		B		No	Fitch
3) 1/24/71	Tan House	W	No	Yes	Gross
		B	Yes	Yes	Johnson
4) 1/24/71	Tan Village	W	No	Yes	Gross
		B	Yes	No	Johnson
5) 7/14/71	Tan Village	W	No	Yes	Murphy
		B	Yes	No	Wimberly
6) 2/7/71	Americana	W	No	Yes	Gross
		B	Yes	Yes	Johnson
7) 1/6/71	Americana	W	No	Yes	Brandt
		B	Yes	Yes	Johnson (2/7/71)
8) 1/6/71	Americana	W	No	Yes	Smith
		B	Yes	Yes	McMullen
9) 2/7/71	Sunshine	W	No	Yes	Gross
	Gardens	B	Yes	No	Johnson
10) 2/7/71	Tan Plaza	W	No	Yes	Gross
	Int'l	B	Yes	No	Johnson
11) 2/7/71	Tan Plaza	W	No	Yes	Gross
		B	Yes	No	Johnson
12) 1/6/71	Tan Plaza	W	No	No	Smith
	Cont'l	B	Yes	Yes	McMullen
13) 2/7/71	Tan Plaza	W	No	No	Gross
		B	Yes	Yes	Johnson
14) 1/6/71	Tan Plaza	W	No	Yes	Smith
		B	Yes	Yes	McMullen

* The relevant footnote in the actual case indicated that the white member was told that an apartment would become available earlier than the black applicant.
Source: Adapted from Appendix B in the opinion, 370 F.Supp. 643 at 656.

quite reported in a matched framework, so we develop an approximate set of matched pairs from it in Table 11.11.

In their discussion of the case, Baldus and Cole (1980, p. 236) restrict their analysis to whether or not applicants were told an apartment was available. Hence, there are seven pairs (1, 4, 5, 9, 10, 11, 13) in Table 11.10 which are discordant. In only one of those was the black applicant told the apartment was available. The sign test (11.15) calculates the probability that only zero or one success occurs in seven independent tosses of a fair coin, as ($p = 1/2$)

$$.0078 + .0547 = .0625,$$

which is not quite significant at the .05 level if a one-sided test is used. In a footnote Baldus and Cole suggest that the court probably gave the data more weight than it deserved as the two-sided p-value of the test is .125. However, this analysis has not used all the available information in Table 11.10, as the data on whether or not a credit check was required and any differential in the rent quoted or time when an apartment would become available has not been utilized.

Suppose we score a yes (no) on availability as $+2$ (-2), a no (yes) on whether a credit check is needed as a $+1$ (-1), being told an apartment is available early (late) as $+1$ (-1) and being charged a lower (higher) rent as $+1$ (-1). For each pair in the data in Table 11.11, we can use the information in the opinion (Table 11.10) to obtain a score for the difference in treatment (white minus black). For the first pair, only data on apartment availability is reported for both members. Here the white receives a $+2$, the black a -2 or a difference of $2 - (-2) = +4$. For the second pair the white applicant was told an apartment was not available (-2) but told one would be available early ($+1$). The white applicant's score is $-2 + 1 = -1$, while the black's score is $-2 + (-1) = -3$, so the difference is $+2$. In Table 11.12 we report the scores developed for the differences in treatment between the black and white members of each pair.

Notice that there are *no* concordant pairs, i.e., in no pair did both applicants receive the same treatment. Of the 14 pairs, in only one (the thirteenth) did the black member receive the better treatment. Using the one-sided sign test, the probability that only zero or one success occurs (assuming that both members of the pair had probability 1/2 of receiving the preferable treatment) in 14 independent repetitions is

$$.0001 + .0009 = .001,$$

which is quite significant. The above calculation was obtained from tables

TABLE 11.12.   Difference in Treatment Scores for the Pairs in Table 11.11

Pair	Scores (W,B)	Difference (W − B)	Pair	Scores (W,B)	Difference (W − B)
1	2,−2	+4	8	(3,1)	+2
2	(−1,−3)	+2	9	(3,−3)	+6
3	(3,1)	+2	10	(3,−3)	+6
4	(3,−3)	+6	11	(3,−3)	+6
5	(3,−3)	+6	12	(−1,−3)	+2
6	(3,1)	+2	13	(−1,1)	−2
7	(3,1)	+2	14	(3,1)	+2

of the binomial distribution. The normal approximation (11.15) yields

$$(11.20) \qquad Z = \frac{B - C}{\sqrt{B + C}} = \frac{13 - 1}{\sqrt{14}} = \frac{12}{\sqrt{14}} = 3.207,$$

which corresponds to a one-sided p-value of .0007. This also shows that the normal approximation is reasonably accurate for the matched pairs sign test in small samples.

The preceeding analysis of the data shows that there is a significant difference in the total treatment black applicants received from the defendant compared to similar white applicants. Although Judge Wollenberg did not perform formal statistical significance tests, he may well have incorporated all aspects of the treatment summarized in Table 11.10 and properly gave it reasonable weight.

Comments.   (1) Notice that we did not use the exact scores of treatment differences in Table 11.12 in our analysis. The reason for this is that the scores given each pair in the data were somewhat arbitrary in that whether the requirement of a credit check is precisely equivalent to half that of being told an apartment is not available is subject to question.

(2) When a scoring system such as the one we employed is constructed, ideally one should not have seen the data first. In practice one may need to look at the possible outcomes to classify the degree of differential treatment. However, the scores can be developed without seeing the race of the testers, e.g., by examining some of the data without this information.

(3) Our purpose in discussing this example is to emphasize the importance of preserving the matching in the analysis of the data and to make sure that all relevant information is used in classifying pairs as concordant

or discordant because in misclassifying a discordant pair as a concordant, one loses the pair to the analysis. Of course, misclassifying concordant pairs as discordant also leads to a possible bias as well as an overestimate of the accuracy of the results, since the sample size (number of discordant pairs) is larger than it should be.

b. A claim of discrimination in job evaluation

The U.S. Government categorizes all occupations in grade levels varying from 1 thru 15. Each job title spans several grade levels, e.g., 1–5, 7–15, etc., where the first level is determined by the lowest level of skill needed for a beginning position and the highest level is the furthest one can progress in that occupation. When a new job type (e.g., computer programmer) is created, its grade level structure is determined by analogy to similar jobs and occupations (e.g., mathematician, mathematical statistician).

A black employee in a grade 13 position filed a charge of discrimination in opportunity for advancement. He noted that the proportion of blacks in the newly created sequence was far greater than their proportion in the job series used in setting the grade levels and that blacks had a lower average grade level than whites. In the actual situation, every division of the employer had one senior employee in each of the job types. Because the workload and size of each division varied, the grade of employees in either job varied by division. To assess the comparability of the job levels, a matched data set analogous to the one reported in Table 11.13 was created. Although one difference was +2, we will simplify the analysis by considering it as a +1, i.e., we score pairs in which the comparable level was higher as +1. Similarly, we would score any pair with plaintiff's job title higher as −1.

The data in Table 11.13 has five discordant pairs, all indicating that the plaintiff's job position has the lower grade, i.e., $B = 5$ and $C = 0$. Due to the small sample size (five), the normal form (11.15) should not be used. The exact probability of observing zero successes in five binomial trials with probability $1/2$ of success on each, is $(1/2)^5 = .0313$, a significant result if one-tailed test is used. However, its two-tailed p-value is .063, which slightly exceeds the .05 level. In light of our earlier discussion of statistical significance and remembering that in our use of the matched pairs technique we neglected the size of one larger difference, it is reasonable to conclude that the job titles do not have the same grade level distribution.

Comment. This application also raises an interesting nonstatistical question. When an employer considers two job types as being comparable to one another, how precise should this comparability be? The test statistic (11.15) tests the hypothesis that they are exactly equal, i.e., the differences in grade level should be centered around 0.

Even without the benefit of statistical analysis, the data in Table 11.13 certainly suggest that the grade levels of the comparable job are higher, as in no case did the occupant of the newer job classification have a higher grade level. However, suppose that there had been 40 more divisions and the grade levels of the occupants of both job types were identical in all 40. Although the statistic (11.15) would still be significant, the reader probably would be less convinced that the plaintiff's job is graded lower than the comparable job series. This problem arises because we are testing whether there is any difference between the proportions of the two groups receiving the higher level job rather than assessing the magnitude of the difference between the two. Hence, our analysis is restricted to those pairs exhibiting a difference in treatment (discordant pairs). Unfortunately, there is no simple statistical way out of this dilemma, but reporting the totality of the data (including the concordant pairs) and an estimate of the odds ratio often clarifies the situation. In the present example, the fact that there were five discordant pairs out of ten and the plaintiff's job classification was the lower one in all five indicates that the borderline statistical difference, if the .05 level is adopted, is likely to be meaningful

TABLE 11.13. Grade Levels of Plaintiff's Job Title and the Comparable Job Title (by location)

Division	Plaintiff's Job Level	Comparable Job Level	Difference
I	12	13	+1
II	13	13	0
III	13	14	+1
IV	14	14	0
V	13	13	0
VI	12	14	+2
VII	13	14	+1
VIII	13	13	0
IX	12	13	+1
X	15	15	0

Source: This hypothetical data is adapted from an actual claim.

and should convince an impartial fact-finder to require that the employer explain how the difference arose from legitimate factors. Of course, the task of explaining the data in Table 11.13 presumably would be less difficult than justifying a more significant difference based on a larger number of matched pairs such as the data in Table 11.9. Perhaps the defendant could show that the qualifications of the incumbents of the established job series exceeded the minimum needed for the job and the posts were upgraded to keep them, or that currently they might have to supervise more people and provisions have been made to increase the grade levels of the new job category when the staff has grown sufficiently.

c.   Philip Morris Inc. v. Loew's Theatres[13] and R. J. Reynolds Inc. v. Loew's Theaters:[14] the propriety of an advertising campaign based on results of a matched pair taste comparison test

In 1979, Lorillard, a subsidiary of Loew's Theatres introduced its Triumph brand of low tar cigarettes and commissioned a survey of consumer preference. The survey's results were presented to the public in a sequence of advertisements asserting that in a national taste test the public preferred Triumph to other brands such as Merit (Philip Morris), Marlboro Lights (Philip Morris) and Winston Lights (R. J. Reynolds). Both Philip Morris and R. J. Reynolds sued Lorillard and requested an injunction to stop the advertisements on the grounds that the claims that Triumph was a "national taste test winner" or "beats" the other brands tested "were false and misleading."

The design of the matched pair study and the criticisms of it were described by Judge Sweet in the *Reynolds* opinion as follows:

"The Smoker Study recorded results from so-called 'unidentified paired comparison tests' of Triumph against the other brands. In these tests individuals in 25 shopping malls across the country were stopped and screened to determine membership in the desired class of low tar smokers. Those meeting the criteria were invited to smoke one masked competing cigarette. The participant was then told the tar content of the two cigarettes and asked: 1) '[The code representing Triumph] has 3 mg of tar while [the code representing the competitor] has [x] mg of tar. Taking this into consideration, which would you prefer to smoke?'; and 2) "Comparing the taste of the two cigarettes, how would you say the taste of the [Triumph] you tried compares to [the competitor]?" While the questions were phrased so that the number representing Triumph was always mentioned first, the order in which individual participants smoked the two cigarettes was rotated.

It was contended in the *Philip Morris* hearing that the disclosure of tar content before question 1 (the preference question) in the test unfairly biased the answer in favor of lower tar Triumph. However, the court there found that too little evidence had been adduced on that matter, and held only that Lorillard's own test results from question 2 (the taste question) did not support the advertising claims of taste parity of superiority vis-à-vis the Philip Morris brands, Id., at 856-857. Here Reynolds mounts a broadside attack upon the test methodology itself, in addition to presenting the same type of claim and evidence which prevailed in *Philip Morris,* addressed to the ads and the message they communicate.

The record constitutes, principally, expert testimony and contains no less than 11 consumer surveys in addition to the challenged Lorillard smoker study. Specifically, Reynolds attacks the methodology of the study on the basis of the timing and use of the tar disclosure, the inadequacy of participant exposure to judge the cigarettes, an unrepresentative and biased sample, the probability of interviewer bias, the order bias resulting from the consistent mention of the Triumph code first in the questions to the participants, and suppression of important test results.

Before discussing the several issues of possible bias in the survey, we reproduce the data from the Triumph v. Merit comparison in Exhibit 11.1 and the advertisement in Exhibit 11.2 and show that the judge was statistically correct in his discussion of the ad in the first case involving *Philip Morris*. First, note that the claim, "60% said 3 mg Triumph tastes as good as or better than 8 mg Merit" is based on the data in the bottom half of Exhibit 11.1. In order to obtain the 60% figure the respondents who said "about the same" were added to those who said Triumph tasted better. Had they been added to the persons liking the taste of Merit better, 64% of the sample would have said that Merit tastes as good as or better than Triumph. A proper analysis is based on the discordant pairs treating the persons who said a brand was somewhat better or much better as preferring that brand. The formal statistical test (11.15) is

$$(11.21) \qquad Z = \frac{B - C}{\sqrt{B + C}} = \frac{(45 + 73) - (36 + 93)}{\sqrt{(118 + 129)}}$$

$$= \frac{-11}{\sqrt{247}} = \frac{-11}{15.72} = -.7,$$

clearly a nonsignificant difference. It is interesting that the description of the survey results, which were available to the public, stated that this difference was not significant but still combined the "about the same" category with those preferring Triumph in the data display (see boxes). To

EXHIBIT 11.1.   Results of the Blind Test Comparing Triumph and Merit Non Menthol

Stated below are the results of the blind test comparison of Triumph against Merit. Appearing under the column labeled "Total" is the _number_ of smokers preferring each brand. Appearing under the column labeled "Respondents" is the _percentage_ preferring Triumph and the percentage preferring Merit. In other words 53% of the respondents preferred Triumph, 42% preferred Merit and 5% had no preference. This difference is statistically significant.

	TOTAL #	RESPONDENTS %
Triumph Non-Menthol Vs. Merit Non-Menthol		
PREFER TRIUMPH NON-MENTHOL	173	53
Prefer Merit Non-Menthol	138	42
No Preference	14	5
Total Respondents	325	100

Appearing below is the number of smokers stating that Triumph is...much better tasting, somewhat better tasting, about the same in taste, somewhat worse tasting or much worse tasting than Merit or had no opinion. As in the previous table, the second column contains the _percentages_ expressing these opinions. 60% find the taste of Triumph as good as or better than Merit. This is a significantly larger percentage than the percentage of people stating that Merit tastes better. The difference between those stating Triumph is better tasting and those stating Merit is better tasting is not statistically significant.

	TOTAL #	RESPONDENTS %
Triumph Non-Menthol Vs. Merit Non-Menthol Triumph Is...		
Much Better Tasting	45	14
Somewhat Better Tasting	73	22
About The Same In Taste	77	24
Somewhat Worse Tasting	93	29
Much Worse Tasting	36	11
No Answer	1	*
Total Respondents	325	100

☐ Significant at 95% level of confidence or higher.

☐ *Less than 0.5%.

Source: Appendix C of the opinion in _Philip Morris v. Loew's Theatres Inc._ 511 F.Supp. 855 (1980) p. 866.

EXHIBIT 11.2.   The Advertisement of Triumph Cigarettes at Issue in *Philip Morris Inc. v. Loew's Theatres Inc.*

TRIUMPH BEATS MERIT!

Triumph, at less than half the tar, preferred over Merit.

In rating overall product preference, more smokers independently chose Triumph over Merit. In fact, an amazing 60% said 3 mg Triumph tastes as good or better than 8 mg Merit.

Results showed that Triumph was <u>also</u> preferred over
• 14 mg Winston Lights • 12 mg Marlboro Lights
• 11 mg Vantage.

Now, test for yourself. Compare Triumph with any other so-called "low tar" or "light" cigarette. You'll taste why we named it Triumph. Also available in Menthol.

National Taste Test results available free on request.
Write: National Taste Test P.O. Box 2733, Hillside, New Jersey 07205

Taste the UMPH! in Triumph at only 3 mg tar.

buttress its case, Philip Morris introduced survey evidence, similar to that described in *Eastern Airlines v. New York Airlines* (Section 9.7) which showed that 37% of the readers of the ad believed it established that Triumph tasted better than Merit.

The Reynolds Company faced a more difficult problem as the raw taste test results, reproduced in Exhibit 11.3, show a statistically significant preference for Triumph over Winston Lights when properly analyzed using the test statistic (11.15). Therefore, Reynolds attacked the entire survey methodology and presentation of the results. In order to assess the potential biasing effect of disclosing the tar content of the cigarettes before the taster was asked to express a preference, two variations of the smoker study were carried out. The first one did not mention tar levels prior to the preference question (as a proper survey would have done), while the second study reversed the actual tar content of the cigarettes, i.e., smokers of Winston Lights were told they had the tar content of Merit and vice versa. In contrast to Lorillard's finding of a 66% to 29% preference for Triumph, Reynolds' first variant showed smokers preferred Winstons 54% to 40%. In the reversed tar study, Winstons was favored by a 70% to 26% margin. Clearly, the data indicate that disclosing the tar content prior to a person's response influences the preference stated. Indeed the cigarette described as "low tar" received about a "two thirds" preference proportion in both the original study and in the second variation.

The statistical analysis of these two related cases dealt with the responses to the first two questions asked the tasters in Lorillard's survey, the results of which were made available to the public (see the ad in Exhibit 11.2). Two other questions dealing with the amount of taste and its satisfying quality were also asked. On these questions Reynolds' brands did better than Triumph, but these results were *not* released to members of the public who requested the survey results.

In light of the strong biasing effect of disclosing the tar content, Lorillard's witholding of the taste results and a survey similar to the one in *Philip Morris* showing that a significant portion of readers of the ad (20% to 33%) received the impression that Triumph had a taste victory over its competitors, the judge enjoined Lorillard from using the phrase "overall preference" or any equivalent statement as well as any explicit reference to taste or national percentages based on the smoker study.

The opinion also questioned the propriety of basing a "nationally projectable statistical percentage" on a mall intercept study. The primarily suburban character of mall shoppers makes it unlikely that they can be

RESULTS OF THE BLIND TEST
(comparing Triumph and Winston Lights)

Stated below are the results of the blind test comparison of Triumph against Winston Lights. Appearing under the column labeled "Total" is the _number_ of smokers preferring each brand. Appearing under the column labeled "Respondents" is the _percentage_ preferring Triumph and the percentage preferring Winston Lights. In other words, 66% of the respondents preferred Triumph, 29% preferred Winston Lights and 5% had no preference. This difference is statistically significant.

	TOTAL #	RESPONDENTS %
Triumph Non-Menthol Vs. Winston Lights		
PREFER TRIUMPH NON-MENTHOL	205	66
Prefer Winston Lights	89	29
No Preference/No Answer	16	5
Total Respondents	310	100

Appearing below is the number of smokers stating that Triumph is…much better tasting, somewhat better tasting, about the same in taste, somewhat worse tasting or much worse tasting than Winston Lights. As in the previous table the second column contains the _percentages_ of respondents expressing these opinions. 66% find the taste of Triumph as good as or better than Winston Lights. This is a significantly larger percentage than the percentage of people stating that Winston Lights taste better. Similarly 52% say Triumph is better tasting while only 34% say Winston Lights are better tasting. This again is significant.

	TOTAL #	RESPONDENTS %
Triumph Non-Menthol Vs. Winston Lights Triumph Is…		
Much Better Tasting	78	25
Somewhat Better Tasting	84	27
About The Same In Taste	44	14
Somewhat Worse Tasting	78	25
Much Worse Tasting	26	9
No Answer	—	—
Total Respondents	310	100

☐ Significant at 95% level of confidence or higher.

Source: The appendix to the _Philip Morris v. Loew's Theatres_ opinion, 511 F.Supp. 855 (1980) at 863.

638

considered a random sample of the nation's smokers. Therefore, the judge noted that comparative advertising based on such studies deserved greater scrutiny than ads based on proper random samples.

d. The use of a matched pair analysis in a promotion discrimination case: EEOC v. IBM[15]

In this case the defendant used a matched pair study as part of its rebuttal evidence. Black and white employees were paired on the following characteristics:

(1) Seniority: The white matched to the black employee was hired within six months of the black employee's date of hire.

(2) Initial Assignment: Both were hired at the same salary or job level.

(3) Education: Both had the same level of educational attainment (highest degree or diploma earned).

The promotions received by the members of the 178 matched pairs were examined yearly. In none of the eight years was there a significant difference between the promotion rates of both groups. Indeed, in five of the years the black employees had higher promotion rates, while the promotion rate for the white employees exceeded that of black employees in two of the years.

Although it is unlikely that a more refined analysis would have altered the ultimate decision in this case, the matched pair analysis probably did not use all the available information. Often there are several majority employees who are suitable matches for each minority employee, and the progress of the minority member should be compared to that of all similarly qualified majority employees. In Section 7 extensions are given for the analysis of the multiple matched situation. In addition to increasing the power of the test, using multiple matches lessens the possibility that a factor not used as a criteria in the matching process could strongly affect the analysis, as that factor would vary among the set of matched employees.

7. Matched Studies with Multiple Controls

In some situations it may be possible to find several control group members who are appropriate matches for each experimental group member or case and the power of a statistical test, and the precision of the estimated measure of difference between the groups are increased by utilizing all available matches. This increased degree of statistical accuracy may be quite important in epidemiological studies of rare diseases where the number of cases is small or in discrimination litigation where the number of minority employees is small and the issue under study is the equality of pay or promotion rates. Another practical advantage of having several controls for each case is that in one-to-one matched studies, if the data on either member of the pair is missing or unusable for any reason, the information for the other member of the pair is also lost, reducing the size of the sample. In this section we present the formulas for estimating the odds ratio, OR, and testing whether it equals 1, i.e., the rates are equal, for multiply matched case-control studies as well as the Wilcoxon procedure for comparing continuous variables measured on all members of each multiply matched set (case-and several-controls). In order to avoid involved calculations and questions of the accuracy of the large sample approximation, we shall not present formulas for the confidence intervals we report. These are taken from the cited papers and typically are based on results given in the *basic* references at the end of the chapter. We apply the methods to an epidemiologic study of workers exposed to a pesticide, the first case-control study showing DES was a carcinogen, and some hypothetical data from an EEO case. We will use the terminology of case-control studies in describing the methodology.

a.   Multiply matched 0–1 data in case-control studies[16]

The general forma for summarizing data from a multiply matched study is slightly more complex, as we need to record the number of the controls matched to a case who were exposed. If each case is compared to r controls, then the case can be exposed (1) or not (0) and the number of its matches who were exposed can range from 0 to r. The data can be summarized by two rows of data reporting the numbers (n_{1j}) of matched sets in which the case was exposed (1) and j of its r controls were exposed in the first row and the number (n_{0j}) of sets in which the case was *not* exposed (0) and j of its r controls exposed. The general format is presented in Table 11.14 and a numerical illustration based on a Swedish study of compounds typically contaminated by dioxin ("Agent Orange") is given in Table 11.15.

The Mantel-Haenszel estimator of the overall relative risk (odds ratio) is again obtained by considering each matched set as a separate stratum as

TABLE 11.14.   Format for Summarizing the Results of a Multiply Matched Case-Control Study with R Controls per Case

Status of Case	No. of Controls Who Were Exposed					
	0	1	2	3	...	R
Exposed	n_{10}	n_{11}	n_{12}	n_{13}		n_{1R}
Not Exposed	n_{00}	n_{01}	n_{02}	n_{03}		n_{0R}

we did in the 1–1 matched pair setting. The resulting formula is

$$(11.22) \qquad O\hat{R} = \frac{\sum_{j=0}^{R} (R - j)n_{1j}}{\sum_{j=1}^{R} jn_{0j}}.$$

An intuitive approach to formula (11.22) follows by realizing that the evidence favoring an increased relative risk comes from the sets where the case is exposed but few of its matched controls are exposed. Similarly, the unexposed cases with some controls who are exposed are evidence of little, if any, risk of exposure. Indeed, if most of the matched sets consist of unexposed cases with several exposed controls, the estimated

TABLE 11.15.   Case-Control Data on Exposure to Phenoxyacetic Acids or Chlorophenols where each Case was Matched to Four Controls

Status of Case	No. of Controls Exposed				
	0	1	2	3	4
Exposed	11	8	0	0	0
Not Exposed	25	6	1	1	0

Source: Adapted from Table 1 of Hardell, L. and Sandstrom, A. (1979). Case Control Study: Soft-tissue Sarcomas and Exposure to Phenoxyacetic Acids or Chlorophenols. *British Journal of Cancer* **39**, 711–717.

odds ratio (11.22) should be less than one, indicating that the agent may be protective.

Formula (11.22) is precisely

$$\frac{\text{the number of unexposed controls for cases who were exposed}}{\text{the number of exposed controls for cases who were unexposed}},$$

(11.23)

which is an intuitive indicator of whether the agent is harmful or protective. If there were no effect of exposure, the OR should be one and the numerator and denominator of (11.23) should be equal (apart from random fluctuation).

Applying formula (11.22) to the data in Table 11.15 yields

(11.24) $$\frac{(4 \times 11) + (3 \times 8)}{6 + (1 \times 2) + (1 \times 3)} = \frac{44 + 24}{11} = 6.18,$$

indicating a substantial risk of exposure to the chemicals studied. In this calculation note that each of the 11 sets in which none of the four controls were exposed contributes a 4 to the numerator, as they indicate a high risk due to exposure. Each of the eight sets where one control was exposed contributes a 3 to the numerator, etc.

The matched sets in which the case and all its controls have the same exposure status, i.e., the n_{1r} sets in which the case and all controls were exposed and the n_{00} sets with the case and all controls unexposed, do not contribute to the estimate (11.22) of overall relative risk, just as the 0–0 and 1–1 pairs did not enter into formulas (11.15) and (11.19).

To derive a test of the null hypothesis that the OR = 1, we organize the matched sets by the number of persons (cases or controls) who are exposed. For each $j = 0, 1, 2, \ldots, r + 1$, let m_j denote the number of such matched sets. First, notice that $m_j = n_{1,j-1} + n_{0,j}$, i.e., the sets with exactly j exposed persons either have the case and $j - 1$ controls exposed or the case is unexposed and j controls are exposed. For each matched set of $r + 1$ persons in which j are exposed, under the null hypothesis that there is no difference between the exposure rate of cases and controls, the probability that the case is exposed is $p = j/(r + 1)$. Indeed, whether (1) or not (0), the case is exposed is a binomial variable with mean $j/(r + 1)$ and variance

(11.25) $$\left[\frac{j}{(r + 1)}\right]\left[1 - \frac{j}{(r + 1)}\right] = \frac{j(r + 1 - j)}{(r + 1)^2}.$$

The mean and variance of the number of exposed controls in all m_j matched sets with j exposed persons has mean $m_j(j/r + 1)$ and variance $m_j j(r + 1 - j)/(r + 1)^2$, and the total number of exposed cases has mean and variance obtained by summing over all j, i.e., over all the sets with different numbers ($j = 0, 1, 2, \dots r$) of exposed persons. Hence, the formal test statistic is

$$Z = \frac{\text{total number of exposed cases} - \text{expected number of exposed cases}}{\text{standard deviation of the number of exposed cases}}$$

(11.26)
$$= \frac{\displaystyle\sum_{j=0}^{r} n_{1j} - \sum_{j=0}^{r} \frac{jm_j}{(r + 1)}}{\sqrt{\dfrac{\left[\displaystyle\sum_{j=0}^{r} j(r + 1 - j)m_j\right]}{(r + 1)^2}}}.$$

We now apply formula (11.26) to the data in Table 11.15. First we note that m_1, the number of matched sets with only one person exposed, is $11 + 6 = 17$. Similarly, $m_2 = 9$, and $m_3 = 1$. The expected number of exposed cases under the null hypothesis, is

(11.27)
$$\sum_{j=0}^{r} \frac{j \cdot m_j}{(r + 1)} = \frac{(17 + 2 \cdot 9 + 3)}{5} = 7.6,$$

while the actual number of exposed cases is 19. The variance of the number of exposed cases is

(11.28)
$$\frac{\left[\displaystyle\sum_{j=0}^{r} j(r + 1 - j)m_j\right]}{(r + 1)^2} = \frac{1 \cdot 4 \cdot 17 + 2 \cdot 3 \cdot 9 + 3 \cdot 2 \cdot 1}{5 \cdot 5}$$
$$= \frac{128}{25} = 5.12.$$

Hence (11.26) becomes

(11.29)
$$Z = \frac{19 - 7.6}{\sqrt{5.12}} = 5.04,$$

indicating a statistically significant excess of exposed controls, which is consistent with the estimated relative risk of 6.18 we obtained earlier (11.24).

Because the workers in the first Swedish study, reported in Table 11.15, were exposed to an impure chemical, a second study was made in the southern part of Sweden of agricultural workers exposed to similar chemicals used in herbicides there, but which did not contain dioxin. Each case was matched to two controls on the basis of age, place of residence and year of death (for the dead cases). Moreover, dead cases were matched to dead controls, so the questionnaire was administered to the next of kin or a close relative to obtain data for that matched triplet. The data is reproduced in Table 11.16. The summary estimate of relative risk (11.22) is 5.1, and an approximate 95% confidence interval for the OR is (2.5, 10.4). As the confidence interval does not contain 1, a test of the null hypothesis (OR = 1) based on (11.26) would also yield a significant result at the .05 level. Since the estimate 6.2 from the previous study lies well within the confidence interval of the second study, one can be more confident that exposure to phenoxy acids and chlorophenols used in herbicides may well constitute a risk factor in the development of soft tissue sarcoma, even when these chemicals are not contaminated with dioxin. Of course, one cannot rule out the possible effect of another covariate, such as exposure to other pesticides, but the result of Cornfield suggests that the fivefold increase in relative risk is unlikely to be completely explained by an omitted factor.

There are a variety of extensions of these results to allow for a variable number of controls per case, i.e., even if one desires to obtain three controls per case, one might only find one or two suitable controls for a particular case. Formulas for confidence intervals for the estimated OR in this situation can be found in the paper by Fleiss (1984).

TABLE 11.16.   Exposure to Phenoxy Acids or Chlorophenols in Matched Triplets (Case and Two Controls) in a Second Study

	No. of Controls Exposed		
Case Exposure Status	0	1	2
Exposed	21	4	0
Not Exposed	76	9	0

Source: Table 2 from Eriksson, M., Hardell, L., Berg, N. O., Moller, T. and Axelson, O. (1981). Soft-tissue Sarcomas and Exposure to Chemical Substances. *British Journal of Industrial Medicine* **38**, 27–33.

Comment. There is some controversy in the epidemiologic literature concerning the advisability of using controls who have recently died of other causes as matches for cases who recently died. While potential problems of differential recall between the study subject and a close relative are eliminated by such matches, dead controls may have higher levels of a covariate, such as smoking, which is associated with the disease under study than live controls have, and this may affect the results of the study. Thus, dead controls need to be selected with special care.

b. *The first case-control study concerning the association between DES and cancer*[17]

In 1970 doctors at Massachusetts General Hospital noticed a cluster of seven cases of a rare vaginal cancer in young women in their twenties. Naturally they were puzzled by such an occurrence and inquired about the cause. One of the mothers of a patient wondered whether her daughter's cancer could be related to the hormone she took during her pregnancy, as DES often prescribed for postpartum suppression of lactation and for preventing miscarriage. The doctors questioned the mothers of the other patients and found that most of them also had taken DES (diethylstilbestrol) during their pregnancy, so this was a factor common to most of the cases.

In order to scientifically check out the apparent association, the investigators matched each of the eight cases with four controls. The controls were identified from birth records of the hospital in which the case was born and were matched by data of birth and type of service (ward or private). Since DES was often prescribed to prevent miscarriage, the mothers of cases were first asked whether they had prior pregnancy loss (which would indicate likely use of DES). The results are presented in Table 11.17, where exposure is whether (1) or not (0) the mother of the case or control had a prior pregnancy loss.

Before analyzing the data in Table 11.17, we note that six of the eight cases were exposed in contrast to two of 32 controls. This strongly suggests that there is an association, but we must carry out the proper *matched* analysis. The estimated odds ratio obtained from formula (11.22) is

$$\widehat{OR} = \frac{21}{2} = 10.5.$$

Of course, the small sample size implies that this estimate has a large

TABLE 11.17.   Frequency of Prior Pregnancy Loss
Among Mothers of Women with
Vaginal Cancer and Mothers of
Matched Controls

	No. of Controls Exposed				
Exposure Status of Case	0	1	2	3	4
Exposed	3	3	0	0	0
Not Exposed	0	2	0	0	0

Source: Adapted from   Table 7.3 of Schlesselman, (1982)
taken from Table 2 in Herbst, A. L., Ulfelder, H. and
Poskanzer, D. C. (1971). Adenocarcinoma of the Vagina: Association of Maternal Stilbestrol Therapy with Tumor Appearance in Young Women. *New England Journal of Medicine* **284**, 878–881.

standard error attached to it. Indeed, Schlesselman (1982) derives the
following 95% confidence interval for OR:

$$95\% \text{ CONF(OR; 1.88, 58.8)}.$$

As the odds ratio and relative risk are virtually identical for small probabilities (see Sec. 5.1), we can summarize the study as showing that our
estimate is a tenfold increase in risk but we can only be highly confident in
saying that the risk of vaginal cancer among young women whose mothers
took DES during pregnancy is at least twice that of women whose mothers did not take DES.

The formal test (11.26) comparing the actual number of exposed cases
with their expected number is

$$(11.30) \quad Z = \frac{6 - \left(\frac{1 \cdot 5}{5} + \frac{2 \cdot 3}{5}\right)}{\sqrt{\dfrac{1 \times 4 \times 5 + 2 \times 3 \times 2)}{25}}} = \frac{3.8}{\sqrt{\dfrac{32}{25}}} = 3.082,$$

a significant result at the usual .05 level.

Comment.   Due to the small sample size, it is safer to use a continuity
correction which brings the numerator close to its expected value of 1/2.

Then the final ratio would be

$$\frac{3.3}{\sqrt{\dfrac{38}{25}}} = \frac{3.3}{1.233} = 2.68,$$

which remains significant at the .05 level (two-sided p-value $= .01$).

The data reported in Table 11.17 refer to whether or not the mother had a prior loss of a pregnancy. A further question assessed whether or not the mother actually had taken DES during the child's pregnancy. That data was even stronger evidence, as seven of the mothers of the eight cases had taken DES, while *none* of the mothers of the 32 controls had done so. Naturally one might have doubts about the validity of a study based on a small number of subjects, however, the estimated relative risk was quite high and there was no difference between the mothers of cases and controls with respect to other potential compounding factors such as smoking, x-ray exposure, etc. Indeed the *lower* limit of a 95% confidence interval for the OR for DES exposure of the cases relative to their controls was 7.59.

Once the original paper was published confirmation of the association came from another study,[18] and a registry of adenocarcinoma of the genital tract commenced in 1972. However, three prospective studies following a total of about 1300 female children of exposed women did not find any increased risk of vaginal cancer, although they did find other abnormalities at higher rates than naturally are expected in young women.

Comment.   At first glance the fact that these seemingly large follow-up studies did not observe any cases of genital tract cancer seems to contradict the case-control study findings, especially as they were based on large sample sizes. However, the *major advantage* of a *case-control study* is that it *requires a much smaller sample* to obtain the same statistical power and is most useful when the disease is rare. The normal rate[19] of vaginal cancer in women (during their first 25 years of life) is only about 8 in 100,000. Thus, the expected number of cases in the prospective studies, assuming the null hypothesis of no association, is

$$.00008 \times 1300 = .104,$$

so only *one* case would have been expected to occur *if the relative risk was ten*. Thus, the fact that the follow-up studies of some exposed daughters failed to observe a single case of a rare cancer only indicates that the disease is rare and does not refute the statistical association obtained in the case-control studies. Indeed, the probability of observing *no* cases when the alternative (RR = 10) is true is given by the Poisson probability (10.3) with $k = 0$, i.e.,

$$P(X = 0) = e^{-1.04} = .353,$$

and if exposure only caused a *fivefold* increased risk, the probability of observing no cases would be .732. Thus, a much larger group of young women would have to be the subjects of a 20-year follow-up study in order to have a study which has a type I error rate of .05 and 90% power (type II error rate = .10). These power considerations show why it is very difficult to detect factors associated with an increased risk of a rare disease in the range of two to three with prospective studies and why case control studies are often the only practical approach.

In Chapter 13 we will review the types of epidemiologic studies, the various concepts of risk which they estimate and discuss how these ideas are used in public policy and courts. Several criteria for assessing the statistical validity of these studies and major problems in carrying them out will also be presented.

c. The Wilcoxon test for multiply matched data

By considering each matched set as a separate strata, as in the Mantel-Haenszel approach in the 1:1 or 1:r matched 0–1 data sets, one can apply the combined Wilcoxon procedure (Section 7.5) to data where one case is matched to several controls when the variable studied is continuous or has many possible values. Even when the number of controls matched to each case varies, the formulas of that section apply. The technique of multiple matching is quite suitable for assessing pay raises or number of promotions received by minority employees relative to majority ones in a large firm. Employees could be matched on year of hire, educational background, job-related prior experience, and initial job assigned (provided initial assignment was not at issue). The method is also useful in epidemiologic studies when data on the amount of duration of exposure to the agent cases and controls had is available. When an agent increases the risk of disease, the cases and controls may also differ with respect to the amount of exposure to it as well as on exposure status, and this information is not utilized in the simple exposed-not exposed dichotomy.

For each matched set of r controls and one case, the estimate of P is the rank of the case (ordering the $r + 1$ numbers in increasing order) among all $(r + 1)$ observations minus 1, divided by r, as we have r case-control comparisons. For instance, if the case is the fourth largest, when compared with four controls it is bigger than three of the four controls so $\bar{P}$ for this set is $3/4 = .75$. The variance of $\bar{P}_i$ from the ith matched set is $(1 + r + 1)/12r = (r + 2)/12r$, as $m = 1$, $n = r$ in formula (7.3).

If we have n matched sets of 1 and r controls, then the summary Wilcoxon procedure is

$$(11.31) \qquad \hat{P}_r = \frac{1}{n} \sum_{i=1}^{n} \bar{P}_i,$$

where $\bar{P}_i$ is the estimate of P obtained from the ith set. As the observations in the matched sets are statistically independent under the null hypothesis of no difference, the sampling variance of $\hat{P}_r$ is

$$(11.32) \qquad V_r = \frac{r + 2}{12r \cdot n},$$

and its standard deviation or sampling error is $V_r^{1/2}$. A test of the null hypothesis $P = 1/2$ is based on the statistic (in its normal form)

$$(11.33) \qquad Z = \frac{\hat{P}_r - \dfrac{1}{2}}{\sqrt{\dfrac{r + 2}{n \cdot 12r}}}.$$

Comment. It should be noted that if $r = 1$, i.e., one has $1:1$ matching, the combined Wilcoxon procedure (11.31) reduces to the sign test, as in each pair the estimate of P is 0 (case has smaller value) or 1 (case has larger value) so that $\hat{P}_r$ is just the proportion of 1's. When $r = 1$ the denominator of (11.32) is

$$\sqrt{\frac{3}{12n}} = \frac{1}{2n},$$

as in the sign test, when it is expressed as the proportion of the total number (n) of comparisons which have a positive sign.

The standard deviation of $\hat{P}_r$, which is in the denominator of (11.33), when expressed in the form

$$(11.34) \qquad \sqrt{\frac{1}{12n}} \sqrt{\frac{r + 2}{r}}$$

enables us to examine the gain in precision of our estimate of P (or power of the test) as r, the number of controls per case increases. The factor $\sqrt{(r + 2)r}$ in (11.34) is $\sqrt{3} = 1.732$ when $r = 1$, $\sqrt{2} = 1.414$ when $r = 2$, 1.291 when $r = 3$, 1.225 when $r = 4$, 1.18 when $r = 5$ and approaches 1 rather slowly as r increases. From these calculations it follows that it is usually *not* worthwhile to obtain more than four matched controls per case unless controls are inexpensive to obtain and one has extremely few cases.

We have discussed the combined Wilcoxon procedure for $1 : r$ matched data sets. In practice, studies often have a variable number of controls, e.g., $r = 1, 2, ..., R$, per case, so we have n_r matched sets of each type to analyze. The overall estimate of P is then obtained by forming the analog of (8.22), i.e.,

$$\bar{P} = \frac{\sum V_r^{-1} \hat{P}_r}{\sum V_r^{-1}},$$

where $\hat{P}_r$ is the estimator obtained from the n_r sets with r controls per case and V_r is the variance of $\hat{P}_r$ given in formula (11.32). We omit the details of the normal form of the test as they are virtually identical to the material discussed in Section 8.5.

We now illustrate the procedure on hypothetical wage data from an employment discrimination case similar to that of *EEOC v. IBM* given in Table 11.18.

The Wilcoxon procedure (11.31) yields a summary estimate of $\hat{P}_r = (2/3)/5 = 2/15 = .1333$, with standard deviation,

$$\sqrt{\frac{r + 2}{n \cdot 12r}} = \sqrt{\frac{5}{5 \cdot 12 \cdot 3}} = \sqrt{\frac{1}{36}} = \frac{1}{6}.$$

The test statistic (11.33) becomes

$$Z = \frac{.1333 - .5000}{.1666} = -2.20,$$

a statistically significant result (at the usual .05 level).

Notice that using the sign test comparing the difference between the minority person and the *average* salary of the corresponding matched controls yields four sets in which the minority (case) received less and one set in which the minority member's salary exceeded the majority average. The one-sided p-value of the sign test is just the probability a fair coin would come up with four or more heads in five independent tosses and

TABLE 11.18. Hypothetical Salaries of Matched Set of Employees Two Years After They Were Initially Hired in the Same Position at the Same Level

Case (Minority)	Controls	(Majority)		$\bar{P}_i$
27,000	28,000	28,500	29,000	0/3
28,500	27,000	29,000	29,250	1/3
32,000	31,250	32,500	33,000	1/3
32,100	32,500	33,000	35,000	0/3
33,000	33,200	33,500	34,000	0/3

equals .1875, which is not significant at the .05 level. Here, the small number of matched pairs again limits the power of the sign test. Moreover, ignoring *all* the possible matches would allow plaintiffs (defendants) to select the highest (lowest) salary of the three matched controls, leading to an inevitable conflict in their conclusion, and courts are correctly suspect of the failure of the parties involved to use all relevant comparisons in equal pay cases.[20]

Finally, we should mention that the Wilcoxon test can be used to show that the groups being compared have a similar distribution of a factor which may be related to the study variable (pay, exposure level) so that the new factor is unlikely to explain a significant difference between the groups. In the next section we will briefly describe how regression analysis can also be used in conjunction with matching to eliminate the effect of a possible covariate not used in the matching process.

Problems

1.* Suppose one forgot that the data in the DES case-control study in Table 11.17 was matched with four controls per case and organized that data in the ordinary 2×2 format.

	Exposed	Unexposed	Total
Case	6	2	8
Control	5	27	32
Total	11	29	40

Calculate the odds ratio and Fisher's exact test. How well does your conclusion agree with the proper analysis given in the text? Why is the example important?

2.* Suppose you were a member of a task force evaluating whether exposure to a chemical increased the risk of a person contracting a relatively rare cancer, i.e., the usual probability of contracting it in a person's lifetime = .002. Would you recommend a case-control or prospective study? Explain what factors would play a role in your decision, assuming that you wish to be able to detect a threefold increase in risk.

3. Using the methodology described in Chapter 10, obtain the approximate sample size required for a prospective study of young women exposed in utero to DES that will have a type I error of .05, a type II error of .10 of detecting a fivefold increase in the risk of contracting vaginal cancer.

Answers to Selected Problems

1. The table is

	Exposed	Unexposed	Total
Case	6	2	8
Control	5	27	32

and the odds ratio estimate is $(6 \times 27)/(2 \times 5) = 16.2$, which is higher than our estimate of 10.5. Similarly, the p-value of Fisher's test is smaller than that of the proper test. This problem is important because it illustrates that proper statistical analysis depends on the way the data is collected or sampled. Neglecting this can lead to a biased estimate of the odds ratio. Usually when the matching is ignored in the analysis the estimated odds ratio is less than the proper estimate.

2. A case-control study would appear to be the most convenient. In fact, it might be possible to launch several such studies in the various areas of the country where the plants using the chemical are located. A historical prospective study would be a realistic possibility if one could reconstruct the data from work histories and contrast the health status of workers exposed to the chemical with other nonexposed employees. The main difficulty might be obtaining information about important covariates such as smoking. However, if the cancer had a long latency period and workers were not very mobile so that the cases were relatively recent, one might be able to obtain reliable results. Some facts one needs to consider are

(a) the time frame of the study, i.e., how long can the study realistically take and the results still be useful?

(b) What type I and type II errors are desired by the policymakers?

(c) The difficulty in obtaining a suitable control or comparison group.

(d) The difficulty in obtaining information about other factors known to be associated with the disease and whether some of the factors are more strongly associated with the disease under study than the relative risk of 5 you need to detect.

8. Other Aspects of the Analysis and Interpretation of Matched Studies

This chapter was devoted to analyzing matched data sets, as matching is one approach to the elimination of the effects of extraneous factors or covariates on our estimate of the parameter (e.g., odds ratio, difference in average salary) of interest. Indeed, stratification can be regarded as group matching, as we form strata of subjects on the basis of their possessing similar values of the relevant covariates. Regression is also used to eliminate the effect of other covariates, and it is reasonable to ask when each method should be used. The answer is not a simple one, in part because they can be used together. This is important because the *interaction* of one or more covariates with the variable of interest, e.g., the synergistic effect of smoking and artificial sweetener consumption or an interaction between sex and seniority in an equal pay study, cannot be estimated from a study in which the covariate was used in the matching process.

In this section we illustrate the use of logistic regression on matched data from the Reye's syndrome pilot study. Then we discuss the criteria that should be considered in the matching process and show how the DES study probably was unfairly criticized for failing to match on a covariate which had not been shown to cause vaginal cancer by itself in the legal literature. In Subsection c we review some of the *assumptions* underlying the methods of this chapter in order to guard against misinterpretation of the results of matched studies. Then we discuss the potential use of matched data in copyright infringement cases. Two cases in which statistical analyses were introduced are described, and a possible use of a matched study as rebuttal evidence in one of them is given. We close this section with matched data from a study concerning the accuracy of screening tests for antibodies to the AIDS virus.

a. Using logistic regression in a matched analysis: the Reye's syndrome study[21]

In response to several previous case-control studies reporting a statistically significant risk of Reye syndrome, a rare but very serious disease in children who had recently taken medications containing salicylate to alleviate symptoms of flu or chicken pox, the U.S. Government carried out a case-control study which went to great lengths to obtain reliable data. Indeed, *four* different control groups were used for comparative purposes: children from the same school, same community, nearby hospital or who were taken to emergency rooms of nearby hospitals. Controls were matched to cases by age and on the basis of having the same antecedent illness within a week of the case. The last two control groups control for the effect of having a sick child on the parents recall of the child's medication use and other salient events such as the seriousness of the antecedent illness (flu or chicken pox).

In this retrospective study the ratio of the odds a case was exposed to salicylate relative to the odds a control was exposed is the parameter of interest. As a previous study indicated that children given medications containing salicylate might have had a more serious antecedent illness, as they often had a higher maximum temperature during the earlier illness, the possible effect of fever and major symptoms were considered in a logistic regression of the matched sets.

Before proceeding to the analysis of the data, we discuss the general model of logistic regression for matched data. We first consider a prospective study where the treated (exposed) group and control group are matched on several variables, $V_1, ..., V_k$ say (e.g., V_1 = age, V_2 = time of the same antecedent illness), and we wish to estimate the effect of the treatment (X_1) controlling for confounding variables $(X_2, X_3, ..., X_p)$ such as fever, coughing, etc. In the prospective framework the probability that a member of the jth matched set gets the disease is

$$(11.35) \qquad P_x = P(D = 1|x_1, ..., x_p) = \frac{e^{\alpha_j+\beta_1X_1+\cdots+\beta_pX_p}}{1 + e^{\alpha_j+\beta_1X_1+\cdots+\beta_pX_p}}$$

so that the log-odds ratio is

$$(11.36) \qquad \log\left(\frac{P_x}{1 - P_x}\right) = \alpha_j + \beta_1X_1 + \cdots + \beta_pX_p.$$

The parameter α_j for the jth matched set reflects the effect of the *variables* used in the matching process, while the β_k, $k = 1, ..., p$ estimate the effect of the other influential variables. Note that if the risk of Reye's syndrome decreased with age, α_j would be higher for the matched sets with younger children, as age was a factor in matching.

When we *compare* the relative odds of disease for an individual with values $X'_1, X'_2, \ldots, X'_p$ for the covariates to those for an individual with values $X_1, \ldots, X_p$, the difference in the log odds of contracting the disease is

$$(11.37) \quad \log OR = \beta_1(X'_1 - X_1) + \beta_2(X'_2 - X_2) + \cdots + \beta_p(X'_p - X_p),$$

provided that both individuals have the *same values* of the *variables* $V_1, \ldots, V_k$ *used in the matching* process.

As we learned previously, the logistic model (11.35) can be used in case-control studies provided that we remember that the parameter P_x no longer represents the probability of exposure, as it is affected by the relative sampling fractions of cases and controls. The estimate of the relative risk of exposure is derived from the log-odds equation (11.37) by setting $X'_1 = 1$ for cases and $X_1 = 0$ for controls so that e^{β_1} is the odds ratio of a case being exposed relative to a control being exposed after accounting for the effect of the variables used in both the matching process and the regression analysis, i.e., $X'_j = X_j$ for $j \neq 1$.

The outcome of the logistic regression which estimated the effects of possible covariates related to the seriousness of the antecedent illness is presented in Table 11.19, which was computed on data for the cases and all controls, as the results were similar in all comparisons of the cases with each of the four control groups. The coefficient of interest is β_1, the log odds ratio of exposure for cases versus controls, which equals 2.95. Conversion to the odds ratio yields

$$\widehat{OR} = e^{2.95} = 19.0,$$

a very meaningful odds ratio. Notice that none of the other covariates have an estimated odds ratio of the same magnitude, and it is very unlikely that a factor not considered in the analysis or matching will have a relative risk and prevalence in the population large enough to explain away the statistical association between salicylate ingestion and Reye's syndrome.

Several interesting conclusions can be drawn from this study:

(1) Contact with a health care provider (X_4) appeared to reduce the risk of exposure and therefore the risk of the child contracting Reye's syndrome. Perhaps the health care providers knew of the earlier studies and recommended medications that did not contain salicylates.

TABLE 11.19. Logistic Regression Fitted to the Reye's Syndrome Pilot Study Data and the Odds Ratios Associated with Each Covariate or Factor

$$\text{Log odds ratio} = 2.9X_1 - 0.50X_2 + 0.73X_3 - 1.32X_4 + 0.03X_5 + -70X_6$$
$$+ 0.34X_7 + 0.18X_8 + 1.32X_9$$

Factor	Variable	Possible Values	Relative Odds Ratio Salicylate Exposure (Controlling for Other Variables
X_1	Case status	Case/control	19.0
X_2	Average daily severity	Mild/moderate/ severe	0.60
X_3	Average daily fever	None/mild/moder- ate/severe	2.07
X_4	Contact any health care provider	Yes/no	2.07
X_5	In bed/absent	Yes/no	1.03
X_6	Headache	Yes/no	2.01
X_7	Muscle aches	Yes/no	1.41
X_8	Sore throat	Yes/no	1.19
X_9	Cough	Yes/no	3.73

Source: The Appendix to Public Health Service Reye's Syndrome Task Force (1985). Public Health Service Study on Reye's Syndrome and Medications. *New England Journal of Medicine* **313**, 849–857.

(2) It might have been useful to incorporate an interaction term X_1X_4 in the regression model, as case-control status might have been affected by whether or not a health care provider was contacted. Had the ratio e^{β_1} been closer to 4.0, the odds ratio the study had been designed to detect with power .90, one would want to incorporate the interaction in our estimate of the effect of exposure to salicylate on getting the disease and there could have been a multicollinearity problem if virtually none of the cases had been in contact with a health care provider.

(3) The odds ratio using formula (11.22), modified for the fact that not all cases were matched to the same number of controls, which did *not*

account for the symptom severity covariates, was 10.4. This shows that adjusting for other potential covariates need not necessarily reduce the estimated relative risk. The effect will depend on the way all the risk factors are distributed in the cases and controls.

(4) The Reye's syndrome study was carried out in order to determine whether a warning label should be put on products containing salicylates such as aspirin. Because the estimated OR was so large, Cornfield's result indicates that the statistically significant and meaningful association between salicylate use and Reye's syndrome is very unlikely to be due to another factor. Furthermore, all four previous studies found an excess risk due to salicylate use. Even though some of them were based on a small number of cases and data was not obtained on all the covariates used in the logistic regression in Table 11.19, the basic consistency of the five studies carried out in different parts of the nation substantiates the association between the disease and exposure to salicylate.

b.   Criteria to be used for selecting the matching characteristics

Since the primary purpose of matching is the elimination of any bias in the estimate of the difference between the experimental and control groups, one should only match on factors known to have an effect on the variable of interest. As we realized in our discussion of the Reye's syndrome study, the effect of other possible factors can be accounted for in the analysis of the data. Thus, in salary discrimination matched study, occupation and seniority should be used in the matching process, as they are typically the major determinants of pay, while in a study of the exposure to asbestos and the risk of future development of lung cancer, smoking pattern and age, both of which effect one's chance of getting the disease should be used in the matching process. One needs to be careful not to use too many factors in the matching because:

(a) Several factors may be highly correlated (e.g., age and duration of exposure), and using all of them makes it more difficult to find appropriate matches, diminishing the size of the available sample.

(b) Matching on a factor which is unrelated to the study variable (e.g., disease), but is positively correlated with exposure in the general population, will lead to a loss of precision in the estimate of the effect of exposure. For example, if a higher fraction of smokers drink coffee than nonsmokers and coffee consumption of mothers is used as a matching factor in a study of the relationship between a pregnant woman's smoking and her child having a birth defect, then having to obtain control mothers who are not coffee drinkers makes it more difficult to find a match for a case. Moreover, matching on coffee consumption will increase the proportion of *concordant* pairs (both case and control are more likely to have the same pattern of exposure to smoking) which are disregarded in the matched analysis.

(c) Matching on a factor makes it impossible to study a possible interaction between that factor and other ones. A way out of this difficulty is to match on whether or not an individual has that factor (e.g., smokes) and incorporate the exposure amount (typical daily consumption) as a covariate in a regression analysis. Then the interaction between the level of the factor and the other risk factors can be estimated.

A useful tool in considering whether or not to use a factor F as a matching factor is to consider a path diagram of the relationship between factor F and exposure (E) and disease (D) as we did in our discussion of the effect of an omitted variable in regression. In each diagram an arrow ($\rightarrow$) represents a causal relation in the sense that factor F increases the risk of exposure (E) or disease (D), while a simultaneous arrow ($\leftarrow\rightarrow$) indicates noncausal statistical association or correlation.

In Figure 11.2a we see that the disease (D) is caused by factor F but *not* by the exposure (E) under study. Because E and F *are correlated positively, failing* to *match* on F or *control* for it in the data analysis will lead to a spurious or exaggerated association between exposure and disease. This type of error probably would occur if smoking were not controlled for in a study of exposure to an agent and lung cancer.

Figure 11.2b illustrates a situation in which both exposure and the factor cause the disease and they are positively correlated. Failure to match or control for F implies that the estimate of association between E and D will be *overestimated* because the effect of F on D will be attributed

FIGURE 11.2.   Two situations in which matching on the factor F is called for. The arrows indicate the direction of the association.
Source: Figure 4.1 in Schlesselman (1982).

to E. This type of bias can occur in health studies of chemical workers when smoking is not controlled for, as a higher fraction of blue collar workers smoke than that of the general population.

On the other hand, if a factor (F) has no effect on a person's chances of getting the disease but is statistically associated with exposure, then it is not necessary to match on F (see Figure 11.3a). Indeed, a regression analysis might attribute some of the effect of exposure to factor (F), yielding an underestimate of the risk of exposure.

Figure 11.3b presents a situation in which both F and E *independently* cause the disease (D). While it is proper to consider matching on F, it is not necessary to do so because factor F is not associated with the exposure variable on which the cases and controls are being compared. Again this situation is similar to multivariate regression where we noted that adding a new explanatory variable which was *unrelated* to the ones already used would not change the estimates of the effects of the previous variables. However, it is useful in such situations to collect information about any factor (F) related to the disease so that one can demonstrate that it is uncorrelated with exposure. Otherwise, the results of a study would be questioned because the situation in Figure 11.2b would apply if E and F were correlated.

The Effect of These Considerations in the DES Study

The situation in Figure 11.3a occurred in the DES study described previously, as mothers who had prior pregnancy loss had a much higher incidence of use of DES. If one matched mothers of cases on this factor (history of prior pregnancy loss), the risk of DES exposure would have been substantially underestimated. An article by Dickson (1982), a lawyer who represented a drug firm in the DES case, suggested that the basic study was flawed because prior pregnancy loss was not controlled for.

FIGURE 11.3.   Two situations in which it is not necessary to match on the factor F.
Source: Figure 4.2 in Schlesselman (1982).

However, he does not provide data showing that prior pregnancy loss of the mother was a *risk factor* for vaginal cancer in a user's daughter *by itself*, much less that it had the high relative risk and prevalence required by Cornfield's result in order to fully explain the development of cancer in the daughters of DES exposed mothers. We next explore timing considerations in the DES-vaginal cancer association.

Since pregnancy loss has been an unfortunate fact of life for many years, if it were a serious risk factor, vaginal cancer in young women would probably not be as rare as it is and the association probably would have been discovered before DES was introduced. Furthermore, in a follow-up study of five cases in New York, not only were *none* of the eight controls exposed, all such cancer cases that occurred in the state of New York between 1950 and 1971 were obtained. For the first 15 years of the period no cases were observed (recall that DES was not prescribed in quantity much before 1950, so cases resulting from its use could only occur in 1965 or later). All five cases occurred in 1966–1971. Since vaginal cancer in young women is very rare, we can assume that the number of cases per year follows a Poisson law. The rate in the 1966–1971 period was one per year, i.e., $\lambda = 1$. Had this rate been in effect during the previous 15 years, i.e., had DES exposure in mothers not affected their daughters, we should have seen about 15 cases in 1950–1965, but we observed zero cases. The probability of observing no cases is

$$e^{-15} = 3 \times 10^{-7} \text{ or less than one in a million.}$$

Since our estimate of λ as 1.0 was based on data and is subject to sampling variability, we should repeat the calculations with values of λ in a range about 1.0. To be conservative, let $\lambda = 1/2$. Then we would have expected to see 7.5 cases during the 1950–1965 era, and the probability of observing no cases during that time is

$$e^{-7.5} = .00055.$$

Thus, the hypothesis that there was a constant rate of vaginal cancer in young women in New York during the 1950–1971 period should logically be rejected in favor of an increased incidence during the period in which the effect of DES exposure could have manifested itself. Time frame considerations, therefore, reinforce the significant association found in the case-control studies.

Comment. Unlike the situation 11.3a, if one matched on *F* when 11.3b was true, one would obtain an unbiased estimate of the association between E and D. However, the sampling error of this estimated association would usually be greater than that of an unmatched study because all the observations for which matches could not be found would be lost to the analysis.

c. Review of the assumptions underlying the analysis of matched data

In describing many methods of data analysis it is easy to gloss over the fact that some assumptions are required for the validity of each method. The underlying model is clearest when regression methods are used, but it is worthwhile to remind ourselves of the assumptions implicit in each type of analysis and to assess how sensitive an inference might be when the data does not strictly satisfy the assumptions made.

The procedures at the beginning of the chapter assumed that the difference between the members of the pair was a constant Δ and that the value of Δ remained the same for all levels of the matching factor. Notice that these assumptions may not be satisfied by the EPA fuel data, as the effect Δ may be related to the size of the car or to its certified level. Although the estimate of the effect Δ will be in error if the assumption of constancy is wrong, the test of the null hypothesis is often valid. As long as the direction of the effect is the same in all pairs, i.e., each difference is centered about a positive number, the three tests will be reasonably powerful. The Wilcoxon test is safer to use than the t-test in such circumstances, as the assumption of normality may be in doubt while the sign test often has low power.

In matched 0–1 response data, one cannot use $(B - C)/N$ to estimate the *difference* between the exposure (promotion) rates of both groups *unless* that difference is the *same at all* levels of the matching factor. This assumption is unlikely to hold, e.g., in the promotion setting the promotion rate may be faster in occupations for which there is greater external labor marker demand. Similarly, in a prospective study the incidence of the disease will often depend on the duration of exposure. However, the test statistic (11.15) is proper because we are testing equality of the promotion rates and we matched on factors which should affect that rate.

Again, in the analysis of matched binary response data, the summary odds ratio B/C estimates the common odds ratio, OR, only when OR is the same at all levels of the matching variable. It is a useful approximate summary measure when the odds ratios do not vary greatly at the various levels of the factors used in the matching process. This assumption can be tested by splitting the data into several (k) subsets (indexed by $i = 1, \ldots k$)

which are relatively homogeneous with respect to the matching variables and computing the odds ratios B_i/C_i for each subset. If the estimates B_i/C_i are all near each other, especially if they are all near 1 (indicating no effect), or almost all on the same side of 1 (indicating an effect), the summary estimate B/C remains quite useful. If the matching factor were duration of exposure (or seniority), one might find that there were virtually no discordant pairs with low values of the factor, as insufficient time elapsed for the disease to develop (or the individual to earn a promotion). Then the overall summary estimate B/C can be computed for the pairs whose matching factor was sufficiently large to yield some discordant pairs and may be a useful summary measure of the relative risk of disease for persons exposed for at least a certain minimum number of years.

Comment. Technically, in the analysis of a matched case-control or promotion study we are implicitly assuming that for each level t of the covariate(s) used in the matching process the odds-ratio is given by

$$(11.38) \qquad \mathrm{OR}(t) = \frac{p_1(t)}{1 - p_1(t)} \cdot \frac{1 - p_0(t)}{p_0(t)},$$

where $p_1(t)[p_0(t)]$ is the probability a case [control] at level t of the matching factor is exposed. If $\mathrm{OR}(t)$ is *constant* for all t then B/C is a valid *estimate* of the odds ratio. Otherwise B/C estimates a weighted average of $\mathrm{OR}(t)$ determined by the values of t of the *cases*. This may well differ from the average of $\mathrm{OR}(t)$ in the general population.

The logistic regression analysis of matched data assumes that

$$(11.39) \qquad \log \frac{p(t)}{1 - p(t)} = \alpha + \beta_1 I + \beta_2 X_2 + \cdots + \beta_k X_k,$$

where $I = 1$ or 0 according, as the subject is a case or control. When there are no covariates in (11.39), the logistic model reduces to the constant odds ratio model (11.38) where e^β is the odds ratio. The logistic model assumes that the effect of all covariates is multiplicative, (i.e., a unit change in any X_j increases the odds ratio by e^{β_j}). This is a fairly stringent assumption, which is why some biostatisticians suggest that several models be used to analyze the data. Fortunately, we are primarily interested in whether β_1 is 0 or not, i.e., or equivalently whether the odds of exposure of cases relative to controls is 1 or not, and quite often an approximate model of the effect of other covariates can achieve a sufficiently accurate adjustment. This is likely to be the case in matched studies, as matching has already eliminated the effect of the other major risk factors.

Even when some of the assumptions underlying a matched analysis are not strictly satisfied by the data, the statistical significance of a difference in the control and experimental group established by a matched study is often valid, although the estimated effect may not be accurate. For example, in the EPA emission study suppose the substitute fuel did not add a constant $\Delta > 0$ but multiplied the emission level by a factor e^{β}. Still each difference d_i, would be centered about a value, Δ_i, which is positive, and the tests discussed in sections 1–3 would detect the higher emission level. As long as the *direction* of the effect or difference does not vary with the level of the matching variable (and covariates in regression analysis) tests of significance should have reasonable power. If the direction of effect changes, then a more complex model is required. In epidemiologic research this should not occur, as it would imply that some exposure to an agent increases the risk of disease but much greater exposure decreases the risk. Of course, the more closely the mathematical model underlying the analysis of data is based on the relevant scientific principles underlying the process generating the data, the more convincing will the ultimate inferences be.

Finally, we note that we have assumed that the variables used in the matching process or regression model are related to the variable of interest and are measured accurately. When a proxy variable is used or there is a substantial measurement error, the same potential bias and errors in variable issues that arise in regression analysis occur in matched studies. The effect of these errors is more pronounced when the matching factor is strongly associated with the outcome of interest. A good review of these issues and references to the literature appears in Chapter 11 of Kelsey, Thompson and Evans (1986).

d. Matched studies in copyright infringement cases

In cases of copyright infringement of published works, a major issue concerns the degree or amount of duplication of the original work that is contained in the alleged infringer. In particular, the fair use doctrine allows others to use some material from the original. Section 107 of the Copyright Act of 1976 specified that the factors to be considered in the determination of fair use versus infringement of a copyright are:

(1) the purpose and character of this use, including whether such use is of a commercial nature or is for nonprofit educational purposes;

(2) the nature of the copyright work;

(3) the amount and substantiality of the portion used in relation to the copyrighted work as a whole; and

(4) the effect of the use upon the potential market for or value of the copyrighted work.

Statistical analysis is relevant to the third factor, as we can estimate the proportion of similar material from proper samples of the two works. Before describing two cases, we note that in one early case, *Callaghan v. Myers* (1888) 128 U.S. 617 at 662, the Supreme Court stated, "one of the most significant evidences of infringement exists frequently in the defendant's volume, namely the copying of errors." Implicitly the Court is assuming that errors in the original work occur at random so that if a subsequent work reproduces a substantial fraction of the errors it presumably copied a similar portion of the entire work. Moreover, the copying of errors suggests that the infringer did not conduct a careful review of the material or synthesize it with other sources, thereby creating a new work.

Financial Information Inc. v. Moody's Investor Services, Inc.[22]

Financial Information, Inc. (FII) charged the defendant, Moody's, with copying the information it gathered and published daily on bonds called for redemption. FII sends its subscribers notices, in the form of index cards, of the bonds called by an issuer, the redemption date, price and agent. In order to compile the information, the employees of FII check public notices and advertisements in over 20 publications. The cost of its service was $279 per year at the time of the suit.

FII claimed that Moody's Municipal Government Manual had copied its call notices from FII's daily cards. Moody's admitted that FII's cards were one source of its information but asserted that they were not its major source so that its limited use of them was permitted under the fair use doctrine.

In 1980, after noticing a coincidence of Moody's publishing errata shortly after FII did, the firm planted one error (a false redemption) which was subsequently picked up by Moody's. An examination of all errors (primarily accidental) made by FII in 1980 and 1981 showed Moody's reproduced seven of the ten errors made in 1980 and eight of eight errors FII made in 1981. While this data is based on matched notices of the same bond redemption, it should *not* be analyzed as a matched study as the FII entries were known to be errors, i.e., only one member of the pair can be considered as variable.[23] Hence, the plaintiff's statistical expert considered each of the 18 redemption notices published by Moody's as an independent binomial variable indicating whether (1) or not (0) the FII error appeared in Moody's and presented a one-sided lower confidence interval[24] for the parameter p, the probability that an error was reproduced. The 95% confidence interval for p based on all 18 errors in both years was

(11.40)   95% CONF(p; .40, 1.0),

i.e., only a value of p *exceeding* .40 could be accepted as a null hypothesis consistent with observing 15 or more reproduced errors out of a total of 18. Hence, we are 95% confident that the fraction of FII's notices reproduced in Moody's is at least .40. This interpretation is similar to the upper confidence interval presented in our discussion of the *Hill* case (Section 4.2). Using similar reasoning he presented a 95% and a 51% confidence interval for p derived from the 1981 data above. These were

(11.41)   95% CONF(p; .68, 1.0)

and

(11.42)   51% CONF(p; .91, 1.0).

The 51% confidence interval was presented, as civil cases are often decided on the "preponderance" of the evidence standard, while the 95% CONF was offered to meet the stronger standard of clear and convincing evidence.

Moody's countered the expert testimony by showing that more than half of all its redemption notices simply could not have been copied from FII's cards due to publication schedules and deadlines. Moreover, it produced evidence that it subscribed to more possible sources of basic information on bond redemption notices than FII and asserted that because its services was more extensive, e.g., bonds were rated for credit-worthiness, it was not in direct competition with FII's.

The district court accepted Moody's claim that the services were not aimed at the same market (in part because the yearly cost of Moody's service was more than double FII's) and rejected FII's statistical argument. In particular, the judge could not "make the leap that 8 of 8 proven instances shows copying 91% of the time" from the 51% CONF (11.42), and he inferred that the two years of data collectively indicated that Moody's copied about 20 to 24 cards during the two-year period.

The appellate court reversed the trial judge on the issue of direct competition and felt that he did not adequately weigh the major piece of statistical evidence, the 95% confidence interval (11.40) for the proportion of all 18 errors replicated by Moody's. The opinion noted that Moody's evidence indicating that it could not have reproduced half of FII's notices did not rebut the inference that they reproduced at least 40% implied by the CONF (11.40). Most statisticians would agree that a confidence interval should have at least 90% probability of containing the true value of the probability, p, and be based on both years of data. Thus, the lower court judge was properly skeptical of the 51% confidence interval (11.42) derived from one year's data but was overly cautious in his interpretation of the data for both years.

Comments.   (a) Since this case was remanded for further proceedings, it is interesting to think about the type of study Moody's might develop to refute FII's data. Here are some ideas:

(1) Examine the original sources for the 17 unintentional errors in the plaintiff's data and show that both services may well have obtained the data from the same erroneous source. If most of the errors came from the original source, e.g., newspaper notice or ad, then the fact that Moody's and FII both published the same error does not necessarily imply either service copied it from the other.

(2) Rather than demonstrating that half of all its redemption notices could not have been taken from FII's daily cards, Moody's might examine the 15 replicates in the plaintiff's study and show that over half of them could not have been copied. This would reduce the sample size available to FII and would decrease the *lower* value of p given by the 95% CONF (11.40).

(3) Rather than relying on the sample of errors, Moody's might conduct a matched pair study by taking a sample of over 100 randomly selected redemption notices and deciding which service published first. Of course, the pairs in which the publication dates are so close that deadlines and schedules indicate that both services might well have obtained the underlying information separately would be considered as ties. The formal statistical analysis would proceed along the lines of our discussion of the EEO comparable grade level and the cigarette advertising cases.

(b) Upon remand the district court found that the cards were not copyrightable because facts cannot be copyrighted and the plaintiff did not show that "independent creation" was involved in compiling its notices. The appellate opinion, 808 F.2d 204 (2nd Cir. 1986) affirmed the lower court's findings. Thus, the statistical aspects played a relatively minor role although a footnote (14 on page 207) of the opinion essentially cites the confidence interval (11.40) as evidence that Moody's did not engage in "wholesale appropriation" of FII's cards.

SAS Institute Inc. v. S & H Computer Systems Inc.[25]

This case dealt with the copyrightability of a substantial revision of a computer software system developed by SAS and whether subsequent products by S & H designed for a different type of computer was so similar to the SAS system that it constituted a violation of the copyright. First, SAS's revised system was deemed copyrightable, as 67% of the lines in its source code were new. This established that the revised version was substantially different from the former version (which was in the public domain).

Before discussing the statistics relevant to the duplication issue, it is important to note that S & H had been a licensee of SAS and therefore had ready access to the software in question. One SAS expert testified that the early source code for the S & H product was substantially based on the SAS code. He supported this opinion by some 44 specific instances showing evidence of direct copying. Another expert testified to a substantial similarity of another portion of the S & H code to that of the SAS system.

S & H argued that the 44 instances of duplication relied on by SAS's statistical expert were trivial in the context of 186,000 lines of code in its software package and disputed a few (four) of the instances of duplication. S & H's expert, however, relied on information provided by the firm's programmers who were not called to testify. In particular, the person who programmed the t-test, one of the 44 examples, was unavailable. Since the t-test requires the calculation of the mean and standard deviation, as well as taking a ratio and comparing the result to a statistical table more detailed than the one presented in Appendix B, almost surely several lines of source code are required to carry out the procedure. Thus, the 44 instances of duplication of procedures may well have involved a much larger number of lines of code. Moreover, the only difference between S & H's program and the one in SAS was that S & H added an IF[26] statement that was never used, suggesting that it was added to make the programs appear different.

Another statistical facet of the case was that there were 70 instances of a particular routine in the SAS program, 69 of which were contained in the S & H product. Finally, S & H included a procedure OBSTIME which had been part of an early version of SAS but later was omitted, except for one accidental occurrence in the SAS system at issue where it was a harmless error. Because of the statistical evidence of duplication, the inclusion of the OBSTIME error and other evidence, the judge found that S & H had infringed on the copyright held by SAS.

Problems

1. In the text we discussed the need for matching or otherwise controlling for the possible effect of another risk factor in an epidemiologic study. Use the same approach to decide which of the factors below should be used as matching variables in an equal pay or promotion study: occupation, educational level, date of hire, age, religion, employee status (e.g., paid monthly, paid weekly on an hours worked basis). Which factors might be considered in a regression analysis and which should not be?

2. In our discussion of the path diagrams 11.1a and 11.1b we assumed that the exposure (E) and the factor (F) were positively correlated in the population. What would be the effect of neglecting to match on F on the estimated association (OR) between exposure and the disease if E and F were *negatively* correlated?

3. Examine the regression coefficients in Table 11.19 for the Reye's syndrome study. Do the *signs* of the coefficients seem plausible to you? Why is this a useful check?

4. Assume the coefficients in the Reye's syndrome regression are medically plausible and the residuals seem to be random. Suppose a representative of the aspirin industry criticized the appropriateness of the logistic model and suggested that a different response function was more appropriate. Do you believe that fitting a new response function, assuming it had the reasonable properties noted in Chapter 8, would alter the ultimate conclusion that salicylate consumption and Reye's syndrome are statistically significantly associated? Explain.

5. Look up other copyright cases to determine what percentage of the material in a work courts require to be new in order that the work be copyrightable. What percentages of direct overlap have implied infringement? What other factors are relevant in addition to the raw percentages?

6.   Both cases discussed in this section dealt with copying well defined items. Other copyright cases have been concerned with alleged copying of directories (telephone or business), popular songs and books. For which, if any of these three topics might a matched analysis be useful? Explain.

7.*   In age discrimination cases involving termination of an employee in the protected age range, plaintiffs may submit data comparing the ages of all terminated employees and their replacements for a one- or two-year time period.

(a) Why is this analysis biased against the defendant? Look up some cases and ascertain what courts have said about such analyses.

(b) Would it be possible to make a comparison of these employee pairs which is more relevant? If so, describe it.

Answers to Selected Problems

2.   Suppose the factor (F) causes the disease but exposure does not. As E and F are negatively related, neglecting to control for F would lead us to underestimate the OR of 1.0 as the nonexposed will have higher levels of F then those exposed.

7.   (a) As one progresses in their career one must grow older. Thus, it would be expected that replacements would be younger (on average) than those they replaced, regardless of whether the first incumbent was promoted or terminated.

(b) One might compare the age of the replacement to the age of the terminee when the terminee *received* the job. This would be a proper statistical comparison. If there was a significant change (to younger replacements) then the employer might be trying to encourage young workers at the expense of older ones.

(e)   Comparing the Diagnostic Accuracy of Screening Tests for Aids Virus Antibodies

In response to a number of transmissions of the AIDS virus via blood transfusions, several relatively quick and easy screening test kits have been developed. In Chapter 11 we will discuss the accuracy of these procedures. Now we illustrate how matched studies are used to compare the rates of accuracy of two test kits. The reason matching is desirable is that the level of antibodies can vary widely among AIDS patients and infected individuals. Moreover, the screening tests themselves may be

TABLE 11.20.   Results of Two Screening Tests for AIDS Antibodies
on Blood Samples from 28 AIDS Patients

| | | Test Kit 1 | |
		Detected (+)	Not Detected (−)
Test	Detected	22	3
Kit 2	Not Detected	0	2

Source: Extracted from Table 1 in Carleson, J. R., Hinrichs, S. H., Yee, J., Gardner, M. B. and Pedersen, N. C. (1986). Evaluation of Three Commercial Screening Tests for AIDS Virus Antibodies. *American Journal of Clinical Pathology*. **86,** 357–359.

less accurate for some subgroups of the population. By using the same blood samples to evaluate the kits, we control these sources of variability when comparing their diagnostic accuracies.

In Table 11.20 we summarize part of a larger study of several test kits which was carried out at the University of California at Davis on blood samples from 28 AIDS patients. Notice that both kits detected AIDS antibodies in 22 patients and failed to detect them in two patients. However, Test 2 detected antibodies in three cases, but Test 1 did not. Before proceeding to a formal statistical analysis, it is interesting to ask which of the screening tests might a person choose to undergo during an operation being screened. Obviously, anyone would choose Test 2.

The test statistic (11.15) is just the sign test, i.e., under the null hypothesis B, the number of discordant (+, −) pairs, has a binomial distribution with parameters 3 and $\frac{1}{2}$. In this problem a two-sided test is called for as both test kits were licensed by the FDA. The p-value of the test statistic is just the probability that three heads *or* three tails would occur when a fair coin is tossed three times and equals $\frac{1}{4}$. Hence, one cannot reject the null hypothesis that the two kits had equal sensitivity in detecting AIDS virus antibodies using the usual criteria for statistical significance, i.e., requiring a p-value less than .05. However, adopting that criteria implies that the *power* of the matched pairs sign statistic (11.15) is *zero*. This is the same issue that arose in the time to promotion issue in the *Capaci* case (see Section 7.3), and reminds us that in small samples, a non-significant result should not be considered as strong evidence in support of the null hypothesis. Only when a statistical test has reasonable power to distinguish the null hypothesis from a realistic alternative is a non-significant result truly meaningful.

Comment. This example illustrates the importance of thinking carefully about the implications of a statistical analysis in determining the Type I and Type II error rates one deems tolerable. The simple answer, of course, is to suggest a larger sample size. However, the investigators were obviously limited by the number of AIDS patients they could legitimately ask to participate. Whenever a new disease occurs, the number of patients available to a study may be inherently small. Hence, one may be unable to obtain a sample of sufficient size for a definitive study. In the present context it was surely reasonable for the FDA to allow blood to be screened by the two tests in order to reduce the risk of AIDS being transmitted. If another small study also indicated that test kit 2 was more sensitive than test kit 1, then an agency might recommend that the second procedure be used when possible.

NOTES

1. Although firm wide statistical data is used in equal pay cases, often the most compelling data is a simple comparison of the plaintiff's salary with comparable employees. In *Fisher v. Dillard University* 499 F.Supp. 525, 26 FEP Cases 184 (E.D. La. 1980) a white assistant professor's salary was compared with the salaries of two black assistant professors in the same department with the same educational background (PhD) and course loads. The plaintiff supplemented this comparison with data indicating a systematic differential between black and white faculty members within each rank who held the same highest degree. The smallness of the total sample size was discounted in the opinion. Indeed, issues of statistical significance typically do not arise in these cases, as the number of matches for one person is too small to carry out formal tests and comparability is crucial. *Jacobs v. College of William and Mary* 517 F.Supp. 791 (E.D. Va. 1980), affirmed 661 F.2d 922 (4th Cir.) noted that two apparently similar jobs, female and male basketball coaches, actually had much different responsibilities, especially in recruiting and bringing in revenue. In *Hein v. Oregon College of Education* 718 F.2d 910 (9th Cir. 1983), the appeals court remanded an equal pay case because the main plaintiff's duties were not comparable to the man who was used as her match or comparison.

2. Regardless of the distribution of the characteristic measured on each member of the pair (x_i, y_i), under the null hypothesis the difference $y_i - x_i$ has a symmetric distribution around 0. Intuitively this follows from the fact that the probability that the event $[x_i = a, y_i = b]$ occurs is the same as that of the event $[x_i = b, y_i = a]$ so that the probability that $d_i = b - a$ is the same as the probability that $d_i = a - b$. Under the alternative, that the y's are shifted by an amount Δ so that the distribution of $y - \Delta$ is the same as that of x, $y - x$ has a distribution about Δ.

3. There are $\binom{n}{2}$ ways to select a pair of differences with distinct members, e.g., d_1 and d_3, and n more ways of selecting the same difference twice.

4. 37 FEP Cases 467 (7th Cir. 1985) affirming 37 FEP Cases 427 (N.D. Ill. 1982).

5. *Federal Register* (1980) **45**, 69816.

6. Kurppa, K., Holmberg, P. C., Kuosma, E. and Saxen, L. (1983). Coffee Consumption and Selected Congenital Malformations: A Nationwide Case Control Study. *American Journal of Public Health* **73**, 1397–1399.

7. 583 F.Supp. 1485 (W.D. Wi. 1985), affirmed 771 F.2d 1035 (7th Cir. 1985).

8. 36 EPD 35,049 (D.C. Ore. 1985).

9. 768 F.2d 385 (D.C. Cir. 1985).

10. Petrocal Waiver (1981) *Federal Register* **46**, 21,695.

11. In large samples both the t- and sign tests have a bivariate normal distribution with correlation $\rho = \sqrt{2/\pi} = .8$. The probability that both standard normal variables exceed 1.645 (corresponding to the .05 significance level) is obtained from the tables in Gupta (1963).

12. 370 F.Supp. 643 (N.D. Ca. 1973), modified 509 F.2d 623 (9th Cir. 1975). The statistical inference was not affected by the appeals court which struck a paragraph from the injunction.

13. 511 F.Supp. 855 (S.D. N.Y. 1980).

14. 511 F.Supp. 867 (S.D. N.Y. 1980).

15. 583 F.Supp. 875 34 FEP Cases 766 (D.C. Md. 1984).

16. The basic references for the material of this section are the texts by Breslow and Day (1980) and Schlesselman (1982).

17. The basic study is due to Herbst, A. L., Ulfelder, H. and Poskanzer, D. C. (1971). Adenocarcinoma of the Vagina: Association of Maternal Silbestrol Therapy with Tumor Appearance in Young Women. *New England Journal of Medicine* **284**, 878–881. We found the discussions of the study in the book by Schlesselman and the article by Colton and Greenberg (1982) quite helpful.

18. Greenwald, P., Barlow, J. J., Nasca, P. C. and Burnett, W. W. (1971). Vaginal Cancer after Maternal Treatment with Synthetic Estrogens. *New England Journal of Medicine* **285**, 390–392.

19. The value was obtained by using the range of estimates (.14 and 1.4 cases per 1000) reported in Colton and Greenberg (1982), who provided further citations to the basic sources.

20. The Ninth Circuit in *Hein v. Oregon College of Education* 718 F.2d 910 (1983) remanded the case to the district court because some of the plaintiffs compared their salary to the highest salary received by any comparable male. The opinion noted that the proper test was "whether the plaintiff is receiving lower wages than the average of wages paid to all employees of the opposite sex performing substantially equal work and similarly situated with respect to any other factors such as seniority which affect the wage scale." Other cases involved several comparisons are: *Heymann v. Tetra Plastics Corporation* 640 F.2d 115 (8th Cir. 1981) at 122 and *Marshall v. Georgia Southwestern College* 489 F.Supp. 1322 (M.D. Ga. 1980). There is some disagreement among these and other decisions concerning the propriety of other factors such as prior salary and/or market forces as explanations of a current salary differential. Relevant cases are cited in *Kouba v. Allstate Insurance Company* 691 F.2d 873 (9th Cir. 1982).

21. Public Health Service Reye's Syndrome Task Force. (1985). Public Health Service Study on Reye's Syndrome and Medications: Report of the Pilot Phase. *New England Journal of Medicine* **313**, 849–857.

22. The appellate opinion appeared in Copyright Law Decisions (1985) 25,744 (2nd Cir. 1985) and the lower court opinion in 1983 Copyright Law Decisions 25,617 (S.D. N.Y. 1983).

23. In a typical matched study, under the null hypothesis both response variables have the same distribution. In the present application we know FII's notice had an error and we are interested in estimating the probability p that Moody's simply copied FII's notice. Hence, for both years we have a sample from a binomial variable with parameters $n = 18$ and a p which is to be estimated.

24. Recall that a confidence interval consists of the values of the parameter (p) that are consistent with the data in the sense that the observed data has a reasonable probability of occurring by chance when the parameter actually equals a number in the confidence inter-

val. Since the present confidence interval is one-sided it is *not* symmetric about the natural estimate of p, $15/18 = .8333$ derived from the data. Remember that the lowest value of p which is consistent with the data is of interest here.

25. Copyright Law Decisions (1985), 25,794 (M.D. Tenn. 1985).

26. An IF statement is used in programming to allow for an option or check. For example, in reading data X_i, $i = 1, ..., 100$ into a computer one can count the number of items read using a state IF the index $i < 100$ continue reading in the data. When the last number X_{100} is read in, the program stops reading in data and goes to the next stage, e.g., computing the mean of the data.

REFERENCES

Books

BRESLOW, N. W. and N. E. DAY (1980). *Statistical Methods in Cancer Research. Volume 1. The Analysis of Case Control Studies.* IARC Scientific Publications No. 32. International Agency for Research on Cancer, Lyon. (The definitive treatment of the subject.)

KAHN, H. A. (1983). *An Introduction to Epidemiologic Methods.* New York: Oxford University Press. (A good survey of the field with illustrations from actual studies.)

KELSEY, J. L., THOMPSON, W. D. and EVANS, A. S. (1986). *Methods in Observational Epidemiology.* New York: Oxford University Press. (This recent book describes the design analysis and interpretation of epidemiologic studies.)

LEHMANN, E. L. (1975). *Nonparametrics: Statistical Methods Based on Ranks.* San Francisco: Holden-Day.

LILIENFELD, A. M. and LILIENFELD, D. E. (1980). *Foundations of Epidemiology,* 2nd ed. New York: Oxford University Press. (A classic test in epidemiology which is quite readable.)

SCHLESSELMAN, J. J. (1982). *Case Control Studies.* New York: Oxford University Press. (An excellent discussion of basic concepts of assessing the strength of an association, the carefulness of the planning and design of a study, as well as the statistical methods used in analyzing the data.)

Articles

COCHRAN, W. G. (1953). Matching in Analytical Studies. *American Journal of Public Health* **43**, 684–691.

COCHRAN, W. G. (1965). The Planning of Observational Studies of Human Populations (with discussion). *Journal of the Royal Statistical Society* Series A **128**, 234–255.

COCHRAN, W. G. (1968). The Effectiveness of Adjustment by Subclassification in Removing Bias in Observational Studies. *Biometrics* **24**, 295–313. (These three articles by the late Professor Cochran present the general ideas underlying observational studies and methods for controlling for confounding factors.

COLTON, T. and GREENBERG, E. R. (1982). Epidemiologic Evidence for Adverse Effects of DES Exposure During Pregnancy. *The American Statistician* **36**, 268–272. (This is a comprehensive survey of health studies related to DES.)

DICKSON, R. L. (1982). Medical Causation by Statistics. *Forum* **17**, 792–808. (An interesting article emphasizing some pitfalls in the use of statistics. It may be overly critical of epidemiologic studies and their use in demonstrating causation, which we discuss in Chapter 13.)

DUNN, S. A. (1986). Defining the Scope of Copyright Protection for Computer Software. *Stanford Law Review* **38**, 497–534.

FLEISS, J. L. (1984). The Mantel-Haenszel Estimator in Case Control Studies with Varying Numbers of Controls Matched to each Case. *American Journal of Epidemiology* **120**, 1–3.

GUPTA, S. S. (1963). Probability Integrals of Multivariate Normal and Multivariate *t*. *Annals of Mathematical Statistics* **34**, 782–828.

ROSENBAUM, P. R. and RUBIN, D. B. (1985). Constructing a Control Group by Multivariate Matched Sampling Methods that Incorporate the Propensity Score. *The American Statistician* **39**, 33–38. (A fine survey of recent advances in matched studies.)

SIEGEL, D. and GREENHOUSE, S. W. (1973). Multiple Relative Risk Functions in Case-Control Studies. *American Journal of Epidemiology* **97**, 324–331. (One of the first papers showing that the logistic model can be used in case-control as well as prospective studies.)

TAYLOR, J. M. G. (1986). Choosing the Number of Controls in a Matched Case-Control Study, Some Sample Size, Power and Efficiency Considerations. *Statistics in Medicine* **5**, 29–36. (This paper presents some power calculations which give guidance in designing the number of controls one should match to a case. In addition to showing that there is little gain once three controls are used, the results indicate that a large number, over 100, matched sets are required to have 80% power to detect an OR of 2.0.)

WALTER, S. D. (1980). Matched Case-Control Studies With a Variable Number of Controls per Case. *Applied Science* **29**, 172–179. (A good presentation of the extension of the material in Section 7a when each case is matched to a variable number of controls. This is important because one may not be able to find the same number (r) controls for each case.)

WILCOXON, F., KATTI, S. K. and WILCOX, R. A. (1970). Critical Values and Probabilities for the Wilcoxon Rank Sum Test and the Wilcoxon Signed Rank Test in *Selected Tables* in Mathematical Statistics. (Harter, H. F. and Owen, D. B., eds.) Chicago: Markham.

Chapter 12

Further Concepts of Statistical Inference: Bayesian Methods and the Likelihood Function

The methods of estimating parameters and testing hypotheses discussed so far have been treated from the frequentist point of view, as we envisage the observed data as one of many possible samples. Indeed, the randomization concept used in Chapters 5 and 7 was imposed on data for an entire population in order to assist our interpretation of the data. While these methods are very useful, they do not enable us to answer all questions of interest. For instance, legal cases are decided by the various evidentiary standards such as preponderance of the evidence, clear and convincing evidence, or beyond a reasonable doubt. These criteria have a probabilistic nature as they refer to a conditional probability, namely,

$$P(\text{guilt } given \text{ the evidence}) = P(G \mid E),$$

where E is the evidence and G denotes guilt (its complement $\overline{G}$ denotes innocence). It is difficult to consider all the evidence in a particular case as a random sample from a general population, as much of it will be unique to the particular situation. An approach to interpreting evidence, some of which can be regarded as statistical while other parts may not be, can be developed using Bayes' Theorem and is called Bayesian inference. This method allows one to combine *prior* beliefs about the defendant's guilt or innocence, whether based on data or on a subjective evaluation of nonstatistical evidence, with statistical data to obtain a summary estimate of $P(G \mid E)$. In this chapter we apply these ideas to the evaluation of medical tests, polygraph tests and identification (paternity) evidence.

We first review Bayes' Theorem and apply it to the evaluation of medical screening tests and draw conclusions for public policy. As the accuracy of polygraph testing and other forms of identification evidence can be analyzed in the same manner, we discuss these applications next.

We then discuss the application of Bayes' Theorem in paternity cases where the important role of the prior probability (π) and various assumptions underlying the calculation of the plausibility of paternity are discussed. In Section 4 we examine why the p-value of the usual test of a hypothesis is *not* the same as the conditional probability of guilt (e.g., paternity) given the evidence (e.g., blood test) and explore probabilistic aspects of evidentiary standards in cases.

The importance of checking the assumptions of all models used in statistical analyses is illustrated in Section 5, where we demonstrate the magnitude of the error that can occur when events are considered as independent when they are not. The impact of such errors in the calculated probability of coincidence used to identify alleged criminals is illustrated on the *Sneed* and *Collins* cases. The same error of assuming dependent events are independent also seriously affects the usual hypothesis tests and confidence intervals as well as Bayesian methods.

Extensions of the basic concepts to allow for uncertainty in our knowledge of the prior probability are discussed in Section 5. The interpretation of $P(G \mid E)$ becomes more complex as it is no longer a fixed number but is a random variable, itself varying with our uncertainty concerning the prior probability of guilt and the sampling variability in the data.

The last section introduces the reader to the concept of a likelihood function, which plots how the probability of an observed set of data changes with the value of the parameter of interest (e.g., if one observes ten minorities among 120 juror selections, the probability of this outcome is a function of the minority fraction in the population). Finally, Bayesian methods are shown to depend on the prior probability and the likelihood.

1. The Use of Bayes' Theorem to Analyze Medical Screening and Related Tests

In order to understand the use of Bayes' Theorem it is helpful to first apply it in a relatively noncontroversial setting, such as medical screening tests. The possible outcomes of the test for persons with and without the

	Have Disease (D)	Do Not Have Disease ($\overline{D}$)
Diagnosed as Being Sick (S)	D ∩ S (correct)	$\overline{D}$ ∩ S (False Positive Error)
Diagnosed as Being Well ($\overline{S}$)	D ∩ $\overline{S}$ (False Negative Error)	$\overline{D}$ ∩ $\overline{S}$ (Correct Decision)

FIGURE 12.1. The four possible classifications of an individual according to their true status and the determination of the screening test.

disease are given in Figure 12.1. Here a certain fraction, π, of the population has a disease. For any patient taking the medical test, the *accuracy* of the test is characterized by the two probabilities of correct diagnosis:

(1) The probability r_1 that the person is diagnosed as having the disease or sick (*S*), given that they truly have the disease (*D*). Thus, r_1 is the *conditional* probability that the person is diagnosed as sick when they have the disease or, in symbols, $P(S \mid D) = r_1$. This probability of correctly classifying a person with the disease is called the *sensitivity* of the diagnostic procedure.

(2) The probability r_2 that a person who does not have the disease ($\overline{D}$) is correctly diagnosed as being disease-free ($\overline{S}$). Again r_2 is the *conditional* probability $P(\overline{S} \mid \overline{D})$ and is called the *specificity* of the diagnostic method.

Suppose that a fraction, π, of persons in a specified population have the disease, and a test is given to a randomly selected person in this population, e.g., a worker in a plant whose employees are given a routine physical exam every year. The main question of interest is: Suppose a person given the test is told the test indicated that they have the disease, what is the probability they actually have it? The key step in the analysis is to realize that the probability of interest is the *conditional* probability

P(patient has disease | the test says they have it) $= P(D \mid S)$,

which is *not* equal to either of the *accuracy probabilities*, which are conditional probabilities *given* knowledge of disease status. We now calculate $P(D \mid S)$. The conditional probability $P(D \mid S)$ can be regarded as the fraction of positive diagnoses that are correct and is called the predictive value of a positive test or PVP.

Recall when the probability $\pi = P(D)$ is known beforehand, $P(D \mid S)$ is obtained using the definition of conditional probability and the total probability theorem given in Chapter 2, i.e.,

$$(12.1) \qquad P(D \mid S) = \frac{P(D \cap S)}{P(S)} = \frac{P(D \cap S)}{P(D \cap S) + P(\overline{D} \cap S)}.$$

We also will use formula (2.6), i.e., $P(D \cap S) = P(D)P(S \mid D)$ and $P(\overline{D} \cap S) = P(\overline{D})P(S \mid \overline{D})$.

In the present application we know the following three probabilities

$$P(D) = \pi, \qquad P(S \mid D) = r_1, \qquad P(\overline{S} \mid \overline{D}) = r_2.$$

Because someone can only be diagnosed as being sick or not,

P(diagnosed as well | one is well) $= 1 - P$(diagnosed sick | one is well),

(12.2a)

i.e.,

$$(12.2b) \qquad P(\overline{S} \mid \overline{D}) = 1 - P(S \mid \overline{D}) = 1 - r_2.$$

Hence,

$$P(D \cap S) = P(D) \, P(S \mid D) = \pi r_1$$

and

$$P(\overline{D} \cap S) = P(\overline{D}) \, P(S \mid \overline{D}) = (1 - \pi)(1 - r_2).$$

From (12.1) we obtain

$$(12.3) \quad P(D \mid S) = \frac{\pi r_1}{\pi r_1 + (1 - \pi)(1 - r_2)} = \frac{\pi r_1}{\pi(r_1 + r_2 - 1) + 1 - r_2}.$$

At this point a numerical example should clarify matters. Suppose $\pi = .05$, i.e., only 5% of the population has the disease and that $r_1 = r_2 = .95$, i.e., the test is 95% accurate. Then the PVP, or the probability that a person the test diagnoses as sick actually has the disease, is

$$\frac{\pi r_1}{\pi(r_1 + r_2 - 1) + 1 - r_2} = \frac{(.05)(.95)}{(.05)(.95 + .95 - 1) + (1 - .95)}$$

$$= \frac{(.05)(.95)}{(.05)(.9) + .05} = .5.$$

Thus, *one half* of the persons diagnosed as having the disease actually have it, which implies that about one half of the persons who are told they have the disease do not have it and will worry needlessly.

The probability $P(\overline{D} \mid S)$ is the proportion of positive diagnoses that are errors and is one minus the *predictive value* of a *positive test* (PVP). Using a similar derivation one can show that

$$(12.4) \qquad P(\overline{D} \mid S) = \frac{P(\overline{D} \cap S)}{P(S)} = \frac{(1 - \pi)(1 - r_2)}{\pi r_1 + (1 - \pi)(1 - r_2)}.$$

The other probabilities of interest are: the probability a person diagnosed as well has the disease, $P(D \mid \overline{S})$, and the probability that a person diagnosed as well is disease-free, $P(\overline{D} \mid \overline{S})$ called the *predictive value* of a *negative test* (PVN). These probabilities can be obtained by our previous reasoning and are given by

$$(12.5) \qquad P(D \mid \overline{S}) = \frac{P(D \cap \overline{S})}{P(\overline{S})} = \frac{\pi(1 - r_1)}{\pi(1 - r_1) + (1 - \pi)r_2},$$

and P(a person diagnosed as well is disease free) or the PVN $=$

$$(12.6) \qquad P(\overline{D} \mid \overline{S}) = \frac{(1 - \pi)r_2}{\pi(1 - r_1) + (1 - \pi)r_2}.$$

Notice that $P(D \mid \overline{S})$ is *one* minus the PVN.

In Figure 12.2(a), we present probabilities for the four possible outcomes of the test reported in Figure 12.1, which describe the situation *before* or *prior* to the administration of the test. Then we present probabilities *after* the test was carried out and the person was diagnosed as having the disease (S) in Fig. 12.2b.

At first glance the result of our numerical calculation is somewhat discouraging, as half the people who were told they had the disease were well. The reason for this is that there were only a small fraction (.05) of all individuals tested who really had the disease. Thus, a small rate of misdiagnosis of disease-free individuals implies that the misdiagnosed disease-free group is a substantial portion of those who are diagnosed as ill.

Let us now assume that the fraction π is larger, say .25, and recalculate $P(D \mid S)$ and $P(\overline{D} \mid S)$. From formulas (12.3) and (12.4) these conditional probabilities are

$$P(D \mid S) = \frac{(.25)(.95)}{(.25)(.95 + .95 - 1) + (1 - .95)} = \frac{.2375}{.225 + .05} = .8636,$$

and

$$P(\overline{D} \mid S) = \frac{(.75)(.05)}{(.25)(.95) + (.75)(.05)} = \frac{.0375}{.0375 + .2375} = .1364.$$

Before (Prior)(a)

$$P(D) = \pi \qquad\qquad P(\bar{D}) = 1-\pi$$

S	$P(D \cap S) = \pi r_1$	$P(\bar{D} \cap S) = (1-\pi)(1-r_2)$
$\bar{S}$	$P(D \cap \bar{S}) = \pi(1-r_1)$	$P(\bar{D} \cap \bar{S}) = (1-\pi)r_2$

After Test (Posterior) Yields S (b)

$$P(D|S) \qquad\qquad P(\bar{D}|S)$$

S	$P(D \cap S|S) = \dfrac{\pi r_1}{\pi r_1 + (1-\pi)(1-r_2)}$	$P(\bar{D} \cap S|S) = \dfrac{(1-\pi)(1-r_2)}{\pi r_1 + (1-\pi)(1-r_2)}$	$P(S|S) = 1$
$\bar{S}$	0	0	$P(\bar{S}|S) = 0$

FIGURE 12.2. Probabilities of the four possible classifications of disease and diagnosis before the test is given and after the test classifies the individual as sick.

Thus, 86.4% of those identified as having the disease actually have it, while only 13.6% of those diagnosed as ill will be false positives. Our two calculations show that as the proportion of the tested populated who have the disease increases, the proportion of persons diagnosed as having the disease who actually have it also increases. This has an important implication for public health policy. When certain subgroups are more susceptible to a disease, public health officials may suggest that medical tests be given only to members of these groups. This strategy enables one to detect the vast majority of cases in the population and avoids alarming many persons who are disease-free.

The relative influence of the accuracy of the test (assuming its sensitivity equals its specificity) and the prior probability (π) on its PVP, $P(D \mid S)$, can be seen from Table 12.1, which gives the posterior probability a person the test indicates has the disease does actually have it. For any fixed value of π, the expected proportion of persons classified as sick who are correctly classified, i.e., the conditional probability $P(D \mid S)$, increases with the accuracy of the test, as one would intuitively expect. Notice that tests which are only 50% accurate are *uninformative*, as the posterior probability is identical to the prior probability.

Comment.   The use of a medical screening test for the HIV virus indicating exposure to AIDS is an application that immediately comes to mind. Because of the nature of the disease and the fact that persons labelled as carriers may well be subject to discrimination of various types, the proper administration of the test, including keeping the results confidential, are of paramount importance. While these issues are not primarily statistical in nature, it is important to keep them in mind when using modern tech-

TABLE 12.1.   The Conditional (or Posterior) Probability That the Individual has the Disease, Given That the Screening Test is Positive as a Function of the Prior Probability (π) and the Accuracy (r) of the Screening Test

Prior Probability	Accuracy								
	.50	.60	.70	.75	.80	.85	.90	.95	.99
.01	.01	.015	.023	.029	.039	.054	.083	.161	.50
.05	.05	.073	.109	.136	.174	.230	.321	.500	.839
.10	.10	.143	.206	.250	.308	.386	.500	.679	.917
.20	.20	.273	.368	.429	.500	.586	.692	.826	.961
.25	.25	.333	.437	.500	.571	.654	.750	.864	.971
.30	.30	.391	.500	.563	.632	.708	.794	.891	.977
.40	.40	.500	.609	.667	.727	.791	.857	.927	.985
.50	.50	.600	.700	.750	.800	.850	.900	.850	.990
.60	.60	.692	.778	.818	.857	.895	.931	.966	.993
.75	.75	.818	.875	.90	.923	.944	.964	.983	.997

Note: Calculated from formula (12.3) assuming both r_1 and r_2 are equal to the accuracy given.

nology to plan public health programs. This is especially true with medical screening tests, as patients with other diseases of lesser seriousness and/ or with less social stigma may have a higher rate of false positive test results because the screening test is less accurate in their situation.[1]

2. Application to the Use of Lie Detectors for Routine Screening of Employees

Although there have been a number of proposals to allow employers to routinely screen employees to assess their propensity to steal, members of Congress have also introduced legislation[2] to limit the use of lie detectors. If we consider propensity to steal as corresponding to having a disease, the result that a polygraph test labels the test-taker as not truthful is analogous to the medical tests indicating the individual has the disease. Thus, the probabilistic characteristics of the results of a polygraph are given by the same analysis. Now, the prior probability (π) is the fraction of employees who are likely to steal,[3] while the sensitivity r_1 is the probability a person with intention to steal is detected by the polygraph and the specificity r_2 is the probability that an honest employee is classified as honest. We will somewhat simplify the problem by assuming that honest employees will tell the truth, while dishonest ones will not, and that the accuracy rates are known. This assumes a greater reliability of lie detection procedures than often is the case in the real world. Several studies of the accuracy of polygraphs suggest that r_1 is in the range .85 to .90, while r_2 is about .75 to .86. For purposes of our discussion, we will take both accuracies equal to .85.

From the column under .85 in Table 12.1 we see that if 10% of the employees are potential stealers, then only 38.6% of the people classified as liars are actually dishonest. Thus, if the test were routinely used, *more than half* of the dismissed employees would be undeservedly fired. Another interesting consequence of Table 12.1 is the perverse effect of a good pre-employment interview and reference check. Suppose that due to a careful selection process only 5% (rather than 10%) of employer A's new hires are potential stealers. If the firm institutes routine lie detector tests, only 23% of those it labels as dishonest actually will be. Thus, nearly 80% of the employees who might be dismissed are *innocent* victims of a *false positive* error.

On the other hand, if employees are given the test only after other indications of stealing or possibly selling trade secrets, etc. have been observed, the prior probability of such an employee being guilty is much greater than .05 or .10, perhaps as high as .5 or even .75, depending on the evidence. In such cases the polygraph may well be useful in confirming or refuting the charge, especially if a top-notch polygraph expert gives the examination.

So far our discussion has assumed that the prior probability (π) is known, so we can obtain the conditional probabilities $P(D \mid S)$, $P(\overline{D} \mid S)$, $P(D \mid \overline{S})$ and $P(\overline{D} \mid \overline{S})$, called the *posterior* probabilities, as they are determined *after* the test has been given. Sometimes these probabilities are not known and must be determined either by direct estimation or by deciding on a probability distribution for the value π. We will discuss these extensions later in Section 5. First we turn to the application of the Bayesian paradigm to help determine paternity and to examine evidentiary standards.

Problems

1. Using formula (12.4) and the values $\pi = .05$, $r_1 = r_2 = .95$, as in the illustrative calculation of $P(D \mid S)$ given by formula (12.3), show that $P(\overline{D} \mid S) = .5$. Why do $P(D \mid S)$ and $P(\overline{D} \mid S)$ sum to 1?

2. Suppose both accuracies of a polygraph when administered routinely in the field by less qualified persons are only about .70 as some experts have suggested.
    (a) How useful will such a test be for routine screening of employees?
    (b) If you were an honest employee in such a firm should you take the routine polygraph test or should you object? Explain the probabilistic reasons underlying your answer.

3.* The discussion in the text focused on $P(D \mid S)$, however, one *minus* the PVN or $P(D \mid \overline{S})$, the proportion of persons classified as not having the disease when they do is quite important. In the context of screening blood for antibodies to the AIDS virus, interpret the meaning of $P(D \mid \overline{S})$ and $1 - P(D \mid S)$.

Answers to Selected Problems

1. $P(\overline{D} \mid S) = (.95)(.05)/[(.95)(.05) + (.05)(.95)] = .5$. As D and $\overline{D}$ are complementary events which exhaust the whole probability space, i.e., one of them must occur, the sum of their probabilities, even calculated conditionally given the occurrence of an event S, still must sum to one.

3. $P(D \mid \bar{S})$ is the probability of a unit of blood that passed the screening test has antibodies to the AIDS virus. Clearly, we desire $P(D \mid \bar{S})$ to be as close to zero as possible. On the otherhand, $P(D \mid S)$ *is* the fraction of blood classified as carrying the infection which actually is contaminated. One minus $P(D \mid S)$ is the fraction of blood that is not used for transfusion because it is screened as carrying antibodies but it is actually free of them. This quantity is of interest to blood banks as it is the fraction of blood they collect but throw away because of a false positive screening result.

3.   Paternity Cases

Paternity suits typically concern questions of financial support or inheritance, although the determination of fatherhood may arise in questions of legitimacy or adultery. Since the genetic characteristics determining blood groups are inherited according to the well-known principles stemming from the $1:2:1$ ratio of dominant, mixed and recessive genotypes due to G. Mendel, one can sometimes exclude a particular man as a possible father on the basis of his blood type if it is incompatible with that of the mother and child. Even if an accused man is not excluded, Bayesian methods can be used to determine the posterior probability that he is the father of the child in question, *provided* that an appropriate prior probability can be established. In this section we first illustrate the ideas using the ABO system of blood groups, which classifies blood into one of four (A, B, AB, O) groups depending on the presence of specific chemical agents (A, B, or A and B) or their absence (O) on the surface of red blood cells. Then we discuss the use of human leukocyte antigen (HLA) types in conjunction with the ABO and other red blood cell systems such as the rhesus (Rh) one, since collectively they have great ability to assist in resolving many questions of paternity.

    We next review some principles of genetic inheritance and apply them to the ABO system. The reason knowledge of gene frequencies is relevant in the determination of paternity is that blood group tests enable us to determine certain genes the father of the child must have. Lack of these genes excludes a male from being the father of the child. On the other hand, if the alleged father can be shown to have the required genetic characteristics and only a small fraction of all men possess them, then this strengthens the case against him, especially if very few other men had access to the mother during the relevant time period and they were *not related* to the accused.

a. Basic genetic principles and the ABO system of blood groups

Before describing the use of serologic tests it may be helpful to review basic genetics. Typically one inherits two genes, one from each parent, for a particular characteristic. When there are only two possible genes, a dominant characteristic, D, and a recessive, d, version, there are three possible *genotypes* a person may have DD, Dd and dd. Since the dominant characteristic determines the manifestation of the characteristic in the offspring, we only observe *two phenotypes,* which we label D+ and D− depending on whether or not the dominant characteristic is manifest, i.e., the genotypes DD and Dd are D+. The classic example of the situation is Mendel's study of yellow and green peas. The *frequencies, p* and *r,* of the genes D and d, in the population can be determined if it is assumed that people mate at random, i.e., the gene does not affect one's choice of mate. This assumption is quite reasonable with regard to blood groups but might not be for genes related to other characteristics such as height. The independent pairing assumption implies that the probability an offspring of a random mating will have the characteristic dd is r^2, as the chance it will inherit the d gene from each parent is r, the frequency of the gene in the population. If we observe a large sample of the population we can determine the fraction, f, of individuals exhibiting the D− characteristic as $r^2 = f$, so $r = \sqrt{f}$. Since there are only two genes, the fraction p of the gene pool held by the dominant gene, D, is $p = 1 - r = 1 - \sqrt{f}$. For example, if we observe that D− individuals form 16% of the population, $r = \sqrt{.16} = .4$, so that recessive gene composes 40% of the gene pool and the dominant gene 60%.

Although we only observe the phenotype of an individual, it should be noted that we expect the fraction p^2 of individuals to have genes DD and 2 pr to have Dd (one dominant and one recessive). Thus, of all dominant phenotypes, only

$$(12.7) \qquad\qquad \frac{p^2}{p^2 + 2pr} = \frac{p}{p + 2r}$$

possess two dominant genes. A short table of the gene frequencies, genotypes, frequencies and proportion of dominant phenotypes who possess two dominant genes is given in Table 12.2.

There are four blood types, A, B, AB and O, which are determined by the presence or absence of an A or B gene. The O type person has neither A nor B. A person's blood type can be determined by testing their red cells for a reaction with antigens for A and B, respectively. The rules for

TABLE 12.2.   The Relationship Between Genotype and Gene Frequencies and the Proportion of Homozygotes Among Dominant Phenotypes

Gene Frequencies in the Population		Genotype Frequencies (%)			Approximate Percentage of Homozygotes Among all D+ Types (DD + Dd)
D	d	DD	Dd	dd	
.99	.01	98%	1.98%	.01%	98%
.90	.10	81%	18%	1%	81.8%
.70	.20	49%	41%	9%	54%
.50	.50	25%	50%	25%	33.3%
.30	.70	9%	42%	49%	18%
.10	.90	1%	18%	81%	5.3%

Source: Adapted from Table 4.4 of Cavalli-Sforza (1977) at 71. The term "homozygote" means that both genes are the same.

the determination of blood group from the test results of antigen testing are given in Table 12.3. It is important to realize that a person with blood group A may have genes AA or AO, either of which will react to the A antigen. Similarly a person with blood group B has either BB or BO genes. The O character is inherited like a recessive gene, only being observed as one's blood group if neither parent transmitted an A or B gene.

Since a child can only inherit a blood type from its parents, in Table 12.4 we present the groups which can occur in children whose parents have the given blood types. In examining the table remember that a per-

TABLE 12.3.   Blood Group Determination from Antigen Tests

Antigen Results		Blood Group
Anti-A	Anti-B	
Positive	Negative	A
Negative	Positive	B
Positive	Positive	AB
Negative	Negative	O

Note: If the blood clumps when mixed with antigen, a positive reaction has occurred.

TABLE 12.4.　The Inheritance of Blood Groups

Blood groups of parents	Blood groups that may occur in children
O × O	O
O × A	O,A
A × A	O,A
O × B	O,B
B × B	O,B
A × B	O,A,B,AB
O × AB	A,B
A × AB	A,B,AB
B × AB	A,B,AB
AB × AB	A,B,AB

Source:　Solomon (1966) at 334.

son of group A phenotype may have the gene pairs AA or AO. In order to use the ABO system in probability calculations, we need the frequencies of the genes determining blood group and these are given in Table 12.5. One can invert the information in Table 12.4 by asking what blood groups a father of a child might have, given knowledge of the blood group of the mother and child and which ones are impossible for him to possess. For example, suppose a mother is type O. If the child is also an O, then the father must have at least one O gene, so he could be an OO, OA or OB. The father could *not* be an AB type. On the other hand, if the child has blood group A then the father must have had the A gene to transmit to the child. So the father must be type A or type AB and could *not* have been an O or B group member. In Table 12.6 we present a list of *exclusions* which can be determined on the basis of the ABO blood groups.

The probability an innocent man will be *excluded* as the possible father by the ABO group test is of primary interest. However, this probability depends on the blood groups of both the mother and child and the gene frequencies of A, B, O in the population. To illustrate the idea, suppose the mother is of group A and the child group B. Then the father must have a B *gene and cannot* be of group O or A. Table 12.5 reports that these two phenotypes constitute 88.4% of the population, so 88.4% of all men would be excluded on this basis. On the other hand, if the mother and child are both group O, only men in the AB group would be excluded. As only 3.4%

TABLE 12.5.   The Proportion of ABO Phenotypes and Genotypes in the Caucasion Population. The Gene Frequencies of A, B and O are $p = .28$, $q = .06$ and $r = .66$, respectively

Genotypes	Phenotype	Proportion in the Population
AA⎱ OA⎰	A	.448
BB⎱ BO⎰	B	.083
OO	O	.436
AB	AB	.034

Source: Adapted from Table 5.2 of Cavalli-Sforza (1977) at 82. We only present the probabilities or proportions of the phenotypes, as these are what are observed in nature and form the data base for the analysis in the text.

of men are in this group, the probability of randomly selected (by the mother) male being excluded in this situation is .034.

The last column in Table 12.6 gives the probability a random man would be excluded solely on the basis of the ABO system. It varies widely, from zero to .86, depending on the blood groups of the mother and child. When a man is not excluded on the basis of the ABO system, we cannot have much confidence that he is the real father. Even the most favorable situation shows that 12% of men would still be included as potential fathers, and some of the mother and child combinations do not exclude any man. Thus, it is necessary to consider a number of red and white blood cell systems in order to obtain a greater *minimum* exclusion probability after tests on all the systems have been carried out.

b.   The use of several blood group systems and the calculation of the plausibility of paternity by Bayes' theorem

In addition to the ABO system, the Rh system with 40 phenotypes can be used in the same manner as the ABO one. Recently, the HLA system for histocompatibility has been extensively studied and gene frequencies for

TABLE 12.6. Exclusion Based on the ABO Blood System

Mother's Phenotype	Child's Phenotype	Blood Group Phenotypes the Father *cannot* have	Conditional Probability a Random Man Would be Excluded
O	O	AB	.034
O	A	O,B	.519
O	B	O,A	.884
O	AB	None	.0
A	O	AB	.034
A	B	O,A	.884
A	A	None	.0
A	AB	O,A	.884
B	A	O,B	.519
B	B	None	.0
B	O	AB	.034
B	AB	O,B	.519
AB	A	None	.0
AB	B	None	.0
AB	AB	O	.436

Source: Author's calculation of the conditional probabilities based on the probabilities (proportions) of the individual phenotypes given in Table 12.5. A table of the exclusions, without their probabilities, is given in Solomon (1966).

at least 18 HLA-A and 18 HLA-B antigens have been determined. Thus, this system is the single most useful one for determining possible paternity. Since the genes determining the ABO, Rh and other red cell marker systems and the HLA system are transmitted independently,[4] we can use them together in paternity probability calculations. As new genetic tests are currently being developed, we will assume that k systems are being used and *each of them has exclusion* probability P_i, $i = 1, ..., k$. Assuming that the genes determining these characteristics *sort independently*, the probability that an accused man selected at random by the mother is *not excluded*, once the total genetic requirements have been determined from the tests on the mother and child, is:

$$(12.8) \quad (1 - P_1) \times (1 - P_2) \times \cdots \times (1 - P_k) = \prod_{i=1}^{k} (1 - P_i),$$

as the probability a man is *not* excluded by the ith system is $(1 - P_i)$.

Using all k systems the probability a random man would be excluded is

(12.9) $$1 - \prod_1^k (1 - P_i).$$

It is important to emphasize that the *exclusion* probabilities, P_i, of the individual systems are *conditional probabilities* determined by the genetic material the child must have inherited from the father *given* the serological tests results on the child and mother.

The probability a randomly selected male is *not excluded*, i.e., is included as a possible father, is given by (12.8) will be denoted by g. If π is the prior probability that the accused is the father, then *after* the tests show he is *not* excluded his probability of being the father is

(12.10) $$\frac{\pi}{\pi + (1 - \pi)g} = \frac{1}{1 + \left(\dfrac{1 - \pi}{\pi}\right)g}.$$

Formula (12.10) is obtained from formula (12.3) by letting D denote the probability that the accused is the father and S denote the event that the test does *not* exclude a random male. We assume $r_1 = 1$, i.e., if the accused is the father he will *not* be excluded. If the accused is not the father there is probability g that he will *not* be excluded so that $1 - r_2 = g$. As the prior probability of the accused being the father is π, the prior probability he is falsely accused is $1 - \pi$ and the result follows from formula (12.3).

Formula (12.10) or a related one is sometimes called the likelihood of paternity, and the symbol W is often used to denote it. However, it may be more useful to denote it by $P(F \mid M)$ to remind us that it is the conditional probability the accused is the father, *given* the genetic *match*, M, and the assumed prior probability (π). We will follow Berry and Geisser (1986) and call it the plausibility of paternity.[5]

Before we illustrate the numerical use of (12.10) we emphasize the basic assumptions underlying the calculation:

(1) The genes in each of the k marker systems are transmitted independently (otherwise the multiplication rule used to determine (12.8) would be incorrect).

(2) The *gene frequencies* in the systems are known and the race of the father can be determined, so the correct gene frequencies can be used.

(3) The possible alternative father(s) can be regarded as a random selection from the same racial group as the alleged father, so his (their) genetic makeup can be calculated from the known gene frequencies.

To illustrate the use of formula (12.10) suppose $g = .02$, i.e., 98% of the men could be excluded. When $\pi = .5$,

$$P(F \mid M) = \frac{1}{(1.02)} = .98,$$

but when $\pi = .2$, as might happen if five men had equal access to the mother during the relevant time period,

$$P(F \mid M) = \frac{1}{1 + \left(\frac{.8}{.2}\right)(.02)} = .926.$$

Because g is so small, both conditional probabilities exceed .90. However, suppose $g = .10$, which still means that 90% of all men can be excluded. Then if $\pi = .5$,

$$P(F \mid M) = \frac{1}{1 + .1} = .909 \simeq .91.$$

However, if $\pi = .2$,

$$P(F \mid M) = \frac{1}{1 + 4(.10)} = .714,$$

a less convincing figure.

We now turn to the way $P(F \mid M)$ is actually calculated in cases and indicate some reasons why its use is controversial. First, the prior probability is almost *always* taken as .5, i.e., the mother is assumed correct 50% of the time. In other words, only one other male is considered as an alternative candidate and, as far as his blood type, he is randomly selected from all men of the relevant race. Under these conditions the conditional probability $P(F \mid M)$ has been interpreted in words by Hummel, reproduced by Krause, Miale, Jennings, Rettberg and Sell (1976), as meaning:

Values of $P(F \mid M)$	Likelihood or Plausibility of Paternity
.998+	Practically proved
.991–.997	Extremely likely
.95–.99	Very likely
.90–.95	Likely
.80–.9	Undecided
less than .8	Not useful

From the previous calculations we realize the importance of both the *prior* probability and the probability g (called the inclusion probability).

When $g = .10$ and our prior probability π changed from .5 to .2, the accused went from a likely father to one for whom the test was not useful. On the other hand, when $g = .02$ even when the prior probability was .2, $P(F \mid M) = .926$, which keeps the accused in the likely category.

Because the above mentioned criteria are not strictly adhered to, a serious problem can arise if the preponderance of the evidence standard is interpreted as meaning that the accused is the father when $P(F \mid M)$ exceeds .5. Since the prior probability is set at .5, whenever g is less than 1, $P(F \mid M)$ is greater than .5. This follows by setting $\pi = .5$ in formula (12.10) which reduces to

$$P(F \mid M) = \frac{1}{1 + g}.$$

As long as $g < 1$, i.e., the test *excludes some fraction* of the population, $P(F \mid M)$ will *exceed* .5, as $1 + g$ will be less than 2. Similarly, if blood systems are used which exclude 90% of all men so $g = .1$, then $P(F \mid M)$ exceeds .9, so *any* nonexcluded male accused by the mother might well be found by a court to be the father.

Although the choice of .5 as the prior probability (π) is referred to as the neutral value (Polesky and Lenz, 1984) using it without checking its appropriateness to the specific case leads to making the determination that because the accused is a member of a sufficiently small fraction, g, of the male population possessing the requisite genetic makeup, the accused is the legal father. If one accepts this criteria, which appears reasonable when the mother had relations with only a few men during the relevant time period, then one must be careful to check that the actual partners of the woman were drawn randomly from the male population and that the accused had half of all relations with her during the appropriate time period. Quite often a woman may know men who are related, e.g., brothers or cousins. As the genetic makeup of relatives of the accused man are more similar to his than the genetic makeup of a random male, the assumption that the genes of the hypothetical alternative father are like a random sample of the gene pool is incorrect. Indeed, the probability of exclusion of a close relative is only about half that of a random man (Salmon and Brocteur, 1978) and errors of paternity determination have resulted by neglecting the "relative" effect (Reisner and Reading, 1983). The plausibility of paternity should prove a useful aid, especially when the court conducts a careful inquiry to first ascertain

(1) whether or not sexual relations between the accused and the mother occurred during the relevant time period and their frequency and

(2) whether or not the mother had relations with other men and if so whether any of the men were related to the accused.

By modifying the prior probability (π) and the inclusion probability, g, to account for this information before calculating (12.10), courts can ensure that a man who is unlucky enough to have the appropriate genetic makeup but who was not sexually involved (or at least not very involved) with the mother is not a victim of a chance coincidence.

Comment. Unfortunately, obtaining information about all possible candidates for fatherhood from the mother may be difficult.[6] Similarly, the accused male may try to deny having relations with the mother during the relevant time frame.

c. Acceptance of blood tests in court

Although blood test evidence was admitted in courts as early as 1931 in Pennsylvania[7] and 1936 in South Dakota,[8] their acceptance became more common after a blood test *excluding* the alleged father was *not* deemed to be conclusive in *Berry v. Chaplin.*[9] After being accused of being responsible for the plaintiff's pregnancy, the actor Charles Chaplin made an agreement with her to pay a stipulated sum of money for her medical care and support during the period of her pregnancy and hospitalization at birth, provided that she and the child would take tests made by competent medical experts to determine the child paternity. The ABO blood groups were Mr. Chaplin (O), mother (A) and child (B), so we know that the accused could *not* be the father, who must have been of type B or AB. Nevertheless, the court felt constrained by a previous opinion[10] which held that the blood tests would not be considered conclusive evidence unless the statute specifically to stated. Thus, the appellate court upheld a jury decision in favor of the mother. The opinion also stated that it was proper for the trial court to have directed the defendant to stand in front of the jury in close proximity to the mother, who held the child in her arms, so that the jurors might study and compare the features of the infant with those of the plaintiff and defendant.

Apparently in response to the adverse publicity and notoriety of the decision, in 1953 the California legislature adopted a statute accepting blood tests excluding the alleged father as conclusive evidence of paternity, except in cases where a husband and wife are cohabitating.[11] The legislature adopted a proposed Uniform Blood Tests Act to determine paternity[12] but omitted the last section of the suggested law which provided: If the experts conclude that the blood tests show the possibility of the alleged father's paternity, admission of this evidence is within the discretion of the court, depending upon the infrequency of the blood type.

Subsequently, the use of blood tests excluding the accused man were accepted as reliable evidence in California, however, acceptance of the inclusion probability was more controversial. In *Dodd v. Heckel*, 84 Cal. App. 31604, 148 Cal. Rptr. 780 (1978), the plaintiff wished to submit blood test evidence based on the medical system that the alleged father was "among the $14\frac{1}{2}$ to 15% of the population that could be the father." The defendant objected to the admission and the judge did not allow it into evidence, as it only showed that the accused was a possible father and that it might unduly influence the jury. The conventional calculation (12.10) yields a conditional probability $P(F \mid M)$ or plausibility of paternity of .87, which would suggest that the accused is likely to be the father, however, this probability would decline to about .69 if the prior probability (π) was 1/4 rather than 1/2. The opinion does not discuss the other evidence in the case, but, as the jury had found the accused was not the father, it is reasonable to assume that a prior probability based on all the evidence in the actual case (which excluded the blood test) was less than .5.

In *Cramer vs. Morrison*,[13] the trial judge did not allow the plaintiff to submit evidence showing that the defendant had a "plausibility of paternity" of .983 based on HLA typing. The appeals court, however, said that the trial court erred in excluding the expert testimony that "there was a 98.3% chance" that the defendant was the father. This assertion was based on the fact that the inclusion probability, g, determined from the HLA system was .017. It means that only 1.7% of all men possess the required genetic characteristics, i.e., a randomly selected man has only a 1.7% chance of possessing the same phenotype as the father. It does *not* mean that the *probability* the defendant is the father is

$$1 - .983 = .017.$$

The conditional probability that an accused man is the father is calculated using formula (12.10) *based on the assumption* that there is prior probability 1/2 he is the father and the alternate is a randomly selected man. This calculation,

$$P(F \mid M) = \frac{1}{1 + g} = \frac{1}{1 + .017} = .983,$$

coincides with the previous calculation because of a mathematical fact that for small values of x, $1/(1 + x)$ can be approximated[14] by $1 - x$.

Since the laws concerning paternity and the admissibility and weight given to blood test evidence vary among the states, we only mention a few interesting developments. The history of the acceptance of blood group evidence in North Carolina parallels that of California. Courts had held that determining parentage is not exclusively a subject for expert evidence, and in *State v. Camp*[15] the state supreme court rejected a court of appeals holding that a blood grouping test establishing *exclusion* was conclusive. In the actual case, the ABO system was used and the mother had type O and the baby type A. Thus, the father must be an A or AB. The accused was a type O. After criticism, including a dissenting opinion, the legislature enacted a new statute.[16]

At this time, blood group tests excluding an accused man from being a possible father are well accepted, e.g., *Little v. Streater*.[17] Legislatures and states have been somewhat reluctant to give the plausibility of paternity dominant weight. In *Crain v. Crain*[18] the court held that the HLA test should be considered along with other evidence, and a Texas court[19] noted that results showing a high probability of parentage standing alone do not necessarily equate with a preponderance of the evidence. On the other hand, a recent case *Machacek v. Voss*[20] upheld a Minnesota statute permitting a temporary award of child support if the plausibility of paternity is at least .92, or 92%.

Comments. (1) Although some commentators (Williford, 1980) have written,

> "The calculation of the likelihood of paternity assumes that the alleged father and a random male with the same characteristics as the alleged father had an equal opportunity to father the child, an assumption which is nearly always incorrect, but which gives the putative father the benefit of the doubt. The defendant is accorded the fullest possible protection: the statute makes the issue of paternity conclusive in his favor if the blood test excludes him, and properly conducted tests for calculating the likelihood of paternity are extremely reliable."

the general claim that the accused male is being given the benefit of the doubt is questionable. While a study in Poland indicated that the prior probability (π) of an accused man being the father was about .70 and another study in the U.S. indicated that it was about .60 (Ellman and Kaye, 1979), these results are based on the assumption that *all accused* men have the same prior probability of being the father. From a statistical view, this assumption that the cases studied can be considered as a random sample from a fairly well-defined population, say men who had sexual relations with an unmarried woman who subsequently became pregnant, is questionable. Indeed, the *Chaplin* case suggests that a woman who had relations with more than one man may well accuse the one who has the greatest ability to pay, rather than the man who most likely is the true father. From a legal view, Ellman and Kaye (1979) note that using a prior probability determined from previous cases would at best be an average figure for all paternity cases in general, and its application in a *particular* case would be debatable. They suggest that evidence such as the frequency with which paternity actions or even breach of contract claims were ultimately sustained in previous cases would be rejected as irrelevant and prejudicial.

(2) On the other hand, some of the criticisms of blood group testing may be too strong. Following the logic of Tribe (1971), Ellman and Kaye (1979) note that even if $g = .05$, the probability a particular accused man is the true father depends on the size of the population to which the inclusion probability applies. They indicate that in a major metropolitan area with two million eligible men, the size of the pool of included men (possible fathers) would be

$$(.05) \times 2 \times 10^6 = 100,000.$$

Implicit in their calculation is the assumption that all two million men are equally likely to have had access to the mother during the relevant time period of about four months. While they are correct in stressing the importance of the number of potential fathers, it seems preferable for a court to try to establish the actual pool of potential fathers and have *all* of them tested. This would ensure that the genetic characteristics of the accused would be compared with the relevant genetic pool. In particular, the problem of relatives as alternative fathers would lessen the bias against the defendant of the calculation (12.10) based on the random man alternative. Indeed, a rather unique case where all possible fathers were tested is described in the next subsection.

d. Related cases and developments

As more blood cell systems and appropriate antigen tests for them are discovered, the probability of exclusion of a falsely accused man on the basis of biological tests for all systems combined becomes quite close to 1.0. These exclusion probabilities are given in Table 12.7, which reports the *average* probability, assuming that the mother and father are ran-

TABLE 12.7. The Average Probability of Exclusion of Non-Father Using Various Blood Systems

System	Chance (%)
Red cell antigens	
MNSs	32.1
Rh	28.0
Kidd	19.0
Duffy	18.0
ABO	17.6
Kell	3.3
Lutheran	3.3
Serum proteins	
Gc	24.7
Hp	17.5
Glm	6.5
Km	6.0
Red cell enzymes	
Phosphoglucomutase	25.3
Erythrocyte acid phosphatase	21.0
Glutamate-pyruvate transaminase	19.0
Glyoxalase	18.4
Esterase D	9.0
Adenylate kinase	4.5
Adenosine deaminase	4.5
HLA	94.0
Total for all systems combined	99.7

Source: Table 1 from Dodd (1986).
Note: The probability reported is an averaged overall possible mother and child combinations, i.e., assuming the parents' genes are randomly selected from the gene pool, there is a well defined probability distribution for possible blood groups of the mother and child. For each such blood group combination there will be a probability (g_i) of excluding a random man. The average of these g_i (weighted by the probability the mother–child combination is in the ith category) is given in the table.

domly selected from their racial group. It is important to distinguish these average probabilities from the *conditional probability* (12.9), which incorporates the mother's blood group in calculation. In this section we illustrate the use of blood group analysis in an unusual rape case and discuss the potential use of DNA-fingerprinting in identification cases.

An Unusual Forensic Application[21]

A severely mentally handicapped young woman, S, aged 16 who was a resident of a special home in England appeared to be pregnant. This came as quite a surprise to the staff of the home due to her extremely limited capability to be by herself.

Due to the potential mother's condition, her pregnancy was terminated and the fetus examined to verify the most likely period of conception and to make serological tests. Because of the limited number (36) of men who possibly could have had access to S and the fact that about 90% of all men could be excluded based on appropriate tests, all 36 were asked to submit to serological tests and all agreed.

The results of the test excluded all but four men and a further enzyme test excluded one more reducing the potential list of suspects to three. The police were happy with the results because their prime suspect was among the three, while the other two had been categorized as "highly unlikely." The prime suspect was another patient in the home who had a less severe mental handicap than S and who could readily move about the home. The net result of the investigation was not a court proceeding but some restriction on this patient's movements within the home. The major value of the blood tests in this case was the elimination of innocent men from the list of suspects.

DNA Fingerprinting

Dodd (1986) reports the use of DNA fingerprinting to identify people. The technique is based on the fact that characteristics of several highly variable genetic loci can be determined simultaneously. In the ABO system, one can inherit only an A or B or neither gene, but in a more highly variable loci, one might have ten possibilities so that the gene frequencies for each phenotype are much smaller than those (p, q, r) reported in Table 12.5. Consequently, if several *independent* loci are analyzed the inclusion probability (g) is of the order of magnitude of one in a billion (a chance match of two persons is about 3×10^{-11}).

The major advantage of this approach is that even close relatives can be distinguished so that paternity and maternity cases can be resolved. A chance match of siblings at all of the loci usually tested is about 6×10^{-6}, which, while much larger than the chance match of two random persons, is extremely small.

The technique was used by the British Immigration Service who first refused entry to a boy from Ghana on the basis that the woman claiming him as her son might not be his mother. The serological tests typically used in paternity cases indicated that only 1% of all women could be his mother and the woman was included in that category. However, the authorities asserted that she might be his aunt so the usual calculation would be erroneous. DNA fingerprinting showed that only six in a million sisters could share all the maternal specific genetic characteristics of the child that the woman possessed. On this basis the mother-son relationship was established and the boy was allowed into the country.

In this section we have assumed that all the tests were carried out accurately. This is obviously the ideal case. A theory incorporating accuracy rates, similar to that presented in Section 2, can be developed, but for many purposes it may be easier to require that the DNA tests be duplicated[22] (by an independent laboratory), as the outcome of a paternity case or rape investigation (based on comparing a stain on the victim's clothes with a suspect's blood or sperm) has far-reaching implications on the people involved.

Comment. The genetic advances described here have profound consequences for society. We have seen that they can do great good by clearing falsely accused persons or allowing a parent and a child to be reunited. On the other hand, errors in the laboratory, the statistical calculations or in the determination of gene frequencies can be quite serious. Discussion in depth of these ethical issues is beyond the purview of this book, but the readers should be aware of them as the ultimate decision on how these methods should be used is a societal one rather than a technical one.

Problems

1.   Assume that a mother has blood type O and the child A. Calculate the plausibility of paternity using formula (12.10). Is it sufficiently high that it should convince a court that the accused is the father of the child at issue? Explain.

2.   Assume that the mother in the previous question had blood type B and the child A. Would this affect your answer?

Answers to Selected Problems

1. From Table 12.6 we see that the exclusion probability is .519 or .52. Hence $g = 1 - .52 = .48$, so $P(F \mid M) = (1 + .48)^{-1} = .68$. In view of the verbal description and the Minnesota .92 criterion, by itself this probability is not very convincing.

2. No. The exclusion probabilities are the same.

4. The Probabilistic Characteristics of Evidentiary Standards and Insights Obtained from the Bayesian Approach

The standard for evaluating various degrees of proof are expressed in terms such as:

(1) the preponderance of the evidence;
(2) clear and convincing evidence;
(3) clear, unequivocal and convincing evidence;
(4) proof beyond a reasonable doubt.

They can be regarded as verbal standards that the conditional probability that an accused person is guilty, given all the evidence, must satisfy in order for a judge to find the accused guilty. The precise interpretation of these terms was examined carefully by Judge Weinstein in his opinion in *U.S. v. Fatico*.[23] We will discuss this opinion in this section and then show how the risks, α and β of the two types of error, convicting an innocent person or failing to convict a guilty one, and the prior probability of guilt affect the ultimate inference. The implications for civil actions are also discussed. In the second subsection, we remind the reader that the *p*-value of a statistical test *cannot* be interpreted as the probability the alternative hypothesis is correct and give examples of this type of misinterpretation. In order to reach this type of conclusion, one needs to incorporate prior probabilities for the truth of the competing hypotheses.

a. U.S. v. Fatico

This case involved the sentence that was to be given defendant Fatico, who pleaded guilty to a conspiracy charge related to receiving stolen goods and who was alleged to be a member of the "Gambino family" a reputedly mafia-like group. To support this allegation, which if true would subject the defendant to a longer sentence than otherwise, the government proposed to rely on the testimony of an FBI agent, which was based on information supplied by an informant whose identity could not be revealed. At the original trial in district court, the judge would not admit this testimony as it appeared to conflict with the Fifth Amendment right to due process and the Sixth Amendment right of confrontation. The court of appeals reversed this aspect of the lower court's decision because there was good reason not to disclose the identity of the informant and the information was subject to corroboration by other means. The opinion[24] discusses the standard of proof needed in sentencing cases, noting cases in which courts required the state to demonstrate that a fact which was *critical to the sentencing decision* had to be established by "clear, unequivocal and convincing evidence" or "clear and convincing evidence," instead of the usual standard of "beyond a reasonable doubt" in criminal cases.

In order to ascertain how other judges assessed the four types of standards of proof, Judge Weinstein surveyed his fellow district court judges whose probabilities, expressed as percentages, are given in Table 12.8. The results in the table indicate that almost all the judges interpreted "preponderance of the evidence" as meaning slightly over 50% and agreed that the four standards given at the beginning of the section were

TABLE 12.8. Probabilities Associated with the Various Standards of Proof by the Judges in the Eastern District of New York

Judge	Preponderance (%)	Clear and convincing (%)	Clear, unequivocal and convincing (%)	Beyond a reasonable doubt (%)
1	50+	60–70	65–75	80
2	50+	67	70	76
3	50+	60	70	85
4	51	65	67	90
5	50+	Standard is elusive and unhelpful		90
6	50+	70+	70+	85
7	50+	70+	80+	95
8	50.1	75	75	85
9	50+	60	90	85
10	51	Cannot estimate numerically		

Source: *U.S. v. Fatico* 458 F.Supp. 388 (1978) at 410.

listed in increasing order of the strength of the evidence needed to establish that they were satisfied. The numerical values of the probabilities, required for the stricter standards such as "beyond a reasonable doubt" varied considerably. Furthermore, the opinion noted that Underwood (1977) had reviewed a number of studies which indicated that judges as well as laymen may not always make the fine distinctions between the four types of evidentiary standards. These studies indicated that more than 50% probability was often required for "preponderance" but that while most persons distinguish between the standards, they assign a relatively small range of numerical probabilities to them.

In evaluating the government's evidence of Mr. Fatico's connection with the "Gambino family" introduced at the subsequent sentencing hearing, which included the additional testimony (not offered at the original trial) of seven *different* agents who relied on a total of 17 *different* informants that the defendant was a member of the "family," as well as independent police observations of the defendant consorting with criminals, Judge Weinstein noted, "Even if one or several of these experienced agents miscalculated the reliability of an informant, the large number of agents and informants greatly reduces the margin for error." He concluded that there was at least an 80% probability that the defendant was a member of an organized crime family and that the government had met its rigorous burden of "clear, unequivocal and convincing evidence."

We now show how the judge's probability assessment can be obtained from the Bayesian paradigm. In particular, we will see that if his prior probability (π) that the defendant was a member of a crime family was at least .20 and the accuracy of an identification by an FBI agent is at least .60, the posterior probability that the defendant is a member of a crime family given the *seven independent* identifications is at least .80.

We shall assume that the accuracy of each agent is r, i.e., the probability that an FBI agent would *correctly* assess the information they received from informants equals r and that the judge has formed a prior probability, π, of the defendant's being a member of a crime family from the evidence introduced at the original trial. From the opinion, it is apparent that based on the evidence submitted at the first trial, the judge put a value less than one half on π. To evaluate the effect of the seven agent identifications, each relying on *independent informants,* we observe that the probability that all seven agents would be correct[25] is r^7, while the probability all would be incorrect is $(1 - r)^7$. Thus, this problem is logically identical to the medical screening problem once we equate the probability of a correct collective identification given guilt with the accuracy r_1, i.e., $r_1 = r^7$, and the probability of an erroneous identification given innocence as $1 - r_2$ with the probability all agents were wrong, i.e., $1 - r_2 = (1 - r)^7$. If we let D denote the event the defendant is a member of a crime family and S the event that seven agents independently identified him as a member, then formula (12.3) yields

$$(12.12) \quad \frac{P(D \cap S)}{P(D \cap S) + P(\overline{D} \cap S)} = \frac{\pi r^7}{\pi r^7 + (1 - \pi)(1 - r)^7},$$

as $P(D \cap S) = \pi r^7$ and $P(\overline{D} \cap S) = (1 - \pi)(1 - r)^7$.

Table 12.9 reports the posterior probability (12.12) for various choices of π and r. Notice that the accuracy of *each agent* must exceed .5 in order for the identification to increase the posterior probability, i.e., to be of any help to the prosecution. However, once the accuracy of an individual identification reaches .65, even if the judge's prior probability is .10, the posterior probability is nearly .90. Once the accuracy of an agent's identification is .75 or more, if seven agents relying on independent information reach the same conclusion, the posterior probability exceeds .99 for any prior probability of at least .10 or more. We see that the judge's conclusion of at least a probability of .80 that the defendant is a member of a crime family given the new evidence is consistent with a belief that, based

TABLE 12.9. Posterior Probability That the Defendant was a Member of a Crime Family Given that Seven Independent Agents so Identified Him as a Function of the Prior Probability (π) and the Accuracy (r) of the Identifications

Prior Probability (π)	Accuracy						
	0.500	0.550	0.600	0.650	0.750	0.800	0.900
0.10	0.100	0.312	0.655	0.894	0.996	0.999	1.000
0.20	0.200	0.505	0.810	0.950	0.998	0.999+	1.000
0.30	0.300	0.636	0.880	0.970	0.999	0.999+	1.000
0.40	0.400	0.731	0.919	0.981	0.999	0.999+	1.000
0.50	0.500	0.802	0.945	0.987	0.999+	0.999+	1.000
0.60	0.600	0.859	0.962	0.991	0.999+	0.999+	1.000
0.70	0.700	0.905	0.976	0.994	0.999+	0.999+	1.000
0.80	0.800	0.942	0.986	0.997	0.999+	0.999+	1.000
0.90	0.900	0.973	0.994	0.999	0.999+	0.999+	1.000

Note: The posterior probabilities were calculated from formula (12.12).

on the prior trial, there was only a .20 probability the defendant was a member of a crime family and each agent is accurate at least 60% of the time.

Comments. 1) Our analysis assumed that each agent's assessment was formed from independent informants as indicated in the formal opinion. Had the agents used the same data or conversed with one another before reaching their conclusions, the assessments would not be statistically independent and the results may be quite different. We explore this point later in Section 7.

2) Our analysis ignored the police observations, as the number of them was not given. If we considered these as the equivalent of one more agent, eight would replace seven in formula (12.12) and the posterior conditional probabilities in Table 12.9 would increase, giving further logical support to Judge Weinstein's conclusion.

3) We assumed that the seven agents who presented testimony were all the agents involved in the identification process. If other, say three, agents who investigated the defendant's criminal ties concluded he was not a member of a crime family, but their testimony was not presented, then our value of r_1 would be incorrect, as r_1 would have been the probability that at least seven out of ten agents made the identification. This would lower the posterior probability given in formula (12.12).

4) One might question our choice of $r_1 = r^7$ and $r_2 = (1 - r)^7$ on the basis of the fact that before the government decided to press the charge it obtained the agents' assessments. Thus, one might wish to incorporate the fact that all the agents agreed. Thus, either they were all correct or all incorrect. As this uniformity of opinion occurs with probability $r^7 + (1 - r)^7$, one could redo the analysis by taking r_1 as $r^7/[r^7 + (1 - r)^7]$ and r_2 as $(1 - r)^7/[r^7 + (1 - r)^7]$. The nature of our conclusions will not be changed, but the precise values of π and r needed to satisfy the condition that the posterior probability exceed .8 would change.

b. Further examination of the meaning of p-values and statistical significance

In the hypothesis testing framework one tests whether or not observed data is *consistent* with what we would expect to observe if the null hypothesis were true. The *p*-value is the probability, calculated assuming the null hypothesis is true, of observing data at least as far from its expected value as the actual data is. This probability is calculated *assum-*

ing the probability distribution specified by the null hypothesis. However, we cannot determine the probability that the null hypothesis is true (or false) from such a calculation. We can only say that if it were true, a very unlikely (or likely) event occurred. This mistake occurred in an opinion which we will discuss in Chapter 14 because it treated scientific evidence quite carefully. We use the following quote as an example of how statistical significance can be misinterpreted even in a well-reasoned opinion:[26]

> The scientific papers and reports will often speak of whether a deviation from the expected numbers of cases is "statistically significant," supporting a hypothesis of causation, or whether the perceived increase is attributable to random variation in the studied population, i.e., to chance. The mathematical tests of significance commonly used in research tend to be stringent; for an increase to be considered "statistically significant," *the probability that it can be attributed to random chance usually must be five percent* or less ($p = 0.05$). In other words, if the level of significance chosen by the researcher is $p = 0.05$, then an observed correlation is "significant" if there is 1 chance in 20—or less—that the increase resulted from chance. . . . Whether a statistical increase or relationship is "significant" depends first upon what arbitrary level of significance a researcher has selected in analyzing the data. A researcher selecting an arbitrary level $p = 0.05$ has determined that where the probability is 1 in 20 that something resulted from random chance (and conversely, that the probability is 19 out of 20 that it did not result from chance), the relationship will be deemed "significant"; where, for instance, the probability is 1 in 19 that events happened by chance ($p = 0.0526$), the relationship will be deemed statistically "insignificant"—even though the probability is 94.73% or 18 chances out of 19 that the observed relationship is not a random event. Though deemed "insignificant" by the researcher, the certainty that the observed increase is related to its hypothetical cause rather than mere chance is still far more likely than not.

The mistake here is interpreting the finding of a nonsignificant result as the probability that it can be attributed to chance and a nonsignificant result as the probability that the data did not arise from chance. The *p*-value of the data is the probability that an event in the set, C, of all possible observations at least as far from the expected value (assuming the null hypothesis) occurred, calculated using the probability distribution determined by the null hypothesis. One *minus* the *p-value* is just the probability of the set $\overline{C}$, the complement of C, again calculated *assuming the null hypothesis is true*. It is *not* the probability that the result did not arise by chance, because all probabilities of events are their probabilities of occurrence under the assumed chance (null hypothesis) model.

To further illustrate the point, suppose we wish to test whether a new coin is fair, i.e., a head has probability $p = 1/2$ of being the side facing upward after a fair toss. If we toss a coin ten times and agree to reject this null hypothesis if 0, 1 or 9, 10 heads occur, the significance level we are working with is .0214. The complement $\overline{C}$ contains the values 2, 3, ..., 8. If any of these occur, we will accept the hypothesis that the coin is fair. From the binomial formula we can calculate $P(C)$ and $P(\overline{C})$ before we do the experiment, assuming either that the coin is fair ($p = 1/2$) *or* assuming the coin is unfair, say $p = .8$. The probability of observing an event in the region C under the alternative hypothesis ($p = .8$) equals .4832 and is the power of the test (two-sided). Again, this is *not* the probability that the alternative is true, it is the probability of observing an event in the critical region, C, when the alternative $p = .8$ is true. In hypothesis testing we desire to find a region C in the sample space which has

(1) a low probability when the null hypothesis is true, and
(2) a high probability when the alternative is true.

Then, if an event in C occurs, we feel confident that the null hypothesis does not explain the data as well as the alternative does, i.e., the observed data is far more likely to occur when the alternative is true than if the original null hypothesis were true.

We should note that later in the same opinion the judge demonstrates his awareness of the problem of testing at a prespecified significance level, α, e.g., $\alpha = .05$, and of sample size considerations when he states[27]

The cold statement that a given relationship is not "statistically significant" cannot be read to mean "there is no probability of a relationship." Whether a correlation between a cause and a group of effects is more likely than not—particularly in a legal sense—is a different question from that answered by tests of statistical significance, which often distinguish narrow differences in degree of probability.

The inherent limitations in the concept of statistical significance are particularly important to the evaluation of statistical studies of relatively small populations, or groups of subjects.

In a large population, random variables tend to cancel each other out, yielding an overall observed distribution that is far more useful in evaluating correlations, relationships and probabilities.

Furthermore, at the end of the previous quote, Judge Jenkins realizes that insisting on significance at a pre-set level, e.g., $\alpha = .05$, is too rigid. This view is consistent with the use of the p-value as described by Judge Higginbotham in *Vuyanich*.

The Bayesian framework begins by placing a prior probability *on the null hypothesis being true* or a prior distribution on the *parameter* of interest. Because it begins with this prior probability, which is updated after the data is observed, we have a new estimate of the probability the null hypothesis is true or on the distribution of the parameter of interest *given* the observed data.

Inherent in the Bayesian approach is a reasonably accurate initial assessment of the prior probability distribution of the parameter of interest. In *Fatico*, this parameter was the probability, π, the defendant belonged to a specific crime family. Thus, the approach is quite useful in applications where there is sufficient prior knowledge. In *Fatico*, the judge had seen the evidence from the first trial and could form his initial assessment. If several judges could have reached much different prior probabilities from the same evidence, then the Bayesian approach may not be appropriate, unless one can show that the result would be the same using each one's prior probability. From Table 12.9, this could have occurred in *Fatico* as long as the prior probabilities exceeded .2 and all judges agreed that each agent would have an accuracy of at least .6.

Problems

1.* (This problem requires some calculation. Readers who are less interested in the computations should read the results and see that they make sense.)

Suppose that the FBI sent N agents to independently check on defendant Fatico and j of them determined he was a crime family member.

(a) Using the binomial formula find the posterior probability that the defendant is a member.

(b) Show that as j (the number of agents making the identification) increases the posterior probability of the defendant being a member increases, provided $r > 1/2$. Does this make sense intuitively? Explain.

(c) From the answer to part (a) show that when only half ($N/2$) of the agents make the identification the posterior probability decreases. Does this make sense intuitively? You can assume N is even for this problem.

(d) How reasonable is the assumption that the accuracy (r) is at least .5? How might one try to verify this fact? How might a defense lawyer try to question it?

2.   Baldus and Cole (1980) present a number of illustrations of the misinterpretation of statistical significance in equal employment cases. Read three of these cases and determine the statistical inaccuracy.

Answer to Selected Problems

1.   (a)

$$\frac{\pi \binom{N}{j} r^j (1 - r)^{N-j}}{\pi \binom{N}{j} r^j (1 - r)^{N-j} + (1 - \pi) \binom{N}{j} (1 - r)^j r^{N-j}}$$

$$= \frac{1}{1 + \dfrac{(1 - \pi)}{\pi} \left(\dfrac{r}{1 - r}\right)^j \left(\dfrac{1 - r}{r}\right)^{N-j}}.$$

   (b) If $r > 1/2$, $r/(1 - r) > 1$. As j increases $(r/(1 - r))^{N-2j}$ decreases, so the *denominator* in the probability (a) above *decreases,* so the probability *increases.* This makes sense, as the greater the agreement of knowledgeable assessors the more confidence we would have in their conclusion.
   (c) If $j < N/2$, $N - 2j > 0$, so $(r/(1 - r))^j$ has less of an effect than $(1 - r)/r)^{N-j}$, i.e., their product $((1 - r)/r)^{N-2j}$ will be *less* than *one,* as $(1 - r)/r < 1$ since $r < 1/2$. Intuitively, if the agents are accurate ($r > 1/2$) and the accused is a member of a crime family, more than half the agents should say so. If only half (or less) identify the accused, the evidence points towards his innocence.

5.   Bayesian Inference when the Prior Probability, π, Is Not Known at the Outset

In our earlier discussion of medical screening and similar procedures such as the polygraph, we assumed that the prior probability or background rate, π, was known. An error in this predetermined value can have a major impact on the ultimate inference, as was evidenced in our analysis of paternity cases. Sometimes we can show, as in our analysis of the FBI identifications in *Fatico,* that the final conclusion will be the same for all reasonable values of π. This is not always the case, so we will discuss two other approaches for incorporating uncertainty in our prior knowledge. The first assumes that each person has the same prior probability π of having the disease. This assumption is appropriate when we cannot distinguish between members of the population to be tested. In this situation we can estimate π from the data and derive a confidence interval for $\hat{C}$, the resulting estimator of $P(D \mid S)$.

The second approach is based on determining a prior distribution for π. While we might not wish to state that the fraction, π, of all persons to be tested who have the disease is .2, we might believe that it is near .2, perhaps evenly spread between .1 and .3. Similarly, a polygraph expert who tests persons accused of crimes might believe that *about* half of all people tested are actually deceptive. Rather than base our analysis on the assumption that $\pi = .5$, one might wish to assume that π has a distribution centered on π with a mode or peak at .5. One such frequency function is

$$(12.13) \qquad\qquad g(\pi) = 6\pi(1 - \pi),$$

which is graphed later in Figure 12.3. By combining this prior distribution π with our observations (data), we obtain a posterior distribution for the conditional probability $P(D \mid S)$ of interest. Section b illustrates this method. Recall that in the classical method of estimation, the estimate (sample mean or proportion) has a sampling distribution which we used to make inferences. The mean (center) of the sampling distribution of the estimate was our estimate of the parameter, and a confidence interval was obtained by considering the appropriate portion of the area under the curve describing its sampling distribution. The Bayesian approach uses the posterior distribution of the parameter which incorporates both the prior knowledge and the sampling variability to draw inferences about the parameter.

a. Estimation of the background rate, π, from the data on persons tested

When the test (medical screening or polygraph) is given to a moderate-sized sample (100 or more) of a large population, the proportion $\bar{p}$ of persons classified as having the disease is available to us. Note that $\bar{p}$ is estimating the probability, p, that a randomly selected person from the population will be classified as having the disease (or as deceptive). In terms of Figure 12.2 we see that

$$(12.14) \quad p = \pi P(S \mid D) + (1 - \pi)P(S \mid \overline{D}) = \pi r_1 + (1 - \pi)(1 - r_2).$$

Equation (12.14) states that the probability a person will be classified by the test in category S (having the disease) is the prior probability (π) they have the disease times the probability this will be accurately assessed *plus* the probability $(1 - \pi)$ they do not have the disease times the probability $(1 - r_2)$ they will be inaccurately assessed. Replacing the probability, p, in (12.14) by the sample proportion $\bar{p}$ and solving for π yields the estimate

$$(12.15) \qquad \hat{\pi} = \frac{\bar{p} + r_2 - 1}{r_1 + r_2 - 1}$$

for the prior probability or background rate of the disease. In turn, substituting $\hat{\pi}$ for π in formula (12.3) yields the estimate

$$(12.16) \qquad \hat{C} = \hat{P}[D \mid S] = \frac{r_1}{r_1 + r_2 - 1}\left(1 - \frac{(1 - r_2)}{\bar{p}}\right)$$

for the posterior probability. It can be shown that for large samples and accuracies r_1 and r_2 in the range .1 to .9 that $\hat{C}$ is a consistent estimator of the posterior conditional probability $P(D \mid S)$ and is approximately normally distributed with standard error[28]

$$(12.17) \qquad \left(\frac{r_1}{r_1 + r_2 - 1}\right)\left(\frac{1 - r_2}{p^2}\right)\sqrt{\frac{p(1 - p)}{n}},$$

where n is the size of the sample tested and p is given by (12.14). In practice one can use the sample proportion $\bar{p}$ for p in making a confidence interval for it, just as we used the sample proportion in making a confidence interval for the success probability in the binomial model.

We now apply these formulas to hypothetical data based on two actual studies.[29] The U.S. Secret Service has tested a substantial number of suspects with a polygraph and found that 50% ($\bar{p} = .5$) of these were classified as deceptive. We will assume that $r_1 = .89$ and $r_2 = .8$ as found in an Office of Technology Assessment (1983) study and that $n = 292$, the sample size of a similar study of Raskin (1986). From (12.16) we find that

$$\hat{C} = \frac{.89}{.89 + .8 - 1}\left(1 - \frac{.2}{.5}\right) = .774.$$

Thus, we would estimate the probability that a person classified as deceptive by the polygraph actually is as .774 or slightly more than three fourths. The standard error due to the estimation of the background rate, obtained from formula (12.17), is

$$\left(\frac{.89}{.69}\right)\left(\frac{.2}{.5 \times .5}\right)\sqrt{\frac{(.5)(.5)}{292}} = .030.$$

In the present application a one-sided confidence interval seems appropriate, i.e., we would like a 95% confidence interval stating that the conditional probability a person classified as being deceptive really is deceptive is *at least x*. Thus, we use the interval of the form

$$P(D \mid S) > .774 - (1.645)(.03) \text{ or } .774 - .049 = .725,$$

i.e.,

$$95\% \text{ CONF}(P(D \mid S); .725, 1.0).$$

Thus, we can be 95% confident that the probability a suspect classified by the U.S. Secret Service as deceptive truly is exceeds .725. Before discussing other implications of formulas (12.16) and (12.17), we emphasize the importance of the assumption that before we test anyone they all have the same but unknown prior probability (π) of truly being deceptive (or possessing the disease in the medical context). This implies that the suspects who are being tested by the Secret Service have similar amounts of evidence against them. In the medical screening example, this assumption means that all persons tested have the same probability of having the disease, e.g., they may be students in a school system at the time the disease affects the town and all can be presumed to have the same probability of being exposed.[30] Finally, we mention that we have assumed that the accuracies r_1 and r_2 are *known*. (When this assumption is relaxed to allow for sampling error in the determination of r_1 and r_2, the standard error of $\hat{C}$ increases.)

In order to assess the effect of the background rate (π) and the accura-

TABLE 12.10. The Estimated Posterior Probability and its Standard Error when $r_1 = .89$, $r_2 = .8$ and $n = 292$

Prior (π)	Expected Proportion ($\bar{p}$)	$\hat{C}$	STD($\hat{C}$)
.8	.752	.947	.0115
.7	.683	.912	.0151
.5	.545	.817	.0253
.4	.476	.748	.0333
.3	.407	.656	.0448
.2	.338	.527	.0625
.1	.269	.331	.0925

Note: The standard error of $\hat{C}$ is denoted by STD($\hat{C}$) and is calculated using formula (12.17).

TABLE 12.11.   The Estimated Posterior Probability and its Standard Error for Various Accuracy Rates When the Prior Probability is .7 or .3 and $n = 292$

Prior Probability $\pi = .7$

Accuracies r_1 r_2	Expected Value of $\bar{p}$	Expected Value of $\hat{C}$	STD($\hat{C}$)
.9 .9	.66	.955	.007
.8 .8	.62	.903	.020
.7 .7	.58	.845	.045
.8 .6	.68	.824	.047

Prior Probability $\pi = .3$

Accuracies r_1 r_2	Expected Value of $\bar{p}$	Expected Value of $\hat{C}$	STD($\hat{C}$)
.9 .9	.34	.794	.027
.8 .8	.38	.632	.052
.7 .7	.42	.500	.086
.8 .6	.52	.308	.086

Note: The expected value of $\bar{p}$ was calculated from formula (12.14), $\hat{C}$ from (12.16) and STD($\hat{C}$) from (12.17).

cies, we present the standard error (12.17) of the estimator (12.16) of the posterior probability in Tables 12.10 and 12.11 for various choices of π. In these tables the sample proportion $\bar{p}$ is taken to equal its expected value p given by (12.14). When both tests are reasonably accurate ($r_1 = .89$, $r_2 = .8$) Table 12.10 shows that the standard error is small, provided the background rate (π) is high, but increases as π decreases. This not only implies that the proportion of positive classifications that are false increases as π decreases, but the *uncertainty* in the estimate, $\hat{C}$, of $P(D \mid S)$ also increases. Thus, the doubts we expressed concerning the utility of polygraph testing (or a single medical screening test) in a population with a low background rate are reinforced when the variability of the estimate $\hat{C}$ is incorporated in our analysis. The results in Table 12.10 depend on the sample size, n, used ($n = 292$). The qualitative conclusions concerning the increases in the standard error of $\hat{C}$ as π decreases remains the same for any sample size (n).

Table 12.11 shows how the *expected value of $\hat{C}$ decreases* while its *standard error increases* as the accuracy of the diagnostic test *decreases* for any prior probability (π) or background rate. Even when the background rate equals .3, we note that the expected value of $\hat{C}$ is .5 when both accuracies equal .7. This means that we should expect 50% of the persons the test yields a positive result for are "false positives." Moreover, the standard error is quite large, .086. It is interesting to compare this standard error to an experiment consisting of tossing a fair coin the same number (292) of times. The sample proportion has expected value .5 and standard deviation

$$\frac{\sqrt{\frac{1}{2} \cdot \frac{1}{2}}}{\sqrt{292}} = .029.$$

Thus, the variability of the result of a diagnostic test or polygraph under these conditions is nearly three times that of tossing a fair coin. The reason for this is that the sampling variability of proportion of all tested persons whose results are "positive," the factor $\sqrt{p(1 - p)/n}$ in formula (12.17) for the standard error of $\hat{C}$ is multiplied by other factors which increase as p and the accuracies r_1 and r_2 decrease.

Comments. (1) The estimation of the prior probability π via formula (12.15) and the subsequent estimate of $P(D \mid S)$ is due to Steinhaus (Finkelstein, 1978; Solomon, 1966), who analyzed Polish paternity cases using these ideas. He did not incorporate the sampling error. As far as its use in an actual paternity case, Ellman and Kaye (1979) question the procedure, as it assumes that the prior probability (π) of the accused man being the father of the child in question is the same for all accused men.

(2) The application of these ideas in polygraph testing is summarized in Raskin (1986), and the standard error calculation is due to the author (1987). Again the assumption that all tested persons have the same prior probability might be questioned. Raskin's sample of 292 persons, however, was limited to persons whom he tested at the request of a defense lawyer so that they are a more homogeneous population than all persons tested by a polygraph expert.

(3) When the prior probability or background rate varies over the population to be tested, one may be able to divide the population into a few homogeneous subgroups and analyze each group separately. Alternatively one may assume that the prior probability varies from subject to subject, i.e., each individual's prior probability (π) can be regarded as one observation from a distribution of π specific to the population tested. The consequences of this approach are discussed next.

b. Bayesian inference based on a prior distribution for π

In order to focus on the main concepts, we will consider the screening test situation where both accuracies r_1 and r_2 are equal (to r). If we knew the value of the prior probability π, then the posterior probability $P(D \mid S)$ is

(12.18) $$P(D \mid S) = \frac{\pi r}{\pi(2r - 1) + 1 - r},$$

as both r_1 and r_2 in formula (12.3) equal r. Now we assume that π has a probability distribution which incorporates our prior beliefs and other evidence.[31] As the conditional probability (12.18) changes with π, it becomes a random variable with its own probability distribution.[32] To understand the role and effect of the prior distribution we examine several special cases.

In Figure 12.3 we graph three prior probability functions

$$g_1(\pi) = 1$$

(12.19) $$g_2(\pi) = 6\pi(1 - \pi)$$

$$g_3(\pi) = 2\pi$$

for the prior probability π, which lies between 0 and 1. Notice that $g_1(\pi)$ has mean 1/2 but gives equal probability to all values of π between 0 and 1.

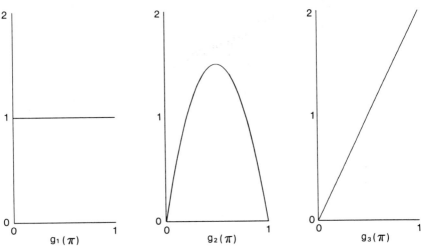

FIGURE 12.3.   Graphs of the three possible prior frequency functions given in Table 12.12 for the proportion, π, of the population possessing the characteristic D.

It can be considered as a prior probability distribution which indicates a lack of prior knowledge, as all possible values of π are given the same weight. The second function $g_2(\pi)$ also has mean 1/2, but it puts greater weight in the neighborhood of .5 than the previous prior. This can be seen formally by noting that the standard deviation of the frequency function $g_2(\pi)$ is .2236, while that of $g_1(\pi)$ is .2887. The third prior distribution gives more weight to larger values[33] of π and has mean 2/3 and standard deviation .2357.

Suppose we obtain a positive result on the screening test and calculate the posterior distribution for $P(D \mid S)$. Intuitively, this posterior distribution should differ from the prior one by putting more weight on higher values for the probability the tested subject has the disease. This is confirmed by examining the posterior distributions graphed in Figure 12.4 corresponding to accuracies $r_1 = r_2 = .8$. The formulas specifying them are presented in Table 12.12 and were derived by letting π have the respective distributions g_1, g_2 and g_3 in (12.19). Of course, had the test

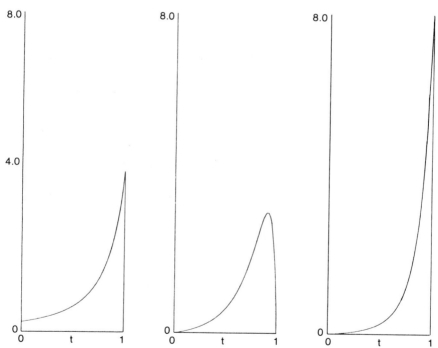

FIGURE 12.4. Posterior density function of the conditional probability $P(D \mid S)$ for the three prior distributions in Figure 12.3 when both accuracy probabilities equal .8.

TABLE 12.12.   Posterior Frequency Function of the Conditional Probability an Individual with a Positive Screening Test Result has the Disease for Each of the Three Prior Frequency Functions

Prior Frequency Function	Corresponding Posterior Frequency Function	
$g_1(\pi) = 1, 0 \le \pi \le 1$	$\dfrac{\dfrac{r}{1-r}}{\left(\dfrac{r}{1-r} - \dfrac{2r-1}{1-r}t\right)^2}$,	$0 < t < 1$
$g_2(\pi) = 6\pi(1 - \pi)$, $0 \le \pi \le 1$	$\dfrac{6t(1-t)\left(\dfrac{r}{1-r}\right)^2}{\left[\dfrac{r}{1-r} - t\left(\dfrac{2r-1}{1-r}\right)\right]^4}$,	$0 < t < 1$
$g_3(\pi) = 2\pi, 0 \le \pi \le 1$	$\dfrac{2t\left(\dfrac{r}{1-r}\right)}{\left[\dfrac{r}{1-r} - t\left(\dfrac{2r-1}{1-r}\right)\right]^3}$,	$0 < t < 1$

result been negative, the posterior distribution would put more weight on the lower probabilities than the prior one, as given the negative outcome the subject is less likely to have the disease than a randomly selected member of the population.

It is important to examine the influence of both the prior distribution and the accuracy r of the test. In Figure 12.5 we see that for the prior distribution $g_2(\pi)$ the posterior distribution has a larger mean or center and is more *concentrated* around its central value when $r = .9$ than when $r = .8$. This makes sense because a test with greater accuracy should leave us with less *uncertainty* in our posterior probability. Indeed, in Section 4 we realized from Table 12.9 that for any fixed value of π, the greater the accuracy, the greater was the posterior probability. Similarly, when we estimated π in the previous subsection we noticed that standard error of the estimate decreased as the accuracy of the test increased, irrespective of the value of π.

The posterior distribution enables us to make statements about $P(D \mid S)$ which are expressed in terms of probabilities by calculating the appropriate probability under the frequency curve, as we did with the normal curve in Chapter 2. Unfortunately, posterior distributions are usually not normally distributed, so the probabilities we need to obtain from them

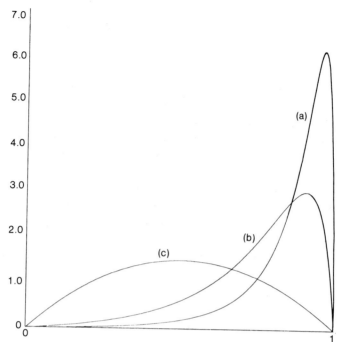

FIGURE 12.5. Posterior frequency functions of the conditional probability $P(D \mid S)$ when both accuracies are .8 and when they are .9 and the prior frequency is $g_2(\pi) = 6\pi(1 - \pi)$. The curve (a) for $r = .9$ is shifted to the right of curve (b) for $r = .8$, indicating that there is a higher probability that the individual has the disease when the accuracy rates of the test is higher. The prior frequency function is curve (c).

have to be specially calculated, i.e., no simple table such as Table A for the normal curve exists.

In our application, the Bayesian *analog* of a *confidence* interval, called the *highest posterior density (HPD) interval*,[34] is quite useful. We will illustrate the one-sided calculation using the prior distributions g_1 and g_3. The reason we want a one-sided interval is that we would like to make a statement analogous to a confidence interval, i.e., we desire to say that given our test result there is probability .9 (90%) that the probability a person for whom the test yielded a positive result has the disease is at least p (the appropriate probability). In Table 12.13 we present the *lower* endpoint of the HPD interval derived from the posterior distributions given in Table 12.12 and graphed in Figure 12.4 which corresponded to the prior distributions g_1, g_2 and g_3. As expected, the lower endpoints are larger when g_3 is the prior than when g_1 is, because g_3 reflects the situation in which we started out with a greater probability that the individual tested had the disease. Recall the mean of g_3 was 2/3, while both g_1 and g_2 had mean 1/2. The 90% HPD $(\pi; .5, 1.0)$ corresponding to the first posterior distribution in Table 12.12 when $g_1(\pi)$ is the prior and $r = .9$ means that after a positive test is observed we place 90% probability on the event "the probability the individual tested has the disease exceeds .5." Had we believed that $g_3(\pi)$ was the prior distribution, we would now put 90% probability on the event "the probability the individual tested has the disease exceeds .806."

When the lower end of the HPD is close to 1, we become more convinced that the individual truly has the disease. Another interesting feature of the results in Table 12.13 is that the lower endpoint is greater when the accuracy r is .9 than when it equals .8. This result makes sense because the effect of a positive result is to shift the prior probability to the right, i.e., the posterior probability density puts more probability on larger values of π than the prior did. The surer we are in the correctness of the positive diagnosis, the greater this change should be.

The same ideas can be used to obtain a posterior distribution for the parameter of interest in other statistical problems. For example, suppose we wish to make inferences about the probability π of success. We might believe that the success probability was about .5 but having some uncertainty we might use the prior distribution g_2. After observing k (e.g., 18) successes in N (e.g., 40) independent replications we could calculate the posterior distribution for the success probability. From it we could obtain

TABLE 12.13. Lower Endpoint of a 90% HPD Interval for the Posterior Probability $P(D \mid S)$ for the Three Prior Distributions g_1, g_2 and g_3

Prior	Lower Endpoint When Both Accuracy Rates = .9	Lower Endpoint When Both Accuracy Rates = .8
g_1	.500	.308
g_2	.687	.493
g_3	.806	.649

Note: When both accuracies equal .9 and the prior $g_1(\pi)$, giving all values between 0 and 1 equal weight is used, the lower endpoint of .5 implies that 90% of the area under the posterior density given in Table 12.12 and Figure 12.4b lies between .5 and 1.0.

a two-sided 95% HPD interval, say, and use it to check[35] whether the value (1/2) was in the interval.

There are several books on Bayesian methods listed in the references for the interested reader. The main advantage of the Bayesian approach is that it enables us to develop a posterior distribution for the parameter of interest after the data has been observed, which cannot be done in the standard framework. Remember that hypothesis tests are based on probabilities of observing the data calculated using the distribution of the statistic (e.g., $\bar{x}$) determined by fixed values of the parameter. On the other hand, the choice of the prior distribution affects our inference. This subjective aspect may make Bayesian methods less acceptable to courts and policymakers. An exploration of the effect of the prior distribution analogous to our discussion of the value of the prior probability (π) inherent in Judge Weinstein's decision in *Fatico* can help to minimize the impact of the choice of prior, as one can decide which of the priors used by the parties is more appropriate.

Comment. As the sample size increases, the effect of the prior on our inference diminishes. This can be seen by reworking the medical test situation by requiring two positive tests, as suggested by Dodd (1986). Then the posterior distribution for $P(D \mid S)$ becomes more concentrated. An interesting illustration of the sample size effect in the context of the binomial model used in the *Swain* jury discrimination case is given in Fienberg and Kadane (1983).

Problems

1. Why might persons who take a polygraph at the request of their defense lawyers have more similar characteristics than all persons who take a polygraph test?

2. Suppose an employer wishes to institute polygraph testing of *all* their employees. Suppose that 10% of the work force are truly deceptive and are potential cheaters. If both accuracies equal .8, find the estimated fraction ($\hat{C}$) of persons classified as deceptive who really are. Find the one-sided upper 95% CONF for $P(D \mid S)$. What implications do your results have for the routine use of the detectors on all employees? How might polygraph testing be a useful adjunct to an employer trying to minimize stealing?

6. The Importance of Checking the Assumptions Underlying the Calculation of a Probability: Implications for Legal Decisionmaking

There are several famous cases involving the faulty use of probability calculations in criminal cases. A common theme underlying these errors is the assumption that two events are *independent* of one another so that the probability that they both occur is the *product* of their respective probabilities of occurrence. Another error is the failure to accurately determine the probabilities of occurrence of each component, and a third error is forgetting that we are interested in the conditional probability of guilt, *given* the evidence, not the probability of the evidence per se.

In this section we first discuss the *Sneed* and *Collins* criminal cases. Then we study more carefully the effect of assuming independence when the events are dependent and illustrate its effect on both Bayesian and classical statistical approaches.

a.   State of New Mexico v. Sneed[36]

The defendant Joe Sneed was charged with the murder of his parents. The admissibility of probabilistic testimony at the jury trial which led to his conviction was challenged on appeal.

The following facts were introduced into evidence:

(1) The defendant had used the name "Robert Crosset" at Yuma, Arizona and at Seaside, California within a week of the night, August 17, 1964, of the murder.

(2) On the morning of August 17, 1964 someone purchased a .22 hand gun from a store in Las Cruces, New Mexico. The store sales register showed that the buyer was Robert Crosset, Box 210, Las Cruces, 5 feet 9 inches, with brown hair and brown eyes.

A professor of Mathematics conducted the following analysis:

(1) He examined telephone books of several western communities and estimated that the books contained about 1,290,000 names. He never found the surname Crosset but found that Robert appeared about once in 30 names. Therefore, he felt that the probability of Crosset being a surname was one in a million, and the probability of Robert being a first name was one in 30. Assuming the choice of first name is independent of one's surname, he concluded that the probability of a randomly selected person having the name George Crosset was one in 30 million.

(2) From the 35 buyers in the store register, he noted that 12 listed

brown hair and brown eyes while 12 of the 35 entries also showed a height between 5′8″ and 5′10″. Hence, he estimated that the probability a person was between 5′8″ and 5′10″ tall and had brown eyes and brown hair was about one in eight. Apparently, he had assumed that height and color of eyes and hair were independent as ◆

$$\frac{12}{35} \times \frac{12}{35} = .1176,$$

which is quite close to 1/8 = .125.

(3) Finally, he testified that the chance that two people would randomly select the same P.O. box number from 1000 numbers was one in 1000 (This calculation is correct if one assumes that an individual is equally likely to select any one of the 1000 numbers).

After estimating these probabilities, the professor multiplied them, obtaining a probability of one in 240 billion, and apparently interpreted it as meaning that the chance that someone else came into the shop and accidentally implicated the suspect as the purchaser of the gun was 1 in 240 billion.

The inference drawn from the mathematician's calculation was that the defendant purchased the gun. The appellate opinion questioned the validity of the calculation because

(1) The choice of characteristics used to define the purchaser was not described. (This is quite important, as the choice of other characteristics might have led to a higher estimated probability.)

(2) The determination of the probabilities was not justified. For example, the choice of one in a million for the probability of the surname Crosset was not explained. Secondly, the exhibits containing the date of purchase of guns from the store only contained ten names rather than 35, so the determination of the probability in step (2) of the professor's analysis was questionable.

(3) The opinion then held "that mathematical odds are not admissible as evidence to identify a defendant in a criminal proceeding so long as the odds are based on estimates, the validity of which have not been demonstrated" and reversed the conviction and ordered a new trial for the defendant.

Comments. (1) The basic thrust of the prosecution using such a calculation is that the probability of locating a person with the defined characteristics is so small that there is a very high probability that only one such person exists and he is the one charged with the crime. This conclusion depends on the size of the population to which this probability applies. Suppose each individual in the nation had a probability of one in 240 billion of being the "purchaser of the gun." As there are about 240 million persons we would expect to find .001 persons with these characteristics[37] in the population. The probability of interest to us, however, is not the probability that one such person exists but the

(12.20) probability there is only one such person *given* that
at least one exists, as we already know that the accused
is a person with the appropriate characteristics.

In the present case, if the prosecution's probability figure is correct, the desired conditional probability (12.20) would[38] be .999, which is rather convincing evidence that the defendant was the purchaser. However, we need to examine the estimation procedure and assumptions of independence made in the calculation. A moment's reflection should make one doubt that first and last names are independent. Not only do parents often think about how a child's name will sound, but different ethnic groups prefer different first names. Since the professor described his probabilistic estimates as conservative, we suggest an alternative method of obtaining an upper 95% CONF for the probability, p, of someone having the name Robert Crosset. Even assuming that the 1,290,000 names in the phone books examined were a random sample of all names in the population and no one had the name Robert Crosset, p would satisfy

$$(1 - p)^n = .05,$$

where $n = 1,290,000$. The solution is obtained as in Chapter 4 and is .0000023. Hence, the upper end of the CONF exceeds one in 30 million figure (.00000033) by a factor of seven. Again a confidence interval for the estimate of the probability of finding a person with the listed buyer's height and hair and eye color characteristics could have been constructed and the upper end of the interval used as an estimate of this probability.

(2) Perhaps more interesting than the statistical flaws are some logical ones. All these probabilities are calculated under the assumption of chance or random selection. Suppose someone wanted to frame the defendant and knew that he used the alias Robert Crosset as well as his height and coloring. Under this assumption there is a probability virtually equal to 1.0 that the defendant would fit the data in the store's register. Thus, one would need to ascertain whether there were other persons who might have a motive for the murder and knew the defendant. Only if this

possibility were eliminated could the calculations made by the prosecution have direct relevance. Furthermore, even if a correct conditional probability (12.20) yielded a probability .99 or higher, it would only show that the defendant purchased the gun, not that it was the gun used or that the defendant used it. Thus, ballistic evidence linking the gun sold by the store on the morning of the murder to the crime should have been submitted by the prosecution.[39]

b.   People v. Collins[40]

This is the classic case used to illustrate the misuse of the multiplication formula (Section 2.3) for independent events. The nonstatistical evidence was summarized in the opinion as follows:

> On June 18, 1964, about 11:30 a.m. Mrs. Juanita Brooks, who had been shopping, was walking home along an alley in the San Pedro area of the City of Los Angeles. She was pulling behind her a wicker basket carryall containing groceries and had her purse on top of the packages. She was using a cane. As she stooped down to pick up an empty carton, she was suddenly pushed to the ground by a person whom she neither saw nor heard approach. She was stunned by the fall and felt some pain. She managed to look up and saw a young woman running from the scene. According to Mrs. Brooks the latter appeared to weigh about 145 pounds, was wearing "something dark," and had hair "between a dark blond and a light blond," but lighter than the color of defendant Janet Collins' hair as it appeared at trial. Immediately after the incident, Mrs. Brooks discovered that her purse, containing between $35 and $40, was missing. About the same time as the robbery, John Bass, who lived on the street at the end of the alley, was in front of his house watering his lawn. His attention was attracted by "a lot of crying and screaming" coming from the alley. As he looked in that direction, he saw a woman run out of the alley and enter a yellow automobile parked across the street from him. He was unable to give the make of the car. The car started off immediately and pulled wide around another parked vehicle so that in the narrow street it passed within six feet of Bass. The latter then saw that it was being driven by a male Negro, wearing a mustache and beard. At the trial Bass identified defendant as the driver of the yellow automobile. However, an attempt was made to impeach his identification by his admission that at the preliminary hearing he testified to an uncertain identification at the police lineup shortly after the attack on Mrs. Brooks, when defendant was beardless.
>
> In his testimony Bass described the woman who ran from the alley as a Caucasian, slightly over five feet tall, of ordinary build, with her hair in a

dark blond ponytail and wearing dark clothing. He further testified that her ponytail was "just like" one which Janet had in a police photograph taken on June 22, 1964.

At the trial a mathematics professor presented the following probabilities of occurrence of the physical characteristics of the alleged assailants given above:

Characteristic	Individual probability
A. Partly yellow automobile	1/10
B. Man with mustache	1/4
C. Girl with ponytail	1/10
D. Girl with blond hair	1/3
E. Negro man with beard	1/10
F. Interracial couple in car	1/1000

Assuming these six characteristics are independently distributed in the population, the expert multiplied them obtaining a probability of one in 12 million that a randomly selected couple would possess these six characteristics. The prosecution emphasized this extremely low probability indicating that it implied that there was a similarly minute chance that a couple other than the defendants had these characteristics.

Before discussing the court's treatment of this testimony, we note that the population of couples to which this probability was not specified by the prosecutor. If only heterosexual pairs residing in the Los Angeles area in 1964 are considered possible suspects, the population might contain about one million couples. If all such pairs in the nation were considered as the possible perpetrators, then there may well have been 60–90 million such couples. Thus we would expect to find "1/12th" of a couple if the probability one in 12 million was applicable to the Los Angeles area but five to eight such couples in the nation. Thus, the implication of the prosecution is contingent on the pool of potential perpetrators.[41]

The opinion noted three basic statistical errors:

(1) The basis for the determination of the probabilities of each of the six component characteristics was not presented.

(2) The independence assumption was not checked. (Indeed, the court observed that black men with beards and men with moustaches are not independent characteristics).

(3) The probability of interest is not the chance of finding a couple with these characteristics in the relevant area but the *conditional probability* of

finding another couple with these same characteristics *given* that Mr. and Mrs. Collins have them, i.e., the probability that this set of six joint characteristics will occur more than once among a population of N couples given that this set occurs at least once.

The court calculated this conditional probability as approximately .4 by assuming that the number N of couples who might have committed the crime equals 12,000,000 and that each independently had a probability of one in 12 million of possessing the six characteristics. This calculation has been questioned by Mosteller and Fairley (1974) because of its choice of N. They show that the conditional probability increases with the size (N) of the pool of suspects. Of course, we really do not know N and can only guess it. As Solomon (1966) notes, the court was not troubled by the use of probability and statistics but the fact that the prosecution employed it in an inadequate evidentiary manner and a logically irrelevant manner (the unconditional rather than the proper conditional probability was presented).

We now turn to a numerical illustration of the effect that lack of independence can have on a probability calculation and then illustrate how this error can occur in other contexts.

c. A mathematical illustration of the effect of dependence among events

In order to study the effect of dependence, we examine its effect on the distribution of the number of positive differences of the sign test described in Chapter 11. We assume that the differences, D, follow a standard normal distribution.

To allow for dependence we assume that the normal random variables are dependent. A simple model assumes that every pair of differences had the same correlation, i.e.,

$$\text{corr}(D_i, D_j) = \rho,$$

where ρ is the common correlation. We know that this means that using any one difference used to predict another will enable us to reduce the variance of the prediction by ρ^2. Thus, a ρ of .3 which implies a reduction of about 10% ($.3^2 = .09$) could be considered moderate. In Table 12.14 we report the probability that all N differences $D_1, ..., D_N$ are positive for various choices of N and ρ. In the usual case of independence this probability is $(1/2)^N$, which approaches zero rather fast. Indeed, if all six differences in a sample of six were positive, a statistically significant result would be observed if a two-sided .05 level test criteria were adopted. Indeed the two-sided p-value would be .032. From Table 12.14 we see that if ρ only equals .1, a small amount of dependence, the p-value doubles, implying a less significant result. When $\rho = .3$, the p-value is in error by a factor of *five*. In all cases, the probability of the event *all differences are positive* calculated under the assumption of independence leads to an underestimate of the true probability in the dependent situation when the correlation between the events is positive.[42]

The above result has immediate relevance to the Collins case, as several of the six characteristics were dependent. While the degree of dependence between the characteristics is unknown, the probabilities presented in Table 12.14 indicate that the one in 12 million figure could easily be one in one or two million. Errors in the determination of the probabilities of the individual characteristics (corresponding to the probability that each difference is positive) could further increase this value.

It should be emphasized that the failure of the assumption of independence affects all inference procedures. The reader can verify this by examining the calculations presented in the *Fatico* case and making an adjustment to the probability all agents reach the same conclusion by multiplying the probabilities used by a factor of five, say, to account for dependence among the agent's sources of information. Of course, Judge

TABLE 12.14.   The Effect of Modest Dependence on the Probability of Obtaining all N Differences Positive for $N = 2, 3, 4$ or 6

Correlation	$N = 2$	$N = 3$	$N = 4$	$N = 6$
Independence ($\rho = 0$)	.250	.125	.0625	.016
$\rho = .1$	.266	.149	.087	.033
$\rho = .2$	.282	.173	.113	.055
$\rho = .25$	.290	.185	.126	.067
$\rho = .3$	.298	.198	.140	.081
$\rho = .4$	.315	.223	.169	.110
$\rho = .5$	.333	.250	.200	.143

Note: The variables $X_1, X_2, ..., X_N$ were assumed to have a standard normal distribution and were equally correlated with correlation coefficient ρ. The probabilities given are just the probability that all of the variables are positive and were obtained from Gupta (1963).

Weinstein's opinion specifically noted that the agents in the case had relied on *independent* informers.

d. *The potential effect of dependence between two screening tests on the interpretation of the results of both of them when blood is examined for antibodies to the AIDS (HIV) virus*

A recent article[43] reported the results of testing blood with two enzyme-linked immunosorbent assays (ELISA) tests to detect antibodies to the AIDS virus. The first ELISA test was based on the H-9 cell line, while the second was derived from the CEM-F cell line. The data is reported, in matched format, in Table 12.15.

The four samples in Table 12.15 that tested positive on both screening tests were retested with the Western blot procedure and were *negative,* i.e., the donors did not have antibodies. Although the persons with one positive and one negative screening test were *not* retested with the Western blot, the authors assumed that they were healthy so the entire sample will be considered as disease-free. This means that the false positive rate of the H-9 ELISA was 4/12,019 = .0034, while that of the CEM-F ELISA was .0044. Thus, the specificity of each test exceeded .995.

An interesting question is whether or not the error classifications of the two tests are statistically independent. If they were independent, then the chance that a healthy individual would test positive on both tests would be

$$(.0034) \times (.0044) = .000015.$$

TABLE 12.15. Positive and Negative Results on a Large Sample of Blood Donations Screened with Two ELISA Tests

| | | H9 ELISA | | |
		Positive(+)	Negative(−)	Total
CEM-F ELISA	Positive	4	49	53
	Negative	37	11,929	11,966
	Total	41	11,978	12,019

Source: Table 1 from Wartick, M. G., McCarroll, D. K. and Wiltbank, J. B. (1987).

This implies that among 12,019 donor samples given both tests we would expect to observe

$$12,019 \times .000015 = .18 \text{ or } .2$$

double-positive results. As there were *four* such classifications, we conclude that the tests are statistically dependent.[44]

Comment. The authors of the study interpreted this dependence between the results of both screening tests as meaning that they detected different populations of donors who would yield false positive results on only one of the tests. I believe further investigation is required before such a conclusion can be established. Indeed, if there were two distinct populations which yield false positive results on each test, one would expect the misclassifications of the two tests to be statistically independent of one another or even negatively correlated.

In order to obtain an idea of the size of the *correlation* between the ELISA-ratios of the two tests, we shall assume that they are normally distributed with correlation ρ. If one fits[45] the data in Table 12.15—assuming that both ELISAs have the same error rate of .004—one obtains an estimate of ρ of .40, while one obtains an estimate for ρ of .49 if one fits the data in Table 12.15 directly.

From our previous discussion of the polygraph and genetic tests for identification, the need for a second confirmatory test is apparent in order to ensure that the PVP (or $P(D \mid S)$) is sufficiently high to be useful. In order to demonstrate this point when populations with a *low* prevalence of AIDS were screened, Allen (1987) evaluated the PVP of a procedure requiring the confirmation of a positive screening test when the prevalence is .1%, i.e., $\pi = .001$ and the misclassification probabilities of the two tests were *independent*. In Table 12.16 we present the expected PVP if the test results were correlated with a ρ equal to .4 or .5. These values were chosen as a result of our analysis of Table 12.15, which is based on the results of two screening tests. The calculation[46] assumed that the accuracy rates, r_1 and r_2, of the screening test both equal .99, while the confirmatory test had perfect sensitivity ($r_1 = 1.0$) and various values of specificity (r_2) ranging from .99 to .999. The results in Table 12.16 show that even when a near perfect confirmatory test ($r_2 = .998$) is used in conjunction with an accurate screening test, a modest degree of dependence reduces the expected predicted value of a test from .98 to .80 or less. This implies that 20% of the persons classified as having the disease

TABLE 12.16. Expected Predictive Value of a Confirmed Positive Result When There is Correlation Between the Two Tests and the Prevalence of Disease is .001

	Expected PVP		
Specificity of Confirmatory Test	$\rho = 0$	$\rho = .4$	$\rho = .5$
.99	.908	.533	.435
.995	.952	.660	.556
.998	.980	.799	.712
.999	.990	.876	.812

Source: The author's calculations, which are similar to those in Allen (1987). The sensitivity and specificity of the screening test were assumed to equal .99, and the confirmatory test had sensitivity 1.0.

may not have it. Thus, the statistical independence of the components of any *multiple* testing procedure should be checked before assuming independence in calculations of the predictive value (positive or negative) of the procedure.

Comments. (1) In some situations a second screening test in lieu of a confirmatory one is deemed sufficient.[47] If the correlation, ρ, between the two screening tests is quite high,[48] the expected PVP can be substantially less than one might expect if one assumed independence. For example, in Table 12.16, if the specificity of the second test also equals .99, the expected PVP would only be .17 if $\rho = .87$. While this is still an improvement over the expected PVP of a single screening test (which is only .09), it clearly is too low to be relied on.

(2) The problem of a low expected PVP is diminished when the prevalence of the disease or trait in the tested group is *not* low. This is one reason why the polygraph may be useful to lawyers defending persons accused of criminal activity even if the results are not admissible in court. The prevalence of illegal activity among such persons is much higher than in the general population.

Problems

1. Read the way probability calculations for purposes of identification were treated in *U.S. v. Massey* 594 F.2d 676 (8th Cir. 1979) and *Hicks v. Scurr* 671 F.2d 255 (8th Cir. 1982). What appears to be the crucial difference in the factual circumstances of the two cases?

2. In *Hicks*, the plaintiff asserted that the probability his fingerprints would match that found at the scene of the murder was one in 30,240 and that he was prejudiced by an expert (for the prosecution) who claimed that the chance of another person having the same fingerprints was one in seven million. The court rejected his claim that this was a violation of due process.
    (a) Formulate a *prior* probability based on the other facts of the case, e.g., there was an eyewitness, and show that the Bayesian approach used in paternity cases would yield a posterior probability of guilt greater than .999 even if the plaintiff's value of the coincidence probability is correct.
    (b) How might one account for the lack of perfect overlap between fingerprints found at the scene and the fingerprints of the actual murderer?
    (c) Does your answer to part (a) make you question the appropriateness of the simple Bayesian calculation?
    (d) What other problems can you see in the fingerprint analysis used in Hicks?

3. Verify that proportions of false positive classifications yielded by each of the ELISA tests are *not* statistically different. Use the statistical test (11.15).

4. Look up the article by Sayers, Beatty and Hanson (1986). From their data does it seem that persons with higher ELISA ratios are more likely to be confirmed as having the disease than those whose ratios are nearer the cutoff value?

Answers to Selected Problems

2. (a) In the present case the prior probability would depend on the accuracy rate of an eyewitness identification. This depends on the facts of the case, such as the amount of light and the length of time the witness

saw the accused. From formula (12.10) we obtain the posterior probability

$$\frac{1}{1 + \dfrac{(1 - \pi)}{\pi} g},$$

where $g = .0000331$. In order for this to be less than .999, $g(1 - \pi)/\pi$ must exceed .001. This implies that $\pi/(1 - \pi)$ must be less than .0331. Further algebra shows that this is equivalent to $\pi(1 + .0331) \le .0331$ or $\pi \le = .032$. Thus, if one believed that the eyewitness had at least a 3% or 4% chance of being correct, the posterior probability would exceed .999.

(c) Yes, we would not wish to credit an eyewitness whom we didn't believe had a reasonably high probability of being correct, e.g., $r \ge .75$. Indeed, the veracity of the eyewitness helps one to overcome the logical distinction in part (b).

(d) The calculation of the posterior probability assumes that the murderer is a random person. In *Hicks* the two robbers were half brothers, so one needs to check whether fingerprint patterns among relatives are more similar than among two randomly chosen people. Otherwise, the calculation could suffer from the same flaw that can occur in paternity cases.

7. The Likelihood Function and its Use in Classical and Bayesian Statistical Inference

Most statistical problems are formulated in terms of drawing a conclusion about one or more parameters of interest. In epidemiologic studies, that parameter usually is the relative risk (or odds ratio) exposed persons have compared to those not exposed to the agent under study. This same parameter is of primary interest in discrimination cases where hiring or promotion rates of minority and majority applicants or employees are compared. In jury discrimination cases one evaluates whether the racial mix of jury venires is consistent with that of the eligible population in the jurisdiction by testing whether the proportion of venire persons is consistent with their fraction, p, in the population. In this chapter we have focused on problems concerning the parameter, π, a particular individual had certain characteristics, such as whether a man's blood group is consistent with that of a particular child. This application differed from previous ones in that the ultimate statistical inference concerns one individual rather than a group or population[49] and we had to introduce a prior probability (π) of that person possessing the characteristics. Although the inferences one can draw using classical and Bayesian methods are presented differently, they both depend on the concept of likelihood. In this section we discuss the concept primarily in the context of the binomial model.

a. The likelihood function and its relation to hypothesis testing

Recall that in testing the hypothesis that the parameter, p, of a binomial distribution $p = .5$ versus $p = .25$, a problem which might occur in testing whether women were fairly represented on a board which should represent the community, we computed the p-value of the data, which is the probability of observing as few or fewer women than were observed to be on the board. The likelihood approach focuses solely on the observed data itself *not* on other possible samples and computes the *probability* of the observed data under the relevant possible values of the parameter. The *ratio* of these two probabilities gives us an idea of their *relative* consistency with the data.

To continue the binomial problem of testing $p_0 = .5$ versus $p_1 = .25$, suppose that three successes are observed in a sample of ten. For any *value* of the parameter p, the probability of three successes in ten tosses is obtained from formula (2.21) and is

$$(12.21) \qquad\qquad \binom{10}{3} p^3(1 - p)^7 = L(\text{data}|p),$$

called the likelihood of the data (three successes in ten trials) as a function of p. It is a function of p, as the value of the likelihood (12.21) varies with p. Intuitively, it is reasonable to conclude that the value p for which the likelihood or *probability of the observed data is largest* is the most plausible value of the parameter. Indeed, this is one way to select an *estimate* of p, which is called the *maximum likelihood* estimate, denoted by $\bar{p}_{m\ell}$. Since it is unreasonable to expect any estimate of p to precisely equal it, we may evaluate the consistency of an hypothesized value of say p, say p_0, with the data by examining the ratio

$$(12.22) \qquad\qquad R(p_0) = \frac{L(\text{data}|p_0)}{L(\text{data}|\bar{p}_{m\ell})}$$

of the probability of the data, assuming p_0 is the value of p to the same probability assuming the parameter (p) equals $\bar{p}_{m\ell}$.

In the binomial example it can be shown that the maximum likelihood estimator $\bar{p}_{m\ell}$ is the *sample proportion* which we have been using to make inferences about the value of p. Again this confirms our intuition as the best estimate of p when three successes occurred in ten independent trials is 3/10. The ratio of the likelihoods (12.22) in our example becomes

$$(12.23) \qquad \frac{p^3(1-p)^7}{(\bar{p}_{m\ell})^3(1-\bar{p}_{m\ell})^7} = \frac{p^3(1-p)^7}{(.3)^3(.7)^7}.$$

This function (12.23) of p is called the relative likelihood function. In Table 12.17 we present the values of the likelihood and relative likelihood for our problem. Notice that the alternative value $p = .25$ has a higher likelihood than the null hypothesis $p = .5$, although the likelihood of the null hypothesis relative to the alternative is (.1172/.2503 = .47) is not so small to cause us (intuitively speaking) to conclude that the data is inconsistent with it. However, had the null hypothesis been $p = .7$, we might well conclude that the data is inconsistent with it, as the value of p as another value ($\bar{p}_{m\ell}$) is far more consistent with the data.

Both confidence intervals and tests of hypothesis are related to the likelihood or relative likelihood function. The *confidence* interval can be

TABLE 12.17. The Likelihood and Relative Likelihood of Observing Three Successes in Ten Independent Trials as a Function of the Probability (p) of Success

p	$L(p) = \binom{10}{3} p^3(1-p)^7$	Relative Likelihood
.05	.0105	.0394
.10	.0574	.2151
.15	.1298	.4865
.20	.2013	.754
.25	.2503	.9382
.30	.2668	1.0
.35	.2552	.9565
.40	.2150	.8058
.45	.1665	.6241
.5	.1172	.4393
.6	.0425	.1593
.7	.0009	.0337
.8	.0008	.0030
.9	.0001−	.0004−

Source: Calculated from formula (12.23).

regarded as those values p of the parameter for which

(12.24) $$R(p) = \frac{L(\text{data}|p)}{L(\text{data}|\bar{p}_{m\ell})} \geq c,$$

where c is a prespecified constant, e.g., 1/4. Similarly, many tests of an hypothesis can be expressed in terms of the ratio of the likelihood under the *null* and alternative hypotheses, i.e.,

(12.25) $$\frac{L(\text{data}|p = p_1)}{L(\text{data}|p = p_0)} = \frac{\text{probability of the data occurring if the alternative is true}}{\text{probability of the data occurring if the null hypotheses is true}}.$$

If this ratio is large we *reject* the null hypothesis in favor of the alternative because the data is not consistent with the null hypothesis, as it has much higher probability of occurring under the alternative.

Comment.   The likelihood ratio (12.25) is the same as the ratio $R(p_1)/R(p_0)$ of the relative likelihoods as the denominators of the *relative* likelihoods for $R(p_1)$ and $R(p_0)$ are the same. An advantage of examining the entire likelihood or relative likelihood function is that it indicates which values of the parameter p assign a relatively high probability to the observed data and hence are consistent with it. In situations where neither the hypothesized null or alternative values are correct, the graph of the relative likelihood function will reveal which one is closer to $\bar{p}_{m\ell}$, which should be near the true value of p.

Unfortunately, one cannot give a simple rule such as the values of p satisfying

(12.26) $$R(p) \geq .333,$$

are consistent with the data and should be regarded like a confidence region because the values of p which will satisfy (12.26) will change with the sample size even if $\bar{p}_{m\ell}$ remains the same, just as the length of a confidence interval decreases with the sample size. To illustrate this we present the relative likelihood function when 15 successes are observed in 50 independent binomial trials, as well as the one corresponding to observing three successes in ten trials in Figure 12.6. Notice that the relative likelihood function based on a sample of 50 is far more peaked.

Kaye (1982) uses the relative likelihood function to analyze the *Hazelwood* data discussed in Chapter 4. Under the binomial model assumed by

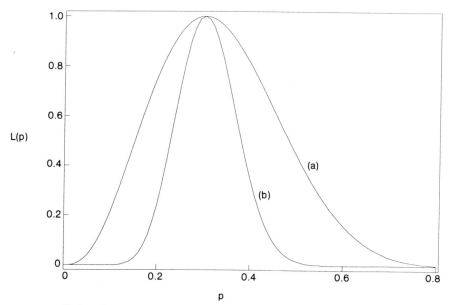

FIGURE 12.6.   The relative likelihood function for data showing three successes in ten trials (a) and for data with 15 successes in 50 trials (b). Both functions reach their maximum at $\bar{p}_{m\ell} = .3$, however, function (a) is more concentrated around .3, as it is based on a larger sample. Notice that the graph stops at $p = .8$ rather than 1.0 because both likelihood functions are essentially zero for values of $p \geqq .8$.

the Supreme Court, he notes that the relative likelihood of the null hypothesis ($p = .057$) for the minority fraction of all teachers residing in the area is only about one fifth. From this he questions the Court's suggestion that the data is consistent with the null hypothesis. His view supports Justice Stevens' demonstration that the blacks were under-represented if a one-sided .05 level criteria were used. Indeed, both the likelihood and hypothesis testing approaches indicate that the hiring data in *Hazelwood* is at least borderline evidence of discrimination. Only if one rigidly adheres to statistical significance at a preset level and ignores the power of the test do the two approaches yield conflicting inferences.

When a parametric model[50] like the binomial model is generally accepted as the appropriate way to examine data, the (relative) likelihood function should prove a useful tool. Although experts may debate whether tests of significance or the likelihood approach are more relevant for practical use, it may be preferable to present both analyses of the data. When the *power* of the statistical test, as well as the *p*-value, are presented in a hearing, along with a likelihood function, a comprehensive and consistent picture should emerge. The only time a null hypothesis will be accepted when its relative likelihood is small and the data seems to be from the alternative, is when the power of the test used is low. This should only arise in situations when the sample size is small or when a test of low power is being used instead of a more powerful procedure.

We conclude this subsection with a summary of the major features of the likelihood function and its relation to significance testing.

(1) Neither the likelihood nor a test of significance is capable of rendering a probability statement about the truth of a null hypotheses. All probability calculations are made assuming a value of the parameter. One needs to incorporate prior knowledge in the Bayesian framework to make a statement concerning the probability the null hypothesis is true *given* the data.

(2) Many tests of an hypothesis against a specific alternative are equivalent to deciding whether the likelihood ratio (12.25) is sufficiently large. This likelihood ratio is a statement of the relative likelihoods of the two hypotheses; these are logically different from probabilities. For instance, suppose we wish to test the null hypotheses $p_0 = .6$ versus $p_1 = .8$ in a binomial model, and we observe three successes in ten trials. From Table 12.17 we calculate the likelihood ratio (12.25) as

$$\frac{L(\text{data} \mid \text{alternative})}{L(\text{data} \mid \text{null hypothesis})} = \frac{.0008}{.0425} = .019 \simeq .02,$$

which would imply that the data is far more likely under the null hypothesis ($p = .6$) than if the alternative were true. The relative likelihood function (Table 12.17) indicates that the data is far more likely to occur when p is in the neighborhood of .3. Thus, the likelihood function shows the direction the data (evidence) is pointing to without any preconceived hypotheses. Moreover, the peakedness or spread of the likelihood function, as in Figure 12.6, reflects the uncertainty due to sampling.

(3) The relative likelihood function is a concise summary of the information obtained from the data and provides a comprehensible picture of it.

(4) The reliability of the likelihood function depends on the sample size on which it is based, just as the length of a confidence interval depends on the sample size.

(5) The likelihood function depends on the model the data is assumed to follow. Use of the binomial model rather than the hypergeometric will

lead to a different likelihood function. Thus, the same type of error we noted in Chapter 5 can occur using the likelihood approach. When the exact model is not known, as is the case with the emissions data in Section 11.5, we can make tests of hypotheses using procedures such as the Wilcoxon or sign tests, which are valid, but we cannot readily calculate the likelihood function.

b. The role of the likelihood concept in the Bayesian paradigm

In order to see the role of the likelihood function in Bayesian data analysis it is useful to re-examine the medical screening problem when both accuracies are equal (to r). If the person is diagnosed as having the disease, then the posterior probability is given by

(12.27) $$P(D \mid S) = \frac{\pi r}{\pi r + (1 - \pi)(1 - r)},$$

where π is the prior probability and is known to us, e.g., $\pi = .5$. Dividing both the numerator and denominator by $(1 - \pi)(1 - r)$, enables us to write (12.27) as

(12.28) $$P[D \mid S] = \frac{\dfrac{\pi}{1 - \pi} \times \dfrac{r}{1 - r}}{1 + \dfrac{\pi}{1 - \pi} \times \dfrac{r}{1 - r}}.$$

Now the factor $r/(1 - r)$ is the likelihood of our observation (the test indicates the person has the disease), since

$$L = \frac{P(\text{data} \mid D)}{P(\text{data} \mid \bar{D})} = \frac{r}{1 - r},$$

as $P(\text{data} \mid D) = r$, the accuracy or probability the test is correct, while $P(\text{data} \mid \bar{D})$ is the probability the test is inaccurate, which is $(1 - r)$. The factor $\pi/(1 - \pi)$ is the prior odds of a person selected from the population having the disease, as π is the prior probability of that person having the disease. Hence the posterior probability (12.28) of a person diagnosed as having the disease actually having it is

(12.29) $$P(D \mid S) = \frac{(\text{prior odds}) \times (\text{likelihood})}{1 + \{(\text{prior odds}) \times (\text{likelihood})\}}.$$

This means that the posterior probability depends only on the *prior probability* and the *likelihood* calculated from the data. Further algebra shows[51]

that the *posterior odds* of having the disease given the test so indicates is

(12.30) $$\frac{P(D \mid S)}{1 - P(D \mid S)} = (\text{prior odds}) \times (\text{likelihood}).$$

Equation (12.30) is a very important summary of a Bayesian analysis, as it states that the posterior odds equals the product of the prior odds and the likelihood.

Although our discussion assumes a fixed value of π, the result (12.30) generalizes to the case when π is assumed to have a distribution, as in Section 5b. Then the posterior distribution of the odds is the product of the prior distribution and the likelihood. Since several papers (Lindley, 1977; Fienberg and Kadane, 1983) have discussed Bayesian methods, their connection with the likelihood and the presentation of a Bayesian analysis in court, we refer the interested reader to them. When a prior distribution can be ascertained, or even if one of several prior distributions can be specified as reasonable, and the data fits a parametric model such as the binomial or normal, then the Bayesian approach is quite useful. Indeed, we saw this in our discussion of the *Fatico* case.

Comment.   One should be careful to avoid forcing *all* statistical problems into one framework. The Bayesian approach is most useful when one knows a substantial amount about the process generating the data and can formulate a sound prior distribution. It is less suitable when one has little background information or when one should not use it on legal grounds. For instance, if a particular minority or ethnic group were disproportionately represented in the population of persons convicted of a particular crime and an accused person was a member of that group, the right of the individual defendant to a fair trial might be severely compromised if one incorporates their group membership in the decision as to their guilt or innocence. Thus, a complete Bayesian analyses could not be carried out as some prior knowledge should not be used.

Recommended Reading

Sometimes parties in a legal action do not submit evidence that one believes they possess. The common sense inference is that this evidence would be adverse to their claim. Lindley and Eggleston (1983) show how the Bayesian approach agrees with our common sense concerning the failure of a party to submit evidence that they possess, i.e., it is most likely to be unfavorable to their claim.

Chapter Review Problem

Suppose that screening tests for recent drug use are 95% accurate. What are the implications of the results of this Chapter for proposed routine mandatory screening of employees? Assume that the prevalence of drug users among employees is in the range of 1% to 5%. How would your answer change if a second test were administered to those individuals who tested positive on the first test? Would you accept a second test which had an accuracy of 95% and whose errors were statistically independent of the first one? Read some of the cases listed in the references and discuss how the risk to the public plays a role in the decisions. Discuss the analogy between the drug testing decisions involving large risk to the public and the evidence needed to show "business necessity" in the equal employment context when public safety may be seriously affected.

NOTES

1. A recent letter from Mendenhill, C. L., Roselle, G. A., Grossman, C. J., Rouster, S. D., Weesner, R. E. and Dumaswala, U. (1986). *Journal of the American Medical Association* **314**, 921–922, noted that persons suffering from liver ailments which often are alcohol related have a higher incidence of false positive AIDS diagnosis. Moreover, women who have been pregnant also appear to have higher false positive rates on the AIDS screening test due to HLA antibodies as noted in Sayers, M. H., Beatty, P. G. and Hansen, J. A. (1986).

2. A summary of the expert testimony at the hearings is given in Holden, C. (1986).

3. We are making a simplifying assumption that a deceptive person is likely to steal and vice versa. By redefining the class D suitably, one can make it more restrictive, so the two categories become virtually identical. For purposes of exposition this is unimportant, but in actual application this distinction is quite important.

4. Quite often when the zygote is formed, the gene transmitted for one characteristic does *not* affect the genes that are transmitted for other characteristics. Thus, one can assume that the probability a person is of type 0 blood group and Rh positive is the product of the individual probabilities. This *independence* assumption must be checked. There is some literature in genetics indicating that genes for the various blood groups are at least pairwise independent (Grunbaum, Selvin, Pace and Block, 1978). Another expression used in genetics is that the genes for the two traits *sort independently.*

5. The term plausibility of paternity is not as strong a phrase as likelihood of paternity. Because of the assumptions that underlie its calculation, in actual cases the term plausibility is more appropriate, as it reminds us to assess the validity of these assumptions before we accept the calculated probability.

6. In the typical paternity case it is unrealistic to expect the mother to volunteer the names of all possible men, and the accused man is likely to understate his involvement with the woman. According to the study by Arthur and Reid (1954) the incidence of false reporting is quite high.

7. *Commonwealth v. Zammarelli,* 17 Pa. D and C. 229 (1931).

8. *State v. Damm,* 64 S.D. 309, 266 N.W. 667 (1936).

9. 74 Cal. App. 21652, 169 P.2d. 442 (1946).

10. Arias v. Kalensikoff, 10 Cal. 2d. 428, 74 P.2d. 442 (1946).

11. See Calif. Evid. Code 621 West. Supp. (1980) and the related cases *Kusior v. Silver*, 54 Cal. 2d. 603, 354 P.2d. 657 (1960) and *County of San Diego v. Brown*, 80 Cal. App. 3d. 297, 145 Cal. Rptr. 483 (1978) cited by Sterlek and Jacobson (1980).

12. Calif. Evid. Code 890–897.

13. 88 Cal. App. 3d. 873, 153 Cal. Rptr. 865 (1979).

14. In general $(1 + x)^{-1} = 1 + x + x^2 + \ldots$ if $x < 1$. For small x, x^2 is quite small so $1 + x$ is a good approximation to $(1 + x)^{-1}$.

15. 286 N.C. 148, 209 S.E. 2d. 754 (1974).

16. N.C. Gen. Stat. 8–50.1 (Cum. Supp. 1979).

17. 452 U.S. 1 (1980). This case held that an indigent defendant in a paternity suit has the right to a blood group test at public expense.

18. 104 Idaho 666, 662 P.2d 538 (1983).

19. *In re* E.G.M. 647 S.W. 2d 74 (Tex. Ct. App. 1983).

20. 361 N.W. 2d. 861 (Minn. 1985). The statute involved is Minn. Stat. 257.62(5) (Supp. 1983).

21. This case is described in Usher and Stapleton (1979).

22. Another practical reason for requesting independent verification of the results of these tests is that the sensitivity and specificity of the diagnostic test which were determined from careful analyses in the laboratory that developed it may be higher than the results of the test when it is used in the field. For example, it has been shown that the accuracy of urinalyses for drugs can be much less in the field than in the certification trials.

23. 458 F.Supp. 388 (E.D. N.Y. 1978) on remand from 579 F.2d 707 (2d Cir. 1978).

24. *supra*, note 23 at 404–411.

25. Since each agent has probability r of being correct under independence, the probability that all of them are is given by the product of the individual probabilities.

26. *Allen v. U.S.*, 588 F.Supp. 247 (1984) at 416.

27. *supra*, note 26 at 417.

28. The derivation of the standard error and conditions needed for the validity of the normal approximation are given in Gastwirth (1987).

29. The studies are reported in Raskin (1986). The sample size of the Secret Service study was not given, so we use the sample size of Raskin's study in our analysis.

30. In the medical diagnosis example, one might stratify the students into those who are in a family with a sick individual already and those who are not directly exposed via the family, and analyze the data for each group separately.

31. The determination of this prior distribution is the most controversial part in the application of Bayesian methods. Quite often, analogous to our treatment of *Fatico*, one can show that several reasonable prior distributions all lead to the same inference.

32. Since $P(D \mid S)$ is a function of π, it will take different values with probabilities determined by the probability distribution of π. While the functional relationship between $P(D \mid S)$ and π is more complex than we have previously seen, the basic idea is similar to the relationship between the distribution of the square (X^2) of a random variable and the distribution of the variable (X) itself.

33. The prior distribution obviously depends on the other background facts specific to each application. There is no reason it will be bell-shaped, much less normal, in all applications.

34. The term appears in Box and Tiao (1980) and is related to the notion that two-sided confidence interval or acceptance region of a test uses the middle portion of the sampling distribution where the density function of the sampling distribution of the estimator (e.g., $\bar{x}$) of the parameter (e.g., mean μ) is highest.

35. This use is analogous to the use of confidence intervals to test an hypothesis discussed in Chapter 3.

36. 414 P.2d. 858 (1966).

37. Here the expected number is np, where n is the sample (whole population) and p is the probability of a match (p = one in 240 billion).

38. The Poisson approximation of Chapter 10 yields this result as follows: P(exactly 1) $= \lambda e^{-\lambda}$ where $\lambda = np$, the expected number. P (at least one) $= 1 - P$(none) $= 1 - e^{-\lambda} = 1 - .999 = .001$. As P(exactly 1) $= .000999$, the conditional probability, which is the ratio of P(exactly 1) to P(at least 1) $= .999$.

39. These arguments are based on the questions raised by Tribe (1971).

40. 68 Cal. 2d. 319, 438 P. 2033 (1968).

41. The reader may note the similarity of this discussion to the pool of potential fathers in paternity cases.

42. If the correlation were negative, the probability that both events occur would be less than the result obtained from the product rule. In most applications, however, the correlation is positive (e.g., scores on the LSAT and law school grades).

43. Wartick, M. G., McCarroll, D. R. and Wiltbank, T. B. (1987).

44. If the tests were positively correlated, a positive result on one would increase the chance of a positive result on the other. An approximation test of the null hypothesis of independence versus the alternative of positive dependence can be based on the Poisson distribution in Chapter 10. Applying the statistic (10.10) yields

$$ Z = \frac{4 - .18}{\sqrt{.18}} = \frac{3.82}{.424} = 9.0. $$

This procedure is an approximate one because we estimated the Poisson parameter λ from the data and used the normal approximation. The authors of the study cited in footnote 43, obtained the same conclusion by a more formal method.

45. The method of fitting is to find the value of ρ which gives the closest value to $P(Z_1 > z_1, Z_2 > z_2) = 4/12,019 = .000333$ where Z_1 and Z_2 are the standardized ELISA ratios and z_1 and z_2 are the critical values of a normal curve. Under the assumption that both error rates are .004, an extended version of Table A shows that $z_1 = z_2 = 2.65$, the upper 99.6th percentile of a standard normal curve. The best fitting ρ was obtained from the tables in Gupta (1963). The estimate of ρ in the more general case was obtained by numerical methods by Dr. M. Goldberg.

46. The formal calculation is similar to that of (12.3). If we let A denote the event that the screening test is positive, B the event that the confirmatory test is positive, so that a person is classified as sick (S) only when $A \cap B$ happens, then

$$ P(D \mid S) = \frac{\pi P(A \cap B \mid D)}{\pi P(A \cap B \mid D) + (1 - \pi)P(A \cap B \mid \bar{D})}. $$

As the sensitivity of the confirmatory test was assumed to be 1.0, the term $\pi P(A \cap B \mid D) = \pi$. The dependence between A and B was assumed to follow the bivariate normal model with the cutoff or critical values set to yield the appropriate specificity. Recall that the confirmatory test is assumed to have very high, but not perfect, specificity.

47. This repeated procedure is sometimes used to check the accuracy of the breathalyzer (Nichols, 1983) and drug tests. References to cases involving drug tests are given at the end of the Chapter and in *Pella v. Adams* 638 F.Supp. 94 (D. Nev. 1986) at 97.

48. Indeed, a high correlation between the results indicate that the test procedure has a high reliability or consistency. This criterion is discussed extensively in the literature on test development cited in Chapter 8.

49. Usually we are concerned with using a sample to obtain knowledge about an entire population or about a difference between two populations. The rationale for using statistical data in a discrimination case involving an individual is that if the relevant group has been treated unfairly (fairly) the general pattern quite likely was applied to the individual.

50. A parametric model is one where the form of the distribution of the characteristic is known and we can calculate probabilities of interest once the parameters are known. For example, a normal distribution is specified once its mean μ and standard deviation σ are given. A binomial distribution is determined once the number (n) of trials and success probability, p, are given.

51. If we let θ denote the prior odds and ℓ the likelihood, then $P(D \mid S) = (\theta\ell)/[1 + (\theta\ell)$, and the odds corresponding to $P(D \mid S)$ are

$$\frac{\theta\ell/[1 + \theta\ell]}{1 - \dfrac{\theta\ell}{1 + \theta\ell}} = \theta\ell$$

as given.

REFERENCES

Books

Box, G. E. P. and Tiao, G. C. (1973). *Bayesian Inference in Statistical Analysis*. Reading, Mass: Addison-Wesley.

Fairley, W. B. and Mosteller, F. (1977). *Statistics and Public* Policy. Reading, Mass: Addison-Wesley.

Finkelstein, M. O. (1978). *Quantitative Methods in the Law*. New York: The Free Press.

Lerner, D. ed. (1958). *Evidence and Inference*. Glencoe, Ill: The Free Press. (An interesting collection of articles by leading scholars from a variety of disciplines on the nature of evidence and the logic underlying the inferential methods used in their areas.)

Lindley, D. V. (1971). *Making Decisions*. London: Wiley.

Lindley, D. V. (1965). *Introduction to Probability and Statistics from a Bayesian Viewpoint*. Cambridge, UK: University Press.

Shafer, G. (1976). *A Mathematical Theory of Evidence*. Princeton: Princeton University Press.

Articles on Statistical Inference and the Admissibility, Relevance and Reliability of Scientific and Probabilistic Evidence

Behringer, J. W. (1986). Introduction to Proposals for a Model Rule on the Admissibility of Scientific Evidence. *Jurimetrics Journal* **26**, 237–239.

Berger, M. A. (1986). A Relevancy Approach to Novel Scientific Evidence. *Jurimetrics Journal* **26**, 245–298.

Boyce, R. N. and McCloskey, K. L. (1982). Legal Application of Standard

Laboratory Tests for the Identification of Seminal Fluid. *Journal of Contemporary Law* **7**, 1–38.

BRAUN, L. J. (1982). Quantitative Analysis and the Law: Probability Theory as a Tool of Evidence in Criminal Trials. *Utah Law Review* 1982, 41–89.

CALLEN, C. R. (1982). Notes on a Grand Illusion: Some Limits on the Use of Bayesian Theory in Evidence Law. *Indiana Law Journal* **57**, 1–44.

CULLISON, A. D. (1969). Probability Analysis of Judicial Factfinding: A Preliminary Analysis of the Subjective Approach. *University of Toledo Law Review* 1969, 538–598.

CULLISON, A. D. (1969). Identification by Probabilities and Trial by Arithmetic (A Lesson in How to be Wrong with Greater Precision). *Houston Law Review* **6**, 471–518.

EGESDAL, S. M. (1986). The *Frye* Doctrine and Relevancy Approach Controversy: An Empirical Evaluation. *Georgetown Law Journal* **74**, 1769–1790. (A recent article reviewing the admissibility of scientific evidence emphasizing the distinction between the relevance of the evidence and the potential problem that jurors may give it too much weight. Recent cases where the jurors were allowed to submit questions to witnesses as well as many cases involving scientific evidence are cited.)

FAIRLEY, W. B. (1973). Probabilistic Analysis of Identification Evidence. *Journal of Legal Studies* **2**, 493–513.

FAIRLEY, W. B. AND MOSTELLER, F. (1974). A Conversation About Collins. *University of Chicago Law Review* **41**, 242–253.

FIENBERG, S. E. AND KADANE, J. B. (1983). The Presentation of Bayesian Statistical Analyses in Legal Proceedings. *The Statistician* **32**, 88–98.

FINKELSTEIN, M. O. AND FAIRLEY, W. B. (1970). A Bayesian Approach to Identification Evidence. *Harvard Law Review* **83**, 489–517.

FINKELSTEIN, M. O. AND FAIRLEY, W. B. (1971). A Comment on "Trial by Mathematics". *Harvard Law Review* **84**, 1801–1809.

GASTWIRTH, J. L. (1988). The Potential Effect of Unchecked Statistical Assumptions: A Fault in *San Luis Obispo Mothers for Peace v. U.S. Nuclear Regulatory Commission*. Manuscript available from the author. (Neglecting possible dependence in a risk assessment is shown to lead to an underestimate of the risk of an accident.)

GIANNELLI, P. C. (1986). Scientific Evidence: A Proposed Amendment to Rule 702. *Jurimetrics Journal* **26**, 260–265.

HANSON, H. J., CAUDILL, S. P. AND BOONE, J. (1985). Crisis in Drug Testing: Results of a CDC Blind Study. *Journal of the American Medical Association* **253**, 2382–2387. (This study showed that of 11 laboratories performing drug tests, only one met the standard that both sensitivity and specificity exceed .8.)

IMWINKELREID, E. J. (1981). A New Era in the Evolution of Scientific Evidence—A Primer on Evaluating the Weight of Scientific Evidence. *William and Mary Law Review* **23**, 261–290.

IMWINKELREID, E. J. (1982). Forensic Hair Analysis: The Case Against the Underemployment of Scientific Evidence. *Washington and Lee Law Review* **39**, 41–67.

JONAKAIT, R. N. (1982). Will Blood Tell? Genetic Markers in Criminal Cases. *Emory Law Journal* **31**, 833–912. (A discussion of the use of blood tests, especially genetic markers in dried blood, emphasizing reliability and accuracy issues.)

JONAKAIT, R. N. (1983). When Blood is Their Argument: Probabilities in Criminal Cases, Genetic Markers, and Once Again, Bayes' Theorem. *University of Illinois Law Forum* 1983, 369–422. (A recent article updating the controversy surrounding Bayes' Theorem and identification evidence. The reader might ask how the prior probability could be determined more accurately in some of the examples rather than totally discounting the Bayesian view.)

KAPLAN, J. (1968). Decision Theory and the Factfinding Process, *Stanford Law Review* **20**, 1065–1092.

KAYE, D. H. (1982). The Numbers Game: Statistical Inference in Discrimination Cases. *Michigan Law Review* **80**, 833–856.

KAYE, D. H. (1983). Statistical Significance and the Burden of Persuasion. *Law and Contemporary Problems* **46**, 13–23. (A basic article on the formulation of judicial decisionmaking in terms of posterior probabilistics or type I and type II errors.)

KINGSTON, C. (1965). Application of Probability Theory in Criminalistics. *Journal of the American Statistical Association* **60**, 70–80.

KRANTZ, P. H. AND MIYAMOTO, J. (1983). Priors and Likelihood Ratios as Evidence. *Journal of the American Statistical Association* **78**, 418–423. (A mathematical article discussing procedures for combining conceptually independent prior knowledge and sample data. The authors demonstrate that in many practical situations binary decision models, such as guilty or innocent, have or do not have the disease, are overly simplistic and that some posterior probability should be assigned to a borderline undecided state.)

LACEY, F. B. (1984). Scientific Evidence. *Jurimetrics Journal* **24**, 254–272.

LEDERER, F. I. (1986). Resolving the Frye Dilemma—a Reliability Approach. *Jurimetrics Journal* **26**, 240–244.

LINDLEY, D. V. (1977a). A Problem in Forensic Sciences. *Biometrika* **64**, 207–213.

LINDLEY, D. V. (1977b). Probability and the Law: *The Statistician* **26**, 203–212. (A readable exposition of the relevance of Bayesian principles to legal issues written by a leading proponent and developer of Bayesian methodology.)

LINDLEY, D. V. AND EGGLESTON, R. (1983). The Problem of Missing Evidence. *Law Quarterly Review* **99**, 86–99. (An interesting analysis of how to interpret the failure of a party to produce evidence available to it.)

NICHOLS, D. H. (1983). Toward a Coordinated Judicial View of the Accuracy of Breath Testing Devices. *North Dakota Law Review* **59**, 329–348. (A useful summary of state laws regarding the admissibility of the results of breathalyzer tests. The author recommends the two-test approach to insure the accuracy of the first test. The effect of the standard error of the estimated blood alcohol level in cases is discussed. The evidentiary problems created when a manufacturer did not notify the police departments who used its device of a defect is also discussed.)

PAGE, T. (1983). On the Meaning of the Preponderance Test in Judicial Regulation of Chemical Hazard. *Law and Contemporary Problems* **46**, 267–283. (This article proposes that the costs of each of the two possible errors in a decision be factored into the criteria used in the preponderance of the evidence standard. Essentially this implies that the critical value of the posterior probability or the likelihood that will be used to decide whether a firm is liable will depend on the total costs to society. A prior distribution on the probability p, the chemical at issue is carcinogenic, is used in the development. The topic of cost benefit analysis in regulation is discussed in Chapter 14.)

PRATT, G. C. (1982). A Judicial Perspective on Opinion Evidence Under the Federal Rules. *Washington and Lee Law Review* **39**, 313–331.

RUBINFELD, D. L. (1985). Econometrics in the Courtroom. *Columbia Law Review* **85**, 1048–1097. (The discussion of statistical evidence and the standard of proof on pages 1050–1054 is pertinent to this chapter.)

SOLOMON, H. (1966). Jurimetrics. In: *Research Papers in Statistics: Festshrift for J. Neyman* (F. N. David, ed.), London: Wiley.

SOLOMON, H. (1982). Measurement and Burden of Evidence. In: *Some Recent Advances in Statistics* (J. Tiago de Oliveira and B. Epstein, eds.). New York: Academic Press.

SPROTT, D. H. AND KALBFLEISCH, J. A. (1968). Use of the Likelihood Function in Inference. *Psychological Bulletin* **64**, 15–22.

STARRS, J. E. (1982). A Still-Life Watercolor: Frye v. United States. *Journal of Forensic Sciences* **27**, 684–692. (A careful review of the facts surrounding the *Frye* case which set the precedent for admissibility of scientific evidence. This article corrects a number of errors which appeared in the previous literature.)

STARRS, J. E. (1986). *Frye v. United States* Restructured and Penalized: A Proposal to Amend Federal Evidence Rule 702. *Jurimetrics Journal* **26**, 249–259.

TRIBE, L. H. (1970). Trial by Mathematics: Precision and Ritual in the Legal Process. *Harvard Law Review* **84**, 1329–1393.

TRIBE, L. H. (1971). A Further Critique of Mathematical Proof. *Harvard Law Review* **84**, 1810–1820.

TUCKER, J. T. III (1984). The Use of Scientific Evidence in Rape Cases. *University of Richmond Law Review* **18**, 851–893. (Provides many references to forensic methods useful in identifying or clearing alleged rapists. Procedures involving polygraph tests, hypnosis and narcoanalysis are also discussed. The author notes these may not be admissible in court but may aid the attorney or investigator.)

UNDERWOOD, B. D. (1977). The Thumb on the Scales of Justice: Burdens of Persuasion in Criminal Cases. *Yale Law Journal* **86**, 1299–1348.

WALDEN, D. E. (1986). *United States v. Downing:* Novel Scientific Evidence and the Rejection of *Frye. Utah Law Review,* 1986, 839–853. (This article describes the opinion in *Downing,* 753 F.2d 1224 (3d Cir. 1985) which adopted a more liberal view of the admissibility of scientific evidence than *Frye.*)

WALTERS, C. M. (1985). Admission of Expert Testimony on Eyewitness Identification. *California Law Review* **73**, 1402–1430.

WEEKS, B. (1975). Bayesian Probability: A Quantitative Technique for the Practicing Attorney. *American Business Law Journal* **13**, 83–102.

Paternity Testing and Related Topics

AICKIN, M. (1984). Some Fallacies in the Computation of Paternity Probabilities. *American Journal of Human Genetics* **36**, 904–915.

AICKIN, M. AND KAYE, D. (1983). Some Mathematical and Legal Considerations in Using Serological Tests to Prove Paternity in *Inclusion Probabilities in Parentage Testing.* (R. H. Walker, ed.). Arlington, Virginia: American Association of Blood Banks.

ARTHUR, R. O. AND REID, J. E. (1954). Utilizing the Lie Detector Technique to Determine the Truth in Disputed Paternity Cases. *Journal of Criminal Law, Criminal and Police Science* **45**, 213–221.

BEAUTYMAN, M. J. (1976). Paternity Actions—A Matter of Opinion or a Trial of the Blood? *Journal of Legal Medicine* **4**(4), 17–25 (see also the letter by Pasternack and the author's reply in the same volume, No. 7, 34–35).

BERRY, D. A. AND GEISSER, S. (1986). Inference in Cases of Disputed Paternity in *Statistics in the Law* (M. H. DeGroot, S. E. Fienberg and J. Kadane, eds.). New York: Wiley. (This paper describes a more refined calculation for obtaining the factor *g* in formula (12.10), which incorporates the probabilities of the different *genotypes* corresponding to the various blood group phenotypes.)

CAVALLI-SFORZA, L. L. (1977). *Elements of Human Genetics.* Menlo Park, Ca: Benjamin/Cummings.

CHAKRABORTY, R., SHAW, M. AND SCHALL, W. J. (1974). Exclusion of Paternity: The Current State of the Art. *American Journal of Human Genetics* **26**, 477–488.

DODD, B. E. (1986). Editorial DNA Fingerprinting in Matters of Family and Crime. *Medicine, Science and Law* **26**, 5–7 (Reprinted from *Nature*).

ELLMAN, I. M., AND KAYE, D. (1979). Probabilities and Proof: Can HLA Testing Prove Paternity? *New York University Law Review* **54**, 1131–1162.

GRUNBAUM, B. W., SELVIN, S., PACE, N. AND BLOCK, D. M. (1978). Frequency Distribution and Discrimination Probability of Twelve Protein Genetic Variants in Human Blood as Functions of Race, Sex and Age. *Journal of Forensic Science* **23**, 577–582.

KRAUSE, H. D., MIALE, J. B., JENNINGS, E. R., RETTBERG, M. H. AND SELL, K. W. (1976). Joint AMA-ABA Guidelines: Present Status of Serologic Testing in Problems of Disputed Parentage. *Family Law Quarterly* **10**, 247–285.

LARSON, M. E., JR. (1974). Blood Test Exclusion in Paternity Litigation: The Uniform Acts and Beyond. *Journal of Family Law* **13**, 713–752.

LEE, C. L. (1975). Current Status of Paternity Testing. *Family Law Quarterly* **9**, 615–633.

LEMMON, L. L. AND MURPHY, L. K. (1985). The Evidentiary Use of the HLA Blood Test in Virginia. *University of Richmond Law Review* **19**, 235–256.

POLESKY, H. F. AND LENZ, S. L. (1984). Parentage Testing: An Interface Between Medicine and Law. *North Dakota Law Review* **60**, 727–740.

PROTOGERE, F. (1981). Use of Human Leukocyte Antigen Test Results to Establish Paternity. *Indiana Law Review* **14**, 831–864.

REISNER, E. G. AND BOLK, T. A. (1981). A Laymen's Guide to the Use of Blood Group Analysis in Paternity Testing. *Journal of Family Law* **20**, 657–675. (A good introduction to blood groups and their use.)

REISNER, E. G. AND MACQUEEN, J. M. (1981). Problems Arising From the Use of the HLA System in Paternity Testing. *Clinical Laboratory Haemetology* **3**, 113–119.

REISNER, E. G. AND READING, P. (1983). Application of Probability of Paternity Calculations to an Alleged Incestuous Relationship. *Journal of Forensic Science* **28**, 1030–1034.

STERLECK, V. L. AND JACOBSON, M. L. (1980). Paternity Testing With the Human Leukocyte Antigen System: A Medicolegal Breakthrough. *Santa Clara Law Review* **20**, 511–531.

TERASAKI, P. (1977). Resolution of 1000 Paternity Cases Not Excluded by ABO Testing. *Journal of Family Law* **16**, 543–567.

USHER, M. A. AND STAPLETON, R. R. (1979). An Unusual Forensic Application of Blood Group Studies. *Medicine, Science and Law* **19**, 165–169.

WALKER, R. H. ED. (1983). *Inclusion Probabilities in Parentage Testing.* Arlington, Va: American Association of Blood Banks.

WIENER, A. S. AND SOCHA, W. W. (1976). Methods Available for Solving Medicolegal Problems of Disputed Parentage. *Journal of Forensic Science* **21**, 42–64.

WILLIFORD, J. W. (1980). The Use of Blood Tests in Actions to Determine Paternity. *Wake Forest Law Review* **16**, 591–606.

Articles Concerning the Polygraph

ALPHER, V. S. AND BLANTON, R. L. (1985). The Accuracy of Lie Detection: Why Lie Tests Based on the Polygraph Should not be Admitted into Evidence. *Law and Psychology Review* **9**, 67–75.

BROOKS, J. (1985). Polygraph Testing: Thoughts of a Skeptical Legislator. *American Psychologist* **40**, 348–354.

CAVOUKIAN, A. AND HESLEGRAVE, R. J. (1980). The Admissibility of Polygraph Evidence in Court: Some Empirical Findings. *Law and Human Behavior* **4**, 117–131. (A report of two experiments assessing the influence of polygraph evidence on mock jurors, indicating that people are not unduly influenced by it.)

GASTWIRTH, J. L. (1987). The Statistical Precision of Medical Screening Procedures: Application to Polygraph and AIDS Antibodies Test Data. *Statistical Science* **2**, 213–222.

HOLDEN, C. (1986). Days May be Numbered for the Polygraphs in the Private Sector. *Science* **232**, 705.

HURD, S. E. (1985). Use of the Polygraph in Screening Job Applicants. *American Business Law Journal* **22**, 529–549.

KAYE, D. H. (1987). The Validity of Tests: Caveat Omnes. *Jurimetrics Journal* **27**, 349–361. (This article discusses the debate between Lykken and Raskin and Kircher on the usefulness of the polygraph.)

KLEINMUTZ, B. AND SZUCKO, J. J. (1984). A Field Study of the Fallibility of Lie Detection. *Nature* **303**, 449–450.

LOWE, R. A. (1981). Regulation of Polygraph Testing in the Employment Context: Suggested Statutory Control on Test Use and Examiner Competence. *University of California Davis Law Review* **15**, 113–131.

LYKKEN, D. T. (1987). The Validity of Tests: Caveat Emptor. *Jurimetrics Journal* **27**, 263–270.

MARKWART, A. AND LYNCH, D. E. (1979). The Effect of Polygraph Evidence on Mock Jury Decisionmaking. *Journal of Police Science and Administration* **4**, 324–332.

OFFICE OF TECHNOLOGY ASSESSMENT (1983). Scientific Validity of Polygraph Testing: A Research Review and Evaluation. Washington, DC: U.S. Government Printing Office.

RASKIN, D. C. (1982). The Scientific Basis of Polygraph Techniques and their Use in the Judicial Process in *Reconstructing the Past: The Role of Psychologists in Criminal Trials* (A. Trankell, ed.). Stockholm: Norstedt and Soners.

RASKIN, D. C. (1986). The Polygraph in 1986: Scientific Professional and Legal Issues Surrounding Application and Acceptance of Polygraph Evidence. *Utah Law Review* 1986, 29–74. (A valuable recent survey of polygraph testing and its acceptance by courts.)

RASKIN, D. C. AND KIRCHER, J. C. (1987). The Validity of Lykken's Criticisms: Fact or Fancy? *Jurimetrics Journal* **27**, 271–277.

SAXE, L., DOUGHERTY, D. AND CROSS, T. (1985). The Validity of Polygraph Testing: Scientific Analysis and Public Controversy. *American Psychologist* **40**, 355–366.

SKOLNICK, J. H. (1960). Scientific Theory and Scientific Evidence: An Analysis of Lie Detection. *Yale Law Review* **70**, 694–728. (One of the first precise treatments of the subject emphasizing the important role of the conditional probability $P(D \mid S)$. References to earlier works are cited.)

TURLICK, J. A. (1980). Courtroom Status of the Polygraph. *Akron Law Review* **14**, 133–153. (Discusses the conditions for polygraph test results to be admissible, focusing primarily on Ohio law.)

WICKER, W. (1953). The Polygraph Truth Test and the Law of the Evidence. *Tennessee Law Review* **22**, 711–727. (An interesting summary of early cases involving the admissibility of polygraph test results, with the author's suggestions to those who wish to obtain judicial approval of the technique. Both improved accuracy and the formulation of adequate standards for polygraph experts are likely to be required prior to widespread acceptance. The reader should compare this article and Skolnick (1960) with the recent literature to decide whether the suggested conditions for acceptance have now been met.)

Screening Tests for Aids Antibodies

ALLEN, J. R. (1987). Scientific and Public Health Rationales for Screening Donated Blood and Plasma for Antibody to LAV/HTLV-III. In: *AIDS:* The *Safety of Blood Products* (Petricciani, J. E., Gust, I. D., Hoppe, P. A. and Krijnen, H. W., eds.) New York: John Wiley. (This article and others in the book provide much basic information concerning AIDS and the safety of the blood supply.)

SAYERS, M. H., BEATTY, P. G. AND HANSEN, J. A. (1986). HLA Antibodies as a Cause of False-positive Reactions in Screening Enzyme Immunoassays for Antibodies to HTLV-III. *Transfusion* **26**, 113–115.

WARTICK, M. G., McCARROLL, D. R. AND WILTBANK, T. B. (1987). A Second Discriminator for Biological False Positive Results in Enzyme-Linked Immunosorbent Assays for Antibodies to Human Immunodeficiency Virus (HTLV-III/LAV). *Transfusion* **27**, 109–111. (This article and Gastwirth (1987) provide further references to studies of the accuracies of screening tests and the predictive values observed in studies of blood donors.)

Drug Tests: Their Accuracy and Legality

BIBLE, J. D. (1986). Screening Workers for Drugs: the Constitutional Implications of Urine Testing in Public Employment. *American Business Law Journal*, **24**, 209–357. (A good survey of cases and the factors affecting the legality of random testing programs).

COHEN, F. AND KING, K. (1987). Drug Testing and Corrections. *Criminal Law Bulletin*, 151–172. (A discussion of drug tests in correctional institutions where special legal standards apply.)

MAZO, D. P. (1987). Yellow Rows of Test Tubes: Due Process Constraints on Discharges of Public Employees Based on Drug Urinalysis Testing. *University of Pennsylvania Law Review*, **135**, 1623–1656.

MORGAN, J. P. (1984). Problems of Urine Screening for Drugs. *Journal of Psychoactive Drugs,* **16**, 305–317. (A discussion of the reliability of drug screening tests. This literature review documents that drug tests have the same problems that the polygraph has when used on populations with *low prevalence* of the characteristics screened for.)

CASES

We list a number of cases concerning drug tests and a few dealing with the polygraph or AIDS testing. Although formal Bayesian reasoning is not utilized by judges, the reader will note that the concepts of reasonable suspicion and probable cause are akin to having an increased prior probability. Other factors such as risk to the public, public trust and how the program of testing affects current employees also enter into the legality of drug screening programs. Most cases, but not all, indicated that the first test should be confirmed.

Schoemaker v. Handel 169 F.Supp. 1089 (D. N.J. 1985).

Turner v. Fraternal Order of Police 500 A.2d 1012 (D.C. 1985).

Higgs v. Wilson 616 F.Supp. 226 (W.D. Ky. 1985).

Wykoff v. Resig 613 F.Supp. 1504 (D. Ind. 1985).

Paranzo v. Coughlin 608 F.Supp. 1504 (S.D. N.Y. 1985).

Jensen v. Lick 589 F.Supp. 35 (D. N.D. 1984).

Smith v. State 250 Ga. 438, 298 S.E. 2d 482 (1983).

Pella v. Adams 638 F.Supp. 94 (D. Nev. 1986).

McDonell v. Hunter 809 F.2d 1302 (8th Cir. 1987) allowed drug testing of prison employees who have regular contact with prisoners provided that it was done by a uniform or systematic selection process, i.e., employees could be randomly chosen or systematically scheduled but they could not be selected subjectively by the supervisory staff. Otherwise, testing was permitted only upon reasonable suspicion. The testing procedure was required to be accurate and reliable.

Local 1277 v. Sunshine Transit Agency 2 IER Cases 579 (C.D. Ca. 1987) found a wholly random drug testing program violated the rights of employees against "unreasonable search and seizure." The opinion noted that a plan based on reasonable suspicion, a lesser standard than probable cause, would be permissible.

Feliciano v. City of Cleveland 2 IER Cases 419 (N.D. Ohio. 1987) found that a surprise testing of a police academy class violated their rights.

Rushton v. Nebraska Public Power 653 F.Supp. 1510 (D. Neb. 1987) upheld drug testing for employees who have unescorted access to protected areas of a nuclear plant. Clearly, safety issues played a role in this case as all employees had a "diminished expectation of privacy" due to the level of security required.

Treasury Employees v. Von Raab 2 IER Cases 15 (5th Cir. 1987) upheld drug testing of new applicants and employees applying for a promotion to "sensitive" posts in the Customs Service. The use of a confirmatory test plus the individuals awareness of the tests *prior* to their application were major considerations in this 2 to 1 decision. The testing program did not apply to current employees who were not applying for promotion.

Recent Cases Concerning Polygraph and AIDS Testing

Morgan v. Harris Trust Co. 43 FEP Cases 881 (N.D. Ill. 1987) upheld polygraph testing of employees of a bank who have access to cash.

Local 1812. AFGE v. U.S. Dept. of State 43 FEP Cases 955 (D.D.C. 1987) upheld testing for AIDS antibodies in applicants for the Foreign Service on the grounds that proper medical facilities were unavailable in many posts and that a medical exam, including blood tests, was already part of the existing procedure.

Anderson v. Philadelphia 3IER Cases 353 (3rd Cir. 1988) upheld polygraph testing for police and correctional officers. The court noted that the lack of scientific consensus concerning the reliability of the tests allows the law enforcement administrator to use them. In this case the privacy rights of individuals were protected as the results were not made public.

Chapter 13

The Main Types of Medical Studies and Their Application in Law and Public Policy

1. Introduction

In previous chapters we illustrated various statistical methods on data from prospective (cohort) and retrospective (case-control) studies. This chapter is devoted to the use of the results of epidemiologic and medical studies in law and public policy. Section 2 of the chapter describes the basic measures of risk used in law and public policy. In contrast with epidemiologic studies which are not based on random samples, so the effect of possible covariates (influential or confounding factors) must be accounted for in the statistical analysis or by using a matched design, clinical trials which are required by the Food and Drug Administration (FDA) to support an application for approval of a new drug can randomly assign patients to the treatment or control (placebo) group. Clinical trials and the use of statistical inferences drawn from them are described in Section 3. We return to the use of observational studies to develop evidence of practical causation in Section 4 and 5, using the clinical trial as a goal for a cohort study. An appendix describes the role of power in the planning of studies. The sample size tables again illustrate why prospective studies of rare diseases that often require well over 1000 persons to be followed for years before a sufficient number of cases develop can be impractical. It is precisely in such situations that case-control studies are most appropriate. Since the next chapter concerns the use of medical statistics as evidence, and we cite many common books and articles, the references for both chapters are given at the end of Chapter 14. They are organized by topic, e.g., clinical trials or the cases and studies relating to a particular agent or disease. All authors of a publication are listed in the reference to it. Sometimes we will refer to an epidemiologic study by the organization that sponsored it or the location where it was carried out. From the year of publication and annotation in the reference the study can readily be identified. Similarly, some sources of data in the tables are identified by the author(s) and date of the publication. The full citation is provided in the list of references. Data from sources not discussed in the text are fully referenced in the tables.

2. Basic Concepts and Measures of Risk

In Chapter 10 we discussed the relationship between rates and probabilities and emphasized the fact that the definition of a rate depends on time and that incidence of a disease is reported in terms such as .005 per person year at risk or 5 per 1000 person years at risk. A probability, on the other hand, refers to the proportion of persons getting a disease in a fixed time interval. It is not exactly a rate as the population size at risk changes during the period. For example, suppose a cohort study follows 1000 recent high school graduates for two years to observe their death by auto accident rates and that 20 die in such accidents in each year. The probability of dying in a car accident in the first year was

$$\frac{20}{1000} = .02,$$

while the probability of being killed in an auto accident in the second year is

$$\frac{20}{980} = .0204.$$

The incidence of accidents during the first year should account for the fact that the *size of the population* at risk changes during the year. When a short time period is involved, e.g., one year, the number of persons exposed during the entire year should be the denominator. This can be approximated by averaging the number of people at the beginning and end of the period. In our example, the incidence rate (IR) in the first year is the ratio of the number of deaths (20) to the average population of $(1000 + 980)/2 = 990$, so that

$$IR = \frac{2}{990} = .0202.$$

From this calculation we see that for practical purposes incidence rates over short time periods can be regarded as probabilities, and we will often do so, however, the reader should note the nature of the denominator, e.g., persons or person-years of exposure when examining incidence rate data.

We will denote the incidence rate of *nonexposed* persons by p_0 and that of *exposed* persons by p_1. The relative risk, R, is p_1/p_0, and essentially is the *ratio* of the probabilities exposed and nonexposed persons have of contracting the disease. As we realized previously in Chapter 5, the relative risk is related to the odds ratio (OR)

(13.1)
$$OR = \frac{\dfrac{p_1}{(1 - p_1)}}{\dfrac{p_0}{(1 - p_0)}},$$

and the two are very close numerically when p_1 and p_0 are small (less than .05 or .10). The *excess* risk or *absolute difference*, $p_1 - p_0$, between the disease probabilities is very important from a public health perspective but is not as useful from an analytic viewpoint, as Cornfield's result demonstrated. The *absolute difference* multiplied by the *number* of exposed individuals yields the expected number of cases that would not occur in the relevant time frame if the exposure were eliminated. From the public health paradigm, the size of the exposed population is at least as important as the risk of disease and the notions of *prevalence* of exposure, i.e., the fraction, f, of the population who are exposed to the agent and *relative risk* are considered jointly in the concept of *attributable risk*, which is defined as follows: The *attributable risk* (AR) is the proportion of *all* cases occurring in the population which are due to exposure to the agent.

The formula for the attributable risk is given by

(13.2)
$$AR = \frac{f(R - 1)}{1 + f(R - 1)},$$

and is derived as follows:

Suppose a fraction, f, of a population of size N are exposed to an agent which has relative risk, R, associated with contracting a specific disease. If the incidence of the disease among nonexposed persons is p_0, we expect

$$NfRp_0 \text{ cases among those exposed}$$

and

$$N(1 - f)p_0 \text{ cases among the nonexposed.}$$

As we expect Nfp_0 cases to occur among the exposed naturally, the expected number of *excess* cases attributed to exposure is

$$(13.3) \qquad NfRp_0 - Nfp_0 = Nf(R - 1)p_0.$$

Hence, the *attributable risk* or fraction of *all* cases due to exposure is

$$(13.4) \qquad \frac{Nf(R - 1)p_0}{NfRp_0 + N(1 - f)p_0} = \frac{f(R - 1)}{1 - f + Rf} = \frac{f(R - 1)}{1 + (R - 1)f}.$$

The concept of attributable risk is important in public health, as it is a measure of the potential effectiveness of a program to reduce the incidence of a disease either by eliminating or sharply limiting exposure of the public to the agent. It also is useful as a guide in planning health research. When the attributable risk of a disease due to one or several factors is near 1.0, say reaches .8 or more, then for practical purposes the main risk factors related to the disease are known, so other diseases, with lower incidence and prevalence rates, might now be given more attention.

Because the attributable risk depends on the fraction of the population who are exposed to an agent as well as the relative risk, agents with a small increased risk, e.g., $R = 1.3$ to which large populations are exposed can create major policy problems. For example, if 80% of the entire nation (population of about 250 million) are exposed to an air pollutant or toxic agent in the grain supply, which has a relative risk of 1.3 of causing a particular form of cancer, then the proportion of all cases occurring after the appropriate latency period that would be due to the agent is

$$\frac{.8(.3)}{1 + (.8)(.3)} = \frac{.24}{1.24} = 19.35\%.$$

If the relative risk, $R = 1.5$, then 28.6% of all cases would be due to the exposure, and if $R = 2.0$, the AR becomes 44.4%. This may help explain the strong public reaction to the finding that EDB was present in amounts greatly exceeding government guidelines in some bakery products a few

TABLE 13.1.   Attributable Risk as a Function of Prevalence (f) and Relative Risk (R) of Exposure

Prevalence (f)	Relative Risk					
	1.0	1.25	1.5	2.0	5.0	10.0
.01	0	.000	.001	.01	.039	.083
.10	0	.024	.048	.091	.286	.474
.20	0	.048	.091	.167	.444	.673
.33	0	.077	.143	.250	.571	.750
.50	0	.111	.200	.333	.666	.818
.75	0	.158	.273	.429	.750	.871
1.00	0	.200	.333	.500	.800	.900

years ago, even though EDB is not that highly carcinogenic.[1] A short table presenting the attributable risk as a function of the relative risk and prevalence of exposure in the population is given in Table 13.1.

One can use similar considerations to assess the potential effectiveness of warning labels and/or a public information campaign. For example, suppose that 75% of all children were given aspirin or other salicylate compounds when they had flu before the Reye's syndrome link was established and that, based on past experience, the institution of warning labels and a public education program would reduce the exposed fraction of children to about .333. Then, assuming an estimated relative risk[2] of 10 the fraction of all cases attributable to salicylate use should decline from .871 to .75. We next estimate the number of cases prevented. Letting p_0 be the normal yearly incidence of the disease, without a preventive program we expect

$$NfRp_0 + N(1 - f)p_0$$

cases per year, where N is the size of the exposed population and f_0 the current prevalence of exposure. The expected decrease in cases due to reducing f from f_0, say, to f_1 is

$$Np_0[R(f_0 - f_1) + (f_1 - f_0)] = Np_0(R - 1)(f_0 - f_1),$$

and the expected fraction of cases occurring now that could be avoided is

$$(13.5) \qquad \frac{(R - 1)(f_0 - f_1)}{f_0R + (1 - f_0)}.$$

In the Reye's syndrome example, R is about 10.0 and $f_0 = .75$ and $f_1 =$

.33, so an educational program should prevent about

$$\frac{(10-1)(.75-.33)}{.75 \cdot 10 + (.25)} = \frac{3.78}{7.75} = .488 \text{ or } 48.8\%$$

of currently observed cases. When the study was planned, about 200 cases occurred each year, an effective program should cut the number of cases to about half that level.

Similar considerations can be used to calculate the expected benefit from reducing the prevalence (f) of a risk factor, e.g., by changing public smoking or dietary habits, on the future incidence of a disease such as cancer.

Comment. We have emphasized the concepts of risk relating to the *incidence* rate rather than the *prevalence* rate, which is the fraction of the population with the disease. The incidence rate refers to newly occurring cases, i.e., those occurring during the previous year, while the prevalence rate includes all persons with the disease regardless of the time they contracted it. Thus, the prevalence rate depends on the duration of the disease as well as its incidence.

Unlike public policy, which is concerned with the health of the entire population, legal cases often focus on the cause or causes of a disease or condition in one or several plaintiffs who allege that the defendant was negligent in improperly exposing them to a toxic agent. Therefore, we are concerned with determining the probability that a case occurring in the exposed group is due to the exposure. Notice that this is a *conditional probability*, as we know that the person has the disease. We call this the *probability due to exposure* (PDE) for cases occurring in the exposed group, and it is given by

(13.6) $$\frac{R-1}{R},$$

where R is the relative risk of disease among exposed persons.

Formula (13.6) is derived as follows: Among all N exposed persons we expect NRp_0 cases. Of these cases Np_0 would be expected to occur naturally, without exposure, and the expected *excess* due to exposure is $N(R-1)p_0$. Therefore the *fraction* of all cases in the exposed group which are due or attributable to the exposure is

$$PDE = \frac{N(R-1)p_0}{NRp_0} = \frac{R-1}{R}.$$

The probability due to exposure measure is important in legal applications because cases are often decided by the preponderance of the evidence standard, i.e., is it more likely than not that the lung cancer of a particular person exposed to benzene or radiation is due to that exposure rather than another cause. If the PDE exceeds one half, the case is more likely than not to have arisen from the exposure. Since a PDE greater than .5 is equivalent to a relative risk, R, of at least 2.0, epidemiologic studies yielding estimated relative risks in the range 1.5 to 2.5 probably will be subject to rigorous scrutiny if offered in court (see McElveen, 1985). On the other hand, when at least two studies which controlled for the other major risk factors yield an estimated R of 5.0 or more and their associated confidence intervals *exclude* 1.0, the results should be difficult to challenge.

Comment.   Although many of the references we cite virtually equate the preponderance of the evidence standard with a more likely than not criteria and use the PDE $> .5$ or $R > 2$ as its mathematical formulation, one should be extremely cautious about making these mathematical criteria stringent requirements. First, as Rubinfeld (1985) notes, there are other factors and circumstances in a particular case that need to be considered by a court (remember, the estimated R is an average over the population). Also, from a public policy view, to require injured persons to demonstrate that exposure to a particular toxic agent doubles the risk of disease before they can receive damages would allow a few unscrupulous producers to expose the public to harmful agents which are known to be weak carcinogens, having relative risks in the range 1.5 to 1.9, with impunity.

We close this section by noting that the effect of a single agent, its attributable risk and PDE are harder to interpret when a disease, e.g., lung cancer, can be caused by more than one toxic agent. One needs to determine how the agents interact. For example, the relative risk of a disease in persons exposed to both agents may be described by several mathematical models. The two most common models assume the effects are either additive or multiplicative.

Suppose that the incidence rate of a disease in persons exposed to *neither* agent (X or Y) is denoted by p_{00}, the rate for persons exposed to agent X but not to Y by p_{10}, the rate for persons exposed to agent Y but not to agent X by p_{01}, while p_{11} denotes the rate for persons exposed to both agents. The notation is summarized in Table 13.2a, and the consequent relative risks $R_x = p_{10}/p_{00}$, $R_y = p_{01}/p_{00}$ and $R_{xy} = p_{11}/p_{00}$ (for persons exposed to both agents) are given in Table 13.2b.

TABLE 13.2. Incidence Rates and Relative Risks for Various Combinations of Exposure of Two Risk Factors, X and Y

		a. Incidence Rates Status With Respect to Agent X		b. Relative Risks Agent Y	
		No (0)	Yes (1)	No (0)	Yes (1)
Exposure Status for Agent X	No (0)	p_{00}	p_{01}	$R = 1.0$	$R_y = p_{01}/p_{00}$
	Yes (1)	p_{10}	p_{11}	$R_x = p_{10}/p_{00}$	$R_{xy} = p_{11}/p_{00}$

Source: This table and our discussion is patterned on Tables 2.16 and 2.18 in Schlesselman (1982).

In the *additive* model, the joint effect of both agents is the *sum* of their individual ones, so the effect of exposure to agent X is $p_{10} - p_{00}$ and the *excess risk* due to exposure to agent X is $(R_x - 1)p_{00}$. Similarly, the excess risk due to exposure to agent Y is $(R_y - 1)p_{00} = p_{01} - p_{00}$ and exposure to both agents has excess risk $(R_{xy} - 1)p_{00}$ or $p_{11} - p_{00}$. If the exposure to one agent does not affect the disease inducing process of the other agent, the *additive* model, which assumes that

(13.7)   the *effect* of exposure to both agents equals the *sum* of their individual effects,

is appropriate.

In terms of the incidence rates, this means that

(13.8) $(p_{11} - p_{00}) = (p_{10} - p_{00}) + (p_{01} - p_{00})$,

and, in terms of the *excess* relative risk (13.7), this means that

(13.9) $(R_{xy} - 1) = (R_{x-1}) + (R_y - 1)$.

When one tries to fit data with the additive model but finds that the effect of exposure to both agents is greater (less) than the sum of their individual effects, we say that the two agents interact positively (negatively). Often positive interactions are called synergistic while negative ones are antagonistic.

Suppose the relative risks of exposure to the separate agents are $R_y = 3.0$, $R_y = 5.0$ and there is no interaction. From (13.9) the additive model predicts that joint exposure would result in a relative risk of

(13.10) $R_{xy} = (R_x - 1) + (R_y - 1) + 1 = 2 + 4 + 1 = 7$

and a corresponding *excess risk* of 6.

Alternatively, one can model the joint effect of exposure to both agents as the *product* of their individual risks, i.e.,

$$(13.11) \qquad R_{xy} = R_x R_y.$$

In terms of the incidence rates p_{00}, p_{01}, p_{10} and p_{11} (13.11) means that

$$(13.12) \qquad \frac{p_{11}}{p_{00}} = \frac{p_{10}}{p_{00}} \times \frac{p_{01}}{p_{00}},$$

i.e., the joint effect is the product of the individual effects, which is why this model is called the multiplicative model. Notice that taking logarithms of (13.11) yields

$$\log R_{xy} = \log R_x + \log R_y$$

so that the multiplicative model of disease risks becomes an *additive model* expressed in terms the logarithms of the relative risk. Since the odds ratio is a close approximation to the relative risk when the incidence rate or probability is small, the *logistic* model of Chapter 8 is often used to analyze data for which the multiplicative model is appropriate.

Several important epidemiologic studies suggest that the multiplicative model fits data quite well. In Table 13.3 we reproduce a table showing the affect of smoking tobacco and exposure to asbestos. Notice that the joint relative risk, R_{xy}, slightly exceeds the product of R_x and R_y. A pictorial representation of these risks is given in Figure 13.1. The risks of oral cancer due to smoking and alcohol consumption also appears to be multiplicative, however, studies of the joint effect exposure to radiation and smoking sometimes fit the additive model (Blot, Akibo and Kato, 1984) and sometimes the multiplicative one (Whittemore and MacMillan, 1983), although recent results favor the multiplicative relationship.

TABLE 13.3.   Age Standardized Lung Cancer Mortality Rate Per 100,000 Man-Years, and Relative Risks for Asbestos Workers, by Smoking Status

	SMR	RR
Nonsmoker (unexposed)	11.3	1.0
Asbestos worker (nonsmoker)	58.4	5.17
Smoker (not exposed to asbestos)	122.6	10.85
Asbestos worker (smoker)	601.6	53.24

Source: Table 8 from Hammond, E. C., Selikoff, I. J. and Seidman, H. (1979).

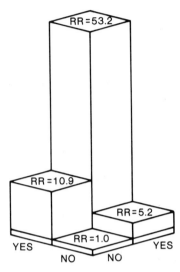

FIGURE 13.1.   Relative risk of death from exposure to asbestos and/or cigarette smoking based on the data in Table 13.3.

The fact that the determination of the relative risk of joint exposures may be model dependent has important implications for health policy. Had the three- and fivefold relative risks in our numerical illustration followed the multiplicative model, R_{xy} would be 15 and the *excess relative risk* 14, which is a far greater risk than that (6) yielded by the additive model. Thus, substantial effort is often spent on testing the goodness of fit of several plausible models to epidemiologic data. Indeed, *a priori* it is difficult to know whether exposure to two risk factors will have an excess risk given by the additive or multiplicative assumption. When the appropriate model and other risk factors are known, one can develop analogs of the attributable risk and probability of causation, however, we shall not explore this area.

Problems

1.*   When planning the Reye's syndrome study it was deemed important to detect a relative risk of 4 or more, and it was assumed that salicylate containing medications were given to about 70% of all children with flu symptoms. Suppose the study had yielded an estimated R of 4.0.

(a) Find the attributable risk of salicylate at the time the study was carried out.

(b) Suppose the government health agencies thought that they could reduce the exposed fraction of children to 20%. How many cases of Reye's syndrome would be expected to be prevented by the warning program?

(c) Now assume that the exposed fraction of children were reduced only by half, i.e., to 35%, what is the expected fraction of cases that would be prevented (again take $R = 4$)? Do you think this result would justify the warning?

(d) Assume the same impact of the warning label and public education program, but assume that $R = 10$, what is the expected number of cases that would be prevented?

2. Discuss the importance of the following concepts from the viewpoint of *public health:*
   incidence rate (or age-adjusted incidence rate)
   attributable risk
   probability of causation due to exposure (PDE)
   expected number of cases avoided
   prevalence of exposure
How do they relate to one another?

3. Table 13.4 presents the results of a study by Rothman and Keller (1972) of the joint effect of alcohol and tobacco on the risk of oral cancer. Using the relative risks in the margin (for each factor) assess whether the multiplicative or additive model fits the data better. Sketch a diagram similar to Figure 13.1 for use in demonstrating your results.

4. Suppose we desired to express the fatal accident rates of recent high school graduates in terms of person-years exposure.
   (a) Calculate the total person years of exposure and the incidence rate. Why is your answer so close to the one-year rate we calculated in the text?
   (b) Can you think of a situation where the multi-year rate might differ meaningfully from the individual year rates? If this might be the case, how should the incidence rate be reported?

Answers to Selected Problems

3. Neither model seems clearly superior to the other. At the highest levels the multiplicative model seems better, as it predicts a risk of 15.6

TABLE 13.4.   The Joint Effect of the Alcohol and Tobacco Consumption on the Risk of Oral Cancer: Relative Risk
by Usage Categories

Alcohol (oz/day)	Tobacco (cigarette equiv./day)				Alcohol (adjusted for tobacco)
	0	1–19	20–39	40+	
0	1.0	1.6	1.6	3.4	1.0
0.1–0.3	1.7	1.9	3.3	3.4	1.8
0.4–1.5	1.9	4.9	4.9	8.2	2.9
1.6+	2.3	4.8	10.0	15.6	4.2
Tobacco risk (adjusted for alcohol)	1.0	1.4	2.4	4.2	

Source: Breslow, N. and Day, N. (1980) cited fully in Chapter 6. They
summarized the results of Rothman, K. J. and Keller, A. Z. (1972). The
Effect of Joint Exposure to Alcohol and Tobacco on Risk of Cancer of the
Mouth and Pharynx. *Journal of Chronic Diseases* **25,** 711–716.
Note: The relative risks are adjusted for age at diagnosis.

for persons in the highest smoking and drinking categories. The additive
model only predicts an R of $4.2 + 4.2 - 1 = 7.4$. In other categories,
however, the additive model yields closer estimates. Finally, we mention
that the estimates of the marginal risks (far-right column for alcohol,
bottom row for tobacco) were obtained from a multiplicative model. The
results do yield a reasonably good agreement between the observed and
expected number of cases in each category (derived from a multiplicative
model) in each category.

4.   (a) We have approximately 990 persons at risk during the first year
and 970 the second for a total of 1960 person years. The incidence rate
would then be $40/1960 = .0204$ or 20.4 deaths per 1000 person years.
There is little difference because the fatal accident rate is essentially the
same in each period.

   (b) If the incidence rate changed during the study period, e.g., a
campaign against drunk driving was conducted, then the multi-year rate
would represent a type of average of the before and after periods. The
individual year rates should be reported rather than the multi-year ones.
This is why medical data is often reported in the form of incidence rates
by five-year age categories. As disease rates change slowly with age, they
can be considered approximately constant for persons within a five-year

age band. They often vary too much to consider the rates over intervals greater than ten years as the same.

3.   Controlled Clinical Trials

a.   Characteristics of a well-planned clinical trial

A clinical trial is a prospective study conducted to evaluate the effect of a treatment relative to an existing treatment (or placebo). Indices of success such as cure or remission rates, survival time, etc. in the treatment group are compared with those of a control group. In order to assure the comparability of the study groups, subjects are randomly assigned to them. Indeed, the randomization can be done by stratifying on major covariates (e.g., age, sex) in order to ensure that the groups are balanced with respect to the major covariates.

In order to minimize other potential biases in diagnosis and reporting of symptoms, a double-blind or double-masked study design in which neither the patients nor their physicians know which drug the patient is being given is often used. This insures that other aspects of the patient's treatment (personal care, timely diagnosis of other problems) are not affected by study group status, so a difference between the treated and control groups (e.g., in the proportions cured) will be due to the true difference between the effectiveness of the drugs. The need for double-blinding is illustrated by a study of the effect of vitamin C on the common cold. Some of the patients became aware of whether they were being treated with vitamin C or the placebo and, as the subjects evaluated the severity and duration of their colds, this unblinding was potentially important. Indeed, among those subjects who learned of their treatment status, vitamin C appeared to have a positive effect, but it showed no benefit over the placebo among subjects who remained unaware of the nature of the pill they took.

A well planned clinical trial will have a protocol, prepared prior to the start of the study, which will specify the objectives of the study, the design and organization of the trial and indicate the steps that will be taken to assure the reliability of the data as well as the techniques that will be used to analyze the data.

In particular the protocol will present:

(1) The major question under investigation and variables used to assess the response of the subjects.

(2) The study population and the criteria to be used in determining eligibility, e.g., persons should be in a certain age range, have a mild (or severe) case of the disease, etc.

(3) The sample size will be determined to have sufficient statistical power to detect a difference between the groups deemed to be of medical interest.

(4) The enrollment of subjects and the procedure for randomly assigning them to the treatment or control group as well as the procedures for follow-up and minimizing attrition (loss) over the course of the trial.

(5) The standardized form of the new drug (its quality, strength and purity) and the dosage which will be administered to all subjects in the treated group. Moreover, the treatment regimen and procedures designed to assess the compliance of the subjects with it should be presented.

(6) How the effect of all drugs will be measured. This will depend on the disease under investigation. To evaluate drugs designed to lower blood pressure, the blood pressure of patients in both groups should be taken at regular intervals and the changes over time in both groups compared. Sometimes the response may be more subjective, such as how someone is feeling or how much energy one has may be the response variables. Well defined, objectively measurable responses are preferable to subjective ones. The length of the trial should be long enough to detect whether or not response has occurred and whether harmful side effects occur. Moreover, the time patients will be monitored after the trial formally ends for possible delayed effects should be specified.

(7) The statistical methods that will be used to analyze the data. Although clinical trials are designed to be ideal studies, it should be noted that:

(a) One must assure that bias does not enter by a failure to double-blind the study.

(b) One needs to assure that the response variable is measured correctly. (In particular, the medical evaluators should not know the treatment status of the individual patients.)

(c) Patients will vary in their compliance with the regimen (one hopes that the randomization process will also make the groups similar with respect to this, but it is wise to obtain information from all patients during their regular visits).

(d) The fact that patients are required to give their informed consent may mean that the study groups may not be truly representative of the general population. (If either the new or old drug may have serious side effects, perhaps patients with mild versions of the disease will participate at a lower rate than persons who have serious cases.)

(e) Inevitably there will be some loss to follow up, i.e., not all subjects will continue in the trial. While some may be lost due to random factors, e.g., moving to a new job, one needs to be concerned that the treated subjects are not withdrawing due to severe side effects or that the control subjects do not learn that they are being given a placebo and drop out.

From a statistical view, the major difference between a clinical trial and a prospective-cohort observational epidemiologic study is that *randomization* is used to allocate patients to the treatment or control group, which tends to produce groups which are comparable with unknown as well as known risk factors and removes any bias of the medical investigator in the assignment process. This contrasts with occupational health studies where one cannot assign workers to jobs with specific exposure levels of a chemical. On the other hand, problems of error in assessing the response and in measuring the amount of the drug actually taken (compliance) are similar to problems of measuring exposure and case status which occur in cohort and case-control studies. The second difference between clinical trials and *some* case-control and historic cohort studies is that the response often is measured or assessed by someone who is unaware of the subject's group status. This diminishes any potential bias which might arise if an investigator is aware of a person's case or control status and subconsciously uses this information in assessing exposure status.

There is a huge literature concerning the analysis data from clinical trials, called survival analysis, the details of which are beyond the scope of this book. The main statistical method used is the Mantel-Haenszel procedure and generalizations that allow for the use of regression analysis to account for relevant covariates. The approach is similar to our discussion of the data in the *Hogan v. Pierce* case in Chapter 6, where the data before each response (cure, remission or death) studied is considered as a separate 2×2 table. At the end of the study period we compare the observed number of responses in all the tables that occurred in the treatment group with its expected value given in Chapter 5.

There is one aspect of survival analysis which allows us to obtain more information than is available from a simple comparison of the proportions of cures in the two groups at the time the study ends. When the status of the subjects is monitored regularly, we can obtain the proportions who died (or survived) in each interval and construct an ogive for mortality.

Often the proportion of persons surviving at least to time t is preferred as a measure. This is just

(13.13)   one minus the fraction of subjects dying by time t *or*
$S(t)$ = the fraction of subjects surviving for at least
time t after treatment,

and $S(t)$ is called the *survival* function.

The estimation of $S(t)$ from data obtained in a clinical trial is more difficult than the formation of the ogive in Chapter 1 because subjects may remain in a five-year study for various amounts of time. The data from a clinical trial is often summarized in the form given in Table 13.5, which presents mortality data from a diabetes trial which assessed the efficacy of several treatment modalities. One of the treatments (tolbutamide) was discovered to have a serious side-effect related to cardiovascular problems.

The data in Table 13.5 and the mortality and survival curves in Figure 13.2 show that after eight years there is a clear difference between the survival patterns of the two groups. They also reveal that throughout all the years of follow-up, patients given tolbutamide did no better than patients just on a restricted diet and a placebo. The data also illustrates the importance of following study subjects for an appropriate length of

TABLE 13.5. Cumulative Mortality from All Causes Per
100 Persons at Risk (by Year of Follow-
Up) and their Standard Errors

Year of Follow-Up	Placebo (Control)	Tolbutamide
1	0.0 (.7)	0.0 (.7)
2	2.1 (1.4)	3.3 (1.4)
3	4.9 (1.8)	6.6 (1.8)
4	6.3 (2.1)	9.3 (2.1)
5	7.0 (2.3)	13.0 (2.3)
6	8.0 (2.5)	14.8 (2.4)
7	8.0 (2.9)	20.3 (3.0)
8	8.0 (3.4)	22.9 (3.4)

Note: Adapted from Table 13 in Cornfield (1971). The data refers to patients who adhered to the treatment regimen. The sample sizes were approximately 143 in the placebo group and 151 in the treated group. The standard errors are given in parentheses.

time. Notice that a significant difference between the mortality rates doesn't appear until the fifth or sixth year.

b.   Drug approval cases

A major use of clinical trials is to substantiate the safety and efficacy of new drugs. The Food and Drug Administration (FDA) requires drug companies to submit at least two well-controlled studies establishing that a drug satisfies this requirement. Typically, efficacy is easier to define and establish with data than safety, as it is virtually impossible to prove a negative such as there are no side effects of the drug. Moreover, the safety of a drug often depends on the severity or criticality of the disease, as more severe side effects are tolerable in the cure of a life-threatening disease than of other illnesses.

In 1962, Congress amended the Food Drug and Cosmetic Act of 1938,

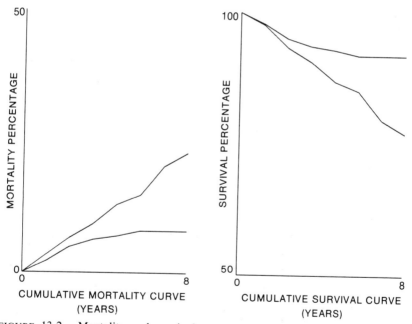

FIGURE 13.2.   Mortality and survival curves comparing the patients receiving tolbutamide with patients on a placebo based on the data in Table 13.5. Notice that the vertical axis for the mortality percentage goes from 0% to 50%, while the vertical axis for the survival curve (the complement of the mortality curve) has a maximum of 100% and a minimum of 50%.

establishing a procedure for the FDA to give premarketing clearance for new drugs to ensure their efficacy as well as their safety. New drug applications (NDAs) had to provide "substantial evidence" that the drug is effective for its intended use. The 1962 act also contained a "grandfather" clause exempting drugs already on the market which were not covered by an effectiveness provision under the 1938 act from the new act.

The term "substantial evidence" is defined in the law to mean "evidence consisting of adequate and well-controlled investigations, including clinical investigations by experts qualified by scientific training and experience to evaluate the effectiveness of the drug involved, on the basis of which it could fairly and responsibly be concluded by such experts that the drug will have the effect it purports or is represented to have..." 21 U.S.C. & 355(d). The act gave the FDA authority to promulgate appropriate regulations. The formal regulations[3] set forth standards for the supporting evidence which are consistent with the guidelines we described. In particular, the protocol or study plan should state the objective of the study, describe an adequate method for selecting the subjects and randomly assigning them to the study groups in order that the groups are comparable in terms of pertinent variables such as, age, sex, severity or duration of the disease and the use of drugs other than the one being tested. The appropriateness of the FDA's criteria were upheld by the U.S. Supreme Court in *Weinberger v. Hynson, Westcott and Dunning* 412 U.S. 609 (1982), which reproduced the criteria in an appendix. The FDA standards also state that uncontrolled studies are not acceptable as the *sole* basis for the approval of effectiveness but may provide corroborative support. However, they do indicate that under certain circumstances the use of historical controls might be appropriate (e.g., a clinic dealing with acute leukemia in children might give patients a new drug and assess its effectiveness by comparing the remission rates obtained with the new drug to historical rates). Of course, the comparability of the control and treatment groups with respect to other influential factors needs to be documented carefully. Currently, at least two well-controlled studies, one of which should be a field study that approximates the actual use of the drug by typical patients, usually are required. We now discuss the use of these standards in cases involving drugs for animals as well as humans, while there may be some differences in the FDA standards for approval of drugs intended for use on animals and those that will be given to humans, the statistical aspects remain the same.

Comment.   The requirement that efficacy be demonstrated in two careful studies may create a problem when the studies are too small to have high power to detect a meaningful effect. Even if each study has 90% power, the probability that both will yield a statistically significant result is .81. In situations where it is difficult to recruit patients, e.g., the disease is rare, this may reduce the probability that an effective drug receives approval. In a small sample study one might only have a power of 75% so the probability that two such studies show significance is $(.75)^2 = .563$. This is why the FDA may grant approval on the basis of only one study in special circumstances, such as the non-availability of other drugs or rareness of the disease.

Masti-Kure Products Co. v. FDA[4]

This case concerned a manufacturer's appeal of FDA's withdrawal of its approval of a new animal drug containing both penicillin and neomycin for use in treating mastitis in lactating cows. The statistical issues in the case concerned the comparability of the control and treatment groups and the propriety of pooling data.

The first study, conducted by the drug company in 1973, compared the cure rates of cows treated with the new combination drug and cows that received *no* treatment at all. The regulatory standards, noted in a footnote of the opinion, specify that a "precise statement of the control group against which the effects of the new treatment modality can be compared" should be given and described three types of control groups

(a) placebo controls (comparing treated animals with controls given an inactive drug, but noted that proper blinding is necessary for valid comparisons),
(b) active dry controls, who receive a known effective drug, and
(c) historical controls.

The FDA claimed that the proper control group would be cows treated with penicillin (or neomycin) *alone,* as they both were known to be effective so that the firm's study did not demonstrate that the new drug was more effective than either drug alone. The court upheld FDA's criticism.

Comment.   Part of the issue here is the interpretation of efficacy. Should a new drug be required to be more effective than other drugs or just of "equal effectiveness"?

TABLE 13.6.   The Number and Fraction of Cows Cured by the New and Old Drugs from *Masti-Kure*. The Data are Organized by the Infections Studied

Control Type	Streptococcus				Staphlococcus			
	Cured	Not Cured	Total	Fraction	Cured	Not Cured	Total	Fraction
Harvey	33	1	34	.97	3	2	5	.60
Cleveland	14	0	14	1.00	1	4	5	.20
Reeves	28	2	30	.93	3	2	5	.60
All Control	75	3	78	.96	7	8	15	.47
Treated (Reeves)	35	1	36	.97	1	0	2	.50

Source: The data is taken from the opinion 587 F.2d 1099 (1979) at 1105-6.

We next describe a study submitted by Masti-Kure where the control cows were given penicillin. In 1974 cows from three herds were used: Harvey, Cleveland and Reeves. The data is summarized in Table 13.6 and suggest that the new drug is about on a par with penicillin alone. The FDA questioned the study because all treated cows were from the Reeves herd, while controls were from all three herds and the herds were subject to differences in management practices, sanitation and general health. The firm did not explain its unbalanced selection of test animals from the three herds, and the appellate court agreed with the FDA's criticism.

Finally, Masti-Kure attempted to combine the results of two studies (one on each infection). The appellate court noted that a combination of multiple studies might be proper provided adequate steps had been taken to assure their comparability and these procedures were described to the FDA.

The design of the 1974 study was clearly poor from a statistical view, as it would have been easy to randomly allocate half of the cows from each herd to the treatment and control groups. If the herd status of a cow was an important covariate and the MH summary test (5.29) was used to analyze the data, the Harvey and Cleveland cows would be ignored in the analysis and the generalizability of the inference of effectiveness (or of equivalent efficacy) to all cows would be questionable. The study apparently failed to consider the power of the statistical test in its design. For the staph comparison, even if pooling all the controls were proper, the difference between 7/15 and 1/2 is not statistically significant; indeed, if the cure rates were the same (1/2), one expects to find 7 or 8 of the 15 control cows cured. Furthermore, if there were herd differences so that the treated group should only be compared with the Reeves cows, the use of only two treated cows from that herd in the staphlococcus part of the clinical trial is clearly subminimal. If one only used cows from the Reeves herd and desired to detect a difference between cure rates of .5 and .6 (the cure rate of the Reeve's control cows), then one should have studied a total of about 780 cows in order for a two-sided test at the .05 level to have 80% power of detecting this difference. Even a one-sided test would require a total of 610 cows in the sample[5] in order to satisfy the 80% power criteria. Obviously, the Masti-Kure study was too small to detect such a difference so that the null hypothesis of "equal effectiveness" was not really being tested in a practical sense.

Comments.   (1) In this case and in *Smith Kline v. FDA*, 587 F.2d 1107 (D.C. Cir. 1978) the method of statistical pooling is not described. In Chapters 5 and 6 we saw that simply adding up the data across all strata is often inappropriate and that the data in each strata should be examined first and the results combined. This allows us to assess whether the results are similar in each strata.

(2) This case also illustrates another advantage of properly designed clinical trials over observational studies. By proper selection of treatment and control cows from each strata (herd), the firm could have created a well balanced data set. If we were comparing promotion rates of minority and majority workers in three occupations requiring specific training, then an unbalanced allocation could occur due to differences in education or training workers received *prior* to joining the employer's staff. Similarly, persons living near the site of a dump possibly contaminated by toxic waste may differ from those living in a different part of town on a pertinent factor (age, diet, smoking pattern), thereby complicating the comparison of the incidence rates of a disease in the two areas.

We next discuss several other FDA cases.

Cooper Laboratories Inc. v. FDA[6]

Here the court accepted FDA's criticisms of a submission by the company, as six of the eight studies it relied on were uncontrolled. Moreover, the two controlled studies were inadequate because the method of selecting controls and assigning subjects to treatment did not assure that the treatment and control groups were comparable with regard to other influential factors.

American Cyanamid Co. v. Young[7]

This case concerned the evidence the firm submitted to support a drug to control fleas on dogs. The drug Proban was alleged to control fleas when administered *twice* weekly. The studies, however, reported data showing that Proban killed fleas up to 24 hours after a dog ingested it, however, no data was submitted on its effectiveness 48 or 72 hours later. Thus, the response to the drug's effect was not measured appropriately. Other deficiencies in the submission were the lack of well-controlled clinical trials including a field experiment designed to assess the effectiveness of a drug under situations approximating its actual use. Finally, several tests did not use the same formula for the drug that was to be marketed.

Comment. From a statistical view, one might test whether or not the various formulations had similar effects, i.e., test the null hypothesis that the *effects* in the various trials were equal. One might use a significance level of .10 or even .20 in order that this test have high power. If the hypothesis of equal effectiveness were accepted, then it would be reasonable to consider the separate studies as testing the same drug. In the actual case, the versions varied in their inert ingredients (excipients), and several witnesses said that the safety and effectiveness of the drug could be affected by the inert ingredient.

Premo Pharmaceutical Laboratories v. U.S.[8]

This case concerned the amount of evidence required by the FDA to document the efficacy of a generic equivalent or a "me too" drug when the drug is claimed to be a copy of an already approved one. The FDA allows an abbreviated application which relies on the safety and the effectiveness test carried out on the original or pioneer drug. Usually the FDA will approve a "me too" drug once it has been shown to be equivalent[9] to the original. However, if the inactive ingredients in the "me too" drug differ from the original, the FDA can require testing of the drug, unless it is shown that the "me too" drug is generally recognized among experts in the evaluation of drug safety and efficacy as being safe and effective and that the drug has been in use for a reasonable time.

Because the excipients in the "me too" drug were different from the already approved one, the FDA required *Premo* to carry out full testing. The district court accepted the firm's evidence of drug equivalence (see Table 13.7) but the FDA did not. The appellate court reversed that part of the opinion because the district court had substituted its opinion on safety

TABLE 13.7. *Bioequivalence Data Used in Premo v. U.S.* Average Number of Micrograms of the Active Ingredient Per Milliliter of Blood Serum

Hours Since Administration	Insulase (New)	Diabinese (Pioneer)
.5	9.4	24.9
1	14.0	31.5
2	23.5	32.9
3	24.7	32.5
4	27.9	29.5
8	26.3	24.9
12	23.6	22.6
24	18.4	18.8
48	11.9	13.4
96	7.3	6.8
168	3.6	3.0
216	0.7	1.0

Source: 475 F.Supp. 52 (S.D.N.Y. 1979) at 56.
Note: The opinion does not report the sample size or details of the study from which the data were derived.

and efficacy for the FDA's. The court should have limited itself to the question of whether the "me too" drug was generally recognized as equivalent to the pioneer. The studies the firm relied on had not been published, and most of the witnesses first learned about the new drug (Insulase) after becoming involved with the lawsuit. Hence, none could testify that the new drug was generally recognized as safe and effective as the therapeutic equivalent of the standard drug (Diabinese).

Comment.   If one looks at the data in Table 13.7 the bioequivalence of the drugs seems questionable. The pioneer drug has a higher level of absorption and reaches its maximum level sooner than the new drug. The only aspect in which the two drugs appear to be quite similar is in the way their effect decays after four hours after administration.

In the Matter of Oral Proteolytic Enzymes[10]

The FDA withdrew approval of five oral proteolytic enzymes (OPEs) which were supposed to be effective in controlling edema and inflammation associated with medical and dental procedures because they were not supported by adequate studies. The decision reiterated the criteria of two sound clinical studies, noting that the results of a single trial have been accepted only in special circumstances such as: where the disease is very rare so it is difficult to obtain subjects for two studies, the disease process is expensive to study, or the one study is large and multicentered and the disease is fatal and no alternative therapy exists.

The following statistical issues arose at the hearing:

(1) Patients in several of the studies offered as evidence of efficacy used a concomitant-medication or treatment along with the OPE or placebo. The drug firms argued that the randomization process would balance the proportions of concomitant-medication users in the control and treated groups. The FDA argued that this could compromise the comparability of the two groups, especially as the firms did not submit data concerning the period patients took the concomitant-medication or its strength. The decision noted that without this information one was unable to assess the degree of possible confounding between the effect of the OPE and other medication.

(2) The FDA distinguished between clinical and statistical significance of the effectiveness of a drug. For instance, one study found a difference in lip measurements of one centimeter out of a total of 24 centimeters to be statistically significant, but the FDA asserted that this difference was not clinically important. Since statistical significance depends on the sample size, as well as the magnitude of the effect, it is reasonable for the FDA to require both a meaningful and statistically significant difference.

(3) Although a number of studies were submitted into evidence, the drug firms argued that studies *not showing statistically significant* results in favor of OPEs *cannot* detract from the studies showing a significant effect. The FDA objected to the original hearing judge's failure to consider the negative studies. The commissioner's decision did not address the issue as it deemed the firm's major studies defective, primarily because of their failure to assess the effect of concomitant-medication.

Comment. The similarity between the questions raised in this hearing and those which arise in the analysis of data in discrimination cases is noteworthy, as they illustrate the statistical principles common to all studies. In particular,

(1) Whenever possible, data on relevant covariates (seniority and education in EEO cases, concomitant-medication and prior health status in medical studies) should be collected. One can then ascertain whether the groups being compared have similar distributions of these covariates, in

which case the simple comparisons probably would not be seriously affected, or whether the data should be appropriately stratified prior to analysis and/or analyzed by a regression approach.

(2) Again the issue of statistical and practical significance arises. It is preferable for agencies to establish measures of practical effect, such as the four-fifths rule for assessing disparate impact, *prior* to a particular hearing. Even general guidelines could prevent a large proportion of disputes. Moreover, clinical trials could then be designed to have high (at least 80%) power to detect meaningful effects.

(3) In the EEO context courts have avoided the error of the drug firms by not allowing plaintiffs to focus on isolated time periods (analogous to individual studies) showing a difference while ignoring the totality of the data. As we realized in Chapters 6, 7 and 11, some courts made the opposite error of insisting on significance in each year of data or in each occupation, which meant that they required a level of significance less than one in 10,000 for the entire data set, without considering the power of the statistical test. The FDA does not appear to be requiring that each study demonstrate effectiveness. Rather, it seems to advocate the logically correct policy of using all studies to obtain the best estimate of the effectiveness of a drug. Additional problems that occur in combining studies from several clinical trials are that some are more reliable than others and that the patient populations studied may not be homogeneous. For example, if a drug is effective for a well defined subgroup of the population, including studies of other segments of the population would mask its effectiveness for suitable patients. The solution here is to conduct a further clinical trial restricting patients to the subgroups on which the drug showed effectiveness in the earlier study.

c. A misleading advertising case involving the reliability of clinical studies: Proctor and Gamble Co. v. Cheseborough-Pond's Inc.[11]

Both firms produce skin lotions designed for the hands and body rather than the face and they sued each other for misleading comparative advertisements in violation of the Lanham Act 15 U.S.C. Section 1051–1127 (1982). In terms of market share Cheseborough's product Vaseline Intensive Care Lotion (VICL) and Proctor and Gamble's Wondra are two leading lotions. In 1983, in order to increase the market share of Wondra, Proctor and Gamble launched an advertising campaign, claiming that because of its additional amount of glycerin clinical tests established that New Wondra relieves dry skin better than any other leading lotion. On the other hand, Cheseborough's ads claimed that no other product is superior to VICL and, as Judge Goettal observed, "we have a situation in which at least one of the parties must logically be wrong." Thus, the court was asked by both parties to determine whose claim was misleading.

Both sides agreed that large scale clinical tests carried out on a double-blind basis so that neither the subject nor the grader (person evaluating skin condition) knows which product was applied were the most appropriate studies. A problem the court faced was that while graders could determine the relative condition of a person's skin and while each grader was internally consistent, there could be a wide variation *between* graders due, in part, to the verbal descriptions not being precisely translatable into a numerical rating.

Proctor and Gamble conducted a test of four products in 1981 and six in 1983. Persons who had evidence of dry skin were admitted into the study group and randomly assigned a lotion. Proctor and Gamble used only one grader, Dr. Dunlap, to evaluate all subjects. The subjects were not given instructions on how much lotion to use and apparently they were not asked about their pattern of use. The 1981 tests showed that New Wondra scored statistically significantly higher (one-sided .05 level test) than VICL, old Wondra or a placebo. The 1983 test results indicated that New Wondra had the highest average rating but not statistically significantly higher than the other products. For a subset of persons with more severe rough, dry skin (those receiving an initial grade in the upper half), the difference was significant.

The above results were derived from a nonparametric analysis of the data, not fully described in the opinion, which used analysis of covariance (presumably calculated on the after-treatment rating *or* a change in score over the course of treatment). Cheseborough criticized the method of analysis and also asserted that weather conditions should be factored into the analysis. The judge noted that while weather is a relevant factor, its effect on the overall comparison should be negligible because of the random assignment of subjects. He also noted that the assumptions for the analysis of covariance were approximately satisfied. Thus, he concluded that while Proctor and Gamble's tests were far from perfect they were not worthless.

Comments. (1) This opinion recognizes the major advantage of randomization is that the groups should be approximately balanced, even with respect to a factor not originally considered. In most situations and especially with small samples, it is wise to check that the means and standard deviations of the initial skin ratings are similar in all the groups being compared, since the effect of the weather might interact with skin condition, e.g., aggravate the more (or less) serious conditions more (less) severely. If the groups are balanced with respect to the initial scores then the interaction would not seriously compromise the validity of the comparison. The opinion was logically correct in remarking that the weather conditions were similar for all subjects so it was not necessary statistically to consider it as a covariate.

(2) If several graders had been used, the analysis could have been stratified by grader and the results aggregated, which would avoid the problem of grader inconsistency.

(3) The significance of the effect on the subgroup with more serious conditions is diminished by the fact that several tests were made on the same set of data, so the probability that one test is significant is greater than .05. A further study could be made for persons with serious conditions to verify this finding.

We now turn to Cheseborough's study in which 73 subjects used VICL on one hand and Wondra on the other and were instructed to apply the lotion twice daily. The data showed no significant difference between the lotions after the subjects were examined one, three, five, eight and ten days after the initiation of treatment. The analysis of the data apparently ignored the matching aspect, which we know often biases the results towards nonsignificance. Furthermore, the analysis used the first day's ratings in which the subjects could not be expected to display a difference. This, again, biases the results towards a finding of nonsignificance. The opinion also noted a variety of problems such as the scores on all hands improved greatly between days eight and ten and that the trial was carried out for a short time. Since this was a controlled test, each participant was given a measured amount of lotion, the dose administration was quite different from Proctor and Gamble's unlimited system. Proctor and Gamble asserted that the matched pair method could have led to participant confusion, with subjects putting the wrong lotion on each hand.

The opinion concluded that Cheseborough's tests were more questionable than Proctor and Gamble's, however, Cheseborough had offered other studies which also showed no clinically significant difference to support their advertising claim of parity (not superiority) and then noted that whether differences are significant depends on how fine a line is being drawn and that this was a dispute over testing methods and neither side could show deception or bad faith on the part of its competitor. Judge

Goettal found that neither party demonstrated a likelihood of success on the merits of its claim and denied their respective motions for preliminary injunctions. The opinion also raised doubts about the role of courts in such cases where the conditions are not serious and the test measurements are subjective.

Comments. (1) The problem of dose administration and adherence to the treatment regime is quite an important one in *all* clinical trials. In the Cheseborough study, if the bottle containers had been clearly labelled (left or right), it is hard to imagine many subjects getting confused. The vagueness of the dose administration in Proctor and Gamble's trial would be more important in the evaluation of a serious drug, especially if over-medication could create harmful side effects.

(2) Neither study seems to have been planned on the basis of what a clinically meaningful difference would be and what sample sizes are needed to have high power to detect this difference using a .05 level test.

(3) The importance of integrating the analysis with the way the data is collected and the assumptions required for the validity of the analysis appears to have been given low priority by both parties. The matching and the fact that the same persons were being followed in the Cheseborough study may not have been fully considered in the design and data analysis.

(4) The short length of time of the Cheseborough study was noted, but both studies did not follow their subjects for a while after the study was completed. This is usually wise, as one would like to observe how long the improvement lasts and whether any delayed side effects occur.

d. Public policy issues in clinical trials

In order to assure the health of the patients in blinded trials, a review committee monitors its progress. If it becomes apparent that one treatment is superior to the other, they can stop the trial and put all patients on the better drug. The topic of informed consent of patients has received substantial attention (Grundner, 1980, Howard, J. M., DeMets, D. and the BHAT Research Group, 1981) and needs to be considered in planning a study. Individuals should be told the risks involved and that they may not receive a drug or treatment if they are randomly assigned to a control group receiving a placebo. In practice this often means that patients suitable for a study are those for which a preferred therapy does not already exist.

Sometimes there is a tension between the desire of researchers for accurate data and the privacy rights of subjects. Friedman, Furberg and DeMets (1985) mention that this topic arises in recruiting patients. Should the names of potential subjects be given to medical investigators without their knowledge? If a patient doesn't wish to participate should investigators have access to their medical records? Even keep their name and address on file? Similarly, these authors note that at the end of a study it is extremely helpful to know the vital status[12] of subjects who dropped out of the trial and to even try to locate the person. They suggest that the informed consent form given patients at the beginning of the trial state that if they stop participating they give researchers the right to find their vital status from a national death registry or the Social Security system.

This author believes that respondents to surveys as well as patients should be given as much knowledge about all the data that will be collected about them and placed in their file. For purposes of health research, the public has been quite cooperative and response rates are high, so there is little benefit in not informing participants fully. Moreover, much public confidence can be lost by not properly informing study participants. We now turn to two studies which had to be modified in midcourse because of the investigators' proper concern for the health of the patients.

The Diabetic Retinopathy Study

Since diabetic retinopathy had become a leading cause of blindness and visual disability in the U.S., and as the eyesight of a victim of the disease usually degenerates over time, a study of the effect of photocoagulation treatment (either a xenon arc or argon laser) was undertaken in 1971 at the National Eye Institute. Each patient enrolled in the study was required to have a prespecified level of the disease and also to have at least 20/100 vision in each eye. The patients were recruited over a 39-month period and a total of 1758 subjects had entered the study by September 30, 1975. One eye of each patient was treated and the other was left untreated. The eye given the treatment and the modality of treatment (argon or xenon) were determined by randomization. A small group of 16 patients were given a combined argon-xenon treatment, but this treatment ended after six months. These patients were excluded from the analysis.

Although patients were supposed to have at least three years of followup, by late 1975 or early 1976 it became apparent that the treatment was beneficial. In Table 13.8 we report the rates of visual acuity of less than 5/200 (indicating severe deterioration of eyesight) per 100 eyes at risk, as

TABLE 13.8.   Cumulative Incidence Rate of Visual Acuity of 5/200 at
Two or More Consecutive Follow-Up Visits

Months of Follow-Up	Untreated	Treated	Difference	Z-Statistic (5.6)
8	1.3 (1375)	.7 (1375)	.6	1.5
12	3.9 (1279)	2.4 (1283)	1.5	2.1
16	6.7 (989)	3.8 (1001)	2.9	2.9
20	10.8 (775)	5.3 (790)	5.5	4.2
24	16.3 (457)	6.4 (477)	9.9	5.5
28	20.0 (237)	6.4 (259)	13.6	5.9

Source: Table 4 from the Diabetic Retinopathy Research Group (1976). The
number of patients at risk during the period is given in parenthesis.
Note: The rates are expressed in percentages rather than fractions. The
treated group contains all treated eyes regardless of modality.

well as the number of eyes at risk. Although the routine application of the
test for a difference between proportions is not strictly applicable, as the
same persons are being followed, so the tests at each follow-up period are
not independent, it is clear from Table 13.8 that, even making a statistical
allowance for multiple testing and dependence, by two years there is a
clear benefit from treatment.

The medical review committee examined the data and found that patients with higher risk characteristics, such as a high number of new
vessels near the disk, were the main beneficiaries of treatment. In view of
the seriousness of eye degeneration, all subjects were informed of the
results and their implications, all persons in the untreated group with eyes
in the range of beneficial treatment were offered the treatment.

The study was continued in order to assess whether the treatment
remained helpful and whether there were any serious long-term side effects. This clinical trial is important because it demonstrates that statistical methods cannot be mechanically used like a robot without regard to
the particular area of application and potential consequences to the study
subjects. Even though the clinical trial was well planned, medical ethics
compelled a change. This is another reason why criteria such as:

(a) the results should be significant at the .05 level or

(b) a clinical trial should be conducted for at least x years to assess
potential side effects

should be considered as guidelines rather than absolute standards that must be satisfied in order for the results to be useful. Of course, deviations from general guidelines and standards should be explained.

We close this section by describing a controversial study that not only questioned the effectiveness of drugs used to treat diabetes in adults, it showed that one of them (tolbutamide) was harmful.

The University Group Diabetes Program Study

This study concerned the effects of hypoglycemic agents on patients with adult onset diabetes and was conducted in 12 clinics. Patients were randomly assigned to a placebo treatment (just diet) and three different drug regimens: tolbutamide, standard insulin and variable insulin. After a number of years patients on tolbutamide showed a $2\frac{1}{2}$ fold elevation in cardiovascular mortality (Table 1 on pg. 790 of the U.G.D.P. report, *Diabetes,*

TABLE 13.9.   Number of Deaths by Cause Among Persons Adhering to Their Treatment Regimen for Each Treatment Modality

	Placebo	Tolbutamide	Insulin Standard	Insulin Variable
No. at risk of death	143	151	121	92
Cardiovascular causes				
1. Myocardial infarction	0	10	3	0
2. Sudden death	2	2	4	2
3. Other heart disease	1	5	1	0
4. Extracardiac vascular disease	2	5	3	2
Total	5	22	11	4
Noncardiovascular causes				
5. Cancer	4	2	3	0
6. Cause other than 1–5	2	2	1	1
7. Unknown cause	0	0	1	0
All causes	11	26	16	5
Percent dead				
Cardiovascular causes	3.5	14.6	9.1	4.3
All causes	7.7	17.2	13.2	5.4

Source: Table 12 of Cornfield (1971).

Note: Patient received *all* of prescribed study medication in at least 75% of all follow-up periods. A patient was regarded as receiving *all* of his assigned study medication in a given follow-up period if he received medication in the dosage specified for at least 75 days of that three-month period and if he was not receiving any hypoglycemic agent other than his assigned study medication during that period.

1970) and showed no evidence of improved efficacy. After several criticisms were published (Schor, 1971, Feinstein, 1971), Cornfield (1971), and later an entire committee (1975), reanalyzed the data.

Before discussing specific criticisms we present two basic tables from Cornfield's paper concerning patients who adhered to their assigned regimen. Clearly, any effects are best assessed on these patients since the estimated effectiveness of a drug could be diminished by including patients who were supposed to take it regularly but did not.[13] Table 13.9 presents the number of deaths by cause in each group and clearly indicates an increased risk for patients given tolbutamide and perhaps also for those given standard insulin relative to the insulin variable group. The next table (13.10) gives the mortality rates at the end of the follow-up year. They are higher than the percentages in Table 13.9 due to the loss in patients over time, but the mortality percentages reinforce the previous table.

The critics raised a number of points. The major ones for our purposes are

(1) The randomization produced biased groups, in particular the tolbutamide group had greater risk of mortality than the others.

(2) An excess mortality rate did not occur in all clinics and was only due to the results in three or four of the clinics.

TABLE 13.10.   Mortality Rates in Percentages and Their Standard Errors Obtained by Survival Analysis for Patients in the UGDP Study by Year of Follow-Up

Year of Follow-Up	Placebo	Tolbutamide	Insulin Standard	Insulin Variable
All causes				
		Cumulative Mortality		
1	0.0	0.0	1.6	2.0
2	2.1	3.3	2.5	4.1
3	4.9	6.6	4.1	4.1
4	6.3	9.3	7.4	4.1
5	7.0	13.0	9.2	4.1
6	8.0	14.8	10.2	4.1
7	8.0	20.3	15.2	4.1
8	8.0	22.9	15.2	9.8

TABLE 13.10.   (*Continued*)

Year of Follow-Up	Placebo	Tolbutamide	Insulin Standard	Insulin Variable
		Standard Errors		
1	0.7	0.7	0.8	0.9
2	1.4	1.4	1.5	1.7
3	1.8	1.8	2.0	2.2
4	2.1	2.1	2.3	2.6
5	2.3	2.3	2.6	2.8
6	2.5	2.4	2.7	3.1
7	2.9	3.0	3.2	3.6
8	3.4	3.4	3.7	4.3

Cardiovascular causes

		Cumulative Mortality		
1	0.0	0.0	0.8	2.0
2	0.7	2.0	1.7	4.1
3	3.5	4.7	2.5	4.1
4	3.5	7.4	5.0	4.1
5	3.5	11.2	6.8	4.1
6	3.5	13.1	6.8	4.1
7	3.5	17.3	10.3	4.1
8	3.5	20.0	10.3	4.1

		Standard Errors		
1	0.6	0.6	0.7	0.8
2	1.2	1.1	1.2	1.4
3	1.6	1.5	1.7	1.9
4	1.8	1.8	2.0	2.2
5	2.1	2.0	2.3	2.5
6	2.2	2.1	2.4	2.7
7	2.6	2.6	2.8	3.1
8	2.9	2.9	3.2	3.6

Source: Table 13 from Cornfield (1971).
Note: The data reflects the total mortality rates and those due to cardiovascular problems for patients with high adherence. The definition of this category of patient is given in the footnote to Table 13.9.

The second criticism is the same fallacy of requiring a significant differ-ence in each strata that the reader is familiar with. The maximum number of patients given a treatment in any of the participating clinics was 22, so requiring a significant difference in each clinic means that a very low type I error (less than one in a million) is being adopted, which implies a high type II error. One needs to have multicenter studies precisely because only a small number of patients are available to each clinic, especially when patients have to meet the eligibility criteria and agree to participate. The proper procedure is to combine the results across clinics by an appro-priate method such as the Mantel-Haenszel procedure.

To study the distribution of risk factors across the four study groups, Cornfield developed Table 13.11, which reports the number of patients by the number of risk factors they had. It is evident that the tolbutamide patients had a slight disadvantage relative to the other groups. Indeed, a t-test based on

$$(13.14) \quad \frac{\overline{X}_1 - \overline{X}_2}{\sqrt{\text{Var}(\overline{X}_1) + \text{Var}(\overline{X}_2)}} = \frac{.27}{\sqrt{(.083)^2 + (.092)^2}} = \frac{.27}{.124} = 2.18,$$

where X is the number of risk factors a patient had and $\overline{X}$ denotes the

TABLE 13.11.   Distribution of Baseline Risk Factors in the Patients Assigned to Each Treatment Group

No. of Baseline Risk Factors	Placebo	Tolbutamide	Insulin Standard	Insulin Variable
0	28	25	22	15
1	60	50	62	76
2	59	58	60	57
3	26	34	34	30
4	10	17	8	4
5	2	4	8	4
6	0	1	1	1
Total	185	189	195	187
Mean No. of risk factors	1.65	1.92	1.86	1.72
Standard error	0.083	0.092	0.089	0.079

* The eight baseline risk factors considered are age ≥ 55 years, hypertension, history of digitalis use, history of angina pectoris, significant ECG abnormality, cholesterol level ≥ 300 mg/100 ml, relative body weight ≥ 1.25, and arterial calcification.
Source: Table 1 from Cornfield (1971).

group mean, indicates a difference in the average number of risk factors between the tolbutamide and placebo group. Thus, one should allow for this in evaluating the results. Before doing this we note that there were six possible pair-wise comparisons one could make, so the fact that one was significant at the .05 level (two-sided) is *not* that surprising.[14] Even though the imbalances could have arisen by chance, the analysis of the data should account for it, as we are primarily concerned with assessing the effectiveness of the treatment modalities.

In Table 13.12 we report the mortality percentages by number of risk factors from Cornfield (1971). The data suggests that the average number of risk factors may not be as important as having at least four or five of them, however, the patients on tolbutamide had the highest mortality rates for patients with 0, 1 or 2 risk factors, who formed over 75% of the study. The standardized (for the number of risk factors) rates in Table 13.12 still indicate that tolbutamide was twice as risky as the placebo and at least 1.5 times as risky as the insulin treatments. While some risk factors (e.g., smoking) were not known, it is implausible that smoking could explain the entire difference between the standardized rates, especially in a randomized study.

Comments. (1) It would be interesting to see the same data for all patients reported in Tables 13.11 and 13.12 restricted to the patients who

TABLE 13.12. Cardiovascular Mortality Percentages from Each Treatment Class Stratified by Number of Baseline Risk Factors

No. of Baseline Risk Factors	Placebo	Tolbutamide	Insulin Standard	Insulin Variable
0	3.6	8.0	0.0	0.0
1	0.0	6.0	0.0	1.3
2	1.7	8.6	5.0	5.3
3	19.2	17.6	14.7	10.0
4	20.0	35.3	12.5	25.0
5	0.0	25.0	37.5	75.0
6	—	0.0	100.0	100.0
All	4.9	12.2	6.7	6.4
Standardized	5.1	10.9	5.9	7.2

Source: Table 7 from Cornfield (1971).

adhered to their treatment regimen. Indeed, the adherence rate of patients on (variable) insulin appears to be much less than those given other treatments.

(2) In Cornfield's paper the p-values of various tests for balance of the groups with respect to the risk factors are given, and almost none of them were significant at the .05 level. Indeed, if one adjusted the tests on whether the average number of risk factors in the four groups were equal for the number of tests carried out, one would not obtain a significant result at the .05 level. However, the two-tailed p-value[15] would be less than .20. Since we realized that the standardized rates did make a difference, in the conclusions we would have drawn from examining Table 13.10 alone (especially for the group on standard insulin), it is preferable to use a higher type I level such as .20 in tests which *check* for the balance of influential factors in the two groups being compared. If the randomization process has not produced groups that are at least that well balanced, potential covariates should be incorporated into the analysis as in the standardized rate analysis (Table 13.12).

(3) In addition to the statistical issues, there is an inherent conflict between obtaining sufficient information to conclude with virtual certainty that tolbutamide caused the excess cardiovascular deaths and ethical behavior. As Cornfield stated, "in investigations involving human subjects one is not obliged to continue treatment until a conclusive demonstration of the mortal effect of a supposedly therapeutic agent has been achieved, particularly when there is no possibility of demonstrating a positive effect on mortality by continuing." The critics who recommended further study of tolbutamide may not have given adequate weight to the greater risk patients, given this drug would be taken, especially as it was not more effective than already existing treatments for diabetes.

(4) The previous considerations should also have an impact on the way courts treat causation in medical cases. By insisting on virtual certainty of the link between exposure to a toxic agent and the development of a serious disease, courts may prevent injured parties from recovering damages because public health authorities and the medical profession may recommend discontinuance of exposure before a "statistically significant" excess of deaths among those exposed has been documented in two or more studies. When we discuss the judicial treatment of data in actual cases, we will see that there has been substantial variation in the acceptance of statistical evidence of practical causation, although recent cases[16] are showing an awareness of the need to place a reasonable burden of proof on the litigants.

4.   The Use of Observational Studies in Developing Associations Leading to a Determination of Practical Causation

In contrast with clinical trials, many epidemiologic studies observe the incidence or mortality rates of persons exposed to possible toxic agents and compare them to the corresponding rates of nonexposed persons. A major problem faced by these studies is insuring the comparability of the exposed (case) and nonexposed or case and control groups with respect to other relevant factors. Unlike the clinical trial, randomization cannot be used to help balance out covariates. Indeed, how could one assign people the task of smoking one pack of cigarettes per day and expect nonsmokers or two-pack-a-day smokers to comply?

In Chapters 5, 6, and 10 we introduced the reader to cohort (follow-up) studies as well as case-control studies and mentioned correlational or ecologic studies in Chapter 8. We now discuss the role of these studies in establishing a causal link between an agent and a disease. In the next section we present guidelines for assessing the validity of the results obtained from different types of studies.

a.   Criteria for establishing causality

The issue of whether a causal relationship between exposure to an agent and the subsequent development of a disease can be inferred from epidemiologic studies demonstrating a significantly increased risk in an exposed population is somewhat controversial. In part this is due to different views of the evidence needed to establish causation. Some may insist on knowing the biological mechanisms along the entire pathway, from exposure to the manifestation of the disease, before saying that exposure causes a disease. If a strong version of this view is taken, one can always disparage the results of any study asserting that it is only a statistical association or correlation and that another factor could be causing the disease or both exposure and the disease. Although spurious correlations do occur, they are more likely to arise in situations when both variates are measured at the same time[17]—so they may have a common cause—than in studies following people over time which obtain data on relevant covariates. Since almost all health professionals accept the ideas underlying the studies that linked cigarette smoking and lung cancer, we now list six criteria that should usually be satisfied in order that practical causation[18] can be established from statistical studies.

(1) The *strength* of the association, i.e., the magnitude of the relative

risk due to exposure (after the effect of other risk factors have been controlled for). The result of Cornfield (appendix to Chapter 6) is useful in this evaluation.

(2) The *consistency* of the association in several studies. When an increased relative risk is found in studies of different populations, e.g., in different locations, it is less likely that another risk factor can explain the association, as it would have to be present (at about the same level) in all the study populations. The similarity of the estimated relative risks (subject to sampling variability) also indicates consistency.

(3) Biologic or medical credibility. Do the results agree with theories of biologic mechanisms, i.e., is an association compatible with scientific and clinical knowledge?

(4) The time sequence: Exposure should precede the disease by a sufficient length of time to enable the disease to develop subsequent to exposure. This requirement is logically related to the previous one, as it relates the exposure-disease association to a biologically plausible time frame.

(5) An increasing dose-response curve should exist. This means that the relative risk of contracting a disease should increase as the amount, duration or intensity of exposure increases.

(6) The association between an agent and a disease or group of diseases should be reasonably specific. Typically a toxic agent will affect one or several organs of the body rather than every organ. Thus, one would be skeptical of a claim that exposure to an agent increases *all* forms of cancer. In Chapter 10 we saw that exposure to vinyl chloride increased the relative risk of liver cancer *not* all cancers.

When the above six criteria are established from the results of several reliable epidemiologic studies, for practical purposes causality should be regarded as having been established. Unfortunately, we cannot state a minimum number of studies that are needed, as this also depends on the magnitude of the relative risk and soundness of the studies. Rarely would one wish to rely on only one study so that two studies should be considered a practical minimum, and even then it would be helpful if other epidemiologic evidence such as standardized mortality studies or animal experiments are consistent with an increased association.

Comment.   The determination of whether an increasing dose-response relationship exists is sometimes difficult to evaluate. One feels more sure in situations showing an increasing trend, such as in Table 10.1 relating age to the incidence of heart problems or in Table 8.12 relating tumor rates to administered dose, than when an increase is not apparent. However, the estimated amount of exposure is subject to more error than the simple classification of exposed or not, and the effects of long-term exposure to a low dose or a short-term exposure to a high dose may not be comparable. Animal experiments are often useful in studying this issue, especially when exposure produces an excess risk (e.g., $R > 2$). Similarly, a finding of *no* excess risk is supported when there is no evidence of a dose-response curve. An example of such a negative (in the medical sense) finding is the given in Table 13.13 showing that coffee consumption by Finnish mothers was not related to birth defects. Apparently it is a coincidence that the highest relative risks were observed in mothers who drank one to three cups per day, but even these were not statistically significant and of small magnitude.

On the other hand, the Reye's syndrome studies did not show a strong relationship between the amount of aspirin taken for the relief of symptoms and the subsequent development of Reye's syndrome. Perhaps, once a certain dosage is administered a child becomes more susceptible to the disease. Because of the high relative risk of salicylate users relative to those using other medications, no one has seriously questioned the relationship on dose-response grounds.

TABLE 13.13.   Relative Risk for Congenital Malformations According to Coffee Consumption During Pregnancy

Malformation	Relative Risk (95% CONF) Number of Cups Per Day		
	None	1–3	4 or more
Central nervous system	1.0	1.4 (.8,2.8)	1.0 (.5,2.1)
Orofacial	1.0	1.0 (.6,1.5)	1.0 (.6,1.6)
Skeletal	1.0	1.2 (.7,1.9)	1.0 (.6,1.7)
Cardiovascular	1.0	1.2 (.7,2.2)	.8 (.4,1.4)
All	1.0	1.2 (.9,1.5)	1.0 (.7,1.3)

Source: Table 4 from Kurppa, K., Holmberg, P. C., Kuosma, E. and Saxen, L. (1983). Coffee Consumption During Pregnancy and Selected Congenital Malformations. *American Journal of Public Health* **73**, 1397–1399. The estimates were based on 465 matched pairs discordant with respect to coffee consumption.

*b. The role of various types of epidemiologic studies in uncovering
causes of disease*

The discovery of the determinants of a disease such as cancer often consists of following up a cluster of cases of a rare cancer, such as the cluster of cases of vaginal cancer in young women in Boston or noticing a relatively high incidence of cancer in a particular location. While a prospective cohort study is most similar to a clinical trial, it is often impractical to carry out, as one needs to follow the subjects for the latent period of the disease, which may be 20 years. Moreover, the sample size required (see appendix for details) to detect an excess risk of 2, say, may be quite large. Therefore, historical cohort studies tracing persons who worked in a plant 20 to 30 years ago, standardized incidence and mortality studies (Chapter 10) or case-control studies are often used.

A major problem in these studies is obtaining data on relevant covariates. The standardized mortality and incidence calculations used in occupational health studies implicitly assume that workers in the various occupations have a similar distribution of these covariates as the general population. While this is often a reasonable assumption, e.g., in Milgram's (1982) study of leukemia (Table 10.7), one cannot obtain information on covariates from the census data used to obtain the number of workers who are exposed. Additionally, one is assuming that all workers in an occupation were exposed and, as we saw in chapter 10, if nonexposed persons are considered as exposed, the power of these studies is reduced, leading to an underestimate of the risk.

By obtaining exposure data from company records *historical cohort* studies often yield more reliable data than standardized mortality studies using persons recorded as employed in the occupation in the census as the exposed group. This is especially true when persons have been individually monitored as the Hanford atomic plant workers are for radiation and somewhat less so when workers are assigned exposure estimates based on their job titles at various times or from measurements made at the work site, as all workers in the same job or location are assumed to have received an estimated average exposure. More seriously, historical cohort studies may not obtain reliable data on important covariates such as smoking. An exception to this may occur in studies of diseases with a long latency period. One can start the study before the disease occurs in the members of the cohort so that relevant information can be obtained from the study subjects. Of course, one can often assess the possible effect of a covariate via Cornfield's result. Finally, case-control studies can also be carried out, but, again, obtaining accurate information on exposures that occurred long ago can be difficult.

When a disease follows exposure within a relatively short time period, it is easier to initiate a true prospective cohort study, especially if there is a readily available large population, e.g., school children, workers in a large plant, or persons receiving medical care through a large health maintenance organization. Even so, unless that incidence rate is at least 5%, the size of the cohort needed will be large so that case control studies are more convenient to carry out. Furthermore, case-control studies using incident (new) cases are usually more reliable than those using prevalent (all existing) cases, as the patients are more likely to be available for interview so the data on covariates is more likely to be accurate. Information from close relatives or friends provided for extremely sick or recently deceased cases is usually subject to more error than that obtained from a direct personal interview.

Blot, Fraumeni, Mason and Hoover (1979) describe the various ways mortality data can be used to generate hypotheses for more careful studies of risk factors associated with long latency periods. For example, the age-adjusted lung cancer mortality rates by region of the country and degree of urbanization in Table 13.14 indicated the highest mortality from this cancer occurred in urban areas of the southeast. A more detailed

TABLE 13.14.   Average Annual Age-Adjusted Lung Cancer Mortality Rates (per 100,000 population) 1950–1969 Among Whites by Sex, Region and Degree of Urbanization

| Sex | Region | % of Population in Urban Areas | | | |
		0–24.9	25–49.9	50–74.9	75+
Male	Northeast	32.8	35.2	37.7	43.5
	Southeast	29.1	32.4	37.7	46.0
	Mountain	23.0	23.9	26.8	30.4
	Far West	32.0	32.8	34.2	40.7
Female	Northeast	5.9	5.6	5.6	6.7
	Southeast	5.1	5.1	6.0	6.8
	Mountain	4.3	4.6	5.1	5.6
	Far West	5.7	6.2	6.2	7.7

Source: Taken from Table 1 of Blot, Fraumeni, Mason and Hoover (1979), who report the data for all seven regions of the U.S.

correlation study regressed the age-adjusted county cancer rates on socio-economic indices and the industrial composition of the county. These regression results indicated a positive statistical association between lung cancer mortality rates and chemical, petroleum and paper manufacturing industries, suggesting an industrial component.

To follow up the statistical association, an analysis of death certificates and a case-control study were carried out. The case-control study showed that working in shipyards during World War II significantly increased one's risk of lung cancer. The increased risk was not explained by smoking or other occupations held. The overall relative risk obtained by logistic regression was 1.6 with a

$$95\% \text{ CONF}(R; 1.1, 2.1),$$

implying a statistically significant excess risk (at the .05 level for a two-sided test). There was an indication of a synergistic effect between smoking and having worked in shipyards, which is probably due to the use of asbestos in the shipyards. This example shows how the correlation method developed useful clues about the cause of a cancer, but the factor which caused the excess risk was not exposure to toxic agents at one's current occupation but at a previous one. Since the industries whose employees display higher than average mortality from lung cancer are those in which it is reasonable for former shipyard workers to seek employment, the original association is logically plausible.

Comments. (1) The pattern of industrial mobility of persons employed in the shipyards might be obtainable from the continuous work history sample of the Social Security Administration, which is a longitudinal sample of worker earnings, employers and location. If a substantial majority of the shipyard workers subsequently went to work in the industries now showing an increased risk of lung cancer, then we would have more confidence that the increased risk is due to past exposure to asbestos in shipyards rather than exposure to a substance used in the current work place.

(2) It is important to emphasize the difference between a statistical correlation found in a study based on aggregate data like the regression analysis just described which cannot adjust for the factors which vary among individuals and a statistical correlation obtained from a case-control or prospective cohort study which is based on data on *individuals*. Increased relative risks found in these studies, which have controlled for the other major risk factors, should be regarded as more solid evidence of

a causal relation, especially when the studies satisfy the criteria for reliability mentioned in Section 5. Most of the humorous correlations which
have become part of our folklore, e.g., relating stock prices to the height
of the hemlines in women's fashions, are based on aggregate not individual data and are not specific (e.g., the change in the price of ATT or IBM
stock tomorrow has not been shown to be correlated with the length of the
skirt worn by a particular woman, such as the firm's chief officer or
spouse).

Since the soundest evidence of an association is usually based on carefully conducted case-control and/or cohort studies, in the next section we
present some criteria for assessing their reliability and indicate where
problems are likely to occur.

Problems

1.   The purpose of this problem is to illustrate the difficulty in determining whether there is a statistical association between two variables, especially a dose-response relationship, when the data is coarsely grouped.
    After receiving reports of infant illness in houses in which a noxious
air contaminant was suspected, a study of the level of formaldehyde and
smoke in the homes of the cases was conducted. Table 13.15 reports data
relating the presence or absence of a smoker in the home and formaldehyde concentration.
    (a) Use the procedures of Section 8.8 to test whether there is a dose-
response association between the presence of a smoker and the formaldehyde concentration in a home.
    (b) Since only the presence or absence of a smoker was reported,

TABLE 13.15.   Smoking Status Inside Homes by Con-
               centration of Formaldehyde

Formaldehyde Concentration	Smokers Absent	Smokers Present
Less than .10	14	4
.11 to .34	12	11
.35 to .80	18	11
Greater than .80	8	7

Source: Table 2 from Woodbury, M. A. and Lenz, C. (1983).

TABLE 13.16. Smoking Status and Formaldehyde Levels in Interiors of Home

| Formaldehyde Level | Smoker Status | | | |
	Present	Absent	All	Fraction Present
Less than .10 ppm	4	14	18	.222
Greater than .10 ppm	29	38	67	.433
Total	33	52	85	.388

Source: Adapted from Table 2 from Woodbury, M. A. and Lenz, C. (1983).

perhaps one should classify the houses as having normal ($<$ .10 ppm) formaldehyde concentration or above normal ($>$ .10 ppm) concentration. The resulting 2 × 2 table is given in Table 13.16. Using the method of Chapter 5 decide whether the proportions of homes with a smoker present is the same for normal and above-normal formaldehyde levels.

(c) Does anything bother you about the data on smokers? Explain.

(d) In Chapter 8 we realized that the age of the building materials was strongly correlated with the level of formaldehyde in the home. What type of statistical analysis does this suggest to you as being appropriate for the study of the relationship between smoking and formaldehyde concentration?

2.* (a) Use an appropriate statistical test to show that the difference in mortality rates between the control and tolbutamide groups after the fifth year is statistically significant (use a two-sided .10 level criterion).

(b) Why is it statistically *incorrect* to look at the data in Table 13.5 in order to decide which year to use for comparative purposes?

(c) Why is the problem you identified in part (b) not severe enough to negate the inference that patients treated with tolbutamide had a higher mortality rate than the control group?

(d) If the number of patients in the trial at the beginning and end of each year were available, which statistical procedure avoids the problem in part (b). Why?

Answers to Selected Problems

1. (a) The test statistic (8.53) does not yield a significant result at the two-sided .05 level.

(b) The usual test (5.6) for a difference in proportions shows a significant difference at the two-sided .05 level.

(c) The data on the presence or absence of a smoker may be inadequate, as the number of smokers and their typical daily smoking pattern while at home should be considered. If one cannot obtain detailed information on cigarette consumption, one might give each smoker a score (1 if away from home during the day, 2 if at home most of the day) to develop a rough index of the number of eight-hour time units a smoker was usually present in the house each day. Then the correlation between formaldehyde concentration and the smoking index could be computed.

(d) With the present data, logistic regression should be used relating the dependent variable presence (1) or absence (0) of a smoker to formaldehyde concentration and age of the building material. If an amount of smoking index and the measured formaldehyde level were available for each unit, multiple regression would be more appropriate, as the formaldehyde concentration could be related to age of the building and the index reflecting the amount of smoking in the unit.

2.   (a) Here, we will use the test statistic (5.6) which is really

$$Z = \frac{\bar{p}_1 - \bar{p}_2}{\text{standard error } (\bar{p}_1 - \bar{p}_2)}.$$

The standard error of $(\bar{p}_1 - \bar{p}_2)$ is the square root of the sum of their individual variances, i.e., $\sqrt{(2.3)^2 + (2.3)^2} = \sqrt{10.58} = 3.25$. Hence, $Z = (13 - 7)/3.25 = 1.85$, corresponding to a two-sided p-value of .064, which would be significant at the .10 level but not at the .05 level.

(b) When one examines the data first, essentially one is testing the differences at the end of all years and selecting the one with the largest difference for the formal test. Hence, one is making several tests on the same set of data. In the present example the tests are highly dependent, as the same set of subjects are being followed, which makes the calculation of the p-value of the multiple testing procedure more complex than in the case of independent tests. Since the p-value of a multiple testing procedure is larger than the most significant individual test, using the most significant single test exaggerates the significance of the difference between the groups.

(c) The multiple comparison issue is not severe enough to reduce the previous analysis to insignificance, as the differences grew larger over time, i.e., the most significant test (the lowest p-value) will occur at the end of the last (eighth) year and the p-value of the test comparing the death rate of patients given tolbutamide with that of the placebo control group is less than .001. Moreover, we would expect the comparison made after the longest time period to be the most meaningful one, as one needs to follow patients for a sufficient time period in order that any difference between the treatments can be observed. Of course, it is preferable to decide beforehand when the data will be analyzed and there are procedures which adjust the p-values for multiple testing.

(d) The Mantel-Haenszel procedure can be used to combine the eight 2×2 tables for all the years. The number of persons in each group at the beginning of the year correspond to n_1 and n_2, and the number of deaths in each group to a and b, respectively. When there are departures during the year, the average number of persons in each group participating in the study during the year are used in place of n_1 and n_2.

5.   Assessing Epidemiologic Studies[19]

In this section we describe some questions one should ask when reading the results of cohort and case-control studies. Although cohort studies have the advantage of providing a direct estimate of the incidence rate as well as the relative risk (recall case-control studies only yield an estimate of the odds ratio, which closely approximates the relative risk for low probabilities), they require much larger samples, so the next subsection will discuss sources of bias and how they can be minimized in case-control studies. The considerations we discuss here mainly apply to analytic or confirmatory studies whose focus is the estimation of a prespecified possible association rather than exploratory studies which are initiated to see whether a larger study would be worthwhile. We illustrate the ideas by discussing two careful studies as well as a poorly executed study associated with the Dalkon shield IUD and its relevance to subsequent litigation.

a.   Assessing a cohort study

(1) Was the design a prospective or historical one or a mixture of both?

(2) How is exposure defined and estimated? Are the criteria well defined so that two independent reviewers of the raw data would classify the same individuals as exposed and place them in the same exposure category (e.g., low, medium, high)?

(3) How are the unexposed or control group members selected? Are

they an external group, such as persons of similar age and sex, as the exposed and residing in the same geographical area, or are they an internal comparison group, such as workers in the same plant who are not exposed to the agent under study? What matching criteria are used if a matched study is carried out, or what selection process is carried out to assure that the age-sex distribution of the exposed and unexposed groups are similar?

(4) What are the main outcome variables (incidence of a disease, death from a disease)? Is the definition of outcome clear, i.e., are the criteria for diagnosis of the disease clear and reproducible?

(5) How is the follow-up of study subjects carried out? What steps are being taken to ensure that occurrences of the disease among exposed and nonexposed group members are *equally likely* to be diagnosed properly? Are all persons followed for the same time period, or are subjects followed until a particular ending date so individuals are followed for varying time lengths? Is the time period of the study long enough to detect an increased incidence of the disease if it has a latency period, i.e., are a sufficient number of persons followed for an appropriate number of years?

(6) What potential confounding variables (covariates) are considered? Are all *known factors* which are causal or suspected to be causal among the covariates? How reliable is the information about them? Is it obtained from employer records, subject interview?

(7) What are the potential selection and observation biases and how is their possible effect controlled?

(8) What quality control steps are taken? Are subsamples of diagnoses and exposure classifications checked by an independent health scientist?

(9) What is the rationale for the choice of sample size? What role did power considerations or the expected precision of the final estimate of relative risk play in determining the sample size?

b. Statistical analysis and the final report

(1) How are the results presented? If rates, are they appropriately standardized? Are the standard errors of the estimates of relative risk and other important parameters given?

(2) Are the methods used to estimate the relative risk and obtain a confidence interval for it described? If matching is used, is a proper matched analysis used?

(3) What methods (stratification, logistic regression) are used to adjust

for the effect of potential confounding factors? What checks are made to ensure that the data fit a regression model used in the analysis?

(4) If relevant, what technique is employed to ascertain a dose-response effect of increasing exposure?

(5) If a nonsignificant relative risk (RR) which is greater than 1.0 is obtained, is the power the study had to detect an RR of 1.5 or 2.0 reported? (Indeed, the actual power of the study to detect several reasonable alternative relative risks should be presented.)

(6) Are non-sampling errors and their rates, e.g., nonresponse rate and loss to follow-up, reported and their possible effect on the statistical inference assessed?

(7) Is the effect of potential biases or omitted covariates on the conclusions discussed?

In cohort studies problems may arise through selection and ascertainment biases as well as loss to follow-up. For example, workers who take a job involving exposure to potentially toxic chemicals may be healthier (sometimes companies give them a physical exam) so that the unexposed comparison group may be less healthy (especially if the controls are chosen from the general population rather than employed persons). Similarly, the health of exposed workers may be monitored more closely so that cases of the specific disease occurring in the exposed population are more likely to be reported than those occurring in the nonexposed group. This second ascertainment bias would lead to an overestimate of the risk of exposure.

c. *Assessing case-control studies*

Since many of the criteria are similar to those used in evaluating cohort studies, we shall be brief when there are clear parallels.

(1) Is the study a matched or unmatched design?

(2) How are the cases selected? Is the diagnosis well defined and reproducible by an independent health professional? What are the source pools for cases (hospitals, public health records, doctor referrals), and will they yield all or a representative sample of cases occurring in an area during a predetermined time period?

(3) What procedures are used to select controls who are disease-free? What criteria are used to ensure that they are otherwise comparable to cases (similar age, sex, prior health status), and what sources (population in the area, hospitals, coworkers) are used to obtain them? If hospital controls are used, is another control group also available to avoid possible Berkson's bias?[20]

(4) Is the definition of the main outcome, exposure to the agent under study, defined clearly so that exposure status can be accurately determined?

(5) How is.the exposure history obtained for cases and controls? Are the subjects interviewed themselves or are proxy respondents (friends, relatives used)? Are the procedures sufficiently similar for cases and controls so that all subjects have the same high probability of being correctly assigned the correct exposure status? Is the classification done on the basis of direct measurement, proxy measurement (e.g., distance of a home from the source of the agent) or interview?

(6) Are all relevant covariates considered and is reliable information about them obtained?

(7), (8) and (9) are identical to 7, 8 and 9 for cohort studies.

The criteria concerning the statistical analysis and presentation of the final report are very similar to those for cohort studies. The report of a case-control study should emphasize the suitability of the controls for comparative purposes, what matching criteria were used, how were they verified and how many were selected per case. The data should be presented in a format enabling the reader to independently verify the basic statistical estimates and tests such as those given in formulas (5.6), (5.36), (11.15) and (11.26). Appropriate confidence intervals, p-values and an indication of the power of the study to detect relative risks in the range 1.5 to 2.5 should be given, especially if a nonsignificant result is obtained when an estimated RR exceeds 1.0.

Comment.   Two types of case-control investigations are typically carried out, incidence density studies and cumulative incidence studies. The first one samples *incident* cases as they occur, and controls are selected (sampled from the undiseased population) at that time. While the controls are disease-free when they are chosen, they subsequently may become cases, although this rarely happens to a significant fraction of controls. In cumulative-incidence studies, the cases that occurred during a prespecified time period are sampled (often virtually all cases are used) and controls are selected from persons who remained disease-free throughout the duration of the study. The cumulative density approach is often used in short-term studies. The distinction between the two types of studies does not affect the practical interpretation of the results or the major considerations underlying proper design, data collection and statistical analysis. In particular, information is best obtained from cases as soon after they are diagnosed with the disease as possible in order to maximize the accuracy of the information on exposure and relevant covariates. While the estimated odds ratios for the two types of studies of the same agent could differ slightly, typically they are quite close.

d. Major potential sources of bias and how sound studies limit their influence

We shall discuss the major sources of bias and their control primarily in the context of case-control studies as the main issues are similar in cohort studies, only the major outcome (exposure or disease status) varies. As the previous section emphasized, it is important that

(1) Disease (case) status has been carefully determined.

(2) Exposure status and, when possible, the degree or amount of exposure is estimated accurately. Moreover, the process of ascertaining exposure status should be similar in both groups.

(3) The major confounding factors (covariates) are accounted for in the study plan and in the statistical analysis.

When the above criteria are not satisfied, there is a potential for a serious bias (under- or overestimate) of the true relative risk (RR) or odds ratio (OR). Suppose that some of the cases are misclassified and don't have the disease, i.e., they should have been controls. If there really is no association (OR = 1) this should not have a serious effect; however, if there is an increased OR the exposure rate of these cases will be like that of the controls, so the usual estimate (5.2) will be biased downwards from the true RR. Misclassification of exposure status can cause a serious bias in either direction. For instance, in a 1:1 matched study, suppose no controls but a few cases are classified as exposed when they were not exposed (this can occur if the diagnosing physician believes there is an association and may use exposure as a factor in the diagnostic decision or when all workers in a particular plant are assumed to be exposed to an agent but some have jobs in which they receive virtually no exposure). In formula (11.19), B will be overestimated by the number of unexposed controls matched to these misclassified cases and, similarly, C will be underestimated, implying that B/C overestimates the true OR. Conversely, if proportionately more controls than cases are misclassified as unexposed, then B/C will be a downwardly biased estimate of OR. Breslow and Day (1980, p. 114) present formulas enabling one to determine the difference between the expected values of the observed odds ratio and the true odds ratio for various misclassification rates in the unmatched case. Modest misclassification rates of 10% are shown to reduce a true risk of 3.9 to 2.4, demonstrating the importance of properly determining exposure status.

In Chapter 8 we saw how omitted covariates can lead to an erroneous inference, so we will not present another example. Rather we will discuss a careful study that helped establish the link between salicylate use and Reye's syndrome in children and other studies, indicating how well the researchers considered the above criteria in carrying out each study.

e. Actual studies

The Reye's Syndrome Study

In the Reye's syndrome study, cases were identified through the cooperation of pediatric hospitals and care centers in 11 states. To ensure that the cases really had the disease, specific diagnostic criteria were established and the cases had to be at the second or greater stage of the disease which also minimized the possibility of misdiagnosis. Critics (Eichenwald, 1983) of the previous studies suggested that a liver biopsy should also be required (only 16% of the cases in the study used as the basis for a proposed regulation concerning a warning label had been biopsied) however, an invasive procedure might weaken a child, so the Public Health Service (PHS) arranged for an independent panel of physicians to review the hospital records and confirm the diagnosis. (Only two of the original 29 cases were subsequently reclassified by the panel.) Moreover, an independent study of previous instances of misdiagnosis showed that it occurred primarily in the less serious cases of the disease, which were excluded from this study.

In order to obtain reliable information on exposure, the respondents were *shown color pictures* of virtually all brands of relevant medications to aid their recall. Whenever possible, they were asked to show the actual medication (container) to the interviewer, so the lot number and expiration date of the medication could be recorded, as well as verifying the child's exposure.

In the Westat (1984) report of the methodology used in collecting the pilot study data, it was noted that care providers of the cases were interviewed about four days sooner than those of the controls and this might induce a degree of recall bias. Some delay is inevitable, as suitable controls matched to a case can only be selected *after* the case has been enrolled in the study. The aids to recall noted above undoubtedly rendered this four-day difference minimal. Moreover, advertising research

(Kirsh, Berger and Belford, 1962) indicates that brand names of recently purchased items are recalled accurately. Indeed, the pilot study also conducted reinterviews of about 19 care providers who administered a total of 40 medications. The reinterviews matched on 37 of the 40. There was, however, greater variation in recall of the dose administered. Reinterview studies are important, as care providers of cases are involved in a more salient event than care providers of the controls, which might make them try harder to recall medications given and other circumstances surrounding the antecedent illness.

The PHS Reye's syndrome study faced some special problems. First, aspirin is the medication of choice for the treatment of arthritic and rheumatic diseases, so cases and controls with such ailments should not be used, as they might have taken medications with salicylate for these illnesses rather than the antecedent flu. Secondly, one needs to determine that the medications were given *prior* to the onset of Reye's syndrome. Hence, ascertaining the date of the child's original illness and when they received medication is very important. School absence records are quite useful in this regard, which is why school controls were used in previous studies (cited in the references at the end of Chapter 14). Moreover, one should check that cases and controls actually had a relevant prodromal illness (flu or chicken pox). Since such diseases tend to travel rapidly through a community or school, matching on time of the antecedent disease and basic symptoms probably ensures that the case and its controls had a similar illness. Earlier studies indicated that aspirin use was related to the severity or highest fever of the antecedent disease. Thus, the investigators had to develop reasonable measures of severity for use as a covariate in the logistic regression (Table 11.19) which incorporated several other variables too.

In the Reye's syndrome and coffee consumption (see Section 11.4b) studies, the exposure status was obtained by direct interview or observation and validated. Studies which cannot do this show that a proxy or substitute measure are likely to be more controversial. For example, the electromagnetic radiation study in Chapter 5 used the proximity of a home to a major source, which reflects one's potential for exposure rather than actual exposure. Similar problems may well occur in the Agent Orange study as the exposure of soldiers will be determined from the locations of their units at the time various areas of Vietnam were sprayed (defoliated). Thus, the variation in exposure that occurred among the soldiers in each unit will be lost to the analysis. Moreover, the accuracy of the data on the dates and amounts of spraying, as well as the location of the units at those times, will be impossible to verify. This is a potential problem in studies which are carried out with a long time lag between exposure and the outcome (e.g., lung cancer or vaginal cancer in DES daughters). Under such circumstances the degree of exposure usually cannot be determined precisely. Since random errors of misclassification tend to make estimates of the RR downwardly biased, when the relative risk one is trying to detect is small (between 1.5 to 2.5), as in the Agent orange study (most soldiers received less exposure than the pesticide workers in the Swedish studies discussed in Chapter 11), the results of the study are almost inevitably going to be debatable.

One of the best known cohort studies which gave a false sense of security which later proved erroneous was that of Fleisher, Viles, Gade and Drinker (1945) who studied cancer in shipyard workers exposed to asbestos. The workers were followed for ten years and no harmful effect was found. However, the latency period required for lung cancer to develop is about 20 years. Later studies showed that exposure to asbestos dust is quite toxic (Doll, 1955, Selikoff, Churg and Hammond, 1964) and, as we saw earlier, smoking and asbestos exposure are *multiplicative* in their effect.

Cohort studies can yield an overestimate of the relative risk when the exposed group is followed more carefully than the unexposed group, as almost all cases of the diseases occurring among those exposed will be ascertained, while some cases occurring in the unexposed group are likely to be missed. For instance, suppose we follow 1000 persons in each group for 20 years. Assume that the normal probability of getting the illness during that period is .05. However, assume that we have perfect follow-up procedures for the exposed group, but only 80% of the cases occurring in the unexposed (control) group are found. Even if exposure has *no* effect, i.e., we would expect 50 cases to occur in each group, due to differential ascertainment the expected data would be that in Table 13.17. The relative risk estimate would be

$$\frac{\dfrac{50}{1000}}{\dfrac{40}{1000}} = \frac{5}{4} = 1.25.$$

In this example, 1.25 would not be statistically significant, using the statistic (5.6), but if the sample sizes had been 10,000 an estimated RR of 1.25 would have been statistically significant. The same type of bias can occur

TABLE 13.17. Hypothetical Expected Data Assuming .05 Incidence Probability with only 80% of Cases Occurring in the Control Group Ascertained

	Size of Chort	Expected Cases	Expected Estimated Rate
Exposed	1000	50	.05
Control	1000	40	.04

in case-control studies. If persons who are exposed to an agent (usually a drug) are observed regularly by their doctor, then they may be more likely to be diagnosed as cases than nonexposed individuals. When a retrospective study is subsequently undertaken, exposed persons will form a higher fraction of diagnosed cases than of all cases. This is an example of selection bias, as the cases used in the case-control study are not a representative collection of all cases occurring in the population. With serious diseases, like Reye's syndrome at the second or greater stage, almost all cases are likely to receive medical attention, so with proper surveillance of all hospitals in a region one can obtain virtually all the cases and avoid this type of bias.

When the criticism of possible selection bias is raised, one should not automatically disregard the study. Rather, one should attempt to assess what are reasonable differential rates of disease ascertainment in a cohort study or rates of becoming diagnosed cases available for a retrospective study and assess numerically what is the magnitude of their possible effect. Again, if the strength of association is high (RR > 4 or 5), modest selection biases are not likely to reduce it to insignificance. As Lillienfeld and Lillienfeld (1980) point out, an increasing dose-response curve is evidence that selection bias is not serious, as the rates of selection bias would have to vary across the levels of response in accordance with the pattern observed in the relative risks. This is unlikely to happen in most settings.

The use of several control groups, as in the Reye's pilot study, also limits the possible effect of selection bias. While it is possible for one of the control groups to have a higher or lower or fraction of exposed members due to a selection bias (or unknown covariate), which then lowers or raises the estimated RR, this is unlikely to occur in all groups. Hospital controls should be used with special care, as the agent under study may be associated with other diseases as well as the disease under investigation. For example, smoking is associated with lung cancer and heart disease. If a case-control study of the possible association of smoking and another type of cancer used hospitalized heart patients as the control group, then the relative risk of smoking on the cancer incidence will be underestimated. In addition, Berkson's bias, mentioned in the last section, can occur when hospital controls are used. One way to check the representatives of a control group is to compare its distribution of relevant characteristics with that of the general population. Similarly, one can compare the demographic characteristics of the controls with that of the cases, as the Public Health Service's Reye's syndrome study (1985) did in their Table 1, to assure that factors such as age were similarly distributed in both groups.

An Asbestos Study

We next discuss a classic historical cohort study (Selikoff, Churg and Hammond, 1964) that helped establish the link between exposure to asbestos and lung cancer. The investigators obtained data on 632 men who were members of the Asbestos Union in the New York-New Jersey region as of December 31, 1942 and followed them for 20 years. Because of the long latency period between exposure to asbestos and the development of cancer, the workers were included in the analysis only after 20 years had elapsed since their first exposure. Of the 632 workers, 339 had their first exposure at least 20 years prior to the start of the study, while 293 reached that state during the 20-year follow-up.

Table 13.18 summarizes the results of the study. Notice that the data is reported in five-year intervals. This is important because the risk of disease should be approximately constant over *each* interval of analysis and as the cohort ages the risk of developing cancer increases. The expected number of deaths for all causes and deaths from cancer of the lung and pleura were obtained using national age-adjusted mortality rates.

Over the entire period, the relative risk of exposed workers dying from lung cancer was 6.8 times that expected, assuming the workers had the prevailing rate of lung cancer in the general population. Moreover, this increased relative risk seems fairly constant over five-year intervals.

The data on deaths from all causes illustrates:

(1) the importance of studying the relation of exposure and a *specific* disease or set of diseases and
(2) the healthy worker effect.

TABLE 13.18. Observed and Expected Number of Deaths Among
632 Workers Exposed to Asbestos Dust for 20 Years
or More

| | Five-Year Time Periods | | | | Total |
	1943–47	1948–52	1953–57	1958–62	1943–62
All Deaths					
Observed	28.0	54.0	85.0	88.0	255.0
Expected	39.7	50.8	56.6	54.4	203.5
Risk Ratio	.71	1.06	1.50	1.62	1.25
(O/E)					
Lung Cancer					
Observed	6.0	8.0	13.0	18.0	45.0
Expected	.8	1.4	2.0	2.4	6.6
Risk Ratio	7.5	5.7	6.5	7.5	6.8

Source: Table 3 from Selikoff, Churg and Hammond (1964).

Had one not suspected that lung cancer was the major disease connected
with asbestos exposure (there was also evidence that the risk of colon-
rectal cancers increased too) and only had examined deaths from *all
causes* during the *first five-year* period, one might have thought asbestos
exposure could be beneficial. Again this reminds us that the working
population is healthier than the general population and to make sure that
the time individual subjects are followed is sufficiently long. In this study,
the 632 workers were studied for a total of 8737.5 man-years, or an average of 13.8 years, *after* they had met the requirement of having their first
exposure to asbestos at least 20 years ago.

As in many *historical* cohort studies, it was difficult to obtain information on all relevant covariates. As smoking is the major cause of lung
cancer, the authors compared the smoking behavior of 320 of the 377
survivors (obtained from a survey in 1962) and compared it with that of
the general male population (determined from a different sample survey).
In each age category about 10% to 15% more of the asbestos workers
were smokers than that of the general population. From Cornfield's result
(appendix to Chapter 6), it is clear that this increased prevalence (in the
range of 1.2 to 1.6 times the general population) is much less than that
required (6.8) to fully explain the association.

The authors proceeded with a cautious calculation, assuming all the workers smoked, to show that smoking could not explain the increased association. We will estimate the effect of smoking by modifying the expected values of cancer deaths occurring in the cohort from the data which indicated that in 1962 approximately 75% of the workers smoked in contrast to 60% of all males. Let r denote the age-adjusted lung cancer death rate of a nonsmoking, nonexposed male. Using the fact that the risk of lung cancer for smokers is about ten times that of nonsmokers, the rate of lung cancer in any group would be

(13.14)   (nonsmoking fraction $\times$ r) + (smoking fraction $\times$ 10r).

Thus, the expected national rate would be

(13.15) $.4r + (.6)\ 10r = 6.4r.$

For the asbestos workers, (13.14) yields

(13.16) $.25r + (.75)\ 10r = 7.75r.$

To adjust the number of lung cancer cases expected in the exposed cohort in Table 13.18 due to its additional smokers, we multiply the original values by $7.75/6.4 = 1.21$. This leads to adjusting the *relative risks* by dividing them by 1.21, so the increased risk of 6.8 would be reduced to $6.8/1.21 = 5.62$ if the difference in smoking habits of the entire cohort studied and all men in the U.S. was correctly estimated using the smoking behavior of the workers alive in 1962.

Comments.   (1) The above calculation (see problem 2) is useful in evaluating the possible effect of an omitted covariate. It highlights the fact that the impact of an omitted variable or factor depends on the *difference* between the proportions of the two groups being compared who possess the factor, as well as the relative risk attributed to the factor. Recall that randomization is used in clinical trials in order to ensure that the groups have similar proportions of various possible covariates (even ones that are not suspected).

(2) Enterline (1976) noted that quite often death rates differ from local (city or state) rates. In particular, New York and New Jersey have a higher incidence of mortality from lung cancer than the national average. Therefore, the expected values in Table 13.18 may be too low. However, we have made an adjustment for smoking, so one should check that the rate of smoking in the local area did not exceed the national rate before making a further adjustment, as the increased local rate of lung cancer may simply reflect the excess rate of smoking in the local region, and

making two adjustments would be an overcorrection leading to an under-estimate of the risk of asbestos. The main points that Enterline makes in the article are useful in that they emphasize the comparability of the exposed and control groups and the similarity of the process of disease status ascertainment. In particular, he notes that when death certificate information in cases is validated (as it should be) one must be careful when computing the expected number of cases from vital statistics based on the raw death certificate information. Thus, one might make the basic SMR comparison just using information from the death certificates of the cases. This is another reason why several studies in different regions are usually required to establish practical causation from exposure. The distribution of covariates, as well as the reliability of the death certificate information, will vary from place to place.

(3) If possible, a control group of nonexposed workers in the same region of the country (often white collar workers of the same employers) can be used. Then the case diagnosis or cause of death information can be verified for nearly all subjects in the study.

An Example of a Poorly Conducted Study: The First Dalkon Shield Study and its Impact in *Hawkinson v. A. H. Robins*[21]

We end this section with an example illustrating the importance of properly planning a study, having proper follow-up of the subjects, continuing the study for a sufficient time period and reporting the standard errors of the estimates of the parameters of interest. The first article on the Dalkon shield (Davis, 1970) reported the results of a study conducted at the Johns Hopkins Clinic beginning in August 1968. The data were analyzed at the end of one year (Sept. 1969). Of the 640 women who had the device inserted to prevent pregnancy, 5 pregnancies, 9 removals for unspecified medical reasons and 3 for personal reasons occurred. This data from the article is presented in Table 13.19, which was based on 3549 women-months of observation. Notice that this implies that women were enrolled in this study throughout the course of the year, as the average number of months a subject was followed is

$$\frac{3549}{640} = 5.5.$$

The data reported in Table 13.19 estimates the rate of pregnancy at the end of one year of follow-up. No indication of the standard error of the estimated 1.1% of pregnancies is presented. (Contrast this to Cornfield's presentation of the UGDP survival study results in Table 13.10.) It is clear that relatively few women could have had the IUD in place for a full year, which implies that the true standard errors of the estimated rates or percentages in Table 13.19 are quite large.

The original article compared the 1.1% rate of unwanted pregnancy to similar rates in an FDA Advisory Committee Report, which gave rates (at the end of one year) of .7% for combined oral contraceptives, 1.4% for sequential orals, 2.7% for the loop and 2.8% for the double coil. Because the sample sizes of the other studies were not presented, one cannot make a definitive statistical test of whether there was a significant difference between the pregnancy rates of Davis' study and the others, however, the 1.1% rate is unlikely to be significantly different from the 1.4% rate for sequentials, as claimed in the article.

In order to have a reliable study of the efficiency and safety of a drug or device, one needs to have some idea of how long it will be used and what possible side effects it may generate. Then subjects can be followed for an appropriate time period. One suggestion of Tietze (1967) was that a study of contraceptive devices follow patients for at least one year, and one may question why this guideline was not adopted by Dr. Davis. When the A. H. Robins drug firm, which purchased the Shield in 1970 and marketed it extensively on the basis of the results in Table 13.19, believed that the government might regulate medical devices, it consulted Dr. Chermos about planning a study. According to the opinion in *Hawkinson v. A. H.*

TABLE 13.19. Experience of 640 Shield IUD Users in the Johns Hopkins Study (rates at one year of use)

	Number	Estimated Rate (at one year)
Pregnancy	5	1.1
Expulsion	10	2.3
Removals	12	2.6

Source: Adapted from Table 1 of Davis (1970). The Shield Intrauterine Device. *American Journal of Obstetrics and Gynecology* **106,** 455–456.
Note: This is the published data. As explained in the text, most of the study participants were not observed for 12 months.

Robins Co., he recommended that a sample of 2000 women be followed for at least two years.

The reason the length of time subjects are followed is so important is that early favorably results can be misleading. In the UGDP clinical trial, no deaths from heart problems occurred until after the first year among patients on tolbutamide, but later many did. In the present situation suppose that a risk of pregnancy only occurs after a woman wears the IUD for six months or more. Then the women who had been followed for less than six months contribute no information about this risk. Similarly, if one is concerned about possible side effects, such as pelvic infections, and if these don't occur until at least a year has elapsed, then Dr. Davis' study could not detect them. In order to give the reader an idea of the time needed for the device to fail or for users to develop a serious infection as a side effect, we present Table 13.20, which gives the approximate time each plaintiff in *Hawkinson* used the Dalkon shield prior to having her medical difficulty. While this is not a scientific analysis, as plaintiffs are

TABLE 13.20. Date of Insertion of the Dalkon Shield, Date of Subsequent Medical Problem and Approximate Time Between Them for 13 Plaintiffs in *Hawkinson v. A. H. Robins Co.*

Plaintiff	Insertion Date	Date of Pregnancy (P) or Infection (I)	Months in between
J.H.J.	8/23/73	3/74 (P)	7
J.V.*	3/4/71 replaced 6/8/71	12/72 (P)	17
X.G.*	6/71	1/72 (P)	16
R.W.	6/5/73	4/30/78 (I)	58
E.F.	4/21/72	5/74 (I)	25
L.P.	5/73	8/15/75 (I)	27
M.C.	6/23/72	4/15/73 (I)	9
D.W.	1972	1/77 (I)	54
M.D.	7/6/72	8/1/80 (I)	73
S.S.*	1/73	1/74 (I)	12
D.C.*	1/74	10/74 or 11/78 (I)	?
B.F.	8/10/73	4/29/75 (I)	20

Source: Derived by the author from the opinion. Only plaintiffs' initials are given for reasons of privacy. Those with asterisks (*) were not awarded damages for reasons given in the opinion.

not a random sample of users, the data does suggest that a two-year follow-up period is probably the *minimum* needed. Before we discuss part of the legal decision in *Hawkinson,* we make the following remarks about the study.

Statistical Comments. (1) The wisdom of the sample size recommendation of Dr. Chremos is confirmed by applying the approximate formula given in Friedman, Furberg and DeMets (1985, p. 102) when one desires to test a null hypotheses of a probability of .02 against a two-sided alternative of .03 or .01 and desires both type I and type II errors to equal .05. This yields a sample size of 1600, to which an extra 10% to 20% should be added to allow for loss to follow-up, removals of the device, etc.

(2) When Dr. Davis compared his 1.1% rate of pregnancy against the percentages in the FDA report, he did not discuss the comparability of the study groups with respect to relevant covariates such as the proportion of the women who were married or had a live-in boyfriend, general health status or prior pregnancy history. This should be contrasted with the asbestos study, which assessed the possible effect that a higher fraction of smokers amongst the exposed groups might have on its conclusion.

(3) Little information is given about the number of persons who left the study. This is important, as apparently the risk of accidental pregnancy increases after about six months, and pelvic inflammatory disease (PID) seems to require at least nine months to develop.

General Comments. (1) Coincidentally, the article following that of Dr. Davis in the same issue of the journal dealt with a *four-year* follow-up study of monkeys who had IUDs inserted in them.

(2) When the results of a study are used in an advertisement it is reasonable to expect that if the ad indicates a useful life of x years, the study should have shown that the product is safe and effective to use for x years.

In the *Hawkinson* case, plaintiffs charged *Robins* with negligence because of its failure to warn of the inherent dangers of the shield, misrepresentation of its product to the public, as well as breach of warranty and fraudulent concealment. In its September 1970 patient information brochure the firm asserted that its product prevented 99% of pregnancies "as do most oral contraceptives", and answered the question "How long can I wear the Shield?" with, "Women have worn the IUD's for 5 years or longer, but many authorities recommend changing to a new one after 2 years." It also mentioned the safety of IUDs.

   Prior to *Robins* purchase of the shield on June 12, 1970 from the Dalkon Corporation, its medical director, Dr. Clark, saw further data from the study we discussed covering a longer, 14-month period. Out of 832 patients, 26 pregnancies had occurred. This could only happen if there were a substantial fraction of early pregnancies among the $832 - 640 = 192$ new entrants to the study or more pregnancies occurred in the 600 or so women still in the study. Even a crude calculation

$$\frac{26}{832} = 3.1\%,$$

which ignores drop-outs, etc., indicates that the 1.1% figure is unreliable. As Judge Matsch notes, "that apparent difference from the reported pregnancy rate of 1.1% did not generate any concern at Robins." He found that the statements Robins made in its patient information and similar ones in its progress report to doctors were not true and found the firm guilty of misrepresentation, but not of fraudulent misrepresentation or fraudulent concealment. He did find that the firm had not tested the product adequately and was negligent in failing to warn of the risks and in its failure to disclose its lack of knowledge. In addition

   (1) The opinion noted that if a woman just became pregnant that would not constitute a breach of warranty, as the device was not presented as 100% effective, but the firm did represent that those who used the device would not be subject to added risks above the normal risks of pregnancy.

   (2) The literature showing a relationship between IUD use and PID was cited. The judge found that while the plaintiffs might not be required to demonstrate that the shield causes a higher incidence of PID than other IUDs, he found that it did.

   (3) He then analyzed each plaintiff's case using the preponderance of the evidence standard, noting that medical science cannot tell us with certainty whether the shield produced a specific illness in a particular woman. Most of the plaintiffs were awarded compensation.

Problems

1. In a previous Reye's syndrome study published in 1982, 160 cases of stage 1 or greater were approached. Of these 25 (16%) refused to participate, while 38 (24%) could not be matched to a suitable control. More-

over, 56% of the cases were at stage 1, which presumably are subject to a greater chance of misdiagnosis.

(a) How might the data on the 38 unmatched cases been used to support (or weaken) the conclusion of the study?

(b) Do you feel that the 16% rate of refusal could have created a sufficient bias to affect the study (look up the results of the study)?

(c) What checks does the article report concerning the similarity of level of recall of case and control care providers?

(d) Can you think of an explanation for the greater estimates of relative risk, RR, obtained from the hospital and emergency room controls in the PHS (1985) pilot study?

2. Our estimate of the effect of smoking on the asbestos workers was based on a survey of workers alive in 1962 and may be an underestimate of the smoking pattern of workers, especially ones who had 20 years of exposure at the start of the study. Therefore it is prudent to assume that 80% to 85% of the workers were smokers. Calculate the relative risk adjusted for the smoking differential under these assumptions. Is the resulting risk of asbestos exposure still meaningful?

Project

The 1982 study was the fourth in a series that indicated an increased risk of Reye's syndrome in conjunction with prior use of salicylate to treat symptoms of flu or chicken pox several weeks earlier. On the basis of this study and an FDA re-analysis of the data, the Department of Health and Human Services proposed a regulation requiring a warning label. After reviewing the studies and critics of it (Eichenwald 1983), the administration conducted the pilot study during the 1983–1984 flu season to be followed by a two-year major study. The preliminary results were announced in early 1985 and an official warning label will be required as of the fall of 1986.

Review the history of the studies and the ensuing court case,[22] then write a report on the history, giving your own views concerning:

(a) The major study was planned to detect a relative risk, RR, of 4.0 or more. What factors would you use to determine the choice of RR deemed important?

(b) At what date, if any, does the totality of evidence indicate a warning label was justified? Explain your reasoning.

We end this chapter with a final

Comment on the Reye's Syndrome Study.[23]   After the publication of the
results of the Reye's syndrome 1984 study, the *New England Journal of
Medicine* in its April 3, 1986 issue published two letters questioning the
methodology of the study and the Public Health Service's response. The
pilot study was carried out during 1984 and the preliminary findings were
announced in early 1985. As a consequence, the pharmaceutical industry
began a voluntary campaign warning consumers of the association between aspirin use and Reye's syndrome. One letter that questioned the
pilot study's results stated,

"There are no data to determine whether the parents of cases, who had
heard the publicity about Reye's syndrome, were as likely to mention aspirin when they were unsure of the exact medication used as were the parents
of the controls."

Although this could be a possible factor affecting the results, since the
data were collected in 1984 *prior* to the publicity and the study verified
about 70% of the medications administered to the subjects, it is highly

TABLE 13.21.   Reported Cases and Incidence of Reye's Syndrome (RS) in the United States, 1974 and
1977–1985

Year	Predominant Influenza Strains	RS Cases	Incidence	Case Fatality Rate (%)
1974	B	379	0.58	41
1977	B	454	0.71	42
1978	A (H3N2)	236	0.37	29
1979	A (H1N1)	389	0.62	32
1980	B	555	0.88	23
1981	A (H3N2)	297	0.47	30
1982	B	213	0.34	35
1983	A (H3N2)	198	0.32	31
1984	A (H1N1) and B	204	0.33	26
1985	A (H3N2)	98	0.16	32

Source: *Morbidity and Mortality Weekly Report* (1986) **35,** 67.
Note: Incidence refers to cases/100,000 population under 18 years of
age. As the data for 1985 was preliminary, we increased the original
count of 91 to 98, as the ratio of the final 1984 count to the preliminary
1984 count was 204/190 = 1.074.

unlikely that the prevalence of this "knew about a possible linkage but did not recall what medication they administered" phenomena would have been ten to 20 times greater among the case parents than among parents of the controls. Thus, Cornfield's result implies that this could not explain the high relative risk observed in the study. Moreover, the prior studies all indicated an increased risk of Reye's syndrome following aspirin use.

As a result of the publicity about the possible linkage between aspirin use and Reye's syndrome, one would expect that parents would give children less aspirin and more non-aspirin products in 1985. Hence, if the association found in the study was valid, we would expect to observe a decline in cases. In Table 13.21 we report the incidence of Reye's syndrome for a number of years (with an adjustment to account for the preliminary nature of the 1985 data). Notice that between 1984 and 1985 the number of cases declined from 204 to 98, the *largest* percentage decline between consecutive years in the table. Moreover, the adjusted 1985 count is not more than one half of the number of cases that occurred in a year with the same predominant flu strain, A(H3N2).

Appendix.   Sample Sizes Required for Studies Comparing Proportions

In this section we give a brief introduction to the determination of the desirable size of the samples of each of the two groups being compared. We assume that the outcome being measured has a binary nature, e.g., developed (1) or did not develop (0) the disease during a fixed time period, or was (1) or was not (0) exposed to the chemical agent under investigation. While the results of this section will be illustrated on health studies, they will also be useful in assessing the power of the tests of proportions when they are applied to hiring and promotion data in equal employment cases (Chapters 5 and 6).

The test of whether two population proportions (probabilities) p_1 and p_2 are equal is based on the statistic (5.6),

$$(13A.1) \qquad Z = \frac{\bar{p}_1 - \bar{p}_2}{\sqrt{\bar{p}(1 - \bar{p})\left(\dfrac{1}{n_1} + \dfrac{1}{n_2}\right)}},$$

where n_1 and n_2 are the sample sizes of each group, p_1 and p_2, the respective sample proportions and

$$(13A.2) \qquad \bar{p} = \frac{n_1}{n_1 + n_2}\,\bar{p}_1 + \frac{n_2}{n_1 + n_2}\,\bar{p}_2$$

is the proportion of 1's in the combined sample which would estimate the underlying probability of response (1) if the null hypothesis that $p_1 = p_2$ is correct.

Using the normal approximation for the sampling distributions of $\bar{p}_1$ and $\bar{p}_2$ and assuming that the sample sizes n_1 and n_2 will be equal (as can be accomplished in clinical studies), the total sample size needed ($N = 2n$, where $n_1 = n_2 = n$) for the test statistic (13A.1) to have Type I error α and power $1 - \beta$ (or type II error β) to detect a difference $\delta = p_2 - p_1$ between the underlying probabilities is given by

$$(13A.3) \quad N = \frac{2(Z_\alpha \sqrt{2\bar{p}(1 - \bar{p})} + Z_\beta \sqrt{p_1(1 - p_1) + p_2(1 - p_2)})^2}{\delta^2}.$$

The points Z_α and Z_β are the appropriate critical values of the normal curve.

To illustrate the use of formula (13A.3), suppose that the usual five-year survival probability of persons afflicted with a particular cancer is .5. A new drug has been successful in animal experiments and will be given to humans in a controlled clinical trial. The medical experts suggest that the drug should increase the five-year survival probability to about .70–.75. Therefore, we will plan a clinical trial to detect a difference

$$\delta = .70 - .50 = .20,$$

using a one-sided test because the drug has had prior success. We will set $\alpha = .05$ and $\beta = .10$. Thus, we have only a 5% chance of saying the drug does work if it has the same results as the existing treatment and a 90% chance of concluding that the drug works if it really does increase a patient's five-year survival probability to .7. Thus, $Z_\alpha = 1.645$, $Z_\beta = 1.282$, $p_1 = .5$, $p_2 = .7$ and $\bar{p} = .6$ (as $n_1 = n_2 = n$). Formula (13A.2) yields

$$N = \frac{2((1.645) \sqrt{2(.6)(.4)} + (1.282) \sqrt{(.5)(.5) + (.3)(.7)})^2}{(.2)^2}$$

$$(13A.4)$$

$$= \frac{2(1.14 + .87)^2}{.04} = 208.1 \text{ or } 209.$$

If we wanted a test having the same power and type I error to detect a difference δ of .1, rather than .2, the required sample size would increase by a factor of four, as the denominator $(.2)^2$ in (13A.4) would be replaced by $(.1)^2$.

Before we present a short table of sample sizes, we note that formula

(13A.3) depends strongly on the difference $\delta = p_2 - p_1$ between the underlying probabilities. This implies that the sample size needed to *detect* an increased relative risk of a rare disease from a cohort study will be very large. For example, if the normal cumulative incidence rate of a disease is .01 (during a five-year period) and exposure to chemical X doubles one's risk, $p_2 = .02$, so $\delta = .01$ and $\delta^2 = .0001$. Thus, the total sample size needed in each group will exceed 10,000 in order to have reasonably low type I and type II errors. For many occupational cohort studies it may be impossible to find 10,000 exposed workers for whom we can obtain a suitable control group.

In Table 13.A1 we present a table of the approximate sample sizes needed to attain 90% power using a test with type I error $\alpha = .05$. The sizes given in Table 13A.1 show that it is difficult to detect a doubling of a risk corresponding to a small probability of developing a particular disease during a period of time over which it is reasonable to follow individuals. In contrast, a retrospective case-control study compares the proportions of both groups who are exposed to the agent. These proportions often estimate probabilities which are in the range .2 to .8 so that the difference δ between the case and control proportions often exceed .1. If the proportion of the control group who are exposed to the agent is very small (less than .05) or quite large (greater than .90 or .95), the sample size needed to detect a relative risk of 2 will be quite large. The reason for this is that the *absolute difference* between the exposure proportions in the two groups is very small. This result can be understood by considering the situation in which virtually everyone is exposed to the agent. Even if the agent is harmful, especially in larger than normal doses, one might obtain data with 100% of the cases and 99% of the controls exposed. Such data is clearly not convincing evidence of an association.

Since the usefulness of a case-control study will depend on the exposure rate (π_0) of the control group (usually a sample of the nondiseased population), the sample size formulas are somewhat more complex and we refer the interested reader to the references. In Table 13A.2 we present the sample sizes for a case-control study with the same number of controls as cases for a range of relative risks and control exposure rates. The results in Table 13A.2 indicate that a moderate sized case-control study can detect relative risks of three or more but that risks of two or less remain quite difficult to detect since one may not be able to study a sufficient number of cases. The use of several controls (e.g., two to four) per case does enable one to rely on slightly fewer cases; however, a major advantage of using multiple controls is that it ensures against the loss of

TABLE 13A.1.   Approximate Total Sample Size for Comparing Various Proportions in Two Groups with Significance Level $\alpha = .05$ and Power $(1 - \beta) = .90$

True Proportions		Sample Size for one-sided .05 level test	Sample Size for two-sided .05 level test
Group 1 $(p)_1$	Group 2 (p_2)		
0.60	0.50	850	1040
	0.40	210	260
	0.30	90	120
	0.20	50	60
0.50	0.40	850	1040
	0.30	210	250
	0.25	130	160
	0.20	90	110
0.40	0.30	780	960
	0.25	330	410
	0.20	180	220
0.30	0.20	640	790
	0.15	270	330
	0.10	140	170
0.20	0.15	1980	2430
	0.10	440	540
	0.05	170	200
0.10	0.05	950	1170

Source: Table 7.3 of Friedman, Furberg and DeMets (1985), *Fundamentals of Clinical Trials*, 2nd ed.

Note: The sample sizes were based on formula (13A.3) and then rounded up to the nearest 10. The reader will note that the sample size needed to detect the difference between the proportions $p_1 = .5$, $p_2 = .7$ is the same as that needed to detect the difference between $p_1 = .5$ and $p_2 = .3$.

data, especially in matched studies, and provides some protection against the possibility of an imbalance in the distribution of an unsuspected covariate in the cases and controls.

The advantage of the case-control approach relative to a cohort study can be seen by comparing the sample size (1170) needed to detect a difference between $p_1 = .10$ and $p_2 = .05$ using a two-sided test ($\alpha = .05$) with a type II error of .10 (from Table 13A.1) with that needed (about 200

TABLE 13A.2.   Sample Sizes Required for the Cases and Controls in an Unmatched Case-Control Study to Achieve 90% Power When a Two-Sided Test at the .05 Level is Used.

Relative Risk	Control Group Exposure Rate (π_0)						
	.10	.20	.30	.50	.70	.80	.90
1.5	1217	714	568	518	668	911	1684
2.0	378	229	188	182	248	347	658
3.0	133	85	73	77	113	163	319
5.0	54	37	34	40	64	96	194

Source: Taken from Appendix A: Case Control Sample Size in Schlesselman (1982) *Case Control Studies.*

to 400 if $.2 < \pi_0 < .8$) to detect a relative risk of 2.0 from a case-control study (from Table 13A.2).

The sample size tables are presented here for the purpose of introducing their magnitudes to the reader. In practice one should use a range of possible values of the relative risk and possible exposure rates and even consider a somewhat lesser power (.75 or .8) than what might be desireable (.9). Similarly, in planning a clinical trial one might assume various plausible values for p_1 and p_2 and hence δ. In both situations, it is wise to allow for some loss of data due to nonresponse, unusable observations, etc. and, in long-term cohort studies or clinical trials, some dropouts. The appropriate increase in the sample sizes depends on prior experience with similar studies, so no simple rule can be stated.

Finally, we note that the magnitude of the difference (δ) between, or ratio (R) of, the probabilities being compared that is deemed important to detect is primarily a function of the subject with area and expected use of the study results. If a large segment of the population may contract the disease or be exposed to a suspected carcinogen, a modest increase in the five-year survival rate (or in the risk of getting the disease) may be important.

NOTES

1. See Ames, B. N., Magaw, R. and Gold, L. S. (1987). Ranking Possible Carcinogenic Hazards. *Science* **236,** 271–280. On the other hand, the OSHA assessment of the potential harm from exposure to ethyl dibromide (EDB) *Federal Register* (1983) **48,** 45956–46003 noted that it also decreased the sperm count of exposed workers.

2. Which is a typical value obtained in the studies listed at the end of this chapter as well as the one discussed in Chapter 11.

3. 21 C.F.R. 130.12(a)(5)(k). Also see the description of the information required in an application issued by the FDA in *Federal Register* (1985) **50**, 7494–7497.

4. 587 F.2d 1099 (D.C. Cir. 1979).

5. These results were obtained from Table 7.3 in Friedman, Furberg and DeMets (1985).

6. 501 F.2d 772 (2nd Cir. 1974).

7. *Food and Drug Decisions*, 38,328 (D.C. Cir. 1985).

8. 475 F.Supp. 52 (S.D.N.Y. 1977) reversed in part in 629 F.2d 795 (2nd Cir. 1980).

9. Two forms of a drug are considered equivalent if they deliver the same total dosage over a reasonable time period (e.g., 24 hours) and reach similar maximum dose levels at about the same time.

10. The FDA decision of May 30, 1985 is reported in *Food and Drug Decisions*, 38,318. It was upheld in *Warner-Lambert v. Heckler, Food and Drug Decisions* 38,346 (3rd Cir. 1986).

11. 588 F.Supp. 1082 (S.D.N.Y. 1981).

12. Vital status refers to whether a person is still living or not. If the subject died it may be helpful to researchers to learn the cause of death to ascertain whether it was related to the illness.

13. It would be unreasonable to consider a drug ineffective if a sizeable fraction of patients assigned to use it did not take it according to the instructions, especially if including these study subjects would mask an effect that is observed when those who took it reasonably regularly are compared to the controls who took a placebo.

14. We have four groups, so we can make $\binom{4}{2} = 6$ pairwise (e.g., placebo-insulin, insulin-tolbutamide, etc.) comparisons. If the tests were statistically independent, the chance that *at least one* would be significant at the .05 level would be $1 - (.95)^6 = 1 - .735 = .265$. The fact that the tests are dependent (the same groups are being compared to one another) would lower the p-value calculated under the assumption of independence, but the adjustment for dependence would not decrease the p-value of .265 to the .05 level. Nevertheless, it is still wise to account for an apparent imbalance in the statistical analysis. Indeed, preliminary tests checking that the data is balanced with respect to a covariates should generally use a higher significance level than .05, e.g., a two-sided level of .10 or even .20 should be considered.

15. Although six tests at the .05 level were made, the correlation among them makes the p-value less than its value of .265, assuming the six tests were independent.

16. *Ferebee v. Chevron Chemical Co.* 736 F.2d 1529 (D.C. Cir. 1984).

17. Such studies are often called cross-sectional studies, as they are based on a taking a sample or cross section of the population.

18. We use the term "practical causation" to distinguish it from causation to a medical or scientific certainty and legal theories of causation.

19. The major reference for this section is the article by Colton and Greenberg (1982).

20. Berkson's bias is a type of selection bias which may occur when hospital patients are used in case-control studies and the probabilities of hospitalization of patients with the disease under study and those ill with diseases used to define the control group differ. Suppose there is no association (RR = 1.0) between exposure to agent X and the study disease in the population, e.g., 50% of all cases and controls are exposed to agent X. Suppose that all cases of the study disease go to hospitals, while only half those with the control diseases go to the hospital, but persons with the control disease who were exposed to agent X have a higher probability of being admitted to the hospital. The data will estimate a negative association (RR < 1) between agent X and the study disease, even when the true RR = 1. This could happen if workers in the plants where agent X is used have better medical insurance than other residents of the area.

21.   595 F.Supp. 1290 (D. Co. 1984).

22.   *Public Citizen Research Group v. FDA and the Aspirin Institute, Food and Drug Decisions* 38,280 (D.C. Cir. 1984).

23.   The reader should be aware of the fact the author was a statistical consultant to the Office of Management and Budget (OMB) while the Reye's syndrome pilot study was planned and carried out. The views expressed here are solely those of the author, who was not associated with OMB when the 1986 letters were published.

The Use of Statistical and Epidemiologic Evidence in Tort Cases and Public Policy

Chapter 14

This chapter is devoted to a variety of uses of health studies in cases involving the compensation of persons who are harmed by exposure to toxic agents and regulating work place exposure to harmful agents. The first section is a brief introduction to some of the relevant legal theories. The next several sections are devoted to the acceptance of statistical findings in Worker's Compensation and tort (negligence, failure to warn, product liability) cases involving diseases with short and long latency periods. Because the reliability of statistical studies of short latency diseases and injuries is easier to demonstrate (e.g., toxic shock, birth defects, resulting from use of a contraceptive method) they have been more readily accepted than studies of long latency diseases. We discuss the use of radiation studies in Section 4. The last section provides an introduction to the use of statistics in regulatory analysis. At the end of the chapter the references are organized by topic, e.g., cases involving a particular agent or disease. All the authors of an article are listed in the references. Sometimes we will refer to an epidemiologic study in the text by the organization conducting it or the state in which it was carried out. From the year of publication and the annotation in the references, the specific reference should be clear.

1.   Uses of Statistical Evidence in Tort Cases Alleging Harm Caused by Exposure to a Chemical or Medical Device

Tort law is concerned with the protection of people (plaintiffs) from various types of harm resulting from the conduct of others (defendants). Statistical data and reasoning are used in cases in which the plaintiff claims he or she was hurt by a device or toxic agent manufactured by or controlled by (in the case of a toxic agent) the defendant, as the plaintiff needs to show that the stated harm is more likely than not to be due to the defendant's conduct (product, chemical). In this section we briefly describe some of the legal approaches to cases which have called on statistical evidence in the course of their proof that the plaintiff's harm was caused[1] wholly or substantially by the defendant. We mention some cases and related issues to provide background for the following three sections, which discuss some data sets used in actual cases.

There are three major legal theories often relied upon in product liability cases:

(a) The *negligence* of a manufacturer or supplier who has failed to exercise reasonable care in the design, manufacturing process, testing and repair of the product or has not provided adequate warning of the potential hazards involved with reasonable use of the product.

(b) *Breach of warranty* is the failure of a product to conform to the expressed or implied representations made on behalf of the product by the manufacturer

(c) *Strict liability* is based on the concept that one who sells a product in a defective condition, so that it is unreasonably dangerous to the consumer or user, is subject to liability for the harm it causes to the user if the seller is in the business of selling the product and the product reaches the consumer without substantial change in the condition in which it is sold. Strict liability may also be applicable to products deemed inherently dangerous.

From reading a number of cases there seem to be several possible criteria or levels of proof that courts may require of a plaintiff attempting to prove a claim of negligence. Sometimes proof that the harm would not have occurred "but for" the defendant's conduct or defective produce needs to be presented. Courts may interpret this as meaning that it is virtually certain that the harm resulted from the defendant's behavior, however, many courts allow legal causation to be established when the plaintiff can show that the defendant's conduct was a substantial factor in or made a substantial contribution to the occurrence of the harmful event. When only one factor could be responsible for the excess risk, the preponderance of the evidence or "more likely than not" standard of proof has been interpreted, as the PDE measure should exceed 1/2, i.e., the relative risk of exposure or use of a drug or device is at least two.[2] This criteria is less reasonable when multiple causes are possible, as it is impossible to determine with certainty which one of the causes is responsible for a particular person's disease.

As the author is a statistician, not a lawyer, references to the legal literature are provided for the evidentary standards required in different jurisdictions and under various laws. In the next section we will see that worker's compensation laws require a lesser standard of proof, i.e., if an employer subjects a worker to a significantly increased risk, the worker may be eligible for benefits even when the RR from exposure is less than 2.0. An interesting case which discusses the interrelationship between federal regulations, the worker compensation systems and state tort law is *Silkwood v. Kerr McGee Corp.*[3]. The district court allowed Ms. Silkwood's father to proceed on the alternative theories of negligence and strict liability since plutonium is an inherently dangerous product.

The acceptance of epidemiologic statistics has been easier in cases where the harm (illness) follows exposure to a drug or chemical or use of a defective device within a short period of time. Some claims involving diseases with long latency periods have been barred by the expiration of a statute of limitations period. In several cases involving vaginal cancer in DES exposed daughters, courts[4] decided that the limitations period commenced at the time of original exposure. As this cancer only occurs 15 to 20 years later under this criteria, young women are precluded from suing. Other courts[5] have interpreted the limitations period as beginning at the time when a person knew or with reasonable diligence should have known about the possible role of the defendant's product or activity in the development of their disease.

An illuminating case on this point is *Snow v. A. H. Robins,*[6] which concerned plaintiff's accidental pregnancy and subsequent abortion due to failure of her Dalkon shield IUD. A lower court had granted Robins Co. summary judgement and was partially reversed by the appeals court. Because the suit was filed eight years after the event and the plaintiff knew it had occurred when the IUD was *in situ* and had mentioned that the IUD was responsible for the abortion to her doctor, the one-year statute of limitations in California applied. However, the plaintiff had only learned that the company might have misrepresented pregnancy rates occurring with the Dalkon shield and concealed the fact that the shield had higher rates than competitive contraceptive devices when she listened to a "60 Minutes" TV program in April 1981. Therefore, she was allowed to sue on the grounds of fraudulent concealment. The appellate opinion noted that "but for" the concealment (if proved at trial) of the data, plaintiff would not have used the device and the subsequent events would not have happened.

Statistical studies have played a role in establishing the time a manufacturer should take action to remedy a product or make an appropriate warning of potential hazards connected with use of the product. Indeed, many of the asbestos cases concern the date the major manufacturers knew of the link between exposure and lung cancer etc.

In recent DES cases such as *Bichler v. Eli Lilly Co.*[7] and *Needham v. White Laboratories* 639 F.2d 394 (7th Cir. 1983) defendants have not seriously disputed the plaintiff's use of the epidemiologic studies we discussed in Chapter 11 as showing that DES exposure was the legal cause of their cancer, but firms have asserted they could not have been aware of the problem in 1950.

The *Needham** case was a trifurcated trial. First, a jury panel was created to determine whether the statute of limitations (two years) prevented the plaintiff from sueing, as her case was diagnosed on March 1, 1974 but the suit was filed on March 22, 1976 (plaintiff's mother took DES in 1952). The appellate opinion noted that the limitations period did not commence until the plaintiff learned of the injury and had reason to know that someone is or may be responsible for it, rather than the date the disease was diagnosed. Then a new jury heard the liability and damages aspects of the case. The lower court decision in favor of the plaintiff was reversed and a new trial ordered because some of the evidence the plaintiff offered was not admissible. The drug firm's defense was that in 1952 it did not know of the propensity of DES to cause cancer and that it should not be held liable. The opinion noted that if White knew or should have known of the cancer risk, White would be liable to Needham for its failure to warn. Therefore, evidence that DES was ineffective in preventing miscarriage, which was introduced by plaintiff, was not relevant to the ultimate issue to be decided. Moreover, a list of articles that the plaintiff's expert said discussed the possibility of a relationship between estrogen and cancer, which was admitted by the trial court, was deemed inadmissible because he admitted that he had not read all of them and some of the articles did not discuss the relationship between estrogen and cancer.

* See the recent decision 847 F.2d 355 (7th Cir. 1988).

Comment. This opinion did not raise questions about the causal relationship between DES and cancer, rather it focused on the time the defendant should have known about a potential hazard and warned users. Since there is evidence that DES causes cancer in animals (Tomatis, 1978), whether or not the producers tested DES on animals prior[8] to introducing it may be important. The adequacy of any studies made by the drug firms, e.g., were multi-generational animal studies made, may also bear on the negligence determination. While we should not expect the studies carried out in 1950 to satisfy current statistical standards, it is reasonable for us to expect drug firms marketing a product whose effect could involve an embryo to assess its effect on the fetus.

Another aspect of negligence cases concerns the propriety of submitting evidence of a defendant's conduct after the event, e.g., modifying the product, putting a warning label or notice on it, or even withdrawing the product from the market. Rule 407 of the Federal Rules of Evidence state, ''When after an event, measures are taken which if taken previously would have made the event less likely to occur, evidence of the subsequent measures is not admissible to prove negligence or culpability with the event. This rule does not require the exclusion of evidence of subsequent measures when offered for another purpose such as proving ownership, control, or feasibility of precautionary measures, if controverted or impeachment.'' The Eight Circuit's decision in *De Luryea v. Winthrop Laboratories*[9] noted that a lower court erred in admitting evidence of a subsequent change in the drug warning label but did not examine the prejudicial effect of the evidence. In *Kehm v. Proctor and Gamble*[10] the same circuit upheld the propriety of introducing evidence of the firm's withdrawal of Rely Tampons after it learned of the results of CDC's studies (see Section 3a). In *Kehm,* the defendant asserted that it submitted the evidence to show good faith towards consumers, but the voluntary nature of the withdrawal was disputed during the trial. Judge Lay's concurring opinion in *Kehm* notes that the Fourth Circuit in *Werner v. Upjohn Co.* 628 F.2d 848, 858 (1980) applies rule 407 to strict liability cases, while the Seventh Circuit in *Lolie v. Ohio Brass Co.* 502 F.2d 741 (7th Cir. 1974) allowed such evidence, as plaintiff must show that the product has not lived up to the required safety standard. He concludes that a product may be rendered unreasonably dangerous by the manufacturer's failure to provide an appropriate warning. The public policy rationale for Rule 407 in negligence cases is to encourage producers to improve the safety of their products as soon as they learn of a problem, in order to minimize the possibility of further harm to the public. Rule 407 is designed to protect the responsible manufacturers from liability at a time (prior to his becoming aware of the problem) when the problem was not foreseeable.[11]

Comment. We have emphasized the importance of considerations of time in both epidemiologic data (exposure must precede the illness) and the analysis of equal employment data. It is interesting to contrast the way some courts accept post-charge data in EEO cases or limit plaintiff's data to a 180-day period prior to the charge plus the post-charge period[12] with their concern with post-event modification of products in negligence suits.

Finally, we mention a nonstatistical issue arising in claims involving long latency periods, for example, the DES and asbestos case—the plaintiff needs to name a specific defendant responsible for the harm. Many DES daughters, none of whom could have read the drug manufacturer's name on the medicine at the time her mother took DES,[13] have sued Eli Lilly, the main producer, or several manufacturers including Lilly, because they don't know which one made the DES ingested by their mother. Some courts have fashioned remedies for DES victims on the basis of alternative theories of market share or enterprise liability and have allowed the plaintiff to sue a group of manufacturers. The major case allowing market share liability was *Sindell v. Abbott Laboratories,* 26 Cal 3d 588, 607 P.2d 924 (1979). Related theories of alternative liability and concert of action were allowed in *Abel v. Eli Lilly Co.* 343 N.W.2d 164 (Mich. 1984). In *Collins v. Eli Lilly* 116 Wis.2d 166, 342 NW.2d 37 (1984), the Wisconsin supreme court rejected market share liability but reversed a lower court's granting of summary judgement for the defendant and allowed the plaintiff to proceed on a risk contribution theory. On the other hand, some courts have granted summary judgement for the defendant firms when the plaintiff cannot identify the manufacturer.[14]

The market share theory assesses each producer its market share of any damages, while a risk contribution theory, as in *Collins,* also takes into consideration factors such as the scientific tests or clinical trials a manufacturer made on the safety and efficacy of the drug or device, its role in obtaining FDA approval of the drug, whether it continued to market the drug after it knew it was unsafe and whether it took steps to reduce the risk in addition to market share. Thus, statistical considerations of the adequacy of the clinical trials and animal studies made by the manufacturers may be relevant in the allocation of any damages the plaintiff is awarded under the risk contribution theory if the defendants are found liable.

2. The Use of Epidemiologic Statistics in Worker's Compensation Cases

a. Legal background and cases concerned with exposure to a single agent

In standard tort litigation, the plaintiff is typically required to demonstrate by a preponderance of the evidence that the defendant caused the specific injury or damage. Worker's compensation cases and special laws such as the Longshoremen's Act, 33 U.S.C. 901-950, or the Black Lung Benefits Act, however, require a lesser burden of proof of causation, in part because of the humanitarian nature of the act *O'Keeffe v. Smith Associates,* 380 U.S. 359 at 362 (1965) and in part because workers accepting benefits under special compensation laws often forgo the right to obtain greater financial sums through the legal system. Thus, the Black Lung Benefits Act contains built-in presumptions which enable the miner with complex pneumoconiosis or a related disease to obtain benefits once he has met their requirements. For instance, if a miner with the disease can show that he worked in coal mining for at least ten years, then he qualifies for benefits unless the company employing him can rebut the presumption by demonstrating with substantial evidence that his disease had a different cause. Miners who are totally disabled due to a lung disease and have worked for at least 15 years in the mines automatically qualify for benefits, i.e., the assumption that exposure to dust, etc. in the mines caused the lung problem is irrebuttable. In *Usery v. Turner Elkhorn Mining* 428 U.S.1 (1976), the Supreme Court upheld the constitutionality of the law in part by approving the reliance of the legislative branch on medical data showing that pneumoconiosis is rare in the general population but occurs in 10% to 20% of miners. Therefore, it was rational for Congress to create the presumptions.

From a statistical view the most interesting cases are those involving diseases which can arise naturally but have a higher incidence of occurring from or being aggravated by exposure to a toxic agent on the job. In a classic case, *Grain Handling Co. v. Sweeny,*[15] Judge Learned Hand considered the definition of an occupational disease under the act. He noted that the compensation law did not cover diseases of ordinary life, per se, but only when work place conditions caused an aggravated case (the plaintiff had tuberculosis which was made worse by exposure to grain dust).

The criteria needed to establish a claim under many worker compensation statutes was clarified by the Supreme Court in *U.S. Indus./Fed. Sheet Metal Inc. v. Director, Office of Worker's Compensation Programs,* 455 U.S. 608 (1982). An employee should offer evidence of (1) a specific physical or mental impairment and (2) a condition at work that could have caused the impairment. Once this has been done many compensation statutes[16] invoke a presumption that such claims are covered, absent substantial evidence to the contrary. The role of epidemiologic data is to demonstrate that a condition at work, typically exposure to a chemical, increased one's risk of contracting claimant's disease. For example, several studies have shown that workers exposed to benzene have an increased incidence of leukemia.[17] This sufficed to satisfy the second step of the claimant's proof of eligibility in *Compton v. Pennsylvania Avenue Gulf Service Center.*[18] It is important to note that the employee need not (and could not) demonstrate that his disease *definitely* arose from workplace exposure, only that he was a member of the population to which the study results pertained.

Many state laws distinguish between known occupationally related diseases, victims of which automatically qualify for benefits, and other diseases which require the plaintiff to offer evidence of how the workplace caused or aggravated the disease. The role of epidemiologic evidence can be seen from the *Powell v. State Workmen's Compensation Commissioner* 273 S.E.2d (1980) case in which the claimant, the wife of a deceased employee, filed for dependency benefits asserting that her husband's lung cancer was due to his occupational exposure to asbestos. The state claimed that lung cancer occurs in the general public and, as the employee did not have pneumoconiosis, this disease, which primarily occurs in miners, could not have been a contributing factor, so his lung cancer was not due to his work. The court noted that the West Virginia statute gave six criteria that should be considered in determining whether a disease should be regarded as occupational:

(1) There should be a direct causal connection under which work is performed and the disease.

(2) The disease can be seen to have followed as a natural consequence of work exposure.

(3) It can be fairly traced to employment as its proximate cause.

(4) It does not come from a hazard to which workers would have been *equally* exposed to outside employment (italics added).

(5) It is incidental to the nature of employment.

(6) It must appear to have had its origin in a risk connected with employment and be a consequence of employment, although it need not have been foreseen before its contraction.

The court cited the medical literature which indicated that adenocarcinoma, the type of lung cancer the employee had, is the predominant cell type of lung cancer associated with exposure to asbestos (e.g., Hasan, Nash and Kazemi (1978), Asbestos Exposure and Related Neoplasia, *American Journal of Medicine* **65,** 649) and epidemiologic studies showing that the degree of increased risk depends on the type of fiber and the duration and level of exposure (e.g., *IARC Working Group on the Evaluation of the Carcinogenic Risk of Chemicals to Man: Asbestos, 14,* Int'l Agency for Research on Cancer Monographs 1106 (1977)). The court stated that the law did not require that employment conditions be shown to be the exclusive or sole cause of the disease or to negate all possible non-occupational causes and that if studies clearly link a disease to a particular workplace hazard, a *prima facie* case of causation arises when the claimant was exposed to the hazard and suffers from the disease to which it is connected.

The opinion also cited a previous case[19] concerning the denial of benefits to a widow of a worker who died of acute leukemia. In that case the plaintiff did *not* submit proof of a causal connection between leukemia and the particular chemicals in the workplace. Thus, the court followed the criteria listed above by insisting on a study establishing an increased relative risk between exposure to an agent and a specific illness or group of diseases. Furthermore, the decision noted, "whether a disease appears causally related to employment in the eyes of the rational mind will turn on the state of current scientific knowledge."

Comment. The issue of cigarette smoking was touched on in the *Powell* opinion when the court said that a claimant did not have to negate all other possible causes, but the opinion noted that smoking might be relevant in determining whether the statutory standards were met. Thus, the comparative risks of two or more exposures may enter into future deliberations.

b.   Worker's compensation cases involving multiple causation

In Utah, occupationally caused diseases are compensated under a different law,[20] as the basic worker compensation program was constructed to cover only accidental injuries. The requirements for compensation are similar to those in West Virginia. A vexing problem for the courts appears to arise from diseases which have multiple causes and the standard of proof required to establish causation, i.e., preponderance of the evidence or beyond a reasonable doubt, may determine the outcome.

In an early case *Garner v. Hecla Mining,* 19 Utah 2d 367, 431 P.2d 794 (1967) a split decision upheld the denial of benefits to a widow whose husband worked in and around uranium mines for many years. The plaintiff submitted evidence that uranium miners have a much higher incidence of lung cancer than non-miners and that the hazardous agent is radon gas. Since radon gas is changed in the human body to lead-210, the degree of exposure to radon gas can be estimated from the amount of lead-210 in a person's bones. Upon autopsy, Mr. Garner had 34 times as much lead as the average non-miner. Moreover, the Hecla Mine had $2\frac{1}{2}$ times the recommended working level approved by the Federal government. The plaintiff's expert stated that these facts indicated that there was a high possibility that Mr. Garner's death resulted from lung cancer caused by radon gas. The Utah supreme court accepted the statistical evidence and the result that the high incidence "would indicate in the same ratio the higher probability than otherwise that such was the cause of the disease" but concluded, "it nevertheless falls short of compelling a finding that such was the cause in an individual case." The opinion noted that if smokers had an excess incidence of 50% it would not logically imply that a particular case of lung cancer was due to smoking. Indeed, Mr. Garner had smoked a pack of cigarettes a day for 20 years. The dissenting opinion asserted that the commission required the plaintiff to prove beyond a reasonable doubt that radon gas caused his cancer rather than by the preponderance of the evidence or the more likely than not standard and had imposed a level of proof upon the plaintiff that was not required by statute or prior cases.

Comments   (1) This case shows how the PDE measure might have clarified the issues. If r_1 were the relative risk due to exposure to radon and r_2 that due to smoking, the fraction of cases among exposed persons attributable to one of the agents would depend on whether the risks followed the additive or multiplicative model. Alternatively, one might have taken the view that if r_1 exceeded r_2, then the PDE exceeded .5. Another possible approach might consider whether r_1 was greater than 2 or 3 and if so conclude that radon was likely to have made a substantial contribution to the development of plaintiff's disease.

(2) Recent cases have considered the extent of exposure to the job-related factors associated with the disease as well as other potentially injurious substances, the latency period of the disease and the employee's age at the time the disease occurred. For example, see

(a) *Christensen v. Vanadian Corp. of Am.* No. 78009904 (Indus. Comm. of Utah, Mar 31, 1982). The risk of the decedent's having developed lung cancer from radiation exposure was greater than having contracted it from smoking.

(b) *Page v. Prestressed Concrete Co.* 399 So., 2d 657, 659 (La. Ct. App. 1981). A claim is compensable when medical evidence shows a majority of cases of the disease are caused by an employment-related exposure and smoking only aggravates the condition.

(c) *McAllister v. WCAB,* 39 Cal 2d 708, 405 P.2d 313 (1968). Although smoking a pack a day for 42 years increased the decedent's chance of contracting lung cancer, the likelihood that his 33-year employment as a firefighter was a contributory cause was great enough to warrant full compensation.

We close this section with the results of a cohort study of uranium miners exposed to radon and cigarette smoking which will be useful in other discussions of the effect of radon as well as illuminating the multiple causation problem. Radon is a radioactive gas generated by the decay of uranium, which itself decays through the production of radioactive "radon daughter" alpha and beta particles in addition to gamma radiation. Exposure to radon daughters is measured in terms of working levels (WL). One WL represents the amount of radon daughters that emit 1.3×10^5 mev[21] of potential alpha energy. Cumulative exposure is measured in working level months (WLM), one of which represents the total dose received from exposure to 1 WL for 170 hours.

The Public Health Service (PHS) measured radon daughter levels in uranium mines from 1951 thru 1968 and gave medical exams to 3362 white males who had worked underground in the mines for a period of at least one month prior to January 1, 1964. The miners were interviewed to obtain their smoking history. The data contains exposure history to radon, including the dates when a miner's estimated cumulative exposure reached levels of 60, 120, 240, 350, 600, 800, 1800 and 3720 WLM, pro-

TABLE 14.1. Number (N) of Lung Cancer and Persons Months (PM) of Observation Time of the Miners Classified by Radiation Exposure (WLM) and Smoking Status

WLM*		Pack-Years of Cigarette Smoking				
		0–9	10–19	20–29	30+	Total
0–21	N	1	8(9)	3	4(5)	16(18)
	PM	197,790	57,292	26,716	14,176	295,974
22–119	N	1	3(4)	5(3)	9(8)	18(16)
	PM	62,305	27,752	19,475	16,246	125,778
120–359	N	4	7	4	8	22
	PM	59,865	32,180	22,825	18,132	130,002
360–839	N	4	3	7	24	38
	PM	46,241	32,170	22,009	21,254	121,674
840–1799	N	3	6	11	18	38
	PM	30,881	21,598	16,634	16,910	86,023
1800+	N	7(6)	12	20	23	62
	PM	15,421	12,115	11,305	10,166	49,007
Total	N	19(18)	29(44)	50(46)	86	194
	PM	412,503	189,107	118,964	96,884	811,458

Source: Table 1 from Whittemore, A. S. and Halpern, J. (1985).
Note: Pack-years and WLM evaluated at age t represent cumulative exposures achieved at age t-120 months. One pack-year equals 365 packs of cigarettes. Numbers in parentheses are cases when miners with borderline exposures were classified in adjacent cells.

vided these dates occurred prior to 1969. Cumulative exposures past 1969 were not estimated. The data on the 194 lung cancer cases observed in the cohort through 1977 were analyzed by Whittemore and Halpern (1985), who provide many references to prior analyses of this and related data sets.

The basic data is presented in Table 14.1, which reports the number of deaths classified by radon exposure and smoking categories. The crude incidence rates for each category are presented in Table 14.2, where it can be seen that generally there is an increasing dose-response relationship for either risk factor, i.e., for each WLM category the incidence tends to increase as smoking increases (read across the table), while for each smoking category the incidence rates increase with increasing WLM exposure (read down each column). This analysis is overly simplistic, however, as both pack years of smoking and working-life exposure (WLM)

TABLE 14.2.   Incidence per 10,000 Working Months for the Data in Table 14.1 Classified by Radiation and Smoking Status

| WLM | Smoking Status | | | | |
	0–9	10–19	20–29	30+	Total
0–21	.051	1.396	1.123	2.822	.54
22–119	.161	1.081	2.567	5.540	1.43
120–359	.501	2.175	1.752	4.412	1.69
360–839	.865	.933	3.181	11.292	3.12
840–1799	.971	2.778	6.613	10.645	4.417
1800+	4.539	9.905	17.69	22.62	12.65
Total	.461	2.13	4.20	8.88	2.39

Source: These crude incidence rates were calculated by the author from the data in Whittemore and Halpern (1985) presented in Table 14.1.

are positively associated with age. Thus, the low incidence in the first category (little radiation and little or no smoking) is due, in part, to the relative youth of these miners. Moreover, the allowable exposure levels in (WLM) decreased sharply over time due to government regulation so that age and date of first employment also affect the WLM for each miner. In order to account for these factors, Whittemore and Halpern (1985) fit a model to the data which assumes a multiplicative relationship between the two risks, adjusting for birth cohort (indicating when a person might have started working in the mines) and age. The resulting estimated risk for each exposure class in relation to the first category (lowest WLM, lowest smoking) are given in Table 14.3, which also reports their standard errors and shows how the multiplicative model is used. We note that the relative risk (11.52) of the highest radiation exposure level is nearly *twice* that of the highest smoking category. However, the risk of the second lowest smoking category (10–19 pack years) is of the same order of magnitude as the fourth highest radon exposure class.

Comments.   (1) The results of this study appear to support the dissenting judge's view in the *Garner* case, as the date of the case suggests that Mr. Garner was employed for a number of years when miners were exposed to high radon levels, while his pack years (20) were on the border between the second and third smoking classes in Table 14.2.

(2) In view of the current allowable exposure limits (.2 WLM/year), if

TABLE 14.3.   Estimated Relative Risk of the Joint Effect of Smoking and Radiation Obtained by Fitting a Multiplicative Model

$$\text{Model RR} = \beta_{Ri}\beta_{sj},$$

where β_{ri} is the risk due to being in the ith radiation exposure category and β_{sj} the risk from being in the jth smoking category. All risks are relative to the nonexposed group (the upper left entry in Table 14.2).

Parameter	Estimate	Standard Error
R2	1.94	.71
R3	2.13	.75
R4	3.41	1.09
R5	4.53	1.46
R6	11.52	3.52
S1	3.38	.98
S2	4.12	1.19
S3	6.24	1.72

Illustrative Use:

The estimated relative risk of a moderate smoker (10–19 pack years—group 2) exposed to 1000 WLM (radiation category 5) is

$$\beta_{R5}\beta_{S2} = 4.53 \times 4.12 = 18.7$$

Source: Table 3 of Whittemore and Halpern (1985).
Note: The categories are numbered in increasing order of the exposure levels in Table 14.2. These estimates of the relative risks are also adjusted for age and cohort effects, so they are a more appropriate summary of the original data than the crude rates in Table 14.2.

uranium mining remains a viable industry, new entrants who smoke heavily may be contributing a greater proportion of the risk of lung cancer themselves than they acquire from working the mines, even if background radiation is included. (see problem 1).

Problems

1.   From the results in Table 14.3, explain the logic behind comment 2, assuming a background WLM of .2 WLM/year or less.

2.   (a) Suppose you were representing a person who contracted lung cancer and had worked for 20 years in a factory where he was exposed to

benzene. Consult the studies mentioned in the article by Blot (1984) and develop evidence showing that the worker should qualify for compensation.

(b) If the worker was a heavy smoker, would this affect your argument? What effect would the criteria required "preponderance of the evidence" or "substantial contributing cause" affect your likelihood of success?

3.   The data in Table 14.1 was based on cumulative exposure ten years before the time of death or when the last data was collected. Why is this a sounder procedure than using current exposure levels?

Answers to Selected Problems

1.   The estimated relative risk 3.38 for the 10–19 pack-year smokers exceeds those of the second and third radiation exposure categories, which are about 2.0, implying that moderate to heavy smoking appears to generate a greater risk of lung cancer than low levels of exposure to radiation.

3.   Lung cancer has a long latency period and ten years is about the minimum time between exposure and subsequent development of the disease. Cases occurring only five years after exposure most probably arose from another prior exposure or occurred naturally.

3.   Diseases with a Short Latency Period

Case-control studies of diseases which occur shortly after exposure are readily carried out because exposure to the agent under investigation can be verified and appropriate controls are often available. Thus, the reliability of these studies is more easily established than studies of diseases with a long latency period. We begin the section with a review of the studies linking Toxic Shock Syndrome (TSS) with tampon use (especially highly absorbent ones) and their use in subsequent product liability cases. We then discuss a recent case, *Wells v. Ortho Pharmaceutical*[22] which concerned the possible effect spermicide use in early pregnancy had on birth defects in the baby. Because Judge Shoob carefully considered and evaluated the conflicting studies, leading him ultimately to rely on medical testimony rather than the studies, and was properly concerned with the relationship of exposure (spermicide use) and a particular type of birth defect (limb reduction) rather than all defects, the case and its surrounding facts are well worth studying. We close the section by citing other examples of the use of studies of short latency period illnesses, especially vaccine-related problems.

a.   The toxic shock studies and their use in legal cases

In November 1978, Todd, Fishaut, Kapral and Welsh (1978) described TSS as an acute disease produced by the *Staphylococcus aurelis* bacterium which occurred in seven children aged 8 to 17. Between July 15, 1979 and January 5, 1980 seven patients with similar symptoms were hospitalized in Madison, WI. Since six of those patients were women who were menstruating at the time the illness began, the Wisconsin Division of Health notified physicians about the symptoms of the disease and its apparent association with menses and initiated a surveillance system which identified cases for further study. We will describe the results of the case-control studies carried out in Wisconsin, Utah, Minnesota and by the Center for Disease Control (CDC) in Atlanta.

The Wisconsin study, by Davis, Chesney, Wand and LaVenture (1980), studied 38 patients whose symptoms met a well defined case definition, which included laboratory analyses to exclude similar bacterial diseases whenever possible. Of the 38 cases, 37 were female and 35 were able to menstruate. These cases were matched to three menstruating controls of similar age (within two years).

The article reporting the study stated that 34 of the 35 cases used tampons, in contrast to 80 of the 105 controls. Although a matched analysis was carried out, the data were not reported in a matched format. The test of significance yielded a value equivalent[23] to the normalized test (11.26) which is significant at the .01 level (two-sided test, *p*-value = .006). An estimate of the odds ratio can be derived indirectly using formula (11.23). Since only one case was not exposed to tampon use, the estimate will be lowest if its three controls were exposed. Then 77 of the 102 controls matched to the cases would be exposed so that a conservative estimate of the OR obtained from (11.23) equals

$$OR = \frac{77}{3} = 25.6.$$

Of course, a 95% confidence interval would be quite wide, as the sample size is small.

The CDC's *Morbidity and Mortality Weekly Report* (MMWR) issued June 27, 1980 described the Wisconsin study, one of its own studies and a small study in Utah. In CDC's study, 50 cases were matched to one control who was selected by asking the case to name a friend. All of the cases were exposed, while 43 of the 50 controls were. Thus, there were seven discordant pairs, and the sign test (11.5) gives an exact one-sided *p*-value of

$$\left(\frac{1}{2}\right)^7 = .0078,$$

which implies a significant result at the two-sided .05 level test criteria typically used in the medical literature.

The Utah study compared 12 cases with 40 unmatched controls and found that all the cases used tampons, in contrast with 32 of the 40 controls. This difference is not statistically significant, as Fisher's exact test yields a *p*-value of about .13. Nevertheless, the data is logically consistent with the other studies, as a higher fraction of cases then controls were exposed and the number of cases is so small that the power of the test is low.

At this time the studies had not found a difference in brand use, however, only the Wisconsin study investigated this question and the data were not given in the published version, so we don't know whether or not there was a nearly significant result (which in a small sample study would at least be suggestive). In early September 1980, the CDC carried out a second study using community controls rather than friends of cases, as in its first study. The preliminary results were announced on September 19, 1980 and showed that *all* 50 cases used tampons, in contrast to 124 of the 150 matched controls. The test statistic (11.26) yielded a two-sided *p*-value of .006. As no cases were unexposed, the odds ratio would be estimated as infinite, so no estimate was presented.[24] More relevant to subsequent developments was the fact that when the data was restricted to tampon users and brand use was studied, the risk of users of Rely relative to users of other brands was 7.9 with a 95% confidence interval of 2.8 to 22.2. This is an underestimate of the risk of using Rely relative to non-users. In fact, 71% of the cases used Rely. The association of Rely brand with TSS was also supported by preliminary results from Minnesota, where 10 of 29 cases (35%) used Rely tampons while only 9 of 50 controls (18%) did. Furthermore, in the complete Utah study carried out at the same time but published in 1981, Rely users formed 63% of the cases but only 24% of the controls. On September 23, 1980, Proctor and Gamble Co. voluntarily withdrew its Rely tampon from the market.

It is important to emphasize data collected *prior* to the removal of the Rely brand, as the accompanying publicity could influence the response given to the brand use question and even the diagnosis of the disease. The major tri-state study, carried out in Iowa, Wisconsin and Minnesota (1982) should be mentioned, as it compared each of 80 cases with two matched controls. It found an overall risk of TSS of 18 for tampon users relative to non-users. In Table 14.4 we present the odds-ratios, 95% confidence intervals and *p*-values for the case-control comparisons. Notice that all brands of tampons had an elevated relative risk but only three (Rely, Kotex, Playtex) reached statistical significance. When comparisons were made between users of Rely and users of any other brand, users of Rely had a risk $2\frac{1}{2}$ times that of other brands.

In order to study other possible factors, such as duration and intensity of menses, continuous or intermittent use of tampons, the fluid capacity (absorbency) of the tampon, as well as the brand, a logistic regression analysis of the data was carried out. It showed that *absorbency* was the major factor, with low absorbency tampons having a RR of about 4 while high absorbency ones had RRs of 8 to 10. Moreover, only the Rely brand had a statistically significant risk (RR about 3) over and above the absor-

TABLE 14.4.   Estimated Odds Ratios and Associated Confidence Intervals from the Tri-State Study

Use Comparison	OR	95% CONF	*p*-value of the test of significance
Any tampon vs. none	18.01	3.94– 82.26	<.001
Rely vs. none	27.15	5.87–125.48	<.001
Kotex vs. none	16.18	1.91–136.64	.01
Playtex vs. none	15.17	2.63– 87.52	.002
Other vs. none	6.75	.64– 70.33	.11
Tampax vs. none	5.92	.82– 42.44	.076
All Non-Rely vs. none	12.24	2.28– 66.00	<.004
Rely vs. All other tampons	2.49	1.31– 4.71	.005

Source: Table 2 from the Tri-state study results (1982).
Note: The brand user comparisons were based on cases and controls who used one brand exclusively or none at all. The *p*-values are for two-sided tests of the null hypothesis OR = 1.0.

bency factor. Thus, the study showed that absorbency was the major characteristic of tampons related to subsequent development of TSS.

All of the studies cited were criticized in an article by Harvey, Horwitz and Feinstein (1982). These authors noted that the interviewers knew the case-control status of the subject being interviewed, and this *could* lead to a bias in the answers to the exposure questions. They also present an example of a case who was misdiagnosed and suggest that others might also have been in error, perhaps due to vagueness in specifying the disease, and suggest that the publicity by the state health agencies could have influenced the reporting and diagnosis of cases, i.e., patients with symptoms similar to TSS might be diagnosed as cases by doctors when they learned the woman was a tampon user. Moreover, they noted that in the three studies done earlier (by June 1980) only two found a statistically increased risk, and no association was found for the highly absorbent brands in these studies. Finally, they raise doubts about the criteria used to select cases, because a sizeable fraction of reported cases were not used in the Wisconsin and first CDC study.

The questions raised by the critics are important, however:

(1) The issue of possible systematic misdiagnosis cannot legitimately be raised by a single error. A sample of cases should be reviewed by an independent group of qualified health professionals, as in the Reye's syndrome study.

(2) There is an inherent contradiction in criticizing a study for having an imprecise case definition and also for excluding some reported cases. Presumably a "tight criteria" will screen out a portion of reported cases. Almost any reasonable criteria will lead to some errors of this type.

(3) While the issue of tampon use being used as a criteria for a case of TSS to be diagnosed and/or reported is important, only those cases who would *not* have been diagnosed as having TSS *without* the fact that they used tampons should be excluded. Again, a proper sample of case records should be studied to decide the potential affect this might have on the results. As noted by Hulka (1982), to reduce the estimated relative risk to 1.0, about 90% of the cases would have to be eliminated or have erroneous exposure data. The reasoning behind this assertion is similar to Cornfield's result, which implies that another factor is unlikely to explain the association between tampons (especially the highly absorbent ones) and TSS. Moreover, the high fraction of Rely users among the cases occurred in the CDC, Wisconsin and Utah studies, which were based on data

TABLE 14.5.   Number and Percent of Users of Major Tampon Brands Among Cases and
Control in Three Studies

Brand	CDC (1980c)		Utah (1981)		Tri-State (1982)	
	Cases	Controls	Cases	Controls	Cases	Controls
All	42	114	24	59	59	116
Rely	30 (71.4)	30 (26.3)	15 (62.5)	14 (23.7)	31 (52.5)	34 (29.3)
Kotex	1 (2.5)	13 (11.4)	2 (8.3)	17 (28.8)	4 (6.8)	10 (8.6)
Playtex	8 (19.0)	30 (26.3)	2 (8.3)	7 (11.9)	13 (22.0)	26 (22.4)
Tampax	2 (4.8)	29 (25.4)	5 (20.8)	18 (30.5)	8 (13.6)	37 (31.9)
Others	1 (2.4)	12 (10.5)	0	3 (5.1)	3 (5.1)	9 (7.8)

Source: The years refer to the data of publication of the article reporting the result. The CDC data is
from Table 2 of their reports. The full citations for the three studies are given in the references. Our
percentages may differ slightly from those in the original sources due to differences in rounding.

gathered *before* Rely was taken off the market as well as in the tri-state
study, which also was concerned with cases occurring prior to the withdrawal. The percentages of cases and controls using different brands are
reported in Table 14.5. Notice that the proportions of cases and controls
using Rely in the three studied are similar. The effect of the recall was
studied in a subsequent article by Davis and Vergeront (1982). While it
had an effect, it was not substantial enough to alter the major policy
conclusion.

(4) As we remarked previously, the fact that the first (preliminary)
Utah study did not yield statistical significance was due to the small
number (12) of cases available. Its result was consistent with an increased
risk of TSS for tampon users (see Problem 1). Of course, had the Utah
study evidenced less risk of exposure, combining it with the other studies
would reduce the estimated summary relative risk due to tampon use.

(5) The final Utah study (1981) restricted its analysis to single brand
users so that recall bias due to publicity should be minimized. Moreover,
the cases were interviewed within four months of illness, so their recall
should be reliable, as regular users of a specific brand have accurate recall
(Kirsch, Berger and Belford, 1962).

Since cases of TSS still occur and medical research is continuing (see
Davis, Cherney and Vergeront (1984)), hopefully the ultimate biological
cause will be discovered. However, an indication of the effect of the
publicity concerning TSS and its relationship to Rely and other highly

TABLE 14.6.   The Number of Toxic Shock Syndrome Cases by
Year (1979–1984)

Year	Cases Occurring in Conjunction With Menstruation	Other Cases
1979	242	27
1980	812	60
1981	469	98
1982	289	88
1983	244	93
1984	181	70

Source: Centers for Disease Control (1986). Annual Summary for 1984. *Morbidity and Mortality Weekly Report* **33**, 64.

absorbent tampon brands can be seen in the data on cases of TSS reported to CDC given in Table 14.6. Since the publicity and the withdrawal of Rely from the marketplace, reported menstrual cases have *decreased* noticeably. This confirms the effect of the publicity and removal of the Rely brand from the marketplace as well as the validity of the statistical association.

We now turn to the role the studies have played in court cases, bearing in mind that Rule 407 of evidence in negligence cases usually bars the introduction of evidence of subsequent remedial measures in negligence cases, *Robus v. Bridgeport,* 191 Conn. 62, 463 A.2d 252 (1983). However, the rule may not apply in strict liability cases.

Kehm v. Proctor and Gamble Co.[25]

The husband of a woman who died of TSS sued the manufacturer for failure to warn potential users of the risk of contracting TSS. The appellate opinion emphasized that in a failure to warn case liability does not depend on whether there is a risk to a substantial number of people, but on whether the manufacturer knew or should have known that there were even a few persons who could not use its product without serious injury and did not warn them properly.

Rely was first test-marketed in 1974 and by the end of 1979 it was marketed nationally, and over half a billion Rely tampons had been sold. On August 8, 1980 Proctor and Gamble received a responsible report of a TSS caused death of a Rely user and on August 21, 1980 it learned of the small Minnesota study showing Rely users had twice the incidence of TSS as users of other tampons. As we know, on September 19, 1980 the second CDC study confirming this result was published.

Mrs. Kehm began using Rely tampons on September 2, 1980, noticed the first symptoms on September 3, 1980 and died on September 6, 1980. The plaintiff sued on the grounds that the manufacturer knew of the problem and did not provide a proper warning and also claimed that the cause was the CMC chips used in the products. Proctor and Gamble contended that it had no duty to warn, as the tampons were not unreasonably dangerous and that Mrs. Kehm did not have TSS and even if she did, her death was due to a unique susceptability to TSS not her use of Rely.

A major issue in this and similar cases is the admissibility of statistical evidence derived from studies and surveys. The defendant claimed that it should have the right to examine the persons interviewed to assess the reliability of the data and determine whether the biases its expert, Dr. Feinstein, a coauthor of the article (1982) which criticized the studies, had noticed could undermine the validity of the findings. The court confirmed the exception to the hearsay rule allowing factual data from public agencies to be used as evidence. Not only did the opinion cite previous cases[26] in which data were used, it noted that in the present case allowing respondents to be cross-examined would threaten their privacy and would inhibit public health agencies in their future data collection activities. Moreover, the defendant had the opportunity to challenge the methodology and findings of the studies as well as presenting its own evidence.

The appeals court upheld the admissibility of the results of the studies, showing the statistical relationship between tampon use and the incidence of TSS as well as documents indicating that the manufacturer knew of the Rely-TSS risk prior to the time Mrs. Kehm fell ill. Thus, the jury award of $300,000 for compensation, was upheld. While we cannot assess the impact of the results of the study on the jurors in the case, the magnitude of the increased risk probably did affect their assessment of the safety of the product.

Comment. Although the main issue in the *Kehm* case was whether or not the defendant provided a timely warning, we note that the increase in reported cases between 1979 and 1980 in Table 14.6 coincides with the national marketing of the brand. In conjunction with the decline in cases after the product was withdrawn, it is difficult to suggest another cause of the increase in TSS cases.

Comment on Data Access and the Rights of Respondents. The issue of access to the underlying data source is a basic one in scientific research, however, it is not necessary to reinterview the original respondents. Quite often the data, with identifying information removed, can be made available to all parties for independent reanalysis. If it is desirable to check the coding and original diagnoses, copies of a sample of records can be made available, with identifying information removed. If necessary, the data can be released to an appropriate party under protective order. Apparently, this was done in a case involving Reye's syndrome, when CDC objected to releasing the original data.[27] This is necessary in order to protect the rights of the respondents, who are promised anonymity and confidentiality, as well as the rights of the public to obtain the most accurate estimate of risk and to protect a manufacturer and the public from a poorly conducted study. Unlike large sample surveys, the cases in a health study, especially those who died from the disease, can often be easily identified from knowing the city they lived in and the time when the study was made (since there may well have been obituary notice). On the other hand, it is advisable for government agencies and others who analyze data to make the computer tapes of nonindividually identifiable data available for reanalysis by others. A recent report[28] discusses the advantage of such data sharing, giving at least one example where a computer or methodological error was made. The study results were significantly changed when these mistakes were corrected. On the other hand, sometimes additional information is added to that provided by the respondents, e.g., tax return information is added to census sample survey data, in which participation is *voluntary,* without their consent or knowledge. This added information may make it easier to identify a survey respondent. The author[29] believes doing this is unfair to the people who cooperated with the research. Moreover, as respondents are unaware of the total content of their file, any misuse of the information is virtually impossible to detect. Since this method of adding information to research data is not typically used in health research, this should not limit the availability of nonidentifiable data for independent review.

We now turn to other legal cases concerning victims of TSS who used other brands of high absorbency tampons.

Ellis v. International Playtex[30]

The Fourth Circuit reversed a lower court opinion absolving the manufacturer from liability because the epidemiologic data was not admitted into evidence. In order to prevail on the legal theories used in the case (implied warranty and negligence), the plaintiff had to prove that

(1) Mrs. Ellis had TSS.
(2) TSS is causally related to tampon use.
(3) The Playtex tampon used by her was responsible for the toxic infection.
(4) Playtex knew of the dangers inherent in its product.

Mrs. Ellis' menstrual period started on May 22, 1981, and she used Playtex super deodorant tampons. On Monday, May 25, 1981, she felt ill and went to bed; on Wednesday she died. The issue of whether or not Mrs. Ellis had TSS was debated by medical experts on both sides.

To demonstrate causation the plaintiff sought to introduce the tri-state and second CDC studies which linked TSS to tampon use. The second CDC study is very relevant, as it showed that the more absorbent tampons had a higher statistical association with TSS. Moreover, the CDC data showed that most TSS cases began on the second day of the victim's menstrual cycle.

The opinion also discussed the reasons the defendant used to convince the district judge to deny the plaintiff the right to place the studies into evidence. These concerned the failure of the studies to use all cases, the fact that several months may have passed between the date of illness and the interview, that doctor's reports were used to identify cases rather than the health investigators making their own examination and that the possibility of future litigation might bias the answers of the cases. The opinion notes the impossibility of interviewing all victims of a disease immediately after they became ill. Indeed, a number of similar cases have to occur before a study will or should be undertaken. There was no evidence presented showing that a time lag of a few months would make the data unreliable, and we know that analyses based on data for single brand users would not be seriously affected by a short time lag. The opinion went on to state that diagnosis of the attending doctor should be reliable, as a sick patient has every reason to speak candidly to their physician. Finally, it noted that possible bias due to the prospect of litigation was just speculation, especially as cases have an interest in providing accurate answers, so proper care and preventive measures can be taken or discovered.

Comment. The criticism of the studies offered by the defendant in this case are quite similar to those offered by Proctor and Gamble in the previous case, and the reasons for a statistician's skepticism of them are the same, especially in light of the data in Table 14.4.

McGowan v. University of Scranton and Tampax, Inc.[31]

This case concerned the applicable statute of limitations period. Ms. McGowan died suddenly on October 13, 1978 while a student at the University of Scranton. Nine months later her parents sued the university and its infirmary nurse, alleging negligence in the medical care their daughter received. In June 1980, the chief pathologist of the hospital at which Ms. McGowan died wrote the parents that TSS might have caused their daughter's death after he read the CDC report. Subsequently, the plaintiffs learned that Ms. McGowan was experiencing menses and was using Tampax super tampons.

The plaintiffs amended their complaint on July 13, 1981, 33 months after the tragedy, but the district court granted Tampax's motion for summary judgement, holding that a two-year statute of limitations applied and was tolled from the date of Ms. McGowan's death. The appellate opinion noted that while the original article describing TSS appeared in 1978, there was nothing in the record showing that the plaintiffs should have known of the connection between TSS and her disease before June 1980 when they became aware of the CDC report. Thus, the court remanded the case to see whether the McGowans could reasonably have discovered the connection between tampons and their daughter's death prior to July 13, 1979, as only that fact would make their case against Tampax exceed the statute of limitations.

Comments. (1) This case is interesting because of its focus on the relationship between the date of a scientific discovery, its dissemination to the public and the running of a statute of limitations period.[32] Similar considerations are involved in determining when a defendant should have known of an inherent defect in a product. In a drug case, presumably the date of one or more consumer complaints or publication of relevant scientific studies will determine when they should have been aware of problems unless the original testing of the product was flawed.

(2) As a result of a jury verdict against it in *O'Gilvie v. Playtex Int'l.* 609 F.Supp 817 (D. Kan. 1985), the company strengthened its warning and promised to take its super-absorbent brands off the market. The opinion does not report whether epidemiologic studies were presented, but we will presume they were as the jury found that a warning statement

that an "association" between tampon use and TSS had been found was inadequate. Furthermore, the jury found that 1) the company knew or should have known of the increased risk of TSS users of Playtex super deodorant tampons were exposed to, 2) super absorbent tampons had an increased risk relative to other tampons, 3) the tampons used by the deceased caused or contributed to the cause of her case of TSS and 4) that the failure to adequately warn was reckless.

The new label will state that use of the tampons contributes to the cause of TSS. When he upheld the jury's punitive damages award of $10,000,000, Judge Kelly stated he would consider reducing it if the manufacturer removed the highly absorbent tampons from the market. After the company made its announcement of changing the product by removing the polyacrylate fiber from their tampons and stated that it would carry out a program to educate the public about TSS, the judge reduced the portion of the total award to $1,350,000.

The appellate court 821 F.2d 1438 (10th Cir. 1987) affirmed the decision concerning the firm's liability and reinstated punitive damages. The opinion noted that the defendant knew of the studies demonstrating the relationship of high absorbancy to TSS but continued marketing its high absorbancy brand while other firms modified their products. The majority opinion did not accept the defendant's claim that it could not be found liable as its warning label met the requirements set by the FDA as these were only minimal standards. Hence, a jury could find that a prudent manufacturer should provide a stronger warning than the minimum. The non-statistical aspects of the case are noteworthy as the victim's doctor misdiagnosed early symptoms of TSS and her sister testified that she typically used a different manufacturer's product.

The latest CDC (1987) study of TSS cases occurring in 1983–1984 confirmed the association between tampon absorbancy and TSS. While all tampon users had an increased risk, Playtex users had the highest risk of the brands studied which supports the *O'Gilvie* decisions.

b. Wells v. Ortho Pharmaceutical Corp.[33]*: the relationship between spermicide use during pregnancy and birth defects*

The parents of Katie Wells brought this suit to recover damages arising from multiple birth defects suffered by her. The two main issues to be resolved were

(1) Whether the spermicide (Ortho-Gynol Contraceptive Jelly) made

by the defendant and allegedly used by the mother several months before and several weeks after the child was conceived, proximately caused these birth defects and

(2) Whether defendant negligently failed to warn the mother that increased risk of birth defects accompanied use of the product.

The major pieces of evidence were the testimony of expert witnesses and the interpretations of various studies and related medical factors. The opinion reminds us that the plaintiff needs to show that to "a reasonable degree of medical certainty" the defendant's product was responsible, citing *Parrott v. Chatham County Hospital Auth.* 145 Ga. App. 113, 115 (1978) and that the plaintiffs could not recover damages if there was only a "bare possibility" that the spermicide caused the defects or that other theories of causation were equally plausible, citing *Maddox v. Houston County Hospital Auth.* 158 Ga. App. 283 (1981).

Before discussing the studies, we review some background information. Although the plaintiffs used a diaphragm and the spermacide in accordance with the instructions they received from a nurse in July 1980, the mother became pregnant in October 1980. On July 1, 1981 Katie Wells was born with the following birth defects

(1) a cleft lip;
(2) an abnormal formation and shortening of her right hand;
(3) the absence of the distal joint on her right finger;
(4) the complete lack of a left arm;
(5) only partial development of the left clavicle and shoulder.

Later the baby suffered from an optic nerve problem, leaving her 90% blind in the right eye.

It is useful to consider the statistical data available prior to July 1980 separately from later studies, as a defendant's duty to warn prior to the time of exposure depends primarily on studies existing at that time. After reviewing the early literature, we will discuss the presentations of both sides, including later studies. Then we will return to a more detailed examination of the additional studies and other available evidence.

The first detailed study appears to be that of Oechsli (1976), who studied the effect of contraceptive failure on the subsequent development of the child. In particular, prior research had led to a suspicion that oral contraceptive use and the rhythm method might be associated with increased incidence of some types of birth defects and/or spontaneous abortion.

The study followed almost all pregnant women who received prenatal care with East San Francisco Bay Area Kaiser Permananete, San Francisco Bay Area facilities from late 1959 through September 1966. Out of about 20,500 pregnancies, 14,517 women agreed to participate. Because participants belonged to a group health program, it was possible to follow the children for five years after birth. Indeed a number of birth defects were first observed in children three- or four-years-old. The study was an exploratory one, as many statistical comparisons were made. Therefore, a few statistically significant results could occur by chance, so we will not report the formal *p*-values associated with the individual tests. Although the Oechsli report considered a number of indices of problem pregnancy, we only present the data on fetal loss and birth defects in Table 14.7. The significant difference between the percentages of babies born with birth defects of white jelly users (8.8%) who discontinued use *after* their last menstrual period, LMP, and those who discontinued use *before* their LMP (5.5%) is not replicated among blacks (see problem 1). Oechsli (1976 p. 10) summarized his finding as follows:

> "It is difficult to reach a clear-cut conclusion regarding the consequences of jelly-foam-suppository use or failure. The increased frequency of defects found in the white group raises a definite suspicion. The fact that these defects were more likely to be of moderate severity (diagnosable between three months and five years) in the failure group as compared with the discontinued user group, coupled with the fact that most of this excess was made up of congenital heart disease cases, tends to confirm that something real was found. The findings that the effect could not be replicated with the other races, that it was not accompanied by an increase in minor anomalies, and that the defects found were not associated with use of any particular preparation combine to suggest that the finding in the white group may have been a statistical fluke. Conversely, one should seriously consider the possibility that the finding represents the working of a factor socially or biologically linked to ethnicity. On balance, I would conclude that the findings raise a serious suspicion that there may be deleterious effects from jelly-foam-suppository use. Further research is strongly indicated. One should note that if there is a real effect and that the birth defect resulting is of the sort indicated (atrial or pulmonic stenosis) only a study which followed the children for about five years would find the effect since most of these diagnoses are made after the first year of life."

The next study was conducted in Canada by Smith, Defoe, Miller and Bannister (1977) and focused on limb deformities. Each *one* of 93 babies

TABLE 14.7. Number of Pregnancies, Live Births and the Percent of Live Births and Birth Defects Classified by Contraceptive Use and Race of Mother

WHITE

Contraceptive Use	Pregnancies	% with Fetal Loss	Live Births	% with Birth Defects
All Women	9600	5.33	9088	4.60
Non-users of contraceptive method	2718	5.05	2581	4.73
Discontinued use of contraceptive method after last menstrual period (LMP)	3589	5.88	3378	4.48
Continued use after last menstrual period (LMP)	3293	4.98	3129	4.63
Jelly Users				
Discontinued use before LMP	271	5.17	257	5.45
Discontinued use after LMP	285	4.55	272	8.82

BLACK

Contraceptive Use	Pregnancies	% with Fetal Loss	Live Births	% with Birth Defects
All Women	3418	6.70	3189	3.79
Non-users of contraceptive method	969	8.15	890	3.37
Discontinued use of contraceptive method after last menstrual period (LMP)	1086	6.35	1017	4.13
Continued use after last menstrual period (LMP)	1363	5.94	1282	3.82
Jelly Users				
Discontinued use before LMP	294	6.80	274	3.65
Discontinued use after LMP	395	5.82	323	3.49

Source: Extracted from Tables 2 and 3 from Oechsli (1976).

TABLE 14.8.   The Exposure Data for Births with a Limb Defect and Their Controls in the Canadian Study

| | Exposure Pattern | | |
	Used Spermicide	Did Not Use Spermicide	Total
Cases	11	82	93
Normal controls	4	89	93
Controls (other defects)	4	89	93

Source: Table 2 from Smith, Dafoe, Miller and Bannister (1977).

with a limb defect were matched to two controls on the basis of birth data (within two weeks) age of the mother (+ 3 years), residence, parity of the mother and, whenever possible, on the sex of the child. Again a number of statistical tests were carried out in the study, so again it is possible that a significant result could occur by chance. Unfortunately, the matched data set was not published, but we reproduce the data in Table 14.8. Considering all the controls as one group of size 186, the difference between the proportions of limb defects occurring in the cases and controls is statistically significant using the test (5.6). Indeed, the two-sided p-value = .036 and the estimated odds ratio = 2.98. (The article does not give an estimated OR or RR.) The study mentioned that some of the preparations contained substances known to be carcinogenic in animals. Apparently some spermicides contained phenylmercuric acetate, which an FDA panel deemed unsafe in the early 1970s. The fraction of spermicide users in this study whose spermicide contained this compound was not available. Therefore, we should consider the estimated RR of 2.98 as being an overestimate. Because the article was an exploratory study, it did not reach a definite conclusion but indicated that the data suggested an association between limb reduction defects and spermicide use.

In a third study Harlap, Shiono and Ramcharan (1980) studied fetal loss among participants in the Kaiser Permananete Plan. The study group seems to include patients from the group studied by Oechsli but may include patients from a larger number of clinics. The only part of this article cited in the opinion is the statement, "Previous reports (citing Oechsli) of an excess risk associated with spermicides are not brought out by this study." The relevant data from the study is reported in Table 14.9.

TABLE 14.9. Number of Women Using Contraceptive Methods and the Standardized Fetal Loss, Rates and Ratios, Classified by Time the Method was Used

| | Method | | | |
	Oral	IUD	Chemical	Total (All Methods)
Used Only Prior to LMP				
Women	8412	1442	1410	15,907
Fetal Loss	351	68	35	703
Rate	40.6	45.5	46.7	42.8
Ratio	1.00	1.00	1.00	1.00
Continued Use after LMP				
Women	781	365	773	3,750
Fetal Loss	34	35	41	192
Rate	47.6	98.2	53.3	52.1
Ratio	1.24	2.11	1.16	1.28

Source: Extracted from Table 4 of Harlap, Shiono and Ramcharan (1980).
Note: The rate was in the average daily rate per 100,000 women at risk, while the ratio reports observed/expected numbers, where the expected figure is adjusted to account for maternal age and days of observation. Thus, it differs slightly from a simple ratio of the two rates.

Notice that the standardized fetal loss rate of chemical users past their LMP is only 1.16 times that of users who stopped prior to their LMP. We next turn to the presentation of the plaintiff's and defendant's experts, who discussed these and other studies at length, along with relevant medical considerations and animal studies.

The main expert for the plaintiff, Dr. Buehler (M.D.), was an expert in limb defects and emphasized that the mother used the contraceptive jelly *after* the baby was conceived *during* the time limb buds are formed in the fetus. He examined the baby for genetic birth defects, which tend to be symmetric, as well as drug related ones. Moreover, he stated that the limb defects were due to vascular disruption but would not reach the same conclusion about the cause of the cleft lip and eye problems. In addition to previous studies, he mentioned the results of a Seattle study (1981) which indicated that children born to white women who had obtained a vaginal spermicide within ten months prior to conception had a greater risk of birth defects (RR = 2.2) than non-users, an animal study (Buttar, 1982) and another study of emergency room patients (1982) which indicated that the risk of spontaneous abortion for mothers who had used spermicides was 1.8 times that of non-users. Moreover, the association was slightly stronger (RR = 2.1) for users who had filled their last prescription within 12 weeks of the estimated date of pregnancy.

The defendant's experts criticized the studies that had shown an increased relative risk and relied on studies which had not found an increased risk. The most well known expert for the defense was Professor Stolley. He cited a further study (unpublished) by Harlap and an article by Mills (1982) which indicated to him that Oechsli's (1976) result was a "statistical fluke." He mentioned that the statistical association in the Canadian (1977) study was not striking and criticized the 1981 Seattle study as having used a loosely defined criterion of exposure. He also noted that the variety of birth defects formed in that study was biologically implausible.

The Seattle study (1981) studied the incidence of birth defects among 763 live-born infants of white women who had received a prescription for a vaginal spermicide within 600 days of the child's conception and a comparison group of 3902 infants. All patients were members of a group health cooperative in Seattle. The pharmacy stocked spermicides containing one of two active ingredients octoxynol (80% of the spermicides) and nonoxynol-9 (20%). Both these chemicals are non-ionic surfactants used in many spermicides. Indeed, the defendant's product contained octoxynol, although both parties agreed that the all non-ionic agents would have similar properties.

Results from the 1981 study are reported in Table 14.10. The study also made comparisons which showed that maternal age is unlikely to be an explanatory factor. The data in Table 14.10 indicates that limb defects and hypospadias are possibly related to spermicide use.

Professor Stolley discussed other studies which did not find an increased risk, which we now summarize. One study asked all women who had a confirmed pregnancy with a Kaiser Permanente facility in Northern California between 1974 and 1977 to fill out a questionnaire concerning their contraceptive use during the preceding 12 months. The brand used and the time use was discontinued were also reported. A total of 34,660 women participated in the study, of whom 3,146 had used a spermicide prior to conception but not after their LMP and 2,282 who continued to use a spermicide after their LMP. In Table 14.11 we report the data from this Northern California (1982) study comparing the malformation rates of

TABLE 14.10.   Prevalence of Specific Congenital Disorders Among Live-born Infants According to Vaginal Spermicide Use from the Seattle Study

	Users (763)		Non-Users (3902)	
	Number of Children with Disorder	Prevalence Rate (per 1000)	Number of Children with Disorder	Prevalence Rate (per 1000)
Any defect	17	22	10	39
Limb reduction	3	3.9	1	.3
Hypospadias	2	2.6	0	0.0
Chromosome abnormality	3*	3.9	1	.3
Heart anomaly	1	1.3	9	2.3

*All cases were Down's syndrome.
Source: Adapted from Table 3 of the Seattle study.

spermicide users with users of other contraceptive methods. We also present the confidence intervals and power of the test to detect a relative risk of 2.0. The study included all pregnancy outcomes for which information on malformations was available. Furthermore, diagnoses were confirmed by an independent study of a sample of records.

Comment.   This study differed from the one by Oechsli, as it did not follow the children for a number of years to ascertain further defects. Even so, the percentage of children with birth defects was substantially higher than the rates given in Table 14.7 from Oechsli's study (although the 1982 study noted that many of the malformations were minor). A comparison of the rates of major defects, including those of the limbs, showed *no* increased risk. The article noted that the spermicide users were older, more educated, drank less alcohol and smoked less than the users of other methods but did not differ with respect to the proportion of persons with a previous abortion or child with a birth defect. The data was analyzed by a multiple logistic model, which yielded similar estimates of relative risk, although the details of this analysis were not presented in the published article. The study also noted its limitations and concluded with, "the results of this study show no association between spermicide use around the time of conception and congenital anomalies. A woman who thinks she might be pregnant ought to have a pregnancy test before continuing to use contraceptives." Nonetheless, the study's data indicate the

TABLE 14.11. Rates of Various Birth Defects in Spermicide Users of Other Contraceptive Methods by Time of Use

Users of Contraceptive Methods before LMP

	Spermicide Users (3,146)		Other Users (13,148)		Relative Risk of Spermicide Users	Confidence Interval	Power
	Number	Rate per 1000	Number	Rate per 1000			
All Defects	415	131.9	1665	126.6	1.04	(.94,1.15)	.99+
Cardiovascular	21	6.68	78	5.93	1.13	(.66,1.84)	.99+
Limb	89	28.29	347	26.39	1.07	(.84,1.35)	.99+
MUsculoskeletal	12	3.81	46	3.50	1.09	(.53,2.09)	.63

Users of Contraceptive Methods after LMP

	Spermicide Users (2,282)		Other Users (2,831)		Relative Risk of Spermicide Users	Confidence Interval	Power
	Number	Rate per 1000	Number	Rate per 1000			
All Defects	294	128.8	360	127.2	1.01	(.87,1.17)	.99+
Cardiovascular	13	5.7	23	8.12	.70	(.33,1.44)	.46
Limb	75	32.87	75	26.49	1.24	(.89,1.72)	.98
MUsculoskeletal	5	2.19	18	5.65	.39	(.11,1.11)	.25

Source: Extracted from Tables 1 and 3 of Mills, Harley, Reed and Berender (1982).

accidental exposure to spermicides after conception is probably not teratogenic.

The second study of a cohort of pregnancies from 13 collaborating hospitals (1982) also found no excess of birth defects in a study of 462 exposed (the exposed group members all used spermicide after the LMP) and 49,820 nonexposed mothers in a collaborative study of births in 12 hospitals during the 1958–1965 period. Relevant data from that study is reported in Table 14.12. Of most significance are the following facts:

(1) There was no increased incidence of birth defects. Indeed, the estimated RR was .9 with a 95% confidence interval of (.6, 1.6).

(2) The patients were interviewed during their pregnancy prior to the birth of the baby and data on drug use were recorded at each antenatal visit.

The findings were as follows: "We conclude that there is no satisfactory evidence to indicate that spermicides increase the overall risk of major birth defects. It is possible, however, that spermicides increase the risk of certain specific malformations. Our own study is not large enough to exclude such a possibility. To evaluate it, further studies are needed." This is statistically quite important, as the *power* of the study to detect limb defects was low. Indeed, at a 1983 FDA meeting Dr. Shapiro, one of the authors of the 1982 article, had noted the problem of power and

TABLE 14.12. Number of Birth Defects and Rate of Defects per 1000 Births in the Exposed and Unexposed Groups in the Collaborative Study

	Exposed (462)		Not Exposed (49,820)		Crude Ratio	Adjusted Ratio (RR)	95% C.I.
	Number	Rate per 1000	Number	Rate per 1000			
All	23	50	2254	46	1.1	1.1	(.7–1.6)
Major	10	22	1383	28	.8	.9	(.4–1.6)
Minor	13	28	885	18	1.6	1.2	(.7–2.2)
Musculoskeletal	3	6.5	392	7.9	.8	1.1	(.2–3.1)
Hypospadias	1	2.2	186	3.7	.6	.6	(0–3.4)
Club foot	3	6.5	189	3.7	1.7	1.6	(.3–4.8)
LRD	0		68	1.36	0	0	

Source: Table 1 from the Collaborative Perinatal Project (1982).

stated, "I'm not for one moment claiming that this study rules out an increase in the risk of specific birth defects." Because the defendant's expert had placed greater confidence in the study by Dr. Shapiro and his colleagues than they had, the court discounted his conclusion.

Another interesting aspect of the case was the testimony on behalf of the defendant of a coauthor, Dr. Watkins, of the 1981 Seattle study, who criticized it on the following grounds:

(1) Whether the mothers who were presumed to be exposed actually used the spermicide was unclear.

(2) Its small size

(3) The fact that several disparate conditions were grouped together and

(4) The mothers were presumed to be exposed if they had obtained a prescription for vaginal spermicide within 600 days of conception, which was not a sufficiently specific exposure criteria.

While the criticisms relating to whether the women used their pre-scribed drug raises questions about the accuracy of the exposure data, the vast majority of people who obtain prescriptions get them filled and use the drug, so the degree of uncertainty in exposure status *may* not be that important. Of course, it would have been preferable for the study team to have interviewed a sample (say 10%) of the exposed group to check this out. Still it seems more reasonable to ask the critics to offer some data to support their criticism. In particular, a sample of patients could have been followed to assess their rate of using prescriptions for contraceptive drugs. This witness did cite one instance where a presumed user had actually planned to have her baby, however, he remained a coauthor of the study. Indeed, the court doubted his credibility because he signed his name to the article and had not mentioned its flaws to the public or scientific community in the four years prior to the trial.

Comments. (1) The above discussion illustrates the importance to both parties of presenting experts who can be regarded as being unbiased. The testimony of one of the plaintiff's experts was also given little weight because he had become interested in the general area after his wife had a spontaneous abortion after using a spermicide manufactured by the de-fendant.

(2) Another defense witness was the firm's Director of Medical Affairs. He testified that Ortho had an "extensive capability for keeping up with scientific literature" and he commented on the various studies. He stated that the Canadian study results were "not striking" because the authors

essentially reported a negative finding (recall they did not claim to establish a causal relationship) and that the spermicides used in Canada may have contained active ingredients which were approved for use in Canada but not in the United States. Although he had not heard of the Oechsli study until after the lawsuit was filed, he felt that the population studied probably included many "high risk" patients rendering it "essentially invalid." He also commented on some of the animal studies concerning absorption of the basic chemicals. All of these studies were published in 1980 or after.

(3) It is interesting to note that the 1981 study of the Seattle group distinguished between women who continued use after their LMP and those who discontinued prior to their LMP, which was an important issue in this case. In view of the fact that many women could have discontinued use during a 600-day period, they might not have exposed the fetus to the spermicide. Thus, this study may have less relevance than some of the others. Indeed, the time frame of possible exposure is more relevant than the issue of whether a sizeable fraction of people did not use the prescriptions they presumably paid for.

Judge Shoob's opinion is quite carefully documented and considers the two issues concerning whether a warning was appropriate prior to mid-1980 and whether any of the child's birth defects were due to her mother's use of spermicide. The opinion found that the drug firm should have placed a warning label prior to 1980, because the defendant had actual or constructive knowledge of studies indicating an increased risk of the product well before the mother obtained her prescription. Thus, the firm was liable under the theory of strict liability under Georgia law. The opinion relied on the plaintiff's experts, one of whom said that the first study (1976) should have prompted a warning but did allow that a warning might have been delayed until the second study appeared in 1977.

The reasoning underlying the findings concerning the defects of the child are quite illuminating. First, we are reminded that only the defects of the plaintiff are at issue, so the plaintiff does not have the burden of demonstrating that the product creates a statistically significant risk in a large population. The judge felt that the epidemiologic studies considered as a whole were inconclusive and relied on the medical testimony of Dr. Buehler, who linked the time of exposure to the time the child's limbs were forming. Thus, the court found that the spermicide caused the defects in the child's left shoulder, arm and right hand but *not* the cleft lip and eye disorder.

Comment. Throughout the book we have emphasized the relationship between statistical data and the subject matter so that the conclusions drawn should make sense in the context of the application, especially with the natural time sequence. It is difficult to question the logic of the opinion concerning the failure to warn issue. Suppose we accept Oechsli's study as an exploratory one, leading us to test the hypothesis that spermicide is (or is not) related to limb defects. Then this would be the primary hypothesis of concern to us in our review of the Canadian study (even though the Canadian authors were unaware of the Oechsli report). The significant risk found in the 1977 study should logically lead us to reject the null (no increased risk) hypothesis.

The 1980 study by Harlap, Shiono and Ramcharam did *not* concern birth defects but focused on fetal loss. Moreover, the data in Table 14.9 suggest that users of spermicides who continued use past their LMP might well have had a slightly increased risk of fetal loss relative to those who stopped use prior to the LMP. While this was not a statistically significant increased risk, the study also reported that women who started to use a spermicide after the LMP also had a nonsignificant increased risk of fetal loss (RR = 1.20). Since we are primarily concerned with the effect of exposure after conception on the plaintiff, and both comparisons with the discontinued users indicate a slightly increased risk of fetal loss, it is hard to understand how this study refutes the findings of the 1977 Canadian study concerning limb defects or the 1976 study of Oechsli, especially as toxic agents tend to cause specific injuries so that an agent associated with a particular birth defect should not necessarily be expected to cause other defects or fetal loss.

We now discuss other epidemiologic evidence, including a study mentioned in a letter to the editor appearing in the same journal issue as the 1982 collaborative Perinatal Project study. The letter by Dr. Oakley noted the results of a case-control study by Polednak, Janerich and Glebatis (1982), who interviewed 715 women in upstate New York whose child had a birth defect. We report the matched data for several categories of defects in Table 14.13. Notice that no particular defect shows a statistically significantly increased risk, however, limb reduction defects *slightly* exceeded their expected number (6 to 4.5). Dr. Oakley (1982) concluded that a causal relationship between spermicide use and birth defects had not been established when the Seattle (1981), Collaborative Project (1982) and New York (1982) studies were considered together. He felt that the total sample size of all the studies was large enough to rule out a greater than

TABLE 14.13.   Data on the Matched Pairs and the Estimated Risk of and Test of Statistical Significance for Various Limb Defects in the New York Study

Birth Defect	Number of Matched Pairs of Each Type				Estimated OR	Two-sided p-value
	(1, 1)	(1, 0)	(0, 1)	(0, 0)		
Limb reduction	1	6	3	98	2.0	.508
Hypospadias	0	8	2	89	4.0	.344
Cardiovascular	1	6	10	87	.6	.454
Multiple defects	0	2	6	92	.33	.290

Source: Table 10 from Polednak, Janerich and Glebatis (1982).

twofold increase in the risk of any birth defect (all malformations) and spermicide use but stated that additional studies would be needed to exclude lower level risks and that it would be possible to establish a small increase in total defects or an increase in a particular defect in future studies. Thus, the opinion's characterization of the epidemiologic evidence as inconclusive seems quite justified.

On the other hand, it should be noted that all but one of the studies yielded an estimate of the relative risk of spermicide use among continuers and limb defects which was greater than 1.0. Thus, the findings of all six studies do suggest a somewhat increased risk of limb defects due to spermicide exposure but the relative risk is likely to be less than 2.

The above conclusion has to be taken with greater than normal caution because of the possibility of an important covariate which could easily explain an increased risk of the magnitudes 1.2 to 2.0 obtained in the studies. In particular, the 1977 Canadian study indicated that tranquilizer use (especially in the first trimester of pregnancy) and a threatened abortion apparently had RRs of limb defects similar to that of spermicide use (see Table 14.14). In view of this finding, it is somewhat surprising that these factors were *not considered* in any of the subsequent studies. Thus, in spite of all the studies, the whole topic still seems scientifically unresolved, confirming Judge Shoob's conclusion that the studies were inconclusive.

Finally we note:

(1) Had the time sequence of the studies been reversed, i.e., had the results of the Collaborative Perinatal Project (1982) and Northern California (1982) studies appeared in 1976 and 1977, while those studies appeared

TABLE 14.14.   The Association with Birth Defects of Several Possible Toxic Agents from the Canadian Study

| | Number of Exposed | | | | |
Exposure	Cases ($N = 93$)	First Control Group ($N = 93$)	Second Control Group ($N = 93$)	Estimated OR	Two-sided p-value
Tranquilizer Use (1st trimester)	14	5	6	2.82	.02
Antihistamines (1st trimester)	8	2	4	2.82	.10
Threatened abortion	24	10	13	2.14	.01
Oral contraceptives	35	50	41	.78	.38

Source: Table 2 from Smith, Dafoe, Miller and Banister (1977). The p-values were calculated from the Chi-square test results given in the paper when cases were compared with all controls. Similarly, the OR estimate was obtained by applying formula (5.2). In all computations the matching could not be considered, as the original paper did not report the data in the matched format.

in 1982, it is questionable that the firm would have had the same duty to warn purchasers of the product in 1980 of a danger in continuing use past the LMP.

(2) The data from the New York (1982) study in Table 14.13 remind us that in *small samples* an apparently meaningful estimated OR can have high probability of occurrence by random chance. Among the nine discordant pairs, the case was exposed in six and the control in three. The estimated OR from formula (11.19) is $6/3 = 2$. However, the probability of observing six or more ones in a binomial random variable with $n = 9$, $p = 1/2$, is .254, which is not even close to the usual levels of significance.

(3) These studies also indicate the difficulty in assessing increased risks which are *less than twofold* in cohort studies of rare diseases, as the sample sizes required to have adequate power (90% or more) to conclude that a nonsignificant observed RR greater than 1.0 can safely be interpreted as *no increased risk is very large*.

(4) A recent study by Mitchell, Cotte and Shapiro (1986) demonstrates the importance of the questionnaire design in obtaining full information on drugs taken during pregnancy. In particular, data from respondents who were asked about specific drug (by name) was more accurate than persons asked an open-ended question about the drugs they took. The article also noted that about 20% of patients receive drugs from sources other than their primary care doctor or health plan. Thus, the sole use of the health plan prescription records in several of the studies relied on in the *Wells* case can be a major source of misclassification of exposure status.

c. Other applications

Epidemiologic studies have been used in cases involving side effects of vaccines and in the regulation of drugs, e.g., determining whether a warning label should be mandated. We now briefly describe those topics.

After courts, e.g., *Reyes v. Wyeth* 498 F.2d 1264 (5th Cir. *cert. den.* 419 U.S. 869 (1974)) found vaccines to be an inherently dangerous product, requiring an appropriate warning to the patient or their physician, manufacturers began to have difficulty obtaining liability insurance. In 1976 when the government began its swine flu immunization program to protect the public against a possible epidemic, the government assumed liability for any personal injury or wrongful death attributable to the vaccine. This was done to obtain the cooperation of drug manufacturers as well as the public.

In order to buttress their proof of causality, many plaintiffs relied on a large study carried out by CDC (1979). When the vaccination program began on October 1, 1976, it incorporated a surveillance program, and by December 2 over 35 million doses had been administered and two clusters of Guillain-Barre syndrome (GBS) in recipients occurred in different states. By December 15, preliminary data indicated that the vaccinated population had seven times the risk of GBS than the non-vaccinated, so the immunization program was terminated on December 16, 1976 and all cases of GBS occurring from October 1, 1975 thru January 31, 1977 that were reported to the CDC formed the basis of the CDC study (1979) that was relied on to determine compensation under the law. The study showed that

(1) The relative risk of contracting the disease was about four the first week after injection, rose to nearly 16 during the third week after injection and then declined to about 2 by six to ten weeks and was not significantly greater than 1.0 ten weeks or more after injection.

(2) The relative risk varied by age group as follows: 18–24 years RR = 3.7; 25–44 years RR = 12.2, 45–64 years RR = 6.8 and persons 64 and older had an RR of 5.2

On the basis of the study the government did not contest claims concerning GBS occurring within ten weeks of the vaccination. In general, courts have found that persons whose disease occurred more than ten weeks after they received the vaccine were not eligible for compensation, as their diseases were most likely due to other causes.

A number of these cases are discussed in the articles by Hall and Silbergeld (1983), McElveen and Eddy (1984) and Black and Lillienfeld

(1984) listed in the references. Therefore, we only mention a few cases in which the CDC study played a role:

Alvarez v. U.S. 495 F.Supp. 1188 (D.C. Colo. 1980). The plaintiff's disease developed seven months later and her claim was denied.

Cook v. U.S. 545 F.Supp. 306 (N.D. Ca. 1982). The court denied plaintiff's claim in part because the disease occurred 12.5 weeks after vaccination. The opinion is well worth reading, as it discusses the potential effect of the under-reporting of cases which occurred after the vaccination program and its associated surveillance of the general population were stopped. Judge Schwarzer chose the methods most consistent with the medical knowledge concerning the latency period of similar illnesses and reactions.

Sulesky v. U.S. 545 F.Supp. 426 (S.D. W. Va. 1980). This is one of the few cases in which a plaintiff obtained compensation, although she received her innoculation more (14) than ten weeks before the disease manifested itself. Judge Haden noted the importance of the normal rate of GBS which was used to compare the incidence of GBS during the swine flu period. The CDC study estimated a *background* rate of .22 cases per million persons per week. However, a subsequent study of GBS during an outbreak of "Russian" flu yielded an estimate of .095 cases per million persons per week. Since .24 cases per million persons occurred during the 13th thru 17th weeks after vaccination in the CDC study, Judge Haden realized that the assumed background rate is the critical element in deciding whether the relative risk was sufficiently large to justify a person's eligibility and decided that the studies did not prove or disprove the plaintiff's claim. He gave the benefit of the doubt to the plaintiff.

Carroll v. U.S. 625 F.Supp. 1 (D. Md. 1982). The plaintiff was 29-years-old and in excellent health when he received a flu shot on October 18, 1976. Within a week he experienced a tingling sensation in his legs and felt quite tired. In December 1976 his physician diagnosed his problem as an upper respiratory infection but his feelings of fatigue continued. Only on December 30, 1977 was his condition diagnosed as GBS. Although the government contended that had the plaintiff seemed ill with GBS, he would have seen a neurologist and been diagnosed in the fall of 1976. Judge Harvey noted that the plaintiff had a stoic attitude to medical care and that his case was relatively mild in its early stages. Therefore, he found that the plaintiffs' case commenced within the ten-week period.

Comments. (1) It is interesting to compare the opinions in *Cook* and *Sulesky*, where both judges had to select an appropriate background rate from several offered by the experts. In *Cook*, the judge decided that, regardless of the choice of base rate, the relative risk of getting the disease 13 weeks after receiving the vaccine was less than 2.0, so the PDE was less than one half, i.e. there was less than a 50% chance that the plaintiff's disease was due to the vaccine. It should be noted that the local area background rate of about .29 per million was presented in this case. Hence, if it was chosen as the reference rate, the CDC rate of .24 per million 13 to 17 weeks after exposure would *not* be excessive. Local rates were *not* available in *Sulesky*, so there was more uncertainty about the background or normal rate in the case, so the judge relied on the medical testimony rather than the epidemiologic study. Moreover, the plaintiff was 30-years-old and belonged to the age bracket with the highest relative risk. It is plausible that the time it would take for the effect of an exposure with an average RR of 12 to dampen down to 1.0 would be longer than for an exposure with an RR of 4.0. Unfortunately, the CDC study did *not* examine the time a person was at an increased risk by age category.

(2) There is a public policy question inherent in the strict adherence to the criteria of the PDE exceeding one half (or the RR exceeding 2.0). If the vaccine had increased everyone's risk by 1.9 and if the CDC national background rate is correct, there would have been

$$.9 \times .24 = .22$$

excess cases per million persons or about nine (8.8) cases among the 40 million persons vaccinated, but *none* of these victims of GBS would receive compensation. Since it is also in the general public interest to have almost everyone vaccinated against a serious contagious disease, it may be preferable to compensate all victims of side effects occurring in a reasonable time frame in order to encourage the population to take the vaccine.

(3) The use of a strict ten week cutoff period may also be questioned, because the decay of the attack rate is gradual and probably does not jump from an RR of 2.0 to 1.0 in a few days. This is especially relevant when the estimated decline of the risk over time does not incorporate other potential covariates such as age and prior health status.

Problems

1. At the time Rely was taken off the market the results of four case-control studies on tampon use and TSS had been published by CDC.

Although some of the studies used matching, we will ignore it (only because all the data was not published in a matched format). The data is given in Table 14.15

(a) Compute the MH test statistic and summary odds ratio using the methods of Chapter 5.

(b) The first CDC study included cases diagnosed a year or more prior to the study, while the second study used recent cases, so interviews were carried out within two months of the disease. Do the results appear similar? What implication does this have on the accuracy of recall about product use? About brand use?

2. Compare the rate of birth defects among white users of contraceptive jelly in Table 14.7 who continued use after their LMP with all other women. The data is given in the following table.

	Births with Serious Defect	Births without Serious Defect	Total
Users of Jelly after LMP	24	248	272
All others	418	8398	8816
Total	442	8646	9088

(a) Calculate an appropriate test statistic and an estimate of the odds ratio.

(b) Create a similar table for the data on blacks in Table 14.7 and carry out the same test and estimate.

(c) Do you think the effect of spermicide use is similar in both groups?

(d) Regardless of your answer to (c), compute the Mantel-Haenzel summary odds-ratio estimate. In the present context would it be a good approximation to the relative risk measure? Explain.

3. Suppose you were hired by the defendant firm in the *Wells* case.

(a) How might you have buttressed its criticism of the Oechsli and Canadian studies concerning the chemical content of the spermicides they studied.

(b) What further information from the various studies might help you rebut the association between spermicide use and limb reduction defects found in the Canadian data?

TABLE 14.15.   Unmatched 2 × 2 Tables for Case-Control Studies on TSS and Tampon Use Available Prior to the Withdrawal of Rely Tampons

	Used Tampons	Did Not Use	Total
CDC Study			
Cases	50	0	50
Controls	43	7	50
Wisconsin			
Cases	30	1	31
Controls	71	22	93
Utah			
Cases	12	0	12
Controls	32	8	40
Second CDC Study			
Cases	50	0	50
Controls	124	26	150

Source: The information for the first three studies appeared in the *Morbidity and Mortality Weekly Report* issue of June 27, 1980, **29**, 297–299. The last data set appeared in the same journal on September 19, 1980, **29**, 441–445.

4.   Suppose you were hired by the plaintiff in the Wells case. What questions might you raise concerning the validity of the Northern California (1982) study?

5.   Suppose you were asked to participate in a task force designing two studies, one case-control and one cohort to resolve the issue of contraceptive use and birth defects.

(a) How would you determine the sample size?

(b) What covariates would you consider and how would you obtain and validate this information?

(c) What statistical techniques might be usable and what checks would you ask your statistician to perform?

(d) What steps would you take to ensure that your study could withstand the scrutiny of a careful examination?

4.   Diseases with Long Latency Periods

The determination of exposure status and level of exposure is far more difficult and subject to greater possible error in studies of diseases which take many years to develop than in studies of recent exposures. As a result, there is more skepticism of the results of epidemiologic studies and the estimated relative risk (RR) and proportion of cases in the exposed population due to exposure (PDE) measures estimated from these studies. The large sample size required for studies to have high statistical power to detect important but modest increases in the relative risk (1.5 to 2.5) of exposure also creates difficulties for policymakers in regulating exposure levels of the population to carcinogenic chemicals, as adequate human data is often unavailable. Hence, results from human populations or animals exposed to high levels of the chemical must be used to estimate the effect of low doses by extrapolation techniques, known as risk analysis or risk assessment.

The best known toxic agents with documented harmful health effects may well be cigarette smoking, asbestos and radiation exposure. In this section we will describe the role of statistical evidence in some cases involving radiation exposure. The radiation studies will be described in conjunction with the cases. References to the literature on asbestos litigation are given at the end of the chapter. Then we present a brief introduction to risk analysis, which is often an issue in cases involving the propriety of regulations, which are the subject of the last section of the chapter.

a. Cases involving alleged radiation induced cancers

1) Allen v. U.S.[34]

From January 1951 through July 1962, the United States carried out numerous tests of atomic weapons in southern Nevada. While efforts were made by the Atomic Energy Commission (AEC) to keep nearby populated areas from being exposed to the radioactivity released by the explosions, residents of areas in the path of natural winds from the test site were exposed to higher than normal levels of radiation. Plaintiffs downwind of the test site who resided in the exposed areas in Utah and Arizona sued the United States for exposing them to the excess radiation. Before discussing some of the studies introduced at the trial, we should mention that prior studies of persons exposed to high levels of radiation, such as the A bomb survivors and radiologists, had demonstrated an increase in leukemia, cancer of the thyroid, lung and digestive organs in both sexes and breast cancer in women. Later in this section we will see that estimating low dose effects from studies of persons exposed to high doses of radiation or any toxic agent is quite difficult and incorporates a number of assumptions which may be difficult to verify, so we focus on studies

TABLE 14.16. Basic Data on Number and Incidence of Leukemia and Other Cancers in Children up to 15 Years of Age in the Utah Study: Observed Deaths from Leukemia and Other Cancers and Person-Years in the High-Exposure and Low Exposure Cohorts of Both Sexes According to Counties With High and Low Fallout

Area	Low-Exposure Cohort, 1944–1950			High-Exposure Cohort, 1951–1958			Low-Exposure Cohort, 1959–1975		
	Leukemia Deaths	Deaths From Other Cancers	Person-Yr	Leukemia Deaths	Deaths From Other Cancers	Person-Yr	Leukemia Deaths	Deaths From Other Cancers	Person-Yr
Total state	51	71	1,426,174	184	194*	4,623,432	122	121	3,604,416
High-fallout counties	7	21	330,177	32	21	724,531	10	15	451,408
Low-fallout counties	44	50	1,095,997	152	165	3,898,901	112	106	3,153,008

*Includes 8 cases with county of residence unknown.
Source: Table 2 from Lyon, Klauber, Gardner and Udall (1979).

directed to ascertaining the effect of the radiation produced by the test bombs on the individuals residing in the exposed areas.

The first study concerned childhood leukemia and cancer was conducted by Lyon, Klauber, Gardner and Udall (1979). From fallout maps of 26 of the roughly 100 nuclear tests carried out during the 1951–1958 period, parts of Utah were identified as high fallout areas, while the remainder of the state was considered as a low fallout region.

A high exposure cohort was defined as all persons under age 15 during 1951 through 1958. These children had the potential for being exposed to the radiation from the tests. Persons under age 15 during 1944 through 1950 formed one low exposed cohort. A child born in 1945 would be included in this low exposed cohort until reaching the age of six (1951), when the child became exposed to higher levels of radiation. A second cohort of low exposed children were those born in 1959 or later (after the tests ended). In Tables 14.16 and 14.17 we reproduce the number of

TABLE 14.17. Standardized Leukemia Mortality Ratios (SMR) for the High-Exposure Cohort as Compared to the Low-Exposure Cohort for Utah and High-Fallout and Low-Fallout Counties

Area	Sex	Observed Deaths*	Expected Deaths†	SMR†	Confidence Interval§	
					Low	Upper
Utah	M	89	57.8	1.54¶	1.00	2.37
	F	95	74.1	1.28	0.93	1.76
Totals		184	131.9	1.40‖	1.08	1.82
High-fallout	M	16	5.6	2.88	0.96	8.60
counties	F	16	7.5	2.12	0.63	7.11
Totals		32	13.1	2.44¶	1.18	5.03
Low-fallout	M	73	52.2	1.40	0.84	2.35
counties	F	79	66.7	1.19	0.87	1.63
Totals		152	118.9	1.28	0.97	1.69

*Observed deaths were those occurring in the high-exposure cohort.
†Expected deaths were generated by application of age-specific mortality rates to person-yr at risk in the high-exposure cohort.
‡Tested by the Mantel-Haenszel procedure controlled for age & sex.
§Approximate confidence intervals.
¶$P < 0.05$. P denotes p-value.
‖$P < 0.01$.
Source: Table 4 from Lyon, Klauber, Gardner and Udall (1979).

deaths from leukemia and other cancers in the three cohorts as given in the study and the SMR analysis, which compared the high exposure group with both low exposure cohorts, yielding an RR of about 2 for the highly exposed group (children in the high fallout counties who were in the highly exposed cohort).

Land (1979) criticized the previous study. He created Table 14.18 of deaths from cancer, in the high and low cohorts, classified by whether the cancer was leukemia or not. Although this is not a proper 2 × 2 table, he felt the total person-years in the two low exposure groups combined were close enough to those of the high exposure category, so the difference between this table and the usual one could be ignored. Concerning the results in Table 14.18 Land (1979) remarked, "It is unlikely that radioactive fallout from the Nevada weapons test caused both an increase in leukemia mortality and a decrease in deaths from other childhood cancers; yet this is a possible interpretation of the results of the above analysis. Nothing so specific as an explanation in terms of misdiagnosis of leukemia is required; either or both of the observed associations with fallout exposure could be fortuitous."

Although one should consider age-adjusted rates, we will continue Land's approximate analysis and examine the crude person-year incidence rates derived from the data in Table 14.16 in Table 14.19.

TABLE 14.18. Comparison of Leukemia and Other Childhood Cancer Deaths in the Two Cohorts According to Fallout Level by a Critic of the Utah Study

	Leukemia Deaths			Other Childhood Cancer Deaths		
Fallout Level	Exposure Cohort		Fallout Level	Exposure Cohort		
	High	Low		High	Low
High	32	17	High	21	36
Low	152	156	Low	165	156
Odds ratio	1.93			0.55	
Chi-square	3.68 (P = 0.055)			3.53 (P = 0.060)	

Source: Table 1 from Land (1979).
Note: The chi-square test is a two-sided test based on the square of the test statistic (5.6). P denotes the p-value of a two-sided test.

TABLE 14.19.   Crude Rates Per 10^5 Person-Years of Exposure of Leukemia and Other Cancer Deaths in the Cohorts and Exposure Areas in Table 14.16

	Leukemia		
	Low Exposure Cohort 1944–1950	High Exposure Cohort 1951–1958	Low Exposure Cohort 1959–1975
High Fallout	2.12	4.42	2.22
Low Fallout	4.01	3.90	3.53
	Other Cancer		
	Low Exposure Cohort 1944–1950	High Exposure Cohort 1951–1958	Low Exposure Cohort 1959–1975
High Fallout	6.34	2.90	3.3
Low Fallout	4.66	4.24	3.55

Source: Calculated from Table 14.16. The upper left entry was obtained as $7/330,177 = .0000212 = 2.12 \times 10^{-5}$.

The high fallout area incidence rates indicate that the incidence of leukemia doubled during the A bomb years relative to both its pre- and post-bomb test period rate. The incidence of other cancers seemed to drop by one half after the 1944–1950 period but remained steady thereafter (the difference between 3.3 and 2.9 being of the order of 10%). Thus, Land's possible interpretation that the bomb tests caused "a decrease of other cancers" results from his *combining* the pre-atomic test period, which had a larger incidence of other childhood cancers, with the post-test period, in which the incidence rates of other childhood cancers were similar to that of the test period. While it would be helpful to understand the cause of the apparent excess of other childhood cancers in the high fallout areas in the pre-test period, since the rate of other cancers did not rise substantially in the post-test period, if there is a statistical fluke in the data set it is most likely to be the 21 deaths from other cancers in the high fallout counties during the early time period. The data also indicates a gradual decline over time in the incidence of both types of cancer in the low fallout counties, although the rate of decline is slower for leukemia. Hence, Land's critique of the original study does not explain the data. Moreover, his analysis did not consider the factor of age. An analysis by Chernoff[35] examined the data by five-year age categories and focused on the 10–14-year-olds who had more time to be exposed and had passed the minimal latency period of about two years. He found that the highly exposed children in this age group had the highest leukemia mortality rate. Thus, his analysis also supported the validity of the findings of the original 1979 study.

Several other studies were also cited in the opinion. In particular, the CDC investigated clusters of cancer occurring in Parowan and Paragonah, two places close to the test site, and found an increased incidence of leukemia in children. This finding is important because leukemia had been associated with radiation exposure in health professionals before the bomb tests so that it would be one of the cancers that should be expected to show an increased incidence in exposed persons. The CDC's results were confirmed by a study of Johnson (1984) who focused on the Mormon population in the Southwest (exposed area). Since Mormons have a lower rate of adult cancer, probably due to their lifestyle, as the church urges abstinence from smoking and alcohol, it is proper to consider religion as covariate.[36] His results showed an increased incidence of leukemia in children and adults, thyroid cancer in adults and breast cancer in women.

A substantial portion of the trial was concerned with problems in dosimetry or measurement of the radiation levels that individuals were exposed to. We will not consider this topic, as hard data was not discussed in the opinion, but note that it is very difficult to make such an assessment years after an explosion has occurred when data was not taken at the time of the explosion. This is especially true of radiation, which does not affect all areas uniformly but sometimes clusters in "hot spots."

Comments on the Statistical Evidence.   (1) The data in this case was a form of historical cohort study in which the exposure classification invariably is somewhat imprecise. This usually implies that some highly exposed persons are misclassified as low exposed and vice-versa. As we realized in Chapter 10, this tends to diminish the statistical power of the study.

(2) A recent article by Darby (1985) discusses the difficulties in evaluating the effect of low-dose radiation from high-dose studies. An extensive British literature is cited concerning cancer mortality in children treated with radiation to cure ankylosing spondylitis. A recent study of Smith and Doll (1982) found a very high RR for deaths from tumors of the spinal cord and nerves but also indicated that the dose-response curve for leukemia among the exposed children was rather flat. If this finding is correct, much of the argument about whether the children in southern Utah were exposed to a sufficiently large amount of radiation would not be of particular importance for the case at hand, provided they received the minimal dose consistent with other data showing an increased incidence of leukemia.

(3) The article by Machado, Land and McKay (1987) disputes the results of Johnson (1984) but now finds an increase in childhood leukemia.

The extensive opinion by Judge Jenkins contains a discussion of atomic physics and radiation as well as tort law and the use of probabilistic and statistical evidence. He noted that the FTCA[37] states that the government cannot be responsible for

> "Any claim based upon an act or omission of an employee of the government, exercising due care, in the execution of a statute or regulation, whether or not such statute or regulation be valid, or based upon the exercise or performance or the failure to exercise or perform a discretionary function or duty on the part of a federal agency or an employee of the government, whether or not the discretion involved be abused."

After reviewing the major related legal decisions,[38] the judge concluded that the clause meant that courts should not interfere with high-level executive decisionmaking, but once the decision is made it needs to be carried out with reasonable care. (See the references for some articles concerning the discretionary clause.)

Before discussing the role of the statistical evidence we note that the judge found that the AEC had a duty to protect health and safety during research and production activities.[39] Although the AEC knew radioactive fallout could be produced which would increase radiation exposure among persons living in off-site communities, as well as others, he found that it did not make any effort to monitor and record internal contamination or dosage in off-site residents on a comprehensive person-specific basis. Indeed, the first random sample was not taken until 1957. He also found that the information given the public was inadequate and overly reassuring and was contrary to the existing principles of health physics. Thus, the government was deemed negligent and to have wrongfully breached its legal duty of care to the plaintiffs who, as off-site residents, were placed at risk.

The opinion notes:

(1) The choice of a level of statistical significance, e.g., .05, is arbitrary, so the p-value of a test should be regarded as indicating a degree of confidence in the relationship. (This is consistent with Judge Higginbotham's statement in *Vuyanich* regarding p-value as a sliding scale. The smaller the p-value, the less belief we have in the null hypothesis.)

(2) The simple PDE > .5 criteria is overly simplistic, as only effects

which at least double one's risk of harm would be compensable. Thus, while mathematical probability is an aid in resolving the causation issue in a complex case, it cannot provide the answer by itself.

Therefore, Judge Jenkins required each plaintiff to establish by a preponderance of evidence that

(1) The decedent or living plaintiff had cancer and resided in area that was probably exposed to radiation in significant excess of "background" rates.

(2) The injury was consistent with those known to be caused by ionizing radiation.

(3) The injured person lived in geographical proximity to the test site for some or all of the years of atmospheric testing.

The statistical results and latency period considerations were used in determining whether each plaintiff satisfied the second criteria. Several determinations follow:

(a) Plaintiff K.H. was born in August, 1941 and lived her entire life in an exposed location. When she was 14 in February 1956, she was diagnosed as having leukemia. Her case was attributed to the radiation as were the next examples.

(b) S.N. lived in another exposed area. He was born in June 1946 and was diagnosed with leukemia in March 1959 at the age of 12 and died several months later.

(c) A.B. was 34-years-old when testing began and was diagnosed with leukemia 11 years later. He was exposed to radiation because of his residence and the fact that he observed a particular blast.

Notice that the above cases met the appropriate minimum latency period criteria, evaluated from the date of their first exposure to the appearance of their disease, as well as having a disease that radiation can cause.

(d) G.H. was diagnosed with pancreatic cancer in 1978. This cancer has not been associated with low doses of radiation, although some studies of Japanese bomb victims suffered that high dose radiation levels might increase one's risk. However, cigarette smoking is known to be a leading cause of this cancer and coffee drinking is also a suspected risk factor.[40] As G.H. was a regular smoker ($1\frac{1}{2}$ to 2 packs per day) and a coffee drinker, the preponderance of the evidence is *against* radiation being a substantial factor in his illness.

(e) Plaintiffs D.J.B. and G.T. had ovarian cancer. None of the studies indicated a statistically significant association of radiation and this cancer. As D.J.B. also received medical irradiation, the evidence failed to establish A bomb radiation as a "substantial factor". A footnote in the opinion refers to an estimate PDE of about .2 provided by the plaintiff's expert for D.J.B.'s cancer being due to the bomb radiation. Thus, Judge Jenkins utilized the PDE concept even though he did not require that the PDE for each cancer victim exceed .5 before they would be eligible for relief.

Comments. (1) Occupational studies of workers subject to low levels of radiation are surveyed in Gilbert (1985). While one table in her paper suggests a possible increase in pancreatic cancer, it was not statistically significant. Moreover, smoking and coffee consumption data for the cohort studied apparently were not available.

(2) As women were rarely employed in jobs such as mining and atomic energy plants during the 1950s and 1960s, virtually no occupational studies are available to ascertain the effect of long-term low level exposures on them. Women did work with radium paint in some plants, especially during the second world war.

2) *Johnson v. U.S.*[41]

This suit against the government was brought by four employees who alleged that their cancers were caused by exposure to radiation from luminous dials and other aircraft instrumentation parts in their jobs at Aircraft Instrument Development (AID) Inc. The plaintiffs claimed their cases of lung cancer (D.V.), adult leukemia, specifically chronic granulocytic leukemia (E.J.), rectal (L.M.) and thyroid cancer (B.W.) were due to exposure to radiation.

This case differed from the *Allen* case in two respects: a) the maximum possible amount of radiation the employees were exposed to was considerably less and b) the trial judge did not accept the concept that a PDE of .50 met the criteria that causation be shown to "a reasonable degree of medical certainty" required in Kansas and required stronger evidence of causation.

There were several studies introduced in this case. One of which showed that no significant excess risk appeared in women who worked with radium paint until they received a dose of approximately 1000 rad[42] and that the radiation caused bone cancer and cancer of the paranasal sinuses rather than the ones plaintiffs complained of.

A fundamental ingredient of any analysis of the excess risk employees were exposed to is the dosage that they were subjected to. There was substantial controversy between the parties about the totality of radioactive equipment in the workplace and the amount of exposure. The judge relied on two surveys which showed that the exposure in plants making similar products was probably no more than 500 mrem per year or about the same level as most residents of the city were normally exposed to. Moreover, only two employees of another plant were found to have been exposed to excessive radiation. The defendant's experts estimated the dose levels received by the relevant organs of the plaintiffs. The court accepted these estimated levels for each plaintiff. B.W. (3.2 rem), L.W. (.16), D.V. (.49) and E.J. (.06), which were the lowest estimates introduced during the trial. However, even had he used the larger estimates of 7 rem, each plaintiff would have received far more radiation from natural causes than from these exposure levels. Before discussing the judge's analysis of each plaintiff's case, we note that he understood the nature of the PDE calculation and the importance of accounting for other known covariates. Specifically,[43] Judge Kelly's opinion described an expert for the plaintiff's calculation of the PDE as follows:

> "The statistical approach used by Dr. Morgan is known as a probability of causation calculation. Mathematically, the risk of a certain dose of radiation is divided by the sum of that same risk and the natural risk of cancer. While this is a proper mathematical formula for calculating the probability of events which have happened, and if well founded, which it is not, may be of some interest as regards the risk assessments relating to any exposure, its results are only as valid as the assumptions which go into it. For example, if the dose estimates which are used are not correct, the final result has to be wrong. If one uses the linear hypothesis to produce an answer, that answer is questionable because the quadratic hypothesis produces an entirely different answer. If a particular individual is exposed to the various other carcinogens at a level different from the level at which an average person in the general population is exposed, then the formula's assumed natural rate of cancer is incorrect for that individual and the final answer is again wrong. If a particular person with lung cancer was a heavy smoker, the formula is guaranteed to yield an inaccurate answer unless some allowance is made for the probability that the heavy smoking rather than the radiation could have caused the cancer. When Dr. Morgan confidently used this mathematical formulas to predict that radiation causes lung cancer in a person who has been a heavy smoker for 50 years without including in his calculations this increased risk from smoking, he illustrates how easily this formula can be used to mislead a court, and probably some juries, rather than to solve the question of what really caused a particular plaintiff's cancer. (T.Tr. Vol. 56, pp. 4374–4378)."

Comment.   The data in Table 14.1 concerning the joint effect of radiation and smoking on lung cancer which we discussed does substantiate the above criticism. However, a particular misapplication of statistical methodology should not affect its correct use in other cases.

In his discussion of the individual cases, the judge noted that even for the plaintiffs whose cancer might be due to radiation, latency period considerations indicated that their particular cancer was probably not caused by low-dose exposure. For example, L.W.'s rectal cancer was diagnosed after being employed at AID for $5\frac{3}{4}$ years, but the minimum latency period for that cancer, when it is induced by high levels of radiation, is nine years. Thus, he concluded that even if the cancer was caused by radiation, it must have been due to some other source.

Further Discussion of the Two Radiation and Cancer Cases.   Although the criteria for proof of causation differed in the two cases, both judges incorporated other factors such as the relationship between radiation and the particular cancer, the latency period of the cancer and the behavior of the defendant in complying with its duty in their decision. A major difference between the two cases may be that the law establishing the AEC specified had to protect health and minimize the dangers involved with explosions and research. Since Judge Jenkins found that the AEC was negligent in failing to properly warn the exposed population and not conducting a scientifically sound monitoring system, his use of a lesser standard of proof seems logical. Indeed, it is similar to the Supreme Court's using a higher Type I level in its test of jury discrimination when the race of potential jurors was known to the persons selecting the venire than otherwise (see Section 4.2). However, the Appellate court reversed the original opinion with respect to the warning issue, as it fell under the "discretionary clause" of the FTCA. Also, the burden of producing reliable exposure estimates may have differed in the two cases. In *Johnston*, the plaintiffs made two surprise visits to AID but failed to measure the levels of radiation on one occasion and said that the measurements weren't carried out properly the other time. The judge was skeptical of the estimates created by their experts when relevant data that might have been used to validate them was not taken. On the other hand, the AEC had a responsibility to monitor the radiation exposure created by its testing program, so the judge in *Allen* may have been more skeptical of the government's low exposure estimates created years later.

Parts of the *Johnston* opinion, however, appear to be overly critical of statistical data. In particular, the statement,[44] "This Court finds by common sense that any statistical method which fails to include some obvious possible causative factors must yield a seriously flawed and untrustworthy end result" makes it too easy for critics of a study to suggest a possible "obvious" factor. We know from Cornfield's result that the factor needs to have a relative risk at least as large as the agent under study and must be sufficiently more prevalent in the exposed group relative to the unexposed to completely explain an observed relative risk. Moreover, if several major[45] factors are incorporated in the analysis, adding another covariate will only improve the estimated relative risk of the agent under investigation if it is not highly correlated in the population with the factors already included.

On the other hand, if Judge Kelly's statement is interpreted as meaning that factors which have a reasonable chance, based on prior medical evidence, of being related to the disease should be *considered* in the planning of the study and in the analysis of the data, then it is consistent with our earlier discussion. Some factors may be eliminated by matching, others by an appropriate regression analysis, while data on others may not be collected either because they are highly correlated with other factors which will be obtained, e.g., age and total work experience for male workers, *or* because they are known to have a small effect, such as an RR of 1.2, which will not affect the planned use of the data. Judge Kelly's statement reinforces our previous recommendation that in a definitive study to be used in a major public policy decision, data on any known risk factor should be obtained. It is much easier to justify neglecting it in the final statistical analysis after showing that it is distributed similarly in the groups being compared or by showing it has no effect in a suitable analysis.

b. Risk analysis

Risk analysis consists of a body of methods for estimation of the risk persons assume from being exposed to a toxic agent. The purpose of risk analysis is to assess

(a) how likely is an agent to be detrimental to human health, e.g., be carcinogenic and

(b) if it is likely to be harmful, what is the magnitude of its impact on the population at large and/or the exposed population given current and projected exposures.

As one can imagine, several key factors in a risk assessment require sound data, e.g., the size of the population at risk, the magnitude of the risk, the total exposure *prior* to any action taken to reduce exposure and projected future exposure levels. As reliable data on all these factors is usually *not* available, invariably a number of assumptions are made in the process of preparing a risk analysis. We begin this subsection by summarizing the results of an analysis published by CDC[46] of the effects of radon exposure in homes. Two sets of risk estimates are provided which hopefully bound the true risk.

From the uranium miner studies a high (H) estimate of radiation related deaths of 7.3×10^{-4} per lifetime WL exposure and a low estimate, 3×10^{-4} deaths per lifetime, WL exposure were obtained. The chart for the general population, including homes where a smoker was present, is reproduced in Table 14.20. For nonsmokers, an estimate one sixth of the high estimate should be used.

The table was published after high levels of radon were observed in a sample of 2000 homes in Pennsylvania. Forty percent of the homes had radon levels exceeding the EPA guideline of .02 working levels. For homes in which a smoker is present, with 20 years of exposure at the .02

TABLE 14.20. Risk (Percent) of Persons Dying From Lung Cancer Related to Radon

Deaths per working level month	Years of exposure	Working level				
		0.004	0.02	0.10	0.5	1.0
7.3×10^{-4}	1	0.01	0.06	0.3	2	3
	5	0.05	0.3	2	7	14
	10	0.1	0.6	3	14	28
	20	0.2	1	6	28	57
3.0×10^{-4}	1	0.005	0.02	0.1	0.6	1
	5	0.02	0.1	0.6	3	6
	10	0.05	0.2	1	6	12
	20	0.1	0.5	2	12	23

Source: *Morbidity and Mortality Weekly Report* (1985) **34**, 657–658, citing National Research Council (1980) for the percents based on the 7.3×10^{-4} risk per WL month and the International Commission on Radiological Protection (1981) for the percents based on the 3.0×10^{-4} risk per WL month.
Note: The risks given assume that residents spend 75% of their time indoors. The two basic risk estimates, 7.3×10^{-4} and 3.0×10^{-4} were obtained from the two sources. The risk reported in the table appears to be the attributable risk.

guideline, between .05% and 1% of the exposed persons are expected to die from radiation-related lung cancer. For exposures greater than .02, the estimated risk increases approximately in proportion to the risk at .02 WL. For instance, at ten years of exposure, the risk is .6%, and at .10, a level five times .02, the risk is 5 × .6 = 3.0%. This relationship is called the *linear* model and seems to have been used as the main component of the estimates past .02 WL in Table 14.20. The estimates of .004 WL, *one twentieth* of the .02 WL exposure appear to be about *one fifth* of those at .02 WL. This may be due to the fact that the *normal* background radiation is included, and it is larger than the very low levels of *indoor* exposure.

The major problem in setting "safe limits" from dose-response data is that one needs to fit a curve to dose-response data obtained at reasonable dose levels and *then* find the *dosage* that will yield a probability so small, say one in a million, of getting the disease during one's lifetime. In Chapter 8, we used the logistic curve to model the probability of a response, however, other curves can also be used. For example, a logistic curve can be fit to dosage (measured in logarithms), so the curve is given by the formula

$$(14.1) \qquad F(d) = \frac{1}{1 + e^{\alpha + \beta \log d}},$$

An alternative model, called the probit model, which assumes that the response probability is given by the distribution function of a normal curve, i.e., once value of the mean μ and variance σ are specified, the response probability is given by

$$(14.2) \qquad P\left[Z = \frac{\log d - \mu}{\sigma} < t\right],$$

where Z is a standard normal variable. Because the effect of dosage is measured in logarithms in both models, they are sometimes called the log-logistic and log-normal models as well as logit and probit.

The dose-response curve for the logistic is just the curve of the logistic distribution function given in Figure 8.7, where x is replaced by the logarithm of the dose. The curve for a log-normal response is virtually indistinguishable from the log-logistic, except at the extremes (near 0 and 1). Unfortunately, we cannot usually obtain measurements at does levels corresponding probabilities of 1% or less because the number of subjects required is quite large.

The problem can be illustrated by the calculations of Brown (1983) who fit several dose response curves to the data given in Table 14.21 on liver

TABLE 14.21. Liver Hepatomas in Female Mice Exposed to DDT

Dose Level (ppm in diet)	0	2	10	50	250
Number of rats at level	111	105	124	104	90
Number of rats with tumor	4	4	11	13	60
Response fraction	.036	.038	.089	.125	.667

Source: Personal communication from Dr. Brown who used the data on tumor incidence in female mice in both the parent and first generation offspring from Tomatis, L., Turusov, V., Day, N. and Charles, K. T. (1972). The Effect of Long-Term Exposure to DDT on CF-1 Mice. *International Journal of Cancer* **10**, 489–506.

tumors in mice exposed to DMN (dimethylnitrosamine) for 120 weeks. We report the results of four models Brown fit to the data, the *p*-values of a test of goodness of fit which checks that the model fits the data and the estimated virtually safe dose, the lower endpoint of a 95% confidence interval for the level corresponding to an excess risk of one in a million, in Table 14.22.

Notice that none of the four models can be rejected, even using the 10% significance level, and none of them fits the data much better than the others. However, the estimated safe dose levels differ by factors of ten or more. Indeed, the maximum tolerable dose using the log-normal model is nearly 100 times that obtained from the log logistic. This phenomenon

TABLE 14.22. Comparison of Virtually Safe Doses Leading to an Excess Risk of One in a Million for Various Dose-Response Models Fitted to the Liver Tumor Data in Table 14.21

Model	Allowable ppm in Diet	Prob-value of Goodness of Fit Test
Log-normal	6.8×10^{-1}	.14
Weibull	5.0×10^{-2}	.22
Log-logistic	6.6×10^{-3}	.18
Exponential	2.1×10^{-4}	.16

Source: Table 6 from Brown (1983).

happens quite often and indicates that much larger sample sizes are required to determine the best fitting model.

Comments.   Since we must extrapolate or project *outside of the range* of the data to obtain the dose giving a response rate of one in a million or perhaps one in 100,000 we would like to have data which at least yields a reliable estimate of the dose level at which no more than one percent of the rats respond, i.e., we would like to conclude that if no tumors occur in a sample of size n rats given dose d, we are 95% confident that no more than 1% of rats exposed to dose d will respond (have a tumor). We calculate the upper confidence interval for p as in Section 4.4d from the equation

(14.3) $(1 - p)^n \geq .05.$

Only now, we desire to determine n as we want p to be .01 or less. Hence, the equation is

(14.4) $(.99)^n \leq .05,$

and its solution yields $n = 298$. Thus, we need to have studied about 300 rats at the low dose level d to be 95% confident that no observed tumors corresponds to a risk less than 1%. Even if we obtained a reliable estimate of the dose level, d, corresponding to a 1% probability or lifetime risk of cancer, we still must extrapolate to obtain the dose levels corresponding to risks of the order of one in 10,000 to one in a million.

The data in Table 14.21 also illustrate a related problem. At first glance it seems that the dose level of 2 ppm would be safe, as no more rats at that dose level developed a tumor than those with no exposure. However, models incorporating a fixed threshold (a minimum exposure level needed to cause a tumor) for all rats exposed or a variable threshold (each individual has a minimum tolerable threshold which varies over the population) also yield widely divergent virtually safe doses. Indeed, the estimates in Table 14.22 incorporated the natural or zero dose risk, i.e., the dose response estimates in Table 14.22 refer to the "excess" risk over the natural or zero-dose rate of tumors.

In addition to the basic issue of the shape of the dose response curve at very low exposure levels, other important considerations are:

(1) How is the natural or background rate incorporated in the model? The response functions we discussed assume that $F(0)$ = the probability of a response, (e.g., tumor) equals 0 when the dose is 0. When there is a natural response rate, perhaps from other causes or due to naturally oc-

curring exposure to the agent under study (such as radiation), one wishes to estimate the excess risk due to the exposure above the natural rate. Two different assumptions can be made to incorporate the natural rate:

(a) the response to the natural rate and administered exposure are independent *or*

(b) the doses *add* so the probability of response to dose d is $F(d + d_0)$, where d_0 is the "natural dose".

In conjunction with the concept of no fixed threshold, the additive dose-effect assumption (b) leads to assuming a *linear* approximation in the low dose range, which is why the *linear* extrapolation model is often used. However, other assumptions lead to response curves which approach the origin at a faster or slower rate.

(2) The competing risk problem where an agent capable of producing the cancer under study with a latency period of t years is also capable of producing or promoting other diseases in less than t years.

Ordinary survival methods assume persons leave the cohort studied at random for reasons unrelated to the exposure. As Gail (1975) notes, this assumption is invalid under a competing risk generated by the agent under study. Indeed, the cancer producing capability of the agent under study could be seriously underestimated if it produced other cancers not studied. To illustrate the issue, smoking has been associated with bladder as well as lung cancer. Because the typical age of diagnosis of bladder cancer in women is about 70, while that of lung cancer about 60, the observed incidence of lung cancer in women increased as their smoking habits increased before the observed incidence of bladder cancer (which only recently has begun to show an increase). Perhaps, women who smoked and were susceptible to cancer got lung cancer rather than bladder cancer. Failure to adjust for the competing risk effect in a study of smoking and bladder cancer would lead to an underestimate of the relative risk of smoking.

Problems

1.*   What are the major difficulties encountered in studying the possible harmful effects of exposure to radiation or other toxic agents on the incidence of a relatively rare disease in small human populations?

2.   Read the studies used in the *Allen* case. Which statistical concept is not discussed adequately?

Answers to Selected Problems

1. The size of the exposed population may not be large enough for the statistical test to have sufficient power to distinguish between the null hypothesis of no effect and the alternative of a meaningful increase (RR ≥ 1.5). The exposure levels of each individual in the population are often unavailable, so we cannot assess whether a dose response curve exists nor can we be sure that all persons classified as exposed (unexposed) were exposed (unexposed). Also, the mobility of the population means that members of the study population may leave the area, and we cannot determine whether or not they subsequently developed the disease under investigation.

2. The *power* of the test statistic to detect a meaningful RR, say 1.5 or 2.0, is not given in any of the studies.

5. The Role of Statistical Reasoning and Risk Analysis in the Regulatory Process

When government agencies such as the EPA or OSHA promulgate standards, such as restricting the amount of lead in gasoline or limiting the average amount of a chemical an employee may be exposed to during a day, affected parties (manufacturers, union members or citizen groups) may bring suit to prevent the regulation from taking effect. In this section we will discuss two cases which illustrate the type of review courts give agency decisions. In turn, these decisions guide the agencies in their rule-making process. While courts hesitate to second guess an agency action if the record reflects that all the available information was considered and the regulation has a rational basis, sometimes insufficient data and/or analysis is used by agencies in setting the tolerable thresholds for chemical exposures or, in a subsequent removal of a previous regulation,[47] and courts disallow the regulation or remand[48] it for further consideration. In the first part of this section we provide some background information. Then we will discuss the regulation of vinyl chloride and benzene.

a. Some considerations used in the regulatory process

Different laws require various degrees of balancing the risk of exposure and the ensuring benefits with the costs of regulating exposure. Some laws such as the Delaney clause,[49] which prohibits the use of food additives which have been shown to be carcinogenic in man or animals, do not allow for the consideration of costs or, as Greenhouse (1980) noted, health benefits which may outweigh the risk. The Clean Air Act, 42 U.S.C. §7409 states that standards must be set with the purpose of avoiding risks to human health. Other laws, such as the Federal Environmental Pesticide Control Act, 7 U.S.C. §136(bb) require the regulatory agency to consider economic costs[50] in setting standards. Implicitly, cost factors also enter in deciding what the "best available technology" is when pollution is to be reduced.

In 1981, President Reagan issued Executive Order No. 12291,[51] which provided for the review of proposed regulations by OMB[52] and specified that a regulatory impact analysis based on the net social benefit would be a major factor in the evaluation of future regulations. The methods of cost-benefit analysis are typically used in the preparation of a regulatory impact analysis. The costs of a proposed regulation are usually easier to determine than the benefits, as the price of equipment can be determined. Indirect costs, such as possible loss of export sales if the price of the product might rise substantially as a result of the regulation, are more difficult to estimate. The benefit of a regulation which would reduce the exposure level of the population or a well defined subgroup, such as workers in a particular industry, depends on a risk analysis which estimates the lowered probability of an exposed individual getting the serious disease, the number of persons who will be affected and a monetary value assumed for the value of avoiding the disease. We refer the reader to the books by Mishnan (1976) and Crandall and Lave (1981) and the articles by Leape (1980) and Latin (1982) for further discussion of cost-benefit analysis and its use in regulatory matters.

Although one can consider the decision to regulate in the hypothesis testing framework (see Table 14.23) as in Wehmhoefer (1984), which is similar to the medical screening paradigm of Section 12.1, one should keep in mind that the cost of a regulation can vary greatly with the maximum allowed exposure level. Thus, it may be fairly inexpensive for an industry to reduce worker exposure levels from 50 ppm to 10 ppm, but lowering the levels to 5 ppm may require a major change in the manufacturing process. Courts[53] have approved a regulation which gave some firms in the industry several years in which to fully comply with the new standards.

Comments.   There are several issues which arise in the use of cost-benefit analysis in this context.

TABLE 14.23.   Hypothesis Testing View of Regulatory Decision-Making

True State of Nature	Decision or Action	
	Don't Regulate	Regulate
Substance not harmful (negative net benefit) of regulation)	Correct decision	Type I error (false positive)
Substance harmful (positive net benefit of regulation)	Type II error (false negative)	Correct decision

Note: The null hypothesis is the assumption that the substance is not harmful. A type I error means that the substance is falsely identified as being harmful, perhaps a carcinogen. The usual criteria that P (type I error) ≤ P (type II error) does not necessarily apply in this context.

(1) The monetary value used when the number of cases avoided or lives saved is converted into dollars is obviously quite subjective. This does not affect the use of cost-benefit analysis in prioritizing risks or helping a firm to allocate a fixed amount of money which will be devoted to reducing health risks incurred by its employees but does suggest that dollar estimates and comparisons should not be taken literally but be considered as estimates of the order of magnitudes involved.

(2) The determination of the probability that a disease will occur at low exposure levels usually relies on methods of risk analysis which are fitted to data which often are unable to distinguish between models yielding estimates which can differ by a factor of 100 or more (see Table 14.22).

(3) An ethical dilemma can occur in the occupational health area, as the expected net social benefit depends on the *number* of exposed individuals. If only 500 persons are exposed to chemical (X) which quadruples one's normal lifetime risk (e.g., probability .01) of a fatal cancer, then the excess risk translates to

$$(.04 - .01)(500) = 15$$

extra cases that are expected to occur among the exposed workers. If policymakers assume a case or life is worth three million dollars, then a simple cost-benefit analysis would conclude that the regulation would not be justified if the estimated cost exceeded 45 million dollars.[54] On the other hand, suppose that 10,000 workers were exposed to a different chemical (Y) which had a relative risk of 1.5 of causing the same fatal cancer. Now the expected number of lives saved if the RR were reduced to 1.0 by eliminating or severely reducing exposure is

$$(.015 - .010)(10000) = 50,$$

which justifies an expenditure of 150 million dollars in this industry to reduce the risk to these workers. The point is that calculating the expected net social benefit can result in allowing workers in small industries to be exposed to much greater risks than workers in larger industries. Although from a net social benefit or public health viewpoint more lives are "saved" by regulating chemical Y rather than chemical X, the fairness of allowing some workers to continue being exposed to fourfold increased risks, while reducing the risk of others who face a much lesser increased risk of serious illness, is questionable. Again we are faced with the issue of which measure, absolute or relative effect, is most relevant. Perhaps both measures should be used in assessing the need for a regulation so that no one is required to assume more than an agreed upon increased risk of disease.

(4) Our discussion of cost benefit analysis only considered comparing the expected benefits and costs. One can incorporate the *variability* of the risk assessment process in several ways. For example, one might assume that the dose-response curve was given by one of the best three fitting models so that each of the three estimated VSD levels has probability 1/3 of being correct. This leads to a probability distribution for the number of cases avoided whose variance can be calculated. Thus, one can derive a range, analogous to a confidence interval for the number of cases avoided and hence for the monetary value of lives saved, and could also compare the expected costs, which we assume to be fairly accurately estimable, with the 75th or 90th percentile of the benefit distribution as well as with the expected benefit.

Since it is more enlightening to study the judicial acceptance of the risk assessments made by the regulatory agencies than discussing the details of how a regulatory impact analysis is made, we now turn to two cases.

b. *Society of Plastics Industry Inc. v. O.S.H.A.*[55]

Before discussing the data the agency used to determine its proposed exposure limit, we mention that the opinion opened with a discussion of the role of the court. It emphasized that the determinations of the Secretary (of Labor) will be deemed conclusive if they are supported by substantial evidence in the record considered as a whole. Thus, the purpose of judicial oversight was interpreted as assuring that the agency carried out its task properly and did not in act in an arbitrary or irrational manner, rather than to second guess the agency's analysis of the data.

The industry challenged the standard set in October 1974 which limited the average[56] daily exposure to vinyl chloride of workers to one part per million (ppm). They claimed that the evidence did not support such a low exposure limit as being required for health and safety, the labeling requirements unduly emphasized the carcenogenic properties of vinyl chloride (VC) and that the standard was not technologically feasible. Statistical data primarily relate to the first two aspects.

In its review of the record the court noted that a Russian study in 1949 found liver damage in 15 of 45 workers and that Dow Chemical scientists had elicited liver irregularities in rats and rabbits at VC concentrations of 100 ppm. Consequently, Dow recommended a maximum allowance of 50 ppm in 1961, but the industry adhered to its previous standard of 500 ppm.

Several other studies also indicated problems, but only in 1972 did the industry decide to finance a study. In January 1973, the industry learned of European experiments with rats showing that at the 250 ppm exposure level tumors in the ear canal, kidney and liver were observed (but not at the 50 ppm level). This was kept confidential and not revealed to NIOSH until July, 1973. In the meantime, in 1971 a Goodrich employee in its Louisville plant died of liver cancer, which is quite rare (its normal incidence rate is about one in 50,000 persons per year). Two more employees died of liver cancer in 1973, and in 1974 several other deaths were reported amongst employees exposed to VC in several firms. In April 1974, an emergency standard of 50 ppm was established by the Labor Department. At that hearing "Dow Chemical spoke out for worker safety and urged that industry exposure be reduced to 50 ppm", but the stance of other firms is not mentioned in the opinion.

In April 1974, animal experiments showed that liver cancer was produced in mice at 50 ppm and the Labor Department decided to hold further hearings and promulgated its standards[57] in October 1974, which also allowed for short-term (15 minute) exposure up to 5 ppm and required employers to furnish workers with respiratory equipment and to institute a monitoring program. The data from the mice experiment were as follows: Of 200 mice (100 of each sex) exposed to 50 ppm of VC for 11 months, 100 died, of these 36 were given a post-mortem pathological exam. Thirteen (36%) had liver tumors, 21 (58%) had lung tumors, 9 (25%)

had skin tumors and one mouse developed a kidney tumor. Obviously, several mice had multiple tumors.

The industry pointed out that a Dow Chemical study on its employees had concluded that exposure at levels below 200 ppm did not lead to any adverse effect. That study monitored 335 employees over a seven-year period. However, not all exposed workers were studied, and the missing employees included many of long-term (20 years or more) employment, the most important subgroup to include, as the latency period for liver cancer is about 20 years.

An article on vinyl chloride was published by three employees of Dow Chemical (Ott, Langner and Holder, 1975), which may be an expanded version of the study mentioned in the above OSHA findings. The study reported eight deaths from all malignant neoplasms versus an expected number of 3.2 for highly exposed (200+ ppm) workers. No other exposure category showed an excess risk. Indeed fewer than the expected number of deaths occurred in the intermediate (25 to 200 ppm) and low (less than 25 ppm) exposure categories. No deaths were due to liver cancer. Also, some of the employees were exposed to other chemicals which are carcinogenic at high exposure levels.

The article also reported the duration of exposure for employees in the various exposure categories which we present in Table 14.24. Notice that only 34 employees were exposed for 20 years or longer, the latency period for liver cancer. Even if exposure tripled one's risk of liver cancer, with such a small cohort the expected number of deaths would still be less than 1.0, so the fact that no employee died of liver cancer is not very informative. The study did check the individual cases to see whether smoking, family history or other exposures might have had an effect. One case of leukemia occured in a nonsmoker with no family history of cancer who was exposed to benzene. Again, one cannot use one such case to demonstrate causation, although two other workers also died of leukemia.

The court in the *Plastics* case noted that already 13 exposed employees had died and that toxicological principles often use a one in a hundred safety factor when translating results of animal experiments to humans in setting a "no effect" or virtually safe dose level. Since mice developed liver tumors at 50 ppm and 50/100 = .5, the 1 ppm standard set by OSHA was justified by the evidence.

Comments. (1) The three cases of leukemia were described in an article by Ott, Townsend, Fishbeck and Langner (1978) which continued Dow Chemical's previously cited study. Two had been employed at Dow for

TABLE 14.24.   Duration of Exposure to Vinyl Chloride, by
Level of Exposure, of the Dow Chemical
Workers

Exposure Category	Number of Employees with Cumulative Years of Exposure			
	<1	1–9	10–19	20+
High (exclusively)	73	71	19	0
High	33	64	39	27
Intermediate (exclusively)	32	36	5	0
Intermediate	29	38	6	0
Low (exclusively)	127	50	3	1
Unmeasured	39	44	16	6

Source: Adapted from Table 8 of Ott, Langner and Holder (1975).
Employees were categorized by their highest exposure during their
work history. Therefore, data was reported separately for employees who had also held a job with a lower exposure level in addition
to the job with their highest exposure level.

over ten years, the third had only been employed for 30 months but had
been employed in a saw mill which manufactured veneer, which also has
been associated with leukemia. Thus, the linkage to benzene may be
questionable in that case, which would raise doubts about the significance
of observing two (rather than three) cases when only .8 were expected.
The benzene studies also illustrate the usefulness of animal studies to
indicate carcinogenic properties of chemicals.

(2) Previously, we noted that the fact that the workers were exposed to
several chemicals. This may not have biased the results concerning an
association of benzene and leukemia, as the cancers associated with vinyl
chloride and benzene exposure are different. Nevertheless, some exploration of the data for possible interaction or synergistic effect might have
been useful.

c. *AFL-CIO v. American Petroleum Institute:*[58] *the strength of the
    Benzene-Leukemia Association*

This case involved OSHA's[59] decision to reduce the maximum average
daily exposure of workers to benzene from 10 ppm to 1 ppm. The Occupational Safety and Health Act was passed to ensure safe and healthful

working conditions for everyone and authorized OSHA to promulgate appropriate

> "occupational safety and health standards defined as 'a standard which required conditions or the adoption or use of one or more practices, means, methods, operations or processes, reasonably necessary to provide safe or healthful employment and places of employment.' The Supreme Court's opinion also noted:
> "Where toxic materials or harmful physical agents are concerned, a standard must also comply with §6(b)(5), which provides:
> "The Secretary, in promulgating standards dealing with toxic materials or harmful physical agents under this subsection, shall set the standard which most adequately assures, to the extent feasible, on the basis of the best available evidence, that no employee will suffer material impairment of health or functional capacity even if such employee has regular exposure to the hazard dealt with by such standards for the period of his working life. Development of standards under this subsection shall be based upon research, demonstrations, experiments, and such other information as may be appropriate. In addition to the attainment of the highest degree of health and safety protection for the employee, other considerations shall be the latest available scientific data in the field, the feasibility of the standards, and experience gained under this and other health and safety laws." 84 Stat. 1594, 29 U.S.C. §655(b)(5)."[60]

According to the opinion, the Secretary of Labor had adopted the view that there is no safe level of exposure to a carcinogen so that exposure levels should be set at the lowest technologically feasible level that will not impair the viability of the industry. There was no question concerning the toxicity of benzene, and the opinion cited the history of regulation of benzene, noting that the federal standard was set at the lower (10 ppm) of two possible standards recommended by two different professional organizations. It then discussed early epidemiologic studies showing an increased incidence of leukemia in workers exposed to high levels (100 ppm or more) as well as studies showing that after benzene use ceased in certain industries, the incidence of leukemia declined.

The Court interpreted the law as requiring OSHA to demonstrate that workers in environments meeting the current standard (10 ppm) exposure limit are subject to a significant risk so that a lower standard is appropriate. The two major studies relied on by OSHA (White, Infante and Walker, 1980) will now be described.

An historical cohort study of exposed workers in two plants in Ohio compared their age-adjusted death rates (from leukemia) to the corresponding national age-adjusted rates for white males (almost all of the employees probably were white, as they were employed during the 1940–1949 period) as well as a cohort of glass workers in the same state. The comparison with the national data yielded a SMR = 5.07 (7 observed vs 1.38 expected, p-value < .01) and the comparison with the glass workers yielded an SMR of 4.73 (7 observed vs. 1.48 expected, p-value < .01). Unfortunately, the exposure levels of the workers were not well documented in the 1940s, and the authors of the report had assumed that when new ventilation equipment was installed in 1946 to bring levels down to "safe" limits, the limit was about 10–15 ppm. At that time, however, the "safe" limit was thought to be 100 ppm, so the study did not clearly demonstrate an increased risk near the current 10 ppm standard.

The second study was conducted by Dow Chemical. Men exposed to benzene, employed at any time from 1940 through 1970, were followed, and their vital status was determined as of 1973. Although only .8 of a case of myelocytic leukemia (the type associated with benzene) would be expected to occur among the 594 men, three did. Furthermore, two deaths from anemia occurred, and the three workers who died from leukemia apparently had average exposure levels *less* than 10 ppm, although one worker could have been exposed to 200 ppm earlier in his career. The original OSHA decision[61] did not place much weight on this study because leukemia was not observed among workers exposed to higher dose levels and because chemical workers were exposed to other chemicals known to be carcinogenic (e.g., vinyl chloride).

Comments. (1) Whether the fact that workers exposed to higher levels of benzene did *not* develop leukemia should be used to question the result depends on the number exposed to higher levels, say 20 to 25 ppm or more. Recall that in the entire cohort only .8 cancers were expected, if only one fourth of the workers were in the highly exposed category, then under the null hypothesis of no association we would expect .2 cases and an alternative of a *threefold* relative risk leads us to expect only .6 of a case. Hence, observing no cases would not be surprising, even if benzene exposure tripled one's risk of leukemia. One should make a power analysis as we did with regard to the cohort study of DES daughters in Chapter 11. Only if there is a low type II error (.2 or less) i.e., high power (.8 or more) should we take such criticisms seriously.

(2) In Section 13.4 we noted that the specificity of the association is important. The fact that workers might be exposed to other carcinogens could only explain the results if the Dow workers were exposed to chemi-

cals suspected of causing leukemia. According to the Office of Technology Assessment Report (1981, Table 17 at p. 85) the only two agents causing leukemia that chemical workers might be exposed to are ethylene oxide (ETO) and thorium dioxide. Thus, whether or not Dow's workers were exposed to these chemicals or to radiation should have been checked before ignoring the results.

(3) The estimated individual exposures in the Dow study, as in most historical studies, were subject to error, as they had to be done on the basis of job held rather than individual monitors. As we discussed in Chapter 8, these measurement errors typically lead to an *underestimate* of the association (or correlation) between the dependent variable (disease) and the independent variable (exposure).

The above comments do not affect the Supreme Court opinion, as the judges can only assess the record. Here, we remind the reader of the importance of assessing plausible explanations to make sure that the conditions under which they would account for an increased incidence of disease are met.

On the other hand, studies *not* finding a significant increase risk were also presented. In particular, Thorpe (1974) compared the number of leukemia deaths occurring among 38,000 employees of a petroleum company with age-adjusted European rates and found only 18 deaths compared to an expected 23.2.

The study itself, however, mentioned several possible methodological problems, namely:

(1) The low incidence of leukemia in the general population.

(2) The validity of the diagnosis of the cases of leukemia reported.

(3) The quantitative definition of the extent of exposure to benzene of the population under study.

(4) The inadequacy of the follow-up on annuitants.

(5) Incomplete occupational histories on individuals with a diagnosis of leukemia.

As discussed in Section 13.5, the accuracy of the exposure classification and case diagnosis are central to the validity of the conclusions of a study. As death certificates were used to determine the cases that occurred among the employees, the coding may be in error,[62] e.g., the person may die of a side effect of the treatment but the real cause of death was cancer.

Just looking at the sample size of the Thorpe (1974) study, one might believe it was a definitive analysis. However, it is much more difficult to accurately check the vital status of 38,000 workers spread over several plants in different countries than a smaller group of workers spread over one or two locations in the same area of a country, and determining the exposure levels from job assignments is a difficult task, so the data underlying the analysis might not have been of high quality.

Another important aspect of the opinion was that OSHA had not constructed any risk-benefit analysis or a dose-response curve that would predict with some accuracy the number of cases of leukemia that could be expected to result from exposure at 10 ppm, 1 ppm, or intermediate levels. The lower court opinion, upheld by the Supreme Court, held that OSHA's conclusion "that the benefits of the proposed standard are likely to be appreciable" was unsupported by the record. The opinion did hold that the record did provide substantial evidence that there is some risk of leukemia at 10 ppm and that the risk would decrease of the exposure limit were reduced to 1 ppm.

In contrast, the industry submitted a dose-response curve projecting that the standard could be expected to prevent at most one leukemia and one other cancer death every six years out of a work force of 30,000. OSHA rejected this evidence because it alleged that such a curve could not be developed. The agency did not argue that two lives every six years justified the regulation or that more deaths would be prevented.

Justice Stevens' majority opinion emphasized that the agency need not calculate the exact probability of harm but does have an obligation to find that a significant risk is present before it characterizes a place of employment as unsafe. Moreover, both the majority and dissenting opinions seem to agree that the determination of whether a particular risk is tolerable or not is a policy decision.

The opinion emphasized that OSHA was *not required* to support its finding that a significant risk exists with "anything approaching scientific certainty," substantial evidence would suffice. Moreover, the law allows the Secretary to regulate on the best available evidence and the opinion cited the *Plastics Industry* case and *Synthetic Organic Chemical Manufacturers Ass'n v. Brennan*[63].

One result of the opinion was that OSHA changed its policy which required the "automatic setting of the lowest feasible" exposure level without regard to determining the risk significance.[64] In a subsequent case, *American Textile Manufacturers Institute v. Donovan*,[65] the court found that the agency based its new limit on exposure to cotton dust on appropriate evidence.

According to Hall (1983) these and similar cases indicate that a quantitative analysis showing, with substantial (but not necessarily conclusive) evidence, that the existing standard poses a meaningful risk should pass judicial scrutiny. Some analysis of the benefits to worker health resulting from reduced exposure should also be provided, however, the opinion in the benzene case noted that "the agency is free to choose conservative assumptions in interpreting data with respect to risking error on the side of overprotection rather than underprotection."[66]

Comments. (1) In the previous section we realized that reliable extrapolations are difficult to make. Several models can be used to fit the data often obtained from animal experiments. If one model does not fit better than the others, as is typical, the agency can choose among them. Due to the limited sample sizes used in most experiments, methods need to be developed which utilize the results of experiments on related chemicals in order to determine the most appropriate dose-response curve for use in projecting a "safe" or virtually safe dose (VSD) level. Because several models which fit a dose-response data set equally well can yield much different low-dose extrapolations, the regulating agency will often have substantial freedom in selecting an exposure limit. On the other hand, requiring the regulatory agencies to analyze the data carefully, perhaps with several biologically plausible dose-response models, may aid in determining the VSD as well as presenting the inherent uncertainty in the threshold setting process. Sometimes one of the models may be eliminated due to lack of fit, which should reduce the range of possible VSD levels deemed consistent with the data.

(2) There are two important considerations concerning the set of studies used in regulatory analysis which deserve attention. At first glance, it would seem obvious that all available studies on human populations would be relevant and should be considered, giving the better studies, which measured exposure levels and disease incidence more accurately and followed persons longer and/or had larger statistical power, greater weight in the ultimate decision. The criteria that OSHA established for the admissibility of studies showing a negative result that required a RR of 1.5 to be detectable and the exposed group to have had at least 20 years of exposure were criticized as too stringent by Doll (1985), who advocated the combining of results of several studies. He noted that the final report should be required to present data by duration of exposure to enable readers to assess the role of the latency period but that when studies are totally excluded because they did not meet all of the OSHA criteria, the one significant result observed among many studies may well have been

due to chance (for another example, see the review problem). The overall analysis of several independent studies is called meta-analysis in the statistical literature. To conduct a careful meta-analysis one needs all the relevant studies.

(3) On the other hand, all studies that have been conducted *need not* be submitted to the regulatory agency. For example, suppose there are ten firms in an industry, each of which conducts a study of the effect of chemical X on a particular disease. If all the studies are designed to have 80% power of detecting an increased risk of 50% (RR = 1.5), we expect two of the ten studies to fail to obtain a statistically increased risk. If the firms in the industry can decide whether or not to submit the results of their studies, the proportion of negative findings in the official record will be far greater than their true proportion of all studies of the relationship at issue. This problem is the reverse of the multiple comparison or multiple study problem alluded to by Doll (1985) and discussed above. Therefore, government agencies might wish to ensure that any source submitting a study is committed to submitting all epidemiologic studies it is carrying out. This may not be easy to accomplish, as companies may not conduct studies if they feel they may be hurt by the results. As the alternative to regulating on the basis of human data is to rely on animal experiments, hopefully all firms in industries involving exposure to possibly toxic agents would agree to carry out careful studies of their workers and present the results to the scientific community for review. A way to encourage cooperation by firms, perhaps by limiting their liability for certain penalties or types of damage awards, might be developed.

Both the vinyl chloride and benzene cases illustrate the difficulty of investigating the effect of occupational exposures and establishing a "safe" level. The accurate estimation of the amount of exposure is limited because employees move during their careers and will be exposed to different chemicals at varying exposure levels during their lifetime. Furthermore, estimating the historical exposure levels can only yield an approximate figure, which probably underestimates the total variation in exposure among all workers, as all persons in the same job for the same time will be assumed to have had the same exposure history. This problem is inherent in all historical cohort and case-control studies concerning diseases with a moderate to long latency period when exposure is estimated from employer records on job held.

Of all the applications of statistics and probability we have considered, from an intellectual view, risk analysis and the setting of VSD levels may be the least satisfying. Often a reliable data base of sufficient size is *not* available. Nevertheless, our focus on an explicit statement of the models used in the analysis, an assessment of the fit of the model chosen by the agency to obtain the VSD[67] to the data used and the reasons why some studies were selected as reliable and others were not, should aid the reader in evaluating the thoroughness of the decisionmaking process. Similarly, any cost benefit analysis presented to assess the impact of a regulation should carefully describe the underlying assumptions. Thus, the main use of statistical reasoning in risk assessment and regulatory analysis is the logical thought process of assessing the effect of the various assumptions on the resulting estimates of risk and cost-benefit trade-offs and to emphasize that the uncertainty in these estimates are far greater than in most statistical applications. This last application of statistics was selected to demonstrate the *limitations* of the subject.

Problems

1. Use the principles of statistics to evaluate the statistical evidence regarding the effect of formaldehyde in new mobile homes used in *Troensegaard v. Silvercraft.*[68]

2. Read the *Gulf South Insulation et al. v. Consumer Product Safety Commission* 701 F.2d 1137 (5th Cir. 1983) case. Do you believe the court was too demanding of the agency or do you feel that the commission did not do a thorough analysis? How did the court and the commission differ in the relative weight they gave animal studies? How might a careful discussion of the statistical power of epidemiologic studies have strengthened the logic underlying the original CPSC regulation? How do the issues considered in this case differ from those in *Troensegaard*?

Chapter Review Problems

1.*   The FDA Commissioner's decision on OPE's discussed Section 13.3a was upheld in *Warner-Lambert v. Hechler* 787 F.2d 147 (3rd Cir. 1986). The court rejected the firm's claim that its drug was effective because, out of 240 statistical comparisons made, it found six significant ones (presumably at the two-sided .05 level or one-sided .025 level).

(a) Assuming the 240 comparisons were statistically independent, use the approach we took in analyzing the *Penck* case in Chapter 11 to show that six significant differences is what one might expect to occur if the *null* hypothesis of no effect is true.

(b) Why does the above analysis support the FDA and the court?

(c) About how many "significant results" should have been observed in the 240 tests, at the one-sided .025 level, showing "efficacy", in order to buttress the manufacturer's claim of efficacy?

(d) How might the firm demonstrate that the drug was efficacious in the six subgroups in which it had a "significant" effect, assuming they are well defined segments of the population?

(e) If the firm followed your advice in (d) and the results were favorable to its drug, is it reasonable for the FDA to approve the drug for use by these persons? Explain your logic. Are there any analogies from the cases discussed supporting your answer?

(f) In our discussion of the Oechsli and Canadian studies in the *Wells* case, we noted that many statistical tests were made in both studies, yet we concluded that together they indicated a statistically significant association between limb reduction defects and spermicide use. What is the difference between our statistical reasoning and that of the manufacturer in *Warner Lambert v. Hechler*?

2.* (a) The article by Black and Lillienfeld (1984) discusses the *Cook* and *Sulesky* vaccine cases and is quite critical of the *Cook* decision. Since the same experts were used in both cases and the decisions were different, contrast their analysis of the opinions and ours. Which fact that we cited might explain why the decisions could reasonably disagree?

(b) The same experts were also used in the two radiation cases, *Allen* and *Johnson*, we discussed. Why did their testimony receive such different receptions in these cases?

3. Compare the supporting evidence used by OSHA is regulating ETO from *Public Health Citizen Research Group v. Tyson* 796 F.2d 1479 (D.C. Cir. 1986) with the evidence used by the CPSC in the *Gulf South* case.

Answers to Selected Problems

1. (a, b, c) The number of "significant" results in a binomial variable with $n = 240$ and $p = .05$ (or .025). Thus, we expect 12 (or 6) significance differences. Clearly, the number of observed cases is at or below what is expected under the null hypothesis.

(d) The firm should carry out a second study on these populations if it made sense medically that they might respond better to the treatment.

(e) Yes. A sound study would have shown these people are helped by the drug and did not suffer harmful side effects.

(f) In our discussion we used the first study to form an hypothesis and tested it on the data from the second study. The drug firm did not make a second study to verify that the six significant results in its study were not due to chance.

2. (a) The extra fact was the local background rate. As the California and Michigan rates were higher than the national average, the West Virginia rate was likely to be *less* than the national rate.

NOTES

1. Legal treatises, e.g., W. Prosser (1971) discusses the concept of proximate cause. It differs slightly from the concept of cause in fact and allows for the notions of forseeability and risk/utility analysis. However, the evidentiary requirements for demonstrating legal causation are rooted in the more commonplace torts, such as auto accidents where one can identify who was hurt and who drove the car. It is impossible to demonstrate with 100% certainty that a particular case of lung cancer is due to the individual's exposure to radiation or their smoking. Epidemiologic and statistical evidence does indicate whether or not the exposure in question was likely to have been a major factor in the exposed person's case.

2. See McElveen (1985), who makes this interpretation. On the other hand, Rubinfeld (1985) notes that the issue of preponderance of the evidence in a specific set of circumstances is more complex than whether or not studies show that exposure at least doubles the risk.

3. ERC 1166 (10th Cir. 1985) on remand from 405 U.S. 615 (1984).

4. *Thomas v. Ferndale Laboratory Inc.* 97 Mich. App. 718, 296 N.2d. 160 (1970) and *Diamond v. Squibb* 366 So.2d. 1221 (Florida App. 1979).

5. *Corder v. A. H. Robins Co.* 692 S.W. 2d. 194, Products Liability Reports 10,694 (Texas App. 1985), *Timberlake v. A. H. Robins* 727 F.2d 1363 (5th Cir. 1984), *Anthony v. Abbott Laboratories* 490 A.2d 43 (R.I. Sup.Ct. 1985).

6. 165 Cal. App. 3d. 120 (1985).

7. 79 A.D. 2d. 317 *affirmed* 436 NE 2d. 182, 450 NYS 2d. 776 (1982).

8. A number of studies concerning the effect of DES on humans were cited in the references to Chapter 11. The book by Apfel, R. J. and Fisher, S. M. (1984) *To Do No Harm: DES and the Dilemmas of Modern Medicine*. New Haven: Yale University Press, presents a history of DES experiments. Not only do the authors cite a number of animal studies from the 1930s, they reproduce an editorial from the *Journal of the American Medical Association* (1939) **113**, 2323–2324 which warned against indiscriminate use of estrogens.

9. 697 F.2d 222 (8th Cir. 1983).

10. 724 F.2d 612 (8th Cir. 1983).

11. In *Adams v. Fuqua Industries, Inc.* 820 F.2d 271 (8th Cir. 1987) the issue of whether the product could have been manufactured with a safety device that currently exists is discussed. The opinion cites cases from several circuits which allow both parties to present evidence on feasibility issues.

12. *Adams v. Gaudet* 514 F.Supp. 1086 (W.D. La. 1981). See our earlier discussion of this case and *Capaci* and *Datapoint* in Chapter 6.

13. In fairness to the reader, the author should state his opinion that requiring such plaintiffs to know who was responsible or starting the statute of limitations period at a time prior to their birth is unreasonable. Since defendants in negligence cases are held responsible

only for what was knowledgeable at the time the product was marketed, it seems fair to hold plaintiffs responsible for what they could reasonably know at an appropriate time. Thus, it is sensible to start the statute of limitations period when a DES plaintiff should have known about its connection with vaginal cancer, as in *Needham*. On the other hand, Tennessee's commencement of its ten-year statute of limitations period at the time of purchase was upheld as constitutional in *Mathis v. Eli Lilly Co.* 719 F.2d 134 (1983). Hence, the plaintiff who developed cancer of the cervix 25 years after her mother took DES could not sue.

14. *Ryan v. Eli Lilly Co.* 514 F.Supp. 1004 (D. S.C. 1981).

15. 102 F.2d 464 (2d. Cir) *cert. denied* 308 U.S. 570 (1939).

16. The state laws vary, as we will see when actual cases are discussed.

17. These studies are discussed later in Section 5.

18. 14 Benefits Review Board Service (M.B.) 472 (1981).

19. *Clark v. SWCC* 155 W. Va. 726, 187 S.E. 2d 213 (1973).

20. See the "Developments" (1983) article in the *Utah Law Review*.

21. Million electron volts.

22. 788 F.2d 741 (11th Cir. 1986) *affirming* 615 F.Supp. 262 (N.D. Ga. 1985) in the scientific part relevant to our discussion.

23. The square of the normal, random variable, Z, is a chi-square variable. The chi-square test for a difference in proportions is based on the difference between the observed and expected number of counts. It is just the square of the appropriate normal form statistic (5.6) or (11.26). It is convenient when the null hypothesis is being tested against a two-sided alternative. Clearly, tests based on Z or Z^2 yield the same result. The chi-square test can be generalized to test whether the distribution of a set of numbers among more than two categories fits a set of executed values determined by a suitable null hypothesis. For a discussion of this test, see Mosteller and Rourke (1973) cited at the end of Chapter 9.

24. One can obtain a lower 95% CONF on the odds ratio as Schlesselman (1982) did in his analysis of the DES data we discussed in Chapter 11.

25. *supra* note 10.

26. *supra* note 10 at 618–619. In particular, CDC studies were admitted as evidence in *Reyes v. Wyeth* 498 F.2d 1264 (5th Cir. 1974) and *Givens v. Lederle* 556 F.2d 1341 (5th Cir. 1977).

27. *Bunch v. Dow Chemical Co.* Petition No. 6442 (Circuit Court, Montgomery County, Md). See also Kolata, G. (1985) Dispute Over Access to Reye's Study Data. *Science* **230,** 297–298 and Yolles, B. J., Connors, J. C. and Grufferman, S. (1986) Obtaining Access to Data From Government Sponsored Medical Research. *New England Medical Journal* **315,** 1669–1672. It should be mentioned that a tape of the Ohio data, with identifiers removed, used by the FDA in its earlier proposed warning, was made available to the industry.

28. Fienberg, S. E., Martin, M. E. and Straf, M. eds. (1985). *Sharing Research Data.* Washington: National Academy Press. A related article by Cecil, J. and Boruch, R. (forthcoming) Compelled Disclosure of Research Data: An Early Warning and Suggestions for Psychologists, *Law and Human Behavior* discusses a number of cases involving court ordered disclosure of research data.

29. Gastwirth, J. L. (1986) Comment on Disclosure Limited Data Dissemination by Duncan, G. and Lambert, D. *Journal of the American Statistical Association* **81,** 23–25. References to articles by advocates of the practice of merging data without informing respondents currently carried out by government statistical agencies are also provided. The most recent government guidelines, cited in the references to Chapter 9, now require that respondents be informed when matching is planned.

30. 745 F.2d 292 (4th Cir. 1984).

31. *Products Liability Reporter* **10,** 470 (3rd Cir. 1985).

32. Other cases involving the statute of limitations issue were cited in our discussion of the Dalkon shield and DES cases and related footnotes 4, 5, 6 and 13.

33. *supra,* note 22.

34. 588 F.Supp. 247 (D. Utah 1984). The decision was recently reversed by the court of appeals, 816 F.2d 1417 (10th Cir. 1987) on legal rather than statistical grounds.

35. Chernoff, H. Childhood Leukemia Associated With Fallout From Nuclear Testing: The Study and a Critique.

36. The effect of religion in the etiology of cancer is well known, see Seidman, H. (1970). Cancer Death Rates by Site and Sex for Religious and Socioeconomic Groups in New York City. *Environmental Research* **3**, 234–250. It is not entirely clear that lifestyle factors would affect childhood cancer, although recent studies suggest that passive smoking might increase one's risk of lung cancer.

37. Federal Tort Claims Act 28 USC Section 2680.

38. *Dahelite v. United States.* 346 U.S. 15 73 S.Ct. 956 (1953), *Indian Towing v. United States* 350 U.S. 6 (76 S.Ct. 122 (1955)), *Blessing v. U.S.* 447 F.Supp. 1160 (E.D. Pa. 1978) and *Jackson v. Kelley* 557 F.2d 735 (1977).

39. See the *Allen* opinion, *supra,* note 34 at 350, citing the relevant portion of the Atomic Energy Act.

40. MacMahon, B., Yen, S., Trichopoulous, D., Warren, K. and Nardi, G. (1981). Coffee and Cancer of the Pancreas. *New England Journal of Medicine* **304**, 630–633.

41. 597 F.Supp. 374 (D. Kan. 1984).

42. A *rad* is the most conversely used to describe the radiation dosage. If 100 ergs (units of energy) are deposited in one gram of tissue, that tissue has received on *rad* of radiation. The measurement of dosage is discussed in the *Allen* opinion, *supra* note 34 at 311–318.

43. See the opinion, *supra* note 41, at 394.

44. See the opinion, *supra* note 41, at 412.

45. In the case at hand, the plaintiff's apparent failure to consider smoking the major factor associated with lung cancer does justify the judge's assertion.

46. *Morbidity and Mortality Weekly Report* (1985) **34**, 657–658.

47. *State Farm Mutual Automobile Ins. Co. et. al. v. U.S. Dept. of Transportation* 680 F.2d 206 (D.C. Cir. 1982).

48. *ASARCO, Inc. v. OSHA* 647 F.2d 1 (9th Cir. 1981) remanded for additional findings on "significant risk" required by *Indust. Union v. Am. Petroleum Inst., infra* note 58.

49. 21 U.S.C. Section 376(b)(5)(B) bars food additives which have been shown to cause cancer in animals or man.

50. The Pesticide Control Act bans pesticides that pose "an unreasonable risk to man or the environment taking into account the economic, social and environmental costs of the pesticide".

51. 3 C.F.R. 127 (1978). The first executive order which mentioned the use of risk benefit analysis in regulatory considerations was announced by President Ford. President Carter also adopted the concept in Executive Order 12,044.

52. Office of Management and Budget whose office of Information and Regulatory Analysis (OIRA) reviews proposed regulations for compliance with the executive order.

53. In *Industrial Union Dept., AFL-CIO v. Hodgson,* 499 F.2d 467 at 474 (D.C. Cir. 1974) the court noted that "no precise prediction of increased harm can be made at this time," so it could not conclude that the Labor Department erred when it found that the delay would not subject the employees to additional risk. However, the court found that the decision to allow extra time to all industries, regardless of their ability to implement the lower standard (two instead of five fibers), was not supported by sufficient policy considerations.

54. Of course, regulators are not bound by the simple comparison of benefits to costs, as they are aware of the fragility of the underlying models and assumption. Indeed, many people might question the propriety of calculating the benefits on the basis of an inherently subjective valuation of a human life.

55.   509 F.2d 1301 (2nd Cir. 1975) *cert. denied* 95 S.Ct. 144.
56.   The average exposure was a time-weighted average in which each exposure level is weighted by the length of time a worker is exposed to the agent.
57.   *Federal Register* (1974) **39**, 35890, which reports the data from the various studies.
58.   448 U.S. 607 (1980).
59.   OSHA is the Occupational Safety and Health Agency in the Department of Labor.
60.   *supra*, note 58 at 612.
61.   See the *Federal Register* notice cited, *supra* note 57.
62.   See Barg and Huenther (1983) and Gute and Fulton (1985) for their studies of the accuracy of birth and death certificate information and further references.
63.   503 F.2d 1158, 506 F.2d 385 (3rd Cir. 1983).
64.   See *Federal Register* (1981) 46, 4890.
65.   452 U.S. 490 (1981).
66.   *supra*, note 58 at 657.
67.   Remember the VSD typically is not the estimate of the dose level at which the response probability is sufficiently small so as to yield an insignificant lifetime risk. It is the upper end of a 95% confidence interval for this dosage, which is why it is called the virtually safe dose level.
68.   California Court of Appeals 1st. Dist. No. A029837 (1985).

REFERENCES

Due to the variety of topics discussed in the Chapters 13 and 14 the references are organized by topic. The basic reference texts for case-control studies and epidemiology were given in Chapter 6.

Epidemiologic Evidence, its Reliability and Legal Standards of Proof

BARG, M. S. AND HUENTHER, C. A. (1983). A Study of the Underreporting of Down's Syndrome on Birth Certificates in an Ohio County, 1970–78. *Public Health Reports* **98**, 78–87. (A study showing that less than half the cases of Down's syndrome are indicated on birth certificates, even though over 90% are identified by the time the child leaves the hospital. The variation between hospitals was also noteworthy.)

BLACK, B. AND LILLIENFELD, D. E. (1984). Epidemiologic Proof in Toxic Tort Litigation. *Fordham Law Review* **52**, 732–785.

BLOOM, A. D. ED. (1981). *Guidelines for Studies of Human Populations Exposed to Mutagenic and Reproductive Hazards*. White Plains, NY: March of Dimes Birth Defects Foundation.

BURR, J. C. (1985). Collins v. Eli Lilly and Company: The DES Causation Problem and Risk Contribution Theory. *Wisconsin Women's Law Journal* **1**, 69–96.

COLTON, T. AND GREENBERG, E. R. (1982). Cancer Epidemiology in *Statistics in Medical Research*. (V. Mike and K. E. Stanley, eds.) New York: John Wiley.

CURRAN, W. J. (1983). The Acceptance of Scientific Evidence in the Courts. *New England Journal of Medicine* **309**, 713–714.

DICKSON, R. L. (1982). Medical Causation by Statistics. *The Forum* **17**, 792–808.

DOLL, R. AND WALD, N. J. EDS. (1985). *Interpretation of Negative Epidemiologic Evidence of Carcinogenicity*. Lyon, France: International Agency for Research on Cancer. (In addition to Sir Doll's introductory remarks, the articles by N. E. Day on statistical considerations and the discussions of the data concerning formaldehyde, saccharine and nitrates by leading researchers are well done and balanced.)

DORE, M. (1983). A Commentary on the Use of Epidemiologic Evidence in Establishing Cause in Fact. *Harvard Environmental Law Review* 7, 429–440.

FERN, F. H. AND SICKEL, W. (1985). Evolving Tort Liability Theories: Are They Taking the Pharmaceutical Industry into an Era of Absolute Liability? *St. Louis University Law Journal* 29, 763–785. (The authors, who are pharmacists as well as lawyers, discuss steps drug firms may take to limit their potential liability under market share and related theories of liability. They argue that the underlying rationale of *strict liability* should not apply to ethical pharmaceutical manufacturers.)

GUTE, D. M. AND FULTON, J. P. (1985). Agreement of Occupation and Industry Data on Rhode Island Death Certificates with Two Alternative Sources of Information. *Public Health Reports* 100, 62–72.

HALL, K. L. AND SILBERGELD, E. K. (1983). Reappraising Epidemiology: A Response to Dore. *Harvard Environmental Law Review* 7, 441–448.

HART, H. L. A. AND HONORE, T. (1985). *Causation in the Law*. 2nd ed. Oxford: Clarendon Press.

LAGAKOS, S. W. AND MOSTELLER, F. (1986). Assigned Shares in Compensation for Radiation-Related Cancers. *Risk Analysis* 6, 345–357. (This article and the accompanying commentaries on it are concerned with determining the fraction of cancer cases due to exposure to radiation. The estimated fractions depend on the model used to describe how radiation induces cancer, the covariates used, as well as the accuracy of the data.)

LIEBMAN, J. H. (1984). The Manufacturer's Responsibility to Warn Product Users of Unknowable Dangers. *American Business Law Journal* 21, 403–438. (This article presents a discussion of recent cases concerning how potential liability in various types of tort cases is related to the knowledge of the manufacturer and the feasibility of making a safer product at the time of its manufacture and/or at the time plaintiff incurred harm in its use.)

McELVEEN, J. C. JR. (1985). Reproductive Hazards in the Workplace. *The Forum* 20, 547–579.

McELVEEN, J. C. JR. AND EDDY, P. S. (1984). Cancer and Toxic Substances: The Problem of Causation and the Use of Epidemiology. *Cleveland State Law Review* 1, 29–68.

MOBILIA, M. A. AND ROSSIGNOL, A. M. (1983). The Role of Epidemiology in Determining Causation in Toxic Shock Syndrome. *Jurimetrics Journal* 24, 78–86.

NOTESTEIN, G. Z. (1984). *Toxic Torts*. Colorado Springs: Shepard's/McGraw-Hill. (A comprehensive review of the field. The chapters on burden of proof by

Rudlin and theories of liability by Pollan provide important background information.)

PARNELL, A. H. (1982). Manufacturers of Toxic substances: Tort Liability and Punitive Damages. *The Forum* **17**, 947–968.

PROSSER, W. (1971). *Handbook on the Law of Torts*. St. Paul: West Publishing Co.

RAPPEPORT, J. R. (1985). Reasonable Medical Certainty. *Bulletin American Academy of Psychiatry and the Law* **13**, 5–15. (Discusses the meaning of medical certainty and distinguishes the legal concept from the scientific concept. The author suggests that an appropriate definition of reasonable medical certainty is that level used by the physician when making a diagnosis and initiating treatment.)

ROBINSON, G. O. (1982). Multiple Causation in Tort Law: Reflections on DES Cases. *Virginia Law Review* **68**, 713–769.

ROSENBERG, D. (1984). The Causal Connection in Mass Exposure Cases: A Public Law Vision of the Tort System. *Harvard Law Review* **97**, 849–929.

SMITH, D. (1985). Increased Risk of Harm: A New Standard for Sufficiency of Evidence in Medical Malpractice Cases. *Boston University Law Review* **65**, 275–313.

SMITH, S. J. AND CHANNON, P. S. (1981). The Rising Storm. *The Forum* **17**, 138–165. (Includes a suggested library for lawyers involved in occupational disease litigation.)

STRAND, P. (1983). The Inapplicability of Traditional Tort Analysis to Environmental Risks: The Example of Toxic Waste Pollution Compensation. *Stanford Law Review* **35**, 575–619.

THODE, W. (1977). Tort Analysis Duty—Risk v. Proximate Cause and the Rational Allocation of Functions Between Judge and Jury. *Utah Law Review* *1977*, 1–33. (This article was extensively cited in the *Allen* opinion.)

TILEVITZ, O. E. (1977). Judicial Attitudes Toward Legal Scientific Proof of Cancer Causation. *Columbia Journal of Environmental Law* **3**, 345–381.

TRAUBERMAN, J. (1981). Compensating Victims of Toxic Substances Pollution: An Analysis of Existing Federal Statutes. *Harvard Environmental Law Review* **5**, 1–29.

TRAUBERMAN, J. (1983). Statutory Reform of "Toxic Torts": Relieving Legal Scientific and Economic Burdens on the Chemical Victim. *Harvard Environmental Law Review* **7**, 177–296.

WEHMHOEFER, R. A. (1985). *Statistics in Litigation*. Colorado Springs, Colorado: Shepard's/McGraw-Hill. (The chapters on risk assessment by the author and on medical causation by L. Siderius are relevant to this chapter.)

Clinical Trials References

ALTMAN, D. G. (1985). Comparability of Randomized Groups. *The Statistician* **34**, 125–136. (This article points out that the failure of a difference in the

baseline characteristics of the treatment and control groups to reach significance at the .05 level does *not* imply that the imbalance won't affect the statistical analysis. The point is illustrated on real data. The article reinforces the type
of analysis given in Table 13.12 which showed that the standardized mortality
rates differed.)

CHAPUT DE SAINTONGE, D. M. AND VERE, D. W. (1984). *Current Problems in
Clinical Trials.* Oxford: Blackwell. (A useful collection of articles on all aspects
of clinical trials. Those by Rose, Vere, Cox and Evans are most relevant for our
purposes.)

DUBEY, S. D. (1981). The role of FDA Statisticians in the Efficacy and Safety
Evaluation of New Drugs. In: *Statistics in the Pharmaceutical Industry* (C. R.
Buncher and J. Tsay, eds.). New York: Marcel Dekker. (A careful description
of the criteria used by the FDA in its statistical evaluation of data submitted as
evidence of efficacy and safety of a drug.)

FRIEDMAN, L. M., FURBERG, C. D. AND DeMETS, D. L. (1985). *Fundamentals
of Clinical Trials.* Littleton, Mass: PSG Co. (A basic text covering most aspects
of conducting a clinical trial from recruitment of subjects to methods of statistical analysis.)

MIKE, V. AND STANLEY, K. E., EDS. (1982). *Statistics in Medical Research.*
New York: Wiley. (These proceedings of a symposium is in memory of Professor J. Cornfield and contain many useful articles. The article by F. Mosteller on
the use of statistics in medical research, the sessions on clinical trials and the
communication of the results are relevant.)

SHAPIRO, S. H. AND LOUIS, T. A. (1983). *Clinical Trials: Issues and Approaches.*
New York: Marcel Deker. (A collection of articles emphasizing controversies
in the design and analysis of chemical studies, limitations, the proper analysis
of data and how the final results should be reported.)

TYSTRUP, N., LACKIN, J. M. AND JUHL, E. (1982). *The Randomized Clinical
Trial and Therapeutic Decisions.* New York: Marcel Deker.

Topics in Case Control Studies

DALES, L. G. AND URY, H. K. (1978). An Improper Use of Statistical Significance Testing in Studying Covariables. *International Journal of Epidemiology*
7, 373–375. (This article points out that an imbalance between cases and controls with respect to a covariate need not be of the magnitude that reaches
statistical significance before it can affect the estimated odds ratio.)

EPIDEMIOLOGY WORK GROUP (1981). Guidelines for Documentation of Epidemiologic Studies. *American Journal of Epidemiology* **114**, 609–613. (This report of
a federal interagency group concerned with the consistent evaluation of epidemiologic studies in regulatory decisionmaking and the related commentary describe the major aspects (study design, comparable study and control groups,
data collection and statistical analysis) of a sound epidemiologic study.)

GREENLAND, S. AND THOMAS, D. C. (1982). On the Need for the Rare Disease Assumption in Case Control Studies. *American Journal of Epidemiology* **116**, 547–553. (The authors show that the odds ratio from a cumulative incidence case-control study is a good approximation to the ratio of the incidence rates or the relative risk, provided that the cumulative incidence of developing the disease over the study period is less than .1 and the prevalence of exposure in the population does not vary much during the study.)

GREENLAND, S. AND NEUTRA, R. (1980). Control of Confounding in the Assessment of Medical Technology. *International Journal of Epidemiology* **9**, 361–367.

NEUTRA, R. R. AND DROLETTE, M. E. (1978). Estimating Exposure-Specific Disease Rates from Case-Control Studies Using Bayes Theorem. *American Journal of Epidemiology* **108**, 214–222. (Although case-control studies only yield an estimate of the odds ratio or relative risk, using additional information such as the overall incidence of the disease in the population, one can obtain the exposure-specific incidence rates this paper discusses. This article develops one approach and gives further references.)

SIEGEL, D. G. AND GREENHOUSE, S. W. (1973). Validity in Estimating Relative Risk in Case Control Studies. *Journal of Chronic Diseases* **26**, 218–225. (This paper illustrates the types of biases that may occur when a covariate is not accounted for in the design by matching or stratification or in the analysis. In particular, they evaluate the effect of ignoring the matching in the analysis of data obtained from a matched study.)

Diabetic Retinopathy and Diabetes (UGDP) Studies

COMMITTEE FOR THE ASSESSMENT OF CONTROLLED TRIALS OF HYPOGLYCEMIC AGENTS (1975). Report. *Journal of American Medical Association* **231**, 583–608.

CORNFIELD, J. (1971). The University Group Diabetics Program. *Journal of the American Medical Association* **217**, 1678–1687.

DIABETIC RETINOPATHY STUDY RESEARCH GROUP (1976). Preliminary Report on Effects of Photocoagulation Therapy. American *Journal of Opthalmology* **81**, 383–396.

DIABETIC RETINOPATHY STUDY RESEARCH GROUP (1978). Photocoagulation Treatment of Proliferative Diabetic Retinopathy: The Second Report of Diabetic Retinopathy Findings. *Opthalmology* **85**, 82–106.

EDERER, F., PODGOR, M. J. AND THE DIABETIC RETINOPATHY STUDY RESEARCH GROUP (1984). Assessing Possible Late Treatment Effects in Stopping a Clinical Trial Early: A Case Study. *Controlled Clinical Trials* **5**, 373–381.

FEINSTEIN, A. R. (1971). Clinical Biostatistics, VIII. An Analytic Appraisal of the University Group Diabetes Program (UGDP) Study. *Clinical Pharmacology* **12**, 167–191.

SCHOR, S. (1971). The UGDP: A Statistician Looks at Mortality Results. *Journal of the American Medical Association* **217**, 1671–1675.

THE UNIVERSITY GROUP DIABETES PROGRAM (1970). A Study of the Effects of Hypoglycemic Agents on Vascular Complications in Patients with Adult-Onset Diabetes. *Diabetes* **19**, 747–830.

Worker Compensation and Benefit Laws

ANDERSEN, W. T. (1983). Workmen's Compensation: The Expanding Concept of Partial Disability. *Southern University Law Review* **10**, 49–63.

ARNOLD, M. T. (1981). Gradually Developed Disabilities: A Dilemma for Worker's Compensation. *Akron Law Review* **15**, 13–39.

BLOT, W. J. (1984). Lung Cancer and Occupational Exposures in *Lung Cancer: Causes and Prevention* (M. Mizell and P. Correa eds.). New York: VCH Publications.

DEVELOPMENTS (1983). Utah Workers' Compensation Occupational Disease Laws. *Utah Law Review* **1983**, 573–650.

MCELVEEN, J. C. JR. AND POSTOL, L. P. (1983). Compensating Occupational Disease Victims Under the Longshoremen's and Harbor Worker's Compensation Act. *American University Law Review* **32**, 717–776.

MEISER, C. K. (1982). The Black Lung Benefits Act. *The Forum* **17**, 813–827.

NOTE (1980). Compensating Victims of Occupational Disease. *Harvard Law Review* **93**, 916–937.

PETERS, S. (1979). Occupational Carcinogens and Statutes of Limitations: Resolving Relevant Policy Goals. *Environmental Law* **10**, 113–158.

PRICE, D. N. (1986). Workers Compensation: Coverage, Benefits and Costs. *Social Security Bulletin* **49**, 5–11.

RITTS, L. S. (1979). Occupational Cancer and Statutes of Limitations on Occupational Disease Claims. *Workmen's Compensation Law Review* **5**, 70–117. (An interesting survey of state laws showing the wide variation among them. In particular, some states have special time limits on specific exposures such as radiation. The author recommends a uniform law requiring workers to file a claim within three years of the time they knew or should have, with reasonable diligence, known that their disease was work-related.)

SHEPLER, L. L. (1981). Occupational Disease Claims. *Drake Law Review* **30**, 841–859.

VISCUSI, W. K. (1984). Structuring an Effective Occupational Disease Policy: Victim Compensation and Risk Regulation. *Yale Journal on Regulation* **2**, 53–81. (A further development of a report on toxic tort compensation policies prepared by the author for government regulators.)

Risk Analysis and Regulation References

ANDERSON, E. L. (1983). Quantitative Approaches in Use to Assess Cancer Risk. *Risk Analysis* **3**, 277–295.

ASHFORD, N. A., RYAN, C. W. AND CALDARD, C. C. (1983). A Hard Look at Federal Regulation of Formaldehyde: A New Departure From Reasoned Decision Making. *Harvard Environmental Law Journal* **7**, 297–370.

ARMITAGE, P. (1982). The Assessment of Low Dose Carcinogenicity. *Biometrics Supplement* March **1982**, 119–129. (A useful survey of the issues involved accompanied by a discussion by J. Van Ryzin.)

BARAM, M. S. (1980). Cost-Benefit Analysis: An Inadequate Basis for Health, Safety and Environmental Regulatory Decisionmaking. *Ecology Law Quarterly* **8**, 473–531.

BRAUM, J. K. (1983). Legislating Cost-Benefit Analysis: The Federal Water Pollution Control Set Experience. *Columbia Journal of Environmental Law* **9**, 75–111.

BROWN, C. C. (1983). Learning About Toxicity in Humans: Some Studies on Animals. *Chemtech* **13**, 350–358.

CANN, W. A., JR. (1982). Cost-Benefit Analysis vs. Feasibility Analysis: The Controversy Resolved in the Cotton Dust Case. *Americana Business Law Journal* **20**, 1–35.

CRANDALL, R. AND LAVE, L. (1981). *The Scientific Basis of Health and Safety Regulation.* Washington, D.C.: Brookings.

GREENHOUSE, S. W. (1980). Some Epidemiologic Issues for the 1980's. *American Journal of Epidemiology* **112**, 269–273.

KREWSKI, D. AND BROWN C. (1981). Carcinogenic Risk Assessment: A Guide to the Literature. *Biometrics* **37**, 353–366. (A comprehensive guide to the scientific literature.)

LAYARD, R. (1974). *Cost-Benefit Analysis.* New York: Penguin Books.

LEAPE, J. P. (1980). Quantitative Risk Assessment in Regulation of Environmental Carcinogens. *Harvard Environmental Law Review* **4**, 86–116. (A thorough discussion of many aspects of the risk assessment process, including the relationship of animal studies to humans and the effect of variation in susceptibility among members of the general population.)

LEVENTHAL, H. (1974). Environmental Decisionmaking and the Role of the Courts. *University of Pennsylvania Law Review* **122**, 509–555.

MERRILL, (1984). The Legal System's Response to Scientific Uncertainty: The Role of Judicial Review. *Fundamental and Applied Toxicology* **4**, 418–425.

MISHNAN, E. J. (1976). *Cost-Benefit Analysis.* New York: Praeger.

MORTENSEN, D. G. AND ANDERSON, F. R., JR. (1982). The Benzene Decision: Legal and Scientific Uncertainties Compounded. In: *Legal and Ethical Dilemmas in Occupational Health* (J. S. Lee, and W. H. Rom, eds.). Michigan: Ann Arbor Science.

RICCI, P. F. AND MOLTON, L. S. (1981). Risk and Benefit in Environmental Law. *Science* **214**, 1096–1100.

RODGERS, W. H., JR. (1980). Benefits, Costs and Risks: Oversight of Health and Environmental Decisionmaking. *Harvard Environmental Law Review* **4**, 191–226.

ROGERS, W. H., JR. (1981). Judicial Review of Risk Assessment: The Role of Decision Theory in Unscrambling the Benzene Decision. *Environmental Law* **11**, 301–320.

ROWE, A. (1977). *An Anatomy of Risk*. New York: John Wiley.

ROWE, J. N. AND SPRINGER, J. A. (1986). Asbestos Lung Cancer Risks: Comparison of Animal and Human Extrapolations. *Risk Analysis* **6**, 171–180. (This article shows that the risk estimate obtained from animal studies is less than that obtained from human data. The fact that they differ by a factor of five reflects the uncertainties inherent in the subject.)

ROWE, W. D. (1977). Governmental Regulations of Societal Risks. *George Washington Law Review* **45**, 944–968.

SCHNEIDERMAN, M. A., DECOUFLE, P. AND BROWN, C. C. (1979). Thresholds for Environmental Cancer: Biologic and Statistical Considerations. *Annals of the New York Academy of Sciences* **329**, 92–130.

SCHROEDER, E. P. AND SHAPIRO, S. A. (1984). Responses to Occupational Disease: The Role of Markets, Regulation and Information. *Georgetown Law Journal* **72**, 1231–1309. (A comprehensive survey of the available information about occupational diseases, workers compensation, tort laws and regulatory issues.)

STARR, C. (1969). Social Benefit vs. Technological Risk: What is our Society Willing to Pay for Safety? *Science* **165**, 1232–1238.

WALD, P. M. (1985). Negotiation of Environmental Disputes: A New Role for the Courts? *Columbia Journal of Environmental Law* **10**, 1–33.

WHITTEMORE, A. S. (1986). Epidemiology in Risk Assessment for Regulatory Policy. *Journal of Chronic Diseases* **39**, 1157–1168.

Asbestos References

BLOT, W. J., FRAUMENI, JR. J. F., MASON, T. J. AND HOOVER, R. N. (1979). Developing Clues to Environmental Cancer: A Stepwise Approach With the Use of Cancer Mortality Data. *Environmental Health Perspectives* **32**, 52–58.

DOLL, R. (1955). Mortality From Lung Cancer in Asbestos Workers. *British Journal of Industrial Medicine* **12**, 81–86.

FLEISHER, W. E., VILES, F. J. JR., GADE, R. L. AND DRINKER, P. (1945). A Health Survey of Pipe Covering Operations in Constructing Naval Vessels. *Journal of Industrial Hygiene and Toxicology* **28**, 9–16. (Concluded that asbestos exposure in pipe covering jobs was not harmful, as only three cases of asbestosis occurred among 1074 workers, and all three workers had over 20 years of employment. Less than 100 workers had ten or more years of work in the industry.)

HAMMOND, E. C., SELIKOFF, I. J. AND SEIDMAN, H. (1979). Asbestos Exposure, Cigarette Smoking and Death Rates. *Annals of the New York Academy of Science* **330**, 473–490.

LIDDELL, F. D. K., McDONALD, J. C. AND THOMAS, D. C. (1977). Methods of Cohort Analysis: Appraisal by Application to Asbestos Mining. *Journal of the Royal Statistical Society* Series A, **140**, 469–491.

SARACCI, R. (1977). Asbestos and Lung Cancer: An Analysis of the Epidemiologic Evidence on the Asbestos-Smoking Interaction. *International Journal of Cancer* **20**, 323–331.

SELIKOFF, I. J., HAMMOND, E. C. AND CHURG, J. (1964). Asbestos Exposure, Smoking and Neoplasia. *Journal of the American Medical Association* **188**, 22–26.

SELIKOFF, I. J. AND HAMMOND, E. C. (1978). Asbestos Associated Disease in United States Shipyards. *CA: A Cancer Journal for Clinicians* **28**, 87–99.

Birth Defects and the Wells Case

BUTTAR (1982). Assessment of the Embryotoxic and Teratogenic Potential of Nonoxynol-9 in Rate Upon Vaginal Administration. *The Toxicologist* **2**, 39.

HARLAP, S., SHIONO, P. H. AND RAMCHARAN, S. (1980). Spontaneous Fetal Losses in Women Using Different Contraceptives Around the Time of Conception. *International Journal of Epidemiology* **9**, 49–56.

JICK, H., WALKER, A. M., ROTHMAN, K. J., HUNTER, J. R., HOLMES, L. B., WATKINS, R. N., D'EWART, D. C., DANFORD, S. AND MADSEN, S. (1981). Vaginal Spermicides and Congenital Disorders. *Journal of the American Medical Association* **245**, 1329–1332.

JICK, H., SHIOTA, K., SHEPARD, T. H., HUNTER, J. R., STERGACHIS, A., MADSEN, S. AND PORTER, J. B. (1982). Vaginal Spermicide and Miscarriage Seen Primarily in the Emergency Room. *Teratogenesis, Carcinogenics* and *Mutagenesis* **2**, 205–210.

KHOURY, M. J. AND HOLTZMAN, N. A. (1987). On the Ability of Birth Defects Monitoring to Detect New Teratogens. *American Journal of Epidemiology* **126**, 136–143. (This article shows that the sample sizes needed to detect moderate increases in the risk, such as an RR of two, of rare birth defects are quite large and suggests some ways to improve the monitoring systems currently in use. Their numerical results document the difficulty epidemiological studies have in determining whether an agent causes a moderate increased risk of a specific defect that was manifest in the *Wells* case).

LOUICK, C., MITCHELL, A. A., WERLER, M. M., HANSON, J. W. AND SHAPIRO, S. (1987). Maternal Exposure to Spermicides in Relation to Certain Birth Defects. *New England Journal of Medicine* **317**, 474–478. (This large case-control study, based in Boston and Iowa, of 4580 infants with malformations indicates that spermicide use does not increase the risk of common birth defects such as Down's syndrome, hypospadias or neural-tube defects. The only subgroup of cases that could not be risked out was limb reduction defects of unknown cause for mothers using spermicide in the first trimester of pregnancy. The estimated RR was 1.7 with a 95% CONF (RR; .8, 3.6).

MILLS, J. L., HARLEY, E. E., REED, G. F. AND BERENDER, H. W. (1982). Are Spermicides Teratogenic? *Journal of the American Medical Association* **248**, 2148–2151. (This is the northern California study of Kaiser plan patients.)

OAKLEY, G. P. JR. (1982). Spermicides and Birth Defects. *Journal of the American Medical Association* **247**, 2405.

OECHSLI, F. W. (1976). Studies of the Consequences of Contraceptive Failure. Report under contract from the National Institute of Child Health and Development.

POLEDNAK, A. P., JANERICH, D. T. AND GLEBATIS, D. M. (1982). Birth Weight and Birth Defects in Relation to Maternal Spermicide Use. *Teratology* **26**, 27–38. (This study was carried out in upstate New York.)

QUILLIGAN, E. L. AND KRETCHMAR, N. (1980). *Fetal and Maternal Medicine.* New York: John Wiley. (The chapters on drugs in pregnancy by R. M. Pitkin and teratology by T. H. Shepard and R. J. Lemire are quite relevant.)

ROTHMAN, K. J. (1982). Spermicide Use and Down's Syndrome. *American Journal of Public Health* **72**, 399–401. (A study indicating that maternal spermicide use prior to conception increases the risk (OR = 3.8) of a child having Down's syndrome and congenital heart disease. This result is not relevant to the causation aspect of the Wells case, as the baby did not have Down's syndrome. It might have been relevant to the manufacturer's attitude towards warning customers if subsequent to the publication it did not mention the results or sponsor a further study.)

SHAPIRO, S., STONE, D., HEINONEN, O. P., KAUFMAN, D. W., ROSEBERG, L., MITCHELL, A. A. AND HELNRICH, S. P. (1982). Birth Defects and Vaginal Spermicides. *Journal of the American Medical Association* **247**, 2381–2384. (This is the 12-hospital collaborative Perinatal Project study.)

SMITH, F. S. O., DAFOE, C. S., MILLER, J. R. AND BANISTER, P. (1977). An Epidemiologic Study of Congenital Reduction Deformities of the Limbs. *British Journal of Preventive and Social Medicine* **31**, 39–41.

WARBURTON, D., NEUGUT, R. H., LUSTENBERGER, A., NICHOLAS, A. G., AND KLINE, J. (1987). *New England Journal of Medicine* **317**, 478–482. This study of 13,729 women who were undergoing prenatal chromosome screening matched each of the 154 fetuses with trisomy, an extra chromosome, with four normal controls. The controls were matched to the case on location and maternal age. Other relevant factors such as parity and smoking status of the mother were accounted for by using logistic regression as in the Reyes' syndrome study discussed in Chapter 11. The study yielded an estimated OR of .9 with a 95% CONF (OR; .5, 1.7) for all trisomy and an OR of .8 for Downs' syndrome. In conjunction with the Boston and Iowa study, these results essentially rule out an increased risk of Downs' syndrome as a result of spermicide use.

Dalkon Shield and IUD Case References

DAVIS, H. (1970). The Shield Intrauterine Device. *American Journal of Obstetrics and Gynecology* **106**, 455–456.

PENDERGAST, P. AND HIRSCH, H. L. (1986). The Dalkon Shield in Perspective. *Medicine and Law* **5**, 35–44. (An update on the status of Dalkon shield litigation.)

TICK, E. L. (1983). Beyond the Dalkon Shield: Proving Causation Against IUD Manufacturers for PID Related Injury. *Golden Gate University Law Review* **13**, 639–665.

TIETZE, C. (1967). Intrauterine Contraception: Recommended Procedures for Data Analysis. *Studies in Family Planning* **18** (Supp), 1–6.

TIETZE, C. AND LEWIT, C. (1973). Recommended Procedures for the Statistical Evaluation of Intrauterine Conception. *Studies in Family Planning* **24**, 35–42. (An updating of the previous article.)

VAN DYKE, J. M. (1978). The Dalkon Shield: A "Primer" in IUD Liability. *Western State University Law Review* **6**, 1–52. (The author has represented numerous plaintiffs and cites cases supporting the interpretation of legal cause as a substantial factor, as well as providing a history of A. H. Robins' product development and sales strategy and the subsequent litigation.)

Radiation and Its Relation to Cancer and the Allen Case.

Medical Literature

BECK, H. L. AND KREY, P. W. (1983). Radiation Exposures in Utah From the Nevada Tests. *Science* **220**, 18–24.

BEEBE, G. W. (1981). The Atomic Bomb Survivors and the Problem of Low-Dose Radiation Effects. *American Journal of Epidemiology* **114**, 760–783.

BEIR REPORT (1980). *The Effects on Populations of Exposure to Low Levels of Ionizing Radiation*. Report of the Advisory Committee on the Biological Effects of Ionizing Radiations, Division of Medical Sciences, National Academy of Sciences, National Research Council, Washington, D.C.

BOND, V. P. AND HAMILTON, L. D. (1980). Leukemia in the Nevada Smoky Bomb Test. *Journal of American Medical Association* **244**, 1610.

CALDWELL, C. G., KELLEY, D. B. AND HEATH, C. W. JR. (1980). Leukemia Among Participants in Military Maneuvers at a Nuclear Bomb Test. *Journal of the American Medical Association* **244**, 1575–1578.

DARBY, S. C. AND REISSLAND, J. A. (1981). Low Levels of Ionizing Radiation and Cancer—Are we Underestimating the Risks? *Journal of the Royal Statistical Society* Series A, **144**, 298–331.

DARBY, S. C. (1985). Evaluation of Radiation Risk From Epidemiologic Studies of Populations Exposed at High Doses. *The Statistician* **34**, 59–72.

DARBY, S. C. (1986). Epidemiological Evaluation of Radiation Risk Using Populations Exposed at High Doses. *Health Physics* **31**, 269–281. (This review of the literature explains why studies of persons exposed to low levels of radiation are often unable to detect harmful effects due to their low power. Therefore, risk estimates need to be made from populations exposed to much higher doses, even with the uncertainty inherent in extrapolation.)

GILBERT, E. S. (1985). How Much Can be Learned From Populations Exposed to Low Levels of Radiation? *The Statistician* **34**, 19–30.

INTERNATIONAL COMMISSION ON RADIOLOGICAL PROTECTION (1981). *Limits for Intakes of Radionuclides by Workers.* ICRP Report No. 32.

JABLON, S. AND BAILAR, J. C. III (1980). The Contribution of Ionizing Radiation to Cancer Mortality in the United States. *Preventive Medicine* **9**, 219–226.

JOHNSON, C. J. (1984). Cancer Incidence in an Area of Radioactive Fallout Downwind From the Nevada Test Site. *Journal of the American Medical Association* **251**, 230–236.

LAND, C. (1979). The Hazards of Fallout or of Epidemiologic Research? *New England Journal of Medicine* **300**, 431–432.

LAND, C. D. (1980). Estimating Cancer Risk from Low Doses of Ionizing Radiation. *Science* **209**, 1197–1203.

LAND, C., McKAY, F. W. AND MACHADO, S. G. (1984). Childhood Leukemias and Fallout From the Nevada Nuclear Tests. *Science* **223**, 139–144.

LISCO, H., FINKEL, M. P. AND BRUES, A. M. (1947). Carcinogenic Properties of Radioactive Fission Products and of Plutonium. *Radiology* **49**, 361–363.

LYON, J. L., KLAUBER, M. R., GARDNER, J. W. AND UDALL, K. S. (1979). Childhood Leukemias Associated with Fallout From Nuclear Testing. *New England Journal of Medicine* **300**, 397–402.

MACHADO, S. G., LAND, C. E. AND McKAY, F. W. (1987). Cancer Mortality and Radiation Fallout in Southwestern Utah. *American Journal of Epidemiology* **125**, 44–61. (The authors dispute Caldwell's results on increased mortality. However, they now find an increased risk of childhood leukemia as indicated in Tables 14.17 and 14.19 and by Chernoff's refined analysis.)

MARCH, H. C. (1950). Leukemia in Radiologists in a Twenty-Year Period. *American Journal of Medical Science* **220**, 282–286.

MAUS, E. A. (1983). Health Effects of Ionizing Radiation in the Low Dose Range. *Annals of the New York Academy of Science* **403**, 27–36.

NATIONAL RESEARCH COUNCIL (1980). *The Effects on Populations of Exposure to Low Levels of Ionizing Radiation.* Washington, D.C.: National Academy Press.

OFFICE OF TECHNOLOGY ASSESSMENT (1981). *Technologies for Determining Cancer Risks From the Environment.* Washington, D.C.: U.S. Government Printing Office.

ULRICH, H. (1946). The Incidence of Leukemia in Radiologists. *New England Journal of Medicine* **234**, 45–46. (An analysis of over 30,000 obituary notices in the *Journal* showed an eight-fold relative risk of leukemia for radiologists compared to other doctors.)

YALOW, R. S. (1983). Reappraisal of Potential Risks Associated with Low Level Radiation. *Annals of the New York Academy of Science* **403**, 37–51.

Legal and General Background

BALL, H. (1986). *Justice Downwind.* New York: Oxford University Press. (Discusses the atomic testing program during the 1950s and the *Allen* case from a perspective sympathetic to the residents.)

CHRISTOFFELL, T. AND SCHWARTZMAN, D. (1986). Nuclear Weapons Testing Fallout: Proving Causation for Exposure Injury. *American Journal of Public Health* **76**, 290–292.

DOYLE, C. M. (1982). Government Liability for Nuclear Testing Under FTCA. *University of California at Davis Law Review* **15**, 1003–1028.

DURRETT, D. B. (1982). Nuclear Testing and Inverse Condemnation. *University of California at Davis Law Review* **15**, 1028–1045.

ESTEP, S. D. (1960). Radiation Injuries and Statistics. *Michigan Law Review* **59**, 259–304. (One of the earliest discussions on the mix of technology and law in deciding what injuries should be compensated, the required proof of causation and proper compensation.)

FAVISH, A. (1981). Radiation Injury and the Atomic Vets: Shifting the Burden of Proof on Factual Causation. *Hastings Law Journal* **32**, 933–974.

NOTE (1980). The Application of the Statute of Limitations to Actions for Tortuous Radiation Exposure. *Alabama Law Review* **31**, 509–521.

SCHOLL, D. (1981). The Nevada Proving Grounds: An Asylum for Sovereign Immunity. *Southwestern Law Review* **12**, 627–665.

WYANT, M. F. (1977). The Discretionary Function Exception to Government Tort Liability. *Marquette Law Review* **61**, 163–185.

Reye's Syndrome

CONSENSUS CONFERENCE (1981). Diagnosis and Treatment of Reye's Syndrome. *Journal of the American Medical Association* **246**, 2441–2444.

EICHENWALD, H. Z. (1983). The Aspirin and Reye's Syndrome Controversy. *Infectious Diseases* **13**, 1–5.

HALPIN, T. J., HOLTZHAUER, F. J., CAMPBELL, R. J., HALL, L. J., CORREA-VILLASENOR, A., LANESE, R., RICE, J., HURWITZ, E. S. (1982). Reye's Syndrome and Medication Use. *Journal of the American Medical Association* **248**, 687–691. (The FDA relied on this study to support its first proposed regulation in 1982.)

PUBLIC HEALTH SERVICE (1985). Public Health Service Study on Reye's Syndrome and Medications. *New England Journal of Medicine* **313**, 849–857.

REYE, R. D. K., MORGAN, G. AND BARALS, J. (1963). Encephalopathy and Fatty
Degeneration of the Viscera: A Disease Entity in Childhood. *Lancet* **2,** 749.
STARKO, K. M., RAY, C. G., DOMINGUEZ, B. S., STROMBERG, W. L. AND
WOODALL, D. F. (1980). Reye's Syndrome and Salicylate Use. *Pediatrics* **66,**
859–864.
WESTAT CORP. (1984). *Reye's Syndrome, Final Report.* (Presents the results of
an analysis of the reliability of the basic data such as demographic characteristics of cases and controls, time elapsed between prodromal illness and interview rather than the estimated relative risk. This report illustrates the wisdom
of assessing data *prior* to the analysis of interest.)

Toxic-Shock Syndrome

BERKEY, S. F., HIGHTOWER, A. W., BROOME, C. V. AND REINGOLD, A. L.
(1987). The Relationship of Tampon Characteristics to Menstrual Toxic Shock
Syndrome. *Journal of the American Medical Association* **258,** 917–920. (This is
the latest study from the CDC.)
CENTERS FOR DISEASE CONTROL (1980a). Toxic-Shock Syndrome—United
States. *Morbidity Mortality Weekly Report* **29,** 229–230.
CENTERS FOR DISEASE CONTROL (1980b). Follow-up on Toxic-Shock Syndrome—United States. *Morbidity Mortality Weekly Report* **29,** 297–299.
CENTERS FOR DISEASE CONTROL (1980c). Follow-up on Toxic-Shock Syn-
drome—United States. *Morbidity Mortality Weekly Report* **29,** 441–445.
CENTERS FOR DISEASE CONTROL (1980d). Toxic-Shock Syndrome—Utah. *Mor-
bidity Mortality Weekly Report* **29,** 495–496.
DAVIS, J. P., CHESNEY, P. J., WAND, P. J., LAVENTURE, M., The Investigation
and Laboratory Team (1980). Toxic-Shock Syndrome: Epidemiologic Fea-
tures, Recurrence, Risk Factors, and Prevention. *New England Journal of
Medicine* **303,** 1429–1435.
DAVIS, J. P. AND VERGERONT, J. M. (1982). The Effect of Publicity on the Re-
porting of Toxic-Shock Syndrome in Wisconsin. *Journal of Infectious Diseases*
145, 449–457.
HARVEY, M., HORWITZ, R. I. AND FEINSTEIN, A. R. (1982). Toxic Shock and
Tampons: Evaluation of the Epidemiologic Evidence. *Journal of the American
Medical Association* **248,** 840–846.
HULKA, B. S. (1982). Tampons and Toxic Shock Syndrome. *Journal of the
American Medical Association* **248,** 872–874.
KEHRBERG, M. W., LATHAM, R. H., HASLAM, B. T., HIGHTOWER, A., TANNER,
M., JACOBSON, J. A., BARBOUR, A. G., NOBEL, V. AND SMITH, C. B. (1981).
Risk Factors for Toxic-Shock Syndrome. *American Journal of Epidemiology*
114, 873–879. (This article reports the final results of the Utah study.)
KIRSCH, A. D., BERGER, P. K. AND BELFORD, R. J. III (1962). Are Reports of
Brands Bought Last Reliable and Valid? *Journal of Advertising Research* **2,** 34–
36.

OSTERHOLM, M. T., DAVIS, J. P., GIBSON, R. W., MANDEL, J. S., WINERMEYER, L. A., HELMS, C. M., FORFANG, J. C., RONDEAU, J., VERGERONT, J. M. AND THE INVESTIGATION TEAM (1982). The Tri-State Toxic-Shock Syndrome Study. I. Epidemiologic Findings. *Journal of Infectious Diseases* **145**, 431–440. (This article presents the results of the major tri-state study.)

SHANDS, K. N., SCHMID, G. P., DUN, B. B., BLUM, D., GUIDOTTI, R. J., HARGRETT, N. T., ANDERSON, R. L., HILL, D. I., BROOME, C. V., BAND, J. D., FRASER, D. W. (1980). Toxic-Shock Syndrome in Menstruating Women: Association with Tampon Use and *Staphylococcus aureus* and Clinical Features in 52 Cases. *New England Journal of Medicine* **303**, 1436–1442.

TODD, J., FISHAUT, M., KAPRAL, F., WELCH, T. (1978). Toxic-Shock Syndrome Associated with Phage-Group-1 Staphylococci. *Lancet* **2**, 1116–1118.

Benzene and Vinyl Chloride

AUSTIN, H., DELZELL, E. AND COLE, P. (1988). Benzene and Leukemia a Review of the Literature and a Risk Assessment. *American Journal of Epidemiology,* **127**, 419–439. (A thorough review of the epidemiologic studies and risk assessments derived from them. The authors note the difficulty of obtaining reliable estimates of the excess risk at low dose levels, corresponding to proposed new regulations, using data on persons exposed to much higher doses).

INFANTE, P. F., WHITE, M. C. AND CHEO, K. C. (1984). Assessment of Leukemia Mortality Associated with Occupational Exposure to Benzene. *Risk Analysis* **4**, 9–13.

OTT, M. G., LANGNER, R. R. AND HOLDER, B. B. (1975). Vinyl Chloride Exposure in a Controlled Industrial Environment. *Archives of Environmental Health* **31**, 333–339.

OTT, M. G., FISHBECK, W. A., TOWNSEND, J. C. AND SCHNEIDER, B. S. (1976). A Health Study of Employees Exposed to Vinyl Chloride. *Journal of Occupational Medicine* **18**, 735–738.

OTT, M. G., CARLO, G. L., STEINBERG, S. AND BOND, G. (1985). Mortality Among Employees Engaged in Chemical Manufacturing and Related Activities. *American Journal of Epidemiology* **122**, 311–322. (An update by the health department of Dow Chemical Co. indicating that employees had a favorable overall mortality rate relative to the age-adjusted rational rate. They cite the healthy worker effect and the pre-employment screening exam as possible factors in addition to the lack of major health problems. The highest SMR, 2.1, wɐ found in death from leukemia. Of course, this finding is not statistically independent of their earlier result.)

THORPE, J. J. (1974). Epidemiologic Survey of Leukemia in Persons Potentially Exposed to Benzene. *Journal of Occupational Medicine* **18**, 375–382.

TOWNSEND, J. C., OTT, M. G. AND FISHBECK, W. A. (1978). Health Exam Findings Among Individuals Exposed to Benzene. *Journal of Occupational Medicine* **20**, 543–548.

WHITE, M. C., INFANTE, P. F. AND WALKER, B. JR. (1980). Occupational Exposure to Benzene. *American Journal of Industrial Medicine* **1**, 233–243. (An analysis of the evidence in the record of the benzene case by members of OSHA. They also include some data that become available after the record was closed.)

Vaccine Related References

BREGMAN, J. G. AND HAYNES, N. S. (1984). Guillen-Barre Syndrome and its Relationship to Swine Flu Vaccination in Michigan 1976–77. *American Journal of Epidemiology* **119**, 880–889.
COMMITTEE OF THE INSTITUTE OF MEDICINE (1985). *Vaccine Supply and Innovation.* Washington, D.C.: National Academy Press. (Virtually all the issues involved in vaccine production, testing and development are examined. The liability issue as well as the propriety of giving individuals live vaccine, which may also give immunity to others exposed to the individual when a dead vaccine with less risk of harm to the person vaccinated exists, are explored. Possible changes in the tort system are also discussed.)
LANGMUIR, A. D., BREGMAN, D. J., KURLAND, L. T., NATHANSON, M. AND VICTUR, M. (1984). An Epidemiologic and Clinical Evaluation of Guillen-Barre Syndrome Reported in Association with the Administration of Swine Flu Influenze Vaccines. *American Journal of Epidemiology* **119**, 841–879. (The above article should be read in conjunction with a critical letter of N. Mantel and the authors' rejoinder appearing in the same *Journal* (1985), **121**, 620–623.)
REITZE, A. (1986). Federal Compensation for Vaccine Induced Injuries. *Boston College Environmental Law Review* **13**, 169–214. (This article reviews the medical and legal history of several vaccine programs and questions some of the statistics on adverse reactions to the diptheria, pertussis and tetanus (DPT) vaccines. It concludes that a new method of compensation to persons harmed by a vaccine should be created, with the government assuming the major obligation.)
SCHONBERGER, L. B., BREGMAN, D. J., SULLIVAN-BOLYAI, J. Z., KEENYOLIDE, R. A., ZIEGLER, D. W., RETAILLIERN, H. F., EDDIW, D. L. AND BRYAN, J. A. (1979). Guillen-Barre Syndrome Following Vaccination in the Natural Influenza Immunization Program, U.S. 1976–77. *American Journal of Epidemiology* **110**, 105–123. (This is the study carried out by the CDC which was relied on in most of the legal cases.)

Sample Size Determination

In addition to the texts on case-control studies by Schlesselman (1982) and on clinical trials by Friedman, Furberg and DeMets (1985), we mention the following articles which provide further references.
GAIL, M. H. AND GART, J. J. (1973). The Determination of Sample Sizes for Use With the Exact Conditional Test in 2×2 Comparative Trials. *Biometrics* **29**, 441–448.

GAIL, M. H. (1973). The Determination of Sample Sizes for Trials Involving Several Independent 2 × 2 Tables. *Journal of Chronic Diseases* **26**, 669–673. (This paper is useful when planning a study which will be stratified on an appropriate covariate such as age or smoking pattern.)

GEORGE, S. L. AND DESU, M. M. (1974). Planning the Size and Duration of a Clinical Trial Studying the Time to a Critical Event. *Journal of Chronic Diseases* **27**, 15–24.

LACHIN, J. M. (1981). Introduction to Sample Size Determination and Power Analysis for Clinical Trials. *Controlled Clinical Trials* **2**, 93–113.

O'NEILL, R. T. (1984). Sample Sizes for Estimation of the Odds Ratio In Unmatched Case Control Studies. *American Journal of Epidemiology* **120**, 145–153. (This article gives the sample sizes required to attain a confidence interval for the odds ratio of a prespecified length. The more accurate one desires the estimate, the larger is the sample size required. The sample size also depends on exposure prevalence as in Table 13A.2.)

SCHLESSELMAN, J. J. (1974). Sample Size Requirements in Cohort and Case Control Studies of Disease. *American Journal of Epidemiology* **99**, 381–384. (This was the original article on which Table 13A.2 is based.)

URY, H. K. AND FLEISS, J. L. (1980). On Approximate Sample Sizes for Comparing Two Independent Proportions with the Use of Yates' Correction. *Biometrics* **36**, 347–351.

WALTER, S. D. (1977). Determination of Significant Relative Risks and Optimal Sampling Procedures in Prospective and Retrospective Comparative Studies of Various Sizes. *American Journal of Epidemiology* **105**, 387–397. (This paper obtains the minimum value of the relative risk (or odds ratio) that can be detected with a prespecified power when the sample size is fixed. This problem is important, as the number of exposed individuals may be small, but a study should be carried out due to the potential harm to them. Similarly, for very rare diseases, the number of cases that are expected to occur over a realistic time frame may be small. In doing this type of calculation various powers, e.g., .9 down to .5 might be assumed.)

WEISS, N. S. (1986). *Clinical Epidemiology: The Study of the Outcome of Illness.* New York: Oxford University Press.

Recent Developments and Recommended Reading

As statistical data is continually being used in novel applications and new methods of analysis are being developed, no book can ever be complete. The following list of topics, cases and references should aid the reader interested in pursuing further uses of quantitative reasoning in law and public policy.

The Legal Process

ARKIN, S. D. (1980). Discrimination and Arbitrariness in Capital Punishment: An Analysis of Post-Furman Murder Cases in Dade County, Florida, 1973–1976. *Stanford Law Review* **33**, 75–101.

BALDUS, D. C., PULASKI, C., WOODWORTH, G. AND KYLE, F. D. (1980). Identifying Comparatively Excessive Sentences of Death: A Quantitative Approach. *Stanford Law Review* **33**, 1–74.

BALDUS, D. C., PULASKI, C. AND WOODWORTH, G. (1983). Comparative Review of Death Sentences: An Empirical Study of the Georgia Experience. *Journal of Criminal Law and Criminology* **74**, 661–753.

GELFAND, A. E. AND SOLOMON, H. (1977). Considerations in Building Jury Behavior Models and in Comparing Jury Schemes: An Argument in Favor of 12-Member Juries. *Jurimetrics Journal* **17**, 292–313. (A comprehensive survey of the research on jury verdicts which was stimulated in part, by the Supreme Court decisions: *Williams v. Florida* 399 U.S. (1970), *Apodaca v. Oregon* 40 U.S. 404 (1972) and *Colgrove v. Battin* 413 U.S. 149 (1973) that allowed six member rather than twelve member juries in some circumstances).

GOLDKAMP, J. S. AND GOTTFREDSON, M. R. (1985). *Policy Guidelines for Bail: An Experiment in Court Reform.* Philadelphia: Temple University Press.

GOLDMAN, S. AND LAMB, C., EDS. (1986). *Judicial Conflict and Consensus: Behavioral Studies of American Courts.* Lexington, KY: University Press of Kentucky. (A collection of studies of voting patterns, dissent rates and the factors affecting them.)

HASTIE, R., PENROD, S. D. AND PENNINGTON, N. (1983). *Inside the Jury.* Cambridge: Harvard University Press.

KAYE, D. (1980). Mathematical Models and Legal Realities: Reflections on the Poisson Model of Jury Behavior. *Connecticut Law Review,* **13**, 1–16.

NAGEL, S. (1980). Some Statistical Considerations in Legal Policy Analysis. *Connecticut Law Review,* **13**, 17–32.

SHUBERT, G. (1959). *Quantitative Analysis of Judicial Behavior.* Glencoe, IL: Free Press. (One of the earliest quantitative studies of judicial decision making.)

McClesky v. Kemp 55 U.S.L.W. 41, 4537–4561 (1987) upholding *McClesky v. Zant* 580 F.Supp 338 (N.D. Ga. 1984) and 753 F.2d 877 (11th Cir. 1985). (An important case concerning the relevance of the statistical studies concerning the death sentence. The plaintiff relied on the studies of Baldus and coauthors, however, the majority opinion felt that more evidence specific to the individual case was required to overturn the sentencing procedure in Georgia. The opinions of all the judges are worth reading, and the case will probably produce a number of articles in law reviews.)

Uses of Statistics and Probability in the Legal Setting

CHANEY, E. M. (1986). Computer Simulations: How They Can be Used at Trial and the Arguments for Admissibility. *Indiana Law Review,* **19**, 735–759. (An interesting article illustrating the potential use of computer simulations based on a variety of assumptions. To assure admissibility the assumptions should be accepted in the field and/or shown to fit actual data.)

DeGroot, M. H., Fienberg, S. E., and Kadane, J. P. eds. (1986). *Statistics and the Law,* New York: John Wiley. (A collection of articles on uses of statistics in the law. A pre-print of the article by Berry and Geisser on paternity case was referred to in Chapter 12. The chapters by King on the use of samples in anti-trust cases, Solomon on confidence intervals, Conway and Roberts on reverse regression, along with the comment by Michaelson, give the reader useful insights into these topics.)

Gorey, H. Jr. and Einhorn, H. A. (1986). The Use and Misuse of Economic Evidence in Horizontal Price Fixing Cases. *Journal of Contemporary Law,* **12,** 1–48.

Kaye, D. H. (1987). The Admissibility of Probability Evidence in Criminal Trials–Part II. *Jurimetrics Journal* **27,** 160–172. (A recent article providing further references to cases and relevant literature.)

Kaye, D. H. and Aickin, M. eds. (1986). *Statistical Methods in Discrimination Litigation,* New York: Marcel Dekker.

Schmalbeck, R. (1986). The Trouble With Statistical Evidence. *Law and Contemporary Problems,* **49,** 221–236.

Thompson, J. J. (1986). Liability and Individualized Evidence. *Law and Contemporary Problems,* **49,** 199–220. (This paper and the previous one debate the usefulness and relevance of statistical data.)

AIDS and its Ramifications

Bloom, D. E. and Carliner, G. (1988). The Economic Impact of AIDS in the United States. *Science* **239,** 604–609.

Curran, J. W., Jaffe, H. W., Hardy, A. M., Morgan, W. M., Selik, R. M. and Dondero, T. J. (1988). Epidemiology of HIV Infection and AIDS in the United States. *Science* **239,** 610–616.

Dalton, H. L., Burris, S., The Yale AIDS Law Project eds. (1987). *AIDS and the Law: A Guide for the Public.* New Haven: Yale University Press.

Dickens, B. M. (1988). Legal Rights and Duties in the AIDS Epidemic. *Science* **239,** 580–586. (A survey of the rights infected person's to confidentiality and nondiscrimination and the rights of uninfected individuals to protection from endangerment.)

Doll, R. (1987). Major Epidemics of the 20th Century: from Coronary Thrombosis to AIDS. *Journal of the Royal Statistics Society* Series A. **150,** 373–395.

Dornette, W. H. L. ed. (1987). *AIDS and the Law.* New York: John Wiley.

Gastwirth, J. L. and Hammick, P. A. (1988). Estimation of the Prevalence of a Rare Disease, Preserving the Anonymity of the Subjects by Group Testing; Application to Estimating the Prevalence of AIDS Antibodies in Blood Donors. To appear in the *Journal of Statistical Planning and Inference.* (This article shows that accurate estimates of the prevalence of AIDS can be achieved by testing the combined blood samples of 10 or 20 persons, thereby protecting their anonymity.)

GOSTIN, L. O., CURRAN, W. J. AND CLARK, M. E. (1987). The Case Against Compulsory Casefinding in Controlling AIDS-Testing Screening and Reporting. *American Journal of Law and Medicine* **12**, 7–97.

INSTITUTE OF MEDICINE, NATIONAL ACADEMY OF SCIENCES. (1986). *Confronting AIDS: Directions for Public Health, Health Care and Research*. Washington: National Academy Press.

WALTERS, L. (1988). Ethical Issues in the Prevention and Treatment of HIV Infection and AIDS. *Science* **239**, 597–603.

Miscellaneous

FINNEY, D. J. (1983). Between Medicine and Law. *Statistics in Medicine* **2**, 113–121.

NEWELL, D. J. (1982). The Role of the Statistician as an Expert. *Journal of the Royal Statistical Society,* Series A, **145**, 403–409.

OLDHAM, P. D. AND NEWELL, D. J. (1977). Fluoridation of Water Supplies and Cancer—A Possible Association. *Applied Statistics* **26**, 125–135.

OLDHAM, P. D. (1985). The Fluoridation of the Strathclyde Regional's Water Supply: Opinion of Lord Jauncey in *causa McColl v. Strathclyde Regional Council:* A Review. *Journal of the Royal Statistical Society* **148**, 37–44. (These four articles concern a case challenging the safety of water fluoridation in England.)

LANDES, W. M. AND POSNER, R. A. (1987). *The Economic Structure of Tort Law*. Cambridge, Mass: Harvard University Press. (An analysis of tort law from the view that one of its purposes is the promotion of economic efficiency. A number of their arguments rely on statistical data and methods, especially regression analysis.)

KOHN, A. (1986). *False Prophets: Fraud and Error in Science and Medicine*. Oxford, U.K.: Basil Blackwell. (The story of how errors, some honest and some truly dishonest, enter into the scientific literature. The incidents described, though uncommon, justify the need for careful review and independent reanalysis of data used for major public health decisions.)

KOZIARA, K. S., MOSKOW, M. H. AND TANNER, L. D. EDS. (1987). *Working Women; Past, Present and Future*. Washington D.C., Bureau of National Affairs. (A collection of research papers devoted to the status of women in the labor force. In addition to general articles the specific ones on women in management (by Dipboye) in unions (by Needlemen and Tanner) in academia (by Bognanno) and the status of minority women (by Malveaux and Wallace) are pertinent to EEO cases and policy.)

SEXTON, P. C. (1977). *Women and Work*. R and D Monograph 46, U.S. Department of Labor, Washington, DC. (A well organized review of the labor market status of women and the effect of government programs. It provides a substantial amount of background information and summaries of research.)

SHUCK, P. H. (1986). *Agent Orange on Trial: Mass Toxic Disasters in the Courts.* Cambridge, Mass: Belknap Press. (A comprehensive description not only of the trial but of the problems inherent in relying on the current system to deal with major environmental hazards.)

WALKER, M. A. (1987). Interpreting Race and Crime Statistics. *Journal of the Royal Statistical Society,* Series A, **150,** 39–56. (A discussion of statistical problems in official crime statistics and how they affect the interpretation of the data.)

Case Index

B

C

Hawkinson v. A. H. Robins, 595 F.Supp. 1290 (D. Co. 1984), 810, 812
Hazelwood School District v. U.S., 433 U.S. 299, 97 S.Ct. 2736 (1977), xxi, 107, 172, 264
Hein v. Oregon College of Education, 718 F.2d 910 (9th Cir. 1983), 672
Henri's Food Products Co. v. Kraft Inc., 717 F.2d 352 (7th Cir. 1983), 523
Heymann v. Tetra Plastics Corporation, 640 F.2d 115 (8th Cir. 1981), 672
Hicks v. Scurr, 671 F.2d 255 (8th Cir. 1982), 730
Higgs v. Wilson, 616 F.Supp. 226 (W.D. Ky. 1985), 750
Hill v. Texas, 316 U.S. 400 (1942), 88, 154
Hillsborough v. Cromwell, 326 U.S. 620 (1946), 29
Hodgson v. Greyhound Lines Inc., 499 F.2d 859, 391
Hogan v. Pierce, 31 FEP Cases 115 (D.D.C. 1983), xv, 265–266, 299, 316, 319, 321, 767
Holiday Inns, Inc. v. Holiday Out in America, 481 F.2d 445 (5th Cir. 1973), 523

I

Illinois Physicians Union v. Miller, 675 F.2d 151 (7th Cir. 1982), 493
In re Corrugated Container Antitrust Litig., 444 F.Supp. 921 (S.D. Tex 1977), 431
In the Matter of Kents, 34 N.J. 21, 166 A.2d 763 (1961), 30
In re Brooks Building, 391 Pa. 137, A.2d 273 (1958), 30
Indian Towing v. United States, 350 U.S. 6 (76 S.Ct. 122 (1955)), 904
Indust. Union v. Am. Petroleum Inst., 448 U.S. 607 (1980), 904
Industrial Union Dept., AFL-CIO v. Hodgson, 499 F.2d 467 at 474 (D.C. Cir. 1974), 904

J

Jackson v. Kelley, 557 F.2d 735 (1977), 904
Jacobs v. College of William and Mary, 517 F.Supp. 791 (E.D. Va. 1980) *affirmed* 661 F.2d 922 (4th Cir.), 671
Jefferson v. Hackney, 406 U.S. 535 and 546, 524
Jensen v. Lick, 589 F.Supp. 35 (D.N.D. 1984), 750
Johnson v. Perini, No. 76-2259 (D.D.C. June 1, 1978), xv, 218–219, 224, 244
Johnson v. U.S., 597 F.Supp. 374 (D. Kan. 1984), 878
Jones v. Tri-County Electric Cooperative, 515 F.2d 13 (5th Cir. 1975), 168–170, 178, 180–183
Jones v. City of Lubbock, 730 F.2d 233 (5th Cir. 1984), 432
Jurgens v. Thomas, 29 FEP Cases 1561, (N.D. Texas 1982), 96, 97, 108, 222, 435, 455

K

Karcher v. Dagett, 462 U.S. 725 (1983), 28
Kehm v. Proctor and Gamble, 724 F.2d 612 (8th Cir. 1983), 845, 829
Kirkland v. N.Y. Dept. of Correction, 7 FEP Cases 700 (S.D. N.Y. 1974) *modified* 520 F.2d 420 (2d Cir. 1975), 458
Kirkpatrick v. Preisley, 394 U.S. 526 (1969), *affirmed* 407 U.S. 901 (1972), 28, 29
Kirksey v. City of Jackson, 461 F.Supp. 1282 (S.D. Miss. 1978), 431
Kligo v. Bowman Transport, 40 FEP Cases 1415 (11th Cir. 1983), 393
Kouba v. Allstate Insurance Comp., 691 F.2d 873 (9th Cir. 1982), 672
Kusior v. Silver, 54 Cal. 2d. 603, 354 P.2d 657 (1960), 740

L

Langeson v. Anaconda Co., 510 F.2d 307 (6th Cir. 1975), 252
Lewis v. National Labor Relations Board, 750 F.2d 1266, 36 FEP Cases 1388 (5th Cir. 1985), 316

Y

Z

Name Index

Subject Index